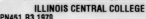

TITANS OF LITERATURE

EDGAR ALLAN POE

TITANS OF LITERATURE

FROM HOMER
TO THE PRESENT

BY BURTON RASCOE

ILLUSTRATED

Essay Index Reprint Series

Illinois Central College
Learning Resouce Center

BOOKS FOR LIBRARIES PRESS
FREEPORT, NEW YORK

41000

First Published 1932
Reprinted 1970

INTERNATIONAL STANDARD BOOK NUMBER:
0-8369-1775-8

LIBRARY OF CONGRESS CATALOG CARD NUMBER:
76-121502

PRINTED IN THE UNITED STATES OF AMERICA

TO THE MEMORY OF

MY FATHER

*

IN books I seek only pleasure through an honest pastime; or, if I study, I seek only the knowledge which tells me how to know myself, and teaches me to die well and to live well. . . . Now the writers of biographies are most suited to my purpose, since they dwell on intentions more than on incidents, more on that which proceeds from within than on that which happens without. . . . For I am not less curious to know the fortunes and the lives of these great teachers of the world than to know the diversity of their teachings and ideas.

MONTAIGNE

CONTENTS

*

CONTENTS

ILLUSTRATIONS

*

TITANS OF
LITERATURE

HOMER *AND GREEK LEGEND*

*

MORE nonsense has been written about the Greeks than about any other race of peoples. This is because their tremendously rich literature has begot a rich literature, rich in nonsense as well as sense. It is a literature that has fertilized all Western literature; and yet, because it was written over a period of many centuries in a changing language that has long since passed out of common use among the descendants of the people who wrote it—just as we no longer speak the language of *Beowulf* or Chaucer—its very sound at different periods is in dispute and the meaning of many of its words still conjectural. So great is the fascination of that literature, however, that commentaries have piled up so great in magnitude about it that no human mind, within one lifetime, could examine and assimilate them all. Discoveries have displaced conjectures; new conjectures have been offered for old ones; in some things we probably know more about Homeric times than Herodotus or Plato knew and in other things, it is likely, I believe, that we know less.

Although the expression "The Greeks" or "The Hellenes" (except as a small tribe in Thessaly) was unknown to Homer and Hesiod, and although Homer and Hesiod had no more in common with Aristotle and Menander than we have with the Anglo-Saxon bards and chroniclers, many writers have no hesitancy in ascribing to the Greeks (a people with a written history at least three thousand years old) qualities as peculiarly Greek and common to all Greeks, which means common to lunkheads out of Theophrastus as well as to Pindaric heroes.

The Greeks have been endowed with impossible virtues and superhuman intelligence; and they have been held responsible for some of the most crack-brained ideas that ever entered the mind of man. That is because their literature has celebrated many virtues, voiced great aspirations, and mirrored great intelligences of great imaginations; and it is also because Greek literature, in parts, is sometimes wholly insupportable and preposterous in its notions.

Nudist cults seek to justify their quite harmless eccentricity (which may or may not have some social or therapeutic value) by saying that their members are seeking to return to the Greek ideal of health and away from our modern unnatural and prurient modesty; and, tangentially, they are right; for, whereas in different periods and in different cities of Greek custom we find extremes of modesty, for a time at least in Sparta it was a civic requirement for youths and maidens to wrestle naked in the open air as part of their state discipline and physical training. Yet the women in Homer are fully and sometimes elaborately clothed; Herodotus speaks of some Lydians and foreigners of his time so modest that the men are ashamed to be seen undressed before one another; and from a passage in Lysias, who was a contemporary of Plato, we know that some Athenian women carried the proprieties to such lengths that not only would they not be seen abroad in the daylight fully clothed but secluded themselves from the sight of men so carefully that they would not even permit their kinsmen to see them.

When a Professor Pangloss seeks to demolish a bugaboo of his own creation, he has no hesitancy about calling in the Greeks to sustain him whenever his argument is weakest; and this is easy enough for him to do because the Greeks, even the best of them, had some ideas that now seem to us silly or erroneous. Greece even in its Golden Age had its Panglosses, and its Pecksniffs, its Podsnaps, its Puritans, its profligates, its retired military colonels, its old dodos, its old soaks, its noisy members of the younger generation and its Babbitts, as well as its men and women of courage, dignity, resourcefulness, intelligence, honor and good sense.

Oscar Wilde before *Reading Gaol* believed he was comporting himself after the best ideals of Greek culture; and, if the best ideals of Greek culture meant to him the ideals, say, of Agathon, the poet playwright who is described by Aristotle, Plato, Xenophon, Aristophanes and Euripides who knew him, then it appears that Wilde was very like Agathon in temperament, character, vices, career and talent, and in the kind and extent of his popularity. Edward Carpenter and John Addington Symonds in their essays on the passionate friendships of men for men and especially between men and boys have plenty to support them from the text of Plato, which is probably the reason why Plato's remarks on love are so generally if vaguely distasteful to most men and women now. And, on the other hand, the *Odyssey* is primarily a parable of early Greek domestic life, of the faithful love of husband and wife which, on the wife's side at least, survived years of separation and against rumors that her husband was dead and against an importunate band of young and vigorous suitors.

There are few scholars or philosophers who can resist the temptation to fob off their less tenable ideas as being ideas in general currency among the Greeks at all times. Things have come to such a pass in this regard that when you encounter a passage anywhere in which a writer says that the Greeks thought thus and so, or the Greeks were like this or that, prick up your ears and be on guard. The writer may be talking sense; he may be making a generalization on good authority. But he also may be pushing an egocentric and insupportable idea and holding the long suffering Greeks responsible for it. The catch in this is that you can cite a passage from some Greek author to prove almost anything you wish to prove, because the Greeks were not "The Greeks" in any too-narrow or peculiar sense, but a race of people bearing many strains, infused with many cultures, rich in varieties and extremes of temperament, homogeneous in the growth and development of their social customs but heterogeneous in character and personality, who produced over a comparatively long period of time a great body of all sorts of literature, much of which is lost to us now and known only in fragments and in references to it in the literature that has come down to us. The storehouse of Greek literature is so rich in substance and variety (though not in bulk) that only English literature among the literatures of the world has surpassed it.

WHEN writers speak of "The Greeks," they usually have in mind not a people, not a community of persons, but an abstraction. Specifically they have in mind an abstract conception of an ideal Greek of the fifth or fourth centuries B.C. More specifically they have in mind their personal vision of what an ideal Athenian was like during a period of about fifty years in three thousand years of Greek history. Needless to say, no such Greek ever existed, quite, in the flesh.

It is incautious to generalize about Greek religion (i.e., to say it was polytheistic) or about what religion meant to the Greeks, because in reading Greek literature chronologically we can see that the recognized religion constantly underwent subtle and profound changes; that some Greeks were polytheists and some were not, even when they were contemporanous; that some Greeks were highly superstitious and some seem to have had no superstitious fears or practices, some were atheistical or skeptical or indifferent, and some were without any religious experience at all. It is not correct to say that the Greeks were healthy, for common colds, pneumonia and malaria for centuries have been endemic in all Hellas; the Greeks of Thessaly appear to have been especially susceptible during a long period to tuberculosis and erysipelas; and at the very outset of their days of the greatest glory of the Athenian city state plagues began to kill them off periodically in alarmingly increasing numbers.

It is incautious to say that the Greeks owed the greatness of their great period in Athens to the fact that they "followed the golden mean," because in their great period there were Greeks in high circles who were licentious, greedy, gluttonous and debauched, who were murderous, belligerent, treacherous, treasonable, extravagant and ignoble. (On the evidence of the practical results of Socrates' teaching it would seem that the Athenians were not unjustified in putting Socrates to death on the charge of corrupting youth; for whereas Plato seems to have nourished his genius by the counsel of Socrates, the favorite pupil, the great hope of Socrates, was Alcibiades. It was in Alcibiades that Socrates hoped to bring his teaching into the full flower of noble action in the person and character of an hereditary prince. And Alcibiades developed into one of the most unconscionable scoundrels in Athenian history, debauched and traitorous. He was disgraced and banished by the Athenians; but not before he had brought about the ruin of Athens. "The whole family," argues Lysias in his oration against Alcibiades the Younger, "is utterly detestable." And Lysias gives pretty good reasons for his assertion, even if we allow much for the extravagances of a speech for the prosecution in ancient times or now.)

The Greeks, in fine, were people. And whatever were their circumstances at any period of their long and varied history, as individuals they differed in character and personality, habits and points of view, quirks of mind and neuroses, virtues and vices as any crowd of persons that swarm into the Grand Central Station in New York between five and six on a week-day afternoon. Incautious scholars, inadequately versed in Greek literature, frequently reiterate the opinion that nervous breakdowns and insanity are largely the result of the conditions of modern urban life, with its hurry and stress and noise and anxieties, and that if we returned to the pure ideals of the Greeks our asylums would close and the psychiatrists would be out of business. But in the time of Greece's greatest glory, nervous breakdowns and insanity were common, and you will find many references to them in the medical treatises of Hippocrates, who was a contemporary of Socrates. The average, everyday Athenian citizen of the great Attic period was, it appears, harassed continually by poverty, worried by debts and petty business cares, bothered by responsibilities involving not only his livelihood but the health and moods of his wife, his children, and his servants, when he had any. Some of them grew erratic, apathetic, listless and incapable of stirring from their beds; some developed manias and delusions—aggravated, it seems, by the priestly quacks whom Hippocrates hated, gentry who regarded "melancholy" or nervous breakdowns and insanity as sacred diseases and tried to cure them by incantations instead of ordering the patients to take rest and quiet and regulate their diet, which was Hippocrates' method of treatment.

The Greeks, I repeat, were people. Hurl a ball of twine into any crowd anywhere and the strand will touch the clothing of people who are in most essentials like the Greeks. In the crowd there might not be any one who, after killing some one, would take the precaution of cutting off the arms and legs or otherwise maiming and crippling the corpse, as a Homeric Greek might do, to prevent the ghost from doing him bodily damage, but there might be many who had beliefs and superstitions akin at least to the beliefs and superstitions of the Greeks.

THE Greeks were people and that, indeed, is what makes a great portion of Greek literature such interesting reading to us. If the Greeks were a race apart, differing in any great essentials from us in thoughts and emotions, we simply would not experience, while reading them, that "emotion of recognition" which is essential for the enjoyment of all imaginative literature. The will to believe is so strong in most of us that we usually can be convinced only when we are emotionally inclined to believe what we read or hear. Therefore, if certain kinds of Greek thought were not something toward which we were already emotionally sympathetic or receptive, these thoughts would be Greek to us in the literal sense of those who cannot read Greek.

But Greek literature and Greek thought and feeling as expressed in that literature are parts of our tradition, parts of the
cultural background of Western civilization. That is why Professor
G. Lowes Dickinson could write in one of the depression years,
1931, a little book (*Plato and His Dialogues*), wherein he drew a
close parallel between the social and political ideas that were in
ferment in Plato's time and ours, because Plato's *The Republic* was
written during a great general economic breakdown in the Grecian
world, when thinkers and visionaries were turning over in their
minds speculations about an ideal arrangement of human relationships and plans for a social and economic organization which would
be ideal, just and sound, and never subject to the hazards of unforeseen misfortune or of human ineptitude. Plato was, in his didactic
writings, very like any one of several dozens of socially minded pub-
licists who began to think critically and emotionally on the social
and economic system in Europe and America after the worldwide
depression that followed the New York Stock Exchange panic of
1929. Aristotle's *Poetics* remains, I think, the best of all available
analyses of literary technique and values, and Aristotle's *Rhetoric*
(at least in the expanded and carefully edited translation of Professor Lane Cooper of Cornell University) remains the most valuable and most practical of all handbooks on the art of writing. The
Oath of Hippocrates (readily obtainable in the handy and invaluable Loeb series of translations) still guides the ethics of physicians
and surgeons in the Western world; and its prohibition of abortion is
still the most generally observed mandate in it, the one to which
physicians usually adhere even when they violate all the others.
Lawyers still model their addresses to juries on speeches by Demosthenes, Aeschines and Lysias, and politicians go to Demosthenes and
Thucydides for phrases and sentiments in golden hyperbole for use
on patriotic occasions.

The two great Greek epics, the *Iliad* and the *Odyssey,* stand
by common consent among the great achievements of the human
spirit, because the stories they tell are so simple, fresh, and human
that no translation whatever, whether it be grandiloquent like Chapman's or pedestrian like William Cullen Bryant's or too sharp and
sophisticated like Pope's, or a trifle smug at times like Lang, Leaf
and Myers', or in unbuttoned, quiet unpoetic prose like Samuel
Butler's, can destroy the charm and interest of them. Although I
know that it is unorthodox and that those Greek scholars, who have
labored years to attain that perfection in Greek which entitles them

to form an exclusive little club of special enjoyment all their own, will not like this, I suspect that Greek is, of all languages, the one that loses least in translation, from poetry or prose; for there is so much substance in Greek literature, and its form is usually so simple and yet so natural, that only the subtleties of the decadence of that literature escape us wholly in translation. And even Lucian's dialogues, which came late in Greek literature, sound as if they might have been written by a contemporary, so like the people we know are the people of the dialogues, so like them in every quirk and accent; and Athenæus has preserved for us from Menander a mordant humorous description of a dinner with one's relatives which might have appeared without change, as it appears in a good translation, in the pages of *The New Yorker* or *Punch*.

Many scholars, since Hedelin and Perrault first raised the question at the beginning of the eighteenth century, have doubted the existence of Homer and have attempted wholly to dissociate the Homer of early Greek tradition from the authorship of the *Iliad* and the *Odyssey*. But the ancients never doubted Homer's authorship of the poems. Herodotus not only believed that Homer was the poet responsible for the form of the epics as he knew them, but that he knew when Homer died. After examining the evidence, I am constrained to cast my lot with Herodotus.

I believe Herodotus was probably right in setting the date when Homer flourished as not earlier than four hundred years before Herodotus' time, even though, when Herodotus wrote that opinion, he knew he was at odds with some of the current critical opinion. Furthermore, I believe that Homer was literate, that is, that he knew how to read and write, that he had traveled a great deal, and that he was an inventive as well as a correlative genius; and this belief of mine too, while controverted by a considerable body of the most modern scholarly opinion, is not only the belief held by Herodotus but by a great number of ancient critics.

Herodotus was an interesting and, in some ways, a peculiar person. He undertook to write a history of the world from ancient times to his own, after much investigation and travel and in his declining years. His purpose was definite: "in order that the actions of men may not be effaced by time, nor the great and wondrous deeds displayed both by Greeks and foreigners deprived of renown, and among other things (to show by the publication of these researches) for what causes men waged war upon each other."

Up until the time of Herodotus (he was a contemporary of Socrates, although about fifteen years older) there had been no attempt in prose to give a true, coherent account of the history of the Greek people. There had been fabulists in prose before him and travelers, like him, bringing back to Athens accounts of the customs, trading practices, engineering and nautical feats, religions and articles of commerce of other nations; but, in the main, the prose fabulists had simply written variations of the more ancient legends perpetuated by the poets and reciters of lays.

Herodotus was born into a skeptical, inquiring and critical age; an age wherein the Athenians, whose cultural development had hitherto been rather provincial and self-sufficient, were beginning to expand their commerce rapidly, enjoy contacts with alien peoples, and learn what they could about the religious rites, philosophy, science and industrial development of other nations. Cultivated Athenians had begun, not only seriously to doubt the divinity of the gods in the Homeric and Hesiodic pantheon, but to doubt the ethical validity of these "Bibles" of the Greeks. Even "impiety" or "blasphemy," although still on the law books and punishable by death, had begun to lose their religious significance and were used for any teaching thought to be contrary to good morals. Euripides was tried for "impiety" for having written the "immoral" line in the *Hippolytus:* "My tongue has sworn but my mind remains unsworn." Euripides was freed on the quite modern plea that those were not his own sentiments or practices but true only to the character he was portraying.

THE higher criticism of Homer and Hesiod had already begun to undermine the authority of the *Iliad* and the *Odyssey* and had already begun to dispute, as we have seen, the authenticity of the legends about the epics and about Homer's connection with them. Once authority is undermined there is a tendency to make a thorough job of it. This iconoclasm was to proceed in the time of Herodotus to a critical review of all the ancient writings showing the divergences from Homer, to a dispute about the time Homer lived and the manner in which the epics came into being. It was to continue on into and beyond the time of Plato, who placed so little reliance upon the authority, ethical responsibility or social value of poets that he would exclude all of them from his ideal Republic and make the writing of poetry a misdemeanor or, in some cases, a high crime punishable by exile or death.

Herodotus was an intellectual heir to this general tendency toward inquiry and reconsideration of the poetic legends regarding Greece's past. He himself had heard, for instance, a version of the story of Paris and Helen from the lips of Egyptian priests, in consonance with the story that had long been accepted and in circulation among the Trojans.

Briefly this story was that Paris, son of Priam, raided Sparta and carried off the treasure and the wife of King Menelaus; that storms drove Paris ashore in Egypt where he, Helen and the looted treasure were held captive by Thonis, governor at the Canopic mouth of the Nile, on the order of King Proteus of Thebes, who had heard about Paris' wrongdoing; that the other Greeks of the Peninsula, hearing of the woe of Menelaus, sent armies to join him in a descent upon Troy to demand the return of Helen and the loot; that the Trojans truthfully denied they harbored either Helen or the loot, and the Greeks, not believing them, laid siege to Troy; that when the Greeks had captured the city, they found that Helen and the treasure were not there; and only then did the Greek give credence to the Trojan story and dispatch Menelaus to Egypt to recover his wife and treasure, which he did.

Now I want to show what a good critic Herodotus was, and how cautious and careful and conscientious. He repeated some whoppers, surely, and his history is studded with preposterous reports to which we need attach but little faith. But there is one peculiarity about Herodotus which should be observed and that is the careful distinction he always made as to (1) what he himself knew to be true after careful investigation, (2) what he had an opinion about—the reasons for his opinion he is usually careful to set forth,—and, (3) what he heard from others and set down, for what it is worth, without any opinion about it at all. Many things were told him about which he could reach no opinion, because he had no means of investigating the facts. That is why, to a superficial reader, he may seem to be credulously accepting many impossible wonders. But, to the careful reader, Herodotus is a thoroughly reliable reporter: his "they say" or "I heard" differs greatly from "my opinion is" and both of these differ greatly from his "I know this to be true."

It is also characteristic of Herodotus that when he cannot know a thing very definitely and offer proof, he says that he has an opinion only when he has investigated a problem pretty thoroughly and therefore believes he has something definite to go on. If he is definite about his opinion and curt in stating it, you can take it, I believe, that he is not just being capricious.

Listen to him then on Homer and Hesiod: "Whence each of the gods sprung, whether they existed always, and of what form they were, was, so to speak, unknown till yesterday. For I am of the opinion that Hesiod and Homer lived four hundred years before my time and not more, and that these were they who framed a theogony for the Greeks and gave names to the gods and assigned to them honors and arts, and declared their several forms. But the poets, said to have been before them, in my opinion were after them."

Herodotus was born in 484 B.C., and thus he places Homer and Hesiod as not earlier than 884 B.C. You will observe that one part of his opinion coincides with the most modern scholastic opinion, that is, that the hymns attributed to Homer and Hesiod in the time of Herodotus (and in the time of George Chapman who translated the *Battle of the Frogs and Mice,* the *Hymn to Apollo,* the *Hymn to Hermes,* the *Hymn to Venus* and shorter lays attributed to Homer) were of a later composition; and that they grew out of the Homeric poems by the efforts of later and lesser poets to compete with Homer and Hesiod.

We know that the texts of the *Iliad* and the *Odyssey* which we have are not exactly the ones familiar to all educated Greeks in the fourth and fifth centuries B.C., and we know that even Plato used one version of some lines when quoting from Homer while Aristotle used a different one, although they were contemporary, and that it is the text Plato knew that has come down to us. So either Aristotle's memory was faulty when he thought he was quoting Homer or in Aristotle's and Plato's time there were editions of Homer which differ as widely in text as the first and second folios of Shakespeare.

It will be my argument that Herodotus was essentially right and that Homer was a real person whose career and whose genius were not too unlike Shakespeare's; that the impress of Homer's individual genius is upon both the *Iliad* and the *Odyssey,* however much he may have lifted and selected and adapted to his uses the material other poets had already worked upon before him. Every one who has read both epics has observed that identical lines occur in both the *Iliad* and the *Odyssey,* although the *Iliad* seems to be a trifle more youthful than the *Odyssey,* and that parts of the *Odyssey* (the eleventh chapter, for instance) are more primitive than other parts, and that the *Odyssey* is not quite one story but two not closely related ones, one of which keeps interrupting the other.

But there is every considerable reason for believing that these two epics, as we have them and as Plato knew them, were the compositions of one man, a comparatively civilized and educated man who could read and write (and not a simple primitive singer of lays accompanied by a lyre), who wrote not a few years, comparatively speaking, after the Trojan war, but several centuries afterward when, to get an audience at all, a poet would have to offer some noticeable improvement upon the outworn lays recited by beggarly bards.

Homer himself was contemptuous of all these "bards" save Demodicus, and so it is sensible not to confuse him with them. They were in Homer's time, at worst, annoyances like the little German band and the hurdy-gurdy with out-of-date tunes today, and at best—when the bards were called upon as entertainers at large banquets—they were sometimes bores because they had only old stuff to offer. So Homer complains. He complains of the dearth of new themes, and the outworn character of the material at hand. He portrays Penelope as exasperated beyond measure by the continual whang-whanging of the pestiferous bard outside her door. It was bad enough, she thought, to have the hundred suitors tearing up the turf in front of her house by spear throwing and quoits and then eating her out of house and home; but the last straw of exasperation was the monotonous twang of the bard: she orders him to be got rid of at once. Again at a large feast of nobles and notables, where the most expensive entertainment would presumably be provided, Homer pictures the host so bored by the bard's recital that he orders the gymnasts out to perform to the music while the recital is going on.

I am constrained, in the face of such evidence as this, not to accept the notion of those scholars who would deprive Homer of his identity and who imagine that the Homeric epics date back to the dim recesses of Greek history when there was no writing and the heroic narratives were handed down by word of mouth. Probably in the tenth century B.C., if the Trojan war really dated that far back, there had already begun to develop recitals of events which took place in that war and these recitals were in verse form usually, so that they might the more easily be memorized.

Such recitals may have been something like the popular folk songs and recitals of our own sophisticated times—"Casey Jones," "Ivan Petruski Skivah" and "Abdul, the Bulbul Ameer," "The Face

on the Barroom Floor," and "Frankie and Johnny," or like the old
Scotch, Celtic and English ballads. But it is my contention that none
of these recitals and ballads, anonymous as they have usually been
and existing in varying versions, was without an original author nor
did they spring spontaneously from the race consciousness of the
people. It took a verse writer, one whose imagination worked easily
and readily and who had a certain technical gift, which differs
slightly from the prosy mind, to write even a "Frankie and Johnny"
and to bring "Sir Patrick Spense" or the song of Ivan Petruski
Skivah and Abdul, the Bulbul Ameer, to their fine haunting technical
perfection, and that even if there were earlier versions to work on
they required a special skill and a special kind of mind to bring
them into being.

I think it is possible that Homer may have been the poet's
nickname or rather what corresponds to our "stage name." The
name attributed to the author of the *Iliad* and the *Odyssey* and the
word for "joined together" are the same (*Homeros*), although this
definition seems to have escaped that vigilant and careful Hellenist,
Gilbert Murray, who follows the old scholars, who give only the
definition "hostage" for *homeros,* a usage that does not occur until
the time of Herodotus. (My Liddell and Scott's Greek lexicon tells
me that, "According to the old Ionic Life of Homer, *homeros* in
the Cumean dialect was *tuphlos,* whence some explain the tradition
of Homer's blindness," *tuphlos* meaning "blind.")

It is probable, also, that Homer was the first to draw the individual and varying versions of the Trojan exploit and its aftermath
together into one continuous and unified narrative, and that his first
effort in this direction was the *Iliad,* which is a unified story, nar-
rating only the principal events of the last few days of a seven
years' siege. This may have been so considerable a success that
Homer was next induced to try to tell another story and at the same
time draw into it a more comprehensive account of the gods, the
underworld, the demigods and monsters and to establish their relationship with the living world. I think it is probable, as Herodotus
believes, that at about the same time another poet, Hesiod, with a
less heroic, less urban and less sophisticated imagination, bucolic
and close to nature, was also trying to get some system into the
confused and confusing popular notions of the nature and character
of the gods.

This, if one grants the premise, was not so much a matter of
invention as a matter of selection, synthesis and judgment, aided

and abetted by a poetic imagination and a fine sense of word values and imagery. A serviceable memory and sure taste, such as Shakespeare or any other great poet has, would draw neatly into the appropriate setting those homely axioms and observations that were already current coin among the people, taking care to give them just that appearance of novelty which would arrest attention and that perfection of syllable which would make them perfect and unforgettable.

It was such a poet, I believe, that Homer was; and, indeed, as Herodotus relates, he did "frame" or "organize" or "put together" a theogony for the Greeks and give names to the gods (that is, rejected the Persian and Egyptian and varying local Doric and Ionic names for the same gods) and assigned to them honors and arts and declared their several forms. I believe, too, that Homer, when he came to write the *Iliad* and later the *Odyssey,* knew the Egyptian, Trojan and Hellenic versions of the siege of Troy and that he could never quite make up his mind which version to choose, the Trojan version or the one prevalent in Sparta, Athens, and in all Hellas generally, and that this indecision caused him never quite to decide which hero he favored, Hector or Achilles. It may have been, of course, that he prepared two versions, one to recite on the Asiatic side of the Ægean and another to recite on the Grecian side. I think it is obvious that he got around a great deal and was known and in popular demand in most of the civilized cities on the borders of the Ægean (somewhat as a great concert artist nowadays), and it may have been as a result of his peregrinations that seven cities later claimed to be his birthplace.

This hypothesis would conform with the name Homer, as a startling, unusual, memorable and onomatopoeic name for his calling, in which he was obviously the most renowned, overshadowing rivals or predecessors like Orpheus, Musaeus, and Bakides. All these names, like Strongfort, Houdini, the Swedish Nightingale, were, in the language of modern producers and impresarios, good names for "billing"; they were memorable and uncommon names, combinations or derivations meant to convey to the prospective audience the nature and quality of the performance. Homer was the poet, composer, recitalist, who had joined together into one stupendous, exciting, marvelous and perfect narrative the story of the Trojan War and the story of the Wanderings of Ulysses. Homeros! Ladies and gentlemen, Homeros!

This explanation also follows very closely the earliest mention of the Homeric epics, mention which has somehow unaccountably confused and puzzled good Greek scholars. The earliest reference to Homer by name and in direct reference to the *Odyssey* is by Pindar (about 500 B.C.), who also speaks of the "Homeridae, singers of stitched lays."

This word "Homeridae" seems to have given a great many scholars, including as recent a commentator as Gilbert Murray, more trouble than it should. The suffix commonly means "of the family (or clan) of," and there are scholars who have believed there were poets claiming to be descendants of Homer and thus claiming proprietary rights in Homer's epics. Or, according to Gilbert Murray, the word may have referred to a clan of minstrels or to minstrels in general. One sees how Professor Murray, even with his usual perspicacity, missed the significance of the suffix; because he admits to only a casual acquaintance with Hippocrates and omits a discussion of Hippocrates from his brilliantly inaccurate but thoroughly enjoyable *Literature of Ancient Greece*.

If Professor Murray had read Hippocrates, his keen eyes would have seen that there were physicians in Hippocrates' time, among whom Hippocrates counted himself one, who called themselves the Asclepiadae. This did not mean that they claimed descent from Asclepius any more than the Freudians of today claim descent from Sigmund Freud. It simply means that these physicians followed a certain diagnostic and therapeutic method, a method, which as Hippocrates explains by inference, was a radical departure from the old methods of healing generally in vogue among the priests.* The Asclepian method, followed and developed by Hippocrates, included not only a general study and investigation of the physiology of the body but of chemistry and physics.

Nor is there much reason for believing, as some scholars are

* Asclepius is mentioned by Homer, *Iliad* 11,729, as having two sons, Podaleirius and Machaon, both of them physicians in the Achaean army. Hesiod tells the story of the birth of Asclepius, making him of semi-divine origin. Pindar in his third Pythian Ode accepts Hesiod's account and expands it. From these accounts I cannot accept the argument of those scholars who would make Asclepius a myth. They forget that deification and semi-deification of mortal men and women is an ancient practice which still obtains in the Roman Catholic church. I accept the testimony of the ancients that Asclepius was a famous physician from Thessalian Trikka. He enjoyed the happy fate of many famous mortals of being made into a god long after his death. The process of the pagan canonization is explained at length in Lewis Richard Farnell's *Greek Hero Cults and Ideas of Immortality*.

inclined to believe, that the Asclepiadae were a clan of hereditary physicians who claimed to be descendants of Asclepius, the god of healing. It seems more likely that Hippocrates, who suffered no supernatural nonsense about him and who was a practicing physician and a trainer of physicians and surgeons, belonged to a school of medical thought or perhaps a clinic or guild which called its members the Asclepiadae. This school or guild to which Hippocrates belonged had a code of ethics and a method that distinguished them from other physicians, especially priestly ones.

The Homeridae, therefore, were singers or reciters who followed Homer's method, as the Delsartians are the followers of the dancing method of Delsarte. A Thespian is still a general term for an actor, as Saw-bones is for a surgeon, but an Ibsenite or a Shavian has a special meaning and has reference to the style or method of Ibsen or Shaw. (One cannot look too closely at modern life to find analogies which will help us to understand the ancients. We are, for instance, inclined to think of "ghost-writing" as a modern institution. Yet it is more than probable that Thucydides wrote Pericles' speeches for him and it was a common practice of Greek historians at the beginning of their careers to put out their work as the work of some person with a well-known name, to insure a better sale through the book sellers.)

Now let me tell you a true story (which the scholars among you know already) of how we came to possess the copies of the *Iliad* and the *Odyssey* that we have. It may shake your faith in the divine order of things or it may confirm your belief that the ways of God are truly inscrutable. Homer was lost and forgotten to the reading world for centuries during the Middle Ages, unknown to the starveling Greeks, even to the few scholars that remained among them. Homer was hearsay to a few Greeks and nothing to the rest of the world. Hebraic and Christian literature, Christian thought, Christian homilies and Christian dialectic had submerged the pagan joy and naïveté and the sweet, simple brilliance of Homer and of all the Greek thought and literature that followed it.

In the late Middle Ages, either through a pious sense of their undetermined responsibility or out of a simple, human devilishness and irrepressible carnality, the monks had preserved, copied and kept hidden many pagan Greek texts—possibly for their own damnable delectation during monotonous and dreary hours, perhaps often

copying and illuminating manuscripts which they could not understand—but Greek literature had passed rather generally out of
knowledge and was known only as it sifted through in the Latin
language which was the literary language and the language of the
Church of Rome. Of pagan writers only Virgil stood out, counte-
nanced, honored and unread, and that was because the Christian
Fathers or Christian sciolists had discovered that in one of the
Eclogues of Virgil (still semi-deified in the hearts of Italian peasants, who had learned Virgil at their grandmothers' knees) there
was an ambiguous passage which might be construed as announcing
the end of paganism and the birth of Christianity. So Virgil was
saved. He took his place as first among the pagans who, through no
fault of his own, was not a Christian; and so was honored by Dante
in deference to the unanimous thought of the time (of those who
had any thoughts on the subject at all) that Virgil was almost as
good as a Christian and a skilled writer of Latin verse to boot.

But of Greek literature there was only oblivion. The man who
was responsible for restoring Homer to the then modern world in
the fourteenth century, A.D., was a fantastic boor, drunkard, cadger
and scoundrel. The man who put him to work translating Homer
was a reformed writer of facetious stories; and the man who had
undertaken to restore the beauties of Greek literature to the world
was a man who could not read a line of Greek to save his neck.

This amazing trio to whom we owe our Homer were: one
Leontius Pilatus, Giovanni Boccaccio and Francesco Petrarca
(known to us as Petrarch). The extraordinary circumstance involving them happened after unusual devastations of the bubonic plague
had reduced Florentian (and all Italian) prosperity to its last gasp,
when Boccaccio had grown old, uncreative and unappreciative of his
own incomparable contribution to world literature and when Petrarch
had foregone the writing of poetry and was a fussy, dominating old
man who had never read the two great geniuses of his own time,
Dante and Boccaccio, even though one of them was a disciple of his
(Petrarch's) new craze for the "Humanities" about which he knew
so little.

Leontius Pilatus (as he called himself) was an eccentric and
amusing adventurer, with an indefinite history probably kept obscure
for reasons known to the police, who showed up in Venice about the
middle of the fourteenth century and earned a living by his wits.
He seems to have had a curious and miscellaneous general culture,
some knowledge (very rare) of classical literature, Greek and

Roman, a propensity for quarreling and drink, for showing off, for insulting people, and for entertaining them. He pretended to come from Thessaly but was really from Calabria, where a bastard Greek was still spoken, and it seems probable that he studied at Athens. He was hairy, uncouth, extremely ugly and personally filthy. He was so weird and interesting a creature that Boccaccio, who had a little money and a home, brought him from Venice to Florence and entertained him for three years. That is, Pilatus appears to have accepted Boccaccio's invitation to his house as a perpetual one and to have come for a visit and stayed three years.

Meanwhile Boccaccio, who was a simple genius who had written immortal stories in the rich and vital Italian of the common spoken language of the time, had an immense respect, amounting almost to idolatry, for Petrarch, an older man who had won fame as a poet and was renowned as something of a Latin scholar. Petrarch made Boccaccio feel ashamed of having written in Italian, the vulgar tongue. Petrarch had, for some reason, become convinced that the way out of the despair of the hard times of the late Middle Ages was to revive the study of Greek, for among the learned men of his time there seemed to be the impression that the forgotten Greek literature held the key to the troubles then confronting the world.

Pilatus, you can well believe, shirked work whenever he could but the time seems to have come when Boccaccio saw a way whereby Pilatus could make some effort toward earning his keep. Pilatus had let it be known that he knew ancient Greek well enough to translate it and that he knew where he could lay hands on a manuscript of Homer. You can imagine with what a thrill Boccaccio received this news. It would mean, if he could get Pilatus to turn Homer into Latin, that his master Petrarch could read Homer and could thus take the first step on his own account in his proposed revival of the Humanities.

So Pilatus translated Homer into crude Latin prose to Petrarch's great joy and to the great joy of the other ignorant but hopeful Humanists Petrarch had gathered around him. There were, according to Petrarch, after the Humanist movement had got well under way, just five persons in all Florence who knew Homer, two in Verona, and one each in Bologna, Mantua and Solmona and none in Rome. It was certain that Boccaccio was one of these only by courtesy, because he confesses that although he tried hard and took many notes he did not understand much of Pilatus' Latin. But an enthusiasm for Homer in Latin spread gradually but surely, reviving an interest in Greek language and literature itself, producing a Greek-Latin lexicon, and bringing about in 1488 the first printed edition of the Greek text of Homer, under the editorship of Demetrius Chalcondyles, a visiting Greek lecturer, brought from Athens to Florence. Other editions, commentaries and scholia on the *Iliad* and *Odyssey* appeared, along with the printing of the Aldine editions published in 1504 and 1517, by which time Homer had become exceedingly popular and the lode for literary miners which has never played out.

It cannot truthfully be said that an enthusiasm for Greek and Latin literature of any kind, except that which was popular and current, ever amounted generally to a passion among the Italians of the Renaissance; for, as James Branch Cabell has written, "literature is a starveling cult kept alive by the literary," who have, it may be added, something of a vested interest in it. Nor was Petrarch or Boccaccio quite aware that in their youth they had produced immortal literature of their own; that Dante, who had died in Petrarch's youth, had produced a classic which was to make him the most perennially popular book-end (with replicas of Rodin's "Thinker" a poor second); and that Boccaccio had produced the book which for centuries would be the one which boys seem first to discover when curiosity begins to stir in them about what it is like to be in bed with a woman. (Montaigne confesses that the *Decameron*, the *Kisses* of Johannes Secundus and *Rabelais* were the books that helped him over the stile of adolescent curiosity.)

I HAVE given, I think, something more than a vague indication of what I believe Homer was like, how he wove the existing narratives of the Greek heroes of his time into sustained epics and breathed new life and spirit into them; how he probably earned a good livelihood going from town to town reciting his epics and permitting copyists to make transcripts of his poems for wealthy men and princes at a handsome fee; and how he founded a "school," not by organizing one but by example, as we speak of the Hemingway school; meaning the kind of writing done by Ernest Hemingway and his imitators. I think it is probable, too, that Homer earned an occasional prize in money in competition with other lyrists at the semi-secular, semi-religious holidays and festivals, as journeyman contestants go from county fair to county fair to compete for prizes or as cowboys go from Cheyenne to Pendleton and Forth Worth to compete at roping, steer-riding and broncho-busting in the rodeos.

That Homer *may* have been a blind and humble bard, begging his bread from door to door and town to town and offering to recite lays for a handout as tramps now offer to saw wood, mow the lawn or dust the rugs, I do not deny. Nor do I deny the possibility that seems to have occurred to some scholars but to have revolted them beyond measure—that the *Iliad* and the *Odyssey*, as we now have them, are the work of an editor or "recensionist," ordered by the tyrant Pisistratus (about 550 B.C.) to prepare official versions of the epics for use at the Festival of the Panathenea.

This was the belief of Pausanias, Cicero and Josephus. The Panathenea was a national celebration, patriotic and religious in character, where the Homeric epics or parts of them were recited, presumably, somewhat as the "Star-Spangled Banner" is played, the Declaration of Independence is read aloud and a prayer offered up, on certain solemn occasions in our national life, like the Fourth of July.

(The piety of such occasions among the Greeks, as among us, must not be stressed too much. It is safe to guess that among the Greeks, who listened to the epics as recited, there were some who had never heard them from beginning to end and didn't want to hear them and whose attention and applause were reflex actions and did not indicate their real sentiments. A national political convention was opened not long ago with a prayer spoken into the microphones, apparently with the idea that God was listening in on the radio, and before a battery of Klieg lights and cameras. When the prayer was concluded it was greeted by applause by the assembled delegates. It should not be assumed—I speak in the manner of a scholar elucidating an obscure point in a Greek text—it should not be assumed that this applause was occasioned by anything notable to which the preacher had called God's attention, so the inference would seem to be that the prayer was so long that the delegates forgot it was a holy petition addressed to God and thought it was a speech to a constituency.)

The more I think of the hypothesis of the recension of the epics under Pisistratus, the more I am inclined to believe there is something in it, especially since it does not invalidate in any way my impression of Homer and his connection with the epics, and only means that Homer was edited as definitive texts of Milton have recently been edited and published for the first time by the Columbia University Press, under the editorship of Frank Allen Patterson and a board of co-editors.

Murray rejects the hypothesis, saying: "The theory, then, that Pisistratus had somehow 'interpolated Homer' was current before Alexandrian times. Why does Aristarchus not mention it? We cannot say clearly. . . ." And he goes on to state the objections to accepting the hypothesis.

But, perhaps we do not have to go to Aristarchus or anybody else and need only to examine the text of the *Odyssey* as we have it. What is the name of Pisistratus doing in the *Odyssey?* He is depicted as the sixth son of Nestor, "peer of the gods in counsel," a young man, companion of Telemachus; and we are shown that he is dutiful, dashing, efficient and energetic, a marvelous charioteer and wise in his youth, as befits a child of Nestor. There is only one Pisistratus in early Greek legend and history and that is the spectacular political genius who, after a long struggle, became master of Athens, developed the naval, military and commercial power of the city state, governed wisely, adorned the city with some magnificent public works, including a temple of Apollo, and instituted the Panathenaic festival. He is said to have been the first person in Greece to collect a library.

Why shouldn't the editor employed by Pisistratus to make the recension of the epic texts, particularly if he were a poet, as he must have been,—why shouldn't he have worked in a flattering tribute to his master, even if Pisistratus did not order it done?

There is no particular anachronism in placing Pisistratus in the text as the companion of the youth Telemachus. It is certain, from *Iliad* xx, 280, that the author of the *Iliad* thought the then reigning king of Troy was a grandson of Æneas, whose parents were Anchises and Venus, according to the myth. If a grandson of Æneas was alive in the time of Homer, there is nothing incredible about Pisistratus' having been in his youth a companion of the youthful Telemachus, son of Ulysses. The poet who did this job of making a coherent and unified epic out of the *Iliad* and the *Odyssey* may have been called Homer, just as Alexandros in the epics was sometimes called Paris because he wore a leopard's skin.

I don't deny these possibilities nor do I deny that Samuel Butler has made out an entertaining and plausible case when he contends at length (in *The Authoress of the Odyssey* and in the notes and prefaces to his own vigorous and superb prose translations of the *Iliad* and the *Odyssey*) that the *Odyssey* was written by a young girl who

lived at the place now called Trapani on the west coast of Sicily, that she introduced herself into the narrative under the name of Nausicaa, and gave herself away as the author by not knowing at which end of a ship the rudder was placed and so, to be safe, placed rudders fore and aft. (Samuel Butler was a valuable social and intellectual irritant, whose mètier in life was to startle the stodgy and the complacent—the "big-wigs," he called them—of Victorian officialdom in almost every sphere of influence, the church, politics, scholarship, education, science and the family; and he did it with gusto in his work on Evolution, his unorthodox investigations of Homer and of Shakespeare's sonnets, his fructifying *Notebooks* and *Erewhon* on which George Bernard Shaw was weaned intellectually, and in his great and mordant study of Victorian family life and education, *The Way of All Flesh*.)

No, I do not deny anything about Homer that can't be proved one way or the other, or that is not contrary to visible evidence; and there is some of this visible evidence which I can account for as having escaped some commentators on Homer only on the ground that, while they have read other commentators, they have not read Homer attentively. Even that fine scholar, whom I admire and whose *The Greek Commonwealth* has meant so much to me and is such fruitful reading in these times, Alfred Zimmern, says that the Athenians of the very richest period of Athenian culture, did not know what beds were as we know them but slept on boards and hides, had no fire in their houses and no sanitary arrangements; whereas, from abundant evidence in the Homeric texts it is certain that Homer was familiar with houses that were two-storied and quite elaborate, with courtyards, open hearths, kitchens, comfortable four-poster beds with bedding, linen sheets, colored silk coverlets and netting to keep out mosquitoes, and with lavatories which had wash basins and hot water, unguents, perfumes and pomades, and water closets draining into cesspools. (See the description of the house and household of King Alcinous in Book VII of the *Odyssey* and of Penelope's house in Books I and III particularly.)

It is to the text of Homer we should go, I think, to clear up the scholastic muddle created by Hedelin and Perrault and pursued into a labyrinth of conjecture by German scholars and their followers in England and America.

On the one side it is argued that each of the epics is the result of a patching together of a great many separate lays, each song, or rhapsody or hymn or narrative having a separate authorship, some of these compositions going back to the very earliest period of Greek history. And yet with such a hypothesis, these same scholars continue to wonder why each of the epics is the artistic and narrative unit it is, written in dactylic hexameters throughout, in good Attic Greek with few archaic words or phrases. The reason is that they have confused the early bards and the common rhapsodists with Homer.

We know what the early bards were like and of what their songs consisted, because Homer tells us. They sang brief and familiar anecdotes or descriptive pieces like the passage describing the shield of Achilles in the *Iliad*. But they did not, I believe, sing whole epics running to fifteen thousand lines or more. In the Eighth book of the *Odyssey*, King Alcinous gives a great banquet in honor of Ulysses. While making preparations for the feast Alcinous says, "We will have Demodocus sing for us; there is no bard his equal whatever the choice of his subject." A servant brings Demodocus, "whom the Muse loved greatly, but had given both good and evil, for although she had endowed him with a divine gift for song, she had made him blind. Pontonous brought a seat for him among the guests, leaning it against a pillar. He hung the lyre for him on a peg over his head, and showed him where to feel for it with his hands. He also set a fair table with a basket of victuals by his side, and a cup of wine from which he might drink whenever he was so disposed."

First, Demodocus sings "The Quarrel of Ulysses and Achilles." It is a brief lay, of which Homer merely says that it recited the "fierce words" that passed between Ulysses and Achilles. This means, I take it, that the recital was in the dithyrambic style or in the fast, stirring rhythm of two dactyls and a spondee, followed by two dactyls and a spondee. It was certainly not in the epic style of Homer. When Demodocus has finished his song, a servant hangs his lyre on a peg for him and sets him on the road in the direction of the athletic games. After the athletic tournament has taken place, Alcinous decides he wants some music and dancing. But Demodocus has left his lyre at Alcinous' house and a servant is sent for it. The occasion now calls for a lighter song than was given at Alcinous' house and Demodocus chooses an appropriate lay, "The Love Affair of Mars and Venus." This recital is not only light; it is humorous and rather bawdy: the immortal gods are depicted as laughing at the words of Mercury who admits that he, too, would sleep with Venus, if he got the chance.

Now this "Love Affair of Mars and Venus," as Homer retells it in the *Odyssey*, is just one hundred lines long. But the point is, Homer *retells* it; he does not give us the song or recital as Demodocus gave it, although he quotes from it. If Homer were merely stringing existing lays together under the general title of the *Odyssey*, he would simply have lifted Demodocus' story verbatim. As it is, neither the story nor the meter was an integral part of the story Homer has to tell, which is "The Wanderings of Ulysses." In these wanderings Ulysses was entertained at a banquet in which a favorite bard sang and Homer is realist enough to describe the bard and tell us what he sang about, but he is also enough of an artist not to stick into his own narrative, unchanged, the whole "Love Affair of Mars and Venus" just as Demodocus sang it. Homer's composition, I take it, was to be read for pleasure as well as heard. In fact, it could scarcely be heard except in a series of recitals.

We also learn from this passage that Demodocus was not considered a social inferior, because at the feast in the evening he is seated with Alcinous and Ulysses. Ulysses cuts a fine slice of his own portion of roast pork and sends it over to Demodocus with the message that, although Demodocus has caused him pain by recalling the quarrel with Achilles, "I salute him none the less; the bards are honored and respected throughout the world, for the Muse teaches them their songs and loves them."

After the meal is over, Ulysses says to Demodocus, "There is no one in the world I admire more than I do you. You must have studied under the Muse, Jove's daughter, and under Apollo, so accurately do you sing of the return of the Achæans and of their sufferings and adventures. If you were not present to see these things, you must have heard of them from some one who was. Now, however, change your song and tell us of the wooden horse which Epeus made with the assistance of Minerva, and which Ulysses got by strategy inside the walls of Troy after filling it with the men who afterwards sacked the city. If you will sing this tale correctly, I shall tell the world how magnificently heaven has endowed you."

Again Homer does not give us Demodocus' exact words; he tells us the substance of Demodocus' version of "The Wooden Horse." Homer in Book IV has already had Menelaus recall the episode of the wooden horse. I think it is possible that Homer *may have been* introducing himself under the name of Demodocus into the *Odyssey* and this possibility gains weight when we realize that, whereas Homer is actually engaged in recounting the woes and adventures of the returning Achæans—the thing for which Ulysses praises Demodocus—Ulysses has not actually heard Demodocus sing anything of the sort. Ulysses has heard Demodocus sing of the love of Mars and Venus and of the quarrel of Ulysses and Achilles, and later he hears him sing "The Wooden Horse." None of these lays has to do with the return of the Achæans.

But it is more probable, I think, that Homer felt himself superior to a bard like Demodocus, although he honored Demodocus above a bard like Phemius, whom we encounter in the first book of the *Odyssey*. Homer was a greater composer, a more accomplished technician and he knew it. He does not sing brief lays or ballads; he is writing a much more ambitious work, a work to be read as well as recited, a work consisting of twenty-four chapters or "books," each book corresponding with a letter in the Greek alphabet and yet one continuous narrative of "The Wanderings of Ulysses."

In the *Iliad,* Homer had already sung one unified theme, "The Wrath of Achilles." In the opening lines of each epic Homer states his theme and in each case, although he amplifies the theme, he sticks to it. The *Iliad* does not relate the history of the Trojan War, which lasted nine years; it has to do with events of the last few days of the siege and specifically with one great dramatic episode which occurred during those eventful days.

Many critics, both ancient and modern, have remarked the fact that whereas the *Iliad* appears to be addressed primarily to men, the *Odyssey* appears to be addressed primarily to women. The *Iliad* certainly is more of a man's book than the *Odyssey*. The one celebrates heroic deeds, courage and loyalty; the other celebrates adventure in times of peace and the virtue of the faithful love of man and wife.

In fact, part of the *Odyssey* seems to have been written less *for* women than *at* them. Homer, in effect, is telling the women who read the *Odyssey* that they should be like Penelope. They, as she did, should remain forever faithful to their lawfully wedded husbands, even when the husband is absent for many years and has been given up for dead. The wife should guard the husband's house and hearth inviolate while he is away, no matter what the circumstances. The husband may come back home after wandering about the world for many years, and he may even admit physical infidelity under certain temptations in which he did not have his heart, and this the wife is asked by Homer not only to believe but to condone and to rejoice that he is back home again, even if, as Ulysses does in the *Odyssey,* he stays home but a few days before he resumes his wandering.

The sub-surface didactic quality of the *Odyssey* is enough, in my mind, to dispose of the ingenious and entertaining hypothesis of Samuel Butler, who contended that the *Odyssey* was written by a woman, or rather more precisely, by a young girl. It might be argued that a young unmarried woman, anxious to appear desirable as a wife or even romantically convinced of the virtue of wifely sacrifice, might have told the story of Penelope and Ulysses pretty much as Homer tells it; but this is arguable, I think, only on the hypothesis that in Greek literature or folk-lore of the time there was a considerable body of legends or parables celebrating the sort of patience Penelope had toward Ulysses. Certainly any mature woman, sufficiently gifted to write an epic, would have had another view of the matter; she might have permitted Penelope to take Ulysses back, she might have kept Penelope's honor inviolate against the importunities of the suitors; she might have made the story, perhaps, a triumph of the moral law; but she would not—no, I think quite honestly, not—she would not have had Penelope receive Ulysses after all those unaccounted-for years, during which time he never communicated with her, without question or recrimination. But it is to the advantage of us male human beings to make it appear to women that Penelope is an ideal toward which all women should strive. And that is why I think Homer wrote the *Odyssey* and that a woman did not.

Nevertheless, the parable of the *Odyssey* does conform to the experience of the race. The human race, not individually but as a whole, seems to have found that it is to the advantage of all concerned for a man and wife to remain faithful and loyal from marriage unto death; that the art of marriage is one of the most difficult but also one of the greatest of all arts; that there is a certain biological frailty in the male which is not so prevalent among women; and that a man's yielding to this frailty is to be condoned as a weakness in no way indicating where his true love lies. And that is what the *Odyssey* is about—about that and about those adventures of the mind and spirit which are necessary if we are to be at all content with the rather unexciting reality we ordinarily find life to be. The *Odyssey* is a story of adventure, or exploration, and of travel, of the seeing of strange sights and of the making of strange encounters, after which the wanderer returns to the peace and quiet of one's declining years.

It should be recalled at this point that, whereas Homer's account of the conduct of Penelope was accepted in Homer's time and later as the "official" version, there were lays and songs and legends, common among the people, which put an entirely new face on the matter. We have these vulgarities only at second hand, but the substance of them is this: that Penelope was not as faithful as she made herself out to be, that Telemachus was distrait because of the scandalous conduct of his mother, and that Penelope made Ulysses believe a story quite as untrue to the facts as the story Ulysses told her.

Homer, as a matter of fact, anticipates or takes into account this universal tendency of the human mind to be at once idealistic and cynical. He does show us Penelope's conduct as being a cause of reproach from the suitors and a cause of anxiety on the part of her son. She flirts outrageously with the suitors, sending them gifts and favors, and writing them notes telling each of them separately that she has him in mind and that it looks as though she will soon be in his arms. This is not only disingenuous; it is, from a masculine point of view, dishonorable. It is what is vulgarly called "teasing." Penelope wants to keep the whole outfit of one hundred suitors on the string, until she can be sure whether her husband is coming back, and if he is not coming back, she can pick out the one she wants.

Good feminists will at once meet this masculine argument by saying, "Why shouldn't Penelope play these tricks on such good-for-nothings as those suitors were? They knew she had a big house and servants and money and, if she were widowed and one of them should marry her, all that money would come to him. They were all taking advantage of a socially and economically unfair custom which permitted the suitor of a widow to press his suit at the widow's expense. As if these scum were doing Penelope a favor! She tried to put them off, tried to discourage them; and yet, day after day, year after year, they clamored about, eating her out of house and home, tearing up her front yard by pitching quoits and throwing spears at marks, spying on her, annoying her, making love to her hired help right under her nose, and doing everything that is unfair, distasteful and dishonorable in a woman's eyes, and all with a bland male assurance that they are doing everything according to law and custom! Law and custom, bah! Man-made law and custom, where women get the worst of it!"

Having stated what I believe to be the logical feminist argument, I regret to say to my male confrères that, although I am resourceful enough in words to word an answer which would sharply put the feminists and all women in their place (or at least it might sound that convincing to males), I have some doubt about my ability or anybody's ability to make the argument stick. Women, since Homer's time, have got rather out of hand. Just how distressingly true this fact was, even in the time of Aristophanes in Athens, I shall tell you in a later chapter: the Athenian males learned that respectable women had minds of their own, even when they tacitly submitted to being kept under lock and key.

There is an incredible (to me) school of thought which argues that there never was a Trojan War. It is difficult to follow this school in all its learned reasonings, its "reconstructions" of the original legends on a stone tablet of which there remains only a fragment with the letter $\tilde{\omega}$ chiseled on it (reconstructed to read, "Now is the time for all good men to come to the aid of their country"), and in its amazing assumption that the human imagination can build up a wholly circumstantial and detailed story with absolutely nothing whatever to work on.

The major outlines of the Trojan War, the forces engaged, the chiefs of the several Greek tribes, the name of the king of Troy, and the outcome of the war do not vary in any of the accounts. The motives vary, yes; and so do some of the details of the various versions of the war. But who shall determine three thousand years hence what the motives were which led to a war in 1914 between Central Europe and the rest of Europe, a war which ultimately drew in the United States of America? Was it a war to "make the world safe for democracy"? Was it a war of revenge for the violation (the rape) of Belgium? Was it a war to restore the ravished daughter of France (Alsace-Lorraine)? Was it a war to avenge the murder of an heir to a throne? Was it a war to provide a new outlet for the products of the Krupps Iron works, the munitions plants of Sir Basil Zaharoff, and to insure the hegemony of the rich of all countries concerned?

Well, yes, to every question, and no, to them all also. But the fact remains that there was a war in 1914 and it lasted over four years, bankrupting all the nations involved in it. There has been a great deal written about it. There have been poems, novels, plays, histories, economic treatises, commentaries, state documents—floods of printed matter relating to it. But suppose something should happen to wipe out all of the existing printed matter relating to the Great War of 1914 except a few fragments, or recollections of what had been printed before the catastrophe? Supposing that upon the basis of these recollections of the oldest inhabitants a literature should grow up, telling of Nicholas, Czar of all the Russias; Wilhelm II, Emperor of Germany; Ferdinand, King of the Bulgarians; Franz-Josef, Emperor of Austria and King of Hungary; Albert, King of the Belgians; George V, King of England, Ireland, Wales, Emperor of India, etc.; Wilson, headman of the United States of America; Clemenceau, chieftain of France; Victor Emmanuel, King of Italy; Ferdinand, King of Rumania, and so on. Because the data would be insufficient to reconstruct the whole war, would it be sensible to deny that such a person as Woodrow Wilson and such a person as Kaiser Wilhelm ever existed and to lay the creation of such names and personages to the vagaries of popular imagination?

No, and there is good reason to believe that the Trojan War was an actual occurrence. In fact, there is no other cogent reason for its having remained so vivid and so painful in the minds of the Greeks for centuries afterward. It was a war undoubtedly which made all of the Greek city states of Thessaly and the Peloponnesus allies against the great Asiatic city state of Troy. The cause, whatever the occasion might have been, for such a war, must have been momentous. The actuaries and economists have a ready explanation, which has plausibility: Troy commanded the Hellespont and the Hellespont was a trade-route for the Greek city states to Asia. Trade with the East had already developed in the Hellenic city states to such a point where every favorable advantage must be taken advantage of, because these city states were more than self-sustaining: their prosperity depended upon the sale of goods by export. The easiest way to the East was, in bad weather, through the Hellespont. And Troy commanded that.

The economists, picturing this possibility, say there was no Priam, no Paris, no Helen, no Menelaus, no anybody we can name; there was merely an economic necessity for the combined Greek city states to force a free entry to Asia through the Hellespont. With the greatest respect to all economists, bosh! Navigation of the Ægean and the Mediterranean, for at least a thousand years before the latest date set for the Trojan War, was a well established science. They could not account for the Æolian winds, or the strange cross-current blasts which came at certain seasons from the region behind the mouth of the Nile. but they knew when they happened and allowed for them. Even in the time of Pericles and later, navigation was stopped in the Ægean during certain seasons, and Athens had no foreigners or tourists and the Piræus was closed against the weather. The Phœnicians, the Cretans, the Minoans had developed commerce and industry to a magnificently flourishing condition when Athens was probably not a city at all but a place where some neighboring farmers could take refuge when predatory, nomadic tribes swept down upon them.

The literal excursus of the "economic determination" theory of the War of Troy, then, doesn't seem to be quite sensible. What is more likely, it seems, was that Troy was at one time a city of much greater wealth, power and magnificence than any city on the mainland in the Hellenic peninsula. Such city states in Asiatic Europe had become established in strength and power by rapacity and expropriation. That is, the nomadic tribes, living by plunder, subjugated the peaceful, agricultural groups and made them pay tribute in the form of a levy on their produce. Long before Athens was anything more than a village, Sparta was something of a commercial city. The legends have it that Paris, son of Priam, King of Troy, paid a visit to Menelaus, King of Sparta, and abused hospitality by robbing Menelaus of his treasure and taking his wife, Helen, also. You must remember that, at the time, value was reckoned in terms of women as well as in terms of oxen or measures of wheat and corn. Paris could hardly have done this without the help of a retinue of soldiers he brought along with him. But Menelaus was probably a "king" only insofar as he was headsman of a clan or several clans in Sparta and may not have been able to offer much resistance.

Whatever actually happened, this invasion of Greek territory by the Trojans solidified Greek national feeling for the first time. All the tribesmen of the Greek city states on the west side of the Ægean united in a war against Troy and did not cease until they had razed the city. Troy had shown itself to be not only a threat but a menace. And so Athens, Sparta, Thebes, Corinth, Salamis, Pharis, Cnossus, Cos, Argos, the Phoceans, Phacians, Bœotians, Locrians, and all the rest enumerated in Book II of the *Iliad*, were allied against Troy.

The fighting which takes place in the *Iliad* is of two kinds, the individual combats of champions and mass warfare, with bows and arrows, swords and spears. Some have argued that this shows that parts of the *Iliad* go back to the days when warfare was conducted only by individual combats between champions chosen to represent the two sides. But there is nothing to prove that the hero contests were ever the sole means of deciding a dispute. In the Biblical history of the Jews, we know of the contest between David and Goliath; but the hero contests did not finally settle matters; and the warfare on the plains of Troy was probably conducted somewhat as it is described in the *Iliad*. The hero contests are more romantic and dramatic than mass warfare and therefore would appeal more to the imaginations of the chroniclers.

The climax of the *Iliad* is the fight between Hector and Achilles. Achilles was the great champion of the Argive forces; but he had quarreled with Agamemnon, commander-in-chief of the Argives and had refused to fight because Agamemnon had reserved for himself a girl taken captive in some raid after Achilles had claimed her. But the wrath of Achilles is finally aroused when his best friend, Patroclus, is killed by Euphorbus, who struck Patroclus in the back with a spear when Patroclus and Hector were fighting. Achilles girds on his armor to meet the challenge of Hector and at this point the dramatic suspense of the *Iliad* reaches and sustains its highest pitch until the combat is over.

We are given the touching scene of the farewell of Hector to his wife Andromache and his little son. In Andromache's speech and actions we are made to realize the real tragedy that war is to women. She, an adoring and dutiful wife and mother, will be widowed by the war, her home destroyed and she herself will become a slave, disposed of like other chattels, by the victors. We are told how Hector looked in his brazen armor, his plumed helmet and his bronze greaves, carrying his polished shield and spear. We are also given an elaborate description of the famous shield of Achilles, forged for him by Vulcan. Hector sees Achilles approaching from afar and fright seizes him. (The Greeks of Homer's time saw nothing weak or effeminate in fright or tears; their strongest heroes tremble with fear and weep easily.)

The Trojans, both men and women, are watching the outcome of this contest from the city walls, and the Argive hosts are lined up on the plain in expectation also. As Achilles gets closer, Hector takes to his heels, with Achilles after him. Achilles chases him three times around the walled city before Hector summons enough courage to give fight. They stand ground and Achilles hurls his spear but misses. Hector hurls his spear in return and it strikes the shield of Achilles and glances off. Hector draws his sword for close combat but Minerva returns Achilles' spear to him and Achilles hurls it again and pierces Hector's neck. As Hector dies he begs Achilles not to mutilate his corpse, but to send his body home for decent burial. His parents, he says, will richly reward Achilles in treasures of gold and bronze.

The full significance of Achilles' refusal to grant Hector's plea may not be appreciated unless the modern reader realizes that superstition governs Achilles' actions. On the face of his action in mutilating the body and dragging it by the heels in the wake of his chariot, it would seem that he is merely satisfying his revenge in a gruesome manner. But it is more than that. Mutilation of the body of an enemy was a common precaution among primitive people against the harm that might be caused by the ghost. A crippled corpse was a crippled ghost.

On the other hand, the belief in the desirability of decent burial with proper religious rites gave Homer an opportunity to present another touching and beautiful dramatic incident: the one in which the aged Priam goes alone at night through the Argive lines to plead for the body of his son. His speech is so simple, so honest, so tender and so eloquent that Achilles consents to accept the ransom (half of which he promises to the shade of Patroclus) and delivers up the body of Hector, washed and anointed and laid out in splendor. The *Iliad* ends with the funeral rites for Hector after the body has been brought back through the city gates to Troy.

The history of Greece was one of frequent and exhausting wars, against invaders from Persia and the North and also among the Greek tribes and city states for supremacy or commercial advantage or simple plunder and expropriation. The Trojan War had been a long and disruptive one, and the women, we can be sure, were heartily sick of war. The war had meant woe and suffering and Homer does not neglect to emphasize this even in the *Iliad*. In the *Odyssey* he yields to what must have been a common Greek feeling, that peace is to be preferred to war, and that life can be interesting and exciting without so much fighting.

In the *Iliad* and the *Odyssey* Homer performed a service for the Greeks which was both secular and religious. He established, by example, the Greek concepts of honor, loyalty, valor, family devotion, paternal love and destructive beauty; but he also assigned to the familiar gods their several functions and protectorates. And he wrote two epics which stand unrivaled in interest and perfection.

About Hesiod and what he was like I have no definite opinion. In *Works and Days* Hesiod says he was a farmer and a very poor one, as farmers immemorially have been; that his soil was thin and rocky and had to be tended with back-breaking toil to extract a bare living out of it; that he lived on the slope of Mount Helicon where the weather is bad in summer and worse in winter; that it is usually rainy when one needs sunshine and there is usually a drought when one's crops need rain; that winter freezes him, food is scarce, his neighbors are mean skin-flints and a grubby lot, pests kill his cattle, rheumatism gets into his joints, members of his family or hired help fall ill, poverty is awful and it is hard to make ends meet.

There are, Hesiod tells us, some compensations for living on a farm, and he undertakes to enumerate them and to provide counsel on how to get the most out of the soil and get the most out of life. He gives astrological information and bits of advice, in a fashion not unlike the farmers' almanacs of our own time. He also tries to write religious exegesis and recount stories of the gods.

But, whether Hesiod really was a farmer or not or whether he ever lived on a farm except in his youth (he tells us he gave up farming for poetry), I cannot say. For analogy I turn to modern writers on bucolic themes and I find most of them living in the cities, whatever their attitude toward farm life appears to be from their writings.

Hesiod may have been a poet like Virgil, who wrote his *Eclogues* at the command of the Emperor Augustus as propaganda for a back-to-the-farm movement when Rome was suffering from a scarcity of food caused by an influx into the city of farmers who had abandoned their farms. That is, Hesiod may have lived a safe distance from the toil he hated. That he earned a living mainly by his compositions I have no doubt. He may have had a patron in a prince or well-to-do merchant, or he may have earned his keep in a vagabond existence as a traveling bard or rhapsodist.

The scholars help one little in an attempt to arrive at an opinion about Hesiod, and Hesiod does not help much himself. Although he writes in the first person at times, he does not reveal himself, I think, as clearly as Homer does. Moreover, Hesiod is something of a bore. In translations his thoughts and images come through as uninspired and prosaic; his catalogues of the gods are wearingly statistical and confusing; and only the glimpses he gives of common traits in men redeem him from the platitudes he scatters about and which must have already been ancient when he was a lad.

The *Theogony* has a few bright spots in it, particularly when it reveals the earlier conceptions of heroic and godly themes, later handled by the dramatists; but nobody in all these years seems to have thought very much of the *Theogony* because it has been but little quoted and the text comes to us in a neglected and wretched condition. The *Theogony* picks up in interest toward the end with a list of goddesses who have had love affairs with mortals, but Hesiod does not go into details enough to pique one's interest. I agree with the verdict of Quintilian that "Hesiod rarely rises and a great part of him is occupied with mere names."

In some special respects, not poetical but historical and anthropological, Hesiod is particularly illuminating and probably for that reason more interest should be taken in him by the scholars; for there is reason to believe that Hesiod, with the common folk at least, was more popular in his time than Homer was in his. The legendary life of Hesiod shows that the people loved him to the point of idolatry; his *Theogony* was probably much more of a Bible to the early Greeks than Homer; and his account of the creation of the world should bear an intrinsic interest comparable to the anonymous Hebraic account in Genesis. The *Theogony* may have been among the first attempts of the very ancient Greeks to personify phenomena of nature and to give names of gods to abstractions. In Hesiod the qualities of human nature have already begun to be reflected as parables of the gods, such as the story of Prometheus and Pandora.

Again, we learn from Hesiod many details of common life in Hesiod's time. We know from Hesiod, for instance, that the Bœotian farmer raised surplus crops for exchange and that he shipped corn and wine to other countries in exchange for merchandise he wanted, and so was not a simple peasant consuming only the produce of his own labor. Therefore Hesiod considered it part of the instruction he proposed to give to farmers that he should teach them about commerce and navigation as well as how to avoid litigation, lay in the best crops, keep on friendly terms with the neighbors and get the best out of life.

It is from this, I suspect, that Hesiod may have been subsidized by some king or prince to write the *Works and Days,* just as the Department of Agriculture sends out to farmers information on tick eradication, crop rotation, pest extermination, etc., because it is economically as well as socially to the best advantage of the state that the farmers should prosper and be contented. Prosperity of the farmers beyond their homegrown simple needs in Hesiod's time meant that masters of the regions, in return for military protection, redress in law courts and other benefits, could exact more taxes.

The legendary life of Hesiod has it that he was one of two sons of a man of property in Ascra in Bœotia; that his younger brother, Perses, by bribing the probate or surrogate judges in the distribution of the estate, beat him out of his share; that his later rough treatment of his native village in his verses was prompted by resentment and revenge for these wrongs; that he served as a priest of the Muses on Mount Helicon; that he entered the poetical contest in the funeral games in honor of Amphidamas in Chalcis and won a tripod, whereat a corruption of the original text "Victor in song a tripod bore away" was misread as "Victor in song over Homer the divine" and gave rise to the erroneous story that he once contested with and defeated Homer. Further, that he misinterpreted a warning from the oracle of Delphi and in attempting to shun it went to the very spot he was warned to keep away from; that while there as a guest in a house, his companion violated the sister of his host, in consequence of which she hanged herself; that the brothers slew Hesiod's companion and Hesiod also for connivance and threw the bodies into the sea; that Hesiod's body was washed up on the shore ("brought to shore by dolphins") and recognized, whereupon an infuriated populace razed the house of the brothers, and deeming Hesiod guiltless, murdered them and threw the bodies into the sea.

Most modern scholars scoff at this account; but I see no reason for not accepting it as being probably, in essentials, true. It is the only account we have and it is not fabulous in the sense of showing godly intervention, and not impossible.

SOPHOCLES *AND GREEK DRAMA*

*

FROM the time of Homer and Hesiod down to the age of
Pericles, if we are to take the evidence of Greek literature, the
more enlightened, or the more sophisticated the Greeks became,
the more superstitions they developed. Homer, besides being a
poetic genius, was a highly civilized and rational human being in
comparison with Pythagoras, who flourished in Athens about 350
years later. But, along with superstitions, the Greeks developed neuroses and strange fears, intimations of immortality, a penchant for
dispute and litigation, individualistic poetry, erotic verse, knock-
about farce, cutting satire and drama of great showmanship and
genius.

In Homer's time the gods were familiar spirits, possessing the
weaknesses and attributes of mortals. They were invisible usually,
but were capable of assuming various shapes in their intercourse
with living men and women. The mind of Homer was serene and
untroubled by those ghostly apprehensions which became the subject of the doleful meditations of the later writers of elegiac verse.
Homer believed in the immortality of the soul, not only of "heroes"
as some have argued, but of all persons of whatever kind and degree; but his idea of immortality was that it was a simple transposition wherein the wraiths or ghosts lived in an underworld region
of darkness surrounded by the wraiths of their former friends and
possessions and sustained by meat and drink offerings made by the
living. Those dead whose bodies had not been buried beneath the
earth chattered and screamed and wailed through the air, but they
were not in torment. The Greeks of Homer's time had not conceived
the idea of hell as a punishment for sins on earth.

37

These early Greeks were without a sense of sin, a sense which became the main preoccupation of mystical philosophers like Pythagoras (and no doubt a common worry) three and a half centuries afterward. Homer had a lively sense of honor and of what was the right thing to do in any given circumstance—an ethical obligation which must be met, even if death were the issue of it. Hector knew, and Andromache knew, that when Hector went forth to battle with Achilles he would not come back alive. Homer is so explicit on this point that he commits the artistic offense, which is frequent with him, of telling what is going to happen before it happens. We call it an artistic offense now, but Homer did not consider it so and therefore it was not one in his time. When we realize that Hector did know he was foredoomed to death, we can realize that it was not funny to Homer or to his audience that this great Trojan hero should tremble violently in the knees at the sight of Achilles and let Achilles chase him three times around the walls of Troy before giving fight. And we can also realize that Hector considered it his duty to fight even what he knew to be a losing battle.

In Homer's time and antecedently, the gods were not always (if ever) just snatched out of the air, even if the Greeks did personify in various gods the abstract qualities of Love (Aphrodite), Wisdom (Minerva), Power in Heaven (Zeus), Strength (Hercules), *et cetera*. They also made gods out of human beings, by way of honoring them for virtues they displayed in the community in which they lived. Anthropologists and philologists, ever since some German pedant raised the question, have been trying to determine what a "hero" Ἥρως was to the Greeks.

Well, I think a "hero" was a hero as you and I and any literate person understands the word—an eminent man, a man who excelled in one particular talent or phase of character, some one who once did something unusual. Many scholars have tried to associate the word with "noble," that is, with qualities which distinguish a kingly or princely person from some one of inferior circumstances; but this does not hold good, because the Greeks created a god out of a physically powerful lunk-head like Hercules and out of a quick and dextrous thief like Mercury.

In fact, I am not sure (and no one can be sure) that Minerva, Zeus, Apollo and the rest of the gods in the Greek theogony may not have existed in the flesh or that those were not real names. Minerva may have been some especially wise woman in a Greek tribe, so wise that her fame spread and her name came to be identified with Wisdom. Aphrodite may have been some particularly beautiful woman in a Greek tribe, so beautiful that her name came to be identified with Beauty.

If we (and I speak of average people) wish to pay a pretty woman a compliment, we do not say she looks like Venus or like Beauty; we say she looks like one of the famous beauties of the stage or screen whom she might somewhat resemble. If we are somewhat self-consciously proud of our culture, we may say she looks like a Botticelli, a Guido or a Romney or like Madame de Lespinasse, Marie Antoinette, the Empress Josephine or some famous beauty with whose portrait we are familiar—but a portrait of a person, not of an abstract quality. And that, I think, has been a constant psychological attribute among people since the dawn of the human race. It is only when people lose innocence of mind that they become over-subtle and begin to refine the human gods out of existence and substitute strange complexities.

THOSE anthropologists who try to establish religious cults as having existed among the early Greeks before the Greeks were intelligent enough to respect personal achievement among themselves have a strange method of reasoning. A child may fear the dark but he attaches no religious significance to the dark until some one tells him fibs—that there is a bogey-man in the dark. But a child, before he acquires any "religious" notions (such as that the bogey-man will get him if he does not behave in the fashion his elders wish him to behave) or before he has any particular concern with anything except his immediate surroundings, his appetites, pains and pleasures, *does* imitate other children and try to emulate the special achievements of these children; a child creates "heroes" and "heroines" among his playmates even if only in the field of hop-scotch. If the anthropologists had thought of this, they would have less trouble with the Greek word Ἥρως.

It would begin to dawn upon them, I think, that the word ἱερός is allied to it, and is a later refinement of it. Homer used the word "hero" for any person skilled or eminent in any pursuit, whether it be Achilles, the warrior; Demodocus, the minstrel; or Mulius, the herald; but not for a minstrel like Phemius or for a servant or a common soldier. To many of these "heroes" semi-divine parentage was later attributed, and they acquired divinity themselves and were worshiped as "heroes" or local divinities.

Rites consecrated to them were presided over by "hierophants" or priests of a ἱερός, a place consecrated to a god. (Homer used the word ἱερός as anything or place "set aside," marked, earmarked or staked out, such as a plot of land or tent belonging to a hero, or a cow destined to be sacrificed.) In later times Homer's use of the word "hero" disappeared altogether and became used only for gods or demigods, objects of worship, just as long after Homer's time, the word ἱερός was used to designate a sacred place or temple. Sophocles in his old age was appointed priest or hierophant to the "hero" Alon.

ONE of the most amazing statements I have ever encountered in a scholar's work is that one of Gilbert Murray's when he says: "The Mysteries are not mentioned in Homer." It is on a plane with that carelessness wherein, without a "perhaps" or "it is said," Professor Murray says Euripides possessed the first library in Athens, when the evidence is plain there were private libraries in Athens going back to the time of Pisistratus and that in the time of Euripides, private libraries were so common that Plato, only fifty years later, was complaining of the over-production of bad books.

Professor Murray is not unique in this error; all other commentators I have read share it. I mean about the Mysteries. This is astounding because Homer, in the *Odyssey*, devotes one entire book to one of the Mysteries, portrays the rites of celebrating it and what happens, or is supposed to happen, when the celebrant performs the required magic. It is true that Homer does not tell the reader in so many words that this is an Orphic, Plutonian or Proserpinean Mystery; he merely depicts one in operation, tells how Ulysses conferred with Tiresias and got into communication with the dead and how he went about it. He no more thought it necessary to explain that this was a Mystery than Cardinal Mundelein would think it necessary in the midst of an "Asperges" to come out with a placard reading "This is a mass."

That Homer did not mention the Eleusinian Mysteries may have been because they were either too sacred or too popular, as Professor Murray supposes. Or it may have been that it did not suit his artistic purpose to do so. But, yet again, it may have been that he had never heard of them. That, I think, is more likely. Some anthropologists have been puzzled because Homer does not *mention* the Orphic or Eleusinian Mysteries and have concluded, like Farnell, that Homer's reason was didactic: that he was a cool, intellectual aristocrat who sought to discourage "this vain dream of the self-exaltation of man." Farnell carries this curious assumption to the point of asserting that it looks as though Homer "deliberately ignored or really knew nothing of hero-worship, of any apotheosis of men believed to have been once alive on earth." Farnell thinks Homer really knew about it, but did not like the idea. This in the face of the fact that nearly all of the heroes in Homer are described as real persons, but of divine or semi-divine in origin!

Such scholars have got the cart before the horse. Freud comes after Knox and Calvin, not before them. In Homer's time, as I have pointed out in the previous chapter, it is obvious that Asclepius had not been deified: he was merely a well-known physician whose home was Trekka but whose fame had spread about generally. By Plato's time Asclepius had become a full-fledged divinity and we have Plato recording Socrates' last words as being, "Crito, I owe a cock to Asclepius. Will you remember to discharge the debt?" (I am not as certain as some scholars are that this meant that Socrates was remiss in his religious duties and had failed to sacrifice a cock to the god of healing at the proper time. Socrates was not noticeably religious and he had said he was not sure there were any gods. He was, however, an indigent and negligent provider for his family, according to ancient testimony. He may have owed a bill to a butcher named Asclepius for a rooster. Still, it may have been a death-bed jest; for, among the superstitious of the time, it was customary to offer a sacrifice in the form of a fowl to Asclepius if one wished to get well or keep well and alive. Socrates' chances to keep well at the moment were exceedingly slim, no matter how many cocks he lay on the altar of the healing god.)

THE Greek theater at the highest point of its development (which was during the time of Æschylus, Sophocles, Euripides and Aristophanes) and for a considerable time before and after, was a state institution, an amusement and diversion for the people, promoted and supported by the city state, and attended by the whole population, including those slaves and harlots who could afford the lowest admission fee of two obols, or about ten cents. Any free citizen who could not afford, or thought he could not afford, two obols for an admission ticket to the cheapest seats in the theater, had only to make his representation to the city treasurer to be supplied with the money, provided he purchased a ticket with it. That was the law of the city state of Athens.

Everybody, then, went to see the plays of Æschylus, Sophocles, Euripides and Aristophanes. Some scholars have thought that women were not permitted to attend the theater, but Dr. Roy C. Flickinger in his monumental and entertaining study, *The Greek Theatre and Its Drama,* has shown conclusively that there is no reason for this assumption, whereas there is every reason to believe women did attend the theater. Some scholars have also assumed that slaves were not permitted in the theater, forgetful of the Old Oligarch's word that it was impossible to distinguish Athenian slaves from their masters by dress or demeanor, that slaves made and saved money, sometimes having more wealth than their masters, and could buy their freedom and become free citizens, if they were born within the confines of the city state or if they proved to the satisfaction of the agora that they would make worthy citizens. Being a citizen involved duties as well as privileges. One had not only to be ready to take up arms in behalf of the city state, but one had to serve as a member of the assembly at regular intervals and decide on minor cases of equity as well as upon matters of major consequence to the city state. Every free citizen of Athens was a member of the legislative and juridical bodies of the government and could be appointed a member of the administration.

The free citizenry of Athens decided everything, including (and this is quite important to this chapter of this book) to which one among the dramatists the prizes were to be awarded in the annual competition. The function of the free citizens of Athens as jurymen in all things is satirized by Aristophanes who, nevertheless, at the same time, addresses this body in his comedies, cajoling, deriding, and entreating them to award him the prize for the play they are witnessing. (It might be argued, I think, that one of the contributing causes of the downfall of Athens was the abuse of communism within the city state—an abuse Aristophanes ridicules unmercifully. Every citizen was supposed to serve in the assemblies and each one received a fee out of the state treasury for each session in which he served. The Greeks were especially litigious, and as property among them diminished the disputes at law became more numerous. Many Athenian citizens, according to Aristophanes, derived their main or their only source of income from jury service, and since the juries were not restricted in numbers, only those who were too busy at other activities stayed away. The funds of the state treasury were being constantly depleted by the fees paid out in jury service.)

The first theater in Athens was that of Dionysus Eleuthereus, on the slope of the Acropolis. The remains of this theater are in an excellent state of preservation, the stone seats arranged with geometrical precision in a semicircle on the slope of the hill, just as they were originally put there, the foundations of the orchestra, the proscenium, the parascenium and the stage remaining, although without their superstructure of wood and stone and painted scenery. The first seats were made of wood, and the stage also was made of wood. It is probable, according to Dr. Flickinger, that all the plays of Æschylus, Sophocles and Euripides and the comedies of Aristophanes were performed on this site from a wooden stage before an audience which sat on wooden seats. The theater in Athens as we can see it now was completed, it is assumed, during the tenure in office of Lycurgus, finance minister of Athens from 338 to 326 B.C. There is late testimony that the original theater in Athens was on a level site in the old market place and that the audience saw the play from wooden bleachers. According to this story the structure collapsed during a contest between Æschylus, Pratinas and Chœrilus in the Seven Olympiad, 499 B.C., killing many people; whereat it was decided to seek a location where the seats would have the natural support of a hillside.

We do not know how Greek tragedy and Greek comedy originated. Aristotle, who lived at a time when the best of these tragedies and comedies were still being performed, did not know. And all the indefatigable scholarship of the last century has not improved upon Aristotle's knowledge of the historical beginnings of the plays he read and witnessed. In 1826, the German scholar Weckler published his *Satyrspiel* which presumed to account for the derivation of tragedy from the dithyramb, through the "goat song" (*tragoidia*) of the satyr plays. Since Winckler's time an enormous library of conjecture and controversy has been built up; but at long last Roy C. Flickinger and W. S. Burrage independently reach the same sensible conclusion that, whereas all this literature of the origins of tragedy and comedy makes interesting reading for scholars and a pleasant little game for them to play among themselves, it is not to be confused with history. The best and clearest discussion of the problem of the origin of the Greek drama is to be found in the introductory chapter of Professor Flickinger's *The Greek Theatre and Its Drama.*

We do know that the dithyramb was a song in celebration of

the birth of Dionysus, because Plato tells us that much; and it is sensible to take Plato's word on this rather than the word of those modern scholars who assume that he did not know what he was talking about. The dithyramb was, not to put too fine a point on it, a drunken song—not a drinking song, but a drunken one, a song to be sung with the wild and frenzied accents of intoxication. The first extant instance of the words occurs in a fragment of Archilochus (680-640 B.C.), "who declares that he 'knows how, when his heart is crazed with wine, to lead Lord Dionysus' dithyramb.' " It should be observed, Dr. Flickinger remarks, that Archilochus does not say he knows how to write a dithyramb, but how to take part in one as a drunken leader.

Many scholars have tried to connect the occasion of the performance of a dithyramb with the satyr dramas and to imagine that the original festivals were very much like the present day carnivals in Thessaly, Thrace and other parts of Greece; and to trace the derivation of the plays of Æschylus, et al., to these primitive ritualistic performances. But Dr. Flickinger quite rightly, I think, rejects the notion. It may just be possible that the remote origin of the circus, the state fair, the street carnival, the old time burlesque and the old time stock company dramas were the same, but the permutations, if the origin *was* the same, were so numerous and so dissimilar that new species were created.

What the scholars have generally overlooked is that the dithyramb did not die out with the development of the organized drama but persisted certainly down through the third century B.C., and I believe persists today under such various forms as the Russian *kazotsky,* some of the more indecorous and frenzied Spanish dances and the "Charleston," an excited dance usually performed to the fast music of piano, saxophone and drums. I think the cordax, which was a lewd dance among the Greeks, and the bibaxo, a swift dance, were dithyrambic. Theophrastus in characterizing a boorish, vulgar fellow, says that he is the kind that dances the cordax "when not even drunk, and without a mask." Theophrastus, who was a contemporary of Aristotle, merely means to remind us here that there is a place for all things; but he also here gives us the information that in his day there was a place for the cordax, if performed at the right time, in the right condition of being drunk, and while wearing a mask. This is true today. There are certain times, places and circumstances wherein it would not be offensive for even a quite proper person to let down reserve and dance a Charleston; but it would be a disgusting exhibition by the same person in other circumstances.

To say that the origin of plays like the *Medea* of Euripides was in dithyrambic songs and dances sounds as absurd to me as to say that the origin of Shaw's *Man and Superman* was the "can-can." The primitive Greeks, I think, devised numerous ways to amuse themselves and to amuse others, and the inventions which especially caught on were perpetuated, revised and improved from time to time. Dr. Flickinger, trying to restore order in the mêlée of such fighting scholars as Dr. Emil Reisch, Mr. Packard-Cambridge, Professor Wilhelm Schmid, Professor William Ridgeway, and Professor Farnell, says his own view is that satyric drama and tragedy were not in the same line of development, the one from the other, but independent developments. However, he thinks they were independent offshoots of the "Peloponnesian dithyramb," which seems to me to be making an unnecessary concession to the assembled "scholars."

I do know that we have Dionysian or Bacchic (i.e., drunken) songs in the *Bacchæ* of Euripides. There is also a Bacchic dance in Aristophanes, performed by Bacchus or Dionysus himself, who is represented as being drunk and disorderly while doing so—the butt of ridicule by Aristophanes and the audience. To read deep religious and ethical symbolism into such plays is to destroy their sense and meaning.

Moreover, the Greek drama as we know it, although it may have originated as a primitive form of entertainment *on the occasion* of religious festivals, is not and probably never was religious in character. It was secular in the very highest degree, expressing the very antithesis of religious feeling. Even the *Prometheus Bound* of Æschylus, a solemn tragedy, is an atheistical defiance of the tyranny of Zeus and an exaltation of man. In Aristophanes Zeus's name is not only taken in vain: Zeus is laughed at, and the god Dionysus is portrayed as a drunken booby.

Greek drama, both comedy and tragedy, then, was entertainment into which were woven discussions of all sorts of questions, ethical, political, social and simply gossipy. The Athenian Greeks were, during a large part of their history, a disputatious and gossipy people. Everything contrived to make them so: the democratic and communistic organization of the small city state, wherein every adult male free citizen was supposed to spend a certain portion of his time in discussing affairs of state in the agora or assembly, the slave labor which left the citizen a certain amount of leisure, the educational system which developed his nervous coördination and perceptions, and a social system which excluded men from the household, which was regarded as the peculiar province and responsibility of the women.

Wars were frequent, it is true, and political questions were sometimes very pressing. But there were long lulls during which there was nothing more immediate to discuss than the meaning of life, the nature of the universe, the question of fate and heredity in the family of Laius, whether Æschylus was a drunkard or not, and the personal habits and vices of various citizens. What strikes us moderns most particularly about the Greek drama is the singular freedom the dramatists enjoyed. They not only enjoyed freedom; they enjoyed astonishing license. They did not stop at downright libel. Aristophanes, for instance, was afraid of no one; and he did not hesitate to denounce in the harshest criticism and with the most outrageous ridicule such dictators or men at the head of the ship of state as Alcibiades and Cleon at the time when they were in office.

This freedom was possible because public opinion was the most powerful determinant in every political, social and private matter in Athens. The whole ethical system of the Athenian Greeks was built around the query, "What will people think?" and on the realistic assumption that what people thought was important. In Athens the state was the Athenian people. So ingrained was this assumption that there arose a school of teachers of argument and oratory, designed to instruct individuals in the best means of getting along in life, how to influence the opinions of others. These were the sophists: they correspond somewhat to our commercial institutions which undertake to instruct one in sales psychology, how to overcome one's lack of confidence, and how to rise rapidly in one's chosen work.

SOPHOCLES is the title of this chapter, but Sophocles is far from being the hero of it. He represents something—precision, didacticism, the "literary flavor," technic without inspiration, the grand manner without the grand style; and therefore he is the special pet of a certain type of academician, a special pet and bugaboo with which to frighten the unscholarly. Among the remarks attributed to Sophocles that have come down to us is the one that "Æschylus did the right thing without knowing why he did it," leaving the inference plain that Sophocles knew just why and how he did everything. This, I think, marks him as a man of great talent and not a genius like Æschylus, Euripides and Aristophanes. Aristophanes was, I think, the greatest mind of the three. Plato thought so, too, saying that the soul of Aristophanes was the temple of all the Graces, and the one the Graces themselves had especially chosen.

(This regard which Plato had for the genius of Aristophanes, by the way, should be a clew, I think, to the misrepresentation Plato has had all these years in the hands of the sciolists and his interpreters. Even G. Lowes Dickinson, who knows his Plato, has been taken in by this representation and has had an inner, not quite resolved rebellion against it, and, as a result, his recent work, *Plato and His Dialogues,* is a puzzling book. It reads like an address for the defense by a lawyer who believes his client is guilty. Plato, too, in the years of his greatest creative activity, was a humorous writer, an indulgent ironist and satirist, who, not having a gift for constructing plays, cast his ideas in the form of dialogues to be read instead of heard. It was not until long past middle life that he became a didactic writer interested in Utopian theories of the state, and the depression of the times conspired to make him interest himself in political and economic theories, just as the times in which I am writing are making many creative artists turn their attention to the politico-economic system under which we live.)

Two or three phrases about Sophocles have come down to us from Aristotle (who obviously found Euripides more interesting because he quotes Euripides frequently, whereas he quotes Sophocles only rarely) and these phrases have been seized upon by those moral philosophers who, having these phrases, never have considered it necessary to read much of Sophocles.

You can hardly blame them for this; because Sophocles is not very easy reading in any existing translation, and whatever any Greek scholar may say to the contrary, Sophocles presents enormous difficulties when one tries to read him in the original, many more difficulties than Aristophanes presents for example, although Aristophanes abounds in topical allusions that are lost to us now. The reason Sophocles is so hard to read and make anything out of is that he is excessively literary and we do not know exactly what many of his words mean, what whole sentences and strophes in his text mean. We can only guess at them.

What is more, whenever anybody writes about the superior enjoyment of reading Sophocles in the original and advances as the reason that this is because the poetry of Sophocles cannot be rendered into English, that person is a humbug. He may be honest enough in preferring his own translation to that of any one with which he is familiar (most of the English translations of Sophocles seem pretty bad), but this is because he possesses a different temperament and type of mind from that of any of the translators and so prefers his own guess as to what the words mean to the many conflicting guesses of other translators.

It is true, moreover, that the poetry of Sophocles or the poetry of any other Greek poet cannot, as poetry, be rendered adequately into English. But it is also true that, as concerns Greek poetry, even the best of Greek scholars cannot appreciate it *as poetry*. The reason for this is that no living human being and no human being who has lived for two thousand years knows for certain what Greek words sounded like in the time of Sophocles. We know the quantities of various types of Greek poetry, because the late grammarians gave us clews, but they neglected to tell us how any one word was pronounced. Take the small English word, "like." If it were a word in a Greek text, we should be able to say that it was pronounced as "like" or "leek" or "lick" (perhaps) and sometimes in poetry as "likie" or "leekie" or "lickie," but that is as much as anybody can say. Two centuries after Sophocles lived, even the syllabication and stress of classical Greek words were so generally unknown outside of Athens that an Alexandrian scholar, Aristophanes (no relation to the comic dramatist), is supposed to have invented the accents which Greek words now bear, to aid foreigners in the pronunciation of Greek.

How Greek consonants and diphthongs were pronounced during the Classical period was finally agreed upon by the scholars, after violent disputes, wherein, since the Germans were the first in the field, it was established that the diphthongs in Greek were pronounced like diphthongs in German; but about the pronunciation of the consonants as agreed upon I think there is even more room for doubt.

The Germans decided, for instance, that the Greek "Beta" was pronounced like our "B" and the German "B," and this was accepted. But in modern Greek the "Beta" is pronounced like our "V." I see no special reason for the German version of a Greek "B." I believe the Greeks know how to pronounce their own language.

That language has undergone changes, as has ours, but while a line from Chaucer does not look like a line from Edna St. Vincent Millay, Chaucer's "B" is still a "B" and is not pronounced like "W."

SOPHOCLES
(From an idealized bust)

Strabo mentions a city in Gaul on the site of the present city of Vienna and he wrote it "Bienna" (βιέννα). I think he pronounced it "Vienna." The Greek word *Blakikos* (βλκικός) used by Plato to mean "indolent," "spiritless," sounds to me like our word "flaccid," which also means "indolent," "spiritless." The philologists say our "flaccid" comes from the Latin *flaccicus*. But if you pronounce *blakikos* with the "B" like "V" you have a sound like *flaccicus*. I also think our word "vivacious" comes from the Greek word *Bibadso* (βιβαζω), which means "to raise up, exalt," and that the Latin word *vivax*, from which our word is derived, according to the dictionaries, is from the Greek *Bibadso*, which I believe was pronounced something like "vivakso" and that the Latin word *vivax* comes from it. There was a Greek word *Bibasis* (βίβασις), meaning a kind of dance. It was a vivacious dance and I believe it was pronounced "vivasis." I believe our word *velocity* comes, by way of the Latin word *velocitas*, from the Greek word βελος, which means "anything which moves in a swift, darting manner." And so on. I believe there is reason for thinking that in classical Greek literature the Delta (Δ) was sometimes sounded like "t," and the "X" or Chi was sometimes pronounced like our "dz" or like the Greek zeta, and so on. In fine, I think classical Greek was more like modern Greek than like modern German.

Of course, I do not intend to outline a new phonetics of the Greek vocabulary. I also recognize that it is highly expedient to have a standard pronunciation of Greek words and letters, even if the pronunciation is under dispute, in order to prevent anarchy in the teaching of Greek; but also I should like to see less humbug among those who can read classical Greek with comparative ease and who can get some sort of sense out of difficult passages in Greek. No one can appreciate Greek poetry, as poetry, in quite the same way as a sensitive and cultivated American or English reader can appreciate Keats, Shelley or Emily Dickinson—and it is absurd to pretend that one can.

In truth, the thing which is hindering the revival of an interest in classical literature more than anything else is the paucity of good translations from the Greek, translations in which the sense of the original is conveyed in the living language of the day—not the stilted Baboo English of editorial writers for the London *Spectator* or the nerveless clichés of the editorial pages of American newspapers. There are good and bad translations and those teachers of Greek and Latin who have a regard for the survival of their profession should be vigilant in making discriminations between them. There are a few good translations in the old Bohn library, for instance, but the one volume of *Lucian's Dialogues* by Howard Williams is worse than no translation at all. It is not in English, although the words are English. One simply can't read it, whereas Lucian is one of the most readable writers that ever lived. In the Loeb Classics, the translator of Lucian is Professor A. M. Harmon of Princeton and this translation is very good indeed. It is not as spirited as those few translations of dialogues by Lucian which Dryden did; but at least Professor Harmon can write English and is aware of the world about him. He is courageous, for instance, to translate *cordax* (κορδαξ) as "the can-can" but not courageous enough to translate it "the hootchie-cootchie," which I think the cordax undoubtedly was like. The Fowler translation of Lucian in four volumes, published by the Oxford University Press, is still better than Harmon's.

When Eastern American colleges begin, as some already have, to drop Latin as a requirement for the Bachelor of Arts degree and to ignore the importance of Greek and Latin as the mediums in which two great literatures were written, the trouble has been, I think, with the teachers of Greek and Latin who have failed to make Greek and Latin literature interesting. It is nonsense for them to advance the old argument that Greek and Latin offer good mental training and exercise and help one to increase one's vocabulary. Learning to diagram Greek verbs is a bore and benefits no one; and to learn Greek and Latin in order to acquire a vocabulary is a very roundabout way of doing it when there are plenty of English dictionaries available. Greek and Latin literature is either interesting *as literature* or it is not worth preserving. People will soon even cease to be interested in translations from the Greek and Latin if the conspiracy to falsify the texts with dreary, expurgated and euphemistic translations continues.

Nevertheless I would not minimize or delimit or fail to honor on my own account those scholars and pedants or even those pettifogging sciolists and patient copyists, who, despite their many errors, their childish bickerings, their little jealousies which make them so human, their transparent arrogances which ill conceal their lack of assurance about things so much in doubt, for all these, even the least among them, have contributed their share to the perpetuation of the rich testimony of the value of human life, its dignity, its absurdity, its adventure and its disappointments, its passion and its calm, its tragedy and its comedy, its humor, pathos, striving, courage, defeat and occasional triumph—that is mirrored in Greek literature.

I should only ask my betters among Greek scholars who really love Greek literature, as literature, to be less patient than I am forced to be with those of their colleagues who undertake to interpret Greek literature to us. If Sophocles were the prig Professor Irving Babbitt makes him out to be, I could not bear to read Sophocles. If he were that public statue of "Civic Virtue" by a particularly tasteless artist, which some homiletic writers make him out to be, he would never have won twenty dramatic prizes in Athens as against five by Euripides and fifteen by Æschylus, because the prizes were conferred by acclamation by the whole free populace of Athens; not by special critics or the *aristoi* but by a popular vote wherein the taste of the cobbler in the top gallery counted as much as the vote of Pericles in the pit.

If Sophocles won the prize in any other manner, a new problem concerning Sophocles arises for the scholars; for the drama prize was a national competition in which the audience decided the winner on the final day of the several in which the dramatic offerings were produced. And if there was any tampering with the votes, as for instance on that occasion when Sophocles defeated Æschylus for the first time, it can only be concluded that Sophocles, who was a rich manufacturer of arms, had greased some palms among the Athenians. This, I am not quite ready to believe, because Sophocles, within his limits, was an excellent showman, a poet-playwright who touched the imaginations of his audience and dug deep into their emotions. He must have done so: he was the most popular of playwrights in the great period of Attic drama. His *Œdipus, the King* seems to have been as popular as *Ben Hur* or *Abie's Irish Rose.* The peculiar appeal of Sophocles to the Athenian populace is a mystery I propose to unravel. The reasons for it do not come through in most of the existing translations, and these reasons are further obscured by the interpretations that have been put upon Sophocles' talents by the commentators.

Aristotle did not really *like* Sophocles and Professor Gilbert Murray, although he tries hard to keep it back, also does not really *like* Sophocles, as witness these statements: "Sophocles is the one Greek writer who is 'classical' in the vulgar sense—almost in the same sense as Virgil and Milton. Even his exquisite diction, which is such a marked advance on the stiff magnificence of his predeces-

sor, betrays the lesser man in the greater artist. Æschylus' superhuman speech seems like natural superhuman speech. It is just
the language that Prometheus would talk, that an ideal Agamemnon
or Atossa might talk in their great moments. But neither Prometheus
nor Œdipus nor Electra, nor any one but an Attic poet of the highest culture, would talk as Sophocles makes them. It is this characteristic which has established Sophocles as the perfect model, not
only for Aristotle, but in general for critics and grammarians; while
the poets have been left to admire Æschylus, who 'wrote in a state
of intoxication,' and Euripides, who broke himself against the bars
both of life and of poetry."

SOPHOCLES was popular with Athenian audiences, as I shall show,
for almost precisely the same reason that *Abie's Irish Rose* was
popular with American audiences. And it is not to be assumed that
the Athenian audience was one whit above the theater-going population of America in intelligence. Even the champions of Sophocles
admit that *Œdipus, the King* was Sophocles' masterpiece—and
Œdipus, the King failed to win the prize.

All this is plain enough in Aristotle, who is so consistently misread by some commentators on Sophocles that I cannot think they
have read either Aristotle or Sophocles but have only read Schlegel
who had read Longinus on Aristotle. Aristotle is quite explicit on
these points, as any one, without consulting the text, can discover
for himself by reading Professor Lane Cooper's *The Poetics of
Aristotle: Its Meaning and Influence* in the "Our Debt to Greece
and Rome" series or Professor Roy C. Flickinger's *The Greek
Theatre and Its Drama.* One of Aristotle's objections to both Sophocles and Euripides was that they both departed from the strict rules
governing the construction of tragedy and sacrificed their artistic
consciences to pander to the popular taste—Euripides more flagrantly in some cases than Sophocles, for reasons which should be
so obvious that Aristotle does not think it necessary to state them.

Professors Cooper and Flickinger know what Aristotle was talking about, but there is a tradition, following Schlegel's panegyric on
Sophocles, which results in such absurdities as this statement of
Professor Irving Babbitt in *Rousseau and Romanticism:* "For the
best type of Greek humanist, a Sophocles, let us say, decorum was
a vital and immediate thing.... Sophocles is more ethical than
Euripides for the simple reason that he views life with more imaginative wholeness.... The Ismene and Antigone of Sophocles are

both ethical; but Ismene would abide by the law of the state, whereas Antigone opposes to this law something more universal—the 'unwritten law of heaven.' This insight of Antigone into a moral order that is set not only above her ordinary self but above the convention of her time and country is something very immediate, something achieved, as I shall try to show more fully later, with the aid of the imagination."

That sounds like one of the burlesque sophistical statements in Aristophanes at which Athenian audiences roared. The character of Antigone, as represented by Sophocles, was only a poetic realization and interpretation of a character whose actions and fate were already familiar to the Greek audience; her defiance of the convention of her time and country, to the Athenian audience which first saw Sophocles' play, was precisely the sort of defiance of the convention of her time and country as Little Eva displayed in *Uncle Tom's Cabin*. There was no ethical problem there involved, so far as the Athenians were concerned, that was as knotty as the ethical problem of *Abie's Irish Rose* to a New York audience of Roman Catholics and orthodox Jews.

Consider the plot of the *Antigone*. Antigone and Ismene are sisters of Polynices, who has been slain while leading an insurrection against his country, in the remote antiquity of the Greeks. Creon, King of Thebes, orders that no one shall bury the body of Polynices but that it shall be exposed to be devoured by the dogs as a lesson to traitors. As I pointed out in the chapter on Homer, one of the strongest of all religious or superstitious feelings among the Greeks was that a corpse should have proper burial beneath the soil and a prayer said over it, lest the ghost of the departed never reach either the Abode of the Dead or the Isle of the Blessed, but fly about distracted in the air.

As complete interment was not always possible, as for instance in war, it later was deemed sufficient that a handful of earth should be sprinkled over the body and a prayer said—a practice which still survives in Christian burial. Antigone, who loved her brother very much, determines to disobey the edict of Creon and draws her sister, Ismene, into her plot. Ismene is hesitant and afraid of the consequences of defying Creon. Antigone gets by the guards and sprinkles the handful of dust over Polynices' body and Ismene, who has gone with her but who has not performed the act, is seized with her. Both are charged with defying the law.

In Antigone's celebrated speech—the most celebrated speech in

Greek tragedy—she gives a dozen or more reasons for her act, all of which boil down simply to a woman's "because," which as any modern woman knows or any Athenian woman knew is the most potent of all reasons for any action a woman does that is of high consequences. Ismene's fiancé is Hæmon, son of Creon. Hæmon intercedes for the girls. But Creon is put into a difficult situation: either he must condemn the girls, although they are his nieces and one of them is the fiancée of his son, or he must admit that his edicts are either meaningless or are capable of being unequally applied. He is in the position of a modern judge whose own son has been brought before him on a charge of robbery: the judge must either hear the case and pronounce sentence according to the law or resign forever from the bench. Creon orders both of them sealed up in a cave without bread or water. Antigone hangs herself and Ismene dies before Hæmon, who has defied his father, can break down the walls and rescue her. Hæmon thereupon kills himself.

This is a play conforming to Aristotle's definition of tragedy, as a representation of action designed to excite pity and terror and so to purge the emotions. It is not, strictly speaking, the resounding of an ethical problem at all. Not as "profound" in that sense as *Abie's Irish Rose*. The story of that modern play is the courtship and marriage of a Jewish boy and an Irish Catholic girl. There are violent objections to the marriage on both sides—for reasons religious, racial and economic. Deep prejudices are involved. Every one knows that it is a more serious matter with an orthodox Jew for his son to marry a Catholic and a more serious matter with a devout Catholic for his child to marry a Jew than it was among the Athenians of Sophocles' time for a girl to defy a tyrant.

Antigone's defiance was not a serious matter with the Athenians at all. They were citizens of a democracy and opposed to tyrants. They were opposed to the Creon of the play from the first and heart and soul with Antigone, Ismene and Hæmon. Creon was what would be called the "heavy," or villain, of modern melodrama. The Athenians enjoyed the *Antigone* for precisely the reason it was designed: they could cry over the fate of Antigone. After they had a good cry they felt better. That is all there is to Aristotle's famous doctrine of the "purging of the emotions of pity and terror" by means of tragedy. Aristotle was the son of a physician and had probably learned from his father the psychological value to the health of an occasional good cry. Those *Kinder-Kirche-Küche* German scholars who imagine that Athenian women did not attend the theater are simply silly: there would be no point in most of the plays of Sophocles and Euripides if there were no women in the audience; and it is practically certain that if the Athenian dramatists wrote only for stag audiences the plays would never have arisen above the obscene farces of the Old Comedy period preceding Aristophanes, at least two of whose comedies were especially designed to appeal to women.

I repeat, the ethical problem involved in Antigone's defiance was settled, as far as the Athenian audience was concerned, as soon as the theme was announced in the prologue. The *Antigone* is superior to *Abie's Irish Rose* because of art, image, story and universality, not because of ethical content. The Athenians knew the story already. In fact, they knew all the stories about the family of Laius, the family of Alcmæon, and the family of Orestes. These stories were not only the common property of the playwrights before Sophocles but the conventions made them choose these plots rather than invent new ones. Aristotle is quite explicit on this point: "Of old the poets adopted any casual fables; but now the most beautiful tragedies are composed about a few families; as for instance, about Alcmæon, Œdipus, Orestes, Meleager, Tyestes, and Telephus, and such other persons as happen either to have suffered or done things of a dreadful nature. The tragedy, therefore, which is most beautiful according to art, is of this construction."

The favorite source of tragic plots and the one made use of by nearly all of the dramatists was the legend of the descendants of Laius. The legends concerning this family corresponded very closely to the legends built up by "scientific investigators" about the notorious Jukes family so dear to American eugenists. The Jukes, as you may remember, were supposed to be a notoriously incestuous family in northern New York, whose descendants turned out very badly, according to the "reports," becoming parricides, murderers, imbeciles, epileptics, common criminals and prostitutes. This was also the Greek story of the incestuous descendants of Laius: they were parricides like Œdipus and Orestes, adulterous murderers like Clytemnestra, epileptics like Orestes, common criminals like Eteocles.

According to the legend, Laius, King of Thebes, married Jocasta (called Epicasta by Homer), but was warned by an oracle against having children and told that if he did so, his son would slay him. Laius and Jocasta refrained from having children until they both got drunk one night at a festival and failed to take precautions. A son was born to them, but the child was immediately turned over

to servants to be exposed to death on a hillside, the tendons of his
heel pierced and tied around the ankles with a thong

A servant of Polybus, king of the adjoining city state of
Corinth, found the infant and brought it to the wife of Polybus who
was childless. The royal pair reared the child as their son and heir.
This child they called Œdipus, or "Swollen-foot," on account of the
deformity caused when the child's ankle was pierced. When Œdipus
was grown to young manhood, at a large dinner one night he over-
heard some of his father's guests casting doubts on his real parentage, and he resolved next day to consult the oracle of Delphi
about it.

The oracle evaded the question at issue but advised Œdipus
not to return to his native land, for if he did so he would kill his
father and marry his mother. Œdipus nevertheless set out for
Thebes. On the road from Delphi in his chariot his way was im-
peded by an old man on foot with a small retinue of attendants.
The charioteer cried out to the old man to make way for a prince
of the royal blood. The old man replied that he was of royal blood
himself and in fact a king, and he refused to make way. A fight
ensued in which Œdipus not only killed the old man but his whole
body of retainers. This old man, although Œdipus did not learn it
till long afterward, was his father, Laius, on his way to consult the
oracle at Delphi about a rumor he had heard that his son was still
alive.

The preposterous improbabilities of this legend increase as the
story went on, although none of the improbabilities ever deterred
the Athenian dramatists. Having killed his father, Œdipus resumed
his way toward Thebes. In the absence of Laius, Juno, who was
always hostile to Thebes, sent the Sphinx to ravage the territory.
The Sphinx was a monster with the face of a woman, the breast,
feet and tail of a lion and the wings of a bird, and had been taught
riddles by the Muses. The Sphinx propounded a riddle to the Thebans, "What is it that has a voice, goes on four feet in the morning,
on two at noon, and on three in the evening?" The oracle said that
the Thebans would not be rid of the Sphinx until they solved her
riddle. Whenever they failed the Sphinx carried off and devoured
one of the citizens.

Finally when Hæmon,* son of Creon, was devoured by the

* The reader will remember that in Sophocles' *Antigone* Hæmon killed
himself. This is just one of those little inconsistencies so common in Greek
mythology and drama. Don't worry about it.

Sphinx (Creon had succeeded to the throne on the unexplained and uninvestigated death of Laius), Creon announced he would yield the throne and the hand of his sister in marriage to whoever would solve the Sphinx's riddle. Œdipus, who had reached the city by this time, stepped forward and answered the Sphinx: "It is Man; when an infant he creeps on all fours; in manhood he walks on two feet; and in old age he carries a staff." The Sphinx thereupon expired. Œdipus became king of Thebes and unknowingly married his own mother Jocasta, who was the sister of Creon. Thereafter dire things began to happen to Œdipus, to his wife and their children, and to all those who had married into the family, such as Electra, Agamemnon, Ægisthus, and Clytemnestra.

The history of this family or of members of other families who had married into it was considered by the Greeks, as the above quotation from Aristotle shows, the only proper source of material for tragedy. The convention for tragedy was the unhappy ending. Aristotle is explicit on this point: "It is necessary that the plot which is well constructed shall be single rather than two-fold, though some say it should be the latter, and that the change should not be into prosperity from adversity, but on the contrary into adversity from prosperity, not through depravity, but through some great error, either of such a character as we have mentioned [Œdipus] or rather better than worse."

If moral philosophers like Irving Babbitt had read Aristotle and the Greek dramatists carefully or even casually, they would have realized that it is to Euripides that they should refer in support of their doctrine of the "will to refrain." It was Euripides, not Sophocles, who held people responsible for the consequences of their actions. And it was precisely for this reason that Euripides was unpopular with Athenian audiences and Sophocles was popular. Sophocles gave them a good cry, but did not remind them that they themselves might suffer the consequences of their own wrongdoing. Sophocles was the Pollyanna of Greek drama; Euripides shook up their complacencies. Euripides also helped vastly to change the point of view of the Greeks; for, although he was not very popular in his lifetime, for several centuries after his death his were the most popular of all Greek tragedies, not only in Athens, but in Ephesus, Delphi, Megapolis, Eretria, Pergamum and Epidaurus.

To Sophocles was attributed the statement, "Euripides depicts people as they are; I depict them as they ought to be." It is certain that Euripides was in constant revolt, not only against the conven-

tions of Attic tragedy, but against the amiable and flabby ethical
content of plays like those which had held the boards since the death
of Æschylus. And there were literally hundreds of these plays. Only
a handful of these dramas have come down to us; but Sophocles is
said to have written 123 plays, Euripides 93, Æschylus more than a
hundred, Menander 109, and among the prize-winning playwriters
at Athens were Aristias, Theodektas, Achæus, Aphareus, Eutes,
Nothippus, Poluphrasmon, Cratinus, and Carcinus.

SOPHOCLES, according to Aristotle, originated nothing and contributed nothing new to the theater except the painted backdrop
curtain. Æschylus had been the real genius and was called the
father of tragedy, for having first increased the number of players
from one recitalist and a chorus to two players, thus giving action
to the spectacle instead of its being a simple recitation with music
as it had been before Æschylus' time. Sophocles developed the technique to perfection without innovations and without bringing a
fresh point of view. His plays were about the sort of thing Ben
Jonson's plays would have been about if they had been written by
Dr. Samuel Johnson instead of by the erudite and belligerent
Elizabethan. Euripides brought something new, fresh, realistic and
disturbing to the theater, and his example was adopted by all dramatists who followed him—Agathon, Menander and the rest. He
brought reality to the stage, and Attic drama was never to go back
to the unrealities of Sophocles.

It is to be remembered that Aristotle's objections to Euripides
are technical and not ethical or esthetic, and that Aristotle's technical criticism has to do with specific points in relation to tragedy.
Aristotle was a professional teacher, and in the *Poetics* to those
among his pupils who aspired to playwriting he was giving practical,
technical advice on the construction of plays, a field in which
Sophocles excelled. There was one bad technical fault about some
of Euripides' plays, which Aristotle specifically objected to—and
that was the abuse of the "god from the machine" to close a play.
Aristotle considered it a concession to the groundlings in the audience, in the same way that we should consider the tacking on of a
superfluous happy ending at the close of a realistic tragedy of
modern life.

I think Aristotle knew why Euripides did this but did not think
it necessary to explain it to his pupils; and because Aristotle did
not explain why, innumerable pedants and moral philosophers who

quote pedants have almost completely misunderstood Euripides and the real nature of his genius.

Professor Murray is perspicacious enough to see the compulsion Euripides' genius put upon him, but he is frankly puzzled by some of Euripides' plays and admits he does not understand what the *Hippolytus*, the *Alcestis* and the *Bacchæ* are about. He would understand these plays if he realized that (1) Euripides was a very daring innovator in dramatic technique, language and point of view, and (2) he had to make his living by writing plays; he had no other source of income, as had Sophocles, who possessed considerable property and a factory turning out a profitable line of shields, greaves, spears, helmets, swords and other implements of warfare.

Euripides began his playwriting career by imitating Æschylus; developed his own startling style and method; found that style and method too much for the Athenians at first; lost the prize several times with his best efforts; made concessions with his endings, without falsifying his vision, to get his plays produced; offended the audience again by having a dissembling and dishonest character in the *Hippolytus* talk as such a character would; was charged with impiety for this; got very embittered and wrote the *Bacchæ*, insulting not only the audience but also the patron god of the drama, Dionysus (this was the only time Dionysus ever was brought upon the stage in tragedy and his effigy was sitting out in front of the stage, presumably witnessing and presiding over the play); retired from Athens to the court of Archelaus in Macedon, where he lived surrounded by his friends, Agaton, the dramatist; Timotheus, the musician; Xeuxis, the painter; and Thucydides, the historian; all of whom had fled the hectic life of Athens.

There in the peace and quiet of his declining years he grew soft, sweet and amiable, as Shakespeare did, and wrote the romantic, untroubling plays, *Helena* and *Andromeda*, full of nice music and fine sentiments. (It must be remembered that an Athenian tragedy was more like a modern opera than it is like a modern play; the author had to write both the words and the music, and he was also supposed to act the principal rôle, at least on the occasion of his first offering in the prize competition. Thus Æschylus played the part of Prometheus in *Prometheus Bound,* and Sophocles and Euripides in youth and middle age were actors in the plays they wrote.)

ÆSCHYLUS was born of a noble family in Eleusis in Attica in 525 B.C. He was provided with a good education under the tutelage of private instructors, which means that, among other things, he learned "music," a term used in his youth to embrace "numbers" or the various forms of poetic diction as well as the music of the harp, flute, clarinet and voice. In his youth, theatrical performances were a simple, declamatory affair, wherein brief legends were woven into narratives in iambic and trochaic meter, instead of the dactylic hexameters of epic poetry. These compositions were recited to music by one performer and a chorus. The chorus was the principal feature of the performance and remained, through the time of Æschylus, Sophocles and Euripides, the one indispensable element of the tragic drama. The chorus was in costume and the early playlet was a spectacle, performed twice a year at the festival of Dionysus, or god of wine.

Æschylus in his youth tried his hand at various types of poetry, even amatory verse, and at the age of twenty-five he submitted his first attempt as a tragic dramatist. We have no fragment of this play and do not know what it was about, but the legend is that Æschylus took part in it as an actor. When next we hear of him he is a soldier and a hero at the Battle of Marathon, receiving public commendation for his bravery. Indeed, if Æschylus wrote the epitaph attributed to him, he considered himself more of a soldier than a dramatist, or at least believed his service as a soldier had been of greater benefit to the state than his work as a dramatist. The epitaph reads (Walter Leaf's translation, in *Little Poems from the Greek*):

> I, Æschylus of Athens, buried lie,
> Euphorion's son, in Gela's fruitful land:
> My worth the long-haired Mede can testify,
> And the renowned Marathonian strand.

Ten years after the Battle of Marathon he fought in the Battle of Salamis and a year later served with Athenian troops in Platæa. Both between wars and afterward he engaged in writing and acting both satyr-plays and tragedies. We haven't much real information about what satyr-plays were like, except that they were some kind of spectacle involving words and music, wherein the performers wore goat-like costumes, with masks and tails, and that they differed from the comus-plays, where the performers wore masks, were made up like Silenus and his crew of roisterers and had the phallic symbol (a ridiculously large leather object) sewed to their costumes at the groins. The distinction between the satyr-play and the tragedy, I believe, was that the latter was more elevated in character, just as the satyr-play was more refined than the comus-play.

In 472 B.C. Æschylus won the prize at the Dionysiac festival with a tetrology consisting of the *Persæ,* which we have, and the *Phineus,* the *Glaucus Potniensis* and another play, all three of which have been lost. The *Persæ* was the second play of the tetrology. If Aristotle is correct, Æschylus had already revolutionized tragedy by the time he composed this work of his maturity and had not only written a play with more than one character and a chorus, but had chosen almost contemporary historical subjects for heroic treatment—a new departure also. Æschylus had taken part in the Battle of Salamis, which had shattered the power and threat of the Persian invaders and had insured for a while the supremacy of Athens. Æschylus laid his scene at the court of the Persian King, Xerxes, invested it with oriental splendor, invoked the Ghost of Darius, and celebrated in brooding and heroic grandeur the struggle between the Orient and Greece.

The highest point of Æschylus' achievement was the *Prometheus Bound,* which may have been one of a trilogy which included *Prometheus Unbound* and *Prometheus the Fire-Bringer,* both of which have been lost. The last named may have been the first play in the trilogy. The *Prometheus Bound* is one of such grandeur of conception, such intelligent understanding of human motives, such simple majesty and force that it is impressive in any translation, even Anna Swanwick's, and is touchingly beautiful in the poetic rendition by Elizabeth Barrett Browning. Reading this poetic version of the *Prometheus Bound* by Mrs. Browning, which I came across quite by accident when I was fourteen years of age, was my first encounter with Greek literature. It awoke in me a consuming interest in, and curiosity about, Greek drama, prose and poetry. I read Mrs. Browning's version so many times I committed it to memory, not by intention but by attention—the whole play, from beginning to end. It recounts how Prometheus defied Zeus' orders and brought mortals the great gift of fire and how, because of this impious act, he was chained to a precipice in the Caucasus where an eagle descended every day to eat out his heart, which grew back again. Prometheus foretells the time when Zeus will be overthrown by a higher moral force just as Zeus had overthrown Chronos. It is thus a thrilling but irreverent play, human and majestic.

Some time during Æschylus' career he seems to have introduced a reference to the Mysteries into one of his plays in a way which was considered a profanation. The audience rose up and was about to mob him when Æschylus' brother, who was acting in the drama with Æschylus, lifted his robe, showing the stump of his own arm lost in the Battle of Salamis, and indicated that both he and Æschylus had fought there. This quieted the mob and saved his brother's life.

It may have been at this same competition that the young Sophocles defeated Æschylus for the first time. At any rate, Æschylus seems to have been embittered by the treatment he had been accorded and by the ingratitude of the Athenians, and to have left the city and taken up residence at the court of Hiero, Prince of Syracuse. It seems probable that while he was in Syracuse he composed his Orestean tetrology and that these four plays were not only performed at Syracuse but that copies of them were sent back to Athens and there produced by his brother, Aminias.

Æschylus died at the age of sixty-nine in Gela. No details of his private life have come down to us, although there are many references in antiquity to his intemperance. He was accused of doing all of his writing while under the influence of wine, which may well have been true: there is intoxication of some sort in his sublime conceptions, whether induced by wine or whatever means. But that, as Athenæus reports to have been common gossip, Æschylus was always so drunk he did not know what he was writing (the interpretation put upon Sophocles' remark, "Æschylus does the right thing without knowing why he does it") is probably exaggerated.

SOPHOCLES was born in the village of Colonnus, about a mile from Athens in 495 B.C. His father was a rich man, a manufacturer of arms. Sophocles was noted for his personal beauty in his youth and for his skill in athletics. It is reported that when he was sixteen years of age he was selected to lead the chorus of boys who performed the pæan of triumph when news was brought to the city of the victory of Salamis. It is certain that he received the best education available at his time. The occasion of his submitting his first dramatic composition to an Athenian audience was on the sacred holiday declared by Cimon when he ordered the remains of Theseus transferred from the island of Scyros to Athens. Sophocles was then only twenty-five years old. In this competition Sophocles was pitting his fledgling talent against the impressive talent of the veteran Æschylus.

The awarding of this prize, which went to Sophocles, was

irregular. The customary procedure was to award the prize by acclamation or vote of the entire audience. On this occasion the judges who counted the votes were joined by Cimon and his nine generals, who performed the libations to Dionysus and sat down with the judges. Instead of referring the decision to the audience, Cimon and his nine generals awarded the prize themselves. When it is remembered that Sophocles' father was a rich munitions manufacturer, there is at least some slight room for doubt that this irregular award, dominated by Cimon and his associates, was strictly on the merits of the dramas involved. If we had the play which Sophocles submitted and the play Æschylus submitted, our doubts might or might not be removed.

At all events, this victory launched Sophocles on a successful playwriting career. He continued to write for the theater for sixty-three years, winning the first prize nineteen times, the second prize more frequently, and he never sank to third prize. However, Sophocles did not devote his entire time to the theater. He succeded to the ownership and managment of the munitions plant; at the age of fifty-seven he was awarded the commission of a full-fledged general (although he was without previous experience as a soldier) in the unimportant war against Samos; and in his old age he was appointed hierophant of the temple to the hero, Alon. His life for the most part was serene; his career coincided with one of the most peaceful and prosperous interludes in Athenian history. He was deferred to and respected, as a rich, genial, pious, amiable citizen, well liked by all.

Toward the very end of his life there occurred the only events which gave him sorrow. Civil dissension followed the close of the Peloponnesian War and affairs of the city-state of Athens began to take on a desperate and disordered character. Added to this, the domestic life of Sophocles was clouded by disagreeable matters. He had for some time been the provider for a *hetaira* (literally, "lady-friend"), named Theoris and the discovery of this brought to an end his tranquillity. His son, Iophon, brought suit to have him committed or declared incompetent to manage his business affairs, evidently fearing that the property would fall into the hands of Theoris. The old man convinced the judges of his sanity, it appears, either by reading a composition he had just written or by reciting one of the most famous passages from his plays and the case was dismissed. He died when the Athenians were being besieged by the Lacedæ-monians. The era of peace and prosperity which Athens had enjoyed was at an end; and new ideas were already occupying thoughtful men's minds.

EURIPIDES, who was fifteen years younger than Sophocles, was destined to come to maturity toward the close of that old era and to be a child of the new. Euripides was born of a middle class family in Phyla, a borough of Athens, in 480 B.C., on the day of the victory of the Greeks at Salamis. Whether his mother was an herb-peddler or vegetable woman or not, as Aristophanes and others have it, does not matter in the least; nor do I see why Professor Murray and others are so anxious to prove that she was not, and that she was, instead the daughter of a noble family. I think she was a vegetable woman and that she probably peddled lettuce and leeks from door to door. That is what Aristophanes, a contemporary, said she was; and what Theophrastus only a little later repeated. This does not mean that she was a vegetable woman all her life; it merely means that at one time or another she had sold vegetables. She may have done so only when she was a young and pretty girl, before Mnesarchides, a petty functionary of the state, who seems also to have owned some land, married her. It was not until Philochorus, an Alexandrian critic and grammarian, started to work on the matter several centuries later that the notion took root, which Professor Murray accepts, that the mother of Euripides was of noble ancestry. After denying that Kleito was a "green-groceress" and asserting unequivocally that she was "of noble family," Professor Murray immediately says, with a surprising turn of mind, "Our evidence suggests that her relation toward her son was one of exceptional intimacy and influence; and motherly love certainly forms a strong element in his dramas." What a sequitur! As if the relations of vegetable women toward their sons are without intimacy or influence; and as if sons decline to love mothers who happen to be vegetable women!

As Euripides grew into young manhood, fortune must have accrued in some way to his father, because one of Euripides' tutors was Prodicus, whose tuition fee was notoriously high. He was also a pupil of Anaxagoras and Protagoras, the philosophers. I believe Protagoras, who is the subject of and a character in one of the *Dialogues* of Plato, exerted the strongest influence upon his mind. Among Euripides' intimates as a youth was Socrates, also a pupil of Anaxagoras. Although I find no authority for it, there is reason to believe, from a passage in Aristotle, that Socrates, besides being a

SOPHOCLES AND GREEK DRAMA

sculptor and a philosopher, produced a few literary compositions and that he may have invented the dialogue form which was developed by Xenophon and Plato and expanded to embrace scenes of common life by Lucian.

It is known that Socrates composed some verses and that he played the lyre. But in distinguishing the different forms of literary composition—the epic, the elegies, the rhapsody, *et cetera,* Aristotle also distinguishes between the "Mimes of Sophron and the Dialogues of Socrates." He doesn't say, "the Dialogues of Plato"; but "the Dialogues of Socrates."

We know what the mimes are, because we have some of the mimes of Herondas: they are very short playlets in dialogue form reciting one episode—the forerunner of the modern short story or one-act play. These mimes were played on a small stage or at private residences by two or three actors (usually female) in costume. They are distinguished from the "Dialogues of Socrates," as we know them through Plato, by the fact that the Socratic dialogues are on disputations and elevated subjects and the cast of characters in them is made up of men in ordinary dress. The Mimes seem to have been designed especially for the amusement of woman; they are about domestic affairs.

There is also a well established story that Socrates helped Euripides in the composition of his early plays. I see no reason to doubt this, because Athenæus quotes Moresimachus and Callias on the subject; but they indicate no more than that Socrates may have read Euripides' manuscript and offered him suggestions for improvement.

It appears that Euripides first thought of becoming an athlete and that at the age of seventeen he was crowned as a victor in the Eleusinian and Thesean contests; but by the time he was twenty-five, he had won third prize in the annual dramatic contests with his satyr-drama the *Plœiades.* This play has not come down to us; but I suspect it may have been an ebullient and extravagant youthful composition—because the curve of his career is so like that of Shakespeare's.

It will be observed that the first composition he submitted in the competition was a satyr-play and not a tragedy. I think the reason some of the commentators cannot make out the meaning of several plays by Euripides is that they think these plays are trage-dies, whereas they are, in reality, satyr plays. Moreover, they naïvely imagine that a Greek tragedy is mournful or serious throughout, whereas nothing is more certain than that passages in tragedies like the *Medea* and *Elektra* of Euripides and the *Philocetes* of Sophocles are intended as "comic relief," and to read and translate them otherwise is to miss both the meaning and the effect of the plays.

Just as Aristophanes knew how to space and time his comic bits so that the laughter of the audience would not interfere with the progress of the play and so that the audience would not be exhausted with laughter before the play was concluded, so also the tragic dramatists knew the importance of occasionally releasing the tension of the audience, before the climax was reached, by interspersing scenes and speeches to make them smile or laugh. Any practiced playwright nowadays knows that unrelieved tragedy defeats its own end before the third act. It exhausts the audience. A comedy which "packs too many laughs" in the first and second acts, disappoints the audience in the third, no matter how funny the third act is: the audience has laughed itself out before the third act is reached.

That Euripides' early and throughout his life displayed some of the aberrations of genius I think there can be no doubt. Genius is an abnormality in the first place and like a harelip or club-foot it does not prevent a man from being as foolish or limited as other people in many respects, outside the province of his genius. In that genius he may be supreme and still be unable to add up a column of figures, undependable as a friend, or unable to get along with his wife.

Euripides' private life was unhappy. He divorced his first wife, Melito, for adultery; and he was equally unfortunate in regard to his second wife, whom he also divorced for the same reason. This private emotion had its effect on his plays; as why, indeed, should it not? He depicted his first wife, I think, in his portrait of Helen in the *Orestes* and he depicted himself in the character of Agamemnon, the husband whom Clytemnestra had cuckolded in his absence and who was murdered by his wife and her paramour. It is important to note that he does not idealize Agamemnon; for Euripides makes saints out of no one whatever. He depicts Menelaus, husband of Helen, as an amiable, indecisive weakling, slightly ridiculous because he had taken his wife back after she had once made a fool out of him, and intimates that she would do it again and again.

Euripides is the first dramatist on record who specialized in

depicting the minds and emotions of women and the intricate problem of sexual relationships. In the *Orestes* there is an unrivaled
scene between Helen and Electra. Helen has sneaked back at night
into the palace of Menelaus after her historic flight with Paris,
knowing full well that Menelaus will forgive her and wishing to
avoid being seen by the women of Sparta, who certainly would not
think any too well of her. She is discovered by Electra, a vixenish
and self-righteous woman, who tells Helen just what she thinks of
her. The claws come out on both sides of this cat fight. Helen's
retort is to the effect that Electra is an old maid and badly in need
of a man and that if she had had the opportunity she would have
eloped with Paris, too; but, alas, she is too unattractive to cause
a man like Paris to fall head over heels in love with her, as he did
with Helen. The quarrel proceeds while Orestes, the epileptic brother
whom Electra had persuaded to murder their adulterous mother, is
raving in an adjoining room. Both women are full of venom and
sarcasm, but Helen is perfectly assured that Menelaus will forgive
her and indulge her in everything, and what is more Electra is sure
of it too and is bitterly cynical about women like her mother and
Helen.

Now, the extraordinary thing is that Euripides' experience with
his wife (or with his two wives, if the *Orestes* was written after his
second marriage) helped him to understand women, apparently;
for his portrait of Helen is sympathetic, not bitter or distorted.
Helen is the heroine of the *Orestes*. She is mischievous, calculating,
self-assured, hypocritical and selfish; but she is beautiful, charming,
gracious, winning—and she does no one any particular harm of her
own accord, even if what she did in following her heart brought
"woes unnumbered to the tribes of Greece."

In the *Orestes* and the *Elektra* there are incomparably subtle
delineations of women. And Euripides is equally successful in characterizing men. Euripides during his high creative period is set
against the idealistic representations of life in plays like those of
Sophocles. His revolt is a burning conviction that such false representations of life corrupt men and make real honor and integrity a
mockery. The people of Athens had been seeing plays like those of
Sophocles and his predecessors for years—these elevating plays;
and look what condition the city and its inhabitants were in! Wars,
which had been glorified in the plays, had depleted the treasury,
reduced a large part of the population to beggary; the rabble ruled;
profiteers spouted platitudes and mulcted the populace—all because

of a false and self-deceiving sense of reality inculcated by the romantic poets.

Euripides and most of his fellow citizens had been reduced to poverty by these wars that had been so celebrated in epic poetry and in the theater, and he began to examine the legends with a critical and realistic eye. As a dramatist he was compelled to follow these legends, because that was the convention and apparently one of the conditions on which plays were admitted into the competition. (It is probable that the theme or themes which the competing dramatists might treat in their plays were given out before the competitors started to work.) Very well, Euripides would follow these legends, but he would have something new to say about them. Incest was incest, murder was murder, adultery was adultery, and blood-feuds were multiple murders—there was nothing glorious about any of them. He would show there wasn't.

We know, in a way, how his plays were received. At first, no doubt, with amazement but interest, resentment but admiration; with the old conservatives, whose occupation it is to conserve invalid ideas, ranting and denouncing him—just as Ibsen was much later to raise a hurricane by having a mature and spirited woman leave her house and home, because she refused any longer to be treated as a brainless doll by her husband. Euripides not only gave the populace something new to think about on social, sexual and domestic themes, but about corrupt politics in a democracy, the selfishness of kings and dictators, the incompetence of the heads of state, and the hypocrisy of demogogues.

The staid citizenry began to bait him. He was brought to dock on a charge of impiety but was released. He had been living, it appears, on the seashore at Salamis, writing his plays in a cave facing the sea, whence he had fled the noise and bickerings of the city; but now he accepted an invitation to go to the court of Archelaus in Macedonia, where he continued to write until his death, 406 B.C., in his seventy-fifth year.

Professor Murray seems to think the *Bacchæ* was composed in Macedonia; but I feel sure that this play was written during a period of special bitterness in his middle-age, that it was submitted to the judges for production and rejected. This play cannot be understood as anything except a violent and merciless satire, cutting five or six different ways at once, without a hero—everybody in it is satirized, even Tiresias and Cadmus (always treated with tender respect by dramatists and poets), even Dionysus (the patron god in whose honor the play competitions were held). The Teetotaler, Pentheus, whom some have tried to establish as the hero of the play, is a hypocrite of the worst sort. He is aroused against the women who are following the new god, Dionysus, in his Asiatic rites of intoxication; but when he learns that these women who are gathered on the hillside are also riotously indulging in sexual orgies, his ears prick up at once; he wishes to disguise himself and take a peek, even if it is a profanation of sacred rites, an act as serious as if he, a male, invaded the temple of Ceres kept sacred by vestal virgins.

The venerable Cadmus and the blind prophet Tiresias are brought upon the stage very drunk, with vine leaves in their white hair and in their hands the thymas, sacred to the rites of Dionysus (Bacchus). They are in haste to join the drinking orgy of the women, and Cadmus undertakes to lead Tiresias. Pentheus' own mother is in the crowd of rioting women and when they discover Pentheus peeking at them from a tree where he has concealed himself among the branches, they uproot the tree, and tear him limb from limb. His own mother, very drunk, seizes his severed head, thinking they have slain a lion.

In the last scene of this gruesome tragedy Pentheus' mother comes on the stage bearing her son's head in her hands and babbling drunkenly about having killed a lion. Not until Dionysus shakes her and makes her come to her senses does she realize what it really is she has in her hands. Euripides closes the play with a concession to the populace, but nothing could save it from the preliminary condemnation of the judges. Nevertheless, after the death of Euripides, the *Bacchæ* was produced and it continued to hold the boards for many years.

ONE of the most important dates in the history of Greek literature is the year 486 B.C., when comedy received official sanction and prizes began to be awarded for it in the annual competition of plays at the City Dionysia. This was about thirty years before the birth of Aristophanes, the greatest genius of the genre whose work has come down to us.

These play competitions were held twice a year, during the Lenæan festival in December or January and during the Dionysiac festival in March or April. Both of these were religious festivals; but you will hardly appreciate their character unless you disabuse your minds of the ordinary connotations of the adjective "religious." From our modern point of view these religious festivals of the

Greeks were the very occasions when the Greeks ceased, for the time being, to be religious. During the Dionysiac festival, the image of the god Dionysus was removed from the temple to games and theatrical performances—an action symbolical of the god's holiday from his august office and of his mingling with the people. It was an occasion of revelry, wherein all ordinary duties and obligations were in abeyance. Business was suspended, slaves were free to address and mingle with their masters on a plane of equality, prisoners were released from jail, every one was privileged to indulge in open criticism and jest without fear of punishment or suits for libel, and, more important, all or nearly all of the ordinary rules of decorum were suspended. Every one in the city, high-born and slaves alike, whose age and temperament permitted them to do so, gave themselves over to revelry and drinking, flirtations and promiscuous love-making. In the New Comedy after the Old Comedy of Aristophanes and his contemporaries, the untoward outcome of these periods of license formed one of the trite themes of comedy; for they were, it appears, invariably followed by a great number of illegitimate births and other problems affecting domestic peace and household economy.

From the fact that comedy was not permitted at the Lenæan festival until about 442 B.C., while tragedy had long enjoyed the boards there, I suspect that the Lenæan festival was somewhat more solemn than the Dionysiac festival. Lenæus was one of the many names for Bacchus. Dionysus was another. But I think that Lenæus may have been a corruption of Linus, who appears to have been a musician and poet who flourished about 1200 B.C., and who later acquired semi-divinity. Homer mentions the song of Linus as being a dirge or lament sung by the grape-pickers at work in harvest time. It was evidently a plaintive melody, perhaps like the *Song of the Volga Boatman* or the Russian and Magyar folk-songs we have now. In legend, Linus was a beautiful youth, torn to pieces by wild dogs, and as well (by an incongruity permissible in legends) the poet-musician who invented the music form of the songs mourning his death. The class of Linus songs also appears to have embraced laments for the death of spring, destroyed by the summer heat. In Homer, the Linus song is sung by a boy with a harp, as he moves along in measured tread with the women while they bear baskets of grapes on their heads from the vineyards. The song ended in the shrill cry "Ai! Linus!"

It is my belief, supported by suggestions from Aristotle and by internal evidence from the plays of Æschylus, that the dithyramb was a development of the Linus song, if the Linus song was not actually a dithyramb. The mournful quality of it was ennobled and refined by Phrynichus and Æschylus, I believe, and erected into the chorus style and convention by Sophocles and Euripides, which Aristophanes parodied in *The Clouds*. Aristophanes says the dithyrambic poets got paid for writing such phrases as these: "the rapid flight of the moist clouds, which veil the brightness of day," "the waving locks of the hundred-headed Typho," "the impetuous tempests, which float through the heavens, like birds of prey with aërial wings, loaded with mists." In other words, Aristophanes decries the fact that versifiers drew money for such highfalutin phrases.

THE above is only conjecture, of course, because very little is known really about the origin and development of either tragedy or comedy beyond the bare suggestions Aristotle gives us. According to one tradition, comedy was invented by Thespis, a native of Icara, a village near Athens, in the middle of the sixth century B.C. Up to that time the Bacchic festivals were largely occasions for merry pranks and buffooneries of men and boys in carnival costumes who followed in the wake of the Dionysiac procession. In this procession was carried the image of the god and also the phallic symbol of fructification. The carnival costumes were of various kinds, then as now; some revelers were made up to resemble roosters, crows, frogs, beetles, lions and goats. Apparently the goat costume became the favorite. The sallies of song and jest at first, it appears, were extemporaneous; but gradually certain of these ribald and merry songs became formalized and were sung in chorus.

To Thespis, who appears to have been an actor, a musician and a dancer, as well as a poet who took part in these Bacchic festivals professionally, was anciently attributed the idea of making a stationary spectacle of the spontaneous and exhausting rounds of pranks. He appears to have written a "show," trained and rehearsed a chorus with songs of his own composition, built a sort of stage and came forward in his own person, with his face smeared in comic fashion with vermilion, and to have recited lampoons. He interspersed his recital with music and dancing by his buffoonish chorus. Phrynichus, a pupil of Thespis and a predecessor and older contemporary of Æschylus, seems to have turned from the light-hearted satiric entertainments of Thespis and to have used the same form, but for a more solemn kind of performance, based upon the dithyramb.

So it is probable that tragedy and comedy developed simultaneously and side by side. Indeed, the first tragedies, so-called, were tetrologies, in which the first three plays were tragic and the last satyric or humorous. When there were only three plays, in a series on one theme by a single dramatist, the third was a satyr play or comedy.

But comedy or burlesque also developed on its own, and it does not appear that Aristophanes ever tried his hand at tragedy. Instead, as a young man, he wrote very low comedies of the sort which were "for men only" and not performed in the regular theaters. This information does not occur in any of the biographies of him; but it is something he tells us about himself in *The Clouds*.

From a parabasis in *The Clouds* we learn that in his youth Aristophanes wrote two skits for male audiences only. They were *The Young Man* and *The Debauchee*. He says they were well received. Later he wrote comedies presentable for audiences made up of women and children as well as men; but he was not yet thirty, which was the age a comic playwright had to attain before he could participate in the prize competition, and so his comedies appeared under other names. When he attained the full maturity required by the rules of the competition and offered under his own name *The Knights,* he had, he tells us, greatly refined not only his own method, but the methods employed by others to provoke laughs. In *The Clouds,* in his address to the audience beseeching them to vote him the prize for the play they are witnessing, he says he is writing for a refined and respectable audience.

"Observe," he says, "the modest demeanor of my comedy. She has not sewn on a piece of hanging leather, thick and reddened at the end [the phallus] to cause laughter among the children; she does not make fun of the bald-headed men, nor does she dance the hootchie-cootchie for them; no old man is seen who, while uttering his lines, batters his questioner with a slap-stick to make his poor jokes seem funnier. She does not rush upon the scene carrying a torch and screaming 'Tra-la, tra-la!' [in burlesque of the spring song dances]."

In fact, Aristophanes did not, even in his time, resort to the low devices used by his predecessors and still used by burlesque comedians in our own day. His wit is subtle; his satire is cutting; and his humor based upon profound understanding of human nature.

More than Æschylus, Sophocles, or Euripides, Aristophanes is acceptable and understandable to us now. There is more universality to his genius. His *Lysistrata* is an almost literal translation and with very few changes in the text was presented to American audiences all over the country in 1931, enjoying enormous popularity. Attempts to revive productions of Sophocles and Euripides by little theater groups and dramatic societies in colleges have been mournful failures. The lines of the chorus and actors of the plays of Sophocles and Euripides were sung and declaimed to the music of a full primitive orchestra, which was made up of musicians playing such instruments as the hydraulic organ, the flute, the clarinet, the trumpet, the triangle, castanets, drums, the lyre, the nine-stringed enneachord and such now unidentified instruments as the phœnices, pectides, magadides, sambucæ, clepsiambi, and scindapsi. We do not know what this music was like; hence a performance of Sophocles or Euripides, without music, is about as spiritless as a performance of *The Magic Flute* would be without the music. The humor and sense of Aristophanes' dialogues and choruses, however, are imperishable. There are other plays by Aristophanes besides the *Lysistrata,* notably *The Clouds, The Knights* and *The Birds,* which might easily be popular with contemporary audiences with very few changes in translation and adaptation.

Let us take, for instance, *The Clouds.* Too serious-minded commentators have mistaken the nature of this play and so, to that extent, have misunderstood the nature of comedy altogether. They have considered it a vicious and unwarranted attack on Socrates, and have even gone so far as to allege that Aristophanes was in league with the enemies of Socrates and aided and abetted them in the prosecution which resulted in Socrates' being put to death, although the condemnation of Socrates did not occur until thirty years after *The Clouds* was produced. This is nonsense: Socrates and Aristophanes were friends; and Plato, who almost worshiped Socrates and would not have tolerated an enemy of Socrates, paid Aristophanes the highest critical tribute he ever bestowed on any playwright and made him a sympathetic character and friend of Socrates in one of the *Dialogues.*

To believe that Aristophanes was an enemy of Socrates on the evidence of *The Clouds* or an enemy of Euripides on the evidence of *The Birds* is to believe that the Messrs. George S. Kaufman, Morris Ryskind and Ira Gershwin, the authors of the Pulitzer Prize Play for 1931, *Of Thee I Sing,* were enemies of President Hoover and

Vice-President Curtis. To believe that the Socrates of the older play was supposed to be a portrait of the philosopher and an exact representation of his ideas and function is to believe that the character of Vice-President Throttlebottom in *Of Thee I Sing* is supposed to be an exact representation of the ideas and function of a Vice-President.

In *The Clouds* Aristophanes satirizes the weaknesses of human nature, particularly the weaknesses of the Athenians in the audience. He uses Socrates as an occasion and as a symbol, just as he uses Strepsiades as a type of well-to-do person who is tight-fisted and has a spendthrift son. Phidippides (doubtless a caricature Alcibiades, because of Alcibiades' fondness for chariot racing) has run his father, Strepsiades, deeply into debt by his extravagance in maintaining a stable of racing horses. Strepsiades hears there is a school of teachers in town where students are taught how to win lawsuits. That is just the thing he is after, because bailiffs are hounding him. He joins the school of Socrates, who teaches profound things while seated in a basket which is suspended in the air, his "head always in the clouds."

The early lessons are perplexing to Strepsiades, who is impatient to skip everything in order to get to the main object of his studies—which is to win lawsuits, particularly those in which he is in the wrong. He has not yet been ushered into the presence of Socrates before he utters a sentence which probably convulsed the audience. A disciple is showing him a map and pointing to a spot which he says is Athens. "Athens!" replies Strepsiades. "You must be mistaken: I see no court sitting." This is a jest at the litigiousness of the Athenians, a habit which kept all of the courts almost continually in session.

Socrates comes in, recites some comic hocus-pocus and begins to interrogate Strepsiades. This dialogue ensues:

Socrates: Come, tell me what kind of mind you have; it is important that I should know this, that I may order my batteries against you in a new fashion.

Strepsiades: Great gods! Are you going to assault me?

Socrates: No. I only wish to ask you some questions. Have you any memory?

Strepsiades: That depends: if anything is owed me, my memory is excellent: but if I owe, alas! I have no memory whatever.

Socrates: Have you a natural gift for speaking?

Strepsiades: For speaking, no; for cheating, yes.

The catechism continues in like vein. Strepsiades has made it plain that he wants to learn "one of your two methods of reasoning, the one whose object is not to repay anything," and later, still impatient, he says he does not want to learn oratory, he wants to learn how to beat his debts. Still Socrates continues to ask him Socratic questions on all sorts of subjects until Strepsiades cries out: "But I have told you a thousand times what I want. I don't want to pay my creditors!"

Strepsiades is too stupid to learn what Socrates has to teach, so he sends his son to learn in his place. The son learns quickly and with zest. He learns from Socrates that turn about is fair play, which Phidippides interprets to mean that, if his father beat him for his own good when he was young, it is now time for him to beat his father for his father's own good. He proceeds to do so. The revolt of youth under Socrates is too much for Strepsiades and, in a rage, he burns down Socrates' house.

On this slender frame-work of plot, Aristophanes has made subtly comical observations on human nature that are laughable in the extreme. He has also worked into it many jesting allusions to people alive at the time the play was written, who were probably in the audience. A well founded story comes down that on the occasion when *The Clouds* was first presented Socrates arose and remained standing throughout the performance so that the audience would recognize the original caricature on the stage. Socrates knew it was all in good fun, and he doubtless enjoyed the play as much as anybody.

This was true also, I believe, of the so-called "attacks" of Aristophanes on Euripides. Professor Murray, who has a strong and justifiable partisanship for Euripides as against Sophocles, is taken in by the grammarian's tradition that Aristophanes was bitterly opposed to Socrates and Euripides; and although Professor Murray realizes that Euripides made such an impression upon Aristophanes that he knew most of Euripides' plays by heart, nevertheless he cannot quite be fair to Aristophanes. "We do not know of any personal cause of enmity between the two men," writes Professor Murray, "but it is a fact that in a degree far surpassing the other comic writers, Aristophanes can never get Euripides out of his head. One might be content with the fact that Euripides was just the man to see how vulgar and unreal most of the comedians' views were, and that Aristophanes was acute enough to see that he saw it. But it remains a curious thing that Aristophanes, in the first place, irritates Euripides to a noteworthy extent—so much so that Cratinus invented a word 'Euripidoaristophanize' to describe the style of the two."

The point, which Professor Murray fails to see, is that Aristophanes admired Euripides above all other dramatists, and took advantage of the "license of speech" of the Dionysiac ceremonies to advertise his friend by jest. He parodies lines from thirty-three plays by Euripides. He doesn't parody the work of Iophon, the tragic dramatist, in *The Frogs,* because he doesn't consider Iophon worthy of his mettle; he dismisses Iophon with a jest which every Athenian appreciated. He merely has Dionysus wonder what sort of play Iophon would produce without his father's help. Iophon was the son of Sophocles. Iophon won one prize in the dramatic competition, with a play, now lost, in which the story current was that Sophocles had written most of it and moreover had bribed the judges.

These bribes were not easy except in a case like that in which Sophocles was awarded his first dramatic prize, an occasion when Cleon and his nine generals usurped the function of the judges. The judges were elected to office by popular vote, and their duty was to count the votes cast in favor of each dramatist or to count the hands held up by the audience.

Both tragic and comic dramatists commonly practiced devious subtle flatteries of the audience to win their votes; but Aristophanes denounces another means used to win votes which apparently was common. Those dramatists who could afford it employed ushers to pass up and down the aisles distributing figs and dates free of charge. Aristophanes in one of his choruses says he never does this sort of thing, but lets his plays stand on their merits. In another play he parodies the device by having ushers throw pebbles at the audience.

It is actually true, or at least I have found it so, that Aristophanes is more amusing to read than any modern comedy writer, more amusing even than the Shaw of *Androcles and the Lion,* which is close to Aristophanes. Aristophanes in style and method often catered to the groundlings with low buffooneries and with jokes on scatological subjects; but such concessions were necessary in his time, as some concessions are in ours, to gain the suffrance of large and heterogeneous audiences, upon whose pleasure his livelihood depended. In *Androcles and the Lion* Shaw uses some of the low comedy devices used by Aristophanes. The subtler satiric comedies produced by the motion picture companies in Hollywood fail utterly to attract paying audiences unless they are interspersed with the old reliable slap-stick stuff; and the humor of the lower grade burlesque houses depends largely upon scatological and indecent jokes to please the audience.

It was a great disappointment to Aristophanes that the play he considered his masterpiece, *The Clouds,* did not win a prize, not even the third one, when it was originally presented. He offered it again the next year. You may be sure that in the second offering of his play he stuck in some low "gags" and that he continued to do so. Toward the last he became more and more vulgar, because with the passing of Athenian Democracy and the establishment of the oligarchy it became increasingly dangerous to satirize political figures or public men of power and influence.

WE KNOW less about Aristophanes than we know about Homer. What we know is what he tells us about himself in his plays and what we have from a few records. The date of his birth was placed by the early scholiasts (incorrectly, I think) at 456 B.C. This date was arrived at from calculations backward from the first recorded play of his to be produced at the two annual competitions. The rules required that a comic poet to be thirty years of age before he could have a play produced, and *The Babylonians* was produced in 426 B.C.

But Aristophanes wrote at least two plays for small audiences and entered three plays, *The Banqueters (Daitales), The Babylonians* and *The Acharnians,* in the contests under the names of actors in the company, before he produced *The Knights* under his own name in 424. This would make his birth 454, by the assumptions and calculations of the scholiasts.

(A point overlooked by the scholiasts and later scholars is that the explanation Aristophanes gives in *The Knights* for not having produced a play under his own name hitherto may not have had reference to the age requirement for the prize competition at all. Aristophanes was a native of Ægina and it may have been that he had not attained full Athenian citizenship until after the production of *The Acharnians.* Aliens were not allowed to compete for the dramatic prizes at the Dionysia and Lenæa, which were official city festivals. Lysias, the orator, a resident alien from Syracuse, did not attain full citizenship until he was 55 years old, although he had been an active Athenian patriot [within the limits of participation in city affairs possible to an alien] for thirty years. Immediately upon attaining his citizenship Lysias impeached Eratosthenes, one of the Thirty, for murder. This act prompted an inspection of his citizenship by his enemies, which resulted in the discovery of a technical irregularity whereby he lost his citizenship. Thereafter he could not plead in the law courts or deliver public speeches; so in his profession as an orator he had to content himself with writing speeches for others to deliver. Lysias and Aristophanes were almost exact contemporaries. The fragment from a lost play by Eupolis, complaining of competition by "foreigners," may have been an unsuccessful rival's attempt to have Aristophanes disqualified for the competition.)

Aristophanes, then, probably was born about 454 B.C. He was a native of Ægina or the son of a native of Ægina, but he attained full citizenship in Athens and became one of the most zealous of patriots. As Aristophanes was growing into young manhood, the Golden Age of Pericles, which all told lasted only about thirty years, came to an end. After the repulse of the Persians in 479 B.C., the Piræus had been fortified and Athens rebuilt; Athens had become the center of power of the Greek peninsula under Cimon, Aristides and Themistocles, and the alliance of the city-states for war against the Persians had resulted in the piling up of a large war defense fund in Delphi. When Pericles rose to power, he transferred this treasure to Athens and began to spend it for large public works, such as the Parthenon and the temple of Zeus. The arts expanded under such expenditures. City rivalry resulted in a war between Corinth and Athens, with the victory for the latter in 458 B.C. Then the Grecian city-states began a series of wars among themselves, which developed into the Peloponnesian War, with Sparta at the head of an alliance designed to wrest sovereignty in commerce away from Athens.

Aristophanes' *The Babylonians* was produced four years after the death of Pericles. This comedy contained a savage arraignment of Cleon, a city official who held office in the Athenian democracy somewhat similar to that of a mayor of New York City. It is a mistake to confound Cleon with a "tyrant" or ruler, because his was an elective office and his power was limited to the influence he could count on among politicians and the ward-heelers among the different classes of voters—the Pentacosiodimni, who were worth five hundred minæ or more; the Equites or Knights who were worth three hundred minæ and were obliged each to maintain a calvary horse; the

Zeugutæ or small tradesmen; and the Thetes or poor people. Cleon seems to have been a demogogue of about the same caliber as William Hale ("Big Bill") Thompson, former mayor of Chicago.

In this connection, by the way, it is interesting to observe that Cleon, although smarting under the attacks upon him, did not dare risk the disfavor of the people by protesting against the free use of lampoon, criticism and invective enjoyed by the comic dramatists during the license period of the Lenæan and Dionysian festivals, *against himself*. Instead he instigated charges against Aristophanes for *ridiculing the city* during the Dionysia, on occasion when the Ægean was open for navigation and the town full of foreigners. Aristophanes was cleared of the charges and next year renewed the attack in *The Acharnians,* which was produced at the Lenæa and won first prize in the competition. The Lenæa occurred in December or January when the Piræus was closed to traffic and there could be no tourist trade in the theater. Consequently in that play Aristophanes takes an opportunity to say: "Spectators, be not angered; although I am a beggar, I dare in a comedy to speak before the people of Athens concerning the public weal; comedy too can sometimes discern what is right. I may not please, but I shall say what is true. Besides, Cleon shall not be able to accuse me of attacking Athens before strangers: we are by ourselves at the festival of the Lenæa."

In *The Acharnians* Aristophanes introduces himself in the character of Dicæopolis, who makes the above speech and he speaks throughout in his own person. Dicæopolis is as much of a caricature of himself as the character of Euripides in the same play is a caricature of Euripides. Failure to recognize this has misled even Professor Murray, who did not see that the sort of fun Aristophanes makes of himself is the same as the fun he makes of his friend Euripides.

When *The Acharnians* was produced the Peloponnesian War had been in progress five years; Athens was beleaguered; the farmers from the surrounding country and the Athenians with country estates had long been cooped up in the city, which was rapidly becoming extremely impoverished. Dicæopolis, who (like Aristophanes) owned some land outside the city, has been reduced to beggary by what he considers a nonsensical war. He dreams of getting back to the freedom of his farm, away from the crowded city with its bribing and bribe-taking demagogues, corrupt politicians, tiresome litigants, docile and stupid rabble and insolent slaves whose masters now fear to punish them lest they desert to the enemy. Dicæopolis has no interest in a war which is simply draining the wealth and life-blood of the city to no purpose, and tries to persuade the Athenians to conclude a peace at any price. He fails at this because Cleon succeeds in beguiling the people with assurances that victory is at hand. Dicæopolis thereupon concludes a private peace treaty with Sparta. That, you will admit, is an original and funny idea. The play concludes with a burlesque of a rustic feast at Dicæopolis' country estate where he and his family now enjoy the blessings of peace.

In *The Acharnians* Aristophanes makes use of the chorus to further the action and act as an interlocutor for the other characters. He also uses it for his direct speeches to the audience, as distinct from the speeches he makes in the person of Dicæopolis, who is a caricature of himself. The political speeches of the chorus in the comedies of Aristophanes correspond somewhat to the modern campaign editorials of the partisan press. The attacks which Aristophanes renewed upon Cleon and his henchmen, in *The Knights* (produced at Dionysian festival in the year following *The Acharnians*), are of two kinds, the rollicking buffoonery of the dialogue and the strident invective of the chorus. In the chorus he attacks Cleon for cowardice as a soldier, for bribery and extortion, incompetence, duplicity and demagoguery. But the Cleon of the play is mainly a bewildered and simple-minded buffoon, always trying to justify himself. In *The Acharnians* Aristophanes declares his intention to be that of driving Cleon out of office, and with *The Knights* he succeeded. That masterpiece of satire won first prize and Cleon lost the next election.

Next year Aristophanes presented what he thought was his masterpiece, *The Clouds* (already described) and it was rejected. We have this rejected play and a part of the address to the audience, which figured in the version of the play which Aristophanes resubmitted the following year. In this address or parabasis, Aristophanes states his intentions and temperament: he levels his satire only at persons in power and with influence (i.e., at persons who can stand it best) and not at weaklings or helpless people who cannot defend themselves. "I attacked Cleon to his face," he says, "when he was all-powerful, and now I have no desire to kick him when he is down. My rivals, on the contrary, once that this wretched Hyperbolus has given them the cue, have never ceased setting upon both him and his mother. First Eupolis presented his *Maricas*, which was simply my *Knights* which this plagiarist clumsily refurbished by adding to the piece an old drunken woman, so that she might dance the cootch. It was an old idea, taken from Phrynichus, who caused this old hag to be devoured by a monster from the deep." And in other plays Aristophanes reiterates that he never takes a mean advantage or attacks the helpless.

The use which Aristophanes makes of the chorus in *The Clouds* and *The Frogs* should have shown the scholiasts and commentators what was Aristophanes' real attitude toward Socrates and Euripides, even if there were no further internal evidence in the plays that these "attacks" were merely friendly jocosities. In all of his political satires Aristophanes uses the chorus and parabasis to step out of his character as a humorist and make direct, serious accusations, exaggerated perhaps, but unequivocal statements of his opinions. In *The Clouds* he never uses the chorus or parabasis in that fashion. He uses one chorus as a judge of two arguments between Just Discourse and Unjust Discourse, swaying first from the one to the other and siding finally with Just Discourse; and he uses the other chorus to make his point clear that the real object of his attack is people like Strepsiades and his son, not Socrates: "Whither does the passion of evil lead! Here is a perverse old man, who wants to cheat his creditors; but some mishap, which will speedily punish this rogue for his shameful schemings, cannot fail to overtake him from today. . . . When we see a man conceive a passion for what is evil, we strike him with some terrible disgrace, so that he may learn to fear the gods." And in *The Frogs,* that marvelous comedy wherein Aristophanes exhibits his genius for parody and humor at its best in a long delicious jibe at Euripides, he dispenses with the chorus almost altogether, using it merely as an accessory to the comedy in the croakings of the frogs and as a beautiful medium for the dithyramb in another.

I think the records we have about the date of Euripides' death are incorrect, because the evidence is plain in *The Frogs* that while Sophocles is only recently dead Euripides is still alive. Aristophanes observes the decorum of mourning and does not parody Sophocles; and he is reverent toward the memory of Æschylus.

Aristophanes varied his themes with the years, revealing an extraordinary fertility and originality. He satirized the Athenian vice of litigation in *The Wasps* and renewed his attack on war in *The Peace* and *Lysistrata*. In *The Plutus* and in two plays that have been lost he satirized the quest of old men for means of rejuvenation. He wrote a gorgeous imaginative comedy, full of fun and poetry in

The Birds and several plays, incluring the *Thesmosporiazusæ* on the emancipation of women and the *Ecclesiazusæ* (the "Suffragettes"). He died at an advanced age, but in what year or where, we do not know. He left a son, Araros, to carry on the work of two unfinished plays but nothing has come down to us as to whether or not his son was a success.

There is nothing whatever in the text of Aristophanes to justify the libelous assertion of Professor Murray that "as a rule he attacks only the poor and the leaders of the poor." The reverse is the truth: he attacked the powerful Cleon and the war profiteers with all the power of his genius for invective; he attacked Alcibiades who was of one of the wealthiest families in all Greece and politically powerful; he attacked the oligarchs and the archons, the men in high places always, never the poor or defenseless. He satirized common vices, vulgarities and stupidities but in the way of amicable satire; he was never mean or vicious about it. Professor Murray has been misled by the scholastic tradition which makes Aristophanes a member of the aristocracy. There is not a particle of evidence for this. There is considerable evidence in the text of his plays that he was a hard-working playwright, depending entirely upon his talents for a living in a time when Athens was poor and a playwright's income was small at best. Several times in his plays Aristophanes shows his anxiety lest he die in poverty, because of the callous fickleness of the audience. The land he owned outside of Athens must have been a liability instead of an asset during most of his life because of the Peloponnesian War.

In his later years, however, he had been productive and inventive enough to give his followers in the Middle Comedy and the New the clews for the development of a new form of comedy—the comedy of manners in which the chorus was dispensed with altogether. This type of comedy was developed by Menander, whose work we know only in a few fragments and in crude adaptation by Latin comedy writers. Menander enjoyed an immense artistic and popular reputation, and it is our misfortune that we have so little of his work to go on and none whatever to justify the honor in which he was held by his contemporaries and by later critics. Plato said his verse was like "a rivulet of oil, noiselessly running." Plutarch and Cæsar praised him extravagantly.

THIS book is about literature and not about philosophy, but I cannot forbear to interject some heterodox opinions on the subject of

Plato for the very patent reason that I consider the *Dialogues* of Plato to be excellent literature and not a philosophy, certainly not a system of philosophy at all. For nearly a quarter of a century now, off and on, I have been reading Plato in translation with the still unshakable conviction I had when I first read him—that is, that these dialogues were written primarily as entertainment for the mind and not as a vehicle of philosophy, that most of these dialogues are humorous playlets, full of irony, satire and sheer fun, and that even the famous *Apology of Socrates* is a work of creative imagination of the highest type.

Plato was a playwright manqué, a dramatic artist forced by the calamitous events of his time to abandon the idea of writing for the theater and forced to develop as a medium of expression the intimate dialogue form for small audiences. Even this he had to abandon in late middle life because Athenian democracy was in a state of collapse; the treasury was empty; Plato had been not only reduced to poverty, but actually sold into slavery, and he was forced to earn his livelihood, when he was freed, as teacher and by writing books on "the way out" of the terrible political and economic mess all Greece had fallen into.

Plato is an example of the creative artist whose genius was directed into uncongenial channels by the adverse circumstances of his environment. His fate was somewhat like Milton's in this regard. Milton planned *Paradise Lost* as a drama and had to turn it into the epic form because the Roundheads closed the theaters. Like Plato, Milton was forced to engage in the political and social discussions that were rife in his time and to use his energy as a polemicist in transient matters. In both instances the audiences and the times made the men; the men did not make or mold the audiences and the times.

Plato traced his descent on his father's side from Codrus, King of Attica, and on his mother's side from Solon, "the law-giver" of Athens. Like Aristophanes he was born at Ægina, but before the birth of Plato the island had become subject to Athens and Plato thus did not have to acquire Athenian citizenship. His father was Ariston, a wealthy landed proprietor of the highest aristocracy, who was also probably engaged in commerce. He sent his son, baptized Aristocles, to Athens to be educated. There Aristocles acquired the nickname "Plato" in his youth, in reference either to the width of his shoulders or the width of his brow. Thereafter he used that name always. He was tall, thin, never in very good health, inclined to a stoop which became pronounced as he grew older. The portrait busts we have of him are idealizations by artists who never saw him.

In Athens Plato's tutors were Draco in music and painting; Dionysius in grammar and literature; Ariston, the wrestler, in gymnastics. He appears to have met Socrates when he was about twenty and to have listened to his discourses for a while, but not to have become intimate with him until about seven years later. Meanwhile he studied mathematics under the great geometrist, Euclid, whose fame was just beginning to spread; he traveled to Italy and to Egypt, learning something about the Pythagoreans in Italy and something about the Iris and Osiris priesthood in Egypt. From the fact that he introduces Prodicus into one of his dialogues it seems probable that he was once a pupil of that famous sophist who charged an admission fee of fifty drachmæ (about 400 grams of gold) for his lectures. He served in three military expeditions, one against Tanagra, one against Corinth and one against Delium.

In his youth he wrote some agreeable amatory and epigrammatic verse, some of which we have. (See *The Greek Anthology,* with the Greek text and translation by W. R. Paton, in the Loeb Classical Library.) His knowledge of verse and music enabled him to become choregus of a play which was backed by the wealthy patron, Dion. A choregus corresponds to our director of an opera or musical comedy. What the name of the play was we do not know.

When he was about twenty-five, Plato resumed his association with Socrates, who seems to have acquired a large following among rich young men of the town, chief of whom was Alcibiades. The city-state then was tottering on the brink of economic collapse, plundered as it had been by the corrupt politicians of a decaying democracy. A plague had ravaged the city, and the two annual theatrical competitions were for a long time suspended. There arose, as a result of this, a form of intimate dramatic composition, known merely as "Dialogues," which I persist in believing were invented either by Socrates or Alexamenus.* If Epimarchus, the comic poet, invented the form, a long example of which we have in Diogenes Laërtius, he wrote his dialogues in verse, whereas Socrates, Xenophon, Plato and Aristotle wrote theirs in prose. The sample of Epimarchus' verse is a dialogue in verse on the First Principle, the existence of the gods, and the nature of the matter. Professor Murray, whose chapter on Plato in *Ancient Greek Literature* is the most heterodox, most brilliant and most acute in that volume and the best extant essay on

---

* Cf. *An Aristotelian Theory of Comedy* by Lane Cooper.

Plato, in my opinion, believes that Plato wrote mimes in the early period of his career as a writer and describes the *Laches* and the *Greater Hippias* as mimes. But Professor Murray, who realizes that these dialogues are literary and not philosophical, fails to make the distinction which Aristotle makes between the two forms of entertainment, the mime and the dialogue. (I have pointed out the difference between the two above.)

The Aristophanic quality of the early dialogues of Plato is so obvious that only an entirely humorless pedant, searching for enclitics instead of reading literature, or an entirely humorless writer of homilies, intent upon Platonic support for his platitudes, could fail to perceive and enjoy the fun of them. Hippias in the dialogue which bears his name is a creature like Strepsiades in *The Clouds:* he is so stupid he cannot grasp the simplest ideas. Plato adds to his comic character by making him a prissy fellow, shocked at the "coarse" language Socrates teases him with.

To read those early dialogues, or indeed most of them, for deep esoteric meanings, foreshadowing Christian doctrine, for instance, seems nonsensical to me. It is proposed by homiletic "philosophers," like Paul Elmer More, that we are to read a profound esoteric philosophy into a dialogue where Socrates tells a whore how to get the most money out of her patrons! That dialogue is a mordant satire, like Thomas Dekker's mock advice to young spendthrifts and profligates in *The Gull's Handbook*. It is proposed by "philosophers" that we are to find Christian doctrine hidden somewhere in a dialogue, the large part of which is given over to a discussion of the cures for an alcoholic hang-over. Moreover (and this is the thing *all* of the commentators except John Jay Chapman and G. Lowes Dickinson have gone wrong on—even John Addington Symonds and Edward Carpenter who defend the fact with a hypocritical obscurantism), I decline to regard the discussion of Love in the *Lysis* and the *Symposium* as what you might call elevating in the moral sense of our day and time. It is a refinement, true enough, but a refinement of precisely the sort of love that Aristophanes inveighed against. Aristophanes called it an unnatural vice. I'm not sure that anything is unnatural, or that anything except excess is a vice; but it will not do to gloss over the things Plato plainly says and pretend he means something else very remote from what is before our eyes.

The *Lysis* was written in the lifetime of Socrates as were the dialogues before it. According to Diogenes Lærtius, Socrates witnessed a performance of it by a company of actors, and after the performance exclaimed, "By Hercules! How many things does this young man report of me!" Scholiasts have tried to discredit this story on the grounds that, although Socrates said this, he was not referring to words Plato put into Socrates' mouth but to Plato's ornate style as contrasted with Socrates' simple diction! I can find no modern scholar who has observed that the Dialogues of Plato were written to be performed.

When Plato was about twenty-eight years old, an event occurred which profoundly affected his life: the condemnation and death of Socrates. It was followed in dire succession by the loss of Plato's own fortune, the economic collapse of Athens, the voluntary exile of Plato, his seizure as a political agitator, his being sold into slavery and his being redeemed by one of his former enemies. The whole fantastic and illogical issue of the catastrophes which befell him was enough to unsettle for all time whatever philosophical sureties about life he had maintained. And they did; for never thereafter was Plato, even in his most didactic works, quite conclusive about anything and such philosophy as he had might be reduced to the single question: "And?"

Gilbert Murray is so succinct, sensible and just about the trial of Socrates that I wish to quote him entire on the subject (from *Ancient Greek Literature*):

"The chief point to realize is that the accusers were not villains, nor the judges necessarily 'lice' as M. Aurelius tersely puts it. Socrates had always been surrounded by young men of leisure, drawn mainly from the richer and more dissolute classes. He had in a sense 'corrupted' them: they had felt the destructive side of his moral teaching, and had failed to grasp his real aim. His political influence was markedly skeptical. He was no oligarch; his oldest apostle Chairephon fought beside Thrasybulus at Phyle; but he had analyzed and destroyed the sacred principle of Democracy as well as every other convention. The city had barely recovered from the bloody reign of his close disciples Critias and Charmides; could never recover from the treason of his 'beloved' Alcibiades. The religious terrors of the people were keenly awake—confusedly occupied with oligarchic plots, religious sins and divine vengeance.

"Of his accusers, the poet Meletus was probably a fanatic, who objected to the Divine Sign. He was a weak man; he had been intimidated by the Thirty into executing an illegal arrest at their orders—the same arrest, according to the legend of the Socratics, which Socrates had refused to perform. Lycon seems to have been an average respectable politician; the Socratics have nothing against him except that he was once the master's professed friend. These men could hardly have got a conviction against Socrates in the ordinary condition of public feeling; but now they were supported by Anytus. A little later in the same year, when Meletus attempted another prosecution for impiety against Andokides, in opposition to Anytus, he failed to get a fifth of the votes. Anytus was one of the heroes of the Restored Democracy, one of the best of that generous band. As an outlaw at Phyle he had saved the lives of bitter oligarchs who had fallen into the hands of his men. When victorious he was one of the authors of the amnesty. He left the men who held his confiscated property undisturbed in enjoyment of it.

"He had had relations with Socrates before. He was a tanner, a plain well-to-do tradesman, himself; but he had set his heart on the future of his only son, and was prepared to make for that object any sacrifice except that which he was asked. The son wished to follow Socrates. He herded with young aristocrats of doubtful principles and suspected loyalty; he refused to go into his father's business. Socrates, not tactfully, had pleaded his cause. Had Socrates had his way, or Anytus his, all might have been well. As it was, the young man was left rebellious and hankering; when his father became an outlaw for freedom's sake, he stayed in the city with Socrates and the tyrants; he became ultimately a hopeless drunkard. As the old tradesman fought his way back through the bloody streets of the Piræus, he thought how the same satyr-faced sophist was still in Athens, as happy under the tyrants as under the constitution, always gibing and probing, and discussing ambiguous subjects with his ruined son. It needed little to convince him that here was a center of pestilence to be uprooted. The death of Socrates was a true tragedy. Both men were noble, both ready to die for their beliefs; it is only the nobler and greater who has been in the end triumphant."

Plato rushed to his master's defense when the charge was lodged against him. He offered to plead for Socrates but was disqualified by the judges. Then he offered his fortune to redeem Socrates, but either Socrates declined this or the judges reminded Plato that Socrates was charged with a capital offense. Plato attended Socrates in jail while the latter was awaiting trial and there, no doubt, made notes on their discussions of the values of life, in the company of Crito, Phædo and other sophists and philosophers. Plato was not present on the day Socrates drank the poison. He appears to have been ill; at least he gives that excuse for his absence. But it might have been dangerous for him to remain in the city. He went to Megara to visit Euclid, traveled for a while and visited the court of Dionysius the Elder, tyrant of Syracuse. There he seems to have become involved in some way in a court intrigue, as a result of which he was seized for stirring up trouble and sold as a slave to a resident of Ægina, his birthplace. There he was redeemed by one Anniceris of Cyrene for thirty minæ. Plato's friends raised this price to buy Plato's freedom from Anniceris and the latter was so touched by this devotion that he set Plato free and bestowed upon him the money raised to purchase his freedom. With this money Plato returned to Athens where he had title to some land just outside the city, and there he built a house and two gardens which he turned into an open air school for pay and called it the Academy. This school had Aristotle as its most famous and most successful pupil. (Other famous pupils included Zenocrates, Demosthenes and Theophrastus. There were at least two women, Lasthena and Axiothea, who studied at the Academy.) Plato taught at the Academy, except for brief residences abroad, for the rest of his life. He died in 347 B.C. at the age of eighty. He had never married and had no natural heirs. He willed his property to his friend and pupil, Adiamantus, who buried Plato's remains in the garden of the Academy, which survived as a sort of university for several centuries.

In the quiet of the Academy, Plato composed his dream of a Utopian communistic state, *The Republic,* his monumental and unfinished work on the *Laws* and other works in kind, a discussion of which is not germane to this book. With Plato's death the grandeur that was Greece had but little while to live; the glory that was Rome was just beginning. Professor Murray says with much reason, "He is the greatest master of Greek prose style, perhaps of prose style altogether, that ever lived." It seems rather frightful that this marvelous prose style, all these years, has been so generally misunderstood and misinterpreted.

VIRGIL *AND LATIN LITERATURE*

*

WITH the death of Plato, the enrichment of Greek literature by no means came to an end. Its period of high creativeness simply died out to be replaced by refinements, criticism and happy eccentricity. The Greek language possessed a much greater vitality and enjoyed much greater longevity than Latin. It had an unbroken history as a medium for prose and poetry from Homer's time until about the middle of the fifteenth century A.D. Latin, which was only a dialect of Latium when Plato was alive, ceased to be the literary language of Rome under Hadrian and ceased to be even the vulgar language of Rome in the seventh century A.D. At the dawn of the Christian era, Greek was so dominant as a universal language in the western world that it was chosen by the disciples and evangelists of Jesus Christ as the medium in which to record the biography—and to propagate the teachings—of the inspirer and founder of the new religion. Long after the supremacy of Athens had vanished and Greek nationality had disintegrated, Greek was the language of culture and international commerce. The great industrial city of Alexandria in Egypt became the center of learning after Athens, and in the great library founded by Ptolemy I—a storehouse so vast that nine hundred clerks were employed to care for its million manuscripts—commentaries and exegeses, grammars and texts in Greek grew to enormous proportions.

What the world lost in the final destruction of the library at Alexandria we shall never know, but it is certain that many "immortal" masterpieces, not only in Greek but in other languages, perished forever with it. It had been founded by the first Ptolemy in the third century B.C., and lavishly endowed by his successors in order to attract men of science and learning to the city. The library was partially destroyed by the army of Julius Cæsar during the siege of Alexandria and in 389 A.D. the Emperor Theodosius the Great, a Christian monarch, ordered its complete destruction as a hot-bed of paganism.

Some of the finest examples of Greek literature that have come down to us have reached us by accident. The only source we have had for fragments of a great body of the finest Greek verse has been a sort of cook-book compiled by a starveling Egyptian named, or nicknamed, Athenaëus, who compiled his curious miscellany called *The Deipnosophists, or the Banquet of the Learned* some time around 225 A.D. The carelessness of some Egyptian embalmers in using Greek manuscripts as wadding to fill out a mummy case resulted in the recovery, not so long ago, of portions of lost plays by Menander, some poems by Sappho and other priceless treasures.

In this literature that has perished there were probably many works of prose and poetry which we should find more interesting even than we find some of the undoubted masterpieces that have survived. After Plato and Aristotle, a highly sophisticated literature flourished for several centuries in Athens. If we did not have to judge the comedies of Philemon, Diphilius, Alexis and Menander through the crude Latin adaptations of them by Plautus and Terence we should probably find them as near to us in spirit and as subtle and amusing as the best of modern plays. The first prose romances and adventure stories were written in Greek; and Roman historians in the decadence of the Roman empire chose Greek as their medium instead of Latin.

Alongside Greek epic and dramatic poetry, which might be considered to be largely group expressions, objective and somewhat impersonal in accent and mood, there had flourished a highly individual and subjective poetry from about 650 B.C., through the so-called classical period; and this sort of poetry continued to be produced for several centuries after the death of Plato. It first appeared, so far as we can make out, in the Ægean Islands, such as Cos and Lesbos, where a high degree of civilization had been reached when the Greek city-states were mere crude settlements and where luxury, ease and learning long survived after the military power of these islands had passed to the more virile and aggressive mixed races of the Hellenic Peninsula.

Sappho, for instance, as early as 650 B.C., enjoyed an education and training in verse writing and music, a freedom of expression and spirit that was never quite possible to an Athenian woman at any time during the whole history of Athenian culture. She was a genius, but the important thing was that the conditions under which she lived made it possible for that genius to bear fruit. This was never possible to a woman in Athens until modern times. The courtesans and hetairæ there enjoyed the companionship and conversation of the leading men of the city, and the famous hetaira, Aspasia, appears to have exercised considerable influence upon the political thought of Pericles and his party; but more than three hundred years before Aspasia lived, Sappho not only wrote poetry but apparently founded a school of poetesses. She invented some thirty-odd verse forms, including the verse form which bears her name and in which she stands preëminent over a host of poets who have since tried the form.

The reason why so little of the personal and subjective Greek poetry has come down to us (what we have is mainly to be found in the compilation of *The Greek Anthology,* available in the Greek text and with an English translation in the Loeb Classical Library) may have been two-fold. It may have been because those who were responsible for the preservation and transmission of literature were, first, men and, second, moralists. As men they would have a natural, if unconscious, prejudice against genius in a woman as startling, as original and feminine as Sappho's. As moralists they could hardly help feeling that the themes—many of them joyous, sensual and erotic—were subversive. On the other hand, it is true that much of this subjective impersonal poetry from Sappho on down through Bion, Boschus, Anacreon to Theocritus is, from the severest standards, second-rate, however humanly touching or pleasing we find it.

THIS second-rate poetry of the Greeks, however, as we shall see later on, furnished the models for the highest form of literature the Romans produced. The reason becomes apparent when we observe that the whole development of Greek thought and temperament as well as the social and political atmosphere differed from that of Rome, whereas Greek literary forms were imposed upon Roman habits of mind.

The Latin language, as it was developed under the Roman Republic and as it came to its finest prose perfection in Cicero and to its highest poetic development in Virgil and Horace was, in the last analysis, a language of dissimulation and of both conscious and unconscious hypocrisy. Except in a very few instances, as in Cæsar,

Lucretius and some of the minor poets, Latin literature is, for the most part, simply not to be trusted to express the author's genuine feelings, emotions or convictions. The very best Latin literature has none of the honest, direct, simple ingenuousness of the Greek. Latin literature is indeed a monument of disingenuousness from the pernicious effects of which we have never quite escaped. It is often literary in the worst sense, a medium of artificial grace and manners. The legend is familiar that Roman soothsayers winked at each other as they passed in the street; but Roman orators and Roman literary men must have winked at each other with no less a consciousness of the essential disharmony between their words and what they knew and felt.

To see why this was so, we need only to trace the parallelism between the growth of the so-called Golden Age of Latin as a literary language and the growth of the Roman state. The Roman state, even before the Cæsars, never was a democracy in the sense that the Athenian city-state was a democracy. The *Res Publica* ("the affairs of the people") were essentially the business of a small handful of rich men. The Roman state was essentially a *plunderbund,* the greatest by far the world has ever seen. When the Roman army conquered Germanic, Frankish, Gallic and Britannic tribes, the generals of the army enslaved the strongest men, looted the land and established military outposts among the tribes, not for colonization but for the exaction of tribute. When the commercial rivalry of Carthage threatened the maritime commerce of Rome, Rome put forth its greatest effort in long, protracted wars and finally looted the city and razed it to the ground.

Now, a *plunderbund,* such as the Roman state was, necessarily rested upon the base of an enslaved population both at home and abroad. Many of these slaves in the households of the patrician families of Rome, particularly slaves from Greek city-states, Alexandria and the Asiatic coast of the Mediterranean, were much better educated, more civilized, indeed, than their masters. Therefore the education of the Roman children of the wealthy class was largely turned over to the household slaves. Just as the children of the wealthy families of Russia under the old régime were taught French and kept rather ignorant of Russian, so at Rome the children of the wealthy were brought up to read and speak Greek, as the language of cultivation and refinement.

This naturally widened the gap between the ruling class and the proletariat. That word, "proletariat" (*proletarius*) was a Latin invention. (The Athenian Greeks had no equivalent for the word, because, although there was a lower class in Athens it was not large enough to constitute a problem in a city wherein no one was very wealthy.) With the growth of the slave population and of the proletariat, the anxiety of the wealthy people of Rome became a downright neurosis. They lay awake nights in fear of another uprising of the slaves which was once abortively accomplished under a slave leader, Spartacus. An ominous note of fear ran through their correspondence. They did not dare express their fright in words, so they developed codes and innuendoes for inquiries and assurances about the slaves.

With this anxiety over a possible revolt of the slaves and proletarians, the ruling class was ceaselessly attempting to provide the lower orders with diversions, such as circuses, chariot races, and gladiatorial combats, and to provide them with literary placebos in exactly the same way as "the interests" of today keep highly paid "public relations counsels" and propagandists busy justifying the ways of the wealthy with the people. The difference, however, between the propaganda of the wealthy class of Rome and the propaganda of American public relations counsels, is that no one ever mistakes the latter for literature; whereas the former *was* literature, a development of a disingenuous habit of thinking. (It may have been a result of this habit of thinking that there was no one word affirmative, no "Yes" in classical Latin. If a Roman were asked, "Will you be at home tonight?" he had to answer, "I shall be at home tonight" or "I shall not be at home tonight." The effort to supply the missing affirmative in the languages derived from Latin, resulted in the *hoc* for "yes" in the south of France and the use of *ille* in the north; hence, the "Langue d'Oc," or the language which used *hoc* for yes and the "Langue d'Oïl," the language which used *oïl,* a combination of *hoc* and *ille* for "yes.")

From all this, the enormous difference between the medium Homer used and the medium Virgil used in the writing of epics becomes apparent. Homer wrote in the "vulgar" or common colloquial speech, because there was no other speech in his day. His vivid and expressive word combinations like *Duparis* (literally, "Hard-luck-Paris") and *gynamanes* (literally, "woman-crazy") have the freshness of the colloquial speech of the uneducated of today. Virgil's language was a refined, polished, literary language, differing greatly from the language of the *vulgus,* or the vulgar tongue. It also differed vastly from the language employed by the writers of Latin comedy, the topical verse writers and the popular poets, such as Catullus, Martial and Propertius. (The curious may find it instructive to read the late Keith Preston's dissertation on the *Sermo Amatorius in Roman Comedy* and the work of Volkmar Hoelzer and Maximilian Heinemann on Roman slang and erotic innuendo.)

The demogoguery which the genius of Greek literature would not and did not let creep into that literature, however much it flourished for a time in the assembly and the market place, is actually the keynote of the character of the great bulk of Latin literature, especially the more or less "official" or classical literature. It is simply impossible to take Cicero's words at their face value, even when he is writing his most intimate letters to his dearest friend; for he wrote more for effect than from his heart. An "attitude" had taken the place of character in his personality, as it had in the personality of most of the men in public life. In one of the purest of Roman spirits, Virgil, this necessity for an attitude, which was at times wilfully and consciously deceptive, resulted in a strange, dull, confused, and unsustained epic, the *Æneid,* part of which is sheer genius triumphing over false material and part of which is hack-work, uninspired and shoddy. Virgil was required, by the nature of the job he undertook, to have elevated thoughts about matters which were not particularly elevating. That he was never satisfied with the epic, never quite completed his revisions of it and left instructions for the manuscript to be destroyed after his death, is quite understandable: his heart was never altogether in it, in the same way, for instance, that Homer's heart was in the *Iliad* and the *Odyssey,* or the hearts of the writers of the Synoptic Gospels were in their work.

The genius of the Roman mind reached its highest felicity of expression, I think, in Horace—a felicity which at its base is simply an amiable cynicism, a determination to accept things as they are, without passion, without rancor, without heroic impulses or exalted idealism. Horace, after he reached maturity, had an unparalleled serenity of mind. No Greek—not even Sophocles—ever approached him in moderation and decorum of speech. Son of a freedman though he was, no Roman emperor or patrician ever approached him in the quality we call gentility. And this was not so much the result of the practice of the official Roman philosophy of Stoicism (a philosophy he ridiculed) as an attitude of compromise taken by a middle-aged poet after an intense youth during which he aspired to "dislodge the stars with his uplifted head." Horace was the finest product of a literary medium and of a national habit of mind. He was also the product of a socio-political civilization which we must either consider to have been pragmatic or malign. And if we consider it pragmatic from the fact that it nourished and developed the most perdurable of all institutions, so far, the Roman Catholic Church, we must remind ourselves that as a civilization it was one of the briefest in the history of the world. The mental habits of the Roman poets, prose writers and orators were such as could persist only when removed from common life to the expression of ultramondaine concerns: the Roman habit of dissimulation reached its apogee in (if we can guess) the Sybilline books and (as we know) in the *De Civitatis Dei* of St. Augustine, in the rituals of the church, in the impalpable intricacies and dialectic of the *Summa* of St. Thomas Aquinas, and in other sonorous fuddlements to lead, scare and direct the simple-minded, trusting and superstitious.

THE LATIN language as we know it seems to be a combination of the Pelasgian and Oscan tongues which were modified and influenced by Greek forms. The Pelasgian-Oscan combination resulted in the Etruscan language about which we are beginning to know a little, but not much. All that we know for certain is that, after many tribal wars, the Indo-Germanic peoples which had invaded and settled Italy in remote Italian antiquity, the Etruscans, Umbrians, Sabines, Oscans and Pelasgians, divided the territory among themselves and that the tribes located around the present site of Rome on the Tiber finally achieved the ascendancy.

It is possible that, in the effacement of the Etruscans (who appear to have been an artistic race) and of the Pelasgians (who appear to have been peaceful and agricultural), there perished the chance for the development of a civilization in Italy at least equal to the civilization of the Greeks. But the strongest and (so it would seem) the most mendacious and callous tribes dominate. The Punic Wars were fought in a manner which do not redound to the glory of the victors; the Germanic, Britannic and Gallic tribes were subjugated by the clement, realistic, and fair-minded Julius Cæsar, whose very virtues caused his almost immediate extinction at the hands of a rabble-rousing element of assassins and double-dealers; and the educated participants in the unparalleled prosperity which came so quickly and easily from military conquest and plunder never quite achieved the courage of that prosperity. They could neither look it in the face, nor accept it for what it was. They could not even, like good, sensible Jesuits, justify the means by accepting the ends: they had to wish away the means and deny that the ends themselves existed. Like a nation of profiteers and *nouveaux riches,* suddenly enriched beyond any possible dreams of the hardy founders of the Roman Republic, they could not quite get used to their good fortune. And so we have in Latin literature an army of sycophants, among the literate and literary folk, making not at all convincing heroes out of brigands and opportunists; and, on the other hand, an army of well-paid literary persons undermining the very foundations of the prosperity the nation enjoyed by an unconscionable amount of false literary drivel about the joys of the simple life.

Perseus, Juvenal and Seneca seem to me, after a very careful examination and revision of all their utterances and of what is available about their careers, simply abominable fellows. They were lice of the worst order, and the fact that they drew sustenance and support from amiable scoundrels (mere opportunists and lucky cheaters in a universal system in Rome) while denouncing the rich and flattering the poor only adds to the despicable qualities I find in them. The security of their patrons depended not upon the flattering and sentimentalizing of the masses but upon their continued well-being and prosperity, their creation and consumption of luxury goods; but this they did not know, and, thinking they were carrying on the spirit of the rugged Cato, they denounced the growing tendency of Romans to take baths on nights other than Saturday, to use silks and dye stuffs, to decorate and beautify their homes, buy decorative as well as useful objects, to enjoy the theater and the library, and otherwise to make use, by rapid turnover, of the great wealth that had fallen into their hands.

In other words, they traduced the men they were working for; and in buttering their own bread they did it with sand. I know of no sweeter justice in history than when Nero told Seneca to take himself off. That was Nero's "You are through, Seneca," after that appalling racketeer had consummated some piece of double-crossing which not even Nero, a tolerant fellow, could stomach. When Nero commanded Seneca to commit suicide, Seneca no longer had any honor left (that was a quality Nero never demanded in his sycophants); but what was worse, he didn't have ordinary prudence.

A much greater man, a much decenter man than Seneca, Petronius, who succeeded Seneca as literary counselor to Nero, witnessed what he witnessed, wrote his *Satyricon,* and, when the time came when he was out of favor, cut his wrists and died peacefully in his bath. The *Satyricon* is a humorous-minded man's picture of the cultural pretensions of his patron: Seneca, who had grown extremely wealthy in the same job, is pictured as adjuring children against the sin of avarice—the last sin of which any child is ever guilty!

Latin literature properly began with the work of Livius Andronicus, a Greek slave from Tarentum, whose plays were first exhibited in Rome about 240 B.C., after the conclusion of the first Punic War. Rome at that time was in a comparatively crude state of civilization. Elsewhere there was real civilization. Callimachus and Apollonius, poets of the Greek decadence, were gathered around Eratosthenes, head of the great library in Alexandria, who was making his first measurements of the circumference of the earth; Archimedes, the physicist and mathematician, was developing in Syracuse his data on the physical sciences; Berosus was writing the history of the vanished glory of Babylon; and Hebraic scholars in Jerusalem were patiently expanding the small body of doctrine which was later to affect the thought of the world.

LIVIUS ANDRONICUS was a man of learning and talent who had been taken prisoner by the marauding Roman armies during the first Punic War and, in accordance with the custom of the time, had been awarded as a slave to an army captain, M. Livius Salinator, in whose household it was his duty to act as tutor for Salinator's children. It was sometimes the custom of wealthy Romans to reward slaves like Livius Andronicus for loyalty and faithful service by granting them their freedom. Andronicus appears to have merited this favor from his master by translating the *Odyssey* into Latin. This translation was used in the Roman schools. Horace tells us that he was flogged by his schoolmaster when he was a boy for failure to memorize given passages from it. It survives only in some quoted fragments.

But the main work of Andronicus after he obtained his freedom was in the composition of tragedies based upon Greek models. These were not particularly successful when they were produced; but they did serve one purpose; they revealed the fact that the Romans had no taste for tragedies. After Andronicus, several poets, notably Ennius and Attius, wrote tragedies which were produced, but they merely proved what the response of the Roman audience to the plays of Andronicus indicated, namely that the Romans, practical and utilitarian, were without the esthetic sensibility necessary for the enjoyment of tragedy. Later writers, among them Seneca, wrote tragedies, but they were written to be read, not enacted.

The Romans did like comedy, however, and the Roman playwrights developed this form of art to such an extent that they are commonly credited with the invention of satire. I can find no real grounds for attributing the invention of satire to the Romans, because there is not a single jest, satirical convention or comic rôle in Latin comedy which has not its equivalent in Greek. Even the Fescennine verses, obscene and scurrilous, from which Roman satire has been supposed by many scholars to have been derived, were the sort of improvisations recited during the early Dionysiac festivals in Greece. The *fascinium* was the Latin equivalent of the Greek phallus, carried in holiday processions, and, as in Greece, its presence was the occasion for lewd jokes among the peasantry. It was the emblem of fertility, but there was no mistake in the minds of the rustic rabble about what it was supposed to represent. As in Greece, the phallic procession was the occasion for the composition and recital of comic verses about the sexual prowess, or lack of it, the habits, vices and personalities of people in the neighborhood. In Greece, the custom received an official sanction under which, during that special period of the year, one could lampoon, satirize and criticize to one's heart's content without fear of punishment or reprisals. The license enjoyed by Aristophanes was possible because of the official sanction given the free use of scurrility during the holiday seasons, and, because his audience demanded it, his plays are occasionally marred by simply filthy jokes about the sexual vices of real persons in Athens, naming the victims by name. In Etruria, and later in Rome, a similar custom developed. This custom was revived in Rome, incidentally, in the fifteenth century, with the *pasquinade*.

"According to Mazocchi," writes Edward Hutton in his biography of Pietro Aretino, "Pasquino was a schoolmaster with a bitter tongue, and lived in Rome in the fifteenth century. But, at the end of that century, and especially in those early years of the beginning of the sixteenth, this name had been transferred to an antique and mutilated statue which had been recently excavated and set up at the corner of the Piazza Navona. To this statue it had been the custom to affix learned squibs on the papal government and famous persons generally. Pasquin had lately taken a partner in the form of another statue excavated in the Campus Martius, and popularly known as Marforio (*a feor Martius*). The regular form of 'pasquinade' now became that of a dialogue of question and answer in which Marforio was usually the questioner. These pasquinades became famous all over Europe. Pasquin, indeed, is of the modern world and is a sign of the return of free satire, anonymous and violent and often as vulgar and salacious as anything in antiquity. He is not really of the people; he is the creation of the learned, of scholars and men of letters."

But the pasquinade survives in Italy today; and Fescennine verse survives among the common people of our own country in pretty much its original form in the old comic valentine. Even the date (or approximately the date), on which it was proper for the Etruscan, Greek and Roman people to have fun with one another with verses caricaturing or libeling them, survives in St. Valentine's Day. (For years I received a comic valentine on St. Valentine's Day from H. L. Mencken, with libelous drawings in color supposed to represent me, and with verses deriding me as a wife-beater, a spendthrift, a guzzler, a dude, a tightwad, a usurer and a hypocrite; so apparently the custom of sending comic valentines still survives in Baltimore, Maryland, on a scale large enough to justify the manufacture of such jokes for sale.)

These folk customs sometimes survive long after the meaning of them has been forgotten. Murray Godwin, writing about the settlement of Polish factory workers on the outskirts of Detroit in the May, 1932, issue of the *North American Review,* tells about a peculiar ceremony that takes place among the Poles on the day after Easter Sunday: "Men and boys armed with switches cut from saplings invaded the homes of neighbors who had unmarried daughters living with them. Up the stairs they went, and into the chambers occupied by the girls, hoping to catch the latter in bed and there to exercise the day's privilege of applying the ceremonial rod to their lightly clothed forms. Refreshments were set out for these friendly flogging parties, and the affair was carried off gayly, with much laughter and shouting but with little smart. For the rest of the day parties of male youngsters patrolled the streets, switching the girls they met or exacting tribute in pennies for desisting. . . . Where this custom derives from I do not know. No Pole I asked was able to tell me. . . . The custom survived the more lustily, perhaps, because it lacked even the shadow of a rational excuse."

THE antique Latin Fescennine verses were composed in a singsong meter like, "The queen was in her parlor, eating bread and honey." Since that was the meter which Livius Andronicus used

in his translation of the *Odyssey*, we can imagine how far from the
original his version was.

That early verse form, called the Saturnian meter, was extremely important, however, in the history of Latin literature. It was
perennially popular. One of the last examples preserved for us is this
jeu d'esprit addressed by the Emperor Hadrian to the poet Florus:

> *Ego nolo Florus esse*
> *Ambulare per tabernas*
> *Latitare per popinas*
> *Culius pati rotundos*

and **Florus' reply:**

> *Ego nolo Cæsar esse*
> *Ambulare per Britannos*
> *Scythicas pati pruinas.*

Flexible, limpid, cadenced and sonorous with the sonority inherent in Latin nouns, this Saturnian meter gave birth to all that is
beautiful, touching, graceful, witty and impressive in Latin poetry
—to the exquisite poems of Catullus, the passionate lyrics of Ovid,
the fine didactic poems of Horace, the elegance of Propertius and
the biting epigrams of Martial. It was a vehicle for somber moods as
well as festive or satirical ones, and those early Saturnian verse
forms were the direct progenitors of such Latin church hymns as

> *Dies iræ, dies illa*
> *Solvet sæclum in favilla,* etc.,

and

> *Stabat mater dolorosa*
> *Luxta crucem lacrymosa,*
> *Dum pendebat filius,*
> *Cuius animam gementem,*
> *Contristantem et dolentem*
> *Pertransvit gladius.*

It is to be found in Catullus'

> *Cum suis vivat valeatque mœchis,*
> *quos simul complexa tenet trecentos,*
> *mullum amans verve, sed identidem omnium*
> *illa rumpens.*

And in the famous and beautiful lines addressed by the Emperor Hadrian to his soul:

Animula, vagula, blandula,
Hospes comesque corporis,
Quæ nunc abibis in loca?
Pallidula, rigida, nudula
Nec ut soles dabis jocos.

The more official Latin poetry of Virgil, though, was another matter. Like the official prose, it was from the head rather than from the heart, and the Romans were especially hard-headed. "The typical Roman," writes H. W. Garrod, compiler of the *Oxford Book of Latin Verse*, "was what we call a 'dull man.'" What is more, the Roman prided himself on this quality of dullness and hard-headedness. Emphasis was put on the practical and utilitarian by the leaders of the state. In the days of the elder Cato the official attitude was one of pride in simplicity, in stern stoic virtues; and hatred of luxury and effeminacy, of anything soft and beautiful.

This convention of rugged simplicity continued when there was no longer any reason for it and to that extent falsified the literature of the so-called classical period, that period of about one hundred and sixty years, from the first appearance of Cicero in public life to the death of Augustus. Within an amazingly short period of time, wars of conquest and plunder had enriched the upper classes in Rome to a degree unparalleled in the history of the world. Engineering and architecture flourished. Even from the earliest days the Romans had built their city with an eye to cleanliness and sanitation. They had built a subterranean sewerage system, insured a continuous supply of clear water, not only for household use but for public baths and drinking fountains; and such improvements rapidly expanded under the prosperous days of the Republic.

In the Rome of Cicero's time, the private homes of the wealthy were built and maintained on a scale beyond the means and imaginations of American millionaires and Hollywood motion picture stars. Cicero, who was not particularly wealthy as wealth went in his time, entertained Cæsar on one occasion almost informally. Cæsar dropped in for dinner on short notice, with his retinue of two thousand men! Cicero describes the occasion in words which show that he was not overwhelmed, in a letter to Atticus, xiii, 52 (translation from Rogers and Harley's *The Life of Rome*):

"The great man stayed with Philippus on Christmas Day till a little after noon. He saw no one. Accounts with Balbus, doubtless. Then a walk along the shore of the Bay. Bath here about 2:00 P.M. Listened to 'Lines on Mamurra' (not a letter altered). Anointed and scented, he sat down to dinner. He started with a pill. So he ate and drank *sans peur;* and 'so sweetly' too. The entertainment was handsome and tasteful, and what is more,

> ...all credit to the cook
> Though Wit, you know, was the best sauce he took.

His *clientele* I entertained in three dining rooms, and right royally. His valets and grooms wanted for nothing: his secretaries were entertained correctly. In a word, we seemed 'mighty fine fellows.' Still, he is not the sort of guest to whom you say, 'Delighted to see you the next time you pass this way!' Once is enough. Conversation? Oh, *rien de serieux; belles lettres* the whole time. *Que voulez-vous?* He was amused, and it was all to his taste. He said he would stay one day at Pozzuoli, and another at Baiæ. Now you know all about my entertainment—or perhaps I should call it a *logement;*—a plaguey nuisance, as I say, though not so very terrible. I am staying here for a little. Then Tusculum."

Private residences and country homes of the wealthy few had indoor and outdoor swimming pools, steam baths, showers, solariums, gymnasiums, indoor and outdoor tennis courts, libraries, enormous dining rooms, guest rooms fitted out with every luxury and living quarters for anywhere from forty to four hundred servants. A man's wealth was estimated by the number of slaves he kept; and Cicero, who inveighed against ostentation, sneered at a man whose cook also doubled in the household as steward. The price paid for slaves varied from about a hundred dollars for unskilled laborers and drudges to thousands of dollars for grammarians, flute-girls, harlequins, eunuchs and handsome boys to wait at table.

"The first Romans," writes Walton Brooks McDaniel in his *Roman Private Life and Its Survivals,* "had no such superfluity of unpaid assistance as wealthier citizens of the Empire were to have. It was not, indeed, until the conquests of the second century B.C. had brought countless prisoners of war in servitude to Rome that the institution of slavery got its stranglehold upon the people. Thenceforth, there was an increasing degradation of free labor. By the close of the Republic, in fact, all manual occupations, most of the trades and even some of what we now term the professions, such as medicine and surgery, were largely in the hands of slaves and ex-slaves, and it meant social debasement for a freeman of birth and education to compete with them, even if he could with any financial profit....

"The personal attentions of ubiquitous, obsequious menials are sure in any age to impair the fiber of manhood and induce in womanhood false standards of luxury and pride. Roman children of sterling ancestry in the close confines of the home had constant and unescapable contacts with at least the alien and often the immoral ideas and conduct of men and women debased by servitude. Slaves had every inducement to pamper their young charges and encourage an egotism that spells ruin. . . ."

The Roman *paterfamilias* was absolute master in his own home. He disinherited his children, divorced his wife, or punished his slaves cruelly, with or without cause. Punishment of slaves ranged from simple flogging to crucifixion. They were often chained to their work, whether at the grinding of corn or while doing the duty of night-watchman. "The food and clothing apportioned a slave," writes McDaniel, "would suffice to keep him efficient as a worker, but no more. While denied, of course, the use of the dress of citizenship, slaves would look in general like the very poor among the free. History tells us of a bill in the senate which proposed to put them all in uniform, but it failed to pass, through fear that a recognition of their numerical preponderance would lead to dangerous uprising such as several times nearly wrecked the state anyway. There were, indeed, many masters who subscribed to the statement that a man had as many enemies as he had servitors."

AGAINST such a socio-economic background Virgil undertook to write an epic which should celebrate this culmination of Roman civilization as something beautiful and divine. The thing was impossible. No one with a spark of humor would have attempted it. Horace, an affectionate friend of Virgil's, wrote a whole thesis in verse, *Ars Poetica,* showing why heroic poetry was an anomaly in Rome and why even the famous Roman "gravity" was a misnomer; it was in reality the mask of a shrewd business man driving a hard bargain. Greek youths were taught to do things worthy of praise, wrote Horace, whereas Roman youths were taught only the principles of success in terms of money.

Virgil had a false history to work on and a false nobility to flatter or, at least, to please. Not only did every patrician house have its family history filled with imaginary leaders and preposterous deeds, because of the traditional cult of family and clan worship, but every plebeian house which had risen in a short time to the wealth, and, thence, to the privileges of the old nobility, hastened to vie with the old nobility in its supply of "noble" ancestors. False genealogies abounded in families only one or two generations removed from slavery and sons of wealthy freedmen concocted family histories filled with preposterous accounts of triumphs and imaginary consulships. The funeral orations over the biers of wealthy Romans, paid for and preserved at great cost, for many centuries baffled historians by references to consulships which could not be traced in official records, until it finally became apparent that these family "histories" could not be regarded as historical at all. There was hardly a true assertion in any one of them.

The barrier of caste between the hereditary nobility, who had actually contributed political leadership to the state, and the lower classes, which merely furnished children for service in the army, disappeared after the first Punic War, and the barrier of class, separating the rich from the poor, took its place. Life must go on among the stay-at-home citizens when the warriors are at war; and the merchants, manufacturers, landlords and bankers of Rome no more missed their opportunities than they do today. The great fleet of galleys, equipped with the new Roman invention of the grappling hooks, by means of which Rome was to challenge the supremacy of Carthage in maritime warfare, had to be built at great cost; provisions for the troops had to be packed and boxed and transport arranged; carts and wagons, arrows, shields, spears, greaves, shoes, helmets, underwear, saddles, harness, mattocks, hardware of all kinds, portable kitchens, cranes, derricks, battering-rams—all had to be manufactured for the armies; horses and livestock had to be purchased by commission agents; state warrants had to be issued which were discounted by bankers. All these things provided opportunities for the rapid amassing of wealth by the shrewd and the corrupt. Profiteers and grafters abounded.

What is more, the old line leaders, returning from the wars, found these profiteers so well established in wealth and power that they could not dislodge them without turning the soldiers against them and starting a civil war; and they had found by one terrible experience that a civil war wrecks the state and impoverishes everybody. The profiteers effected the passage of the Licinian and Ogulnian laws giving wealthy plebes (lower class citizens of Rome who were not called upon to offer military service to the state) political and religious equality with the old-line nobles.

The result was a vast increase in the number of "nobles" whose only qualification for nobility was wealth, however acquired. With the increase in their numbers their power increased also and soon they controlled the political situation as well as the economic resources. They had, of course, to keep the army placated, which they did with liberal gifts and grants, and they found it convenient, as the economic rulers in modern societies do, to keep in the background and let the nominal rule be in the hands of the popular military leaders.

THE Roman Republic, therefore, in its most momentous days, was not a democracy at all, although it had some of the forms of a democracy. The Roman Senate, originally a body of patricians dedicated more or less to the general welfare of the state, became an organization of wealthy landlords, bankers, manufacturers, profiteers or representatives of this class who held office and exercised power not for the general weal but for special privileges. It became a trading body dividing up concessions, contracts and semi-state revenues among themselves.

There was a second legislative body, the Assembly. Originally it was a popular assembly by which the free citizens below patrician rank could register their opinions and act as a check upon the power of the Senate. But after the rise of the plebeian "aristocracy," the Assembly lost all pretense of representing the common man.

There were no longer any "common people" in the sense that we use the term to indicate the vast body of voters who elect their representatives and government administrators in America. There were only the very rich and the very poor and a vast enslaved population. The Assembly was filled with grafters in the pay of the rich. No democracy, no representative government in the true sense ever existed in the Roman Republic, and after a comparatively few years, even the pretense to one ceased to be made; a dictatorship passed almost imperceptibly into a monarchy, dependent for its security upon the temper of the army and upon the opportunities it afforded the wealthy class.

The rapacity of this wealthy class is unexampled in the history of the world. The "splendor" of Rome took the form of extravagances in the scale of living on the part of the millionaires, wherein each tried to outdo the other. The Seneca, who is still called a "philosopher" in the textbooks because of the insincere trash he wrote, built a palace larger than Nero's and entertained there on a scale to excite the jealousy of the Emperor to whom he was indebted for the vast concessions he had in Italy and Gaul. In order to maintain this ostentation, Seneca was in continual need of cash; and so merciless was he in his exactions of tribute that he nearly precipitated a revolt in Gaul. His avarice and ambitions finally became too much for Nero, who sent troops to surround his house and a message commanding him to commit suicide. Seneca did this with a sickening exhibition of false heroics: he wrote an "apology" in imitation of Plato's *Apology of Socrates,* cut his veins in his bath, and (final touch) drank hemlock, as Socrates was ordered to do.

In Virgil's time there were landlords like the millionaire Crassus, who derived his enormous income from the rent of jerry-built slums. No poor man in Rome had a home of his own. He lived and raised his family in top-heavy structures, several stories high, built of wood, which were not only insanitary and breeders of disease, but horrible firetraps as well. The grasping landlords never repaired these warrens; there were no laws governing the responsibility of the owners, no insurance, no adequate protection. Once a fire started a whole block or a whole district might burn, with great loss of life and the complete destruction of everything the tenants owned. Crassus bethought himself of a ghoulish racket in connection with this, the idea for which came to him as a result of the frequency of fires in the slums. "Crassus," writes Plutarch, "observed how liable the city was to fires, and how frequently houses collapsed, disasters due to the top-heaviness of the buildings and to over-crowding. To meet such occasions, he included in his staff of slaves men who were carpenters and masons, and he continued to collect them till he had five hundred or more. He then speculated by buying houses which were on fire, and others that adjoined them; and he usually bought them very cheap because of the anxiety and distress of the owners. In this way he came to own a large part of Rome at the time." Apparently ownership of a house also indicated ownership of the land on which it was built.

To get the real picture of the society into which Virgil was born, one must remember that, alongside of this vast wealth in the hands of a few and this awful poverty of the great mass of the population, there was a convention of moral censoriousness unequaled anywhere except possibly among the early Puritans of the Massachusetts Bay Colony. Surviving from the early days there was an honorary office, available only to old men of long and honorable service to the welfare of the city, and aspired to because of the peculiar advantages adhering to it—the office of censor.

The censor was responsible only to his conscience, and he could annul marriages, deprive men of property, actually put men and women to death for whatever he happened to consider moral turpitude. It was also an office in which old men, with the fires of youth burnt out in them, could indulge in the most distressing perversities. The most famous of these censors was Marcus Porcus Cato, and even in the most laudatory accounts of him, one sees that he was a most intolerable and intolerant scoundrel. Plutarch, who paints an idealized portrait of him as a patriarch and as an example of the rugged Roman virtues of simplicity, plain living, hard work and distaste for frills, nevertheless shows us, almost against his will, that Cato was a heartless skinflint, callous, avaricious, and a hypocritical old goat with women. He drove his slaves out to starve when they were grown too old and decrepit for heavy work and sold off others when they fell ill or weak, instead of caring for them in recognition of their long service, as some other Romans of ordinary decency of feeling did. But that wasn't Cato's way: to do that would have been, to him, weakness and sentimentality. It was not good business. Then again, as censor, he threw out of the Senate Manilius who would have been the next consul, for having "in the presence of his daughter, and in open day, kissed his wife." And yet the old Censor's conduct with the young female slaves of his own household after the death of his wife was scandalous to such a degree that his son was forced to act to save the family reputation and cause the old lecher to marry a young woman he had seduced. Such moral hypocrisy was almost universal. Prostitution among the poor and profligacy among the rich were so common that no other literature in the Occident refers so often to sexual vices as does Latin literature. Yet there was an "official" literature consisting of fictions about the rugged simplicity of the Roman people, the sanctity of the Roman home and the high destiny of S.P.Q.R. (the Senate and People of Rome).

PUBLIUS VIRGILIUS MARO was born on October 15, in the year 70 B.C., on a small farm owned by his father near the village of Mantua in Cisalpine Gaul. He was therefore by birth not a citizen of Rome, because the full franchise of Roman citizenship did not extend to Mantua until 49 B.C. Nor do we know how or when Virgil attained full citizenship. Virgil's father was apparently well-to-do because the boy received a liberal education, not only under slave tutors but in the special schools of Cremona, Milan and Naples. He read Greek literature avidly, studied philosophy under a disciple of Epicurus and specialized in chemistry and medicine. He appears to have intended to become a veterinary and, according to Donatus, his first employment was in that capacity in the stables of the Emperor

Augustus. Because this story was elaborated in the legends about Virgil in the Middle Ages, when he was considered a sorcerer, that is no reason why we should doubt it as many scholars are inclined to do. It would explain, for one thing, how an unknown Mantuan of low birth got so easily and quickly to the ear of Augustus. The Emperor was more of a lover of horses than a lover of literature.

Virgil appears to have assumed the *toga virilis* (indicating his growth into manhood) at the unusually early age of sixteen. But this was probably for the reason that his health was bad; he was of a studious disposition, and he could not partake in athletic games. He was shy and bashful, delicate and retiring. He early developed conspicuous symptoms of tuberculosis of the lungs and, as he grew older, suffered frequent hemorrhages. He went to Rome in his early twenties to make his way in some sort of profession, but his health was unequal to the strain of competition in the city and he retired to his father's country home. When he was twenty-six years old he was a victim of the rapacious and inequitable system upon which the Roman state was founded. After the battle of Philippi, the whole region in which he lived was expropriated and divided among the legionaries of the victorious Octavius and Antony. Virgil saw his estate seized and turned over to supporters of Octavius and Antony, for no other reason than that the old republican party in the neighboring city of Cremona had supported Brutus.

The governor of the region who was responsible for the work of expropriation was a man who had grown wealthy by choosing to run with the lucky political party. His name was Asinius Pollio. He became governor of Cisalpine Gaul. He was a tyrannical and oppressive governor, exacting the last penny of tribute from the region, but he fancied himself something of a scholar, orator, and literary man; and when Virgil's plight came to his notice, he gave the young man a letter of introduction to the millionaire patron of the arts, Mæcenas, in Rome. (You will observe that he did nothing for Virgil on his own accord beyond this at the time, although it was in his power to do so. It was not until Virgil had become established as a poet with a reputation that Pollio undertook to patronize him.)

There are two men of wealth in Rome about whom we have never heard quite enough. One of them is Mæcenas and the other is Atticus, the wise and patient friend of Cicero. More and more, the honorable qualities, the inherent decency, the quiet humor of these two men impress themselves upon one. I am almost inclined to believe that those two men and Cæsar (whose essential intellectual integrity and emotional honesty stand out above the demagoguery and hypocrisy of the time) were the great men of their period.

Popular and scholastic legend has made of Mæcenas a man of great wealth who patronized the poets Virgil and Horace, and therefore a Mæcenas in our language is, say, a man like Otto Kahn, who takes pleasure in endowing the opera and aiding other artistic enterprises. But Mæcenas was not, as wealth went in Rome, a wealthy man. He was a member of the equestrian class; he owned some property in Rome and he appears to have been engaged in some commercial enterprises; but his household retinue was small, his private life rather austere for the times, and his security was largely dependent upon the sound political and commercial advice he could offer the Emperor Augustus. He was an adviser rather than an active politician.

In 36 B.C., Mæcenas accompanied Octavius into Sicily but was sent back to administer affairs in Rome; and during the campaign at Actium he was named vice-regent, in which capacity he crushed the conspiracy of Lepidus. But he did enjoy (and he must have merited it) the unlimited confidence of Octavius Augustus, who entrusted him with the official signet with authority to open and to alter and reply to all official letters. His moral authority over Augustus also appears to have been considerable. He dissuaded him from many acts of revenge and exploitation; and he appears to have been the person responsible for inculcating in Augustus ideas of clemency, conciliation and diplomacy instead of the heartlessness and ruthlessness which had been characteristic of the Emperor during the early years of his reign. Ten years after the Battle of Actium there was a rupture between Augustus and Mæcenas, as the result of which Mæcenas was deprived of his official position, as administrator of Rome and Italy. (This office corresponded more to the modern presidency of a corporation than to a governorship; or probably it might be compared to the administration of the budgetary affairs of German cities, or of Toledo, Ohio.) What caused the break is uncertain. It seems, unhappily, to have been domestic in nature. The wife of Mæcenas, Terentia, and the Emperor Augustus appear to have become too intimate for the complete concord of the two families; and although there was no divorce, Mæcenas retired from court life to his unpretentious palace on the Esquiline (a by no means fashionable neighborhood, since it had once been a burial ground and was considered unwholesome) and there lived out his years, surrounded by his friends, Virgil, Horace, Propertius and Varius, and the most brilliant circle of Rome. (From Horace's ode on the marriage of Mæcenas we know that Mæcenas married late in life a gay young woman, with pretty legs and feet, who "danced," which was something the sedater matrons of Rome did not do. And Mæcenas was much older than Augustus.)

How Virgil so quickly became a man of property, with a definite and rather considerable income, after only a few years in Rome remains a mystery. It is nonsense to imagine that Mæcenas gave him a large sum of money out of hand: millionaires, then or now, don't do that. Millionaires sometimes subsidize a writer but only in recognition of definite services received or on the promise of work which will redound to the interest or glory of the patron. Besides, Virgil never seems to have received any patronage from Mæcenas in the form of gifts, such as Mæcenas bestowed upon Horace for having dedicated verses to him. The Sabine farm, indeed, which Mæcenas gave Horace, was a piece of unproductive property which Mæcenas was anxious to get rid of but could not sell, and which was costing him too much money to keep up. Horace could afford to live on the farm with a housekeeper and two or three slaves, because of the income he derived from his writings and from his patrimony. It was a very modest existence at best, not at all comparable to the scale of living Virgil was able to maintain; for Horace's needs were simple and his tastes never luxurious.

There was a story that in Rome Virgil engaged for a while in some commercial pursuit, the nature of which is not disclosed. If he was a veterinary whose skill had commended itself to Augustus, the Emperor may have put him in the way of making some money by investment or in commissions, in gratitude, say, for having saved the life of one of his favorite horses. It is hard to account for the fact that, in a comparatively short time after his arrival in Rome as a dispossessed farmer's son, he owned valuable property in Rome, Naples, and Mantua—unless he was an exceedingly shrewd business man or had been put in for a quick turn in the market by the Emperor or some of his supporters. Rome had a stock exchange for the sale of shares in commercial enterprises as well as for dealing in futures in grain and other commodities.

At all events we know that, through the good offices of Mæcenas, Virgil succeeded in having the paternal property in Mantua restored to him. He returned there for a year or so and devoted his time to the composition of pastoral poetry. It was then, I believe, from the biographical and other evidence at hand, that he conceived an idea which he was able to sell to Mæcenas, the confidential adviser to Augustus.

He had been writing some poetry reciting the charms of country life, in imitation of Hesiod and Theocritus. A peculiar situation had arisen making the time ripe for the propagation of such poetry. An acute food shortage was developing in Rome. The reason is easy to see. In the middle and south of Italy the lands had long been held by private inheritance which the Roman law had upheld; but the rich lands to the north of Rome, extending to the Alps, had been declared the property of the state by Julius Cæsar who began the system of expropriating the land in this region from the original settlers and dividing it among his legionaries as a form of payment for their services. This system had continued and the property had been shifted three times by the time Augustus came into power: once by Julius Cæsar, once by Marc Antony when he held the authority over that domain, and again by Augustus after he had defeated Antony at Actium. In this disruptive shifting of farm ownerships, farms went into decay. Soldiers were not any too good as farmers in the first place; in the second place many of them retained titles by absentee landlordism; and in the third place no one felt like making permanent improvements in property which might be seized in the next shift of the wind in politics.

Farming, then, all over Italy and particularly in the North was in a very bad way. Rome was overcrowded with families who had abandoned their farms and with families whose farms had been taken away from them. Famine loomed as an imminent possibility. Augustus had restored order and under the wise counsel of Mæcenas a temperate and peaceful reign seemed at hand. But before prosperity could be restored it was necessary not only to get people back to the farms, but to make it seem worth while for them to do so.

It is quite definite that Virgil was commissioned by Augustus, at the instance of Mæcenas, to busy himself with the manufacture of poems which would celebrate the glories of the simple life, the beauties of agricultural pursuits, the wholesomeness of plain living. It is not to be imagined that Virgil undertook this task with his tongue in his cheek. He had been writing pastoral poetry before he was officially commissioned to write it. Indeed, it is not at all unlikely that the hard-headed and quite Philistine Augustus asked to see some of Virgil's samples when Mæcenas was urging upon Augustus the economic advantages of disseminating some pastoral poetry among the masses.

Living on a farm suited Virgil because of the delicate condition of his health. He was, moreover, interested in the dialects of the Mantuan district and eager to introduce to his people a form hitherto unknown among them—a form derived largely from the *Idylls* of Theocritus. He called his poems *Eclogues*. The truth was, however, that he actually knew very little about farm life and never did learn much about it. Horace, in an ode, gently chided him about this and made unmalicious fun of Virgil's knowledge of agriculture. Many of the *Eclogues* are, from a realistic point of view, absurd. He made no attempt to disguise the fact that he was imitating Theocritus. As a result he substituted names and transferred the locale of the Theocratean poems, thereby making Sicilian shepherds out of Italian dirt farmers. The people whose simple life he celebrated in pastoral verse never were pastoral and they never have been. Pastoral poetry is a lonely poetry wherein the shepherd poet (David, for instance, and Theocritus) beguiles his loneliness with plaintive or sportive imaginings. The Italians of the countryside were rough, ready, rude and gregarious.

Nevertheless these *Eclogues* were popular. They were delicate, wistful, and easy to memorize. The Fifth Eclogue in which two shepherds honor the memory of a dead companion, one by singing his epitaph and the other by singing his apotheosis, was an especial favorite, the more so in that it was supposed to refer to the assassination and deification of Julius Cæsar, who had become a great popular hero, and whose memory was reverenced by the people.

After Virgil had published a few of his *Eclogues* he must have been stung by the infinitely delicate criticism of his friend Horace who merely remarks about the "elegance" of Virgil's rural scenes, an adjective Horace knew could not appropriately describe any actual rural scene in all Italy. (It must be noted here that publication of verse in Rome took two forms: verses were copied and sold in bookshops and they were also recited in the theater, sometimes to musical accompaniment and sometimes not. The recital of a bit of verse in the theater was like a song number in modern vaudeville; it was a feature on a bill which included a variety of entertainment. The Romans did not care for tragedy, but they liked comedy and variety performances: they perfected the art of vaudeville.) At all events Virgil turned from the immediate scenes visualized through the glasses of Theocritus and wrote the Fourth Eclogue, in which he abandoned his model and achieved a high degree of originality— such originality, as a matter of fact, that this poem was the most famous of all his works, not only in his own time but throughout the Middle Ages.

The Fourth Eclogue is a miniature epic. It sings of the Perusian wars and the conflict between Antony and Octavius which were brought to a peaceful conclusion by the Treaty of Brundisium. The poet calls upon the Cumean Sibyl for verification of the fact that famine has been succeeded by prosperity, that granaries once empty now are filled, and that the reign of fabled golden age—the age of Saturn—is at hand. (It turned out to be almost as short-lived as the New Era of Prosperity believed to have begun under the presidency of Calvin Coolidge in America; but this did not hurt the immediate and lasting success of the poem.) As a matter of fact, the Fourth Eclogue is obscure and its very obscurity was what contributed to its success. The whole of the Mediterranean world, with the exception of Rome and to a certain extent, Alexandria, was in a state of economic collapse. Brooding philosophers were turning inward from the growing misery of the great mass of the population of the world; religious cults were spreading which dwelt on the idea of death and immortality as an escape from the wretchedness of living; the moody Jews of Palestine, with a racial culture developed by a communal plight extending over a long period as a subject race, were developing the idea and the hope of a Messiah who should lead them to prosperity either in this world or the next. In this eclogue Virgil had to paraphrase the Sibylline oracles which the later Christian fathers found to parallel so closely lines from the prophecies of Isaiah that they took Virgil to their hearts and conferred upon him a sort of pre-Christian sainthood, differentiating him from other "pagans."

The parallels found by the Christian bishops were these:

> *Jam redit et Virgo, redeunt Saturnia regna;*
> *Jam nova progenies cœlo demittitur alto—*
> *Te duce, si qua manent sceleris vestigia nostri,*
> *Ittita perpetua solvent formidine terras—*
> *Pacatumque reget patriis virtutibus orbem*
>
> IV. ECLOGUE, v.6.

Behold a virgin shall conceive, and bear a son.—

ISAIAH, vii, 14.

"Of the increase of his government and peace there shall be no end, upon the throne of David, and upon his kingdom, to order it, and to establish it with justice from henceforth even forever."—Isaiah, ix., 7.

Concerning this eclogue, Gibbon writes (*The Decline and Fall of the Roman Empire,* chapter XX):

"Forty years before the birth of Christ the Mantuan bard, as if inspired by the celestial muse of Isaiah, had celebrated, with all the pomp of oriental metaphor, the return of the virgin, the fall of the serpent, the approaching birth of a god-like child, the offspring of the great Jupiter, who should expiate the guilt of human kind, and govern the peaceful universe with the virtues of his father; the rise and appearance of a heavenly race, a primitive nation throughout the world: and the gradual restoration of the innocence and felicity of the golden age. The poet was perhaps unconscious of the secret sense and object of these sublime predictions, which have been so unworthily applied to the infant son of a consul or a triumvir: but, if a more splendid, and indeed specious, interpretation of the fourth eclogue contributed to the conversion of the first Christian emperor, Virgil may deserve to rank among the most successful missionaries of the gospel."

Beneath the suave irony of that passage, it is obvious that Gibbon also misread the eclogue, accepting the mistranslation that had been so long current. The *Virgo* of Virgil does not refer to the Virgin Mary nor yet to Cæsar's half-sister, Octavia, who married Antony, as Heyne and other scholars have figured out. (Octavia, widow of Marcellus, was with child by her deceased husband when the eclogue was written.) The *Virgo* of the eclogue is the Virgo of the astrological chart and so is the *Saturnia*. The combination of Virgo under Saturn in astrology is deemed especially benign: the reign of Saturn is rare, occurring only one year in every twenty-nine. Saturn is beneficent only under certain combinations, but when Saturn is in Virgo, in the jargon of the astrologers, the good results enumerated by Virgil are supposed to ensue. Virgil was an amateur astrologer, as he indicates in several passages in the *Georgics;* and astrology, which had been brought to Rome from the Babylonians, was extremely popular. Professional astrologers and diviners infested the streets of Rome, dressed in their symbolic costumes familiar now to every one, and pursued a lively trade, because the Romans, while never religiously inclined, were especially superstitious, believing in lucky signs, charms, malign days of the year (as for instance the Ides of March) and what not.

The Tenth Eclogue is interesting in that it is the earliest indication we have of Virgil's views of love. It is also indicative of the attitude he is to take as a poet throughout his career. His poetry shows us that love meant very little in his life, and passion meant to him nothing at all. He never celebrates a mistress of his own, like

Catullus, Tibullus, Horace and Propertius. He describes the experience of love only in the third person. In choosing a Greek model to imitate he took the humblest, sweetest natured, most retiring of all Greek lyric writers, Theocritus, who also largely chose to deal with passion at second-hand.

With the success of the *Eclogues,* Virgil appears to have been commissioned to write more poems which would aid in a back-to-the-farm movement. To this end he began to study the Italian peasant farmers and brings his subjects closer to their hearts and homes. After three years in Mantua, however (with frequent trips to Rome where he was the guest of Mæcenas and a figure in the literary circle which included Horace, Plotius and Varius), the moist climate of the district aggravated his pulmonary condition and he moved to Naples. He also had a villa in Sicily and an apartment in Rome on the same street on the Esquiline where Mæcenas and Horace had their residences.

WITH the composition of his second volume of bucolic poetry Virgil changed from Theocritus to Hesiod as a model, purposing to write an Italian equivalent of the *Works and Days.* The *Georgics* are definitely didactic. They undertake to tell the Italian farmer how to get the most produce out of his land, how to take care of his orchards, how to tell the signs of the weather, how to cultivate bees, and (most important of all to Virgil, who was a veterinary) how to feed, tend and doctor horses and cattle. Along with this he gave a history of agriculture and a spirited account of the Battle of Pharsalia, retold the legend of Orpheus and Eurydice and the story of Aristæus, described horse and chariot racing, told of the prodigies at the death of Julius Cæsar, described a bleak winter in Scythia—and celebrated the joys of country life.

Thomson's *The Seasons* and Philips' *Cyder* are imitations in English poetry of the *Georgics.* These didactic poems by Virgil have had a great critical success with modern scholars who probably haven't taken the trouble to read them critically but are eager to pass along the torch of error. They have been praised in the most fulsome panegyrics. They are dull imitations of a dull model and not even the delicate and precise quality of the language Virgil uses can make them more entertaining to a modern reader of Latin than Thomson's *The Seasons.* They are actually less entertaining than a good contemporary almanac, the modern equivalent of what Virgil intended them to be.

The reason for the general overestimation of the *Georgics* in the standard literary histories and commentaries is easy to seek. The *Georgics* are the least read, least known of Virgil's work. Every scholar worth his salt knows that the *Æneid* is a very unsatisfactory performance, even as an epic. Few of them go as far as Niebuhr, who said this epic was a complete failure and a false idea in the first place (although I agree with Niebuhr), but even the most fervent apologists for Virgil qualify their praise with so many reservations as to destroy their carefully built up estimation of the epic as a whole. They turn almost too readily, and as if with a feeling of relief, to the *Georgics,* praise of which is safe because nobody reads the *Georgics* any more for pleasure—nor, one suspects, for any other reason.

But the *Georgics* and the *Eclogues* were as popular with the Roman populace and peasants in Virgil's time as Edgar Guest's poems are with newspaper readers today. The Sixth Eclogue, called the *Silenus,* which gives a short vulgarization of Epicurean philosophy, was recited in the theater by the celebrated actress of mimes, Cytheris, to the great applause of the whole audience, including Cicero. And the *Æneid,* published by the order of Augustus after Virgil's death, simply had to be admired under the reign of Augustus whether one really liked it or not. (Isolated passages from it, by the way, are wholly admirable, lofty sentiment couched in the most appropriate words.) Moreover, Virgil's reputation was kept alive throughout the Middle Ages by two factitious circumstances: on the one side he was regarded as the pagan poet intrusted by God to announce the birth of Christ, and on the other side he was regarded as a sorcerer, because of the pharmacology of the Eighth Eclogue and because of the passage in the sixth book of the *Æneid* which seemed to indicate his acquaintance with the nether world. (Dante subscribed to this popular belief, wherefore he chose Virgil as his guide through Hell.)

Virgil was ten years writing the *Æneid* and he never finished his revision of it. This epic was not, like the bucolic poems, a commissioned work. When Virgil was about forty years of age and living most of the year in Naples, he gave out the information to his circle of literary friends on one of his visits to Rome that he was writing an epic which he hoped might be to Latin literature what the *Iliad* was to Greek literature. The hero was to be Æneas, son of Venus and Anchises, and the epic should tell of the wanderings of Æneas after the battle of Troy, his visit to the court of Dido, Queen of

Carthage, his arrival in Italy at the mouth of the Tiber; his war with Turnus, his marriage with Lavinia, daughter of King Latinus and the founding, growth and glory of Rome.

The greatest curiosity about the work was aroused long before anybody at Rome had seen any of it. Then, on one occasion, Virgil showed to the poet Propertius the passage from the *Æneid* describing the shield of Æneas, a skillful imitation of Homer's shield of Achilles. Propertius was enthusiastic and passed the word around that Virgil was writing an epic which would eclipse the *Iliad*. News of the work penetrated to the field headquarters of Augustus, who was engaged in a military expedition against the Cantabrians, in a remote corner of his empire. He sent a messenger at once to Virgil asking the privilege of reading it. Virgil did not comply with the request. Augustus kept writing until Virgil finally wrote, "I have of late received from you frequent letters. With regard to my Æneas, if, by Hercules, it were worth your listening to, I would willingly send it. But so vast is the undertaking that I almost appear to myself to have commenced such a work from some defect in judgment or understanding; especially since, as you know, other and far higher studies are required for such a performance."

About a year later, however, after the return of Augustus to Rome, Virgil took some of the manuscript with him to read to the Emperor and his sister, Octavia, who had recently lost her only son, Marcellus, whom Augustus had adopted and who would have been his heir. Virgil chose to let them hear the sixth book and he recited it himself. His voice was soft, musical, delicately modulated; his bearing *spiritual* because of the ravages of tuberculosis; his articulation perfect. When he came to the passage in which he alludes to the death of the beloved youth Marcellus, he withheld the name till he came to the line, *"Tu Marcellus eris—manibus date lilia plenis."* The break in that line, the catch in the throat, the tender eloquence of the whole passage caused Octavia to break down. The success of the passage was complete. Octavia is said to have directed the immediate payment to Virgil of ten thousand sesterces for each verse in the celebrated passage. (Under Augustus a sesterces was a brass coin the exchange value of which was estimated to be worth four asses.) If this story is true, Virgil received the highest price for literary work, per line, that any one ever received anywhere.

After the success of this recital, Virgil returned to Naples, enlarged his already magnificent library and continued his labor.

It was arduous for him, because his lungs continued to waste away, and he was subject to frequent headaches and fainting spells. He had a librarian, a freedman named Eros, who helped him in research, and an amanuensis, who took down his lines as he composed them. These dictated lines Virgil subjected to infinite revision.

WHEN, in his fiftieth year, Virgil completed the *Æneid,* he went to Athens, prepared to spend three years there in patient revision of the epic; but, after he had been in the city only a few months Augustus passed through on his way back to Italy from a visit to his eastern domain. Augustus invited Virgil to accompany him back to Rome in the imperial squadron. Virgil was very ill but accepted the invitation. He was weakened by sea-sickness on the trip and when the emperor's vessel touched at Brundisium he was too ill to proceed. He was removed from the ship and cared for in the seaport town; but within a few days he died. With him were his friends, Varius and Plotius Tucca, whom he instructed to burn the *Æneid* as not measuring up to the standard he had set for himself in writing it.

Augustus rescinded this death-bed wish and commanded Varius and Tucca to edit and revise the poem but to make no additions of their own. They cut out twenty-two lines in the second book, in a passage about Æneas and Helen; and transposed books two and three. The transposition remains but the excised lines were restored.

Virgil willed his considerable wealth largely to his brother, but included specific bequests to Mæcenas, Varius and Tucca. He also expressed a dying wish that his remains be buried at Naples. This wish Augustus himself carried out, causing a tomb to be built which is still to be seen about two miles north of the city. Throughout his life Virgil had been "sweet" and *pius* (which is not exactly the same as pious). Horace had a warm affection for him; Augustus deferred to him; Mæcenas honored him. The pleasing quality of his personality doubtless contributed much to the view taken of his work.

The plain fact, however, is that Æneas is not a hero as Virgil depicts him; he is cold, smug, unfeeling, uninteresting. Turnus whom Æneas defeats is the only human and appealing character in the book, except Dido, and there is little imagination in the creation of this queen who is supposed to represent the historic Cleopatra. Pope is right in saying that the epic is a political tract, meant to strengthen the popularity of Augustus and to flatter the vanity of Virgil's countrymen. Some of the lines connecting Iulus allusively with Julius Cæsar are not only bombastic but downright funny. The mythology often creaks. Moreover, some of the best individual lines in the poem are lifted hardly with a change from Ennius and Catullus. The poem is, in fact, almost a mosaic of bits from other poets, Homer, Arctinus, Euphorion, Apollonius Rhodius, Pacuvius, Attius, Nævius, Lucilius, Varius and Lucretius. (Macrobrius has ferreted out all these borrowings.) The choice of Virgil, as the Latin poet whose work is most generally taught beginners, is explainable: Virgil's language is pure, in the two senses of that word, a rarity among Latin poets. He is considered safer for the morals of the young, less likely to excite the classroom blush or pique the adolescent fancy than Catullus, Tibullus, Propertius or even Horace. But the defect of this quality which Virgil had in such perfection is that Virgil is likely to spoil a beginner's interest in Latin poetry altogether.

Horace, now, is another matter. Horace invented the term *urbanitas* to describe a special disposition, mood and quality of mind, which is a compound of good humor, tact, intelligence and quiet acceptance of reality. *Urbanitas* is the exact opposite of *rusticatas,* which indicates the rude, direct, insensitive behavior of the peasant. In urbanity I am inclined to believe that Horace has never had an equal in the whole world of classical literature, just as I am inclined to believe there never was a truer wit, a more knowing mind, a cleverer literary artist than Horace. If Virgil is overestimated by the classical scholars, Horace is incredibly underestimated by them, even by those who love, honor and appreciate him. Even Professor Tenney Frank, that brilliant, serene and perceptive scholar and fine stylist whose *Catullus and Horace* is such a joy, even Professor Frank is not quite unrestrained enough in his praise of Horace to please me. For what he is, a perfect artist always, a perfectly adjusted man, a gentleman in the very best sense of that word, and a civilized intelligence, Horace is perfect. There is not a flaw in him. He is one of the greatest writers of humor the world has ever known. Never a perpetrator of the rude jocularity or the slap-stick fun of comic writers, like Plautus and Terence, he strikes always at the humor of the mind, at those delicately apprehended incongruities of life. He mocks so slyly at pretense and pomposity that his victims rarely know they are being made fun of. There was a convention in Latin poetry of the sharp transposition of mood and cadence in the last line, to achieve a smarting, stinging wit. It was a convention in which the better Latin poets excelled. One of the most famous is Carmina LVIII of Catullus:

> *Cæli, Lesbia nostra, Lesbia illa,*
> *illa Lesbia, quam Cattulus unam*
> *plus quam se atque suos amavit omnes,*
> *nunc in quadriuviis et angiportis*
> *glubit magnanimis Remi nepotes*

"Cælius, our Lesbia, that Lesbia whom Catullus loved more than himself and all things, now on the street-corners and alley-ways *glubit* the high-minded descendants of Remus."

After the lovely, noble beginning of that poem, Catullus achieves the ferocious bitterness of that word *glubit* and the infinite sarcasm about the "high-minded descendants of Remus."

Heinrich Heine excelled in this form, as witness this perfect example,

> *Nur einmal möcht ich dich sehen,*
> *Und sinken vor dir aufs Knie;*
> *Und sterbend zu dir sprechen:*
> *"Madam, ich liebe sie!"*

Translated with remarkable ingenuity by Louis Untermeyer (*Poems of Heinrich Heine*):

> Oh, once, only once, might I see thee
> Ere I break these fetters in shards,
> And kneel to thee dying and murmur:
> "Madam, my best regards."

It is a form used with excellent effect in our own time by Edna St. Vincent Millay, Dorothy Parker and Samuel Hoffenstein.

Horace was a master at this form, but he subtilized it, hiding (except to the wary eye) the sly malice or the ironic point within the elaborate phrases themselves. An enemy of all false art and all false sentiment, he could imitate the elevated too "poetic" style to such perfection that only an adroit use of a word would give away the humor, the joke, of his comprehensive criticism. Just as Max Beerbohm's *Enoch Soames* is a criticism of a whole tradition of English letters, so also is any satire by Horace a criticism of a whole system of thought or attitude of mind.

Sometimes he achieved this effect by a false humility (when Horace is deferential toward an inferior but popular poet, you may be quite sure it is a false humility because Horace knew his genius, his talent and his limitations to a degree rare in poets) as when, addressing Antonius Iulus, he writes, "You, a poet of sublimer style, shall sing of Cæsar, whenever, graceful in his well-earned laurel, he shall drag the fierce Syngambri along the sacred hill; Cæsar, than whom nothing greater or better the fates and indulgent gods ever bestowed on the earth, nor will bestow, though the times should return their primitive gold. You shall sing both the festal days, and the public rejoicings on account of the prayed-for return of the brave Augustus, and the forum free from law-suits."

In the original, of which this is a literal translation by Smart, that whole passage is a parody of the phraseology and the sentiment of the "sublime" style of Latin poetry, so superbly done that only the witty reference to the numerous law-suits among the "rejoicing" Romans, serves to point the burlesque and sarcasm of the tribute. And the poem does not end with that line: it goes right on to a mock heroic conclusion with Horace never cracking a smile.

Horace was serene, but he was a man of so much pride and honor that he would permit no one, however exalted, to impose upon or take advantage of him. Augustus he considered a pompous nit-wit, a dull, uninteresting fellow, and so kept him at a distance, complying grudgingly with the Emperor's repeated requests for a poem written especially for him by sending a poem which showed there was no sycophancy in the soul of Horace. When he saw how Augustus took it, he sent him others. He even rebuked Mæcenas on one occasion for presuming too much. Mæcenas had written to Horace summoning him to Rome and had hinted at the gratitude Horace should have for Mæcenas' patronage. Horace replied (I use the translation of Professor Tenney Frank in *Catullus and Horace*):

"My debt to you is great and I gladly acknowledge it, but I am not as young as I was, and to care for my health I must remain away from Rome till spring. If this seems ingratitude, I will submit to your judgment and give back the estate. In the fable the fox lost his liberty by feeding too well in the corn-bin. Have I done so? Telemachus wisely refused the gifts of Menelaus which he could not properly use. There is also a story of a tradesman of Rome who accepted from a patron an estate which destroyed his happiness. He saw the mistake and gave back the gift. The moral is obvious."

Professor Frank remarks, "Horace does not remind Mæcenas that after all his Sabine farm was only a fair return for the home which the state had confiscated, but he doubtless wrote with that thought in mind. Horace's pride, of which Augustus had complained, was not a thing for any one, not even Mæcenas, to disregard. The publication of this frank epistle is proof enough that Mæcenas was the kind of sportsman who could appreciate the poet's temper." That Horace's temper when aroused could steel him to deadly, subtle malice is to be seen in the seemingly casual comparison of himself to Telemachus and of Mæcenas to Menelaus. To the old husband of a young and flirtatious wife about whom there was talk, the reference to Menelaus was not altogether fortuitous.

THE biography and critical study of Horace by Professor Frank in that masterpiece of scholarly revivification, *Catullus and Horace,* is such a detailed and perfect thing that I hesitate to venture my own briefer account of a personality which Professor Frank has realized so adequately. But as any one who has read that book will immediately recognize how much I am indebted to it, perhaps my presumption is not too great.

In his later years Horace was no doubt what some women would call a selfish old bachelor, because he would not, or at least did not, marry and, although he seems to have had a mistress or so, his passion was easily requited and he considered the emotion of love pretty much of a nuisance. In his amatory verse (they can hardly be called love poems) he is never distressed, jealous, petulant, recriminative, or revengeful like the emotional Catullus. In love, as a matter of fact, he usually makes fun of himself, telling how he was left in the lurch, discomfited, or deserted for another. He protests, in fact, too much: it is obvious that he was more beloved by women than either Catullus or Propertius; that he was, indeed, more or less pursued by them. He liked women and women liked him, but he was not a fool about them. He was fickle because his passion never went very deep; his being brooked in love did not hurt or madden him as it did Catullus. The Ninth Ode of the Third Book of his Odes, the dialogue with Lydia, is a light and delicious treatment of his attitude toward love; and it shows why women loved him: he could make love with grace.

During the Roman holiday season in December, corresponding to our Christmas and to the Lenæa of the Greeks, it was the custom of slaves and masters to exchange places for the day, and the slaves were privileged to scold, abuse and criticize their masters on that occasion. In Satire VII, of the Third Book of Satires, Horace imagines his slave, Davus, as taking advantage of the occasion to call his master to account. Among other things, Davus says that Horace is lazy, weak-willed and drinks too much; that when he is in the country he yearns for the city and when in the city yearns for the country; that he writes verses praising the rugged virtues of the ancient Romans whereas he knows perfectly well that he could not abide living among such people for a minute; and that moreover, prating of freedom, he is never free: he is enslaved by passion for a married woman; that when he makes furtive rendezvous with her he quakes with fear and is so apprehensive as to be a ridiculous disappointment as a lover; that he congratulates himself on not being an adulterer but is not only because he is too scared to carry his projects through. "A woman demands five talents of you, plagues you and after turning you out of doors, douses you (from a window above) with a pitcher of cold water: she calls you again (and you obey). Rescue your neck from this vile yoke; say to yourself, 'I am free, I am free.' You are not able to do so because a harsh master oppresses your mind, claps the spurs to your jaded appetite, and forces you on though reluctant."

We know almost as much about the character and personality of Horace, his daily life, thoughts, sentiments and feelings, as we know about Samuel Pepys. He was the most personal of classical poets. He was almost incomparably frank about himself, probably for the reason that he found it inexpedient and quite useless to be less frank about himself than he was about the ruling society of vainglorious Babbitts who made Rome under Augustus and the twelve Cæsars the Los Angeles of the ancient world. His urbanity and disabused intelligence, however, did not prevent his lashing out with the stinging whip of his invective against bad manners, stupidities, cruelty, hypocrisy, pretense, and depravity.

HORACE's full Latin name was Quintus Horatius Flaccus. He was born on the eighth of December, 65 B.C., near Venusia on a small farm where the roar of the Aufidus could be heard. He writes in Satires I. vi., "I am descended from a freedman; thus I am one whom everybody feels free to high-hat. . . . I cannot reckon myself a lucky fellow for having become your friend; for it was not by accident I met you. That best of men, Virgil, long ago, and afterward Varius, told you about me. When I first came into your presence I spoke a few words in a broken manner (for childish backwardness prevented me from speaking more); I did not tell you that I was the son of an illustrious father: I did not pretend that I rode about the country on a Satureian horse, but plainly what I was. You answer, as your custom is, in a few words; and I leave; you reinvited me nine months later and commanded me to be in the number of your friends. I esteem it a great thing that I pleased you, who distinguished probity from baseness, not by the illustriousness of a father, but by purity of heart and feelings. . . . If I live undefiled and innocent, dear to my friends, my father was the cause of this, who, though a poor man on a lean farm, was unwilling to send me to school under Flavius, where grand youths, sprung from great centurions, with satchels and tablets swung over their left arms, used to go with money in their hands the very day it was due, but had the spirit to bring me to Rome, to be taught those arts which any Roman knight and senator can teach his own children."

The rest of the satire is a beautiful tribute to the memory of his father. Horace tells us his father dressed him well, as a boy, but he also guarded the youth's mind as well as his body, teaching him to be civil, unashamed of his station and occupation; he did not spoil him or encourage him to be idle or dissipated but upright and full of self-respect. Therefore Horace did not associate with the gilded youths of his own generation but with boys of his own class. Least of all would he associate with the sort of youths who were ashamed of their fathers because of the newness of their wealth: his manners and ways of thinking were far different. He goes on to say that, as the result of this early training, he can, even though no longer poor, go about on a bob-tailed mule, unaccompanied, if he wishes, whereas others cannot make a trip to the country without a coach, horses and attendants.

Horace's father was an agent who collected the money from purchasers at auction sales, a business he developed and continued after the purchase of the small estate near Venusia. In this work he learned there were often persons at the auctions who wanted some article put up for sale, but did not have the immediate cash for it. He offered to lend money for these purchases at interest. From this he developed a regular banking business, lending money on collateral mortgages, discounting government warrants and paying interest on cash deposited with him. Horace was himself instructed in this business and assisted his father; as heir to the banking business, he always drew an income from it, although he apparently relegated to freedman agents the business his father established.

Horace appears to have lost his father about the time he reached manhood's estate, for he never speaks of his association with him after that time. When he was twenty-one he went to Athens to study.

While he was there Julius Cæsar was assassinated and, as a young radical, Horace joined the Republican party, enlisted in the army of Brutus and served under him as a military tribune until the battle of Philippi. In later years he made fun of his career as a soldier, saying that he distinguished himself at Philippi as the best runner in his outfit: showing his heels to them all in flight.

When Horace returned to Rome, the situation had changed for him indeed. His personal property was confiscated and his father's estate also. He was penniless. He had learned, he said, at Athens how to distinguish a straight line from a curve, but that was about all he knew of practical affairs. With a sum of money (secured from where he does not say) he purchased a clerkship under a quæstor, for one could *buy* a job in Rome in those days. On this small income he lived in a rather poverty-stricken manner until he began to think of earning a little money on the side by writing verse. His verses came to the attention of Virgil through Horace's friend, Varius, and Virgil introduced him to Mæcenas. He apparently made no impression upon Mæcenas at first, but nine months later Mæcenas was getting up a small crowd of literary men to accompany him on a diplomatic mission to Antony's headquarters in Brundisium and he invited Horace to come along. In the entourage, besides Horace, were Virgil, Varius and Appollodorus. "One may imagine Horace in his dusty office enjoying in anticipation this month's vacation with the foremost political and literary men of the day," writes Professor Frank. "What conversation there would be over the cups, when the policies of empire would be argued! It turned out otherwise. The great men were quite discreet; it might as well have been some fishing trip. In his diary of the journey (Sat. 1, 5) Horace succeeds very well in conveying the impression of the conventional twaddle about wine, mosquitoes, rough roads, bad inns and a small-town boxing match. When he returned and all his friends gathered about him to hear the report of his marvelous vacation, he had very little to tell, and presently he jotted down his account of the succession of nothings as a joke on himself."

Soon enough, however, he showed that, if he could not hear witty and interesting conversation in the circle of Mæcenas, he could supply it; and he actually became the chief figure of the group, though perhaps more deference was paid Virgil on the latter's occasional trips up from Naples.

When he was a young man Horace was short and stocky, but well-formed and with a heavy growth of black hair which came

down low on his narrow forehead. As he grew older he expanded
into a roly-poly little fellow, partially bald, fastidious in all things
—dress, speech, person, tastes. He fell victim to a variety of minor
ills, probably because he never took any exercise, read and wrote a
lot, loafed and drank wine in great quantities. He had trouble with
his eyes and smeared them with a black ointment; he was short of
breath; he had especially sensitive nostrils and could not bear the
smell of garlic. On one occasion he wrote a whole poem to Mæcenas
gently begging him to give up his taste for garlic. He also never
laughed and did not like to hear people laugh out loud. He disliked
talkative persons.

THROUGH the good offices of Mæcenas, Horace was sufficiently
advanced in favor and attention to give up his clerkship and, in one
way or another, soon became a man of modest property. When he
was about twenty-eight, Mæcenas gave him the Sabine farm, situ-
ated twenty-eight miles from Rome, a place such as Horace had
probably audibly yearned for, as a retreat where he could pursue
his literary labors, away from the distractions of Rome. The farm,
as I said before, was in wretched farming country and probably an
expense to Mæcenas. It had a house on it, facing the sea, however,
and some woods around it, a brook, and several good springs, including a favorite one, which Professor Frank says is still flowing.
Norman Douglas in *Old Calabria* reports that the region is now
denuded of forests and the land poorer than ever; the whole district
is practically abandoned because it has also become, since Horace's
time, highly malarial. Horace used to complain of the gnats and
mosquitoes but apparently in his time the mosquitoes were not of the
malaria-carrying kind, although he knew of the malaria in Apulia.

It is not my intention to follow the whole career of Horace.
One may do so with great enjoyment by reading Professor Frank's
study already referred to, or go into it more extensively by reading
all of the extant work (not too much remains) of Horace, in Latin
if one can; if not, preferably in a good literal prose translation like
Smart's. Professor Frank has shown conclusively that Horace, aside
from his literary reputation as a wit and a master of graceful
satires, letters in verse, and odes, is also one of the greatest lyric
writers that ever lived.

Toward the last Horace is gently complaining that the advanc-
ing years are robbing him of everything—his mirth, his gallantry,
his revelings and his play. Worse still, he says, they are depriving

him of his ability to write verse. He died at the age of fifty-seven, after a long illness, and his ashes were buried in Rome near the tomb of Mæcenas. At fifty-seven he had lived a full life and a perfectly adjusted one. He knew the worth of his verses, and the centuries have not belied him: "I have completed a monument more lasting than brass, and more sublime than the regal elevation of the pyramids . . . I shall not wholly die . . . I shall continually be renewed in the praises of posterity . . . I, exalted from low degree, shall be acknowledged as having originally adapted Æolic verse to Italian measures. Melpomene, assume that pride which your merits have acquired, and willingly crown my hair with Delphic laurel."

Horace, the son of a freedman, was the finest product of imperial Rome. With him might be named also Lucretius, Catullus and Propertius and the very modern Martial (a Roman equivalent of the newspaper columnist) as the best there was in the imagination and spirit of Rome, beyond the Roman genius in organization and administration. The glory that was Rome, grounded on an evil and inequitable social and economic system, was engulfed and devastated in a remarkably short while by a rapid decline of prosperity, by plagues, by disease, by stagnation, and by the wholesale turning away from this world to the next of an enslaved and impoverished population. The insincerities of Cicero, the deification of Cæsar, the glamour which Virgil attempted to throw over all that opportunistic culture, went down rapidly. The Roman genius for organization and administration survived only in the religion that arose out of the sorrows and aspirations of the Palestinian, Alexandrian and Roman rabble.

DANTE *AND THE MEDIEVAL MIND*

*

"THE *Divine Comedy* is like a forest of truth," writes Henry Dwight Sedgwick in his *Dante,* "in which a thousand men climb a thousand trees, and, each man, as he mounts nearer toward heaven, fondly believes that he had chosen the poet's tree of life."

The innocent incongruity of that image is the comical one presented to me by the commentators on Dante who seek to perpetuate the fallacy that Dante is still worth reading. I see Matthew Arnold shinning up one tree, Macaulay up another, Carlyle up another, George Saintsbury up still another and so on and so on, no less than a thousand of them up a thousand trees, all jabbering about the ineffable beauties of a dreary catalogue of names and vices and about the "grand style" of a poem that, by any sensible standards whatever, is no more worthy of admiration than a carved replica of the Battleship Maine assembled inside of a bottle.

Professor Borghese once accounted for the comparative infertility of Italian literature since the days of Dante by saying that the peak of achievement was reached in the first great work in the Italian language, the *Divine Comedy,* and that the genius of the country had never been able to live up to it. I repeated Professor Borghese's remark to an irreverent Italian of great scholarship and discrimination who said, "No. The real trouble is that Italian literature has never been able to live it down."

The *Divine Comedy,* like the Holy Roman Empire, which Dante admired and which was neither Holy nor Roman nor yet an empire, is not an epic; it is not divine; it is not a comedy; nor, except in a few isolated passages, is it poetry. It is not a story; there is no pleasing figure in it performing heroic actions. The

128

Inferno is not even elevated treatment of an elevated subject; it is a petulant act of revenge. Of the three books, the *Purgatorio* (least regarded by most of the commentators) has by far the better claim to one's interest and critical consideration—but as a moral discourse, not as poetry. And even as a unified moral discourse it lacks the dignity, the humanity, the sheer ethical appositeness or the poetical grandeur of one of the least poetical of all the books of the Old Testament, *Deuteronomy*. Even as allegory it is not as sublime in conception as *Pilgrim's Progress*.

Parts of the *Paradiso* are curious enough to repay the time spent in reading it; but in the *Paradiso,* even more than in the *Inferno,* Dante displays the unhealthy state of his mind, which is simply that of a weak voluptuary tortured by a medieval conscience. The "testimony," the spiritual experience of Dante, is, in character and spirit, exactly like that of the derelicts of the Bowery mission who achieve grace every Sunday night and fall out of it again on Monday. The plight of these derelicts is a subject for pity, irony and pathos, and is capable of being transmuted into poetry of the highest order; but Dante, describing himself in a similar plight, is either arrogant and complacent, or whining and maudlin.

Whatever truth there is in the *Divine Comedy* is manifest, eternal and apprehended by everybody. And it always has been. This truth is, that if you give yourself over to the sins and vices, the time will come, very likely, when you will find life somewhat unpleasant. Your health will break under it; people won't like or trust you; and there will be tumult and torment in your soul. If you repent of your ways in time and take yourself in hand, lead a simple and active life, are kind, beneficent, forgiving and obedient in the ways of God, you are apt to find life less vexing than formerly.

The truth, such as it is, of the allegory of the poem, as regards the Beatrice motive, is that the pure spiritual ideal of womanhood refines the grosser nature of the male; and, as regards the lady-at-the-window motive (which Dante explains as personifying Philosophy), the allegory is that reading and meditation keep one out of mischief. Dante is not consistent in this, because the virtue he insists upon more than anything else is activity, of whatever kind: it is better, he says, in effect, to be a scoundrel than to be what the French call an "honest" man. In the third canto of the *Inferno,* Virgil and Dante come into the vestibule of Hell. Here there are "sighs and clamors and shrill wailings" from "uncouth tongues," "utterances horrible, words of despondency and tones of wrath, high voices and hoarse and sounds of hands as well." Dante is horror-stricken and asks Virgil who these miserable people are. Virgil answers:

> ... These miserable ways
> They hold, the most unhappy souls of those
> Who lived without disgrace and without praise.
> Commingled are they with that caitiff choir
> Of angels who rebelled not, yet to God
> Were faithless; all for self was their desire.
> Heaven refuses them, lest they should stain
> Its glory; and deep hell admits them not,
> Lest even the damned from them some glory gain.

"Their fame on earth is as a breath of glass."

—*Translation by Jefferson Butler Fletcher.*

In that passage Dante rules out of consideration the average man and about ninety-eight per cent of the human race. The average man and the human race have repaid the compliment. Not only was Dante never popular, but he has never, in any age, been generally read even by men whose profession or recreation is literature. The cult of Dante has been kept alive by a small band of scholars in each generation who treat the *Divine Comedy* as a sort of crossword puzzle—and his name has been kept alive because replicas of the portrait bust in the Naples museum have been perennially popular book-ends. Boccaccio, who wrote the first biography of Dante and was among the first to insist that Dante had performed a great service in writing a lofty poem in the Florentine idiom instead of in Latin, makes it plain, nevertheless, that he did not understand the *Commedia* and got very little out of it; and by a curious eventuality the *Commedia* (or *Divine Comedy,* as Boccaccio was the first to call it) has enjoyed a more fervent devotion among English critics than among the first rate Italian critics.

George Saintsbury is ordinarily a sensible, straightforward man, impatient of humbug, blunt in his criticism of Arnold and Macaulay, deep-voiced, clear, vibrant, intelligent and humorous-minded. But his essay on "Dante and the Grand Style" (in Volume III of the *Collected Essays*) is such a perfect example of critical mumbo-jumbo that it has been generally classed as the best essay on Dante in modern times. To say the insupportable in the terms of an ulti-

DANTE ALIGHIERI
(Engraved by Raphael Morghen)

matum had been just what the Dante specialists had been striving for; and that is what Saintsbury achieved. Dubiety had marked their utterances; reservations had canceled much of the force of their argument. They had sought to persuade when their own words showed that they themselves were not convinced, as when John Jay Chapman, after saying that there is no work in the English language which approaches the style of Dante for concision and laconicism, says, "Dante is not only concise, but logical, deductive, prone to ratiocination." That is like saying, "He is not only short, but undersized, stocky and ten feet tall." Any one who is prone to ratiocination cannot, by the very nature of his complaint, be laconic or concise.

How this error about Dante's brevity and concision got started would be interesting to trace; but it is to be found perpetuated in nearly every discussion of him. And Dante is one of the longest-winded writers in the history of literature. He is verbose and redundant. Would a concise writer have used all those adjectives to describe the hub-bub in the corridor of Hell?

Let us take an example of the inconclusive proof of Saintsbury's contentions about the style of Dante:

"Perhaps the three or four words *E quella non ridea* at the beginning of the Twenty-first (Canto of the *Paradiso*) are Dante's tersest and most concentrated triumph." Having said this he appends a footnote saying, "They rank near to if not level with the two 'jewels four words long' of 'The rest is silence' and *'ego de mona kateudo,'* four well-known words giving the most absolutely uncommon effect, which seem to me the triumph of poetry in Shakespeare and Sappho."

The "and she smiled not" of Dante is in no way comparable to the Sapphic and the Shakespearean "jewels four words long." Shakespeare and Sappho both used their four words to cap and round off what had gone before. In fact, Sappho's jewel is not quite comparable to Shakespeare's, which are the dying words of Hamlet, the words which are often used as the "curtain line" of that stupendous tragedy. The ordinary reader, I suspect, is less familiar with the "Night-song" of Sappho, so I quote it entire:

> Δέδυκε μὲν ἀ σέλαννα
> καὶ Πληΐαδες, μέσαι δὲ
> νύκτες, παρὰ δ' ἔρχετ' ὥρα,
> ἔγω δὲ μόνα κατεύδω.

The moon is gone
And the Pleiads set,
    Midnight is nigh;
Time passes on,
And passes; yet
    Alone I lie.

—Tr. J. M. Edmonds, *Lyra Græca*, Vol. 1.
Loeb Classical Library.

The force of *Ego de mona Kateudo* is somewhat lost in the translation. The literal meaning is nearer to: "And I have to go to bed alone." It is the poignant disappointment of a young woman who has waited for a lover who has failed to keep his tryst.

Now, the "And she smiled not" of Dante caps nothing. In fact Beatrice continues at great length to explain why she doesn't smile:

Already on my lady's face anew
    Mine eyes were fastened, and with them my mind;
    And from all other objects this withdrew.
And she smiled not; but "If I smile," she said,
    Addressing me, "verily wouldst thou become
    Like Semele, when ashes she was made;
Because my beauty, which along the stair
    Of the eternal palace kindleth more,
    As thou hast seen, the higher our mounting there,
If it be tempered not, so far transcends
    In its effulgency thy mortal power
    That this were as a leaf the thunder rends.
We are uplifted to the seventh light,
    Which now beneath the burning Lion's breast
    Is raying downward mingled with his might.
Whither thine eyes look be thy mind addressed,
    And let those be as mirrors to the shape
    That in this mirror shall be manifest."

—Canto XXI, tr. Fletcher.

Dante continues about that failure of Beatrice to smile for no less than 120 lines and returns to it in the Twenty-third Canto! Is that "Dante's tersest and most concentrated triumph"? Is that the sort of thing we are asked to believe is on or near the level of "The rest is silence," *"ego de mona kateudo?"* As a matter of fact, the whole passage is a conscious imitation and elaboration of *Genesis* xviii: 6-19.

The most celebrated passage in the *Divine Comedy* also contains the most familiar Dantean line (with the exception, possibly, of the "All hope abandon ye who enter here"). The passage is the reply of Francesca to Dante when he encountered her in Hell. It will be remembered that Francesca is condemned to Hell because of her incestuous love for her brother, Paolo.

> ... There is no greater woe
> Than recollection of the happy time
> In wretchedness; and this thy Sage doth know
> But if in these so great affection seeks
> To see laid bare the first root of our love
> I can but do as one who weeps and speaks.
> For pleasure on a day of Lancelot
> We two were reading, how love mastered him.
> We were alone; misgivings had we not.
> And oftentimes that which we read would call
> Our eyes to meeting and make play our faces;
> But one part only brought us to our fall.
> When we had read there how the longed-for smile
> Was kissed by such a lover, this one then,
> Who parts not from me this eternal while,
> Kissed me upon my mouth all tremblingly.
> A Gallehaut was the book, and he who wrote it.
> That day we read no further, I and he."

—INFERNO, Canto V., tr. Fletcher.

About this passage there can be little doubt: it is a lovely thing. The sweet Francesca's simple account of how she and her brother incurred their guilt, is simple, direct, circumstantial. They were reading a romance about Lancelot and Guinevere: the hero in the story kissed the heroine when she smiled with love. This vicarious thrill inflamed the two children.

The pregnant sentence which closes this confession is beautiful and effective and so poetically *novel* as to merit much of the praise that has been given it. But it is taken as a supreme example of Dante's power of suggestion, of his ability to say slightly less than he means and thus to heighten the force of his suggestion. But, in all conscience, what more could he have made Francesca say? What more would even a tenth-rate poet have added to that recital? Dante has almost no sense of character and almost no power of expressing character; but in that passage he does rise to the level of keeping Francesca in character, in the situation he evokes, by having her say no more than she does. Remember that this is a young child in Hell; that she is confronted by the impressive personages, Virgil and Dante, one of whom, Dante, asks her how it happened that she and her brother committed their sin. She answers simply. She was not asked to give details, and no poet with any taste whatever would have continued beyond the point where her recital ended. If she had said, "We put the book aside" it would have been less effective because lacking in the conclusiveness of the suggestion, "We read no more that day." But this happy choice of words, innumerable examples of which can be found in the prose fiction of Ernest Hemingway and F. Scott Fitzgerald, is hardly enough to justify the claim that Dante was a master of the "grand style" in the sense that we use that phrase in connection with Homer, Shakespeare, Æschylus and some of the anonymous writers of the Bible.

Let us quote more from Saintsbury, who seems to have become mildly demented in commenting upon the grand style of Dante, saying that Dante possessed more than Homer or Milton, and pointing to Dante's choice of the adjective *livido* ("livid") in describing the pass of "livid rock" which leads to the Circle of Envy!

"No place is fuller of our evidence [of the grand style] than the opening of the *Purgatorio:* indeed the first two Cantos are almost compact of it. The immense sense of *relief* which the poet has managed to communicate to his readers expresses itself in no relaxation of style: but only in a greater glow and brightness."

If Dante began the *Purgatorio* with the words of an apartment lease, it would have been an immense relief after the Thirty-four cantos with its catalogue of names which varies in unpleasantness, piling up of such adjectives as "loathsome," "sinful," "horrendous," "bloody," "dolorous," "foul," "scabby," "vile," "repugnant," "monstrous," "filthy," "slimy," "ulcerous," "stinking," "scaly," etc., etc.

The truth is that there is very little evidence in Dante of that sublimity, restraint, simplicity and understanding of human motives evident in Homer, in Æschylus, in Euripides, in the Bible and in Shakespeare. In the *Divine Comedy* are to be found more examples of bad taste than in the work of any other writer of reputation. Boccaccio, attempting to honor the memory of Dante, compares him to a peacock. The peacock, he reminds us, has a voice that is "horrible to hear." And, writes Boccaccio, "Who cries out more horribly than he, when in the bitterest fiction he censures the faults of many who are living, and chastises those of the dead? Certainly none. By his demonstrations he in the same breath terrifies the good and casts down the wicked. Therefore, as far as this point concerns us, he truly may be said to have a horrible voice."

Boccaccio's true feeling about Dante and about Dante's style comes out in that passage. Boccaccio didn't like all that screaming; and he did not think it good taste for Dante to censure with bitter fiction (untruths) the characters of living people or to heap insults upon the dead; and, moreover, he did not think it good taste to "terrify the good." Dante's vulgarities are appalling; and he is guilty of so many lapses that I call attention only to the whole of Canto XXII of the *Inferno* and particularly to the last line, "And he had made a bugle of his backside." In Aristophanes, in Rabelais, in Shakespeare even, such an image would be all right, but in a poet celebrated as "sublime" or "divine," it is simply tawdry, cheap and dirty.

A moment ago I called attention to the fact that Dante has almost no sense of character and he resorts to mere cataloguing. He also has no critical appreciation of poetry and very little discrimination. In Canto IV, he lists the poets in the order of their greatness as Virgil, Homer, Horace, Ovid and Lucan! He says nothing about the quality of the poems of any of these. Let's take two typical passages:

> From here He wrested our first parent's shade
>   And that of his son Abel, and of Noah
>   Of Moses, voice of Law himself obeyed;
> Abraham patriarch and David king;
>   Israel with his father and his sons
>   And Rachel, won by so long traveling.

and

> I saw Electra in great company,
>   In which I noted Hector and Æneas,
>   And full armed Cæsar of the falcon eye;
> And with Camilla, over opposite,
>   Penthesilea; and saw the Latian king
>   Beside Lavinia, his daughter, sit.
> I saw the Brutus that drove Tarquin off;
>   Lucretia, Julia, Martia, and Cornelia:
>   Saw Saladin stand lonely and aloof.

What does Dante tell you about any of those historical characters? Nothing. There are pages of such stuff, with no more poetry in them than there is in a telephone directory. What is illuminating about saying, "Helen, for sake of whom men sinned such length of days; and see the great Achilles, who strove with Love to the very end. See Paris, Tristan." That is juvenile, pedestrian, uninspired and dull. And when he gets into his catalogue of minor politicians in Florence whom he wishes to revenge himself upon by placing them in Hell, his imagination does not even rise under the ordinary stimulus of hate; all he is capable of is a list of names, spaced with just enough words to pad out his lines.

FINALLY there is no philosophical unity in the *Divine Comedy*. A few minutes ago I pointed out that in some passages Dante urges his readers to repent of their sins and seek the glory of God in the peace of the spirit and in other passages he condemns those who do this. There is a frightful dichotomy in his mind, caused by the hysterical nature of his balked ambition and by his inability to reconcile the Christian virtues of humility and resignation with his own arrogant pride, sadism, cruelty and revengefulness.

Therefore, there is throughout the three books a false note and often a false tone; an unconscious hypocrisy, a lamentable failure at elementary self-understanding. In Dante was the culmination of the medieval attitude in conflict with the rising spirit of the Renaissance. Part of his mind voiced the almost universal tendency of the Middle Ages to regard this life only as a preparation for the next, to renounce worldly things that one might enter the Kingdom of Heaven; and another part of his mind was incessantly involved in worldly ambitions of the most impatient and sordid kind, ambitions which led him into political intrigue, party disloyalty and finally what was no less than downright treason.

If Benedict Arnold was a traitor, Dante was certainly one. The nature of Dante's betrayal of Florence was more flagrant than Arnold's betrayal of his country. Dante sought not only to restore himself and his exiled fellow aristocrats to power in Florence, but, failing in this after many years, he connived with a German emperor to invade Italy and try to take Florence. It was his hope that his native city, which he professed to love, a city in which the nearest form in Italy to a republic had been established, would become a dependency, paying tribute to an alien government. And when patriotic Florentines repulsed the army of the Hapsburg, Henry VII, and prevented his subduing all Italy and crippling the power of the Pope, Dante went into a perfect fury of rage.

He had staked everything on the German subjugation of his "beloved" Florence. He had written a "theological" treatise *De Monarchia*, which is a specious argument intending to show that kings rule by divine right, and that in kings only (not in the Pope) the word and wishes of God are made manifest. (This document for centuries had a most pernicious effect in limiting the liberties of the people and hampering the spiritual work of the Roman Catholic church. It became the bible of every upstart king in Europe, helped to precipitate wars between rival monarchs who were asserting their "divine right" to certain possessions, control of trade routes, and tax revenues; and it was the principal authority on which even the more recent monarchs relied for proof of their omniscience.) Here is the letter that Dante wrote the German monarch:

"Dost thou not know, most excellent of princes, and from the watch tower of highest exaltation dost thou not perceive where the fox of this stench skulks in safety from the hunters? For the culprit drinketh not of the headlong Po, nor of thy Tiber, but her jaws do ever pollute the streams of the torrent of Arno; and (knowest thou perchance) this dire plague is named Florence? She is the viper that turns upon the entrails of her mother. She is the sick sheep that infects the flock of her lord in contagion. . . . In truth, with the fierceness of a viper she is striving to rend her mother, for she hath sharpened the horns of rebellion against Rome, who created her in her image and after her likeness." (*Dante's Letters,* Temple Classics.)

To the princes of Italy, exiled or in power in Genoa, Venice, and Rome, he wrote a letter trying to scare them into acceptance of the Hapsburg's rule of all Italy, filling his letter full of apocalyptic prophecies: "The strong lion of the tribe of Judah hath lifted up his merciful ears, and, taking pity on the wail of universal captivity, hath raised up a second Moses to snatch his people from the burdens of the Egyptians, leading them to a land that floweth with milk and honey. . . . Awake, then all ye dwellers in Italy and arise before your king since ye are destined not only to obey his command, but, as free-born children, to follow his guidance."

That is undoubtedly paranoiac. Rome submitted to Henry VII and so did Lombardy; but he was so badly defeated in the siege of Florence that any hope of restoring even the semblance of the old, vicious and ineffective "Holy Roman Empire" went glimmering. And it should have failed. Florence was beginning to expand as a prosperous city, soon to have the freest, the most lenient government any community had had for centuries; the plastic arts were to develop there as they had never developed anywhere, before or since.

And who was this Dante who was urging the subjection of this city to a foreign king? Well, he was an erratic, undependable, disloyal politician who had quite properly been kicked out of his party and out of the city. Let us examine his life.

By common consent of all Dante commentators the best biography of Dante is still the one Boccaccio wrote not many years after Dante's death. Boccaccio was nine years old when Dante died and therefore he could not have seen him, because Dante died in exile; but he knew the poet's two sons and also many Florentines who knew Dante and his family. Boccaccio wrote the biography after he himself had given up the sort of writing which had made him famous, had renounced his career as a story-teller and had come under the influence of Petrarch who, in his old age, had renounced his own poetry and undertaken to revive the study of the Greek and Latin classics. Petrarch had a contempt for Dante as a poet, and, according to Thomas Caldecot Chubb (*The Life of Giovanni Boccaccio,* page 192), Boccaccio tried unsuccessfully to convince Petrarch of Dante's eminence. Chubb believes Boccaccio's *Life of Dante* was propaganda. It is, in part, a fulsome thing; and, in part, it is a work which shows that Boccaccio has moments of regret that he has turned his back upon the free, joyous, spirited work of his youth. It is, therefore, a curious document. Half the time he seems trying very hard to convince himself of Dante's excellence, and at the same time he cannot hide his inner contempt for the character of the man. He knew Dante was a Guelf who had turned Ghibelline *but who had done so only after he had been exiled by the Guelfs;* he knew Dante was deceitful and in his exile was engaged in very reprehensible intrigue; he knew Dante was boastful, arrogant, boorishly ill-natured; he knew that while Dante was singing of his great spiritual love for Beatrice he indulged in bouts of low debauchery not only in his youth but in his maturity; he knew Dante condemned others in the vilest and most unrestrained manner for doing the very things he never checked himself in doing; and Boccaccio knew that Dante's "spirituality" was somehow vaguely distasteful to healthy men like himself and that Dante's epic was a literary "monument" whose meaning was destined to be disputed by scholars and whose merits were not to be perceived by the generality at all.

From Boccaccio we learn that Dante's own story of his ancestry was that he was descended on the one side from the Roman family, the Frangipani, and from the Aldigheri of Ferrara, and that in his veins flowed the blood of the famous Elisei family of knights who founded the city of Florence. In the marriage of an Elisei to a famous Aldigheri beauty, the husband "caused his descendants to

relinquish the title Elisei and take as their patronymic Aligheri"
(from which the "d" had been dropped).

Of this noble and wealthy family Dante Aligheri was born
in Florence in 1265. The Aligheri had allied themselves with the
Guelf faction in the political party strife for the control of Florence.
These two parties were somewhat like the Republican and Democratic parties in America, one of them prevailing at the elections for
a while and then the other. Their party strife was intense, but it
was not a family feud as it is sometimes erroneously supposed to
have been. Originally the Guelfs, in principle, believed that the
superior authority should reside in the Pope, whereas the Ghibellines
believed that the superior power should reside in the Emperor, in
the loose and cumbersome state of mind (rather than a real organization) called the Holy Roman Empire. But in Florence, even
by the time Dante was born, the real distinctions were hardly discern-
ible; a Guelf might or might not give his allegiance to a Roman
Pope, and a Ghibelline might or might not give his allegiance to a
German Emperor. (Clement V was proclaimed Pope the year Dante
was born, and a year later Clement had put Charles of Anjou on
the throne of Naples; but two years later still Clement died and
dissension was so great that there was no Pope for nearly three
years. And Frederick II, son of Barbarossa, in 1265 was on the
crusade in which he took Jerusalem.)

Florence, at the time of Dante's birth, was already emerging
into an independent city-state, with a democratic form of government developing, in which there was to be no allegiance either to
Roman Pope or German Emperor because neither functionary had
a stable existence. The population was to remain Catholic in religion,
but, although Dante was never aware of it as long as he lived, the
old order was passing even before Dante was born. Florence was
a walled city on a strategic trade route between middle and lower
Italy and the Germanic and Gallic cities. It demanded and received
revenue from commerce coming into or passing through the city;
it was rapidly developing into a wealthy manufacturing and commercial center, with a thriving trade in wool and a strong and influential banking system. The fight for the political control of the city
was a fight for the vote of the thriving merchant class, tradesmen,
guild workers and laborers. About the only distinction between the
two parties in Florence was that there were more old line nobles
among the Guelfs, because these nobles had owed their ancestral
wealth to papal grants and prerogatives. But this meant little more

than does the fact that the old New York families are mostly Republican in politics whereas the city is run by Democrats.

DANTE'S father was a lawyer and active in politics. He encouraged his son to study the liberal arts rather than go into commerce, which was a career sought even by the sons of nobles. Boccaccio tells us that Dante studied Virgil, Horace, Ovid and Statius, "and every other famous poet," by which he means not only the Greek poets whose work was available to Dante in Latin translations but the renowned poets of the Middle Ages, the writers of the *chansons de geste,* Bertran de Born, Arnaud Daniel, Guraud de Bornelh, Huon de Villeneuve, Colin Muset, Rutebeuf and Guillaume le Venier. (In the *Purgatorio* Dante ventures upon a critical estimate of these poets, and with his inveterate habit of picking the wrong things to admire, placed the ornate and gummy Arnaud Daniel at the top of the list. "He [Daniel] surpassed all others in romances and love poems, say what they may, those fools who think that Guraud de Bornelh is his superior." Joseph Bédier describes Daniel's rhymes as so "lugubriously opulent" as to be clogged and meaningless, whereas Guraud de Bornelh aspired to write poems "which my grandson could understand and in which all the world could take pleasure": He was not only the most popular poet of his time, but later critics also have united in nullifying Dante's judgment.)

Meanwhile an event had already happened in Dante's life which he was vastly to magnify in importance until his remembrance of the event came to have a dominating influence upon his ideas and his poetry. There was a neighbor of the Aligheri family, named Folco Portinari, who invited all his friends and their families to his home at a May Day feast when Dante was nine years old. Folco had a daughter, a year younger than Dante (according to Dante), named Beatrice, affectionately called Bice. "Her features," writes Boccaccio, "were most delicate and perfectly proportioned, and, in addition to their beauty, full of such pure loveliness that many thought her almost a little angel. She, then, such as I picture her, or it may have been far more beautiful, appeared at this feast to the eyes of our Dante; not, I suppose for the first time, but for the first time to inspire him with love. And he, though still a child, received the lovely image of her into his heart with so great affection that it never left him from that day forward so long as he lived."

Now there need not be any doubt that Beatrice Potinari existed. Nor need there be any doubt that Dante and she met at this feast, or at some other one, and that Dante fell in love with her, as boys of that age do sometimes fall in love with little girls, dumbly and without the courage to speak to them. Nearly all of us can remember the first person we fell in love with, and we can remember how poignant, selfless, wondrous and deep that love seemed, and was. We can also remember that in those impressionable days we were destined to experience that same sort of love several times, perhaps not on each occasion with equal depth and poignancy, but sufficiently so to make us alternately happy and vaguely disconsolate.

But the great significance which Dante afterward attached to this common experience of mankind was a poetical convention among the poets of the Middle Ages. Even the age he sets for Beatrice at the date of their first meeting was a literary convention. The heroines of the *chansons de geste* are nearly all eight or eight-and-a-half years old and inconceivably beautiful. What is more they always remain young, no matter if the heroes, who fight over them and die for them, and the husbands, who finally win them, live to be a hundred.

Another thing to bear in mind in accounting for the literary influences of Dante's time is that the poetry of the trouveres and the minstrel songs had run the full course of its inspiration before Dante was born, and had become formalized, sophisticated and in a state of decadence. Moreover, the joyous quality had gone out of it. That sort of poetry, writes Fr. Funck-Brentano in his history, *The Middle Ages* (in his translation by Elizabeth O'Neill), "reached its apogee in the second half of the twelfth century. In the thirteenth the poetic vein loses its richness. By dint of harping continuously on the same theme, the troubadours arrive in the end at a conception of love, refined and subtilized to such a degree that it has no longer in it anything of this world. Through the religious reaction which follows the Albigensian Crusade, the improvisation is transferred gradually into a hymn of purified love which becomes a hymn to the Virgin, who is the purest, fairest, gentlest of all women."

Dante was the literary heir to this old poetry of the *Langue d'oc*. It was the only living poetic tradition in Southern Europe. Latin was taught in the schools; it was the language of the mass, of church ritual and of church hymns; but it had long ceased to be spoken and in Dante's time was known only to the educated few. Dante's native language was the Tuscan dialect of the Latin-root language in which "si" was used for "yes." And because Dante wrote the *Divine Comedy* in that Florentine idiom and because Boccaccio and Petrarch followed him in the use of that common speech, Italian reached the honorable state of being recognized as a literary medium.

Dante was heir also to the pessimism of the Middle Ages, which was darkest just before the dawn of the Renaissance. Political and social life were in a state of transition; the last barons in their feudal castles were giving way to the rule of the cities; the idea of empire was crumbling; the wretchedness, poverty and monotony which had sent hordes of peasant warriors on crusades against the Saracens in the Holy Land had also, inadvertently, widened the horizon of the crusaders by bringing them into contact with older cultures and traditions.

In Dante's time the social, economic and political conditions which had fostered the only living literature of the Middle Ages had practically disappeared; but conventions and traditions die hard and sometimes notions survive the more persistently when they are utterly without support of logic. In Florence, in the last quarter of the thirteenth century, there was no sense whatever in a young man's carrying in his heart an unexpressed (as well as unrequited) passion for a young woman of his own class, race and religion who lived in the same neighborhood. Therefore, it is not to be believed that Dante actually did. But it was the poetic fashion of the time for young blades to have an "unattainable" object of their devotion, even if they had to invent one, to whom they should indite verses and whom they might worship at a distance, in a purely spiritual way, and whore around to their hearts' content.

In the early feudal days this convention did have some reason for being. The trouveres and troubadours, the wandering minstrels, were vagabond entertainers depending upon the alms and favor of the barons. Some feudal lords had their own minstrels among their retainers, but they ate and slept with the servants. They could not address the ladies of the castle directly or on terms of equality; but, nevertheless, they had to please the ladies as much as the lords, if they wished to be kept in food and shelter. Hence they turned from celebrating the heroic virtues and resplendent qualities of the noble lords in poems, which the wives of those noble lords must have heard with many a secret smile or snicker, to the composition of verses celebrating the beauty of the wives and daughters of their masters.

They had to be very discreet about this. Even if a noble lady were as beautiful as the trouvere's verses proclaimed, the trouvere who wrote the song or the troubadour who sang it could not pay these compliments directly to the lady without making it clear to all concerned, especially to the husband, that this was an impersonal matter with the poet: the poet was content to lay down his life for his master's lady, and nothing would please him better in this world or the next than to sing her praises without expecting anything in return.

Out of this literary convention arose the romantic convention of the *cavaliere servente,* the cavalier servant of a great lady, the devoted knight who dedicated his life (within limits) to the service of the lady of his heart, asking no further reward than an occasional glance or (almost too much to hope for) a smile. Dante with his taste for mixing up allegory, allusion, symbolism and personification makes a deep puzzle out of the lady's smile in the *Paradiso*. George Saintsbury never understood the puzzle, so he made Dante's use of it a shining example of Dante's "grand style."

Dante does not seem to have been poignantly reminded of Beatrice until she died at the age of twenty-four. When he thought about it, this love for Beatrice may have been very real to him. Once established in the mind of a sensitive neurotic, such as Dante was, the pose, the attitude, the idea may easily have become paramount. In his case we know it did. His imagination fed on it. He tortured himself with the idea. He personified ideal, spiritual love in Beatrice. She was the force which was to redeem him from his grosser nature. It took a great deal of redeeming and was a task never quite accomplished. Therefore we have the spectacle of Dante in his youth, a rich and attractive, disdainful and full-blooded fellow, carousing with Forese Donati, with the sort of women who went about in the streets of Florence "with breasts and nipples bare" (*Purgatorio XXIV*) and probably crying into his cups over "the pure lost love of his heart," and writing poems somewhat like Dowson's which has the refrain, "I have been faithful to thee, Cynara, in my fashion."

Boccaccio describes Dante's personal appearance in these words: "Our poet was of moderate height, and, after reaching maturity, was accustomed to walk somewhat bowed, with a slow and gentle pace, clad always in such somber, sober dress as befitted his ripe years. His face was long, his nose aquiline, and his eyes rather large than small. His jaws were large, and the lower lip protruded beyond the upper. His complexion was dark, his hair and beard thick, black and curled, and his expression ever melancholy and thoughtful."

He goes on to show that Dante was vain of his appearance of somber thoughtfulness and tells that once when he passed some women he heard them talking in an undertone among themselves about him and saying, "He is the man who goes down to hell and returns with tidings about those below," and that Dante was pleased with this, "smiling a little as if content that they should hold such an opinion."

Boccaccio gives another example of Dante's means of drawing attention to himself (without saying that Dante did this from vanity). In Siena one day there was a great tournament going on during a festival. There was music and dancing, applause and laughter. There were games and dances among the young fellows and pretty girls. Dante took a conspicuous position at this festival at three o'clock in the afternoon, opened a book and read in it, without moving his position, until six o'clock. Some one asked him how he could do this, without being distracted by the festivities. He replied (no doubt in a languid manner of mild surprise) that he was not aware there had been a festival going on!

This pose of remoteness was not constant with him. He and his bosom friend, Forese Donati, sought the taverns and the *lupanars* and exchanged bawdy sonnets, some of which still exist, describing their drunken escapades. Guido Cavalcanti in a sonnet and Leonardo Bruni in a life of Dante, as well as Boccaccio, tell us that Dante would alternate between studies and sprees, and they gravely refer to his "baseness" and "abjectness" in debauchery. But this is not to be taken that Dante was necessarily more self-indulgent than any other young man of a sensual nature. In fact, the finest, freshest, the only humane work he ever did, the *Vita Nuova,* was written during this time.

The age at which Beatrice married indicates more definitely that the "eight years," which Dante placed as her age at their first encounter, was a fiction invented by him to comply with the poetic convention. If she were eight when Dante was nine, she married at the unusually late age of twenty-one. She was married in 1287 to Simone de' Bardi, a Florentine banker. She died three years later.

According to Boccaccio, "Dante was thrown into such sorrow, such grief and tears, that many of those nearest him, both relatives and friends, believed that death alone would end them. . . . Not an hour passed without groans and sighs, and an abundant quantity of tears. His eyes seemed two copious springs of welling water, so that most men wondered whence he received moisture enough for his weeping. . . . He became outwardly almost a savage thing to look upon—lean, unshaven, and almost utterly transformed from

which he was wont to be formerly." Friends and relatives began to
wait upon him, trying to comfort and console him. Given abnormally to self-pity, Dante no doubt reveled in this. Real grief is
never expressed in such demonstrations. Dante was false and theatrical in everything he did.

Shortly after the death of Beatrice his grief seems to have been
assuaged for we find him married and already proving a great trial
to his wife. Boccaccio accounts for his marriage by saying that his
friends and relatives, seeking to console him, found a young girl
for him and persuaded him to marry her. I don't think we need this
explanation. All we need to believe is that he had already met a
young woman, Gemma Donati, sister of his chum, Forese Donati,
and when he was about thirty he married her for one reason or
none. Anyway, he seems to have decided it was about time for him
to settle down.

Boccaccio who, in his later years when he wrote the life of
Dante, had become an inveterate woman hater gives a queer account of Dante's domestic life. Gemma bore Dante two sons and
two daughters, but they seem to have quarreled violently all the
time and finally to have separated, Dante going to live in one house
while she lived in another. It seems that Gemma was jealous of
Dante and that he had given her ample cause to be. But, nevertheless, he resented her questionings. "He who was free to laugh or
weep, to sigh or sing, as sweet or bitter passions moved him, now
does not dare, for he must needs give account to his lady, not only
of greater things, but even of every little sigh, explaining what produced it, whence it came and whither it went. For she takes his
light-heartedness as evidence of love for another, and his sadness,
of hatred for herself." And she was probably right.

"Accustomed to pursue his sacred studies far into the night,
as often was his pleasure, he discoursed with kings, emperors, and
other most exalted princes, disputed with philosophers and delighted
in the most agreeable poets; and, through listening to the sufferings
of others, he allayed his own." Oh, naïve or disingenuous Boccaccio!
Gemma Aligheri knew that in staying out night after night Dante
was not seeing kings, emperors, philosophers and princes, for there
were no kings, emperors or philosophers in the city and only a few
uninteresting princes. "But now he is bound to withdraw from this
illustrious company whenever his lady wishes him to listen to the
talk of such women as she chooses, with whom he must not only
agree against his pleasure, but whom he must praise, if he would

not add to his troubles." In other words, Dante did not like his wife's friends.

The tension between Dante and his wife grew; he sulked and kept to his study; he would go for days without speaking to either her or the children; he stormed and grew hysterical at the least excuse. Then Boccaccio leads up to another disclosure cautiously, "And now I come to things that cannot be evaded." He evades saying it outright but implies clearly enough that Gemma found love elsewhere. And Boccaccio cannot be fair to her. "Who doubts that the judgment of people concerns itself with one's wife, as to whether she be fair or no? And if she be reputed beautiful, who doubts that she straightway will have many admirers, who will importunately besiege her fickle mind, one with his good looks, another with his noble birth, this one with marvelous flattery, that one with presents, and still another with his pleasing ways? What is desired by many is hardly defended from every one, and the purity of women need be overthrown but once to make themselves infamous and their husbands forever miserable."

Well, Dante is not the only one in the world who discovered he could not eat his cake and have it too. Nor is he the only husband in the world who, claiming every freedom of movement for himself, including as many extra-marital affairs as interested him, was nevertheless extremely jealous and, in time, with cause. Romantic notions about ideal love in conflict with a sensual and self-indulgent nature combined in Dante to cause a deal of misery. Idealists are usually disagreeable people, and Dante was certainly a disagreeable person, on every count, in all the things that come to us about him in his own work or in the work of his biographers. He had a maniacal temper. Once in Romagna he seems to have thrown rocks at a feeble old woman who was talking against the Ghibellines; and Boccaccio says that it was a common report that he would throw rocks at old women and at children, too, who disagreed with him.

Dante published his *Vita Nuova* when he was about thirty, and when he was about that age he also wrote his treatise in Latin *De Vulgaria Eloquentia* ("On the Vulgar Tongue"), giving cogent reasons why it should be adopted generally as the literary language, and thus preparing the way for the composition of the great work which should make him famous (for it seems that he had early made up his mind that he would some day write something which would place him alongside his idol, Virgil). This treatise is an excellent

one, and in it Dante is the first (in writing) to distinguish the
Langue d'oc, the *Langue d'oil* and the Italian language which used
"si" for "yes."

But meanwhile he had also gone into politics. "Domestic cares,"
writes Boccaccio, "drew Dante to public ones, where the vain hon-
ours that are attached to state positions so bewildered him that,
without noting whence he had come and whither he was bound
[Boccaccio means to say that Dante didn't know whether he was
coming or going], with free rein he almost completely surrendered
himself to the management of these matters." Boccaccio says that
Dante had the final word on everything in Florence; but this is an
exaggeration: Dante was only an alderman. To be elected to the
board he had to enroll in a guild, because that was the law in the
democratic city-state of Florence, and he chose the guild of Physicians and Apothecaries. In the Board of Aldermen or Priors was
invested the supreme executive office of the city.

One of Dante's first official acts, it appears, was to concur in
the order banishing a man who had been one of his best friends,
Guido Cavalcanti. From this I think we may infer much about his
character, still without damning him utterly—yet. The details of
Dante's political life are meager and conflicting: moreover, they are
intensely partisan. Thus Henry Dwight Sedgwick says, "Pope Boniface VII, scheming to get the city in his clutches, made an unscru-
pulous bargain with the Neri and sent a blackguardly French prince,
Charles of Valois, with a body of men-at-arms to do what he called
bringing about peace and order. Prince Charles promptly put the
Neri in power; and they, with equal promptitude, treated Florence
like a conquered city." There seems to be a mistaken partisanship
in this. Boniface VII was no such villain as that passage would
imply: he was an extremely able organizer who almost brought
about the unification of Italy through the states of the church. His
one mistake was his choice of Charles of Valois, brother of King
Philip IV of France, to champion the papal cause. Boniface sent
Charles to Florence to mediate between the Neri and Bianchi in
Florence.

"The White party was in power," says the *Oxford History of
Medieval and Modern Italy,* "and although its members were loyal
Guelfs they did not wish to embroil Florence in a war which did
not concern her. The Blacks, on the other hand, were ready to fight
Boniface's battles; and they persuaded the Pope that their rivals
were not merely non-interventionists but secret Ghibellines who

would strengthen the hands of Aragon and make Florence a refuge for the Colonna. Boniface therefore regarded the situation in Florence as a partisan and not as an arbiter. The result of Charles' mediation was that the White went into exile, and there joined hands with their former enemies, the exiled Florentine Ghibellines."

As Boccaccio says, things were happening so fast that Dante did not know whether he was coming or going. Elected to the aldermanic board as a Guelf, his partisanship was with Boniface. But he seems to have been thrown out not by the Bianchi but by the Neri who were allied to his Guelf party. Sedgwick says, "Dante's patriotic opposition to the Pope had marked him for vengeance; he was summoned to trial on trumped-up charges of corruption and of actions hostile to the Pope." But Dante was on the Pope's side! And Dante was not charged with corruption by the Boniface faction, but by his own party, the Guelfs. He was apparently standing charge for corruption when Charles of Valois arrived, and, under trial, he had gone over to the Bianchi. The Neri triumphed and the Bianchi were driven out. Dante was condemned to perpetual exile. He joined the Ghibellines and began his years of secret work trying to get alien princes, and finally a German king, to war upon his native city and reduce it to vassalage. He was, therefore, not only a turncoat but a traitor; not even a party man but an undependable, characterless opportunist. Boccaccio cannot disguise his contempt for Dante's political career, try as he may.

Dante's real property was confiscated by the Florentine government but his wife and children did not suffer. His wife had considerable property of her own, and she was able to live in easy circumstances and provide a good education for her two sons and dowries for her daughters. She and Dante had not been living under the same roof for some time before his exile, so it is not to be supposed that either of them was distressed much by the greater separation.

"Condemned to leave his wife, his little children, his friends, the beautiful city of his youth and his forefathers, which he loved so passionately, and to roam, poor, despised, begging alms at the courts of princes," writes Henry Dwight Sedgwick, and that is the popular legend with Dante apologists.

The truth seems quite otherwise: Dante lived in luxury at the courts of princes who, even when they were exiled, seem to have had palaces to go to and to have got away with enough swag to keep them comfortable; he went to Paris and spent some time there in study and in theological disputations; he visited Padua where he watched Giotto at work on the frescoes of the Arena Chapel; and he was a guest for a long time in Verona with the immensely wealthy and powerful prince, Can Grande della Scalla, who provided him with money and offered him a place to work in ease and comfort. Count Guido Novello sent him on a diplomatic mission to the Doge of Venice, and although he seems to have taught the poetic composition for a while in Ravenna, he never appears to have suffered any hardships whatever. He was eager to get back to Florence, but to wield political power there, not because he "passionately" loved his city. He had no friends in the city and was not concerned about his children. He was so shifty in his schemes that he even fell out with his fellow exiles, the Ghibellines, and failing in his efforts to unite the princes of Italy in a war for the conquest of Florence, he addressed himself directly to Henry, Count of Luxembourg, who became King of the Romans in 1308. It was to him that Dante turned with frantic enthusiasm and paranoiac ideas. It was to him, a German count, that Dante addressed the *De Monarchia*.

This document put ideas into Henry's head. Henry was practically a king without a country; he had a few dominions of his own and was a German lord of French-speaking provinces in an empire that had only a nominal existence; and he had been elected King of Rome in Luxembourg. He aspired to receive the crown in Rome. All the advantages seemed to favor him. The papacy had been transferred to Avignon after the death of Boniface VIII and a French Pope, Benedict XI, held precarious spiritual dominion and no temporal dominion at all. Italy had no secular or religious head.

Henry crossed the Alps, *De Monarchia* in his hands, with a dream of reviving the imperial power. The French Pope favored his expedition! This means that the man in the office which traditionally asserted the sovereignty of the papacy over the mundane kings was actually welcoming the appearance of a king who would (if his plans met successful issue) cripple the power of the papacy even further than it had been crippled. The exiled Italian nobility of both the Guelf and Ghibelline parties gave Henry aid; all were hoping that under Henry's triumph their privileges and fortunes would be restored and they would rule the roost again. Henry encouraged them in this, sending envoys to them all saying that once he was crowned Emperor of Rome, the Italian nobility would rule with him as members of the imperial household. None was more enthusiastic about the prospect than Dante, as his letters at the time prove. He was itching to squat as a prior in Florence with all the graft that went with the job.

But two things prevented Henry's triumph: Henry and his supporters were broke, and democratic governments in Florence, Milan, Genoa and Venice were under way. Henry couldn't make imperial progress unless somebody paid the bill. So he began to levy heavy taxation on cities in Italy. In Milan, in 1311, a revolution broke out when the German soldiers descended upon the town to demand heavy taxes. Moreover, Henry and his soldiers did not understand Italian ways and Italian conditions: they were inconsiderate, rude and boorish, and presently every Italian began to hate all Germans on sight. Rebellion broke out in Cremona, and Henry in reprisal put the wrong people to death. In Rome, opposing Henry's entry, was John of Anjou, brother of King Robert of Naples; and the stupid Henry did not know John was his enemy until he was fired upon as he crossed the Ponte Molle, and he had to be crowned in St. John Lateran, because John of Anjou denied him access to St. Peter's (*Italy, Medieval and Modern,* by E. M. Jamison, C. M. Ady, K. D. Vernon and C. Sanford Terry).

When Henry sent his army against Florence to exact tribute in the name of the Holy Roman Empire, every man jack of the citizenry of Florence forgot local political differences, swarmed to the defense of the city and not only defeated Henry's forces, but ended forever that fantastic simulacrum of phantom power called the Holy Roman Empire. After that the ancient rivalry between the Pope and Emperor was gone. The decline of the papacy set in, held under the thumb of the French kings. The Middle Ages were ended; new theories of civilization and progress—theories Dante had fought all his life—were in the ascendancy.

Dante was once offered release from the exile inflicted upon him but he made so many exactions that the offer was withdrawn. In his exile he saw to it that copies of the *Divine Comedy* were circulated in Florence and it would seem that a large part of the composition was written for no other purpose except to get even with his enemies, and he seems to have had no friends in Florence. He sent cantos to Can Grande della Scala as he finished them and Scala had them copied.

Guido Novella da Polente, lord of Ravenna, hearing that Dante was in the Romagna, went to see him and invited him to come and live with him. Guido was a scholar, a cultivated man and a patron of letters, and he also sent to Florence for Dante's two sons and his daughter, Beatrice, to join their father on Guido's estate. He organized a school and taught in it; and dedicated his leisure to the composition of occasional bucolic poems. In these surroundings Dante died at the age of fifty-six. The last thirteen cantos of the *Paradiso* had not been received by Can Grande della Scala when Dante died, and it appears that it was several months before his sons found them among his papers.

Dante died in 1321 but it was not until fifty-two years later that any real interest began to be taken in him, and then chiefly because of the labors of a man who admitted that he could only understand the simple parts and left the deeper meaning "to the search of men of understanding." This first Dante enthusiast was Boccaccio, who, some nineteen years before, had written a life of Dante which met with no success and which increased Dante's fame very little. Dante's fame had spread somewhat in other cities of Italy, but the Florentines would have nothing of him. They did not quickly forget that he called the city a viper, a stinking fox, a sick sheep, fouling the River Arno and infecting the whole of Italy, or that he was a traitor abetting the city's enemy.

But seventy-one years after the decree of exile had been pronounced against Dante, condemning him to be burned to death if he should attempt to regain power in the city, the old party fights had been forgotten and the expanding, prosperous city was becoming what we now might call culture-conscious. "With the increasing fame of his book," Thomas Caldecot Chubb writes in his *Life of Boccaccio,* "Dante followers sprang up. Imitators and writers of rhymed eulogies came into being. Annotators and interpreters appeared. . . . Private tutors seeking employment gave as one of their qualifications that they could 'also expound Dante.' Soon a definite Dante cult was flourishing."

In the summer of 1373 a petition was made before the Council of the Captain of the People that an expounder of Dante should be hired out of the public purse, at a salary of one hundred gold florins, for a period of one year, for the benefit of all those citizens "who wish to attain virtue, as well as for their children and posterity, to be instructed in the book of Dante—from which even the unlettered can learn how to avoid evil and how to acquire good quite as much as eloquence of language." A vote was taken and the petition was called 186 to 19. Boccaccio was chosen for the post. (An interesting detailed account of the founding of this public lecture-ship on Dante, together with an analysis of Boccaccio's naïve "interpretation" is to be found in Chubb's life of Boccaccio.)

But even with public lectures provided by Dante's native city, Dante was never an author read, loved, memorized and remembered like Ariosto. He became an institution instead, an unread but generally praised "classic." Ariosto, on the other hand, the great epic genius of the Italian language (I am happy to have Benedetto Croce's agreement with me in this: Signor Croce ranks Ariosto with Shakespeare and Corneille), has been neglected by English scholars and critics but not by Italian critics and least of all by the Italian people. In New York City in the Italian quarter, until the depression of 1930, the performance of the whole of the *Orlando Furioso* in cycles was an annual affair at a marionette theater, attended by all classes of Italians with enraptured pleasure. But who, among the Italians, reads Dante?

Dante, it seems to me, combined in him all of the unpleasant aspects of the Middle Ages and none of its virtues. He was without kindness, charity, tolerance, gentleness, humility or (though he wrote much of it) love. He was born not long after the Inquisition of Toulouse, at the time of the founding of the order of the Flagellants, and during one of the fanatical crusades against the Mohammedans; and he, too, was cruel, delighting in tortures, revengeful. He had a certain talent, perhaps even a certain genius. He is supposed to have invented the *terza rima* or the rhyme form in which the *Divine Comedy* is written, not a particularly astonishing invention; and the idea and the form of that poem are certainly his. He will undoubtedly live as the author of a curious, perverse and almost unreadable "epic."

But surely the time has come when less nonsense, less fustian, less cant will be written about him by men and women who have any regard for values in literature. To read the *Infero* through at a single sitting is actually an experience so distasteful as to make a sensitive person actually ill. There is nothing elevating about the subject of the *Divine Comedy* and even less about its treatment. Let the English critics, who pride themselves on their knowledge of Italian, turn from the pathological nastiness of Dante to the sweet, serene, joyous, human heart of Ariosto; or, if they must have "divine" theology, to the thrilling heroics of Torquato Tasso. Otherwise, they will only be shinning up the thousand trees Mr. Sedgwick visualizes, each jabbering about his own exclusive qualifications for seeing the truth of Dante. If they wish to do this for the exercise, all right, but let us not confuse it with literature or art or criticism.

BOCCACCIO *AND THE RENAISSANCE*

*

GIOVANNI BOCCACCIO was a bastard born in Paris some time during the year 1313. His father was Boccaccio di Chellino di Buonaiuto, a native of Certaldo, who occupied a position of considerable means and influence as a banker and merchant in Florence at a time when that city was governed by a few wealthy families of the bourgeoisie who had ousted the aristocracy and had imposed political and civil disabilities on all people who numbered a knight among their kin. The elder Boccaccio, we know, was in Paris on some mission as early as 1310, because his son recounts that the elder Boccaccio saw the slaughter of the fifty-four Knights Templars which took place in Paris during that year, and we know also that he remained in Paris until 1313 because in that year he witnessed the execution of Jacques de Molnay, Master of the Templars.

Meanwhile the elder Boccaccio combined business with gallantry and begot a child he named Giovanni, of a French widow whom he speedily deserted. He returned to Florence with his infant son in 1314 and married a young woman named Margherita di Gian Donato de'Martoli whose dowry was attractive and whose social position was secure. This much—and more—we know from those highly personal and now unread allegorical romances Boccaccio wrote before he displayed the actual genius we find in *The Decameron*. His father wished him to learn merchandising and banking (for which the young Boccaccio early manifested a violent distaste) and to that end sent him to Naples as an apprentice in one of the corresponding branches of his spreading enterprises.

In Naples Giovanni learned nothing about buying and selling and the mysteries of brokerage, time loans and interest; but he did learn a great deal about life. Naples, he wrote, was at that time "gay, peaceful, rich, and splendid above any other Italian city, full of fiestas, games and shows. . . . Venus there was indeed a goddess so that more than one who came there a Lucrece returned a Cleopatra." The morals of the city were certainly indulgent, so indulgent indeed that a quaintly acrimonious debate arose between King Robert the Wise and a citizen of Naples over the paternity of a child born to the wife of the citizen. King Robert contended that he was the father of the baby girl inasmuch as he had had knowledge of the mother in one of the gay and abandoned moments of a fiesta nine months previously. The husband contended that, even so, there was still left an element of doubt, inasmuch as he had had intercourse with his wife during the same gala occasion and that the preponderance of evidence was in favor of his paternity inasmuch as he was the younger and more virile of the two.

This child was destined to become the most considerable emotional influence in Boccaccio's life. Boccaccio had fiddled away six years in Naples, making little pretense of learning business; and had finally prevailed upon his father to let him take up something else. The merchant banker had released his son of the obligation of succeeding him as a man of affairs on condition that he prepare himself for the legal profession by the study of canon law. Boccaccio entered into his studies with some enthusiasm at least for the preliminaries, which embraced the study of Greek and Latin; and from his studies he acquired not only a thirst for culture but a knack of writing verses in the Tuscan vernacular.

On Holy Saturday, March 30, 1331, Boccaccio went to ten o'clock Mass—the fashionable hour—in the church of Saint Lorenzo of the Franciscans. On this occasion he saw for the first time the child of disputed parentage mentioned above. She was then seventeen years old, a year younger than Boccaccio, and had been married two years to Count d'Aquino, a collateral descendant of St. Thomas Aquinas. She was tall, slender, vivacious and blonde. Her eyebrows were thin black semi-circles and her complexion was the color of milk. Boccaccio fell instantly in love with her and throughout the services stared at her so persistently that she was obliged to screen her face with a veil.

Next day Boccaccio went to church again and, of course, found her there. But whereas she had been demurely dressed on the morning before, she was on this occasion swathed in green silk and arrayed in jewels. From this Boccaccio deduced that she had come to attract and that his suit would not be in vain. He forthwith set about fashioning verses and planning his attack. He was no Dante whom a smile sufficed and she was no Beatrice content to be worshiped from afar; but the conventions of gallantry at the time required that the lady test the ardency of her lover by a period of keeping him on tenter-hooks; and so it was twenty-four days after their first encounter before she gave him reason to hope for the consummation of his desire.

This Maria d'Aquino, whom Boccaccio in his fiction refers to as Fiammetta, was something of a minx. Her husband's house was on a well-traversed avenue and it was her custom to sit at her window or on the balcony and flirt with the men who pleased her eye among the passersby below. It is probable that Boccaccio, after an ardent courtship, finally gained access to her chambers in some such adventurous manner as is described with variations over and over again in *The Decameron*. Boccaccio was not Maria's first lover, nor was he destined to be her last. Their intimacy lasted a year, when Maria's ardor cooled toward Boccaccio and flamed anew for another suitor. While her husband was absent in Capua she had a rendezvous with her new lover at Baia, a fact which Boccaccio discovered to his great misery.

This betrayal by his Fiammetta hurt Boccaccio so profoundly that there is no intimation that any other woman ever entered his life. Ten years later both Fiammetta and Petrarch's Laura perished in the Black Plague which ravaged all Europe and there is some evidence on which to base the belief that Boccaccio nursed her in her last illness and helped to bury her. Meanwhile, disillusioned in love, Boccaccio was to experience soon thereafter another calamity. His father was ruined by speculation and poverty engulfed the family. His gay friends in Florence and Naples gave him the cold shoulder and he was faced with the problem of turning his talents to profitable use. Distressed in mind, he made a pilgrimage to the tomb of Virgil and there made a vow to devote himself to literature.

Out of his love affair with Maria d'Aquino came the *Filostrato*, a poem in octave-stanzas from which Chaucer drew for *Troilus and Criseyde;* the *Filocolo,* a long and tedious prose work which he wrote to please Maria; the *Teseide,* a narrative in verse concerning the friendship of Palamon and Arcite and their love for the same mistress; the *Ameto,* a prose work reciting his own history in allegory; the *Amorosa Visione,* a long poem written in Dante's meter, telling of his love for Maria (Fiammetta); and the *Fiammetta,* described by Edward Hutton as "the first novel of psychology ever written in Europe." The *Fiammetta* deals with the emotions of a wife who is deserted by her lover. Before Boccaccio wrote *The Decameron* he was also to write what Professor Hutton calls the most mature of his poems, the *Ninfale Fiesolo.*

It was not long after the death of his Fiammetta that Boccaccio returned to Florence and began work upon his great masterpiece, *The Decameron.* Both her death and the plague were still fresh in his mind, for the plan of the book calls for ten fugitives from the plague who gather together in the country and distract their minds from the terror by the telling of stories, and one of these fugitives is Fiammetta. *The Decameron* seems to have been begun in 1348, the year of the Black Plague, and to have been finished in 1353.

In 1350 another great influence came into Boccaccio's life. In that year he went to Padua, as ambassador from the Florentine republic, to recall Petrarch from exile. He already knew Petrarch's sonnets by heart, and he had held him in admiration since his youth. When he met Petrarch, the latter was already engaged upon his great work in the revival of Latin and Greek classical learning, which was to make him known as the father of the Renaissance; and so great was Petrarch's influence upon the younger man that Boccaccio was gradually weaned away from the vernacular in which he had written an indubitable, universal and perennial masterpiece, and was turned into a scholar. Not, however, until he had paid his respects to his great poetic predecessor in Italian in the *Vita Di Dante.* It was Boccaccio who, in his biography, gave to Dante's epic the title it now bears, inserting the adjective *Divine* into Dante's simple title, *The Comedy.*

Curiously enough, as Boccaccio's discipleship of Petrarch progressed, his taste for Italian decreased and he was to end by regretting that he had ever written *The Decameron.* He engaged in scholarly pursuits entirely, writing in Latin heavy treatises which became textbooks of the new Revival of Learning. It was Boccaccio, too, who restored Homer to the modern world. Petrarch owned a copy of the *Iliad* in the original Greek, which he could not read. In 1358 Boccaccio met a Calabrian scribe named Leontius Pilatus who knew

ancient Greek. Although the fellow's manners were gross and offensive, Boccaccio engaged him to live in his house and make a Latin
translation of the *Iliad* for Petrarch. When this great work was finished Boccaccio got Pilatus an appointment to deliver a series of
lectures on Homer at the University of Florence.

Boccaccio died on December 21, 1375, in Certaldo. He was
sixty-two and the last few years of his life had been spent in poverty, bitterness and melancholy, made bearable only by his great
affection for Petrarch. When Petrarch died in 1375 there was nothing left for Boccaccio to live for, and when illness attacked him
the following winter there was no will to live left in him to overcome the effects of disease.

My first acquaintance with *The Decameron* came in early adolescence. Curiosity, says Aristotle, is the strongest urge experienced
by human beings, surpassing love and hunger in intensity and
duration; and curiosity in an adolescent is particularly strong concerning the nature and functions of male and female. Time has
consecrated *The Decameron* as one of the textbooks for adolescents
in such matters, and this is all the more interesting in that it is a
tradition which has evidently been handed down by word of mouth
through the ages. Just the other night I learned, by asking, that
The Decameron had occupied precisely the same place, in the early
education of seven men gathered together, as it had occupied in
mine. And in Montaigne I discover that the books which gave him,
in part, the particular information he sought in his boyhood were
"Boccaccio's *Decameron,* Rabelais, and the *Kisses* of Johannes
Secundus."

Frankly, I must say that, tradition or no tradition, *The Decameron* is disappointing as a textbook of information to the
adolescent confronted with the mysteries of his early sexual prompt-
ings; for the information is of a nature such as he can only regard
as academic and of very little practical use to him. A boy of fifteen
in our day and country is not likely to find all the ruses and subter-
fuges, so ingeniously set forth in *The Decameron* to bring about the
meeting of lovers, quite to his purpose; he has no difficulty in meeting whatever girl upon whom, however transiently, his interest is
fixed; nor is he likely to avail himself of the knowledge of how to
behave after taking refuge in a wine cask on the sudden return of
the husband he has just cuckolded when the husband brings with
him a man who wants to inspect and buy the cask at a certain price

and the wife informs the husband that she has just been offered more money by a man who is now inside examining it: what he wants to know is how to comport himself if, by some remote chance, he should find himself in some situation similar to that in which the chap in Boccaccio found himself just before it was necessary to take refuge in the wine cask. In such information *The Decameron* is deficient. What the adolescent wants to know is this and that, specifically, very little light on which is thrown anywhere by *The Decameron*. And so he learns to avoid the tedious prologues to each story and reads through the hundred tales with the desperate hope of a bio-chemist seeking the meaning of life. In the end he has acquired, quite against his intention, and almost subconsciously, a perception of human nature to mitigate the awful seriousness of adolescence.

When one has lost one's innocence one can return to *The Decameron* with a new interest and a heightened pleasure. Here now are delightful and amusing tales, involving all sorts and specimens of humanity in situations grave and farcical, romantic and lecherous, natural, earthy and unregenerate; here is satire, whimsical or boisterous, directed against friars, monks and nuns of a type plentiful in the Middle Ages, and against women whose concupiscence balks at nothing and in whose "frailty" there is purpose and cunning; here are the plots of all the merry comedies ever written; here are pleasure and voluptuousness, adventure and joy in life, related with relish and gusto.

The Decameron is the highest type, the prose masterpiece, of a literary genre in which mankind has always taken delight and probably always will. It is the genre which produced the *Mimes* of Herondas, the comic episodes of *The Golden Ass of* Apuleius, the Milesian tales (one of which, the *Matron of Ephesus,* was incorporated into the *Satyricon* by Petronius), Rabelais' story of Hans Carvel's ring, the *Facetiæ* of Poggio and on down through Chaucer's *Canterbury Tales* to our own time. It is a genre that is humanizing and refreshing. Man is an aspiring animal and he is constantly glossing the facts of his nature with illusions of perfections toward the attainment of grace and, taking it all in all, he makes a fairly commendable effort to live up to his illusions; but, if there were nothing to remind us, when we see certain imperfections in our own nature, that there are any number of others in the same fix as we are, we should probably find life intolerable. It is a very for-

tunate thing for all of us that there is a *Decameron* to counter-poise
The Divine Comedy.

Some one has pointed out that whereas *The Divine Comedy* was
designed to prepare the reader for the life to come, *The Decameron*
was designed to prepare the reader for the life on earth; and there
you have, I think, the difference between the essence of the Middle
Ages and the essence of the Renaissance. *The Divine Comedy* was
the culmination of the dominant ideas of the Middle Ages, an epoch
that came to an end with the Black Plague. After that wholesale
devastation of Europe, in which three-fourths of the population
died within a year, it was necessary to start life afresh and to give
those who survived something to live for. Millions of people had
been all too precipitately ushered out of this life into the life to
come by a plague supposed to have been brought to Italy by Genoese
galleys; and so it was necessary to bolster up the spirit of the sur-
vivors by creating a new interest in the life vouchsafed them. In
The Decameron, ten fugitives, seven women and three men, turn
their thoughts away from the plague with amusing tales involving
strictly earthly concerns.

The Decameron is one of the greatest impersonal, disinter-
ested and objective works of literature. Nowhere in it does the author's personality obtrude; nowhere is the author's private moral
conviction allowed to color the narrative. This method, of course,
precludes any depth or grandeur in the recital. Every episode is
related with detachment and is therefore related from the outside;
such and such occurred in such and such a manner, we are told,
without any pity or censure, compassion or distaste for the princi-
pals. What would actually be tragedy for the participants becomes
comedy to us. And that is precisely how things turn out in life.
Some one you know, for instance, may be involved in a love en-
tanglement which has a number of ramifications. You have observed
that person and have known him or her to do strange and interesting things under the stress of his or her situation. To that person
these actions are performed under compulsions of the most powerful sort, perhaps anguished in the extreme. But, as you relate the
story of the affair to me it becomes, to both you and me, absurd
or comical. So, too, a story of venery, if told simply as a story, is
amusing or not, depending upon how it is told and whether, as a tale,
it has point; and certainly, if it is a good story with application to
human life, showing up in bold relief some trait of human nature, it

is a story which would be ruined by moralizing, for its whole purpose is to evoke the response of the listener to a fact of common knowledge or common experience. The stories in *The Decameron* throw light upon almost every trait of human nature, including the traits of modesty, chastity and piety.

Although *The Decameron* was famous in manuscript during Boccaccio's lifetime, the first printed edition is without date or printer's name, and is believed to have been published in Florence about 1470. It has since been translated into all Occidental languages, the first English translation appearing in 1620. In 1903 was published a version in more modern English by J. M. Rigg; but while Rigg's version is admirable in many respects it is somewhat stiff, archaic and "literary." The most satisfactory version is that of Frances Winwar, herself a novelist, who endeavored to render Boccaccio's fluid Tuscan vernacular into a correspondingly simple and fluid conversational English.

RABELAIS *AND MEDIEVAL GUSTO*

*

VILLON'S total production bulks very little. All the poems written by, or attributed to, him can easily be read in two or three hours. We cannot spare a line of this poetry, even the lines where the full meaning is lost to us since we do not know what Villon's jesting allusions are, what jibes he is concealing in his incredibly dextrous conveyance of double meanings. We know he is up to tricks and we can only regret that we are not let in on the jokes. We are sure they must be marvelous ones. For myself, I even regret the elision of those lines in the disputed poems which some of his editors think are too shocking to be set in type. Even when one doesn't wholly understand them, Villon's lines are perfect.

Nor does the work of Rabelais bulk large, comparatively; but unless one is a confirmed Rabelaisian, one can easily spare whole chunks of it. The histories of *Gargantua and Pantagruel* are, together, a masterpiece, but it is like that bulky masterpiece of our times, James Joyce's *Ulysses;* it has stretches of dullness which put a terrific strain upon the attention of the reader. It has long passages which seem to be about nothing at all. And, after sweating and tussling with such passages, rummaging through all the books and archives of the sixteenth century, trying to find the meaning of them, the better scholars have come to the sensible conclusion, which an average reader would have on first encountering such passages, that not only do these passages *seem* to be about nothing in particular, but they really are about nothing in particular.

They are the innocent enjoyment of a man playing with words

with the same delight an infant takes in playing with sand on the beach. The child does not examine the sand, grain by grain; he doesn't want to use it for anything; if he fills a bucket of it, he immediately pours it out again and shovels in some more, slowly, patiently and with vast enjoyment. Often Rabelais is like such a child, only he pours in shovelfuls of words instead of sand. The history of *Gargantua and Pantagruel* is a gigantic bucketful of words.

It is also something else: it is a book full of irreverent gusto, lusty, earthy, gross, full of peasant-like animalism, written by a man sick unto death of the pall of medievalism, the curse of ecclesiasticism, the rigmarole of finicky doctrine, disputations accompanied by long faces, formalized literature, the solemn pretences of bigwiggery that are only masks for petty advancement and private gain. "Words," wrote Sarcoë Boturn, "are expressly designed to hide sentiments. They may suggest and often do suggest, but they cannot convey meaning. That is, meaning in the concrete: they cannot express what is actually in the mind so accurately as silence can. Words, though, are convenient noises. Philosophers mumble them with infinite pleasure to themselves but with only confusion to others; tradesmen employ them to cheat one another; politicians howl them with extraordinary effect upon the minds of numbskulls; priests use them with the most eloquence when they least believe in them; poets use them when they are inarticulate, which is often. There is another use for words, but, by your leave, I shall not disclose it, for I am in the business myself (*c'est mon métier*)." Rabelais wished to kill all that: he wished to give meaning to words again. To do away with this evil function of language and give it new life.

If you cannot stand nonsense, if you are a serious-minded person, if you read only "to improve the mind," if you are hot on the trail of the immediate, definite and conclusive solution of the problem of life or even if you are following clews with hope and confidence and enthusiasm, Rabelais is not for you. Rabelais is a protest against all that, a violent, explosive, derisive protest against all that. If you are in that camp, Rabelais is your enemy. But if you are not in that camp, I will tell you this: your enemy will never triumph; the force of numbers is overwhelmingly against him. The majority of people want to be sad and certain, even when there is nothing especially to be sad about and when their certainties are manifestly chimerical, denied by reality on every side. The majority of people like consistency and illusions untouched by doubt; whereas the only consistent men are in the asylums and they alone never for a moment doubt that they are Napoleon or Cæsar or Cromwell or that their wills do prevail.

There are few consistencies in Rabelais and no certainties whatever: the second book of the history of *Gargantua and Pantagruel* was written before the first; each book was written in about two months' time, tossed off without plan or intention, just as they came out of Rabelais' head, obviously never even re-read, polished or corrected. Gargantua and Pantagruel, conceived as giants of Gothic immensity, shrink to mortal dimensions from time to time because of the author's forgetfulness; tag-lines and bits of real or fanciful erudition reappear in the text because Rabelais has forgotten that he has already used them. There is no continued story, characters drop out of nowhere and disappear as suddenly, or appear for two or three chapters and do no reappear until the author happens to think of them again. Conversation, jocosities, parodies, anecdotes, jibes, word-exercises and inventions, stinging satire, pleasing pictures of peasant life, affectionate characterizations of friends, literary criticism, obfuscations—all pour out of the immensely vital, high-strung, volatile mind of Rabelais and race pellmell across the pages in the swiftest course and cadence ever employed by any writer in the world except his incomparable English translator, Sir Thomas Urquhart, that Scot genius at translation who has made Rabelais as much of a figure in English literature as he is in French and much nearer to modern readers of Rabelais in English than to modern readers who know only French.

The history of *Gargantua and Pantagruel* is the uninterrupted flow of a subconscious teeming with ideas, images, desires, experiences, a subconscious flow released by some ecstasy, some intoxication; whether that ecstasy or intoxication was induced by wine (as Rabelais tells us) or by sheer exuberance of spirit, it would be hard to tell. But it is a book written by an intoxicated man, whether intoxicated by alcohol or the divine afflatus. (It should be remembered that many books have been written by intoxicated men, who have drunk, presumably, nothing but water: for instance, the *Apocalypse* of St. John the Divine, the *Religio Medici* of Sir Thomas Browne, the *Anatomy of Melancholy* by Robert Burton, *Gulliver's Travels* by Jonathan Swift, *Die Blechschmiede* by Arno Holz, *Ulysses* by James Joyce, to name a few.)

And, although Rabelais has robust opinions, a genuine humor, and an intelligent and expansive view of life, he is not, as he has been

FRANÇOIS RABELAIS

(From an early mezzotint by Sarrabat)

so often called, a satirist; nor is he enigmatic: he says things plainly and plainly says so:

"Do you believe, upon your conscience, that Homer, whilst he was couching his Iliads and Odysseys had any thought upon those allegories, which Plutarch, Heraclides Ponticus, Eustathius, Cornutus, squeezed out of him? If you trust it, with neither head nor foot do you come near to my opinion, which judgeth them to have been as little dreamed of by Homer, as the gospel sacraments were by Ovid, in his *Metamorphosis;* though a certain gulligut friar, and true bacon-picker, would have undertaken to prove it, if perhaps, he had met with as very fools himself, and as the proverb says, 'a lid worthy of such a kettle.'

"If you give any credit thereto, why do not you the same to these jovial new Chronicles of mine? Albeit, when I did dictate them, I thought thereof no more than you, who possibly were drinking the whilst, as I was. For in the composing of this lordly book, I never lost nor bestowed any more, nor any other time, than what was appointed to serve me for taking my bodily refection, that is, whilst I was eating and drinking. And, indeed, that is the fittest and most proper hour, wherein to write these high matters and deep sentences: as Homer knew very well, the paragon of all the philologues, and Ennius, the father of the Latin poets, as Horace calls him, although a certain sneaking jobbernol alleged that his verses smelled more of the wine than oil.

"So saith a Turlupin or a new start-up grub of my books; but a turd for him. The fragrant odor of the wine, oh! how much more dainty, pleasant, laughing, and delicious it is, than the smell of oil! And I will glory as much when it is said of me, that I have spent more on wine than oil, as did Demosthenes, when it was told him, that his expense on oil was greater than on wine. I truly hold it for an honour and praise to be called and reputed a frolic Gaultier and Robin Goodfellow; for under this name am I welcome in all choice companies of Pantagruelists. It was upbraided to Demosthenes, by an envious, surly knave, that his Orations did smell like the sarpler, or wrapper of a foul and filthy oil vessel. For this cause interpret you all my deeds and sayings, in the perfect sense; reverence the cheese-like brain that feeds you with these faire billevezees, and trifling jollities, and do what lies in you to keep me always merry. Be frolic now, my lads, cheer up your hearts, and joyfully read the rest, with all the ease of your hearts, and profit of your reins. But hearken, joltheads, you viedazes, or dickens take ye, remember to

drink a health to me for the favour again, and I will pledge you instantly, *tout aresmetys."* *

Rabelais, like Villon, in all his work was trying to free us, and
himself to get away, from the awful corruption which official Latin
literature laid as a curse on the expression of human thought and
feeling, the curse of resonant falsity, equivocal clarity, riddles and
conundrums to insure power and to hide the truth from the great
mass of people; away from the conscious hypocrisy of Virgil, Cicero,
Juvenal, Seneca and the *Res Gestæ Divi Augusti;* away from the
infection of this deceitful language which had decayed the minds
of the rabble that had succeeded to it and to the power and which,
with this double disease, had turned the ancient Hebrew songs and
histories and folklore and even the simple message of Jesus into
ugly parodies by expoundings and "interpretations," marginal readings and allegories, and so created a terrifying theology instead of
a religion. Rabelais, like Villon, was trying to get away and did get
away from the *gradum ad absurdum* of that corruption in Dante's
allegory within an allegory, within an allegory, within an allegory.
He was trying to liberate the mind (at least he was *liberating* his
mind) from all that muck, which was a great stench to his nostrils,
a gag to his stomach, a closure to his windpipe. He wanted to
breathe, and breathe he did. He wanted to cast off pretense, have
done with "im-im-pe-e-tum-um in-i-i-i-mi-co-o-o-o-o-o-rum-um" and
chase Pirochole's army out of the vineyard with the staff of the
professional cross. He had had over thirty years of it, in cloister
and monkery, in ecclesiastical college and in medical college, as secretary to an ignorant but astute and intriguing bishop, as medical
attendant upon a harassed and ailing cardinal, as an editor of
learned works and as a proof-reader of unreadable ones—and he
was tired of it. It all came out of him—all that was pent up in him
—in two titanic binges, two gargantuan debauches of the mind.

He had precedents, but never before or since was there such
a binge or one so reckless, unrestrained, destructive, jubilant, sanguine or full of merriment. There have been sad drunks in literature, mournful drunks, critical drunks, weeping drunks, belligerent
drunks, amorous drunks, pious drunks, drunks filled with visions
of grandeur and drunks filled with delusions of omniscience; but
never before or since has there been a drunk like Rabelais, so merry,
so hearty, so careless, so humorous-minded, talkative and free. (Let
me remind you again that I am speaking of drunks and binges as
I was above. We do not know whether Rabelais was an abstemious

man or not. He may have drunk nothing except water, but if he drank nothing but water that would be the most startling miracle of the middle ages; and, moreover, his father had a vineyard.)

In 1494 there was printed in Basle on the first printing press set up in that city (and one of the first printing presses in a world which was soon to become flooded with printed books) a curious satirical book by Sebastian Brant, an inn-keeper's son from Strasburg, who had taken his degree at law at Basle but had become so infatuated with the new invention of printing from movable types that he largely gave up the practice of law for literary and publishing activities. His book was called *Narrenschiff* (The Ship of Fools). It was written in the Swabian dialect. The author conceived of a ship on which there were gathered one hundred and fourteen different kinds of fools, all bound for a Fool's Paradise. The ship never left dock because the author became so engrossed in enumerating the various traits of his assortment of fools that he forgot about the ship until he had exhausted what he had to say. But inasmuch as he meant to employ the voyage only as a narrative background for his satire, it did not matter.

This book had a tremendous success. It begot a vast literature of a similar nature and inspired two works of classic importance, *Praise of Folly* by Erasmus and *Gargantua and Pantagruel*. The *Narrenschiff* was translated into French, English and Latin. In 1497 Basius Ascenius, a Belgian who later became one of the most famous printers in Paris, wrote a sequel to Brant's book in Latin which he called the *Stultiferæ Naves* or "Shiploads of Foolish Women." Other imitations followed in German, Flemish, French and English.

It was the beginning of the revolt against narrow ecclesiastical authority, inquisitorial methods, intolerance, and dead literature in dead languages. (Although Brant was an excellent Latin scholar, he chose to write his almost epoch making satire in his native dialect.) Less popular, perhaps, than Brant's satire but of immensely greater effect upon the minds of the learned, was a book derived from it, the *Praise of Folly*, which Erasmus, a learned Franciscan monk, wrote while recuperating from an attack of lumbago at the house of his friend and fellow philosopher, Sir Thomas More, in England.

Erasmus, who acquired the designation "the educator of Europe," came to maturity at the time of the Protestant revolt against papal authority, a time of violent dissensions and much blood-letting. Erasmus was a man of peace and he was against the practices of the papacy but he was even less attracted by Luther. An ironist, skeptical and aloof, disdaining to take a partisan interest in the strife of the period, he leveled his shafts (as Rabelais did after him) at both the Papists and the Protestants. Nor did he take sides with the kings. While Machiavelli was writing his cynically realistic book of instruction for rulers, *The Prince*, Erasmus was writing his treatise *The Christian Prince* in which he argued that the common rights of humanity were more sacred than the rights of kings and that the Gospels of Jesus Christ should not be kept in an obscure language and taught through "interpretations" but should be available in clear language so that the plowman, the weaver, the worker and the women might read them.

The reception of the *Praise of Folly* convinces me that the theory so often held that Rabelais wrapped his message in an allegory because he was afraid of the Inquisition or the retaliation of the church is without foundation. *Praise of Folly* is a much more direct attack upon the Pope and the practices of the Church than *Gargantua and Pantagruel*, which was published two decades later. Erasmus accuses the Pope and prelates of being grasping and avaricious, frivolous and extravagant, imitating the princes in their vices and luxury, deaf to the pleadings of the poor, careless of the instruction of the masses, putting money above Christ's teachings. But on the authority of Erasmus himself, Pope Adrian VI read the book and laughed and his only comment was "I am glad our Erasmus is in the Moria himself." (*Moria Encomium* was the Latin title of the *Praise of Folly*, which was written in Latin also. It was translated into English by John Wilson in 1668.) The theologians were angry and a lecturer at the University of Louvain wrote Erasmus, "Formerly everyone admired your writings; but now this wretched Moria, like Danus in the play, is upsetting everything." There was complaint from the clergy that Erasmus was destroying the whole Church by his "quips and jokes." But the important thing is that the Church gave him no trouble; it did not retaliate in any way. Forty editions of the work were published in his lifetime; Holbein illustrated it; it was translated into practically every European language; and yet Erasmus came and went, honored everywhere.

Nor can I find that Rabelais suffered any serious inconvenience because of *Gargantua and Pantagruel*, although that book is certainly irreligious and blasphemous. Upon the complaint of the Faculty of Theology of the University of Paris that the book was salacious he made some revisions in it; but in toning down the sexual references he used the space for writing in things more damaging to the respect and authority of the Faculty of Theology; and in 1543, twelve years after the publication of *Pantagruel*, the Faculty of Theology put *Gangantua and Pantagruel* on the list of proscribed books, but this did no more than to give greater advertisement to a book which had already achieved a phenomenal success. The inconvenience to Rabelais was probably no more than the inconvenience to James Branch Cabell when *Jurgen* was suppressed on the complaint of an officer of the New York Society for the Suppression of Vice, until a court declared for the defendants and released the book. In fact, it probably inconvenienced Rabelais less. To proscribe a book in those days merely meant that the presses subject to ecclesiastical authority could not print it and that pious Catholics were enjoined from reading it; but books were surreptitiously published then as now, and some Catholics, then as now, made a point of reading the books listed on the Index Expurgatorius.

The date of the birth of François Rabelais cannot be determined, although scholarly opinion seems to have settled on the year 1495. He was the son of a man who was either an apothecary or an inn-keeper, or both (he may well have conducted an apothecary and an inn) at Chinon in Touraine. His father also owned a vineyard adjoining the Benedictine abbey of Seuilly, and it was at the school in this abbey that young François received the preliminary instruction which was to prepare him for the clergy. At about the age of fifteen he enrolled at the monastery of la Baumette where he made friends among the fellow students who were later to prove reliable and influential, notably Geoffrey d'Estissac, who was to become bishop of Maillezais, and the brothers du Bellay who later rose to power as papal ambassadors, cardinals and soldiers.

It was the custom of students of the time, as we learn from Rabelais' account of the education of Pantagruel, to enjoy a *wanderjahre* of going from one school to another to broaden their minds and to pick up odds and ends of irregular instruction. It seems fairly certain that Rabelais was a brilliant and studious youth, so it is difficult to account for his next step in his education; for he entered the Franciscan monastery at Fontenoy-le-Comte, where "one takes the vow of ignorance instead of the vow of poverty," as he characterized the mendicant order of the followers of St. Francis. The Franciscans, who were called the Cordeliers because they girdled their robes with a rope to indicate their poverty and were also called

the Gray Friars because of the color of their habits, prided themselves on their ignorance, holding it to be heretical to seek too much
after knowledge. Albert Jay Nock and C. R. Wilson, the best of the
Anglo-English biographers of Rabelais, suggest that the choice of
the Franciscan order was not Rabelais' but his parents'; for François was the youngest son and the family was poor. François seems
to have indicated a wish for a higher education (his brother Jamet
was apprenticed to a merchant of Tours), and the Franciscan monastery may have been the only one within the family means.

In due time Rabelais was ordained a priest. But one less fitted
for the clergy could hardly be imagined. The Church did, however,
afford the most rapid means of advancement that was available at
the time for a young and ambitious child of the poor. In France,
at least, commerce had not developed to the extent that it had in
Italy; writing was not a remunerative profession; law was limited
by the extent of ecclesiastical jurisdiction; and only the clergy and
medicine remained.

Just as some men do not discover until after they have been
graduated from West Point and have received their lieutenancy
that they do not like the Army, so Rabelais seems to have been
ordained a priest and rendered subject to Franciscan rule before
he discovered that he did not like the priesthood. He remained
within the order and at the monastery over a considerable period,
perhaps five years, but not as a good Franciscan, because he was
devoted to acquisition of knowledge. In the monastery, however,
he found a kindred soul in a monk named Pierre Amy, or Pierre
Lamy, who had somehow smuggled into his cell a number of books
in Greek, some text-books in Hebrew, and some books on Arabic
and Roman law, which the two conspirators against the Franciscan
ignorance managed to study without detection for a considerable
period of time. Amy and Rabelais, moreover, wrote "fan" letters
to the great scholar Budé, who was secretary to King Francis I,
and they were spurred by his encouragement to indefatigable labors
in the acquisition of knowledge. At Fontenay, Rabelais and Amy
formed a group of intelligent men in the town for discussions of the
intellectual ferment taking place at the time. It was the age of
Columbus, Copernicus, Leonardo da Vinci, Michelangelo, Raphael,
Titian, Dürer, Erasmus, Cervantes and Lope de Vega. Commerce
was expanding through the discovery of new continents, knowledge
was spreading by the new and easy method of publishing books from
movable type.

With the usual stupidity of vested authority, the solemn pedants of the University of Paris decided that this manifestation of a new spirit, active and almost universal, was heretical, revolutionary and inimical to order and good government and, with their customary obtuseness in ascertaining causes, decided that the whole trouble originated in the Humanists and in the study of classical Greek literature encouraged by the Humanists. (By a curious irony, within our own time, there arose a school calling themselves the New Humanists in America, whose chief exponent was Professor Irving Babbitt of Harvard, which tried to stay the progress of democracy by attributing all the evils of modern times to the doctrines of Jean Jacques Rousseau. This evanescent "school" called upon classical Greek literature to support an anachronistic Toryism. One New Humanist, Paul Elmer More, declared that the rights of property were more sacred than human life. Another, T. S. Eliot, came out for "royalism in politics; Catholicism in religion; and classicism in literature." And there were other absurdities.)

The Faculty of Theology at the University of Paris therefore solemnly declared the study of Greek to be heretical. Among the fellow inmates of Amy and Rabelais at Fontenay there were some jealous and envious monks who disclosed to the ecclesiastical authorities that Amy and Rabelais had books in Greek hidden in their cells. The cells were searched and the books confiscated. Amy and Rabelais were disciplined and placed in solitary confinement. Amy escaped from the monastery and made his way to Switzerland where he renounced Catholicism and became a Lutheran.

Rabelais, however, appealed to his old schoolmate, Geoffrey d'Estissac, who had risen rapidly in the world and who now had a palace at Ligugé, where, as Bishop of Maillezais, he presided over the Benedictine Abbey. The Bishop was powerful enough to effect the transfer of Rabelais from the Franciscan to the Benedictine order and, having done so, appointed Rabelais as a canon in the abbey and made him his private secretary.

Meanwhile Rabelais had studied medicine. We must infer this, because we find that on September 16, 1530, he was admitted to the college of medicine at the University of Montpellier, and six weeks later, on November 1, he emerged with his degree of Bachelor of Medicine. He could not possibly have completed a course of studies within that short time, so the only justifiable inference is that he had prepared himself before he went to the university and remained there only long enough to take his examinations and obtain his degree.

After receiving his degree he was awarded an appointment at the university as a lecturer on anatomy. At Montpellier he seems also to have indulged in other seculary activities and may have written a comedy called *The Man Who Married a Dumb Wife*. He was drawing himself more and more away from the Church and more and more into the socio-intellectual current of his time. Geoffrey d'Estissac and his secretary traveled about the diocese, Rabelais soaking in all sorts of images and impressions which he was later to incorporate in his books.

The next we hear of Rabelais he has left the employ of d'Estissac and the Abbey Maillezais and has an established practice as a physician in Lyons. This was when he was thirty-five. In 1532 he published his Latin translations of the medical works of Hippocrates and Galen. This was a labor of love with him and, because the sale of the books did not indemnify the printer for the cost of printing, Rabelais made a vow: "By Jupiter and Styx, by the name I bear I will repair your losses, and I swear to you that Rabelais, known now to few, will soon be in the mouths of all and in the hands of all, so that his fame will be as great abroad as at home."

He had edited for the printer a little book of folk tales called *Les Grandes et Inestimables Chroniques du Grand et Énorme Géant Gargantua*. This book gave him an idea. I take it that he was acquainted with Brant's *Narrenschiff* and with Erasmus' *Praise of Folly*. The latter had been published in Paris in 1511 and had become known to almost the entire literate European world. Genius is a synthesis subjected to a temperament, and out of the world of Rabelais' experience, revolt and knowledge and out of these books mentioned above there was produced in Lyons at the publishing house of the printer Etienne Dolet, to whom he had made his promise, the first installment of *Pantagruel*.

This book, written in haste and apparently set down as it flowed out of his head at all hours of the day and especially while he was eating and drinking, justified his boast to Dolet. Rabelais called his book *The Horrible and Dreadful Feats and Prowesses of the Most Renowned Pantagruel*. He signed it with the pseudonym, Alcofribas Nasier, an anagram of François Rabelais. The success of the book was immediate.

At about the same time he was appointed head physician on the staff of the city hospital of Lyons. He was therefore settled for life—not that his books brought him any money to speak of; most of it went to the printer—but his income was secure. Rabelais never renounced his faith or his order, but he never had an income from the church until the last years of his life when he was made parish priest of Meudon in the diocese of Paris, a charge for which he drew his pay but performed no priestly office, beyond visiting the parish on occasion.

Not long after the publication of *Pantagruel* Rabelais was summoned by his old friend, Jean du Bellay, to accompany him on an important mission, in the combined capacity of personal physician and private secretary. Jean du Bellay was entrusted with a delicate and momentous mission: it was his job to bring about, if possible, a reconciliation between Henry VIII of England and the Holy See, at the behest of his sovereign, Francis I, to whose advantage it was to prevent a rupture between England and Rome and thus to check the power and encroachments of Charles V of Spain. The Spanish monarch was beseeching Pope Clement VII to excommunicate Henry for divorcing his wife, Catherine of Aragon, who was an aunt of Charles V. Francis had prevailed upon Henry not to break with Rome until Clement was sounded out and to this Henry agreed.

While du Bellay was daily interviewing the Pope and the cardinals, Rabelais was enjoying his visit to the ancient capital which had been laid in ruins only a few years before when the soldiers of Charles V sacked the city. He wrote letters to the Bishop of Maillezais about the sights which interested him, and the thing which concerned him least was the possible separation of the English king from the Church of Rome. Jean du Bellay's mission was unsuccessful. Clement excommunicated Henry, thus bringing to a head the seething virus of religious prejudices, and intensifying the clash between Catholics and Protestants.

Meanwhile Rabelais lost his job. It seems that on both of his trips to Italy he was absent without leave and, indeed, without the knowledge of the hospital authorities. In February, 1535, he disappeared again and apparently tipped off some friends that his post was vacant, because three physicians made applications for the job. This was the first that the authorities had heard of it, and they declined to fill the vacancy until March, when they had made sure Rabelais was not coming back. This testifies, I think, to his reputation as a physician—this, and the fact that he incurred the envious enmity of the famous Italian physician, Julius Cæsar Scaliger, who had come to France as physician to the Bishop of Agen.

The next we hear of Rabelais is that he had made another trip to Italy as physician to du Bellay, who on this occasion was visiting Rome to receive the red hat of a cardinal, and also, according to Nock and Wilson, to undermine the political influence of Charles V with the Pope. Rabelais was left behind when du Bellay left Rome in great haste to intercede in a war which was brewing between Charles V and Francis I. The war did develop, but so prompt was du Bellay in fortifying and provisioning the towns that the expedition of Charles' soldiers was frustrated almost from the beginning.

Meanwhile Rabelais left Rome somehow and returned to Montpellier where he produced his second book (first in the order we now have them) of the History of Gargantua and Pantagruel. While in Rome Rabelais appears to have made an effort to get his status recognized which would entitle him to a benefice, but he failed in this and returned to the practice of medicine in Lyons. He engaged in the intellectual disputes of the period, and got in bad odor with the ecclesiastical authorities at the Sorbonne; but, on the whole, lived well, easily and above the battle. It was not until 1551, when he was sixty-six years old, that he received his appointment as curé of Meudon. He kept the office as an absentee shepherd of his flock, remained in Paris and wrote the concluding adventures of Pantagruel.

In these books some of the gayety of his early productions has given way to bitterness. The reason is not far to seek. In his whole lifetime there had been no demonstration of man's cruel stupidity equal to the demonstrations that occurred during the last few years of his life. Men were cutting each other's throats over points of doctrine which could seem to Rabelais not only idiotic, but blindly so. But there was more than that. All his life he had been fighting against the horrible reality of the injustice of man to man, the hatred that sects showed toward each other, the low tricks that men play upon one another for advancement. He had tried to get it out of his mind by writing *Gargantua and Pantagruel,* but this did not solve the problem.

He fled from France to Metz, where he had been offered the position of city physician at a salary three or four times larger than he had ever received. At the same time he was writing to the Cardinal du Bellay for money. We do not know the reason for this. Messrs. Nock and Wilson suggest that he was merely asking for the money left him as a legacy by one of the du Bellay brothers. This, I believe, is the correct interpretation. As a member of the du Bellay household, under the system of patronage then existing, he was entitled to a servant's wages and perhaps these had not been paid. Moreover, in Metz Rabelais had his own household expenses to bear, for there is no evidence to support the conjecture of Nock and Wilson that Rabelais lived in Metz under the patronage of de St.-Ayl and in the latter's house. Moreover, Rabelais had an illegitimate son (and also an illegitimate daughter, if the old legends are correct), who by this time had come of an age when Rabelais may have wished to make some provisions for his education.

Rabelais resided in Metz just one year and on June 24, 1547, he was dismissed from his post as city physician. This dismissal may have been due to political reasons and it may have been due to his irresponsibility. Some biographers of Rabelais piously decline to mention drinking in connection with Rabelais, but it is not necessary to take the word of Rabelais' enemies that he was a "drunken and dissolute" man to accept the possibility that Rabelais' drinking habits made him an undependable city physician. We know from his actions while he was head physician of the city hospital in Lyons that he did not have an acute sense of responsibility in connection with his work; and when he accepted the position as curé of Meudon without performing the office of priest of the parish, we know that his sense of duty was not any too strong.

Rabelais died in Paris on August 9, 1553, and we know nothing of his movements or his life for six years before that date. He may have been in the employ of the Cardinal du Bellay. There was a rumor that he was thrown into jail in Lyons for a time, but the cause of the imprisonment is not mentioned and it probably is an invention of his enemies. There were Rabelaisians or Pantagruelists in Rabelais' lifetime and there were anti-Rabelasians. Rabelais died in a house in the Rue des Jardins and was buried in St. Paul's churchyard.

There were legends about his death. It is said that, after the priest had heard his last confession and administered the viaticum, he asked for his Benedictine habit, saying *"Beati qui moriuntur in domino,"*—"blessed are they who die in a domino (or in the Lord)." And it is also said that he made his last will in the form of a jest: "I possess nothing; the rest I give to the poor." And that when the Cardinal du Bellay sent to ask after his health, he answered, "Tell Monsignor in what a merry mood you find me. I go to seek a great

Perhaps. He is at the magpie's nest, bid him stay there: as for you, you will never be anything but a fool." And that his last words were: "Draw the curtain: the farce is ended." The priest who attended him reported that Rabelais died drunk.

I do not think it is necessary to affirm or deny these legends. They are the sort of legends Rabelais would have enjoyed about himself.

The story of *Gargantua and Pantagruel* can no more be condensed into a few words than can the "story" of the Arabian Nights. It is vaguely about the life and adventures of Grandgousier and his son, Gargantua, and his son's son, Pantagruel, prodigious fellows all, great drinkers, fighters and disputants. Grandgousier is coarse and brutish; Gargantua less so; and Pantagruel is learned, dextrous and cultivated. The book begins with a burlesque genealogy and a burlesque of the sort of poems which are supposed to conceal deep meanings. Rabelais' poem means nothing whatever. Then comes the story of the marvelous birth of Gargantua, who emerged from his mother's womb in the eleventh month, bawling in a big voice heard for miles about, "Some drink! Some drink! Some drink!" Thereafter comes an account of his nursing, the clothes made for him, his early education, his escapades in Paris, his war against Picrochele, and lastly the building of Abbey of Theleme.

The story of the Thelemites is as close as Rabelais comes to disclosing a philosophy. The motto of the Thelemites, who were both men and women, was "Do what thou wilt." An inscription in verse was over the gate of the abbey describing the sort of people not permitted to enter—bigots, hypocrites, lawyers, monks, usurers, drunkards, liars, pensive dotards, lazy slugs, envious, cruel, credulous or stupid people.

> Grace, honour, praise, delight,
> Here sojourn day and night.
> Sound bodies lin'd
> With a good mind.

The residents of the abbey are all honorably married, temperate, wise, witty, charitable, tolerant, gracious, gallant and just. Parodying the rule in certain convents that when any woman comes in, they must immediately sweep the ground she has trod on, in the abbey of Theleme all the rooms are thoroughly washed and cleaned through which any man or woman of religious orders passes through!

The character upon whom Rabelais lavishes the most affection is Friar John of Entommeures, "young, gallant, fresh, lusty, bold, adventurous," a hater of all pretense, mummery, pedantry, bookishness. Friar John is made abbot of the abbey of Theleme. He prides himself that in his abbey they never study at all, "for fear of the mumps." Rabelais uses Friar John as the real wit of all the discussions. When Rabelais introduces his "Prophetical Riddle" in verse, Gargantua says he believes an enigma means "the progress and carrying on of divine truth." Friar John says, "I can conceive no other meaning in it, but a description of a set at tennis in dark and obscure terms." It is through Friar John that Rabelais achieves his greatest satirical effects, directed against all religious practices and especially against monastical institutions.

Rabelais was more a product of the middle ages, I think, than a product of the Renaissance. The Renaissance was essentially an age of refinement, whereas Rabelais is a protest against too much refinement. He had no sympathy with that phase of the Humanistic movement which manifested itself in glosses and commentaries on works in Greek and Latin: he fills his book with burlesque learning, quite often, I think, deliberately making mistakes. It would amuse him to see the Variorum edition of his works, in which scholars have solemnly corrected his errors of scholarship. His errors are so numerous that the notes now bulk larger than the text.

Rabelais was definitely anti-clerical, but he was not sympathetic to the rise of Protestantism either. Some biographers and commentators have wondered why Rabelais never mentions his most eminent contemporary, Martin Luther. Joseph Spencer Kennard has the right of it, I think, in his *The Friar in Fiction*, when he says: "They were both of them friars, one an Augustinian, the other a Franciscan. They both put off the friar's habit and ever after denounced the monks and friars as lazy beggars, cumberers of the earth, sots, libertines. There are passages in the *Table Talk* of Luther as daring in their defiance of the proprieties as anything in the writings of Rabelais. Thus Luther and Rabelais were congenial spirits and the mission of both was the overthrow of the Catholic religion. But with this difference between them, that Rabelais sought destruction pure and simple of Catholicism and Christianity, while Luther's purpose was only to do away with what he held to be the accretions of superstition and paganism, that in ages of ignorance had attached themselves like barnacles to the nucleus of pure religion."

It seems probable to me that when Rabelais first began to write the story of Pantagruel he had no serious purpose whatever; and he may have had no serious purpose at any time. But out of his subconscious poured this tremendously humorous book, making fun of all the follies of his day. And I do not need to remind my readers that there is no good comedy that is not first nourished in the soil of reflection. The term, Rabelaisian humor, has long been current. It is very loosely used. I do not think it can be correctly applied to any literary work of our time.

No account of Rabelais can be complete without mention of his great English translator, Sir Thomas Urquhart. It is one of the paradoxes of literature that Urquhart should have been attracted to Rabelais, and one of the miracles of literature that in Urquhart Rabelais found an English interpreter with a genius akin to his own, who could not merely translate but re-create. Urquhart's translation, completed by Motteaux, makes Rabelais one of the great English classics.

And Sir Thomas was like Rabelais; he delighted to satirize. He was a very bookish man, constantly in debt, a violent partisan, patriot and a Scotsman. His books were seized by his creditors, whereupon he left Scotland after espousing the losing side in the Civil War and wandered in Europe, studying languages and collecting books. He was one of the great race of Elizabethan translators. He is reported to have died of laughter on hearing that Charles II had regained the throne!

VILLON *AND MEDIEVAL MUSIC*

*

THE term "medieval," even in historical usage, indicates a condition of affairs inculcating a point of view rather than a division of time. France was more definitely medieval during the fifteenth century than it was during the fourteenth. Through the attrition of wars, the ravages of the plague and the intellectual domination of a decadent and venal clergy, which was no longer governed by a strong and intelligent central authority, France had slipped out of the sun of the Renaissance back into the murk of the Middle Ages at the beginning of the fifteenth century.

There had been a brief flare up of civilizing activity by the time Charles V came to the throne of France in 1364. Charles V was of the house of Valois, a family that was (if one may roughly characterize the individuals of any family as a group) dashing and eccentric, but cultured, pleasure loving, full of gayety and independence of spirit; and Charles V so loved leisure and ostentatious display that he put less emphasis than his immediate forebears had on wars of plunder and conquest and more on the peaceful pursuit of oppressing his subjects for the wherewithal to enlarge and enrich the visible evidence of his power. He remodeled the Louvre, built royal palaces, liberally patronized the arts of jewelry making, intaglio and cameo carving, painting and the work of the copyists in literature (for books were not yet printed). His library contained eleven hundred volumes, an enormous collection in those days, and it included Latin translations of Plato, Aristotle and Plutarch and the works of Ovid, Livy, Seneca, Petrarch, Boccaccio and the medieval poets who wrote in the emerging French vernacular.

It will be noted that in the library of Charles V there were the books especially popular in the revival of learning, called Humanism, which was initiated in Florence by a former poet and private citizen (not a wealthy prince), Petrarch, and his devoted helper, Boccaccio. But at the beginning of the fifteenth century this Humanistic movement had already degenerated and come to such a pass that there were scholars and poets who offered to confer immortality on all and sundry at so much per head. ("Another characteristic of these Humanists, at any rate of Fifelio and Poggio, was the 'traffic in immortality,' to borrow Voight's expressive term, which they carried on with the princes of Italy. It was founded on the belief, held with equal credulity by both buyer and seller, that the Humanists could confer by their writings immortal glory or everlasting shame" —Arthur Tilley in *The Dawn of the Renaissance*.) Dante had set the shining example to these traffickers in immortality.

The other Valois, the Duc de Berry, the Duke of Anjou, the Duke of Burgundy and Louis II de Bourbon, were all patrons of the more showy arts of architecture and jewelry making. Under their rule as semi-dependent princes, most of the pretty châteaux which still remain in France were built, although some of the costly ones have since been destroyed. The younger brother of Charles V, the Duc de Berry, completed the façade of the cathedral of Bourges and built beautiful palaces at Riom and Poitiers and châteaux at Mehun-sur-Yevre and Bicetre. He was a collector of embroideries, tapestries, rubies and fine examples of the goldsmith's art. He was also a collector of illuminated manuscripts, of which he had more than three hundred. The art of illuminating manuscripts, although begun by the monks back in the darker ages, was just developing in Paris when Dante visited there, and he commented on this art, new to him, in a letter to Can Grande della Scalla. It should be remarked parenthetically that a love of illuminated manuscripts does not imply a love of literature; it implies only a love of illuminated manuscripts, which are costly objects of display.

In this love of artistic possessions, however cultivated that love may have been, was the seed of disaster not only for Valois but for France. In order to build châteaux, palaces and cathedrals, collect gems, jewelry, tapestries and illuminated manuscripts and endow colleges, the princes of the house of Valois had need of money; and to collect it they were exceedingly rapacious in taxing and impoverishing their subjects. Soon they had drawn all the wealth out of their subject lands and had expended it in the unproductive wealth of prettified feudal castles and other means of ostentation. Then these princes began to seek money from one another and thus to fall out among themselves.

ON THE death of Charles V, and under the regency for his twelve-year-old son (Charles VI), the Duc de Berry, the Duke of Anjou, the Duke of Bourbon and the Duke of Burgundy began to dispute the domination of the infant king and the right to taxable areas. Uprisings and civil wars broke out. The richest of the dukes was the Duke of Burgundy, who derived his wealth from Brabant and Flanders and had his court at Brussels and Bruges. His son, Jean sans Peur, took it into his head to assassinate the Duke of Orleans, which he did on the night of November 23, 1407. This murder precipitated a civil war between Orleans and Burgundy, with the Armagnacs, aided by Gascon mercenaries, fighting on the side of Orleans. Raids on Paris by the Burgundians resulted in widespread slaughter of women and children as well as plain citizens and Armagnacs.

Henry V, an ambitious but impoverished king of England, was appealed to by both sides, and seizing the opportunity, he came in on his own account, promising to pay the Duke of Exeter, the Earl of Huntington, and other marshals of large bands of mercenaries out of the ransom he would be able to extract from the plundered towns of France. This was an error of calculation on Henry's part and an error of judgment on the part of his commanders. There wasn't any money to speak of in France, no trade, no commerce and very little food. Henry V, who won the victory over the French at Agincourt which was to make the bulk of France an English dependency for nearly forty years, was heavily in debt throughout his reign. His ambassadors, captains of towns, soldiers in control of France, were unpaid, unfed, unloved. The Earl of Huntington was kept prisoner in France because his government could not pay the 8,157 livres it owed him for his services, and ransom him. Exeter and Hungerford did not receive their wages for Agincourt until the reign of Henry VI. (Arthur Tilley, *The Dawn of the Renaissance.*)

This civil dissension cut France off from communication with Italy. The papacy was without power; the pope was exiled from Rome; Rome itself was comatose and largely in ruins; the real ecclesiastical authority of the Catholic Church, broken by ill-government and by the Protestant movement in Germany, now resided in the theologians of the University of Paris, who drew their income from vast ecclesiastical properties which were now in a precarious state, causing the ecclesiasts to play chameleons of mind and spirit before whatever band of brigands happened to be uppermost in power.

In 1431 the English under the command of the Duke of Bedford ruled the very dirty roost of France and dictated the "papal" policies of the venal ecclesiastics at the University of Paris. These ecclesiastics still held an emotional whip hand over the superstitious French dukes and princes, inciting in them the fear that, behind their ponderous and awful jargon, their vast accumulation of doctrine, and their legal formalism, they (the ecclesiastics) still had the power to work the will and wrath of God.

The naïve and simple peasants, carrying a truer religious feeling in their hearts, began to doubt revealed religion and to suspect that the mitered bishops and cowled monks were something less than vicars of Christ; and, true to the dictates of their hearts, they began to create a religion of their own which they could respect. They found it in the legends of the saints of the Church, about whom an aura of sweetness, kindness and charity had been created, instead of in the God which was represented to them in the persons of the flint-hearted, pompous, mean-spirited bishops of the Church. So great was the disrespect created among the people by a licentious and predatory clergy that whole groups of peasant people had gone over to rival cults of the Catholic Church which had sprung up in the more out-of-the-way places of France, Germany, England and Scotland.

THESE cults were a real and serious menace to the authority of the Church. In some instances, among the more educated, antagonism toward the Church, with its inquisitions, its intolerance, its frightful punishments of the heretical (which included any scientist who disputed the errors of ecclesiastical doctrine in the matter of the physical sciences) took the extreme form of devil-worship. Since the Church had attributed so many pleasant and reasonable things to the devil, very well, they would renounce the Church and go over to the devil. They would do all the things they were forbidden by the ecclesiastical authorities to do, which included believing in the evidence of their senses, enjoying themselves and making love.

This revolt from the ignorance and intolerance of the Church which took the extreme form of devil-worship, in the study of such forbidden books as the *Cabala* and other works of incantation and magic, in the effort to transmute lead into gold, and in parodying rituals of the Mass, found expression in the Faust legends which were later subjected to poetic treatment by Marlowe and Goethe. It also found expression in the legends of the Black Mass, the story of Bluebeard, and the strange history of Gilles de Retz (or de Rais), who as marshal of the French armies, fought by the side of Jeanne d'Arc.

Margaret Alice Murray in her extremely interesting and scholarly work of anthropological research *The Witch-cult in Western Europe* believes that Gilles de Retz and Jeanne d'Arc belonged to the same Dianic cult and that this accounts for the great bond between them. When Jeanne was given permission to choose her escort her choice fell upon Gilles de Retz and he remained with her all day when she was wounded in Paris. This would also account for the fact that both of them were tried for heresy and executed by order of the ecclesiastical court.

I believe that Miss Murray's contentions are, in essentials, true, but she has narrowed her theory of the Dianic cult down too much and given it a formal organization much more definite than it ever had. (The evidence she produces shows that there was not one cult but dozens of them, perhaps hundreds, with no central authority, often with more definite organization than a local one established by a "missionary" from some other community.) If we are able to believe that Jeanne d'Arc and Gilles de Retz were, from a strictly ecclesiastical point of view, justifiably charged and condemned for heresy (and this I am constrained to do on the evidence, without justifying the malign and stupid judges who tried her and without justifying the sort of religion they represented), it is not also necessary to believe that they belonged, as we should say now, to the same church. The difference between the cults they respectively belonged to may have been as great as the difference between the present day Baptists and the cult of Oom, the Omnipotent. Gilles and Jeanne would have the great bond in common that they were members of cults which were distinct from, and opposed to, the reigning ecclesiastical authority—highly secular and powerful—the Catholic Church.

Following Miss Murray and Pierre Champion (who is a great authority on the Middle Ages but who does not perceive that Jeanne *may* have been a member of a witch-cult), I believe that Jeanne was the member of a cult which centered upon the merciful stories of the martyred maids, Sts. Catherine and Margaret in the medieval plays (both of whom had interviews with the devil) and St. Michael, "whom God commanded to represent Him every time he wished to make a great act of resistance." St. Michael, in hallucination or in the form of an actual person in whom Jeanne chose to believe, would have had much more real existence to her and much more divine authority than the fat prelates of a barbarous and degenerate ecclesiastical organization.

Gilles, on the other hand, it is obvious from the records of his trial, belonged to a much more sophisticated and licentious cult. It probably corresponded somewhat to that elaborately ritualistic cult of sadism and devil-worship organized in our own time by Aleister Crowley and patronized by drug addicts and neurasthenics among the aristocracy of wealth in England and America. On two occasions Gilles attempted to enter into a compact with the devil. "He could not decide which religion he would belong to, the old or the new," writes Miss Murray, who considers the Dianic cult older than the Christian religion. "The old religion demanded human sacrifices and he gave them, the new religion regarded murder as mortal sin and he tried to offer expiation; openly he had Christian masses and prayers celebrated with the utmost pomp, secretly he followed the ancient cult; when he was about to remove the bodies of the human victims from the castle of Champtoce, he swore his accomplices to secrecy by the binding oaths of both religions. . . . And infringement of the rights of the Church brought him under ecclesiastical law, and the Church was not slow to take advantage of the position. Had he chosen to resist [the ecclesiastical authority of the University of Paris], his exalted position would have protected him, but he preferred to yield, and like Joan he stood trial on the charge of heresy. The trial did not take long; he was arrested on September 14 and executed on October 26."

Those two examples of states of mind are what we mean by medievalism—the martyrdom of Jeanne d'Arc and the execution of Gilles de Retz, not for murder and blood sacrifice, mind you, but for defiance of ecclesiastical authority. The mystery of the martyrdom of Jeanne d'Arc will probably never be explained. The complete records, ordered and correlated and translated from the original Latin and French documents, have recently been made available for the first time in English by W. P. Barrett under the title *The Trial of Jeanne d'Arc*, together with an essay on the trial by Pierre Champion. This record of the second greatest trial in history will doubtless prove a mine for generations of playwrights and novelists and commentators. It is enough to say of it here with Champion that "it is a drama of the deepest pathos, where innocence and youth were victims of political passions, of theological and juridical knowledge. Formal law triumphs here over candor and intuition."

The trial was precipitated by an eventful happening. A peasant girl from Domremy, fired by a faith in her "voices," believed that she had been called upon to drive the English out of France, became commander of an army of fourteen thousand men and nearly succeeded in her purpose. She defeated the English at Orleans, although they vastly outnumbered her forces; she succeeded in crowning the weak and vacillating Charles VII, King of Poitiers, as King of France at Reims; but her audacity was too great for the weak and somewhat treacherous support she had and she fell into the hands of the English. She had cost the invading English forces much and they feared her power. They handed her over to the ecclesiastical authorities and brought charges of witchcraft against her, thus attempting to wash their hands of culpability should the plain people of France rally to her defense or resent by violence her execution by aliens.

Under intimidation by the English Duke of Bedford and under the eye and authority of Pierre Cauchon, Bishop of Beauvais, who was indebted to the English for indemnification for loss of revenues when he was expelled from Beauvais and who aspired to the archbishopric of Rouen as a reward for his service to the regnant English, the trial proceeded to its foregone conclusion. The burning of that glorious peasant child from Domremy was the evil of the Middle Ages at its worst—an evil compact of gross superstition, decayed theology, ugly and neurotic fears, mercenary motives, and the generally appalling poverty of the masses.

It was into such a world in the year of the martyrdom of Jeanne d'Arc that there was born in Paris a child who was to become one of the greatest poets that ever lived, with a lyric gift of unexampled poignancy, force and beauty, and whose checkered career was destined to stir the imagination of poets, novelists, biographers and historians as much as the career of the Maid of Orleans herself.

THIS child was François de Montcorbier, known to literature as François Villon. He was born of poor and uneducated parents somewhere across the river from the University of Paris. While he was still an infant his father died and the care of him was left to a young and vigorous mother who probably slaved in the poverty-stricken city to support him until at last she was equal to the task no longer. She could not see her child starve, and she remembered that at the University there was a priest in fairly easy circumstances for the times, since he had his benefices from the Church and an income from vineyards and the rents of two houses in the University neighborhood; moreover, this priest was a distant relative of the Montcorbiers.

The child was five years old. Paris, long in the grip of poverty, was now experiencing one of the most terrible winters it had ever known or ever was to know. The countryside was devastated; the food supply had been cut off; forty-five thousand inhabitants died of famine and the plague within a few months; people lived on offal; famished wolves prowled on the outskirts of the city. Even the people who had a little money lived mainly on fish from the Seine, ducks and wild geese from the moats, and on the not yet exhausted wines in the cellars of the thousands of taverns.

It is not too much to presume, I think, that the widowed mother did not seek a friendly priest to adopt her child until the last extremity of her resources had been reached. When she crossed the Seine with the little fellow, it is probable that the effects of undernourishment which were always visible in the frail constitution, nervous and exacerbated temperament and predisposition to disease of the poet in later life, had already worked its havoc in the child's physical conditioning.

The priest to whom she took the child was Guillaume de Villon, chaplain of the University church and professor of canon law. He occupied a house inside the cloister. He not only took pity upon the plight of the mother but became an indulgent, perhaps too indulgent, foster-father. It is probable that he whiled away his lonely evenings reading and telling stories to the child, acquainting him with the poets in Latin and French, giving him as a text-book Eustace Deschamps' *Art de dictier* (which prescribed the rules for composing ballads) and offering him rewards for attempts at verses of his own.

When François de Montcorbier was thirteen years old his name was inscribed on the student rolls of the University as a candidate for the degree of Master of Arts. When he obtained the degree, it would be only after long preparation in ecclesiastical law and doctrine, as well as in the elementary humanities commended by the Church. It would qualify him for benefices, give him standing and open a career to him in the profession of religion.

Before we proceed to the disreputable and uncomfortable ways which François Villon (who adopted his foster-father's name) fell into later on, ways which brought him within an ace of the gibbet as a thief, a homicide, and general outlaw, let us consider if there were not ample motives, special reasons, mitigating circumstances for his choice of a mode of life; and having considered them, thank God for them, because otherwise we should not have had his incomparable poetry. He might have written poetry but not the poignant, personal, perfect poems he wrung out of his genius and his misery.

One thing we know is that he profited very little by his studies at the University, not even in whatever classes in literature were afforded him there; for he knew a little Latin, read Ovid, but, from the evidence, little else. It is not to be assumed that he was "naturally" wayward, but we may believe that he was not subjected to strict discipline by his foster-father, unless we care to argue that he was subjected to a discipline so strict that he revolted violently from it (and this is not a valid assumption because Villon writes of his foster-father as being more than a mother to him, kind, gentle, indulgent). But more important than a lack of discipline in determining his mode of life was the lack of incentive to lead a decent, studious, cautious life. A youth as brilliant, sensitive, knowing and talented as Villon was, could not possibly have regarded a career in the Church and University of his period with anything but violent distaste. In Italy the Pope was impotent; all the authority of the Church resided in the schemings and intrigues of the prelates who controlled the University of Paris, through which the Church revenues were collected and distributed.

In the second place the utter hopelessness of the economic condition of Paris and of all France and the comparatively wealthy condition of the ecclesiastical authorities made theft and burglary comparatively honorable pursuits. Is Villon's alleged career as a pimp for a while to the harlot called, in his ballad about her and his relations with her, the Grosse Margot, as vile and dishonorable as the conduct of Cauchon, Bishop of Beauvais, who burned a child at the stake in hopes of being rewarded with an archbishopric? Besides, I shall show that, contrary to general and accepted belief, Villon was not a pimp.

In the third place, there was a constant feud between "town

and gown," between the poverty-stricken citizens of Paris and the students who were destined for a superior station in the University cloisters. This feud was real and well-grounded; poor lads of the city, sons of simple hucksters and tradesmen, had a contempt for the lads who were able to seek soft berths for themselves in ecclesiastical careers supported by tithes wrung from the sweat of peasants and themselves. Villon early participated in some of the brawls on the side of the students; but before he left the University for good his real companions were of the town and not of the student body. I believe that, consciously or unconsciously, he considered his lot to be with the youths of his own degree and station, and the more disgusted he became with the rigmarole of the University the more definitely he identified himself with the common people of Paris, from which he sprung.

And the common people of Paris, as we have seen, were having a hopeless time of it. Misery prevailed everywhere. Money was scarce, jobs were almost non-existent. Even Guillaume de Villon's comfortable income was cut down to almost nothing; but his tenants could not pay their rent (one tenant paid him no rent for eight years); revenues from his vineyards were intermittent and subject to the invasions of the banditry common at the time; even the stipend he derived from his chaplaincy and professorship probably underwent fluctuations.

BUT François Villon had not only a knack but a genius for writing verse. It was his comfort, his justification of himself; it was his pleasure in creation, and, moreover it was equivalent to pocket-money. He could compose ribald and topical songs and recite them in taverns, and more fortunate fellows would buy wine and food for him. Among all the people of Paris those most likely to have cash from time to time and to be liberal with it were the gentry who had come by it dishonestly. The prudent live frugally and are not disposed to prodigality. The more dishonest a man's source of income, the more prone is he to gestures of wide generosity. And the man who lives by his wits in an enterprise like gambling or illicit trade is likely to be most liberal of all in his tips and largesse and the "treating" of his fellows.

For wine, food and companionship, then, Villon began to desert the cold cloisters of the University and the freezing room he had at his foster-father's house, a room in which he shivered and wrote verses by the light of a guttering candle, his bones aching with chill and his teeth chattering the while. Sneaking out o' nights he would find warmth in the taverns, and companionship with fellows who turned out to be picklocks, sneak-thieves, common thugs and highwaymen. Such fellows would interest him with their careless ease of living, their hearty indifference to fate, their curious and salty slang, their camaraderie, after the dreary lectures on obscure points in ecclesiastical law Villon had to listen to in school. Soon Villon was writing verses, not only about these people he met at the taverns, the roisterers, harlots and vagabonds of Paris, but in their vernacular.

At nineteen Villon had completed the University routine which entitled him to inscribe after his name, Bachelor of Arts, and three years more of servitude (probably to please his foster-father), permitted him to inscribe after his name, Master of Arts, and wear the simple tonsure and cap and gown, which gave him a small fee, various privileges, and an opportunity to further himself in the teaching profession or in the clergy. But by this time he was too far gone in another and, to me, in the circumstances, a decenter way of life. He had probably promised his foster-father to take a degree and lived up to the promise, but having promised no further, he shook the cobwebs of the University from his head and feet forever.

But by doing this, Villon was sacrificing a meager and distasteful security for the insecurity of life as a poet-artist and vagabond. There was one other profession open to a person of his talents, and that was in the company of the strolling players, jugglers, acrobats, musicians and reciters of verses, who produced crude miracle plays; and from what he tells us about himself it seems that for a time he was connected with such a troupe and that he either wrote a miracle play himself or produced it.

But the profession of the strolling players had almost died out in France in Villon's time, although it had flourished in the feudal period which ended with the extinction of the Capets. It was in the days of feudalism that the French language took form, first in the dialects derived from Latin which, owing to the influences of the different regions became the Franco-Provençal of the South, in which the dialect of Limoges became the accepted literary language, and the speech of the Ile-de-France, which became in time the speech of Paris.

Both old French and Provençal were in their beginnings hardly distinguishable from Latin. The famous oath of Strasburg taken by

Louis, son of Louis the Debonair, is like French and like Latin and still unlike either: *"Pro Deo amur et pro Christian Poblo et nostro commun salvament d'ist di en avant, in quant Deus savir et podir, me dunat, si salvarai eo cist meon fradre Karlo et in adiudha et in cadhuna cosa si cum om per dreit son fradre salvar dist."* ("For the love of God and before all Christian people and for our common salvation, from this day forward, insofar as God may grant me knowledge and power, I will aid my brother Charles by assistance and in all things as by right a brother should.")

The influence of the language of the Gallic tribes in the formation of this new French language, or rather, two new French languages, from the Latin was less on the vocabulary and the forms than on the word endings and much less even at this period than was the case in the development of the Germanic and English languages. The earliest civilizing influences among these tribes came through the offices of the Catholic church, which sent priest missionaries out from Rome to Christianize the tribes and bring the people under the wing of the Church. Often these missionary priests were themselves ignorant of Latin and had been taught the mass and rituals only by ear. As a result of these missionaries' residence in areas remote from Rome and because they passed on, by word of mouth, the mass and rituals to converts whom they ordained to assist them in their missionary work, the wording of the mass and rituals sometimes became queer mixtures of Latin, Italian and the dialects of the people among whom the mass was performed. A priest who forgot the Latin words of the mass and who was unable to supply them because he did not know what they meant, would fill in a local dialect word which sounded like it. There exist versions of the mass made up of Latin, Tuscan, low German, high German and Celt.

In the spacious and comparatively peaceful era of the twelfth century, the first written texts of the trouveres begin, with the songs in Provençal of "courteous love" and "fine love," touched upon in this book in the chapter on Dante. These were the love songs written at first by vagabond poets, in the train of the jugglers and tumblers, who entertained the feudal families in their castles. They were songs to the poet's "liege lady," flattering, elevated, remote, asking only to serve the lady without reward until death. Variations on this theme were introduced in the love lyrics; the poets became pensive, sang of death, or their own hard road, their wayward life which has landed them in prison. These poets, singers and strolling players were usually without protection, subject to the whims of the feudal lords and ladies, often robbed of their small pay, and probably robbing others whenever the opportunity afforded. They were like gypsies, in fact *were* gypsies, for the first of the *jongleurs* were Rumanian gypsies carrying strange musical instruments, singing songs and performing tricks, while going from feudal castle to feudal castle and from tournament and festival to tournament and festival and sometimes teaching their art to natives of Italy, France and Spain who would join them.

Along with the songs of "courteous love" and "fine love" which developed so extensively in Provençal were the *chansons populaires,* which Gaston Paris believes came into existence in the region of Poitou, and were not written by the famous or popular trouveres, but by the minstrels. Frequently, these "popular songs" were dance songs, a fact which made necessary the invention of varieties of meter and verse forms to escape monotony. The essential quality of these songs was the refrain. The invention consisted chiefly of new lines to alternate with fixed lines. This invention led to such developments as an Early English macaronic of French, English and Latin like this one:

> *De moy, jeo pry, aves pyte;*
> I falle so doth the lef on the tree
> *Tristando*

> *Tot le mounde longe et le*
> I wolde leve and take thee
> *Zelando*

> *Pur vostre amour, allas, allas,*
> I am worse than I was
> *Per multa*

> *Jeo suy dolorouse en tut manere;*
> Wolde God in youre armes I were
> *Sepulta*

Those are only two verses of a fifteenth century poem and are easy enough to read without translation; they are given to illustrate how the popular songs were formed on the lovely hymns in Latin rhymes written in the early Middle Ages by Thomas Aquinas, Thomas à Celano, Adam of St. Victor, Vernardus of Clairvaux and Cacopone da Todi. The *Comtemptio Vanitas Mundi* of St. Bernard, abbé of Clairvaux, a Burgundian of the eleventh and early twelfth centuries, for instance goes like this (first verse):

> *O miranda vanitas!*
> *O divitiarum*
> *Amor lamentabilis!*
> *O virus amarum!*
> *Cur tot viros inficis*
> *Faciendo carum*
> *Quod pertransit citius*
> *Quam flamma stupparum.*

In that semi-Latin hymn the emergence of the Burgundian dialect is already evident. Translated:

> O emptiness of vanity!
> O lamentable bewitchments of love!
> O virus of lust!
> How strange that man will welcome
> Toil and trouble to gather riches
> Which melt as fast as fire consumes stubble.

The churchly men seeing village girls dancing around the may-pole to the sounds and words of the *chansons populaires,* feared that people might get into the habit of enjoying themselves and put a ban upon such doings. In consequence the popularity of the songs increased, spread in character, became gay, indiscreet, sensuous and sometimes slightly bawdy.

But the simple gayety of the early Middle Ages was passing under the prohibitions of the Church and also under the changing economic conditions. Times became hard; Gothic heaviness weighed on the hearts of men; the plagues decimated the population; people were reminded on every hand of the imminence of death. Pessimism abounded; pictorial representations of the Dance of Death were favorite themes for those who could scrawl or draw.

Even the more courtly and refined poets began to write poems on the quick passing of beauty, wealth and power. One of the earliest of early medieval English lyrics was widely used as a model by poets whose names are forgotten and in it we see the crude original model for Villon's "Ballade of Ladies of Times Gone By" and "Ballade of Lords of Times Gone By":

> Hwer is Paris and Heleyne,
>   That weren so bryht and feyre on bleo?
> Amadas, Tristram and Dideyne,
>   Yseude and alle theo,
> Ector with his scarpe meyne
>   And Cesar riche of worldes feo?
> Heo beoth iglyden ut of the reyne,
>   So the scheft is of the cleo?

Observe how the plaintive note of the English medieval lyric, later to give a wistful sad quality to all the ballads, is effected and sustained by the rhymes "bleo," "theo," "feo" and "cleo." And notice, for a moment, how firm and hard and personal the same theme becomes in the hands of a great genius like Villon:

> Dictes-moy ou, n'en quel pays,
> Est Flora, la belle Romaine;
> Archipiada, ne Thaïs,
> Qui fut sa cousine germaine;
> Echo, parlant quand bruyt on maine
> Dessus rivière ou sus estan,
> Qui beauté eut trop plus qu'humaine?
> Mais ou sont les neiges d'antan!

I append the translation by J. U. Nicolson (*The Complete Works of François Villon*, with an introduction by Lewis Galantière). I find Mr. Nicolson's rendering of this poem more satisfactory than D. G. Rossetti's or John Payne's, both of whom make the poem too "musical," destroying its natural diction which was Villon's great quality, and both of whom make the poem too sentimental. Villon has sweetness in him and love of beauty, even piety; but his grace is a steel-like hardness; he is never, except perhaps in the Ballade of Grosse Margot, sentimental. Swinburne understood Villon perfectly, and he did several excellent translations but he did not translate the *Dead Ladies:*

> Say where, not in what land, may be
> Flora the Roman? Where remain
> Fair Archippa's charms, and she—
> Thaïs—in beauty so germaine?
> Echo, calling afar, in vain,
> Over the rivers and the marshes wan,
> Lovelier once than girls profane?
> But where are the snows of last year gone?

Nicolson's version is not perfect, but it is better than Payne's or Rossetti's. There is nothing sing-song or pretty about Villon's verse; it is exquisitely cadenced, perfectly phrased, but is as natural as his tavern speech, containing always the element of surprise, the perfect phrase of summation in the refrains:

> Ne que monneye qu'on descrie
> *   *   *
> En ceste foy je vueil et mourir
> *   *   *

Bien heureux est qui rien n'y a!

    *   *   *

Autant en emporte ly vens.

    *   *   *

En ce bourdel ou tenons nostre estat.

We left Villon to recall his poetic heritage and we return, appropriately, to find him engaged in a serious street-brawl. On the evening of June 5, 1455, when Villon is twenty-four, he is seated on a stone bench in the Rue St. Jacques, outside the cloister where he made his home with his foster-father. It is a warm night and Villon has just had supper at the She-Mule tavern across the street. Beside him sits "one named Ysabeau," and a priest named Gilles. The character of Ysabeau we may deduce from the words of the Letter of Remission granted by Charles VII permitting Villon to return unpunished to Paris after Villon had fled as a result of the escapade of this summer evening: Ysabeau is given no further name and no further identification than *"une nommée Ysabeau";* and she was not a woman who had much regard for her reputation or she would not be sitting with a fellow like Villon on a stone bench in the student district at nine o'clock at night. (Curfew was at seven; good citizens were in bed by eight in the dimly lighted, badly policed town.)

As he sits there with Gilles and Ysabeau, one Philip Chermoyne, a priest, comes up accompanied by Master Jehan de Mardi. Chermoyne is in a belligerent mood; it is evident that there is bad blood between him and Villon; and Chermoyne has been drinking. Chermoyne says, "By God! I have found you." Villon tries to pacify him, aware of the priest's mood and condition, rises to make room for him on the seat and asks, "Dear fellow, what is wrong?" Chermoyne gives him a shove, forcing him to the sitting position again. Gilles, Mardi and Ysabeau, scenting a brawl, make away from the scene as fast as they can. Chermoyne draws a large dagger from his gown and, before Villon can rise to defend himself, slashes him across the face with it, cutting his lip so badly that thereafter his mouth was badly scarred. Villon whips out his dagger and strikes wildly at his antagonist, hitting him in the groin. Having thus weakened the force of Chermoyne, Villon is eager to call the fight a draw and escape. They wrestle and Villon breaks away. Chermoyne pursues him. To stop Chermoyne's progress, Villon picks up a stone and hurls it at him, catching Chermoyne full in the face with it and knocking him down.

Villon hurries to a barber-surgeon named Fouquet to have his lip dressed. But Fouquet cannot be implicated in this; he will not let Villon depart until he has the wounded man's name and some details of the affair in case he should be questioned by the police. Villon, hastily inventing a name as people do nowadays who are caught in a police raid, give his own name as Michael Mouton (a common name like John Smith), Chermoyne's real name, and his version of the affair. Then Villon hurried away, determined no doubt to keep out of sight for a day or two. But Chermoyne is found by persons passing through the cloister of St. Benoit into which he had chased Villon, picked up and carried to the hospital. But his skull had been cracked or he had bled so profusely from the knife wound in the groin that within a week he was dead. Villon is in his first jam with the forces of law and order. An order is out for his arrest. In fact, two orders; one under the name of François de Montcorbier and another under the name of Michael Mouton, for his real name is known by this time and later it is found that he has used another alias, François de Loges, and also his familiar name, the one everyone knows him by, Villon.

He is away from Paris for a whole year, banished by royal edict under pain of hanging if he returns. Where he went we have no notion, although there have been many conjectures. In the *Grand Testament* there is a "bequest" to Perrot Girart, barber of Bourg-la-Reine, a village not far to the south of Paris, "two basins and a pitcher, since he works so hard for his living. It is just half a dozen years ago since he fed me at his house for a whole week on fat pork—witness the Abbess of Pourras."

There is an obscene allusion in this bequest and Villon is calling attention to a joke he played on his host. The reference to the Abbess of Pourras, according to D. B. Wyndham Lewis, is to a notorious actress whose real name was Huguette de Hamel. "She had taken the religious habit in 1439, had become Abbess of Port-Royal [popularly Pourrais or Pourras] in the Chevreuse valley near Paris, about 1454, and then, by swift degrees had gone completely to the bad. In this year 1455 when Villon knew her or pretended to, her conduct was not the subject of more than local gossip; but by 1463 the scandal had become such that the Abbot of Chaalis, her superior, who had had her placed under observation, degraded her from her office and thrust her into the prison of the abbey of Pont-aux-Dames, in the diocese of Mieux, to cool her hot blood and bring her to penitence and obedience. Among the charges brought against her were that "she attended feasts and revels, disguising herself, with gallants, and behaved in such a manner that the men-at-arms put her into a ballad."

Villon is telling us slyly and without boasting that he spent a week with the notorious abbess in the boarding house of Girart. There is no reason to doubt him. One would be foolish to believe anything Villon said on oath to get out of a scrape or to avoid any unpleasantness, but it is obvious that he keeps his verse inviolately truthful.

How Villon earned a living during his year's absence from Paris we cannot say. Some scholars believe that he joined the Coquillards of Burgundy at this time. The Coquillards was a gangster organization, originally mercenaries who fought for pay against the English and Burgundians and who, thrown out of employment by the Peace of Arras, organized on a smaller scale and lived by plundering the countryside. We know that Villon was a member of a branch of the Coquillards in Paris, because he wrote seven ballads in the jargon of the gangsters, and tells us repeatedly that he was.

It is possible that on the occasion of this absence from Paris he was so reduced in circumstances that he earned a living in the manner described in the "Ballade of François Villon and the Grosse Margot," the ballade which has caused the righteous to shudder more violently than anything else he wrote. Much of the repulsion to English readers is caused by failure to read it carefully and by the mistranslation of "paillard" as "pimp" and by the awful horror of Robert Louis Stevenson that a man should be so depraved as to live on the earnings of a woman.

What Villon says in the poem shows his own horror of the episode strongly enough, but he does not say he was the pimp or procurer for Margot. He merely says that he was the waiter in the "bourdel" and the lover of Margot. He does not drum up trade for her; nor, indeed, is there any reason beyond the word "bourdel" for translating "la belle" by "whore" as Payne translates it or by "harlot" as Nicolson translates it. Margot is fat but she "has a very sweet countenance and behavior" (*tres doulce face et pourtraicture*) and, moreover, she is a "pious creature" whom Villon loves for herself and who loves him. (*Je l'ayme de propre nature, et elle moy, la doulce sade.*) He seems to have loved her when she was one of the "ladies of Paris" and he remembers her with affection but he does not say she was on the town.

And when he was her lover in the "bourdel," he says no more

than that he worked there, served food and wine, and that she slept with him at night; that they were drunken, quarrelsome and lascivious. But it must be remembered that Villon's ideal true love is romantically ideal; that such a love is barred to him by his poverty and even more by his unprepossessing appearance; he must take what he can get and his experiences in love have been particularly disillusioning. He was in love with many women but the name of one of them, Katherine de Vauselles, we know.

About this Katherine de Vauselles there has been a world of tedious research and a world of conjecture. D. B. Wyndham Lewis, Auguste Longnon and Pierre Champion found the name Petru de Vaucello signed to an old receipt, and Lewis "confidentially" identifies him with one Pierre de Vaucel, one of the canons of St. Benoit-le-Bientourne. (He would have been saved all that trouble if he had read Louis Moulton's introduction to the Garnier Frères edition of the Œuvres Complètes of Villon. Moulton writes as though the identification were known to everybody.) From his astonishing discovery, which is astonishing only to himself, and not a discovery, Mr. Lewis deduces that Katherine de Vauselles was a niece of Pierre de Vaucel. But this tells us nothing about Katherine if it were true. If those who spend so many hours looking for signatures among old records in the hope of identifying some one as a relative of some one else who is mentioned in a poem, would spend about ten minutes examining the text of the poems instead, they would not write such prodigious amounts of nonsense.

Whoever was originally responsible for the notion that Katherine de Vauselles was the great love in Villon's life, I don't know; but I do know that he made a completely unreflective and silly mistake and that every biographer after him has repeated and elaborated the mistake. The latest biographer, Lewis, says, "Villon's passion for Katherine de Vauselles is undoubtedly the nearest thing to a pure and steadfast love, free from commercial preoccupations, that he ever experienced" and, like the others, he goes on to identify her with every passage about love in the Testaments, pausing only to doubt the inference of some of the other critics and biographers that when Villon writes a poem with another woman's name in it, he is still celebrating his passion for Katherine de Vauselles.

Well, what is the basis for this romantic conjecture, this wild reading into the poems something that is not there? In the Grand Testament Villon inserts a ballade and a double ballade which are variations of the same theme. It is probable that these two poems,

like others inserted in the great work, were written before he undertook this poetic testimony in 1461. The poems are not "bequests"
any more than is the ballade of Dead Ladies. They are "testaments,"
however, of Villon's experience. And both of them are exercises on
two refrains. One of them is put into the mouth of an old woman
who was a famous beauty in her youth and who has had many
lovers—in years gone by. She is talking to some girls who work in
shops and who indulge in light loves. In the preceding ballade we
have had a description of the poor old woman; every feature of
beauty she once possessed is described and contrasted with her
appearance now. The old woman tells the girls that her real trouble,
the thing that brought her to her state, was that she loved too deeply
and too many times, and because of this she did not demand money
of her lovers to lay by against the time when she would no longer
be desirable. Above all, she says, get the money; be pretty and
agreeable outside, but do not give your heart to men, because to do
so ages you quickly. And then what have you got? Neither beauty
nor money. You are worthless as paper money that will no longer
be legal tender and that nobody will accept.

It is bitter, cynical advice, so bitter and cynical that Villon,
who is no sentimentalist, heaven knows, thinks it is necessary to add
eight stanzas explaining several things. First, he wants to make it
clear that what the old woman advises the girls is not his advice: he
has merely put her speech into verse, following as closely as he can
the actual words as they were taken down by his clerk, Fremin.
He anticipates the objections of some. They will say, "But she was
just an old whore talking to some tarts. She wasn't talking about
good women or true love." Villon answers the objection: "Ah, but
were those poor girls born deflowered and depraved? Certainly not.
Once each and every one of them was pure and innocent, without
reproach. What happened? They all fell in love, one with a student
perhaps, another with a monk, another with a rich young fellow.
They loved in secret, never got married. Then the day came when
lovers tire of each other; the song is done; they part. All too soon
the girls are on the town. Why? Well, it's my belief (although I
mean no disrespect to the sex) that when a woman loves she wants
all mankind to have a share of her love. A rejected woman who is in
love falls into the arms of the nearest available man and then six
lovers at one time do not seem to compensate her for the love she
has lost. She suffers and for one short moment of pleasure suffers a
thousand pains. But, that, as I see it, is the way life is."

Having written that ballade Villon has an idea for another one, a double ballade. This time, he, Villon, a man who has been through the mill, will give some advice to young bucks such as he once was. He tells them to look out for women—all women—stay clear of them. They will only cause you misery; get you into trouble. Look at what happened to men in history. Look at what happened to Samson. Look at what happened to John the Baptist. He is reminded, while thinking of John the Baptist, of something that happened to him once.

> De moy, pauvre, je veuil parler;
> J'en fuz, batu, comme a ru telles,
> Tout nud, ja ne le quiers celer.
> Qui me feit mascher ces groiselles,
> Fors Katherine de Vauselles?
> Noe le tiers ot, qui fut la.

("Take even a poor fellow like me. I'll give you an incident. Once I flayed the way laundresses flay shirts when they are washing them in the river. I give you my word. And I was stark naked when I got the beating. . . . Now, who do you suppose got me into that jam? . . . Katherine de Vauselles, no less. . . . Old Noah himself was the one who did the job.")

Now, long ago, there were commentators who "identified" Katherine with Ysabeau of the brawl which led to Villon's banishment from Paris and Noe (Noah is the correct rendering of Noe, not Noel, as one will discover by looking at the first line of the *Ballade et Oraison* in which Villon speaks of Père Noe, the Father Noah of the Bible) with the priest Chermoyne whom Villon killed. This dubious identification passed out in favor of a romantic and absolutely preposterous one, unanimously adopted by all English critics and biographers (the most sentimental race of scribblers in Christendom). This romantic notion is that Katherine de Vauselles is the only woman Villon ever loved! Villon plainly tells us that he wore his heart on his sleeve; he writes a tender ballade to Frances Martheo whereas he writes none to Katherine Vauselles; and he had affairs with dozens of women, some of whom he remembers tenderly and one of whom he says he really loved, fat Margot.

These romantic commentators declare, on the strength of *"J'en fuz batu,"* that Katherine called in her real lover, Noah, to give Villon a beating after making a rendezvous with the latter. Others still more romantic have conjectured that Katherine had Villon whipped *publicly,* whereas Villon says there were *three* persons present, meaning himself, Noah and Katherine, and moreover he says he was naked when he got whipped.

Let's drop romantic nonsense and use common sense. What is the oldest, the most common of all anecdotes in literature and bar-room talk of discomfiture in love? What else except the story of being caught in *flagrante delicto* by the husband? Or sometimes brother or lover? But the husband is the favorite. If you will turn back to the chapter on Latin literature you will find that Horace uses it as a warning against becoming enslaved by the tender passion. But it was old in Horace's time. It was used by Catullus, Propertius and Martial. It is one of the favorite situations in the *Decameron* and in Poggio, in Brantôme, in *The Book of the Courtier,* in the *Heptameron,* in the *Pentameron.* It is in *The Merry Wives of Wind-sor;* it is the favorite comic device of the Restoration dramatists; it is in Sterne's *Sentimental Journey.* It is in *all* facetious and amorous literature. It is the favorite situation described by men when they are alone and inclined to be smutty. In our times the man who is telling it boasts that he had to run out the back door or down the fire-escape carrying his clothes; or that he was shot at just as he jumped over the fence. Thomas Wolfe uses it in *Look Homeward, Angel.*

Villon tells us that he was caught with Katherine in *flagrante delicto* by Noah de Vauselles; that he did not have a chance to get on his clothes and was beaten within an inch of his life. One thing is pretty certain and that is, if Villon loved Katherine as much as the romantic commentators say he did, he would not have put her full name in the ballade. It would be unheard of in the history of love lyrics, ancient or modern: the custom has been, when names are used at all, to use a pet name or a disguised name to throw readers off the scent. Villon may have thrown in the name, Katherine de Vauselles (Champion, giving us hope of identifying Villon's Kath-erine, says the name of Vauselles or Vaucelles was very common in Paris during the fifteenth century) to make the episode sound more authentic (although there is no reason to believe that such a mis-fortune did not happen to Villon, indeed several times) and gave the husband's name as Noah, that is, an old man.

Such attempts at identification when we do not know the identity of the woman mentioned, as for instance we know the identity of Catullus' Lesbia (a pet name among Latin poets), are idle, because even when we do know that Catullus' Lesbia was the wife of a Roman knight, we know no more about her than what Catullus tells us; and it would make no difference who she was; Catullus' poems to, and about, her would have been just the same. Moreover Lesbia was by no means the only woman in Catullus' life and she may have been in the poems a composite of several women. The savage degrading of a former sweetheart in Catullus' *Carmina XXXVII*, by the way, corresponds very closely to the savage degrading of a former sweetheart in Villon's "Ballade of Fat Margot"; and Villon's *"Pour son amour ceings bouclier et passot"* corresponds closely with Catullus' *"pro qua mihi sunt magna bella pugnata"* in the same situation; both former sweethearts ran public houses at the time given in the poems.

I have written thus at length about Katherine and Margot only for the reason that so many biographers and critics seem not to know how poetry is written. And not understanding this they pervert the nature of poetry itself. There are translators, for instance, who have rendered Villon into archaic English. This is grotesque. The French that Villon used was not archaic to him. On the contrary, it was his pride as an artist, and he says so, that he uses the living language of the Paris streets; he loathed stilted and archaic speech as much as he loathed stilted and archaic sentiments. He created few verse forms (in fact, I am not sure that he created any), but he brought vivid life into the forms he used: he made his readers forget that the strange and beautiful music that he gave them, sometimes bitter, sometimes cynical, sometimes pitying, was imprisoned in severe verse forms. He is communicating his inner experience as faithfully and honestly as he can, in a distillate of the language of the streets. Years later Paul Verlaine, who was a more musical and softer heir to Villon's genius and spirit, describes the art of poetry, ending with the line, "And all the rest is literature." That is, all the rest is false poetry: good poetry does not merely demand a good heart and good intentions; it demands genius.

WE LEFT Villon at the age of twenty-five, banished from Paris. The banishment seems to have lasted for nearly a year, when Charles VII is prevailed upon, through affidavits and petitions, to pardon Villon, convinced that he killed Chermoyne in self-defense. We have the Letter of Remission: it is to be found in all the lengthy, standard biographies of Villon.

We cannot even be sure that Villon was away from Paris during the year of his first banishment. He had already adopted criminal ways; his associates and himself were marked by the police. But it is a trait of the undercover police, whose specialty is the ferreting out of criminals, that they prefer to keep criminals loose, unarrested and under their eyes rather than out of the city.

The reason for this is plain. When a robbery takes place, it is up to the police to find the ones who did it. That is their job. If they fail, they are subjected to severe criticism; the public demands that the perpetrators of crime be brought to justice. So the police permit criminals, even those against whom there are standing charges, to remain in the city; they know the hideouts of the criminals; they keep tabs on their movements; but they do not arrest them. They are waiting for a new crime to develop. Then they know, or think they know, who did the job. They round up all the suspects, or they are tipped off and catch the right one. This means quick work and glory for them, promotions, rewards and honor. If they do not know where the criminals are hiding when a crime is committed, their worries begin. The public expects them to apprehend criminals at once or to say who committed a crime and where he went.

So it does not necessarily follow that because Villon was banished for the death of Chermoyne that Villon was away from Paris for a year, any more than it necessarily follows that, when a warrant is out for the arrest of a New York gangster on a minor charge or a charge that would be difficult to support, the police would dutifully bring him in. The charge against Villon was not murder; it was a simple homicide incurred in a brawl and, moreover, there were no witnesses that could be found. But Villon was known to the Paris constabulary to be a crook, getting his first lessons from seasoned veterans. It is likely that they said to themselves, "This lad will be υp to something really serious pretty soon. It is better to let him keep under cover where we know how to find him."

Therefore, we find Villon near Christmas time in 1456, sitting down in his room at Guillaume de Villon's house and leaving a note in the form of a poem. He is about to skip town again. But before he goes he wants to pay off some old scores. He is in an excited and versifying mood. He calls the note he is about to write the *Lais* or "Will." To English readers it has long been known as "The Little Testament" to distinguish it from his major work of six years later, *Le Grand Testament*. Villon has participated in a crime which will not be discovered until three months later; but he does not know this. He may learn any minute that he is wanted. He is in a remorseful mood.

Also, in leaving this note, he wants to construct, for the benefit of the police, a credible alibi. What more plausible alibi could a poet devise for his leaving town than the alibi that he is suffering from a broken heart, especially if it is done in excellent verse? That is the alibi Villon chooses. But, although he aims to dupe the police, there is this peculiarity about him that, to his perspicacious readers, as well as to himself, he tells the truth. Beginning in a noble and remorseful way, he wishes his good foster-father well, and then grants forgiveness to the cruel lady who has been unfaithful to him (her name, no doubt, is Legion).

Then he proceeds to display that special brand of malicious wit which is his own genius and creation. It is clever; it is good fun; everybody can appreciate a good joke on the other fellow, and Villon contrives to make clever characterizations and jokes about everybody in the underworld except the chief of police. He gets in all the gossip, and in a later ballade he says in all the world there is not such good gossip as in Paris or so much of it. The chief of police will like a joke on the captain of the watch and his "flatfeet"; very well, Villon will gratify the chief of police. He's the one he may have to deal with.

He writes at least the first draft of the "Little Testament" in a single night, in one great burst of inspiration. He tells us his feelings and emotions while writing it, and how, when the job is done and he is shivering with cold, the candle has guttered out; he has read the poem over and feels the joy of creating a perfect thing and that he is now ready to lie down to sleep "all muffled, among the mice." Next morning he still approves of what he has written, perhaps making only a few changes; but he needs one more stanza to round the thing off. He describes himself as "black as a scrubbing brush," penniless and hungry, but adds, in effect, "By God, François Villon is a poet and these other fellows who have money and good looks will soon be forgotten while François Villon will not."

He told the truth.

On March 9, 1457, the thing that was bothering Villon's conscience on that December night came out. He had taken up burglary as a profession in a gang under the leadership of the notorious Guy Tabarie. Moreover he had participated in a serious offense. He, Tabarie, Colin de Cayeux and a chap called "Shorty Jack" broke into the chapel of the College of Navarre, picked the lock of the treasure chest and stole the contents, about five hundred gold crowns, a great deal of money in those days—or now.

Colin was a locksmith and he had picked the lock with great

care, closed and re-locked the chest, and covered up the visible evidence of the theft. So carefully was the job done that the authorities at the college never knew the chest had been robbed until they opened it three months after the event to put money into it or to take some out. The police were called and the routine usual with the police in such circumstances was gone through with. Everything was examined, expert opinion was obtained on the nature of the job, as to whether it were an "inside one" or not, the work of amateurs or professionals. They said expert locksmiths had reached the conclusion that the job was done only a night or two before by amateurs, which, as crooks and newspaper reporters know, meant that the police were sure the crime had been committed a long time back by professionals.

But how to apprehend the crooks? That was the question for the police. If it had happened the night before, they would have rounded up all the gangsters, and given them a shellacking, one after another, in the hope that one would squeal. Now, they would have to proceed more cautiously, because not knowing the exact date of the burglary, it would be easy for all of the crooks implicated to establish alibis. Their only chance was through the efforts of a stool pigeon, or a "squeal." No doubt they checked up on the movements of Master François Villon and found that he was out of town, and moreover had been out of town several months. Therefore they *knew* he was mixed up in it. They probably found that Colin de Cayeux was out of town on business also.

In July however Guy Tabarie was hauled in on another job. It seems probable that the police had been watching him closely. It also seems probable that the crime he was caught in this time was a minor one, and that the police, as is their immemorial habit, promised Tabarie immunity from prosecution if he would tell who pulled the big job at the College of Navarre. The college authorities were clamoring for the arrest and punishment of the criminals. Tabarie squealed, naming his accomplices, including Villon: he could do this with a crook's honor because Villon and Colin had skipped and only "Shorty Jack" would "take the rap"; in other words, "Shorty" would be offered up as the victim. Sentence of banishment was pronounced upon Villon and Colin; "Shorty Jack" was sent to jail; and Tabarie was set free. No money was recovered; but justice was done. Within a year Colin is again in jail.

Villon, on the other hand, is on the high-road with about one hundred and twenty-five gold florins in his pocket. It was a lot of money but it would not last a lifetime. Tabarie had told the police that Villon was staying with an uncle, an abbé in Angers, sounding out the possibilities of robbing an old priest who was said to have a fortune in gold locked up in the abbey.

What Villon did and where he went during the five years of his absence from Paris we know only from his *Grand Testament*. At first he probably "enjoyed himself" in that way he was later so bitterly to regret. His regrets are not that he spent his time with light women but that he spent his money on them. His complaint is that one can always get women if one has the money. We know he wandered about in Brittany and Poitou; he tells us that no less than two young ladies taught him the language of Poitou; he visited Dijon and got as far south as the Dauphiné; he spent some time at the court of the Duke of Orleans, who was a patron of the arts and who was a fairly good writer of verse himself.

But the edict of banishment against Villon read "from the Kingdom of France," not just from Paris. He was, therefore, committing a crime by remaining on French soil. The next we hear of him, then, is that he has turned up in Meung in 1461 and has been clapped in jail by Thibault d'Aussigny, bishop of Orleans, who appears to be the only one who took the edict of banishment literally. This churchman objected very strongly to the robbing of churches, and when he caught such a robber, he did plenty to him. Villon's rub with Thibault seems to have been his first real taste of punishment. He was subjected to the water torture, to make him confess other crimes, and then thrown into a foul, underground dungeon of the castle of Meung, and kept there a whole summer on a diet of stale bread and water.

This imprisonment broke Villon's health, reduced him to skin and bones, a hairless, toothless wreck with a hacking cough. It is a wonder that he survived it at all. And no wonder that he hated Thibault more than any person in the world and heaped execration upon him in the *Grand Testament*. For Villon was released from prison not by the clemency of the bishop, but by the accident of a custom of the times. When a new king passed through one of his subject cities for the first time, it was the custom to open the prisons and free all criminals in celebration of the event. The young King Louis XI made a state entry into Meung on October 1, 1461, and Villon, with others, was freed.

A few months later he is back in Paris, "a scarecrow," so changed in appearance that even the police do not recognize him.

Bitter, remorseful, still a child in many ways, he sits down to the one thing in the world he has faith in, the testimony of his life on earth, expressed in verse. He writes his "Great Testament." It is one of the most personal, most intimate, most human documents ever written, and it is matchless poetry. He reviews his life. Although he is only thirty he is an old man; all the vitality that is left in him is in his brain and nerves. Some one has said that one is never a free man until one is free to say what he thinks and that most people never achieve that freedom until it is time for them to make their wills.

That is true of Villon. At thirty he had little more to fear in life, no need to dissemble; death was around the corner; he had been near the gibbet, so near, in fact, that he can describe with macabre humor what he would look like at the end of a rope: he is so thin it might be necessary to tie weights to his feet to stretch his neck; so dry and scrawny he would be pauper pickings to the buzzards. All of his old intimates have gone the way of the evil: Turgis has been boiled in oil, Montigny has swung on the gibbet of Montfaucon, Colin is rotting away in jail; Perrenet de la Barre, a gambler who used crooked dice, Jack the Wolf and Chollet—Villon remembers them all in his Testament, tells their fate, characterizes them in a line or two, makes kindly jests about them. Into the last testament he has the artistic taste, the sense of drama and unity, to mix the sweet with the bitter. Into it go all his moods, laughing or weeping, sardonic or sublime, gross or reverent—and his prevalent mood of hard facing of reality and calling things by their right names.

Mankind seems eternally striving to do two things, to reach the heart of reality and to get away from it. In the one striving there is mysticism, a confusion of motives, a dressing the soul out in fine and fancy garments. In Villon's poetry there is a soul bared; laid utterly naked. And, after all, it is a fine soul, one of the most beautiful in all literature. It is tender, humble, sensitive, frank and honest. With meticulous self-examination he asks himself what crimes he has committed and in honesty he cannot answer that he has committed any; and, unless we regard the occasional violation of the rights of property as a crime, we cannot find that he has. And who in a lifetime is free from that "crime"—in one way or another? Villon says he has tried to understand life and finds that he can't; least of all can he understand himself. He asks all and sundry to forgive him and have pity on him, and in magnificent lines he forgives those who have ever done him any harm and pronounces his benediction on them.

But the poor fellow cannot keep out of trouble. He has no sooner finished the "Great Testament" than he is in jail again. Perhaps he had been in hiding in Paris, and with the innocence of a penitent fresh from the confessional, he may have imagined that he had absolved himself from all charges against him by writing some poetry. We, his debtors in posterity, absolve him, but Master Laurens Poutrel, who had something to do with the bookkeeping at the College of Navarre, did not: Master Poutrel demanded that Villon be locked up and Villon was jugged again. He promises to repay his share of the loot, one hundred and twenty-five crowns, at the rate of forty crowns per annum, and is released.

A few days later he learns that even the innocent can be made to suffer at the hands of the law, if one has ever been up before the police justice or in jail. Past records count against one. A clerk is beaten up by thugs just as Villon is passing by, and he is seized and thrown into the Châtelet. His misdemeanors are recited, his police record is dug up; it is decided that Master François Villon has caused too much trouble. He is condemned to be "strangled and swung from the Paris gibbet." Villon appeals. His case is taken under consideration. Perhaps inquiries are made and it is discovered that this criminal is also a poet; that he had been a guest at the court of Charles, the Duke of Orleans, and had there written some poems which Charles had copied out in his own handwriting; that Charles, a poet himself with considerable talent for formal verse, had honored Villon; that Villon had written some patriotic verses held in high esteem by those in power; that Villon had been freed from prison in Orleans by the Duke and had written a poem in celebration of the birth of the duke's daughter, Marie (the worst poem Villon ever wrote but the one the civil authorities of Paris would probably choose most to admire). In fine, somehow, Villon's sentence was changed. Instead of hanging he is awarded ten years' banishment, and as he is led outside the city gates by the police, it is probable that a sergeant says to him seriously, "And now, kid, stay out."

Apparently Villon did. We hear no more of him. This was on January 8, 1463. We do not know when or where he died. Fifty years later Rabelais has heard stories of him in Touraine, where legends seem to have grown up about him. Rabelais uses these hearsay stories of Villon's reckless bravado in creating the character of Panurge. It was just the sort of figure that he needed to round off his robust microcosm of a book, *The Horrible Deeds and Prowesses of the Well-Renowned Pantagruel, King of the Dipsodes, Son of the Great Giant Gargantua.*

MONTAIGNE *AND THE AVERAGE MAN*

*

RABELAIS had the Gallic spirit, a tonic quality of earthiness and levity which identifies French literature and sets it slightly apart from all other literatures of the world. Villon, Rabelais and Montaigne may be said to have formed the French mind and there is nothing in the subsequent literature of France which is alien to these three writers. In Proust, who aspired to write an Arabian Nights entertainment in terms of the *Memoires* of Saint-Simon, we see the same inner necessity which set Montaigne meticulously to examine, expose and record himself. Verlaine is almost like a reincarnation of Villon, and the rasping, plaintive, sardonic voice of Tristan Corbière is that of the wayward starveling of medieval Paris reëchoing in the rainswept streets of a more modern Montmartre. Ronsard is a lyrical Rabelais; Voltaire is the creator of Gargantua speaking always in the person of Friar John of Entommeures; Renan and Anatole France are heirs to the irony, frankness and freedom of Montaigne and to the surprising turn of thought invented by Rabelais; Molière is the homeliness of Montaigne and the satire of Rabelais done into good theater; Rousseau is a soul tortured by a Calvinistic conscience and eager, like Montaigne, to learn the meaning of existence by examination of self. La Fontaine, Racine, what are they but, in the one case, the concision and condensation, and in the other of the rarification, of the wit of Rabelais? What was the origin of that seeking after truth that is found in the first great psychological novels of Balzac, Flaubert, Stendhal and Zola, but the urge which made Montaigne day after day, over a long period of years, set down even the most trivial matters about himself?

No man is a hero to his valet and Montaigne was valet to himself. Therein lies his greatness: he deigned and dared to proclaim that in no single thing was he a hero. Persons who suffer from a feeling of inferiority should read Montaigne. Whatever they think is holding them back, Montaigne had in double measure. He had, so he tells us, everything wrong with him except his health, and even that went bad on him in his middle life, for he suffered from stone in the kidneys which modern surgery would have relieved. He was undersized; and this seems to have bothered him considerably: "My height is rather below the average. This defect hath not only the drawback of ugliness, but, in addition, that of inconvenience. A beautiful figure, in truth, is the only beauty allowed to men. . . . I am of something lower than middle stature, a defect that not only borders upon deformity, but carries withal a great deal of inconvenience along with it, especially to those who are in command; for the authority which a graceful presence, and a majestic mien beget, is wanting. . . . I am, as to the rest, strong and well knit, my face is not puffed, but full, and my complexion betwixt jovial and melancholic, moderately sanguine and hot." *

One cannot be sure that Le Duc de La Rochefoucauld ever read Montaigne, but we can be sure that Montaigne put something in the air when we find Rochefoucauld writing this sketch of himself as a preface to his *Maximes:*

"I am of medium stature: I am well proportioned and my gestures are easy. My coloring is dark but harmonious. My forehead is high and rather broad; my eyes black, small and deep set; my eyebrows are dark and bushy, but well shaped. I am at a loss what to say of my nose, for it is neither hooked nor aquiline, heavy, nor yet, to my knowledge, sharp; all that I can say of it is that it is large rather than small, and that it is a trifle too long. My mouth is large and my lips are usually fairly red and neither well or ill shaped. My teeth are white and moderately regular. People have told me that my chin is too pronounced. I have just examined myself in the mirror to ascertain the truth of the matter, and I do not quite know what judgment to pronounce. My face is certainly square or oval—I hardly know which. My hair is black, curls naturally and is sufficiently abundant to sustain my pretensions to a fine head.

"My expression is both haughty and sad, which leads most persons to deem me supercilious, although in reality quite the reverse. My gestures are easy, perhaps too easy, for I gesticulate freely when speaking. Such, quite frankly do I consider my exterior, and I fancy one will find that my opinion is not far from the truth. . . ."

— Tr. John Heard.

* Tr. Trechmann, Oxford Univ. Press.

Le Duc de La Rochefoucauld, whose particular responsibility seems to have been the distillation of his experience in terms of epigrams, not for pay, not for advancement, not for anything except a satisfaction to himself, followed Montaigne in subjecting himself to relentless self-scrutiny.

Montaigne, long before Rochefoucauld, realized that it is "easier to understand mankind than to understand a man." Therefore, he set out to understand himself, or rather to reveal himself and let others make what they could out of it.

MICHEL EYQUEM DE MONTAIGNE had one of the most glorious fathers in the history of literature, and, in a way, the famous Essays of Montaigne are a long comparison of the son with the father to the great disadvantage of the son. Montaigne's father was, in many respects, everything Montaigne would like to have been, and failing to be like his father, he celebrated the virtues his father possessed. This, I may remark, is extremely rare. Sons of well-endowed fathers frequently bear toward them a special grudge. The Freudians call it an Œdipus complex and say that it is the result of a sense of rivalry on the part of a son for the love a father enjoys from the son's mother which the son cannot share. But this, I think, is far-fetched. There are only about fifteen years in a man's life or a woman's in which a passional interest is paramount. After that, extreme passion is an aberration. In one's middle years and after, one is happy enough for any eventuality which recalls to one that the only conceivable aim of life is the perpetuation of life—or going through the motions of perpetuating it. After forty the war may not be won or the enthusiasm for it quite diminished; but at least, in general, the motives are clear, the aim is in mind, the outcome (win or lose) is discounted. After forty one may see qualities in one's father that one wishes one had, and to wish it one may have only an esthetic interest.

Montaigne's father was a virgin when he married a Jewess in his thirty-third year on his return from Italy after campaigning as a soldier under Francis I. (The wars of Charles VIII, Louis XII, and Francis I upon Italy were idiotic from a practical standpoint, for they brought no money into the French treasury and ran up a considerable debt, but they did acquaint the victorious French with a civilization from which they were able to learn something.) That a man may remain a virgin until his thirty-third year and that he might remain thereafter a singularly monogamous husband may seem incredible to the youngsters of our generation; but such, it appears, was a fact which Montaigne, who had been deflowered in puberty, had to face. There was no reason for his father's chastity, for the age was especially licentious, beyond a certain fastidiousness in his nature and an inclination toward physical exercise. Montaigne's father was an athlete: he could vault, leap, run, swim, box, fence, dance, play tennis, lift weights and curb a horse in a fashion so expert as to excite the wonder and admiration of his son, Michel, who could do none of these things with any credit to himself.

Montaigne's father, in the report of his adoring son, was grave, humble and modest in his behavior; swart, well-proportioned and well-knit, though of small stature, of pleasing countenance, and capable of miracles of vaulting, running and leaping. He was, it seems, a bundle of wiry nerves all in perfect coördination with his muscles. Such a constitution Montaigne admired because he himself was fumbling, phlegmatic, self-indulgent, weak, unambitious, forgetful, and without any physical prowess whatever. As a youth he was dandified, seeking to make up in clothes the deficiencies he felt about his appearance. The only physical exercise he ever enjoyed was that of horseback riding, and since he tells us that he was pretty good at this, we can take it that he was very good indeed, because there is no man in the history of literature so inclined as Montaigne is to belittle his abilities. He tells us that he has no memory and that he cannot remember things he has read two hours after he has read them, but when he quotes from memory he is much more nearly perfect than scholars who pride themselves on the accuracy of their scholastic attainments. (The late Stuart P. Sherman revealed in an essay that he did not know such a common thing as the authorship of the words, "She walks in beauty ——." Irving Babbitt attributes to Bacon the words of Lucian about there being no beauty without some strangeness in it. Ambrose Bierce said about Brander Matthews: "He is nothing if not accurate; and he is not accurate.") In the glosses on Montaigne there are but few corrections in his scholarship and such few as there are remain equivocal. He had a library of a thousand books and these thousand books he knew intimately. For the rest, he did nothing after forty, except to examine himself for our benefit and report his findings faithfully.

Besides Montaigne, there have been but two men in the history of literature who have had this pressing sense of the value of the true record of what a man sees, thinks, feels, and does—Samuel Pepys and James Boswell. Boswell, who was a great man, had the charming humility of believing he was a mere agent for recording the minutiæ of an intellectual dictator of his period, and he never for a moment realized that his *Life of Samuel Johnson* was vastly superior to anything Johnson had ever written. And Pepys seems to have had only a tenuous apprehension that a record of his most trivial doings was much more important to a fine mind, like Marcel Schwob's, than any of the vainglorious conquests of Alexander the Great.

Lytton Strachey, when he wrote *Landmarks of French Literature,* was still a young man, and it is only on the score of youth that we can excuse him for saying that Montaigne was "neither a great artist, nor a great philosopher; he was not great at all." Strachey, when he wrote that, was under the popular delusion that greatness consists in doing something flamboyantly discreditable, like leading an army against a defenseless people, achieving great wealth by tricks, usury and extortion, or maintaining nonsense by a great show of syllogisms. In his later years, Strachey reversed his position so thoroughly that he discredited the motives which enable one to become a cardinal, a founder of English public school education, an angel to the wounded in war, and a conquerer of barbaric tribes. But, meanwhile, he neglected to revise his verdict that Montaigne was "not great."

Montaigne's greatness is visible in nearly every great work of French prose; he and Rabelais gave final form to the still plastic French language, before the standardizing of it set it under the direction of the French Academy. He invented the familiar essay; he was the father of the spirit of inquiry which produced Voltaire and the French revolution. If the word "philosophy" means anything, Montaigne's philosophy of "loyal enjoyment of being" is as valid as any philosophical system I know. Montaigne aspired to simplicity, clarity, and easiness in writing; he strove to use only those words "which are current in the Paris markets." He was one of the first to espouse the doctrine of equality of the sexes; one of the first to combat that idealization of woman which so hampered the freedom of all women. As Buckle said, "Under the guise of a mere man of the world expressing natural thoughts in a common language, Montaigne concealed a spirit of lofty and audacious inquiry." He immeasurably increased the estimate of the dignity and worth of human life, by showing us the kinship between great spirits and the average man. Montaigne was the first, and almost the last, to search out his soul, "to penetrate the dark profundities of its intricate windings; to choose and lay hold of so many little nimble motions," with complete honesty and fidelity to the record. He was a great artist in the greatest of arts, the art of living.

Let me tell you how easy it is to take Montaigne to your heart: You can scarcely open a page of, say, the translations by E. J. Trechmann or by Thomas Cotton, or of Dr. Armaingaud's text, without coming upon something which causes you to exclaim, "That is like me." I am not so foolish as to imagine that I am very like Montaigne or so careless of the truth as to try to create Montaigne in my image. But Montaigne tells us in one place something that has struck some commentators as trivial but rather curious; he says that at first he did like radishes very much, then he could not eat them at all for a long time, and now he likes radishes again. And, dear reader, that is what happened to me. As a boy I was so fond of radishes that my mother told everybody that I could "eat a barrel of them"; then my taste for radishes vanished for a long period of time; and now I am very fond of them again.

Does that sound trivial? If it does, you are incapable of understanding Montaigne. For that is a paradigm of Montaigne's great contribution to thought. Listen to the great French critic, Jules Lemaître (translated by A. W. Evans in the collection of essays, *Literary Impressions*):

"One of Montaigne's favorite thoughts is that we can have no certain knowledge since nothing is immutable, neither things nor intelligences, and the mind and its object are both borne along in perpetual movement. Ourselves changing, we behold a changing world. And even when the object under observation is for ever fixed in its forms, the mind in which it is reflected is mutable and multifarious, and this is enough to make it impossible for us to be responsible for anything more than our momentary impression.

"How, therefore, could literary criticism constitute itself into a doctrine? Works pass in procession before the mirror of our minds; but, as the procession is long, the mirror becomes modified in the interval, and when by chance the same work returns, it no longer projects the same image.

"Any one can try the experiment on himself. I have adored Corneille, and I have been within an ace of despising Racine; at the present moment I adore Racine and Corneille is almost indifferent to me. The transports into which Musset's verses used to throw me, I can recapture now no longer. I have lived with my ears and eyes filled by Victor Hugo's resonance and enchantments, and today I feel Victor Hugo's soul almost alien from mine. I dare not read again the books that delighted me and captured my tears at the age of fifteen. When I try to be sincere, to express only what I have really felt, I am frightened at seeing how little my impres-

sions of the greatest writers accord with traditional judgments, and I
hesitate to tell all my thought."

In the frank and intimate record Montaigne set down on paper
in the privacy of his library in the Château Montaigne, he observed,
first of all, that his opinions were subject to change—not his fundamental opinions, perhaps, but those opinions to which bigots give so
much weight. He found inconsistencies within himself. He made the
great discovery that life is a living thing; that living is an adventure the outcome of which is happily uncertain.

Michel Eyquem had a vanity: let us forgive him for it. He was
not of the nobility, but he wished to convey the impression that he
was, that he might explode the pretensions of the nobility with better
grace. He added "de Montaigne" to his name and he wrote that his
ancestors had occupied the château for many generations, whereas
his great-grandfather had purchased the estate in 1477 and had
never exercised the right to the name "de Montaigne," nor had
Montaigne's father, Pierre Eyquem. This estate was in Périgord
not far from the flourishing commercial city of Bordeaux, where
Pierre Eyquem was a merchant of wines as well as a landed proprietor.

Pierre Eyquem was of middle-class French stock, with an ad-
mixture of British blood. As a young man he had served as a soldier
in Italy under Francis I, and in his thirty-third year had married
Antoinette de Lopez, a daughter of a Jewish family, whose ancestors
had been driven out of Spain and had embraced the Protestant
faith. (It was usual for Jews to avoid persecution either by becoming
converts to Catholicism or by becoming Huguenots.) There were
nine (or it may have been eleven) children born of this marriage,
of which Michel was the eldest. Michel was born at the château
at high noon on February 28, 1533.

Pierre Eyquem was in every way a remarkable father. An uneducated man himself, he had definite ideas about the proper training and instruction of his children. He wished them to be close to
the soil, to learn peasant ways and be, in all things, humane in their
feelings. He gave Michel a peasant godfather and godmother, and
had him suckled at the breast of a peasant woman. He had ideas
about the "conditioning" of children which should interest the Be-
haviorist psychologists of our time. He forbade corporal punishment and enforced the rule that his children should be taught by
gentle persuasion and not by threats, severe discipline, or anything

which would shock the nervous system. Pierre arranged that his children should be awakened by the sound of music, he "being of the opinion it did trouble and disturb the brains of children suddenly to wake them in the morning, and to snatch them violently and over hastily from sleep." Among his other activities (he was once mayor of Bordeaux) Pierre Eyquem conducted an employment agency and a labor exchange, and through this agency he brought to the château as instructor to his children a German tutor who knew no French but was learned in Latin. Pierre made it a rule that everybody in the household, the servants included, should learn Latin from the German tutor and forbade the use of French before the children until they should have reached six years of age. Mother and father, cook and gardener, nurse and page, dutifully learned Latin.

When at the age of six Michel Eyquem was sent away to the College of Guienne at Bordeaux, he already knew Latin literature and spoke a kind of Latin better than he spoke French. He tells us, however, that he was dull and backward as a child, a dreamer who was never much in danger of mischief because he did nothing whatever. "For, though I was of a strong and healthful constitution, and of a disposition tolerably sweet and tractable; yet I was withal so heavy, idle and indisposed that they could not rouse me from this stupidity to any exercise or recreation nor get me out to play." He envied the ability of other children to excel in athletics but not to the point of emulating them; the only thing he enjoyed in the nature of exercise was horse-back riding.

His father wanted him to be a lawyer and that was the profession in which he was educated. And at the age of twenty-one he had served out an apprenticeship in Toulouse, after leaving school at the age of thirteen, and his father purchased him a magistracy under the system then prevailing. In the following year he accompanied his father, then mayor of Bordeaux, to Paris to plead for the restoration of the privileges of the city which had been abrogated by the king after the salt tax uprising.

Next year he began the practice of law in Bordeaux, but a more important thing happened to him: he met and became the friend of Étienne de la Boëtie, a brilliant young lawyer, for whom he formed a strong attachment which lasted until Boëtie's death six years later while still in his thirties. At this period of his life Montaigne was somewhat dissipated and self-indulgent. He has given us an astonishingly frank account of himself and of his self-indulgences of these years of sowing wild oats. He was bored by his work as a magistrate. But he was of good address, charming in his manner, and a few years later we hear of him as a man respected and admired by the rival monarchs, Henry III and Henry of Navarre, and learn that he was entrusted with various diplomatic missions between the rival factions. He is strangely silent about these years of his life; but he emerged from them with a particular attachment for Henry of Navarre.

Meanwhile Boëtie died, leaving Montaigne his fine library. And at the age of thirty-three Montaigne married François de la Cassaigne, a woman of a middle class family, who brought to him a considerable dowry. She proved to be a perfect mate for him, for she was efficient, cautious and capable: she managed his affairs for him on the estate, which he would surely have let go to the dogs, because he had no business or monetary sense, no knowledge of farming: he was negligent and forgetful; he could not read his own handwriting two days after he had written something; and he was utterly helpless in practical affairs. Of marriage he has written, "Marriage hath for its share, usefulness, justice, honour, and constancy—a flat pleasure but a universal one. Love is founded upon delight alone, and giveth it, truly, of a kind more poignant, more caressive, more vital . . . A man doth not marry for himself, whatever people say; he marries quite as much, for his posterity and his family."

He was not over-faithful to his wife; but his temperament was not very sanguine and he seems to have caused her no distress. From all accounts his marriage was a happy one. "Every strange woman," he writes, "seems to us a comely woman; and every man knows by experience that the continual sight of one another cannot give the pleasure which comes of taking and leaving by fits and starts. As for me, these interruptions fill me with a fresh love towards my family, and restore me in pleasanter fashion to the groove of my home. . . . The fact that happy marriage is so rare is a sign of its value. When we fashion it finely and take it the right way, there is no nobler institution in society."

In this he was following the custom of the good French bourgeois. Six children, all girls, were born of the union, only one of whom reached maturity. In 1568 his father died, leaving him the château and the estate. He spent two years in Paris seeking a high appointment in court; but the most fanatical of religious wars—the war between Catholicism and Protestantism—was brewing at that time and he, being of a peaceable nature, hating all forms of cruelty and intolerance, gave up public life in disgust and retired to his château. In 1572 occurred the dreadful Massacre of St. Bartholomew's Day. Montaigne refused to become embroiled with either side and it was in that year that he determined upon the task which was to occupy him the rest of his life—that of setting down from day to day his comments on what he read and on the things that interested him. In the library of the château he had Latin mottoes from the classics inscribed upon the beams and the walls of his study, such as, "I determine nothing; I do not comprehend things; I suspend judgment; I examine"—"The human race is too greedy of fables"—"Men are tormented by their opinions of things; not by the things themselves."

Beginning first as a mere commentator upon the works he read, he developed a tendency to examine himself, to write about his contacts with the peasants and tradespeople; to set down his impressions of life; and lastly to study carefully and accurately his own nature, making a clinical report of his conduct, his feelings, his ideas. In 1580 he published the first two volumes of these *Essays*. He sent a copy to Henry III, and decided to travel. He made a tour of Switzerland, Germany and Italy. On this trip he kept a diary of the things which interested him. In Bologna he saw a priest attempt to exorcise a devil from a melancholy man, and when Montaigne questioned the priest, he said he had relieved a woman of an unusually large devil only the day before. Montaigne sets down all the priest told him. He witnessed a circumcision and described the ceremony in detail. He encountered, during Lent, a group of Flagellants, men, women, boys and girls, whipping themselves until their bodies were raw and bloody, but apparently without pain. He was received everywhere as a man of high estate and was entertained by cardinals and magistrates. The fame of his *Essays* had preceded him and he was asked by the ecclesiastical authorities to remove certain passages they considered inimical to the Church; whereupon he made changes but only to emphasize the matter objected to.

Nevertheless he conformed always outwardly with Church observances, putting up votive tablets for himself, his wife and daughter at the shrine of Loretto. He was particularly interested in the courtesans and houses of prostitution in Rome and Venice, and he visited many of them, carefully noting down what he saw. He was also suffering from the stone at this time and sought the baths and cures, to no avail.

On his return to France he was elected Mayor of Bordeaux, the office his father had held before him. He made an excellent mayor, instituting many reforms. He was on such intimate terms with Henry of Navarre that, when the latter succeeded to the throne, he twice visited Montaigne at his château. During the plague of 1587 Montaigne absented himself from the city and remained on his estate, an act which has brought severe censure upon him by some commentators and which caused charges of neglect of duty to be lodged against him

He was tired of political life, anyhow, and he probably welcomed the opportunity to be relieved of his post. He had found two devoted disciples in Pierre Charron, an eminent ecclesiastic, and in Mademoiselle Marie de Gournay, a German woman, whom he spoke of as his adopted daughter and who may have been his mistress. It was to Mademoiselle de Gournay that he left the work of editing and revising his unpublished *Essays*.

While he was in Paris superintending the publication of a new edition of the *Essays*, he was thrown into prison on trumped up charges by the Catholic League, but was released within eight hours on the order of Catherine de Medici. On his way home he attended the States General at Blois, but left in time to escape the assassination of the Duc de Guise. He died on September 13, 1592, after long months of pain, from stone. Toward his last years he wrote much about death. But he had a brave attitude toward dissolution:

"Few men die in the opinion that it is their last hour, and there is nothing wherein the flattery of hope does more to delude us. It never ceases to whisper in our ears, others may have been much sicker without dying; my condition is not so desperate as it is thought, and at the worst, God has done some miracles. Which happens by reason that we set too much value upon ourselves. It seems as if the universality of things were in some measure to suffer by our dissolution, and that it did commiserate our condition. For as much as our depraved sight represents things to itself after the same manner, and that we are of opinion they stand in as much need of us as we do of them; like people at sea, to whom mountains, fields, cities, heaven and earth are tossed at the same rate they are."

The greatest single work of Montaigne is the *Apology of Raimond Sebond*. It is a long sustained work of irony; on the surface a vindication of Catholic orthodoxy and in reality an assault upon every conviction, Catholic or Protestant, upon which faith is based. It is the bitterest satire he ever penned, and it was inspired by the fanatical fratricide between Catholics and Huguenots, which within a few years had cost eight hundred thousand lives, left nine towns razed to the ground, two hundred and fifty villages burned, and had turned the whole countryside of France into a shambles. Montaigne's château was twice invaded, but he kept his temper and his counsel and nothing was harmed.

Much ink has since been spilled in argument as to whether Montaigne should have done this or that, whether he should not have espoused a cause and declared himself in the momentous religious and political uprisings of the day. But his eternal question, *"Que sçay je?"* ("What know I?") is the answer. As J. M. Robertson says in his admirable introduction to the Oxford University Press edition of the *Essays of Montaigne,* translated by Trechmann, "The human wisdom of Montaigne had entered into the lifeblood of France and of the world." Plutarch nourished Montaigne, and the genius of Shakespeare fed upon the genius of Plutarch and Montaigne. The quarrel between Huguenot and Catholic has long been dead now: the essays of Montaigne are eternal. With sublime audacity that swart little man, who has described himself so perfectly and minutely to us, has given us all reason to face life with more courage and assurance.

CERVANTES *AND THE SPIRIT OF MOCKERY*

*

CERVANTES is an example which we may always cite in evidence that the period in a man's life at which genius may come to full maturity is unpredictable; for in his youth Cervantes tried his hand at many kinds of writing, both in prose and in verse, and what he wrote was unsuccessful and without distinction. It was not until he was fifty-seven years of age that he began to write the immortal *Don Quixote* which an English critic, Sir Walter Raleigh, did not hesitate to pronounce "the wisest and most splendid book in the world" and which even in a now archaic English translation seems fresher and nearer to us than some of the work of Shakespeare.

Don Quixote is there also to refute the critical doctrine that a great work of art is necessarily planned out, with a definite purpose in mind, the words tested, and the whole brought into unity by prevision and revision. *Don Quixote* started out to be one thing and turned into something which was originally far from the author's purpose. One of the principal characters in the novel, Sancho Panza, did not occur to Cervantes until he was well along with his story and was introduced then only because Cervantes suddenly remembered that in the chivalric romances a knight was always accompanied by a squire. Even after Cervantes had introduced Sancho the vast possibilities which the character offered as a contrast to Don Quixote were not at first perceived by him but grew on him as both characters got out of hand and, in a way, wrote their own story by taking shape, blood, accouterments and soul in his mind.

Don Quixote in literature is what biologists call a *sport*. It is the first and most perfect specimen of a unique genus. No book has been more than superficially like it in all literature. It is so rich in substance that it is possible for several different persons of varying natures to read it and to derive from it dissimilar impressions. Young people ordinarily read it as a fantastic tale of adventure. Persons of mature minds either find it an excitement to laughter at the weaknesses of human nature, the foibles and deceits and duplicities of mankind, a satire upon all that is in this world, or else they find it a book of deep and mellow wisdom moving them nearer to tears than to laughter because of the infinite compassion of Cervantes. And there are those among the elderly who say that, just as some writers cannot be properly appreciated until one has reached the age of forty, Cervantes cannot be thoroughly understood and honored until one has reached the age of sixty and has grown indulgent toward man, undisturbed by the vagaries of fate, and no longer the victim of one's own ego and one's passions. For myself I am not sure I shall reach the age of sixty but there is an additional reason for me to reach that age, if I am to enjoy Cervantes more than now.

Not so long ago (in 1905 to be exact) the renowned Spanish philosopher and critic, Miguel de Unamuno, wrote a book apropos of *Don Quixote*, which was designed to stir up dissatisfaction among the Spaniards with their ruler Alfonso and to lead them away from the mechanization of life with which he thought the new industrialism threatened them. Eight years later he enlarged and revised the work. It is available in an excellent translation into English by Homer P. Earle and is called *The Life of Don Quixote and Sancho*. Unamuno follows the book straight through almost from beginning to end, selecting from nearly every chapter a paragraph or so and commenting upon it. It is a beautiful work of literature itself; but, if you have read *Don Quixote*, you will be astonished to find that Unamuno, basing his work of philosophy on the text of Cervantes, left out nearly everything that Cervantes thought important, and so Unamuno's Cervantes is not my Cervantes nor the Cervantes of many people who read him simply for delight and for the rare humor and rich mockery he displays. Unamuno's whole argument is that people should strive to be *like* Don Quixote as much as possible, which is just what most of us try to avoid: we find that we are all too preposterously like the fellow.

I don't think Cervantes ever had a "serious" purpose in writing *Don Quixote*. He did not have a "serious" type of mind. That was why he was such a failure as a writer in his youth. In his youth pas-

MIGUEL DE CERVANTES
(After the Spanish print engraved by D. F. Selma)

toral romances were all the rage with the reading public. They had succeeded the old books of chivalry, and the poetical romances of heroism and chivalric love; but like the latter these pastoral romances were stilted and artificial compositions about high-born ladies and gallant gentlemen who played at being shepherds and shepherdesses and uttered sentiments of a lofty nature. Cervantes wrote such a romance and called it *Galatea*. It was worse than many of the others of its class and character and was not a success.

One readily understands why it wasn't. Cervantes' keen sense of reality, his natural inclination to humor, burlesque and mockery, his inveterate mischievousness simply would not permit him to keep a straight face long enough to compose such a romance. There are people who naturally see things in a comic light, who cannot comprehend the representations in art of the tragic emotions or of high-flown sentiments. This does not mean that they are incapable of feeling emotions deeply; in fact they feel emotions sometimes with an intensity so poignant that their only defense against themselves is laughter, and not an hysterical laughter, but a comic expression which affords them relief from the tension within.

I will try to give an example of what I mean. Miss Fannie Brice, the comedienne, I am pleased to think is one of the greatest artists our generation has seen on the stage. Hers is a comic genius, a divine sense of the absurdity of things, most especially a sense of the absurdity of false art, bogus sentiment and pretentiousness. She is a technician who can spot with easy certainty the slightest flaw in dramatic technique. Once I sat behind Miss Brice at the theater. The play was a sentimental tragedy of the type of *The Green Hat*. The heroine was called upon to do a great deal of hand-wringing and other theatricals indicating a crushed and much-put-upon heart; she was called upon to speak numerous lines in a throaty voice, indicating that she was keeping back her sobs only because her honor would not permit her to betray what she knew and felt. I happened to glance at Miss Brice during all this and she was making such comical expressions that I choked up with laughter watching her and had to leave the theater for a few minutes, gasping and sputtering. Every gesture, every expression of the tragedienne on the stage was registered by Miss Brice and given just the twist which made the whole thing absurd. I learned from her some months later that she was unconscious of doing this; that it was natural with her and she sometimes forgot that she did it and, without intending to do so, distracted the actors on the stage. As a result, she told me, she usually sat in the last row of the theater or, if she sat closer, she would ask whoever accompanied her to jog her if she started unconsciously making funny faces. On this occasion, her mother called her attention to what she was doing and during the second act they succeeded in getting their seats transferred to the rear of the house.

Cervantes, I think, possessed a type of mind like that. Remarkable ironies have followed because of this. In Chapter XI of *Don Quixote* it amused Cervantes to write a gorgeous burlesque of the pompous style of poetic rhetoric and oratory and of the shallow thinking which imagines that there was once a golden age when everything was perfect and the world was a paradise. This passage was seized upon by the pedants with perfect seriousness. They never suspected that it was a satirical joke. They cited it as a work of noble and lofty thinking; and in nearly all of the manuals of rhetoric which young Spaniards are forced to study it is reproduced as an especially fine example of the grand style! The poor lads have to memorize it. It is supposed to inculcate in them a profound sense of the finer things in life. Yet one should think that nothing could be so obvious as the humorous and satiric intent of the passage. It is the romance-mad Don Quixote who delivers this eulogy of the Golden Age and he delivers it to an audience of goatherds who, mark you, listened to it "all amazed and suspended, with very great attention all the while." Cervantes meant therein to tell us that sheer idiocy, if couched in flowery terms of rhetoric, mystifies and enchants the dumb and ignorant. Let us read this eulogy, in the slightly revised seventeenth century version by Thomas Shelton:

Happy times and fortunate ages were those, whereon our ancestors bestowed the style of golden! not because gold (so much prized in this iron age) was gotten in that happy time without any labours, but because those which lived in that time knew not these two words, "thine" and "mine," in that holy age all things were in common. No man needed, for his ordinary sustenance to do ought else than lift up his hand, and take it from the strong oak, which did liberally invite them to gather his sweet and savoury fruit. The clear fountains and running rivers did offer them these savoury and transparent waters in magnificent abundance. In the clefts of rocks and hollow trees did the careful and discreet bees erect their commonwealth, offering to every hand, without interest, the fertile crop of their sweetest travails. The lofty cork-trees did dismiss of themselves, without any other art than that of their native liberality, their broad and light rinds; wherewithal houses were at first covered, being sustained by rustical stakes, to none other end but for to keep back the inclemencies of the air. All then was peace, all amity, and all concord. As yet the ploughshare presumed not, with rude encounter, to open and search the compassionate bowels of our first mother; for she, without compulsion, offered up, through all of the parts of her fertile and spacious bosom, all that which might satisfy, sustain, and delight those children which it then had. Yea, it was then that the simple and beautiful young shepherdesses went from valley to valley and hill to hill, with their hair sometimes plaited, sometimes dishevelled, without any other apparel than that which was requisite to cover comely that which modesty wills, and ever would have, concealed. . . .

There is more in a like vein; but it is difficult to fathom how any one could miss the satiric intent of that passage. Cervantes, captured by Barbary pirates and held for many years for ransom, knew only too well that among primitive people, untouched by civilization, life is not, and never was, the blissful sort of existence imagined by the poets. Man has never lived without labor or without the fruits of labor; and in primitive times the struggle was harder, more relentless, crueler and more frightening than now or than it was in Cervantes' times. Cervantes, who had suffered more misfortunes than usually fall to the most unlucky men, knew that the conditions of life have always been opposed to vistas of an earthly paradise dreamed by the visionaries.

The career of Miguel de Cervantes Saavedra was one long struggle against adversity, debt, poverty and sheer bad luck. No one in all literature, with the possible exception of De Foe, suffered from so many and such terrific bad breaks. As a soldier of the King of Spain in the decisive battle of Lepanto which put a quietus on the Turkish ambitions in Europe, he was severely wounded in many places and completely lost the use of his left hand; he was taken captive by Algerian bandits and held five years for a ransom which his impoverished family could not pay. He returned to Spain after being ransomed by a Trintarian monk, who did not know Cervantes from Adam but found him with some Spanish nobles whom he had been commissioned to redeem by ransom. On Cervantes' return he found that while ex-soldiers are in high favor when they go away to the wars they are not in favor at all with employers when they return, particularly if they return crippled; and he found himself thrown into jail for bad debts. He wrote no less than thirty plays in a vain effort to emulate the success in riches and glory attained by his great countryman, Lope de Vega; he wrote a pastoral romance after the current formula and got one hundred and forty dollars;

he got a government post and the government was so broke he could not collect his money with any regularity; he got a job with the Royal Treasury and deposited government funds with a banker who went bankrupt, leaving Cervantes to bear the onus and the cost of bad judgment. He wrote the first part of *Don Quixote* in frantic financial desperation and, although it was an immediate and tremendous success—six editions were called for during the first year and translations into foreign languages began almost immediately— there was no adequate copyright protection; his book was pirated right and left and not only did he derive very little money out of it but there was put on the market a "sequel" to it before he had finished writing his own second part; and this "sequel" made money for its author and publisher, but not for Cervantes. A nobleman was stabbed in the apartment house in which he and his wife, his daughter and his niece lived, and all of them were thrown into jail on account of it until he was able to prove that they knew nothing of the slaying. His daughter resorted to harlotry; and through the last years of his life, when his fame was resounding not only through Spain but through all Europe, he was forced to live in the most destitute circumstances, bordering on starvation.

There is a school of modern critics which has given rise to a rather generally accepted idea first enunciated by Whitman—that to have great writers it is necessary to have great audiences and that the conditions and the *mores* of the times may crush and warp genius, making it conform to the social demands of the moment. I cannot find a single instance where I am fully satisfied that this is true. In the case of Mark Twain, usually cited by these critics, I not only do not think he was distracted from his God-sent mission but that he did produce a small body of great and permanent literature which was the best he had in him and was a very good best indeed. And I think Henry James' deficiencies are the deficiencies of talent and character and not the unhappy results of a crude and bourgeois environment from which he found it necessary to flee. He was essentially, as I see it, all that was shoddy and distasteful in the *nouveau riche* aspirations of his time in America—withal that he had a brilliant talent which made an almost magnificent most of very little substance in his fastidious and appallingly self-satisfied middle-class soul. Henry James was the poseur who carried the artificial attitude to high limits of artistic satisfaction; but in all essentials his talent was, in kind, like Oscar Wilde's, and not so pleasingly hard, graceful and sustained in elegance. His art suffered from a lack of that leaven of wit and humor possessed by his English rival and competitor in high-toned romance, George Meredith.

Cervantes certainly had disadvantages in lack of appreciation and encouragement, in the contrary spirit of his times, in social and economic values; yet he produced the "Bible of Spain," the book which to this day is one of the three books, aside from the Bible, foremost in general and perennial demand—the other two being *Pilgrim's Progress*, by John Bunyan, and *The Imitation of Christ*, by Thomas à Kempis. *Don Quixote* has been translated into every known language and dialect. Two years after the first part was published in Spain, Thomas Skelton began work on his famous translation into English; and one hundred years after the first complete edition appeared in Madrid, the Charles Jervas' translation came out in England, helping to start *Don Quixote* on its career as a world classic. The foremost authorities on Cervantes, indeed, are not Spanish but English. The two standard biographies are those of Fitzmaurice-Kelly and Rudolph Schevill, the latter's *Cervantes* superseding the great work of scholarship and research of the former through new discoveries and realignments. (I must confess, however, that Professor Schevill's biography of Cervantes, while rich in new material and careful as well as acute in its judgments, is written without vivacity and is therefore rather difficult to read. I can make no claim whatever to original research in Cervantesana; but whereas the Spanish commentators constantly assert that almost nothing is known about the life of Cervantes, Professor Schevill has shown that, on the contrary, quite a great deal is known.)

Cervantes was a contemporary of Shakespeare and, in fact, the two greatest writers of their respective countries died in the same year. The one came to maturity just when his country, Spain, had passed the apogee of its commercial and maritime greatness and was already on the decline, and the other came to his full flower just at the moment when the British triumph over the Spanish Armada settled for several centuries the rulership of the seas. I have read learned and specious treatises of theorists in literature, who are always ready with profound explanations which explain nothing as concerns the phenomenon of genius, in which I am asked to believe that *Hamlet* and *Coriolanus* and *A Midsummer Night's Dream* and Marlowe's *Dr. Faustus* and Burton's *Anatomy of Melancholy* and Bacon's *Essays* and Chapman's translation of Homer and other classical glories of the Elizabethan period were the direct result of the victory of the English fleet over the Spanish galleons in the

English Channel; that this event led to the expansion of the English mind, causing citizens to wake up and feel their oats, dream new dreams and take on self-assurance and all the panoply of greatness. That would be a very plausible explanation if it could be shown that the Old Testament was produced while the Jews were becoming world-powerful, that Homer wrote in an age of the greatest expansion of the Greeks, that Rabelais got his great burst of energy out of a triumphant France, that De Foe wrote in an age of splendor. It is strange that the same defeat of the Spanish Armada which produced a Shakespeare in England should have caused a Cervantes to flower in Spain. Ah, many deep thoughts which, on analysis, have no sense to them! Cervantes came into the world and wrote a book which was in the main an assault upon "deep thoughts."

A great many people, unfortunately for their own well-being, enjoyment and mental health, know only this much about *Don Quixote,* that in it Cervantes "laughed away" the age of chivalry and that he made his hero charge, with leveled lance, some windmills under the delusion that they were monstrous giants. Lord Byron, the quality of whose mind seems to grow less and less supportable to us year by year (since in so many respects he was like a particularly conceited Hollywood movie actor with a sing-song rhyming talent), was responsible for the first generally false impression. In *Don Juan,* Byron said, "Cervantes smiled Spain's chivalry away... seldom since that day has Spain had heroes.... While Romance could charm, The world gave ground before her bright array; And therefore have his volumes done such harm, That all their glory, as a composition, Was dearly purchased by his land's perdition." Nothing could be more idiotic. Chivalry had been dead two centuries in Spain; what could not be borne was the flood of books, literally thousands of them, celebrating in a stiflingly conventional form and diction the absurdest sort of life it was possible to imagine. The greatest hero Spain ever had was Cervantes himself.

In 1492 a Genoese navigator, with a quaint geographical notion that he could establish a trade route between Spain and India by heading directly west (thus escaping the Mediterranean pirates, the Venetian monopoly, the hazards of going around the Cape, the monsoons of the Bengal ocean and the caravan raids of Berbers, Arabs and Turks), succeeded in persuading the harassed and impoverished Spanish royal family to finance an exploring expedition. The caravel, under the command of Christopher Columbus, never reached India, but it did, eventually, touch land in the fertile islands of the West Indies which Columbus claimed for the Spanish sovereigns. On the return of the voyagers, Columbus and other Spanish soldiers and adventurers set out and discovered the mainland of the western hemisphere, inaugurating an era of discovery, territorial conquest and plunder in Central and South America and Mexico, which was to bring back gold and silver in vast quantities from a dying civilization that had been greater in many respects than its conquerors had ever known. The sixteenth was Spain's great century and, in literature and in the arts, it produced nothing except some fine swords and rapiers of an especially fine-tempered Toledo steel and some sickening imitations of the *Amadis of Gaul*, the *Romance of the Rose*, and medieval French balladry. It was not until the seventeenth century when Spain was politically and commercially on the skids that she produced her two greatest writers, Lope de Vega and Miguel de Cervantes. The first part of *Don Quixote* was published in 1605. J. D. M. Ford in his *Main Currents of Spanish Literature* says, "it is of record that no *new* novel of chivalry was printed" in Spain *after* that date.

Cervantes, like Dickens, had a father whom one may love but not be constrained to admire: he seems to have been a piddling, helpless sort of fellow, with all the graver faults of a pampered son of a family that has fallen suddenly upon evil times and who is forced to make his way in the world, untrained and undisciplined in work or application, and yet fretfully of the opinion that one who is used to luxury and to lording it over people when the family was in funds should be permitted to do so when the family hasn't a sou. In consequence of this sweet and troublesome dementia, Roderigo de Cervantes spent an unconscionably large part of his time in jail for debt, loudly protesting that it was not meet that a *hidalgo* should be treated thus. (Cervantes has the realistic niece of Don Quixote remind the crazy man that one cannot act the *hidalgo*, if one has no money, even if one is by title a *hidalgo;* for it costs money to be a lordly fellow. And Russian grand dukes and grand duchesses, after the Bolshevist revolution, discovered that, whereas many Americans and western Europeans of wealth found them socially charming and invited them to their tables, they also found them economically so grave a disappointment that they rarely stood ready to give them jobs, much less advance them any considerable amount of money.)

Miguel de Unamuno reminds us that the law of the Partida in Spain describes a *hidalgo* or *hijodalgo*, as meaning *hijo de bienes*, or "son of good things"; but that "this term is not to be understood to mean temporal wealth; for there are innumerable poor gentlemen, and innumerable rich men who are not gentlemen." Maybe so; but Roderigo de Cervantes understood it to mean that, being of noble descent, he shouldn't pay his bills; and they clapped him in jail for this opinion. And, incredibly enough, in a way he was right. Years back the nobles had made things easy for themselves and, having the power to do so, had passed a law stating that a *hidalgo* was not required to pay taxes and could not be jailed for his debts. Roderigo asked his judges to look up the law and they did, finding that, indeed, a *hidalgo* could not be imprisoned for debt. After nearly a year they released him, but then it occurred to them that, although the law was as it was on the books, they had no proof that Roderigo was a *hidalgo*. So they clapped him into jail again, until he furnished proof (which was forthcoming) that he was a *hidalgo*.

The next thing for a released *hidalgo* who cannot be imprisoned for debt to do is to establish credit among the tradesmen, and this poor Roderigo was unable to do, for if by law a *hidalgo* may escape his debts, then it is expedient to require cash of him. This put a great strain upon the poor fellow; he had a wife and seven children living in poverty on some mortgaged property in Alcalá while he was making shift to earn a living as a barber-surgeon in the more populous town of Valladolid and there being imprisoned for debt. He seems to have known almost nothing about the profession he was engaged in, his knowledge being confined to what he could get out of a volume on "The Four Diseases" and a copy of Galen's medical dissertations.

Let us pity Cervantes' mother, Leonor de Cortinas who, from the few accounts we have of her, was a patient and capable woman, brave in the face of adversity. It seems probable that when she married Roderigo the latter was a charming, dashing, irresponsible son of the vigorous and wealthy Juan de Cervantes who was a successful lawyer and a city magistrate of Cordova. It would appear that the couple had barely got settled in marriage when a financial depression blasted the fortunes of Juan, sweeping away much of his property and income and thus cutting Roderigo and other dependent sons off from the inheritance that had been settled upon them and forcing them to shift for themselves. The blow to Juan's fortunes appears to have crippled his assurance and to have somewhat unsettled his temper, for the next we hear of him he has only a deputy magistracy in the smaller city of Cuenca. We learn that he was soon dismissed from this position and fined twenty ducats on charges made and substantiated by one Diego Cordido, to the effect that Juan de Cervantes had subjected him to the torture (or, as we would call it, the third degree) unjustly and without cause and had confined him in jail for three months without due process of law.

The formal education of Miguel de Cervantes was negligible and desultory; and although he may have acquired the equivalent of a common school education, it is quite certain, I take it, that he never attended the University at Alcalá, in which city he was born in the year 1547. Some biographers have assumed that he did attend the university although no one has been able to find his name among the records; but Cervantes tells us quite definitely that he knew almost no Latin, and Latin was about the only thing that was taught with any enthusiasm and persistence in the medieval universities.

From a legendary account, corroborated by a semi-autobiographical passage in one of his minor works, it seems probable that as a lad he was a page in the household of Cardinal Guilio Acquiviva. If he was, he would have there been subjected to a certain amount of educational training imposed by the cardinals upon the ignorant and immature servants recruited from semi-noble or *hidalgo* rank, who might be expected to show talent which would later be of service to the prelate. Another member of the household was a youngster of Cervantes' own age, possibly a natural son of the cardinal, and who bore a title. Cervantes was classed as a "relative" in the household, so it was possible for him to become an intimate of the young heir on grounds of social equality. The first fruits of their social equality, however, was a murder charge lodged against Cervantes. The titled youth fell in love with a young woman beneath his social station, to whom marriage was forbidden him by his father. He paid court to her nevertheless and, accompanied by Cervantes one night, sought a rendezvous with her, but while nearing her house two assailants, either brothers of the girl or a rival lover and a friend, fell upon the youths with drawn swords. Cervantes and his companion drew their rapiers and in the fight the two assailants were killed. The victors tried to cover up their part in the affair, but at last, to escape the law, were obliged to take refuge in a monastery and thereafter set out for foreign territory in the garb of monks. Cervantes was then twenty-two and he was not to return to Spain for twelve years. He made his way into France and seems to have served in Flanders in the army of Charles V, and later we pick up his trail definitely in a garrison in Naples where he is enlisted in the army of the alliance of Spain, Venice and the Papacy, and where his brother Roderigo is also a soldier. Two years later, as an officer under the command of Don Juan of Austria and the Duke of Sessa, Cervantes took part in the great and decisive naval battle of Lepanto in which the Spanish Armada captured or destroyed the Turkish fleet comprised of more than two hundred galleys, a squadron of galleasses and sailing ships, and some thirty thousand troops. Cervantes was severely wounded and his left hand was nearly torn off from a blast of lead from a harquebus. He never regained the use of his left hand.

While on garrison duty in Italy, Cervantes visited the various cities on leave and he tells of strolling the streets of Genoa, Venice, Naples and Palermo. On the return of the victorious fleet to the base at Messina, Cervantes was long in a hospital recovering from his wounds, and it was not until spring of the year after the battle that he has fully recovered. He returned to his post and reported for duty, but after one small scouting trip through the Ægean in search of Turkish ships, Cervantes' active soldiering came to an end. He tired of garrison duty and asked for letters of recommendation from Don Juan of Austria and the Duke of Sessa to Philip II in Spain.

This was in Cervantes' thirtieth year. Returning to Spain on a troop ship from Naples, the ship was held up by Algerian pirates off the French Riviera and Cervantes along with a number of others was taken prisoner. A penniless and improvident soldier, whose entire family was poverty-stricken, he had the misfortune to carry in his pockets those letters of recommendation signed by a great duke and a great commander. The letters convinced the pirates that Cervantes was one of the prizes of their haul, which included several nobles and men of property. They fixed Cervantes' ransom at five hundred ducats. There had not been that much cash in the Cervantes family in all its known history.

So Cervantes was fated to remain five years in an Algerian camp as a slave of the pirates who unsuccessfully negotiated with Spain for his release. During those five years, however, his life was fairly easy. Unlike the "common" captives (because they thought his family was very rich) he was not compelled to do backbreaking labor and he says he was never struck by his master. He wrote plays and got up entertainments in which his fellow captives took part and so ingratiated himself that he almost effected the escape of himself and his fellow captors on one occasion without being disciplined for it.

He had seen others crucified and broken on the rack who tried the same thing. To save his fellow captors from punishment he took the blame for the whole affair, saying that it was he who planned the escape.

A monk sent among the pirates to negotiate for the ransom of some Spanish nobles became interested in Cervantes. Through a grant to the mother of Cervantes by the King of about a third of the ransom for Cervantes' services in the army, contributions raised among charitable institutions and through the heroic and self-sacrificing efforts of Cervantes' mother, the five hundred ducats were raised and the monk was sent to bring Cervantes back. Another day and Cervantes would have been bound for Constantinople, there to be sold into slavery in the public mart. His captors were getting impatient and a political change in Algiers made their stay there hazardous. Cervantes was in irons aboard ship when he was delivered.

On his return to Spain Cervantes gave up soldiering for literature and engaged in a furious activity of literary production. He wrote poems, plays, prose romances, and literary criticism. He imitated the popular models, but with no success. He wrote some flattering poems angling for a patron, but without success. He addressed fulsome tribute in verse to Lope de Vega and this got him nothing either. He was in dire straits. His entire family had sacrificed nearly all they had to effect his release; two sisters had contributed dowries. In an effort to get a footing in literary society, he was reduced to writing advertisements in verse form for the books and plays of others and to collaborating with celebrated playwrights as an unidentified "ghost." He had a reputation as a writer for cutting, satirical characterizations in verse and seems to have been called upon to furnish bits of this kind even by the famous Lope de Vega.

His indigence did not deter him from gallantry, and in 1584 he became the father of an illegitimate daughter, borne him by an actress, Anna Francisea de Rojas. This daughter, Isabel, was later to play a considerable part in his life. That same year Cervantes married a widow, Dona Catalina de Palacios, who brought to him a small country estate with an orchard and a vineyard, a comfortably furnished house, a well-stocked larder, a small chicken farm and a going business in the making, bottling and sale of wine. For a considerable time Cervantes seems to have been so gratified at an opportunity to eat regularly that he became a small squire managing his property, which was not far from Madrid, and pursued a leisurely course of writing, or rather of trying to write, for the theater. He wrote, in all, about thirty plays, a few of which were produced; but although he says they were received "without cucumbers and other things that may be thrown, or hisses or catcalls," they brought him little money.

What is worse, his little chicken farm and vineyard ceased to support himself, his wife and his three step-children, and next we find him in the civil service in Seville while his family is left on the farm. In his job in the Service of Supply of the King's army, his duties included the requisitioning of food and farm products, clothing, harness, horses, etc., and the distribution of them to the camps and garrisons and to the port of the Spanish fleet. This was a job which proved much too big for Cervantes; for the King was engaged in no less a project than equipping the Spanish Armada with which he hoped to sweep the English from the seas. His own fleet was swept from the seas instead and meanwhile, as a supply commandant, Cervantes had proved himself singularly inefficient.

First, he was embroiled with a prelate for having taken supplies from property belonging to the church and the ban of excommunication was placed upon him. He succeeded in getting this ban removed only with difficulty (excommunication was less to be feared because of its religious significance than because it deprived one of definite privileges as a free citizen). The defeat of the Armada brought further confusion, Cervantes' accounts became involved, whether through defalcation on his part or simply because of bad bookkeeping, we cannot determine. In a panic he tried to escape to America by asking for a Central or South American appointment. This was refused. Auditors began to investigate his books and found them in hopeless confusion. He had deposited government funds with a Portuguese banker, who promptly failed. Cervantes could not be held responsible for this, but it hastened his dismissal. The final auditing of his books showed that about one thousand dollars could not be accounted for. Cervantes was, therefore, arrested and thrown into jail. He was freed after four months under bail and under promise of restoring the money, which he never did.

His whereabouts from 1597 to 1602 are not known, but in the latter year he is in trouble with the courts again on account of debt. He disappears once more from sight for two more years and turns up, at Valladolid, at the age of fifty-seven with the manuscript of an immortal masterpiece, *Don Quixote*. The book is an immediate and sensational success, but because there was no copyright, pirated editions were brought out and he made but little money out of it.

Next year he and his wife, his daughter, Isabel, his two sisters, and a niece are all cooped up together in a lodging house in a mean street. A duel is fought in front of the house and a noble rake is killed. The whole Cervantes family is lodged in prison as accomplices on the suspicion that the death was brought about through the loose morals of Isabel. The family is released when no evidence is produced connecting them with the affair.

Cervantes continues to write furiously, turning out his next greatest work, the *Exemplary Novels,* which are broad and humorous parodies, rich in observation and in characteristic Cervantesque detail, purporting to be stories of an elevating moral nature, but in reality are stories satirical, non-moral, and rather bawdy. Also, he produces a long and rather uninteresting poem, *Voyage to Parnassus,* in *terza rima.* But all along he is at work on the thing nearest to his heart, the second part of *Don Quixote.* The characters have taken hold of him. He has noted what the critics said about the first part— that it was too diffuse and that some of the adventures are too extravagant. He can learn from the critics; and besides he is an excellent critic himself as is revealed in the chapter on the books in Don Quixote's library with the descriptions of the books which the curate and the barber consign to the flames as having addled the brains of the poor scarecrow. Moreover, he sees now that what he started out to write has become not simply a satirical burlesque but an analogue of all mankind's adventures on this earth. Every character a writer creates is autobiographical, male and female, hero and villain, and into the characters of Don Quixote and Sancho Panza, Cervantes threw all of himself, all his own aspirations and experiences. He will not turn it over to the publishers until he is satisfied with it. He collects some of his plays and publishes them; he does miscellaneous hack work. He is an aging man now, suffering from dropsy, but still full of spirit and with dignity of bearing. At sixty-six, he tells us that he is "a man of aquiline visage, with chestnut hair, smooth and unruffled brow, with sparkling eyes, and a nose arched, although well proportioned, a silver beard, although not twenty years ago it was golden, large moustache, small mouth, teeth not important, for there are but six of them and those in ill condition and worse placed because they do not correspond the one with the other, the body between two extremes, neither large nor small, the complexion bright, rather white than brown, somewhat heavy shouldered, and not very nimble on the feet."

In 1615 he delivers the second part of *Don Quixote* to the printer. That same year, while his fame is known all through Europe and Skelton has already published his famous translation in England, Cervantes was living in distressing poverty. On April 23, 1616, he died and was buried in a grave which cannot be located.

BESIDES *Don Quixote* Cervantes wrote many minor works which need concern only special students; but aside from his great masterpiece, the *Exemplary Novels* are also decidedly worth reading.

Don Quixote, like *Jurgen*, is a comedy of justice and of man's quest for ideals of his own dreaming which, unfortunately, conflict too frequently with workaday reality. Don Quixote, like Cervantes' father, is a poor noble in a poor land, a dry land where rain has eroded all the fine soil to the bare rocks and sand, verdure has largely disappeared and poor nobles as well as peasants are hard put to draw from the soil enough sustenance to maintain their bodies. Even the wealth wrung by the old nobles from the toil of their serfs has disappeared, for gold cannot be eaten, and when there is no real wealth about, gold quickly vanishes and leaves one with property which is more a burden than a source of income. The people become nomad herdsmen instead of agriculturists and subsist on water, wine, a little bread, beef and occasionally mutton or by rare chance a bit of fowl.

We discover one plain *quisada* (or *quesada*), thus impoverished at the age of fifty, living on an inherited estate, with a woman servant of forty and a young niece. He is of "a strong complexion, dry flesh, and withered face." The reality he knows is exceedingly dreary, so he escapes from it by reading books of knighthood. Great words and high sentiments enchanted him. When he read, "The reason of the unreasonableness which against my reason is wrought, doth so weaken my reason, as with all reason I do justly complain of your beauty," or, "The high heavens, which with your divinity do fortify you divinely with the stars, and make you deserveress of the deserts which your greatness deserves," he is in transports like Matthew Arnold reading the exalted nonsense of Dante and Milton. He bought every book of the sort he could lay his hands on, and his acres of arable land gradually went to others for cash that he might buy the books which addled his brain. Instead of looking after his estate, cultivating his garden, he entered into disputes with the village curate (a learned man) and the village barber, as to whether Palmerin of England or Amadis of Gaul was the better knight or whether, after all, Don Galaor, Amadis' brother, was not worth the two of them put together.

Such deep problems sent him into such an orgy of reading and meditation that his "wit was wholly extinguished" and he "fell into one of the strangest conceits that ever madman stumbled on in this world; to wit, it seemed unto him very requisite and behooveful, as well for the augmentation of his honour as also for the benefit of the commonwealth, that he himself should become a knight-errant, and go throughout the world, with his horse and armour, to seek adventures, and practice in person all that he had read was used by knights of yore; revenging of all kinds of injuries, and offering himself to occasions and dangers, which, being once happily achieved, might gain him eternal renown."

Among his heirlooms is a suit of rusty armor, without a helmet or a morion, but he hastily supplies the deficiency with papers pasted together. He has also an old sword, broken at the handle, and he ties and pastes up this weapon. He has a lance, too, but it is fragile. He has a horse, all skin and bones, which he thinks is superior to Alexander's Bucephalus, and he spends four days devising a name for him, finally hitting upon Rosinante as being a name "lofty, full and significant." Next he must have a name more resounding than Mr. Quisada, and remembering that Amadis was not satisfied with the "dry name of Amadis, but added thereunto the name of his kingdom and his country," he calls himself Don Quixote de la Mancha, thereby honoring the province in which he resided.

Thus accoutered against all common sense and reason, Don Quixote sets out. He travels a full day without encountering any injustice which needed to be righted, no dragons to slay, no imperiled virgins to rescue, and comes at last to an inn presided over by a dull practical fellow and servanted by two harlots, who appear to him "two fair maidens or lovely ladies taking their ease at the gate of the castle." He addresses them at length in the most poetically highfalutin terms, and they hear him patiently and kindly and, when he is finished, ask "whether he would have something to eat." Quixote recalls that to maintain his strength he must replenish his belly and does eat; but he is bothered in his conscience that he is not truly a knight and must be dubbed so. He empowers the inn-keeper to dispense this honor and, as inn-keepers immemorially follow the doctrine that "the customer is always right" (so long as he pays his bills), the inn-keeper gave him the prescribed whack over the head with a sword and pronounced the sacred words which an

English monarch so ennobled when in his cups at a feast, he dubbed a side of beef Sir Loin.

Immediately, however, Don Quixote's beautiful misunderstanding of the ways the affairs of this world are conducted become painfully manifest. The inn-keeper presents him with a bill. Don Quixote hasn't a nickel. He had never read "in the histories of knights-errant that they carried any money." That money is required to carry on the pursuits of honor, justice and chivalry had not occurred to Don Quixote. The inn-keeper makes it quite plain that this is the case. And so endeth Don Quixote's first lesson in the evils of this world. He returns home and by "selling one thing, pawning another and making a bad bargain in every case," he rakes up a little money and, being heedless of affairs, quite fails to observe that when you have possessions which seem to you of great value, you can get almost nothing for them when you are forced to dispose of them. On his return home (where he finds his niece and housekeeper, the curate and the barber, not in sympathy with his shenanigans and thoroughly convinced that he was a fool and a madman) he bethinks himself that he is lacking in something; all knights have squires. (One may read into this, perhaps a symbol: that one cannot achieve great deeds of splendor and knightliness unless there is one to do the dirty work and that the only way one can get any one to do this dirty work is to promise him money or glory.)

Quixote has a neighbor, Sancho Panza, "an honest man (if the title of honesty may be given the poor), but one of a very shallow wit" to whom he sold the idea that the wars he was about to make were from the highest ideals and bound to be successful, and, moreover, in Don Quixote's Alexandrian conquests he would reward Sancho with the governorship of the first island that came under his reign. Sancho has a mule, he is tired of his nagging wife, and so, with high hopes, he sets out, squire to the redoubtable Don Quixote de la Mancha.

Their deeds and their discomfitures are told by Cervantes in about three hundred and twenty-five thousand words. I shall not attempt to brief them; for in each adventure, the essence of the humor and the wisdom is in Cervantes' treatment of it, his sub-acid comments, his calm force of understatement, his bland affirmation of what we know, sometimes with anguish, to be the reality of life. When Cervantes describes a muleteer as one "who could not have much good nature in him" and shows him as giving Don Quixote a gratuitous kick in the ribs when the Don has fallen off his horse in full armor and cannot rise, we see what a master of effective under-statement Cervantes is. When he sees a peasant flogging a boy servant, he cries to him to desist in the name of the God that rules and the sun that shines upon us, or by God's grace he will run him through with a lance. The peasant argues that it is his right and privilege to beat a bound-boy; that's the law. Whereupon Don Quixote offers to pay him the sum necessary to redeem the boy—as soon as he can dig up the money. The peasant agrees, waits until the Don is out of sight and beats the daylights out of the poor lad in revenge for having been censured. "Thus," writes Cervantes, "did the valiant Don Quixote right that wrong."

That is the wisdom and the flavor of *Don Quixote*. The sub-acid counsel of it is so humane and merciful and bitter and just that literature was never to know any books comparable to it, in kind, until the *Penguin Island* of Anatole France, *The Crock of Gold* by James Stephens, and the *Jurgen* of James Branch Cabell.

CHAUCER *AND THE ENGLISH SPIRIT*

*

WHEN François Villon was a tractable lad, living in a cloister of the University of Paris, he studied *The Art of Versifying and of Making Ballades and Chants-Royaux* by Eustace Deschamps. The author of this book was born in the same year as Chaucer and became so devoted a friend of the Englishman that he felt privileged to deplore Chaucer's weakness for women and to warn him against the evils of self-indulgence.

Both men were born at the outset of the Hundred Years' War between England and France, and if it should seem strange that an Englishman and a Frenchman living in that unhappy period were close friends, it should be made clear that the Hundred Years' War was a horribly absurd affair wherein an English king, told by his business manager that there was no money to be had anywhere, invaded France after calling in the dukes of the realm and making them a proposition. If they could raise an army of mercenaries he would pay them a specified sum out of the ransom money they were able to extract from captured French towns.

And French kings, equally hard up, would make the same sort of promises to their marshals and princes, and declare war upon England. Meanwhile, free passage through the countries nominally at war was a common granting on either side; and Frenchmen taken prisoners and held for ransom, which the French kings could not pay, civilized the courts of England. On each side these prisoners were given every freedom. The French prisoners organized tournaments, taught the English falconry, balladry and the arts of the chase. It was a game, this century long war, played by kings and princes who used their subjects as pawns of taxation in a stupid game of chess among themselves.

I say "stupid" because the long, desultory wars got them nowhere. They depleted the royal treasuries on both sides, brought about the Peasant Revolt in France and the Wat Tyler Rebellion in England. The economic realities of the time were clear, not to the sovereigns of France and England but to the astute and ingenious gentlemen who founded the Hanseatic League and who traded at all the ports of Christendom and even dealt in ivory, apes and peacocks among the heretics and schismatics. The Easterlings, who were the English representatives and correspondents of the Hanseatic League who gave to English coinage the designation Pound Sterling, had docks and warehouses in the very London neighborhood where Geoffrey Chaucer grew up as a child.

During the Hundred Years' War Chaucer visited France on several occasions of the various "truces" and at none of these times suffered so much inconvenience as when, with a band of archers foraging for food before Reims in Edward II's unsuccessful assault upon that city, he was taken prisoner by French skirmishers and held for ransom at sixteen pounds (computed at about $1,250 nowadays), which the king paid. Jean Froissart, the French historian, author of the famous *Chronicles*, visited England during the Hundred Years' War as the guest of his countrywoman, Queen Phillippa, wife of Edward III, and, by bringing histories of French and Norman heroes into England, gave rise to the notion that England might yet be the nation indistinct from France.

Chaucer and Deschamps were born in 1340. In that year England decided to become English and abolished the law of Englishry, which gave special protection to those of Anglo-Saxon extraction.

But French was still the language of the courts of law, of diplomacy and of the king and his counselors. It was not until Chaucer was sixteen years old that a law was passed requiring all hearings in the Sheriff's Court to be made in the vulgar tongue, that is to say, in the Midland dialect of Anglo-Saxon which Chaucer spoke and used. And not until Chaucer was twenty-two years of age did English become the official language of parliament.

It was not until fifty years after Chaucer's death that the use of French disappeared entirely in England in favor of the Midland Anglo-Saxon dialect in which Chaucer wrote. His poems, so universally known, solidified and formed the language. It was the language that was to dominate England until the expansive Elizabethan period.

It was a language quite difficult for us to follow now, so difficult, indeed, that we cannot read Chaucer, "the father of English literature," without glossaries and (if we read it aloud in mixed company) without a bit of hemming and hawing. You have heard of the crude four and five letter Anglo-Saxon words: Chaucer used nearly all of them.

Long before Chaucer lived, centuries, in fact, before he lived, there was an Anglo-Saxon literature, and also a Celtic literature. There was an "Anglo-Saxon" language and literature so stable, so well-defined, so common that it ceased to function only after the Norman conquest of England in 1066. The Norman conquerors were not French but Vikings with mixed blood, Celtic, Pict and Danish, who used, however, the prevailing dialect of what is now Northern France and Belgium.

The great Anglo-Saxon classic *Beowulf* was written in this pre-Norman language. Let us, please, forget it. Perhaps in college you had a year or so of Anglo-Saxon and had to study it. So did I. The professors who taught it disliked it more thoroughly than I who never mastered it at all. Let's not feel bad about not knowing *Beowulf*. The late Sir Edmund Gosse has absolved us from all feelings of respect that we may imagine we ought to feel toward the epic. It must have caused Sir Edmund great anguish of soul to release us from the necessity of admiring *Beowulf;* for that dreadful composition had so long been, like Magna Carta, a sacred monument which it were treason not to worship; and Sir Edmund became Sir Edmund instead of plain Edmund Gosse by harping on the sacred traditions of Old England. In *More Books on the Table,* Sir Edmund writes apropos of the translation of *Beowulf* into modern English by C. Scott-Moncrieff:

"People have talked as though the author of *Beowulf* was a far-away precursor of Mr. Rudyard Kipling. This is surely a patriotic illusion. There is nothing English about *Beowulf*, so far as I can see, except the curious and agreeable fact that it comes to us composed in the language employed in Merica, that is to say, Leicestershire, about the year 700. Not an English place or person is mentioned in it, except one king who may or may not be English, for I have my doubts about Offa. Whether it is likely that a poem mainly describing the seacoast and maritime adventure should have been conceived in the neighborhood of Ashby-de-la-Zouch I leave to more learned pens than mine. But all the scenes and all the personages are clearly Scandinavian. . . . The landscape is consistently Danish. . . . Judged by any modern standard, the method of *Beowulf* is bewildering in the extreme. The poet seems to have drawn no distinction between the real and the unreal."

After that from the unofficial prose laureate of England, why should you and I beat our brains in an effort to admire *Beowulf?* But the *Canterbury Tales* of Geoffrey Chaucer are perennially fresh, perennially diverting: they are of the stuff of good literature. If one finds these poems difficult to follow in the original, there is an excellent version in modern Anglo-American by William Van Wyck.

CHAUCER was born (so scholars have generally agreed) in 1340, in a tenement near the docks of London, probably close to the foot of the King's Highway. His father, John Chaucer, was a wine merchant who seems to have been high in favor with King Edward III. Kings met on terms of equality in those days with commoners of the prosperous class, and we hear of Henry Picard, a friend of John Chaucer's and also a wine merchant, who entertained in his home Edward III, King John of France, King David of the Scots, the King of Cyprus and the Prince of Wales. The age of chivalry was passing; the country was very poor; and kings and princes as well as knights engaged in trade.

Medieval London was a crude, barbaric and filthy city. The streets, after rains, were deep in mud and muck; sanitary arrangements were almost nil and it was customary to throw one's slops and garbage out of the window. The masses of the poor lived in the utmost squalor; rats and vermin were prevalent, and every one, high and low, suffered from lice. Twice in Chaucer's boyhood the bubonic plague broke out in the walled city of London and spread through the countryside, killing about a fourth of the entire population. London was unpoliced; robberies, stabbings, drunkenness and debauchery were common; the amusements of the people were savage and cruel; and the heads of those who were declared traitors (a broad political indictment) were suspended from pikes on London Bridge and on the Tower, and parts of the corpses of criminals that had been drawn and quartered were exposed as a warning, and of course spreading stench and pestilence.

Nevertheless, there were public schools and lads were flogged by schoolmasters for breaches of discipline and made to study Latin and the elements of arithmetic, reading and writing. French was spoken as much as English in Chaucer's time; and among Chaucer's accomplishments was a fluency in several languages, including Dutch and Italian, which caused him to be chosen for several diplomatic missions.

As a boy Chaucer was a page in the service of the Countess of Ulster, wife of Prince Lionel, who was the son of Edward III. One of the few authentic accounts we have of his early years is an item showing that in 1357 there was awarded to Geoffrey Chaucer a short cloak, a pair of red and black breeches and shoes. He was early brought into contact with court life and with such cultivation as there was in England. He learned to compose verses, ballades and rondels, after the approved verse forms of the time. He wrote a number of poems about unrequited passions; but to do so was a convention, and it is obvious from his later work that he was well versed in venery.

When Edward III organized his large but ineffectual army and invaded France in 1359, Chaucer was a soldier of the king. Service in the army was voluntary; but levies were also made upon the countryside. Archers were the mainstay of the army; but a considerable body of soldiers was made up of Welshmen, armed only with daggers or with long knives—undisciplined and savage troops who caused great anguish to their king by rushing in close on the French archers, hacking and stabbing them instead of taking them prisoner to be held for ransom. The expedition was a costly failure, because the French withdrew within their walled cities and would not give fight, except sporadically. Food was scarce and the invaders nearly starved; more died of lack of nourishment and disease than in combat. Chaucer in command of a small band of archers was taken prisoner and held for ransom, which the king paid.

Throughout his youth Chaucer seems to have been bound out at various times in the service of some noble in Edward's court and because of his natural ability and pleasing personality, together with his gift for rhyming, climbed steadily in court favor. The next we hear of him he is either married to, or living with, one of the ladies of the Countess of Ulster's household, a woman who had at least taken his name, calling herself Phillippa Chaucer. This was the woman who was, or who became, his legal wife, bringing him a considerable fortune, so it is probable that she and Chaucer were married at the time we first hear of her. Phillippa was granted a life pension by the Queen; and she seems to have served as a lady-in-waiting or mistress of the chamber to the wife of John of Gaunt as well as to the Countess of Ulster and the Queen.

Chaucer meanwhile, in 1367, is a servant of Edward III. His task was to wait on tables, make beds and perform other menial tasks under the direction of the chamberlain. He wore livery and slept with other yeomen, two abed in the great hall at Westminster Palace. He had a daily allowance of a portion of bread, a plate of stew and a gallon of beer; he was clothed and shod at the king's expense and given a small allowance of money. A few years later he has risen in the king's favor to the office of squire, and his work seems to have been largely that of entertaining the king and his court, reading and reciting chronicles, writing verses, getting up games and small entertainments, organizing hunts and in general making himself agreeable. His pay was increased; he had a private room and a servant; and his allowance of beer was increased to a gallon and a half a day. His daily companions were French nobles, even King John himself, all held for ransom which the French towns would not pay.

At the age of thirty Chaucer was so highly regarded by the king that he was entrusted with a mission of some sort abroad. He subsequently went to France and Italy on several occasions and all of the trips appear to have been of a commercial rather than a political nature. He was an accountant and probably had some commercial experience under the Easterlings. In 1372 he spent a year in Florence and Genoa, largely in establishing trade relations between Genoa and London. From the Clerk's Tale in the *Canterbury Tales* it would seem that Chaucer may have met Petrarch in Padua. However, Chaucer does not say that *he* learned the story of the Patient Griselda from Petrarch but that the clerk did. And I think it is hardly likely that Petrarch related the story to Chaucer. In 1372 Petrarch was an old man, with but two more years to live. Moreover he had renounced his poems and was very bitter about them. He could not bear to have them mentioned. He was devoting himself to the revival of Greek and Latin learning. That Chaucer met Boccaccio, to whom he owed so much in the nature of plot material, seems to me the more likely although nowhere does he mention Boccaccio. But whether he met Petrarch or Boccaccio or not, it is certain that he became well acquainted with the work of both men and also with a considerable body of Italian literature, including the work of Dante, from whose work he did not hesitate to lift whole passages word for word, translate them and incorporate them into poems of his own.

Besides making two business trips to Italy, and undertaking several missions to France and the Netherlands, he was also sent with two others as ambassador to arrange for the marriage of the young Richard II to the daughter of the king of France, negotiations which did not produce the desired results. His fortunes steadily improved; in 1374 he was made comptroller of customs at the port of London; given a daily grant of a pitcher of wine for life (like the present poet laureate of England, John Masefield, to whom the custom of the post grants a wine allowance, Chaucer later asked to be paid the money equivalent of the wine; and the wine grant was turned into a pension amounting to about $1,000 a year in our money). His first comptrollership was over only wool, skins and leather but a year later he was put in full charge of all customs. His salary was a considerable one for the times; and besides, both he and his wife had pensions from John of Gaunt and from the King. It is estimated that his income was about $5,000 a year at that time.

He had twelve years of uninterrupted prosperity, living in rooms in Aldgate Tower, translating Boethius, writing his *Troilus and Cressida,* the *Legend of Good Women,* the *Parliament of Fowls* and his great work, the *Canterbury Tales.* In his ease and security his genius came to maturity. He was elected to Parliament as Knight of the Shire of Kent, in which county he also held the post of justice of the peace. From the evidence of his poems, he does not seem to have been happily married or always to have lived with his wife. The marriage seems to have been one of convenience, or it may have been a forced marriage. But on the other hand it may have been a normally happy marriage, because divorce was easy for a man to obtain in those days (though not for a woman) and could be had by simple formal repudiation. And Chaucer never divorced his wife.

In his forty-first year, however, he seems to have brought a young unmarried woman, Cecilia Chaumpaigne, to bed with an illegitimate child and he was forced to buy her off and bring up the son as his own. There exists a document whereby Cecilia renounces all claims she has against Geoffrey Chaucer *de raptu meo.* The term *raptu* may have meant rape; but more likely it was simply a seduction under promise of marriage, with the result that she was entitled by law to bring bastardy charges against him. Skeats, the great authority on Chaucer, believes that Chaucer's "little sown Lowis" was his child by Cecilia Chaumpaigne.

In 1387 Chaucer's wife died and in the following year his fortunes began to wane. In the minority of Richard II who, like his father Edward III, had been a friend and patron of Chaucer, the finances of the country were in bad condition. Richard had been extremely extravagant, and the House of Commons shut down on his supplies and refused to permit the transaction of any business for two months, demanding that he get rid of his ministers and chief supporters. Either because Chaucer was a favorite of Richard's or because he mismanaged his office, he was deprived of, or had to give up, his post as comptroller of the customs. Suddenly losing his chief income, we must infer that he had been improvident and extravagant, because within a year he was bankrupt and assigned his pensions to John Scalby, a money-lender.

But when Richard II reached his twentieth birthday in 1389, he suddenly and dramatically asserted himself, having come of legal age to reign, dismissed his chancellor, ordered the arrest, trial and execution of some of his enemies, recalled John of Gaunt, who had gone to Spain in hopes of becoming king of Castile, and appointed Chaucer clerk of the king's works at the Palace of Westminster, at the Tower of London, and at the king's various castles, manors, lodges, parks, stables, gardens and fish-ponds. He empowered Chaucer to draft laborers "with or without all liberties" and to set them to work repairing the roadways, under pain of imprisonment, at wages stipulated by royal order. Chaucer then was, in fact, a contractor, on a salary, and probably with commissions; and he was engaged in rebuilding St. George's Chapel at Windsor, repairing castles, dikes and drains, and in the erection of a grandstand for the Smithfield tournament in 1390.

In that same year Chaucer was twice fallen upon by highway robbers who took everything he had on him, including, it seems, his workmen's payroll. For one reason or another he was deprived of his clerkship and he seems to have fallen upon hard times until the last year of his life. He held no post of importance and no public office except that of Forester in Somerset. In 1394 Richard II granted him a pension of twenty pounds a year; and when Henry IV came to the throne he increased the pension slightly; but the royal treasury was frequently empty and Chaucer had to dun the king repeatedly for the money due him. He was sued by Isabella Buckholt for a debt of about 15 pounds in 1398; the sheriff reported that Chaucer had no attachable assets, and the king granted him letters of protection against arrests, suits and attachments of his property. He also seems to have been under the protection of John of Gaunt, who some scholars believe, was his brother-in-law. The Katherine Synford who married John of Gaunt may have been a sister of Phillippa Chaucer.

As he neared the end of his life, Chaucer became somewhat embittered and wrote poems voicing his distress; but he was never in actual want. He had wealthy and influential friends and G. G. Coulter (author of *Chaucer and His England*) seems to have established the fact that he had a wealthy son or step-son, Thomas Chaucer, who was chief butler to Richard II, Henry IV and Henry V, constable of Wallingford castle, member of Parliament from Oxfordshire, commissioner for the marriage of Henry V, ambassador to France, member of the King's Council and a very rich man.

In 1393 Chaucer wrote the *Treatise on the Astrolabe* to teach his young son, Lowis or Lowys, the "science touching numbers and proportions." On December 24, 1399, he leased a tenement in the garden of St. Mary's Chapel, and in this house he died on October 25, 1400. He was buried in Westminster Abbey.

One of the peculiarities of Chaucer is that, although he lived through troublous and stirring times and participated in them as a soldier, ambassador, business man, court officer, magistrate, member of parliament and poet, it never occurred to him to refer to any of the great events of his day. It was an insane century, the fourteenth: Charles VI was a raving maniac on the throne of France; Timur conquered Persia and subdued part of India; Wenceslas, the drunken and violent king of Bohemia, ruled with a turbulent and bloody hand; the Peasant Revolt broke out with the insurrection of Wat Tyler; the Swiss and Austrians were at war; Wickliffe translated the New Testament into Chaucer's English; Gregory XI returned from Avignon to Rome, ending the long exile of the papacy; the Protestant revolt became widespread; France and England were engaged in a protracted desultory war; the Scots invaded England and the English retaliated by burning Edinburgh; the battle of Chevy Chase was fought; John V, emperor of the Eastern empire, was dethroned by the Turks and his empire made subject to the Ottoman rule; the schism of the papacy took place, two popes reigning, Urban VI and Clement VII, the Black Death ravaged all Europe—and all of these things Chaucer ignored in his writings.

That he did so indicates that he believed that material things are transitory but things of the spirit endure. He was first and foremost a poet, the first and one of the few great poets in English literature. He was a superb story-teller, a matchless technician, a man of great breadth of mind, humorous, realistic, of a happy nature, sanguine, hearty, without illusions. He was a fat little man, accustomed to drinking great quantities of ale and wine. He touched upon every variety of English life. He created immortal characters in the figures of the *Canterbury Tales*. He invented the meter and rhyme scheme he used and, although he drew upon Livy, Æsop, Petrarch, Dante, Boccaccio and a variety of other sources, he made his borrowings indelibly his own. Not all of Chaucer is entertaining or valuable to us now. Perhaps we could easily do without all of his work except the *Canterbury Tales* and some parts of these tales are uninteresting to us. But the spirit of the *Canterbury Tales* is the spirit that is English: it is an earthy spirit, taking delight in all the simple pleasures of life, free-minded, humorous, indulgent and kind.

SHAKESPEARE *THE MIRROR*

*

EVERY one who has thought about Shakespeare at all seems to have had a clear idea as to what Shakespeare was like as a man. This is all the more remarkable in that there remains a modicum of doubt that the Shakespeare who lived and died at Stratford and the author of the poems and plays attributed to Shakespeare are the same person. It is a very dubious doubt and I don't share it for a moment; but because we have so little evidence of Shakespeare's actual existence and so high a general reverence for his writings, the Shakespearean plays have been, as Hugh Kingsmill says, the happy hunting ground for deranged minds; and there has been offered strangely unconvincing but ingenious cipher evidence that not only did Sir Francis Bacon write the Shakespearean plays but that Sir Francis Bacon was the whole Elizabethan Age in literature, having written *The Faërie Queene* attributed to Edmund Spenser and *The Anatomy of Melancholy* attributed to Robert Burton and all the prose and verse of consequence between the two. (The most fantastic of these cipher readings I have seen was one which found the preface verses of *The Anatomy of Melancholy* buried acrostically in *Troilus and Cressida* and the whole of Chapman's translation of Homer buried anacrostically in the type shadings of the first folio edition of *Pericles*.)

Shakespeare's history, like that of Jesus of Nazareth, about whose personality every one seems to have an opinion including the opinion that he did not exist, is largely conjectural and must be taken more or less on faith. A further difficulty involved in an attempt to state with any assurance what sort of man Shakespeare was derives from the fact that he was one of the most impersonal of all writers

250

and among the most reticent of men. Dante and Milton were egois-
tical chatterboxes beside him, baring their souls, and even Euripides,
about whom we know almost nothing, let us know what he thought
about women and the nature of love much more unequivocally than
Shakespeare did. Shakespeare was a mirror of life, not a thinker
on it. It is hazardous to deduce too much from what is apparently
his most personal expression, the Sonnets. It must be remembered
that a sonnet is the literary expression of a poet's *total* experience in
reference to one idea, one image, or one sentiment, and to whomever
it is addressed and whatever it is about, it is but a refinement and
crystallization of that total experience, and hence must not be too
closely identified with one person or taken to say things specifically
so much as generally.

It must not be forgotten that a poet's wares are rhetoric. (Not
so long ago a poet—not a first-rate poet but a poet—died and left
behind him a group of sonnets he had never published. They had
been given to a woman whom he professed to adore and whom, in a
fashion, he probably did. They seemed personal and revealing, and
the recipient consented to the publication of these sonnets, together
with an account of her friendship with the poet and his love for her.
Some of these sonnets were particularly striking in the ardor of their
sentiments and the recipient had been duly touched by them. It
turned out, however, that copies of certain of these more *personal*
sonnets were held by no less than two other women, each of whom
had been assured by the poet that the poems were inspired by, and
meant for, her and her alone.) There is reason for believing that the
Sonnets of Shakespeare are actually less revealing than the plays.
The reason for this is that many of the sonnets are plainly artificial,
and hence the whole sequential history of the emotions they celebrate may have been written as "literature" out of a feeling more
rhetorical than real, in an age when subtle flattery was an important
means of advancement and success.

What we actually know about Shakespeare can be reduced
finally to the scant evidence of a few public documents, some meager
bits about him written by his contemporaries and such testimony
about him as may be deduced from the phrase in his will about "the
second best bed." It was inevitable that about a man whose personal
history was so little known many legends should accumulate, and it
was also inevitable that, in the course of time, most of these legends
should be explained away and new ones offered as substitutes. The
reputation of a scholar is sometimes made upon a single minute

(and wholly unimportant) discovery, and since legends are legends and not facts, the running down of the truth about a legend is sure to stir up that strange clamor of applause and hostility in the learned journals which make a scholar's reputation and a scholar's life exciting.

It was once held that Shakespeare was an ill-educated son of a butcher, that he was chased out of Stratford for deer-poaching on the preserves of a minor aristocrat of the region, that his marriage was a belated one performed under the urgency of impending father-hood, that he held horses in the rain before the doors of the London theater and there formed the connections through which he picked up his skill in the art of the theater, that he was an actor of small bits as well as a playsmith and director and assumed the rôle of the Ghost in *Hamlet* (wherefore the slang expression, "the ghost walks," for Shakespeare was paymaster also to the troupe), that he had some disappointments of the heart in connection with a dark lady, that he had a proscribed attachment for a young man identified only as "Mr. W. H.," that when *Hamlet* was performed he had an income from his work that amounted to the modern equivalent of about twenty thousand dollars a year, that he bought the most pre-tentious house in Stratford and retired there to live out his years in ease and comfort as a gentleman whose station was attested by a coat-of-arms granted by the herald's college, that he died as a result of a drinking bout with his old London cronies, Ben Jonson and Michael Drayton, and that his dislike for his wife, although she had borne him three children, was so venomous that he willed her in malice only his second-best bed.

Shakespearean scholars have argued most of these legends away or revised the old interpretations of them. Professor Joseph Quincy Adams, for instance, has explained the matter of the sec-ond-best bed. The best bed, Professor Adams tells us, in Shakes-peare's time was usually an ornate and rarely used article of furniture. It was reserved for guests, to impress them with one's pos-sessions, like the best silver, the best china, the best linen, and the best bathroom towels which wives bring out for use only on special occasions and in the general use of which the family would be very uncomfortable. Professor Adams reminds us that, at the time Shakespeare made his will, Mrs. Shakespeare was an invalid past sixty and would have wanted especially the bed she was used to. Also, Professor Adams tell us, it is not to be assumed that the bed was all she got from Shakespeare: the law explicitly provided her with a one-third dower right, so the will would not specify the amount in money and chattels she should receive. If it especially designated any one thing, it would be a token of affectionate solicitude. If Mrs. Shakespeare had a particular fondness for the second-best bed, Shakespeare would have made a special provision that she should inherit it, so that in the distribution of the property it would not go to one of his daughters or, in a sale for the distribution of the estate, to some one else; and he did make this provision.

You can share Professor Adams' explanation or you can substitute an opinion of your own. Your view of the matter will largely depend, I imagine, upon what experience you have had with matrimony or with women. If you are male and happily married, even if you manage to live in town most of the time while your wife brings up your children in the suburbs, you will readily assent to Professor Adams' interpretation. If you have cause to have slightly revengeful feelings toward any one woman whatever, you will probably reject Professor Adams' opinion. Nor need you be intimidated by Professor Adams' scholarship; for this business about the second-best bed is not a matter of scholarship but a matter of conjecture.

But aside from the conjectural details, even the meager postulates concerning Shakespeare's history have a certain validity because when we look about us to see how people with certain temperaments and in certain circumstances act, we see that Shakespeare also, apparently, acted in this manner. Thus, it is a very common experience for a young man of talent, energy and ambition to leave the provinces, even if he is encumbered with a wife and children, and go up to the city to try to better his fortune in life. And if he has success, to look toward the time when he can have a home in the country to retire to. It happens all the time. If he can afford it and he usually can somehow, he takes his wife and children with him, perhaps occasionally sending them back in the summer time, or when the pressure of earning a living is too great, to stay with his parents or his wife's parents. Or if he can't afford to have them in town, he may leave them under the roof and protection of one of their parents, sending back to them whatever he can manage out of his earnings and saving toward the time when he can have his family with him.

We don't know for sure whether Mrs. Shakespeare and the children, Susanna, Hamnet and Judith, who were baptized at Stratford, lived in London with Shakespeare all or part of the time during his residence there or lived in Stratford, and, although even the most recent Shakespearean scholar, J. Dover Wilson, author of *The Essential Shakespeare* (1932), assumes like others that Mrs. Shakespeare was never with the poet in London, there is no evidence to support the assumption, and there is just as much reason (rather more I think) for believing she was in London with him as for believing that she was not. That the children were baptized at Stratford proves nothing except that the children were baptized at Stratford: Shakespeare may not have gone to London until after the birth of Susanna (he was only nineteen when Susanna was born), and he may not have gone to London until after the twins, Hamnet and Judith, were born (he was only twenty-two then). Or if it is assumed that Shakespeare had already started his career in London by the time of the birth of the twins, there is no evidence to support the assumption that Mrs. Shakespeare was not in London with him: she may have returned to Stratford as her critical time approached, for reasons obvious to any woman or any father, or she may have returned to Stratford merely for the ceremony of baptism.

Somewhere in the background in London, Shakespeare's wife may have been during all the years Shakespeare spent there. Or she may have remained in Stratford under her father's roof or in a rented house and Shakespeare may have run back to Stratford to see her occasionally. The reason for believing that Shakespeare's married life was as tranquil or as "happy" as marriages usually are, is less to be conjectured from the circumstantial appearance of his relationship with his wife than from the evidence in his poems and his character depictions of his reaction to the marriage relationship. And despite the domestic tragedies of *Hamlet, Macbeth,* and *Othello,* he seems not to have any very strong feelings on the subject of the marriage relation as such. Which means that he never had to justify his emotions subconsciously by expounding his side of the matter obliquely through the medium of poetry.

From Euripides, for instance, we know in our hearts that he had a weakness for women and that women apparently had for him, that his relationship with women was rather stormy and that he took revenge upon the sex by exaggerating their destructive and deadly qualities. From Dante also we know that he was tormented by the medieval ideas of a wholly spiritual love and the demands of his own flesh, shuttling him back and forth from asceticism to debauchery, and that neither lechery nor his aloof great love for Beatrice prevented him from raising a legitimate family. From Milton also we know that Milton believed that a wife should be submissive and obedient in all things to her husband ("Hee for God only, shee for God in Him") and that such ideas apparently drove his first wife from him within a month or so after their marriage, a fact that prompted him to write voluminously on the subject of divorce and the state of marriage, and colored his relationship with his subsequent wives and with his daughters whom he cruelly dominated.

Moreover, if there is one thing about Shakespeare on which commentators agree, it is that he was a pretty easy man to get along with. He was not temperamental and troublesome like Marlowe, overbearing and belligerent like Jonson, envious like Greene or intolerably aware of his genius like Chapman. He was a sweet-tempered man who made friends easily and kept them; he had a natural courtesy and gentleness of manner which endeared him to high and low alike—qualities he had need of as an actor-manager of a theater and as a diplomat who had to keep in the good graces of influential courtiers like Southampton, Rutland and Essex—causing his truculent rival, Jonson, to say he "loved him this side idolatry" and the printer who had published Greene's scurrilous pamphlet against Shakespeare to apologize publicly and say of him, "Myself have seen his demeanour no less civil than he excellent in the quality he professes," i.e., the quality of a gentleman. Shakespeare kept his personal affairs to himself; he was a good listener, quick of wit, a good companion, a good drinker, and a shrewd practical man who took the trouble to learn everything he could about the profession he adopted.

The thing he took most seriously was the business of writing popular and successful plays. That they were as good as they are is because of his genius, but also because the standard already set was high and the competition keen. His references to the art of acting and to the theater are numerous, and he drew many metaphors or similes from this art and from the art of music; but nowhere does he give you a clew that he bothered much about the art of writing, a gift so natural to him that he never thought about it, and so easy for him that he could hardly have been aware that he was the towering genius he was. When he describes or alludes to poets it is to make fun of them. Greene was the only one of his contemporaries who slandered him, and that was because Shakespeare had come up from the provinces with new and taking ideas and a manifest talent and had soon displaced Greene in court and popular favor. One can entertain a definite sympathy with the bitter castigation by Greene, a dying, broken, starving man, of the "upstart" who had made his way quickly in popularity and had elbowed him and other waning talents out of the limelight.

J. Dover Wilson had pointed out that fate contributed mightily to Shakespeare's success, and certainly the times conspired to nourish Shakespeare's genius. When he first began to try out his talents as a poet and a writer for the stage, many of the great men in his calling had set the pace for him and were beginning to drop by the wayside. His fledgling effort, when he was about twenty-five years of age, seems to have been a collaboration, *Titus Andronicus,* and a rather rickety, sophomoric effort it was, with not much to commend it except the lamentable industry of concocting it. His second effort was *A Comedy of Errors,* a rowdy farce comedy derived from Plautus, and his third was *Two Gentlemen of Verona,* a comedy of manners apparently derived from Bartholomew Young's translation of the *Diana Enamorada* of the Italian Jorge de Montemayor, wherein Shakespeare for the first time shows that he has begun to master the tricks of showmanship, to write what is called "good theater." By the time he is twenty-nine he had written, apparently, all within one year of fertile and feverish fecundity, two long and exceedingly popular poems, *Venus and Adonis* and *The Rape of Lucrece,* one play that is not so good, *King Henry VI,* in collaboration with another playwright, and one of the most (if not the most) elfin and charming exercises of the imagination ever visualized on the stage, *A Midsummer Night's Dream,* derived from Chaucer's *Knight's Tale.*

Meanwhile what had happened? John Lyly was still alive but had ceased to write, and he had contributed the euphuisms that Shakespeare was to make so much use of in *As You Like It* and in other plays; Christopher Marlowe, to the sonority of whose "mighty line" Shakespeare owed so much, had just been done to death in some shady piece of business during a tavern brawl; Thomas Kyd, upon whose unpublished play, *Hamlet,* Shakespeare was later to base a version of his own (one theory being that he inherited it as a producer's property and then revised it), and whose *The Spanish Tragedie* was the most popular of all Elizabethan plays, had died following his arrest and torture on a charge of atheism; Greene, who may have collaborated with Shakespeare on *Henry VI,* and whose *Triumph of Time* later gave Shakespeare the idea for *A Winter's Tale,* was going out of fashion, losing his patronage and his grip and actually starving; and Peele and Lodge had ceased to write. And Shakespeare was senior to Jonson, Drayton, Middleton,

Ford, Dekker, and Massinger, who had not yet matured. What a chance for a bright young man, with industry, energy, genius and the sober habits which were probably early forced upon Shakespeare because of delicate health!

That Shakespeare took full advantage of his opportunities we know. For nearly ten years he was an exceedingly busy and popular man, turning out three or four plays a year (writing *The Merry Wives of Windsor* on order for Queen Elizabeth in a fortnight, it appears), directing, acting, and managing a theater. He was so busy and so enthusiastic about his work that he saw little of his writing friends and rivals, pleading fatigue, headaches or incompleted work when they invited him to join them in carouses. The companionship of men had meant much to him, too, and some of his finest passages attest to his understanding of the good-fellowship and tenderness expressed in badinage between men. The legend comes down that Shakespeare, Jonson and their cronies, among whom may have been the Earl of Essex and the Earl of Southampton, used to foregather at the Mermaid Tavern and grow "nobly wild, not mad" over wine; and Thomas Fuller some fifty years after Shakespeare's death set down:

"Many were the wit-combats between him [Shakespeare] and Ben Jonson, which two I behold like a Spaniard great galleon and an English man-of-war; Master Jonson, like the former, was built far higher in learning, solid but slow in his performances. Shakespeare, with the English man-of-war, lesser in bulk, but lighter in sailing, could turn with all tides, tack about, and take advantage of all winds by the quickness of his wit and invention."

I think that Mr. Wilson is right in believing that Shakespeare's first noble patrons were young men, for, as he says, "Play after play of this period contains its party of dashing young bucks." Almost always, he continues, "like young men of whatever rank or period, they hunt in threes, Mercutio, Romeo, and Benvolio; Berowne, Longaville, and Dumain; Antonio, Bassanio, and Gratiano; Petruchio, Lucentio, and Tranio." Well, and Shakespeare was young himself, not so young as the wealthy Earl of Southampton, his first patron, who was ten years younger than Shakespeare, but still a young man full of high spirits, mirth, and wit, or at least with an author's genius to picture and celebrate these qualities. That he put his noble young friends and patrons into plays is easy to believe. In fact, it is difficult to avoid thinking so, because comedies of noble manners were in fashion and they were the only nobles

Shakespeare knew outside of books. He had to flatter or amuse them with caricatures or romantic visions of themselves; and since he knew what would tickle them most he introduced subtleties, topical allusions, digs and japes that are no longer understandable now and, because they are not, have led puzzled research scholars, sweating through piles of documents, dim printing, and weighty tomes in search of the hidden meaning of some purely timely gag and finding it not, resignedly concluding that it is a corruption of the text.

Meanwhile Shakespeare grew older; his gifts matured; a tragic sense of life was borne in on him maybe by one circumstance, maybe by another, or rather more probably by a whole chain of events, including the physical fact that age had crept upon him. Shakespeare, who in his early period had shown great verbal felicity, cleverness, poetic imagination and a good sense of the theater, had written amusing comedies but had created no characters and shown them in the process of growth. This was because his own character had not grown or developed—he was still a sort of playboy in the art of writing.

But suddenly something happened to him. His production slowed down, his plays began to take on weight, he turned to tragedy. His plays instead of being light and airy are anguished and passionate, plumbing the depths of man's ingratitude, treachery, deceitfulness, knavish ambition, hatred, guile, jealousy, lust, or simple, tragic helplessness against the evil forces of nature and the conflict of base and heroic human motives. That Shakespeare himself was near to madness when he wrote *Lear* is, I believe, obvious enough, and he was certainly a sick man when he wrote *Timon of Athens*. I know it is not orthodox to put the unknown date of composition of the unfinished *Timon* before the date of composition of *Lear:* but I have a notion that *Timon* may have preceded *Lear,* for it was apparently written in the first angry reaction of rage and in a wish to wound somebody, the work of a man sick with anger and revulsion but still experiencing the active force of this anger and revulsion, whereas *Lear* is a deeper-seated thing, the result of art brought to bear upon brooding and deep sorrow.

The next, the final stage of Shakespeare's development has been the one, curiously, that has puzzled commentators most. Suddenly in his fifties Shakespeare changes his style, changes his outlook, sweetens his temper and grows mellow and indulgent. From the creation of heroic and tragic men and women, he turns, of all things, to the creation of sweet and innocent, fresh and lovely young girls. This from a man who had been savage and cynical, ruthlessly attacking sentiment and romance, uncovering evil, and showing men mad or near to madness, full of disillusion and despair. A new mood of optimism, of satisfaction in the fact and sight of young and tender love comes into *Pericles* and continues through *Cymbeline, Winter's Tale,* and *The Tempest.* Suddenly Shakespeare is interested in daughters, in Perdita, Miranda, Marina, Florizel and Imogen. Well, says Mr. Wilson, why not? Shakespeare has two daughters and a granddaughter at home, already growing into that age when they would be objects of his attention and interest and solicitude. In them and through them, whatever he had been through, he could find something new, pleasing and comforting, renewing his spirit.

Sir Edmund Chambers and some later scholars, realizing that in the third phase of Shakespeare's productive career he underwent a "complete reversal of standards and values," attribute it to a nervous breakdown and a prolonged recovery following the tension and anxiety that had produced *Timon* and *Lear.* Sir Edmund thinks and Mr. Wilson thinks that prostration followed a period of bitter disappointment and bleak despair and that Shakespeare was nursed back to health by his son-in-law, Dr. Hall, who had married Susanna and that on his recovery in the peaceful presence of Dr. Hall and Susanna and his younger daughter, Judith, he found warm affection again, which served to change his outlook upon life.

This sounds plausible and indeed obvious; but it is well not to make too much of it, because other factors may have entered into this change of attitude. It is not necessary to consider Shakespeare a mere time-server to credit him with having changed his manner to keep in fashion with the demands of the time; for it must be remembered that Shakespeare was an actor (and from some accounts a very good actor, having been named with William Kempe and Richard Burbage as early as 1594 and having been in the list of the principal comedians appearing in Ben Jonson's *Every Man in His Humour* and *Sejamus,* and having been named before Burbage and Heminge in the royal patent of 1603, establishing the King's Company of Players), a producer and a participating member of a syndicate, organized to produce plays. His nervous breakdown, if he had one, then, might merely have resulted from overwork or from financial anxiety attendant upon the hazards of producing plays to meet popular favor in times when the plague was recurring and the political scene in turmoil and fortunes insecure.

When we remember that a popular actor-playwright like George

M. Cohan began his career first by acting in other men's plays, then produced and acted in his own plays, and before he was fifty began to produce plays by other men, either touched up by his hand or enlivened by his direction, we understand what might have happened in Shakespeare's case. Or, to seek another analogy, recall that Owen Davis, an extraordinarily fertile playwright, began his career with lurid melodramas such as *Gertie, the Sewing-Machine Girl* and *Bertha, the Beautiful Cloak Model,* successfully rang all the changes in theatrical fashions, comedy, farce, romantic drama and tragedy, and finally produced the Pulitzer Prize-winning play, *Icebound.* We may see that when Shakespeare returned to Stratford when he was about fifty years of age, he may simply have been in need of a rest, and that while enjoying his rest he tried his hand at the sort of thing the younger dramatists like Beaumont and Fletcher, Middleton and Dekker were writing for the more frivolous demands of the Jacobean court. And try he did with *Pericles,* which was strangely enough one of the most popular of all plays by Shakespeare or his contemporaries, and with *A Winter's Tale,* which is, from an artistic standpoint, one of the greatest plays ever written.

When Shakespeare retired to Stratford he was a grandfather, his daughter Susanna having borne Dr. Hall a daughter. Shortly before he died, his younger daughter Judith, a spinster thirty-one years of age, suddenly married Thomas Quiney, a draper's son, aged twenty-six. The couple did not get the special license required by the ecclesiastical authorities and after they had been summoned twice to comply with the law they still did not obey the summons and were excommunicated by the Bishop of Worcester and the Consistory Court.

Professor Adams thinks the fact that Shakespeare altered his will after Judith's marriage indicated he was distressed by the marriage, the excommunication and the type of man she married. I don't believe this is necessarily true, for after all he left her what amounts nowadays to about fifteen thousand dollars and his "broad silver gilt bowl." It had looked as though Judith were going to remain an old maid and when she married it was necessary to alter the wording of the will.

He left to Susanna the bulk of his estate, including the dwelling in New Place and his equities in the New Globe and Blackfriar theaters and his investment in Stratford tithes, these investments being valued at about fifty thousand dollars. To leave the bulk of his estate to his eldest daughter, with special instructions that she should provide a home for his widow, was in accordance with the custom of the time among those whose ambition it was to found a landed family. This seems to have been Shakespeare's aim, for a long section of the will entailed Susanna's inheritance upon the male heirs of the line forever, and if after seven childbirths Susanna had not borne a son, Susanna's inheritance was to pass to Elizabeth Hall, Shakespeare's niece; and if she produced no sons, to Judith and the son she might bear and his son and son's sons.

Ben Jonson and Michael Drayton used to come up from London to visit Shakespeare, and on one of these occasions, it appears, Shakespeare drank too much, rapidly developed a fever and died within a few days. It may have been that he had been suffering from Bright's disease and had been forbidden to touch alcohol and that disobeying the doctor's orders he suffered the consequences. Or he may have given up alcohol for a long period of time on account of ill-health and fallen off the wagon in his joy at being with Jonson and Drayton.

Shakespeare died, at any rate, when he was fifty-two years old. He remembered his old fellow actors in his will, Richard Burbage, John Heminge and Henry Condell, and his friends in Stratford, Hamnet Sadler (after whom he may have named his son who had died at the age of eleven), William Reynolds, Anthony Nash and John Nash. That he especially remembered Burbage, Heminge and Condell shows I think, how important his career as an actor had been to him, or at least shows his affection for actors.

Shakespeare's body was buried in a wooden coffin in Trinity churchyard, and over the spot a new church was later raised, inclosing and marking the resting places of Shakespeare and his wife and daughter Susanna. The Johnson, or Janssen, brothers, stonemasons of London, were engaged by the family at considerable expense to do a bust of Shakespeare and set up a monument to him in the church; and this they did, modeling the features either from a life or death mask or from their memory of what he looked like. The monument was an elaborate affair in the most expensive bad taste of the period and the bust is smug and complaisant.

Judith's marriage, it seems, turned out badly; her husband was a failure in business, and after becoming involved with the law, he deserted her. Her two sons had died, and thus she could not profit by the provision that Susanna's inheritances should revert to her sons should Susanna fail to have male issue, which was the case. But her father had provided the income of seven thousand five hundred dollars for her and she lived to the ripe old age of seventy-seven. The landed family Shakespeare wished to found never became established; hopes for it died out entirely within fifty years after his death, leaving him without lineal descendants.

Nothing is entirely incredible about the legends which modern Shakespeare scholars unite in rejecting, not even the legend that Shakespeare was prosecuted for poaching on the preserves of Sir Thomas Lucy and afterward took revenge upon Sir Lucy by picturing him as Justice Shallow, with twelve lice rampant on his coat of arms, in the second part of *King Henry the Fourth*. But the trouble about hearsay evidence is that it has a tendency to alter in form and color with each re-telling, even by the same person.

Thus it may have been that Shakespeare in his boyhood was apprenticed to a butcher, but that he was an "illiterate apprentice" is nonsense. Butchers at the time were generally unable to read and write, but it may have been that during school vacations or in after hours Shakespeare worked for a butcher not as an apprentice but for pay; for Shakespeare seems to have taken whatever work at any time was available to him, including the job of teaching school for a while. In Shakespeare's early boyhood his father was apparently well-to-do, a glover and a wool-merchant and at one time holding an office in Stratford similar to that of mayor of an American town or village. John Shakespeare, however, apparently suffered reverses of fortune at about the time of his son's marriage to Ann Hathaway, who was eight years Shakespeare's senior and the daughter of a prosperous middle-class resident of Shottery. This may have strengthened Shakespeare's decision to seek his fortune in the metropolis.

However Shakespeare acquired his education, whether by the good public schooling afforded in Stratford in those days, or by reading and study in Stratford or later in the Earl of Southampton's library in London, to which Florio, the translator, was attached as tutor and where Shakespeare may have also been, it is certain that Shakespeare knew Latin well enough to read Ovid in the original and to base the *Comedy of Errors* on a hitherto untranslated play by Plautus. He knew Plutarch and Montaigne most likely in translations and was familiar with the Geneva version of the Bible. Some one has said that, if Shakespeare knew Plutarch and Montaigne thoroughly, he did not need anything more to make him a well-educated man; and for his purposes certainly those two books and the Bible, and Ovid and Plautus, furnished literary seed enough to fecundate his mind and imagination, already natively alive and impressionable.

The reason Shakespeare got the reputation with some critics for being a hack-writer and mere play-doctor has been explained by research into the way things were done when Shakespeare went up to London and got into show business. The opening of the first playhouse to the public took place in London when Shakespeare was thirteen years old. Hitherto masks and pageants and plays had been the exclusive enjoyment of court nobles and ladies. With the opening of a public theater, the show business became not merely a profession dependent upon noble patronage (although noble patronage still counted for much), but a real business, profitable but hazardous, as it is now.

As in the time of Æschylus, Sophocles and Euripides, who also wrote for the public, the themes selected for presentation were familiar ones. The Athenian audiences knew the outlines of all the plots used by their dramatists for these plots were familiar folklore legends. What they liked to see was how different dramatists treated the same subject. Burlesque and vaudeville and musical comedy artists to this day know that an audience's response to a joke or situation depends largely upon their familiarity with it and their appreciation depends upon the twist given a familiar joke or situation.

This was so in Elizabethan times. As a result, whenever a poet playwright wrote a play that was accepted, the script and all rights to it remained the property of the company that bought it. It was theirs to change or revise in any way whatever. And to a certain extent the value of a play depended upon the number of revisions it could stand. When Shakespeare first tried his hand at play-writing, the most popular playwright was Kyd and the most popular play, *A Spanish Tragedie*, a blood-and-thunder drama. Being in an imitative period, Shakespeare made an attempt at this sort of thing in *Titus Andronicus*. Then Marlowe, using the scripts of old plays in the hands of the player companies, introduced a new treatment; he was a poet of great eloquence, grounded upon a rich knowledge of the Latin poets. Into the fustian of the sanguine plays, Marlowe introduced beauty and dignity, and Shakespeare was later to learn much from him.

The prevailing mood and temper of the plays and pageants of Elizabeth's court, however, had been those created by the niceties of John Lyly with his Nice-Nellyisms which came to be known as euphuisms and euphemisms. The idea was to say things in a round-about way, or delicately, especially those things that had hitherto been said with coarse and earthy Anglo-Saxon bluntness. It was a style Queen Elizabeth approved and followed. It was falsely poetic and lended itself to parody, and parody it Shakespeare did, with just enough original treatment to introduce a new element into the theater—polite comedy, knock-about farces, essentially, subjected to refined treatment. This was Shakespeare's claim to originality of treatment, then. It was a new twist, and immediately popular. He created a fad and a fashion in the theater: hence the jealousy of Greene, on the manuscript of one of whose plays Shakespeare had worked and made a new and shining thing out of it. This wasn't plagiarism; it was the common thing, the thing Greene and the rest had done before Shakespeare.

As an actor-playwright-producer Shakespeare had need con-stantly for new plays, new ideas, new twists. Changing conditions, social and economic, affected not only his thinking but the tastes and desires of the public, as it always does. So it cannot be said that Shakespeare turned from comedy to tragedy, and from tragedy to pastoral romance simply to please his public: it was the way he felt like writing and it was the sort of thing that was in the air. The times and the people produce literature almost as much as the authors themselves. Shakespeare may even have thought he was merely trying to please the public; but at the same time he was really writing what he had in him and what it was in his mind and heart to write. That it was some of the greatest literature that has ever been produced probably never occurred to him, although there is evidence in his early comedies that he knew he was a very clever fellow. And in his later plays, particularly in *Hamlet,* there is evidence that in the art of acting and in the art of writing for the theater he knew what was honest, natural, impressive and touch-ing and that he could not tolerate shallow, false, bombastic utterance.

The English drama, like Greek drama, began as a religious ob-servance. We have seen in the second chapter of this book how the Greek plays took form gradually from early pagan rites. The English drama began with the Miracle plays, which were pantomimes repre-senting events in sacred Christian history. From pantomime and pageant there developed episodes in which the actors were given lines to speak or declaim. This, we see, is analogous to the develop-ment of the motion pictures, from the crude, silent "flickers" with their one-reel episodes, to the six- and eight-reel silent pictures wherein the great Charlie Chaplin developed his extraordinary technic; then from the early trials of the sound-recording devices to the modern "talkies," which are still in an early stage of development.

From the sacred plays, which were popular on religious occasions, as *holy* day or holiday observances, they developed the secular pantomimes and the Morality plays, wherein the Virtues and the Vices were represented by characters in action and in dialogue. One of these Morality plays, *Everyman*, has been revived on several occasions in modern times with considerable success. (The well-known Reinhardt production of *The Miracle* was an elaborate and costly modern version of what the crude early miracle plays were like.)

Poets began to contribute to the declamations and dialogues of the secular plays and, as poets have their profane as well as their sacred natures, the secular plays developed into farces as well as into romances. The authors moved from the presentation of biblical scenes to the representation of historical events still alive in the memories of the audiences, through oral tradition or in some cases through medieval chronicles, and to representations of scenes from common life, in the form of comic masks and pastorals.

This form of entertainment became wearisome like any other too long repeated, and the strolling players who had developed as a profession had to write new stuff, create variety. To this end they searched for plots in Latin and Italian and Anglo-Saxon chronicles. They began to draw upon or adapt comedies from Plautus and Terence and from Italian romances, and to make plays out of the historical characters found in Plutarch, Holinshed, Livy and other historians.

We know what these strolling players were like and what sort of plays they ordinarily produced, even what sort of players they were; and we would know this even if all other sources of information had been lost except Shakespeare's *Hamlet*, for he put one of these plays into his *Hamlet*, and the play itself was only his version of a popular theme that had been used in various versions by just such strolling players before him.

We have a fair knowledge of the history of *Hamlet*. The original source is the *Historia Danica* by Saxo Grammaticus who died about 1220. This history was first printed in Paris in 1514, and in 1570 Francis de Belleforest retold the story in his *Histoires Tragiques*. That the story of Hamlet, Prince of Denmark, as a prose romance was early seized upon by the playwrights in need of plot material we know, because many references to the *Ur-Hamlet,* or early version, have come down to us. As a play *Hamlet* was a great popular favorite. By 1589 the various playing versions of it had become exceedingly numerous. In evidence of this we have a preface by Thomas Nashe to Greene's *Menaphon,* wherein he makes fun of the number of persons, qualified or unqualified, who are feverishly turning out plays, and says this type can "afford you whole Hamlets, I should say handfuls of Tragical speeches."

We know that the *Ur-Hamlet,* that is, the original acting version, belonged to the Lord Chamberlain's company. This means the Chamberlain's company owned what would now be called the copyright to the versions of the tragedy played by that company. From a version written in Kyd's lifetime, Shakespeare, as an actor-playwright, either of the Lord Chamberlain's or the Lord Admiral's players, made his version of the familiar theme. It seems probable that Greene had made an acting version of the play and that it had been performed, but possibly not with entire success; and that Greene's version was turned over to the play-doctor Shakespeare to see what he could do with it.

Greene had died in September, 1592, and Marlowe in May, 1593. Within a short time an unusually severe outbreak of the plague closed all the theaters in London, and it was not until June of the following year that a fresh start was made by the Lord Chamberlain's and the Lord Admiral's players. The new plays they had to offer were *Hamlet, Titus* and *Taming of a Shrew* (sic), according to Henslowe's diary, and Henslowe was the manager of the theater in which these plays were produced. It is rather certain that the *Titus* and *Taming of a Shrew* were Shakespeare's and probably the *Hamlet* was also, although it was not copyrighted until 1602.

Fully to understand what *Hamlet* meant to an Elizabethan audience, we must remember that the play, to them, was not so much about murder as about incest. From early times it was considered incestuous for a man to marry his brother's widow. Not knowing this has caused a modern critic, T. S. Eliot (in an essay in the volume *The Sacred Wood*) to criticize Shakespeare's handling of the theme, by saying that the anguish of Hamlet is insufficiently motivated! Claudius and Gertrude were living adulterously and incestuously; they had murdered Hamlet's father not only to ascend to the throne but to commit incest and to deprive Hamlet of his succession—and still Hamlet's agitation was hardly accounted for! Heaven help us!

Now we must go back for a moment to see how conditions and events conspired for the flowering of Shakespeare's genius as it is expressed, for instance, in *Hamlet*. The popularity of plays and pageants in Elizabethan court circles had become so great and the competition among the playwrights so keen that about 1580 some young university members and graduates began to take an interest in them and look toward the composition of plays as a means of livelihood and advancement, as well as an exercise of their talents. Among these were Robert Greene, Thomas Nash (or Nashe), John Lyly, George Peele, Thomas Whetstone, and Thomas Lodge.

Lyly especially was a man of brilliant talent, sound learning, polish and cultivation. Moreover he was an original: he invented or evolved a new, caressing, subtle style, which, as we have seen, permeated the diction of the court, and infiltrated into the plays. Their separate styles, based upon Latinisms and classical learning but invigorated with good Anglo-Saxon words had their effect upon a still younger man who was a natural singer, a born poet, a sensitive youth with an imagination inflamed by deep reading in Greek and Latin and medieval chronicles—Christopher Marlowe.

Marlowe had read Ovid and Lucian and an early version, probably in English, of *The History of the Damnable Life and Deserved Death of Doctor John Faustus,* and Fortescue's translation of Pedro Mexia's life of Tamburlaine (in Spanish) and probably much else besides; for, when he was only twenty-four years of age his tragedy was produced, which already revealed his "mighty line" in full perfection. This "mighty line" was a free development of the use of blank verse, giving it dignity and grandeur. Hitherto the rhymed couplet had been the fashion, and then the blank verse couplet. It was Marlowe who first showed how blank verse could be developed to its full power in English. His was a tumultuous temperament, alternating apparently with graver moods. His early cadences had a violent crescendo followed by calm iambics. This cadence he developed until it has become one of the chief glories of English literature, a cadence taken over without much variation by Shakespeare.

(I wish to digress at this point to air a vanity. I can lay claim to an important discovery in scholarship, a discovery that had eluded the great scholars and the vaunted commentators on English literature, although my discovery, I learned, was afterwards used as the basis for a thesis for a Ph.D. in English literature. I shouldn't display this vanity if it were not to make a point. The point is that amateurs of good literature can make scholarly discoveries as well as any big-wig professor or don, and often do make the most interesting ones. My discovery was about Marlowe's "mighty line." The finest example of that mighty line had long been taken to be the opening words of Faust's invocation to Helen in the *Tragical History of Dr. Faustus:*

> Was this the face that launched a thousand ships
> And burnt the topless towers of Ilium?

It was my pleasure to point out in 1923 that these two lines are an almost literal translation from the Greek of Lucian. In Lucian's dialogue between Menippus and Mercury, Mercury takes Menippus into the underworld and among various sights of interest shows him the carcass of Helen of Troy, now a repulsive thing, all bones and dry, sunken flesh. Menippus exclaims: "How! Was it for this that all Greece embarked upon a thousand ships and so many brave men perished and so many towns were burned to ashes?")

Well, and Marlowe performed his brief, brilliant function and died miserably; and Shakespeare was on the scene and on the rise. Marlowe was born in the same year that Shakespeare was but his genius matured much more quickly.

Marlowe was the son of a shoemaker, and was educated at Kent's School in Canterbury and at what is now Corpus Christi College, Cambridge. He was, it seems, in early youth much like the young Shelley, an ardent champion of the emancipation of the intellect. He had seen a schoolmate, Francis Kett, burnt at the stake in Norwich for heresy in denying the divinity of Christ, and this apparently influenced him for he, too, was charged with heresy and escaped it only by denial of the charge, but, when he could, he put skepticism in the speeches of his plays. He, like Shakespeare, incurred the envy and jealousy of Greene who, in the same pamphlet in which he derided Shakespeare, charged Marlowe with atheism and loose living. So it is justifiable to infer that Marlowe for a time displaced Greene in popularity.

But Marlowe was not capable of the sober application to work that Shakespeare had and soon was spending his time pretty much in drunken carouses and apparently deriving his income as a paid informer of the secret police, a work that would cause him to associate largely with thieves, cutthroats, pimps and bawds of the underworld. He was stabbed to death in his twenty-ninth year, May 30, 1593, in a drunken quarrel with one Francis Frizer over a division of some money (not over a woman as romantic legend has it) in the presence of two companions, in a room of a house owned by a certain Eleanor Bull, a widow, at Detford Strand, County of Kent.

From the nature of Marlowe's employment at that time, it is probable that the quarrel over the division of the money had to do with Marlowe's share of a theft or robbery. It has always been customary for stool-pigeons to be in the pay of criminals and in the pay of the police at the same time. (We owe, by the way, the final clearing up of the story of Marlowe's slaying to J. Leslie Hotson of Harvard University who found, deciphered and translated the coroner's report concerning Marlowe's death and published his findings in 1925 under the title *The Death of Christopher Marlowe*. All scholars and commentators up to this time had accepted the legend that Marlowe was killed by "a bawdy serving-man" in a quarrel over a whore.)

I wish to take the characters of Hamlet and Falstaff as Shakespeare created them as an illustration of the peculiar quality of Shakespeare's genius. In that lecture written and delivered in French, of which George Moore is justifiably so proud that he has now republished it three times in as many books, Moore says that Hamlet is the hieroglyph and symbol of human intelligence and that Falstaff is the symbol and arabesque of the flesh. I know of no better description of these characters than this. The flesh of Falstaff, says Moore, is animated with a Hamlet-like intelligence; and though both Hamlet and Falstaff are garrulous, Falstaff's garrulity is that of the birds which sing of a sunny morning.

No one before Moore has noticed, I believe, that kinship of spirit between Hamlet and Falstaff. They are both men with a quick sensibility and a rich and superior vocabulary, who are spiritually muddled and indecisive. They are mentally at sea over the crosspurposes of life; they are pessimistic about the designs of nature; they abhor both knaves and fools. And, significantly—to analysts of Shakespeare's genius—they have the same skepticism of feminine chastity, a skepticism which leads them to impugn it without charity and to their own distress. Ophelia is to Hamlet a predestined adulteress, though he has no warrant beyond a generalization from his mother's guilt. Sir John Falstaff sets so little store by wifely virtue that he flatters himself that he, a great tun of guts, "old, cold, withered and of intolerable entrails" can cuckold a countryside, and trying it, gets a bath in the Thames and the bastinado for his pains, the wives, not the husbands, tricking him to grief. No less,

Hamlet bids Ophelia get herself to a nunnery, encompasses her insanity and finally her death; and Falstaff expires either into Hell or into Arthur's bosom, babbling of the great "whore of Babylon." In both cases they treated potentialities as if they were deeds performed, without discounting human factors. Women are kindly and they wink too much among themselves, else they would have long ago delivered, with these two examples, a homily on masculine sentiment.

Hamlet, like Heraclitus, wept at the human spectacle; and Falstaff, like Democritus, laughed at it; therein you have their only essential difference. Each I think is a character creation equal in greatness to the other. And they reflect the artist spirit in Shakespeare, two sides to the same shield, both a mirror of life rather than a commentary on it. If Hamlet was not precisely Shakespeare the man, he was an adumbration of Shakespeare's spirit, and so was Falstaff.

They are two moods in the same person. And they are characteristic. Shakespeare never reached any conclusions about life, seeing it as a growth and diversity, meaningless and yet full of meaning. To live was to him in itself important. And that is wherein the great artist differs from the great philosopher. The great artist is interested in life as it is, whereas the great philosopher is interested in life as he thinks it ought to be or might become. (I except Aristotle as a philosopher in this, because Aristotle's interest was largely an artist's interest and his advice the mere results of his testing of the artist's tools.)

Shakespeare not only was not a philosophical thinker (happily); he did not even understand the philosophical type of mind and caricatured it wherever he had occasion to use a philosopher, as in Polonius. If Shakespeare had been a thinker, like Milton, for example, he would have written didactic plays, and no play of Shakespeare's is didactic. Shakespeare's plays are mirrors of life. And so many-faceted is that mirror and so rich his genius that any one looking into it sees precisely what he wants to see, what he has the gift to see—himself.

VOLTAIRE *THE CRITIC*

*

VOLTAIRE'S *Candide* is a hardy perennial of the publishing business. Hardly a year goes by in which there is not one or more handsome editions of that invigorating and humane, deliciously satirical buffoonery, purchased by an avid public, thus testifying to the undying appeal of the happiest side of Voltaire's genius. Voltaire's spirited history of *The Age of Louis XIV*, so brilliantly and vivaciously written, also enjoys a continuous popularity. The *Philosophical Dictionary*, the light tales like *Zadig*, and perhaps one or two other works are dipped into now and then; but the vast bulk of his writings (he was one of the most prolific writers that ever lived) have sunk into limbo while his personality as a man has had a persistent fascination for transcending some of his most ambitious labors.

His tedious epic, *The Henriade*, is justifiably forgotten; his plays in which he fancied himself superior to Shakespeare gather the dust of oblivion; even the political and philosophical pamphlets, tracts and books which made him the most influential, the most conspicuous man of letters of the eighteenth century, are now read only by amiable, old-fashioned atheists who wish to "argufy" with texts, just as Fundamentalists wish to "argufy" with texts from the Bible. Voltaire's poetry, of which he produced an amazing lot, is now simply unreadable.

And yet there is a new biography of Voltaire almost every year, most of them very entertaining. The wizened hypochondriac, who was given up for dead on his birth, and who died during eighty-four years of incredible vitality, remains a symbol of the defeat

271

of the sickly flesh by the health of the spirit and the jauntiest of all representatives of the war upon intolerance, injustice, cruelty and slavery.

François Arouet, of which name "Voltaire" is an ingenious anagram, was the son of a clerk who worked under the supervision of the great Duc de Saint-Simon, the author of those *Memoirs* to which attention has been so often called in this volume, because like *Main Currents of Nineteenth Century Literature* by Georg Brandes, Gibbon's *Decline and Fall of the Roman Empire* and Boswell's *Life of Samuel Johnson,* it is a work of literary art whose merits as a work of art are sometimes overlooked because it is an historical record.

Voltaire was a precocious child, but a blithe being and not a somber one like so many children with frail constitutions. His adolescence was passed during the latter part of the reign of "The Sun King," who died when Voltaire was twenty-one. His subsequent life was to pass through an age of revolution in which he was one of the most active intellectual leaders. Born in Paris and a Parisian of Parisians, he was educated at the Sorbonne and on his graduation had so made his wit felt that he attracted the attention of the famous but then aged beauty, Nanon de Lenclos, the Aspasia of the Age of Louis XIV, who had been successively the mistress or adored one of the Cardinal Richelieu, Molière, St. Evrémond, and Fontanelle, and who had, by her wit, beauty and general charm, created a salon, somewhat easy in morals, which was the most brilliant in Paris and the envy of duchesses and princesses.

Nanon saw the possibilities in the young Voltaire and in her will left him a legacy with which to purchase a library. He was an impetuous youth, who delighted in his cleverness. Soon he had run up against the self-importance of those in power and, having ridiculed them, was thrown for eleven months into the Bastille as a dangerously seditious writer. He improved his time while incarcerated by writing an epic poem *The Henriade* recounting the deeds of the king who had largely been responsible for a consolidated France. It was patriotic and probably designedly so. On his release from prison he was accepted everywhere in fashionable society as a poet and an intellectual.

Audacity and irreverence, particularly irreverence for the pretensions of the aristocracy, were of the soul of Voltaire and he accepted invitations to the homes of the aristocrats only with the

VOLTAIRE
(From the painting by De La Tour)

mental reservation that he would not cringe or fawn upon them or hold his tongue when they gave lip to imbecility. His life at this early period was a fantasia of imbroglios. He quarreled with friends and enemies alike; he was on terms of social equality with everybody whose name counted for anything in Paris—princes, cardinals, bankers, ecclesiastics, poets, dramatists, actors and actresses; he rushed to the defense, this irreligionist, of the Abbé Desfontaines, who was imprisoned on a charge of sodomy, although Voltaire's suspicion was that the abbé was the victim of a political frame-up; he was favored protégé of young Louis XV and his queen, as well as of the mistress of the prime minister during the regency. He had a particular venom against the Chevalier de Rohan, whom he openly insulted in public during an intermission at the Comédie Française. A brawl was prevented by the opportune fainting of Voltaire's mistress, Mlle. Lecouvreur. A few evenings later while Voltaire was dining at the home of the Duc de Sully, he received a message saying that some one wished to talk to him outside, and when he came out he was horsewhipped by gangsters in the pay of Rohan, who stood by and laughed at his agony.

Voltaire, in his turn, did not bide his time: he went into training, took fencing lessons, and made acquaintance with Paris cutthroats and gangsters. He was determined to catch Rohan in a situation such as Rohan had caught him, and stand by while thugs beat the daylights out of Rohan. But Rohan was more astute in criminal ways than Voltaire: he put detectives on Voltaire's trail who uncovered Voltaire's purpose. As a result of the depositions of the detectives, Voltaire was again thrown into the Bastille and released within two weeks on condition that he leave France. He went to England, where he lived with Lord Bolingbroke (referred to in the chapter on De Foe) for three years. In England Voltaire had a chance to review his exciting career in perspective and to develop a special philosophical line of attack; he met Newton and Addison, studied English parliamentary reforms and returned to France eager to do battle with whatever bogeys confronted him. His *English Letters* were published on his return and as a result his publisher was shut up in the Bastille while he himself enjoyed the favor of the King, who appointed him the royal historian and gentleman-of-the-bedchamber, dual offices entitling him to bed and board for himself and his mistress, Mme. de Châtelet, and giving him a benefice from the royal treasury.

He didn't care for the king's mistress, Mme. de Pompadour, and let the fact be known too patently, as the result of which he was dismissed, only to become the guest of King Stanislas of Poland at the king's French palaces in Luneville and Cirey. Meanwhile he had shown his practical intelligence by the risk of a portion of his savings in a series of speculations in the stock exchange which multiplied his fortune. When Mme. de Châtelet died he was a man of immense paper wealth. Frederick II (known as the Great) of Prussia was very like Voltaire and he had a vanity about his ability to write verse. He wrote to Voltaire whom he had met on an occasion when Voltaire was on a secret diplomatic mission to Prussia, inviting him to come to Potsdam as a member of his entourage. Out of pique perhaps as much as for any reason, Voltaire left France (as if to show the French king where he got off) and became Frederick's court chamberlain. In Prussia Voltaire ruled the intellectual roost, with frequent bitter quarrels with his patron, and feathered his nest financially by making certain secret contracts with the chancellor of the exchequer, until in the end he had to leave Frederick's company and (since he was not welcome in France) take refuge in Switzerland.

Both Louis XV and Frederick II had disillusioned Voltaire. He had hoped to be Machiavelli to either the one or the other of them, but his experience with them led him to the conclusion that kings hold jobs by chance and that most of them are too stupid to profit by any intelligent suggestions regarding their kingly tenure. In his exile in Switzerland Voltaire began to issue his political pamphlets against the church and the monarchy which, as much as the doctrines of Jean-Jacques Rousseau, brought about the Revolution, for the Parisian man in the street shared Voltaire's views as much as the bored duchesses at Versailles and the pleasure resorts of the nobility shared Rousseau's doctrine of the "return to nature."

Voltaire thundered from Switzerland to an ever delighted French audience: his speculative adventures had proved successful, and so at last he acquired a château and an estate at Ferney on the Swiss-French border, where he settled down as the fiery invalid who consecrated his life and his genius to "the execration of the infamy" of religion and of the *ancien régime*. His home, for an outcast officially declared a criminal, was a model of splendor, ease and gentility. There, with one of his many happy mistresses, Madame Denis, he "danced with arms and legs," entertained guests, poured out a constant stream of literature, good, bad and indifferent, but always in good humor, always full of an eager zest for life. To his dying day he could not be sympathetic toward the "back to nature" philosophy of Rousseau. His own philosophy was one of sophistication and intelligence, of intellectual domination over the evils of the flesh and of society; and after a long period of happiness greater perhaps than that enjoyed by any major figure in literature, he returned to Paris to witness the opening performance of his drama, *Irène,* was welcomed back in triumph (for though the Revolution was still to come, he was the idol of the people), and after a visit to the Academy (of which he had been made a member in 1746), he capped a lifetime of triumphs by dying in the very height of his acclaim and glory. In his eighty-fourth year, a frail shadow of a man, toothless and bald but still full of nervous energy, he proposed to the Academy a plan for the reform of the French dictionary, fortified himself with vast quantities of coffee and some opium while working out his plan on paper, and fell mortally ill. Before he died there was an obscene spectacle wherein, for the publicity for the Catholic church, some importunate priests begged the dying and delirious old fighter for a recantation of his religious heresies. They even claimed to have got one from him. But, happily, a short time before this, while quite well and sane, he seems to have anticipated this pressure and to have signed a testament which reads:

"I die adoring God, helping my friends and not hating my enemies, and detesting superstition."

Whatever concessions he may have made to the priests may have been to prevent his body from being cast into the sewer as unhallowed. He died on the evening of May 30, 1778, near midnight. The Archbishop of Paris, not carrying out the notions of the priests who had bothered Voltaire in his last hours, forbade him Christian burial; but his relatives and friends acted quickly and the corpse was interred at Scellières, in a Christian plot where he had a relative in the prior. Two years after the Revolution his body was dug up, exposed to view in all its decomposed horror, and buried, amid great pomp, in the Pantheon.

Voltaire's great gift was a quick intellect and an ability to use French with the lightning flash of an expert duellist, scoring time after time, against the heart of prejudice, injustice, privilege and superstition. He was wit, audacity, courage and intelligence personified. He made the utmost use of his powers and, physical weakling that he was, he was the most lordly figure of his time.

MILTON *THE CONSCIENCE*

*

TAKE an aspirin and a bromide before I utter the most frightful blasphemy that was ever uttered since Dr. Faustus signed his name to an infamous pact with the devil, a pact which released him from the great urgency of following theological disputations to their ultimate, infinite end and gave him permission, almost too late, to go out and chuck a girl under the chin. I am about to say (please hold your breath) that *Paradise Lost* and *Paradise Regained* are horrible examples of what may occur when a man with a displeasing type of mind happens to be an expert versifying technician in what is loosely called the biblical style.

Yet, after having done this, I look into the mirror and see that my face has not blackened, nor have my ears sprouted thorns at the tip; my wife and children come out to my study occasionally and ask if they can get me a sandwich or a glass of milk and do not regard me with terror but with humane indulgence; the pages in my typewriter do not turn sere and crisp and the roller does not melt before my eyes. In fine, nothing has happened except that I have recorded, for good or ill, the true state of my feelings, after much meditation, re-reading, and self-questioning.

They told me (some did), when I was in my twenties, that I would be able to appreciate and enjoy *Paradise Lost* after I had reached the age of forty. I am past forty now and twice within the last six months have I read *Paradise Lost* and *Paradise Regained* through, from beginning to end, and I have much less respect for them now than when I was forced to read them in college.

Milton is lacking, in that epic, in common sense, in true loftiness of feeling, in kindness and generosity and give-and-take, and most of all, he is thoroughly lacking in *style,* grand or common. Milton, as an epic poet, has only the make-up and costume of the grand style: he is lacking in the unpremeditated gestures, in the unconscious revelations of feeling, the soul of *style.*

When J. C. Squire reviewed Logan Pearsall Smith's *Treasury of English Prose,* he swelled up in his most dictatorial magnificence and said that when prose arises to distinction in imagery and rhythm it inevitably falls into the manner of the Authorized Version of the Bible. Mr. Squire's mistake arose from the fact that Mr. Smith had selected for his thesaurus only that prose which bore the nearest resemblance to his own—which is to say, some prize examples of bad prose—and many examples of those instances in which English writers have fallen into the Levantine sonorities of the Old Testament. This *Treasury of English Prose* was made up of a few whimsical, pansy-like confections and a great deal of the prose of the long face, the knitted brow and the patriarchal gesture. It was prose in which the golden-haired lad in lace shirtwaist and velveteen jacket was held hand in hand with the town orator in black long coat and side whiskers. It is, in the main, the language of the monody, the orison, and of the fraternal order initiation. It is the prose of the bedside manner.

It takes no special talent for irreverence to observe (if one is true to one's real response to any stimulus and not so afraid of one's self as to try to disguise it) that the so-called biblical style, nine times in ten, propounds the dubious, the false, the untrue, the bombastic or the commonplace. Too frequently it has the specious solemnity of the *C Sharp Minor Prelude,* the puerile pensiveness of some of Mr. Smith's whimsies, or the maudlin bathos of *The Face on the Barroom Floor.* It soothes the fatuous ear, but it speaks little to the mind. It is an opiate, an anodyne. It brings the comfort of the softness that is near to tears; it rests and tranquilizes; it achieves the inestimable duplicity of making the reader think he is thinking.

To be able by mere arrangement of words to anesthetize a victim and lead him to believe that his vacuous mental wandering is cerebration is, true enough, a triumph. It is the business of the politician and the quack, and on the higher plane, it is the aim, the purpose and the achievement of many good poets and musicians. But it is not inevitably the *métier* of the man who, in the sight of God (or his own self-respect) wishes to put on record what he thinks, knows and feels. Good prose is not always a threnody. Quite often it is a medium of logic, reasoned argument, orderly presentation, irony, satire, humor, fantasy, exact or suggestive description, criticism and analysis.

The convention of grandeur of the Old Testament style is, I think, a pernicious and stultifying one. "Read the Bible" is become as staple an admonition to the literary aspirant as "Don't watch the clock" is to the ambitious under-clerk. The grandeur of the Old Testament itself is unassailable truly, but it is a venerable grandeur arising from the needs and aspirations of a people. When the style of it is imitated (and it is easily imitated) it is, more often than not, the tool of charlatans or of deluded persons who think in pompous platitudes. To the sensitive, it is not always satisfying, even esthetically, because too frequently it shrouds the debatable in oracular cerements.

The real reason for the exaggerated esteem in which the biblical style is held is readily to be found in the simple experiments in the physiology of sensations. An effect of solemnity is obtained in writing, no less than in music, by the simple device of retarding the tempo of the expression. An allegro passage in music or a succession of anapests carrying the thought of a sentence to a swift conclusion is, as we know, described as "light" and "airy" or "vigorous" and "joyous." A largo passage in music, or a sequence of stressed accents in a sentence, particularly when inversion is resorted to, to check the impetus of the idea, is interpreted as "dignified," "solemn," or "profound." We speak accurately of a writer's *restraint*, but we usually mean by this to commend his thought, whereas the restraint really lies in the sentence structure. It is not, inevitably, related to high quality or distinction of thought.

Style, Remy de Gourmont pointed out, is largely governed by respiration and by the circulation of the blood. The enjoyment of a prose style, no less than the style itself, depends upon physiological factors. Thoughts recorded on a brisk walk have invariably about them a certain violence and emphasis of expression. Nietzsche's contempt for what he called "sedentary" philosophers was, in reality, only a contempt for the calmer and more leisured statement of ideas that sedentary writing induces. He himself has told us that practically everything he wrote was jotted down as he strode vigorously along lonely pathways. This accounts for the exultation and the element of violence in most of his writing; it accounts, too, for the fact that the major portion of his work is in the form of aphorisms, sketches, short notes, and that even in his longer essays there is an abruptness and patchiness suggesting an artificial cohesion. His thought, stimulated by exercise and mountain air, was governed in its expression by the rapid circulation of his blood, the swift rhythm of respiration. He was antipathetic to the calm and deliberate elaboration of an idea, an elaboration possible only to a sedentary writer. Reasoned utterance, from the very fact that it is set down as it is evolved, slowly and carefully and between breaths, falls naturally into a leisured tempo. It is never breathless or excited, for the reason that it is never spontaneous, coming with the rapidity of a single exhalation. It would be absurd to maintain that the sentences I have just written, having been composed unhastily and with precision, are for that reason more valid as relative truth than a sudden intuitional perception recorded by Nietzsche as it came to him with an impact or in a flash.

It is unreasonable, moreover, to assert that the leisured style is better than the aphoristic. To state your preference in styles is only to betray the state of your psycho-physical organization. For one's response to style, unless governed by will, is dependent, as much as is the style, upon physiological factors. The preference of youth is invariably for the spontaneous, the staccato, the vibrant, the "joyous." When youth does not reveal this preference it is due either to a weakened constitution, fatigue, phlegm, or to too precocious maturity; in other words to a condition which is not, properly speaking, young. The preference of age is for unemphatic orotundity, for the reason that such expression, being uttered in a state corresponding to the state in which it is received, is grasped and assimilated with the least exertion.

We know that most men "discover" the Bible after they have reached thirty-five. They are, for the most part, men who have in their youth been "brought up" on the Bible, and who have been thrown frequently into contact with its utterances, but have actually made many unsuccessful attempts to read it. The reason is that in their youth they are, not mentally but physiologically, incapable of responding to its patriarchal sonorities. It says nothing to them, not because the context is incomprehensible (for in the Old Testament at least the context is usually simple and explicit) but because the style or rhythmical coördination is not attuned to the pulsating physiological rhythm of youth. It is in the interest of critical common sense that we entertain more valid notions about the agreement of manner and context. It is high time to dissociate the idea of iambics from the idea of the Infinite.

BEFORE I proceed with the virtues which Milton had as a writer (and those virtues are many) I must continue my indictment of the two poems, *Paradise Lost* and *Paradise Regained,* which have been accorded far too much honor. Because Milton wrote two "epics" he is regarded by schoolmasters as having supplied that thing which was lacking in English literature. Greek literature had its Homer; Latin literature had its Virgil; Italian literature had its Dante. Homer set an example. One did not ask whether Virgil and Dante were the equals of Homer; one said "an epic writer is an epic writer; therefore Homer, Virgil and Dante are peers." Milton by writing two "epics" got into that gallery. Worse yet, he is mentioned in the same breath with Shakespeare; nay, even considered superior to Shakespeare, by some critics, who frown severely at Shakespeare's "lapses of taste" and at Shakespeare's great sense of humor.

The error of over-estimating Milton is perpetuated in England and America by the deficiencies of our educational system. Honesty of opinion is not always sought by the faculties of English and American universities but only conformity of opinion. If a man aspires to teach English in an English or American school and prepares himself for that profession by taking courses which lead to a master's degree or a doctor's degree, without which he cannot expect to rise in his profession, he is usually required to have "correct" opinions on all subjects. One of the correct opinions is that Milton ranks with Chaucer and Shakespeare, whereas there is ample reason for classing Milton as a minor poet, inferior not only to some of the great Elizabethans, aside from Shakespeare, but also inferior to Dryden. Even as a prose writer he is not comparable to Robert Burton, Sir Thomas Urquhart, Sir Thomas Browne, Thomas Dekker, Daniel De Foe, Jonathan Swift or John Dryden. There have been a few hardy spirits among critics in England and America, including the renowned scholars, Charles Eliot Norton of Harvard and Bliss Perry, also of Harvard, who have dared to question Milton's eminence. Norton said that even students of literature could disregard *Paradise Regained* altogether and that to read only the first two books of *Paradise Lost* was quite sufficient to give them all they needed to know about the epics.

Also, it may be remarked that few idolaters of Milton have been able to bring themselves to any real enthusiasm for *Paradise Regained*. Even in Milton's lifetime that composition was a source of great irritation to Milton. "Most of us," writes Norman Douglas in *Old Calabria,* "have wondered how it came about that Milton could not endure to hear *Paradise Lost* preferred to *Paradise Regained,* in view of the apparent inferiority of the latter. If we had known what Milton knew, namely, to how large an extent *Paradise Lost* was not the child of his own imagination, and therefore not so precious in his eyes as *Paradise Regained,* we might have understood his prejudice."

The truth is known to many•scholars that *Paradise Lost* is one of the baldest plagiarisms in the history of literature. For many years it was known that it was a pastiche or a mosaic of pilferings from Æschylus, Ovid, Ariosto, Masenius, Cedmon, Vondel, and others, but it was not learned that Milton had stolen the whole scheme of *Paradise Lost* from a little-known Italian contemporary and had translated or transliterated passage after passage almost word for word, until Professor Bliss Perry of Harvard happened to examine the text of a unique copy of *Adamo Canuto* by Serafino della Salandra in the library of the University. The discovery had really been made by an Italian scholar, Francesco Zicari, who published a paper in the Naples, *Album scientifico-artistico-litterario,* in 1845 under the title *Sulla scoverta dell' originale italiano de cui Milton trasse il suc poema paradiso perduto.*

Salandra was an Italian poet-playwright who published a mystery play called *Adamo Canuto* in 1647. "I will now," writes Norman Douglas, "without further preamble, extract from Zicari's article as much as may be sufficient to show ground for his contention that *Paradise Lost* is a transfusion, in general and particular, of this same mystery." Douglas proceeds:

Salandra's central theme is the Universe shattered by the disobedience of the First Man, the origin of our unhappiness and sins. The same with Milton.

Salandra's chief personages are God and His Angels; the first man and woman; the serpent; Satan and His angels. The same with Milton.

Salandra, at the opening of his poem (the prologue), sets forth his argument, and dwells upon the Creative Omnipotence and his works. The same with Milton.

Salandra then describes the council of the rebel angels, their fall from heaven into a desert and sulphurous region, their discourses. Man is enviously spoken of, and his fall by means of stratagem decided upon; it is resolved to reunite in council in Pandemonium or the Abyss, where measures may be adopted to the end that man may become the enemy of God and the prey of hell. The same with Milton.

Salandra personifies Sin and Death, the latter being the child of the former. The same with Milton.

Salandra describes Omnipotence foreseeing the effects of the temptation and fall of man, and preparing his redemption. The same with Milton.

Salandra depicts the site of Paradise and the happy life there. The same with Milton.

Salandra sets forth the miraculous creation of the universe and of man, and the virtues of the forbidden fruit. The same with Milton.

Salandra reports the conversation between Eve and the Serpent; the eating of the forbidden fruit and the despair of our first parents. The same with Milton.

Salandra describes the joy of Death at the discomfiture of Eve; the rejoicings in hell; the grief of Adam; the flight of our first parents, their shame and repentance. The same with Milton.

Salandra anticipates the intercession of the Redeemer, and the overthrow of Sin and Death; he dwells upon the wonders of the Creation, the murder of Abel by his brother Cain, and other human ills; the vices of the Antediluvians, due to the fall of Adam; the infernal gift of war. The same with Milton.

Salandra describes the passion of Jesus Christ, and the comforts which Adam and Eve receive from the angel who announces the coming of the Messiah; lastly, their departure from the earthly paradise. The same with Milton.

That is not all. I refer you to *Old Calabria,* which is a charming and informative book in every respect, written by a true scholar and an incomparable stylist, for the examples, in parallel, of instances where Milton translated Salandra almost word for word. Some of these passages contain phrases which have been pointed out as evidences of Milton's mastery of "the grand style."

The charge which must be brought against Milton is really a serious one. At the age of thirty-three he gave notice in his pamphlet, *The Reason of Church-government Urged Against Prelatry* that, through "labour and intent study (which I take to be my portion in this life) joyn't with the strong propensity of my nature," he intended to "leave something so written to aftertimes, as they should not willingly let die," and that "what the greatest and choycest wits of Athens, Rome, or Modern Italy, and those Hebrews of old did for their country, I in my proportion with this over and above of being a Christian, might doe for mine." (It is obvious that he thought his being a Christian gave him a great advantage over Homer, Æschylus and the authors of the Old Testament.)

After he had advertised his intention, he proceeded in that same pamphlet to condemn all English poetry of his time and before him—the poetry of Chaucer, Spenser, Shakespeare, Marlowe, Donne, Jonson and the rest—as the work of "unskilfull . . . monks and mechanics." Also he criticized Homer, Virgil, and Tasso as being too "diffuse" and held the *Book of Job* to be a "brief model" of the sort of thing he meant to write. He advertised, moreover, that he intended to write a poetic *drama* about an English king or knight who lived before the Norman conquest, in whom he might "lay the pattern of a Christian Hero." He would do for England what Sophocles and Euripides had done for Athens. (It is important to note here that Milton did not mention Æschylus, the Greek dramatist from whom he pilfered so much, and that he voiced no high opinion of Shakespeare as a dramatist, in comparison with the author of the *Apocalypse,* which he describes as "the majestic image of a high and stately Tragedy, shutting up and intermingling her solemn Scenes and Acts with a sevenfold Chorus of halleluja's and harping symphonies.")

He tells us, frankly, that with the sort of gifts and Christian nature that he has, he can write a poetic drama which "may be easily made appear over all kinds of Lyrick poesy" in "the very critical art of composition."

These abilities which he has, he tells us, "wheresoever they may be found, are the inspired guift of God rarely bestow'd, but yet to come (though most abuse) in every Nation: and are of power beside the office of a pulpit, to inbreed and cherish in a great people the seeds of vertu, and publick civility, to ally the perturbations of the mind, and set the affections in right tune, to celebrate in glorious and lofty Hymns the throne and equipage of Gods Almightinesse, and what he works, and what he suffers to be wrought with high providence in his Church, to sing the victorious agonies of Martyrs and Saints, the deeds and triumphs of just and pious Nations doing valiantly through faith against the enemies of Christ, to deplore the general relapses of Kingdoms and States from justice and Gods true worship. Lastly, whatsoever in religion is holy and sublime, in vertu amiable, or grave, whatsoever hath passion or admiration in all the changes of that which is call'd fortune from without, or the wily suttleties and refluxes of mans thoughts from within, all these things with a solid and treatable smoothnesse to point out and describe. Teaching over the whole book of sanctity and vertu through all the instances of example with such delight to those especially of soft and delicious temper who will not so much as look upon Truth herself, unlesse they see her elegantly drest, that whereas the paths of honesty and good life appear now rugged and difficult, though they be indeed easy and pleasant, they would appeare to all men both easy and pleasant though they were rugged and difficult indeed. And what a benefit this would be to our youth and gentry, may be soon guest by what we know of the corruption and bane which they suck in dayly from the writings and interludes of libidinous and ignorant Poetasters, who having scars ever heard of that which is the main consistence of a true poem, the choys of such persons as they ought to introduce, and what is morall and decent to each one, doe for the most part lap up vitious principles in sweet pils to be swallow'd down, and make the tast of vertuous documents harsh and sowr."

He tells us also, with monumental egotism, that, even in his youth while he was in Italy he dashed off some "trifles," which he had "shifted in scarcity of books and other conveniences" and that these trifles were received with "written Encomiums, which the Italian is not forward to bestow on men this side the Alps." (Shakespeare would have been surprised, I think, on reading that passage from Milton. It would never have occurred to him that a poet needed books and other conveniences in order to write poems. Nor, I think, would it have occurred to Shakespeare to put the judgment of Italians above that of his countrymen and to flatter himself that he had been praised by Italians.)

Milton, indeed, promises us a great deal. He resorts to the writer's ancient alibi for not being able at the moment to turn out the sort of thing he would like to write: Milton blames "prelatry" and says that under its "inquisitorious and tyrannical duncery no free and splendid wit can flourish." That excuse is as good, or as bad, as any other: some writers blame democracy, some blame capitalism, some blame this and some blame that: Milton blamed the prelatry, which is amusing to consider, inasmuch as we know well enough that in Milton's time the authority and the influence of the Catholic prelates in England had been vastly curtailed while Protestantism flourished. Moreover, Milton asked for time (no one was urging him): "Neither doe I think it shame to covenant with any knowing reader, that for some few yeers yet I may go on trust with him toward the payment of what I am now indebted, as being a work not to be rays'd from the heat of youth, or the vapours of wine, like that which flows at wast from the pen of some vulgar Amorist, or the trencher fury of a riming parasite, nor to be obtain'd by the invocation of Dame Memory and her Siren daughters, but by devout prayer to that eternall Spirit which can enrich with all utterance and knowledge, and sends out his Seraphim with the hallow'd fire of his Altar to touch and purify the lips of whom he pleases: to this must be added industrious and select reading, steddy observation, insight into all seemly and generous arts and affairs."

Why Milton felt obliged to write so large an order against himself no one can determine. But there it is in one of his long-winded pamphlets, a pamphlet ostensibly about church government but so rambling that the only parts now interesting to us are those parts in which Milton tells us, as if he had been ordered to do so, that he was going to write the greatest single work of literature that was ever written. He was a clever man, an exceedingly clever man, and he had a talent so adroit that he has deceived generations of critics into putting the same valuation upon him as he put upon himself.

But, after so vain a pronouncement, had not the world, to whom Milton so confidently addressed himself, a right to expect something more than a theft from a poor little Italian contemporary, interlarded with transliterations from Æschylus, Ovid, Vondel and others? The classics, as Norman Douglas pointed out, are there for all of us to make what use of them we can (Milton made plenty use of them) but when one steals the work of a contemporary that is not so condonable a matter.

Milton at first advertised that he was going to write a great tragedy around the deeds and personality of one of the early English kings or knights. It is known that he contemplated making King Arthur his hero. He announced, in effect, that his drama would not be homely, like the poems of Chaucer (in Milton's time the notion was general that Chaucer was a monk), nor would it be "mechanical" or "rays'd from the heat of youth, or vapours of wine, like that which flows at wast from the pen of some vulgar Amorist," i.e., like the work of Shakespeare. But at that time he had not seen Salandra's tragedy.

The *Adamo Canuto* of Salandra was not published until six years after the pamphlet, *The Reason of Church-government Urged Against Prelatry.* We do not know how this Italian tragedy came into Milton's hands. Norman Douglas suggests that Milton may have met Salandra during his sojourn in Italy and that Salandra may have given him a manuscript copy, knowing that Milton was a famous and influential man in England, and hoping that Milton would arrange for an English translation of his tragedy. There is also the fact that Milton had correspondents in Italy (he met Grotius in Paris and Galileo in Florence as well as other famous per-

sonages of his time), who may have sent him a copy of the tragedy
when it was published. The *Adamo Canuto* had a very small sale.
Milton was a great English pamphleteer, none of whose work could
go unnoticed, whereas Salandra was an obscure Calabrian monk!
Mark the fact that Salandra was a monk and recall what Milton
wrote about the literature of monks.

"It is certainly an astonishing fact," writes Norman Douglas,
"that no scholar of the stamp of Thayer was acquainted with the
Adamo Canuto and it says much for the isolation of England that,
at a period when poems on the subject of paradise lost were being
scattered broadcast in Italy and elsewhere—when, in short, all
Europe was ringing with the doleful history of Adam and Eve—
Milton could have ventured to speak of his work as 'Things un-
attempted yet in prose or rhyme'—an amazing verse which, by the
way, is literally transcribed out of Ariosto (*Cosa, non detta in prosa
mai, ne in rima*)."

Now what did Milton contribute to *Paradise Lost* that was his
own? He contributed, or worked in, the notion that Man is the highest of God's creatures, Lord of the Universe, and that Woman should
be subservient to man always, never thinking for herself. He embellished Salandra's character of Satan, who, in modern theatrical
parlance, "runs away with the show." And he transliterated Salandra
into austere and stately blank verse.

Much ink has been spilt by interpreters of Milton's "thought"
as embodied in *Paradise Lost*. To me, the most interesting of these
interpretations is *The Modernity of Milton* by Martin A. Larson,
of the department of English at the University of Idaho. Another
good one is the work of a French critic, Denis Seurat, whose *Milton:
Man and Thinker* is now considered a standard commentary. Each
is a work of art in itself: Mr. Larson and M. Seurat have written
charming books about themselves, and about life in general, *apropos
of* Milton. It is therefore not to be wondered at, that their understanding of Milton differs on almost every important point. Both
of them read into *Paradise Lost* many values which I am constrained
to believe Milton did not put there. M. Seurat believes that Milton
made himself the hero of *Paradise Lost* and threw himself "personally into the struggle against Satan" and that from "a reading
of *Paradise Lost* one gathers two inevitable impressions: the greatness of Satan and the greatness of Milton. . . . Milton had Satan in
him and wanted to drive him out. He had felt passion, pride and

sensuality. The deep pleasure he takes in his creation of Satan is a joy." Nearly all critics have agreed that Satan is the real hero of *Paradise Lost*. It is pleasant therefore to hear Mr. Larson's argument that Milton's Satan is not a hero at all, but a villain, and that under Milton's treatment the character of Satan "undergoes a progressive desiccation and degradation."

What interests me most is Milton's treatment of the character of Eve, and his attitude toward women generally. Milton was of the opinion that woman should be submissive to man in all things. His picture of the ideal relationship between man and wife, in his portrayal of Adam and Eve, is that wherein the husband does all of the thinking for the family and the wife yields to him with "coy submission, modest pride." The husband is to seek God, and the wife is to think he is like God.

"Hee for God only, shee for God in him."

With ideas like that, one is not surprised to learn that women found Milton rather trying. His first wife left him within a few months after their marriage and did not return to him for two years. "It seems that in later life," writes Mr. Larson, "Milton became less amiable in attitude toward women and more distrustful of them. In *Paradise Lost* he seems to take a kind of pleasure in humbling Eve before her husband; he makes her play a peculiarly ignominious part in the Fall—one more so than the Bible story would require. He portrays the deceits of Delila, her repulse by Samson, and her unmasking with evident delight. In *Paradise Regained*, Milton makes Satan express scorn for Asmodai's opinion that Christ could be seduced by women and praises Alexander and Scipio, who could be superior to their charms. . . .

"Thus we see that Milton's attitude toward women underwent a complete change during the course of his experience: first, it was a childish admiration for their mere outside; second, it was a high honor, based on heavy requirements exacted from them; and, third, after many years of varied experience, it was a final distrust which bordered on hatred."

That is the truth about the matter, and it comes from a critic wholly prejudiced in Milton's favor. It is pleasant to have this confirmation of my own impression.

Milton was the apotheosis of the Puritan conscience. I do not wish to become metaphysical, but it seems to have been in the supernal scheme of things (or God's design, if you prefer) that poor

Milton should suffer, as a scapegoat, like Christ himself, for the concupiscence and intemperance of man. And that three wives and three daughters should suffer with, and from, him. The ideal of chastity was paramount with him; and yet he was a full-blooded man. His ideal, as we know, caused him great anguish: it is evident throughout his work.

It is a significant fact, I think, that Milton wrote only one love poem in English, *To a Nightingale*. He seemed to regard the English language as an instrument only of austerity and of vicious personal abuse. When he wrote pleasantly or lightly of love, he used Italian —"this is the language Love boasteth as his own." Let no one quote *L'Allegro* to me in refutation of what I have just said, and mention Amaryllis. That poem, like its dark twin, *Il Penseroso,* is a sophomoric composition. Those two poems are literary refinements of adolescent perplexity written by a studious and proper and very gifted young man, picturing to himself the delights of two possible ways of life. In adolescence one is confronted with two conflicting desires—to have a good time and to make something out of one's self. Milton was bothered by this dilemma. He thought it would be nice to have a sweetheart and to "sport" with her, freely and joyously on some river bank. But stern duty and his conscience told him that he ought to be in some dark tower, poring over books and thinking out the meaning of life.

Milton thought out *a* meaning of life and to him it had to do with the Puritan conscience, foreshadowed in *Il Penseroso* and reflected in all his later work. Critics have tried to explain away the Puritan in the most Puritan of poets by showing his literary derivations from the Italian renaissance. But this is because they associate the word "Puritan" with the word "dour." The puritanism of Milton degenerated among the weak and fearful into a strict set of prohibitions. Milton's point always, and eloquently, sustained in the *Areopagitica,* was that the proof of virtue was in the exercise of virtue in a free choice among the widest possible temptations.

Milton is one of the best examples we have of what resolution and purpose, application and self-discipline can enable a man to achieve a goal early perceived in life. Milton not only decided quite early in life that he was going to be one of England's great poets, if not England's greatest, but in the *Lycidas,* in a few of his sonnets, and in the *Samson Agonistes,* he achieved the lesser ambition. In fact, in the minds of some, he achieved it in *Paradise Lost* and

Paradise Regained. But my own conviction is that these two "epics" will, in time, be considered mere curiosities of literature.

JOHN MILTON was born in London on the ninth of December, 1608, eight years before Shakespeare died. He was the son of a man who made his living in the mortgage loan business, but who seems to have had his heart in music and scholarship. His cultural hobbies, however, did not prevent him from being a good provider for his family. The elder Milton pampered his son, John, and supported him until he was thirty-five years old. He gave his children every advantage, and Christopher, a younger brother of John, rose to eminence in the judiciary and became a knight.

John went to St. Paul's school in London and to Christ's College, Cambridge. At college he was nicknamed the "Lady of Christ's." That was not kind, but collegians are usually rude barbarians who have little tolerance with the sort of prig which Milton undoubtedly was. In his religious and sectarian pamphlets, he is discursively autobiographical, often giving us much more about himself than about the subject of his thesis; and in these pamphlets he paints a picture of himself (without intending to do so) that is much more intolerably priggish than Marcus Aurelius is in his *Meditations*. He has been described at that period as beautiful and as of cleanly habits and of "daintiness" in his life and conversation. He had, however, a hysterical temperament; he was feline and utterly without a sense of humor; he displayed the emotions of a prima donna all his life. In his *Apology Against a Pamphlet Called a Modest Confutation,* he loses all sense of proportion, leaves his subject hanging in the air for page after page and tells us what a chaste and well-brought-up person he is, and how far he outshines all other poets in virtue. In that pamphlet those who disagree with him are "vipers," "scavengers," "imbeciles," "illiterates," "dissolute heathen," "frequentors of bordellos," "obscene," "drunken," "fenborn serpents," who write "vomit." One doesn't need to be a Catholic or an Anglo-Catholic to suggest that it was slightly exaggerated to describe the English vicars of Christ of Milton's time as being mired in "a masse of slime and mud" and as participants in "the sloathful, the covetous and ambitious hopes of Church-promotions and fat Bishopricks" in which the Church is "bred up and nuzzl'd in, like a great Python from her youth, to prove the general poyson both of doctrine and good discipline in the Land."

Milton was vain and rebellious as a student at Cambridge, and that is a good sign always in youth. But his rebellion was at once a monumental self-satisfaction and a monumental dissatisfaction with himself. We do not know how or why he early conceived the idea that he was destined to write the greatest work of literature that had ever been written. He was graduated from Cambridge with two degrees, after having written some sonnets in English, Latin and Italian, the *L'Allegro* and *Il Penseroso* and the stately charade to be performed by students, *Comus*.

At twenty-four he left college and went to reside at Horton at Buckinghamshire with his mother who was living in a house there although her husband was in London. For five years Milton did little work. He spent his time in study and in "self-improvement." In college he had written several poems, notably his sonnet on his twenty-third birthday, expressing dissatisfaction that he was getting along in life without having accomplished anything. That is natural enough: all men in their youth feel that time is passing swiftly and that they have not yet become great heroes or great thinkers or great men of wealth.

"Milton at Horton," writes Augustine Birrell in his life of Milton which is to be found in *Obiter Dicta*, "made up his mind to be a great poet—neither more nor less; and with that end in view he toiled unceasingly. A more solemn dedication of a man by himself to the poetical office cannot be imagined. Everything about him became, as it were, pontifical, almost sacramental. A poet's soul must contain the perfect shape of all things good, wise and just. His body must be spotless and without blemish, his life pure, his thoughts high, his studies intense. There was no drinking at the Mermaid for John Milton."

From Horton he begins to write letters to his friends which may be studied as models of the kind of stilted literariness which should be avoided like the plague by all writers; he displays in these letters some woefully inept literary judgments, and he begins in them that conscious or unconscious duplicity which is to characterize him throughout his writing career: never once does he praise the writers to whom he is most indebted, only a few of them does he mention, and he seems deliberately to establish literary progenitors to whom he owed nothing, and (what has astounded his most sympathetic interpreters) he turns upon those Hellenic writers he had praised in his youth with a special venom when he grew older. (See the chapter, "The Evolution of Milton's Thought" in Larson's *The Modernity of Milton*.)

When his mother died, he was twenty-nine, and he obtained money from his father to spend fifteen months of travel and study in Europe. His father must have been liberal, for Milton went as a man of importance and he was received everywhere with that deference accorded a man of letters with two degrees from Cambridge. He met and conversed with famous scholars and scientists in France and Italy, chief of whom was Galileo. He did not kiss the Pope's toe, for he was a bitter and unrelenting Protestant who described the Pope as "a grim wolf" and the Pope's prelates as so many carrion crows. He traveled about, as Birrell says, "in a leisurely manner from city to city, writing Latin verses for his hosts and Italian sonnets in their ladies' albums, buying books and music, and creating, one cannot doubt, an all too flattering impression of an English Protestant." He intended to go to Sicily and Greece, but he was recalled home by the gravity of the situation which was arising in England.

This is not the place for me to unravel the threads of the political and ecclesiastical tangle which had developed when Milton was recalled from Europe. Charles I was a pleasant and cultivated person but he was ill-advised and was ill-fitted for the kingship of a country from which the prosperity of the expansive Elizabethan era had fled and of which the state treasury was empty. Cromwell was an exceedingly capable leader of men, if ruthless, as dictators and good military commanders must be. If I read the economic realities of the period aright, there is little to choose between Charles I and Cromwell. Both men were creatures of a social and economic system which was vicious in many respects and which was impoverishing the people, and that means it was also impoverishing those at the top, although it might not immediately appear so to them.

Cromwell's rule was brief and the Puritan reaction against the Cavaliers was brief also, for it was followed by the most licentious era in English history. Cromwell, by an earnest decimation of a vast section of the population, in England, Scotland and Ireland, in a civil war, brought about a temporary prosperity which was carried over into the reign of Charles II. When there are fewer mouths to feed, the family budget goes further and war has a way of creating an apparent prosperity by laying the cost of war upon future generations. Cromwell is frequently said to have restored to the English people their ancient liberties and to have achieved much for the triumph of democracy. Actually he did little more than disprove

the theory of the divine right of kings; he greatly aided the expropriation of the land by the bankocracy and passed laws which kept
the masses in a more servile condition than before. (See Karl Marx,
Capital, page 798.)

When Milton returned to England he did not participate in
any of the stirring events of the time; civil war broke out and he
opened up a boarding school for boys; he did not become a pamphleteer until his domestic troubles caused him to write his famous
pamphlet, *The Doctrine and Discipline of Divorce Restored to the
Good of Both Sexes*.

It will be observed that Milton was not a disciplined and dispassionate thinker; he was not interested in ideas so much as in
ecclesiastical theory and in theories of moral conduct, and he was
stimulated to write vigorously on those subjects only under private
irritation. Just as his most famous prose work, the *Areopagitica*,
was later on to be written by him out of disappointment because the
Round Heads had closed the theaters as incitements to vice, whereas
his principal ambition was to write great dramatic works which
would be produced on the stage, so were his divorce tracts caused
by his marital troubles.

WHEN he was thirty-five Milton married Mary Powell, a seven-
teen-year-old daughter of a royalist country squire, and brought her
to live at the house in Aldergate Street where he had his school.
She left him in less than a month and returned to her parents.
Milton was undoubtedly a tyrannical husband with very strange
ideas about women: he believed a wife should never express opinions of her own, that she should submit to her husband in all things,
and, moreover, he believed connubial pleasures should be austere
and that a woman should find her greatest pleasure in pleasing her
lord and master. If one is curious about Milton's views of marriage,
one might read Book IX of *Paradise Lost* which describes the fall
of Eve. The book ends:

> ... Thus it shall befall
> Him who to worth in Women overtrusting
> Lets her will rule; restraint she will not brook,
> And left to her self, if evil thence ensue,
> She first his weak indulgence will accuse.
>   Thus they in mutual accusation spent
> The fruitless hours, but neither self-condemning,
> And of their vain contest appear'd no end.

Augustine Birrell suggests that Mrs. Milton, being the young, lively and happy daughter of a rollicking Cavalier, found the dour mode of living of the Puritan poet too great a contrast to the jolly home life she had been used to. He says, with a certain malice, that "silence reigned in the house" and that probably the only noise she heard was that of Milton thrashing his pupils; for "Milton had none of that noble humanitarian spirit which had led Montaigne long years before" to protest against the custom of flogging school-children. But there is proof in Milton's writings that he had a violent and somewhat hysterical temper; and inasmuch as he accuses his wife of "sitting mute and insensate" at the table, it is probable that the half-spirited young woman had to listen to a great deal of dicta-torial nagging and recriminations from him, grew sulky and refused to answer him back and, finally, completely fed up, left him. She ultimately returned to him, after a separation of more than two years, and bore him four daughters. But the iron sank into his soul after that honeymoon experience.

Not long after Mrs. Milton left the poet, he appears to have consoled himself by paying court to a young unmarried woman; and when he wrote the divorce tracts, it is probable that he hoped to obtain a divorce from his wife and marry again. On the subject of divorce he argues with great force, cogency and verbosity that not for adultery alone should a divorce be granted but on any grounds of incompatibility, for irreconcilable differences in religious views or even from a simple realization that a man and wife are not har-moniously suited to one another. But these divorce tracts were unacceptable to all the Protestant sects of the time as well as to the Catholics, and Mrs. Milton would not divorce him. How the reconciliation was brought about we do not know; but I think there is great significance in the fact that when Mrs. Milton returned to the poet's house in London she brought all of the other Powells with her. Her father had been reduced to poverty by the Civil War; and I think that perhaps it was only in this extremity that Mary Milton was forced to return. She bore him four daughters in rapid succession, dying in childbirth at the age of twenty-six.

About the time of Mary Milton's return in 1645, Milton pub-lished his first collection of his poems, the title page of which reads: "Poems of Mr. John Milton, both English and Latin, compos'd at several times/Printed by his true Copies./ The Songs were set in Musick by Mr. Henry Lawes Gentleman of Kings Chapel, and one of His Majesties Private Music." The volume included the ode

On the Morning of Christ's Nativity, L'Allegro, Il Penseroso, and some of his sonnets. In the same year he also brought out *A Mask,* which is usually called the *Comus.* Meanwhile he was furiously engaged in pamphleteering.

In 1649 Milton launched his famous pamphlet *The Tenure of Kings and Magistrates,* "proving that it is lawful, and hath been held so through all the ages, for any who have the power, to call to account a Tyrant or a Wicked King, and after due conviction, to depose, and put him to death, if the ordinary Magistrates have neglected to do so." That was the year of the trial and execution of Charles I, but Milton's pamphlet was not a provoker of that deed; it was an argument after the fact. The pamphlet made so little stir that Charles II did not include Milton among the regicides called to account after the Restoration. Milton was also employed in that year as Latin Secretary to Cromwell's council of state; but he was not Cromwell's secretary, as has erroneously been said, and was not even an active participant in the politics of the time. His job was only a clerkship and came to him because of his linguistic abilities. He was required to translate Latin and Italian dispatches into English.

Meanwhile, following the *Tenure,* Milton became embroiled in prolonged logomachy with the European scholar, Salmasius, on the propriety of beheading a king. Salmasius wrote taking issue with the *Tenure,* whereupon Milton leveled at his critic three pamphlets in rapid succession, including the two tracts on the *Defence of the English People.* It is curious to note that in these pamphlets Milton wrote mainly about himself and descended to the most violent personal abuse: there are some noble passages in them, but also some passages in billingsgate which are without parallel in English literature.

Milton's first wife died in 1653, and three years later he married Catherine Woodstock, who died within less than two years. He appears to have been somewhat happier with Catherine Woodstock, for he wrote a tender, if rather unemotional, sonnet to her memory after her death. In 1663 he married Elizabeth Minshull, who seems to have been little more than a housekeeper for him. By that time he had been totally blind for eleven years; he was working on *Paradise Lost,* requiring his daughters to wait upon him, read to him and take his dictation, and ruling them in such a tyrannical manner that they grew to dislike him intensely. He permitted them no soul or existence of their own.

Milton finished *Paradise Lost* in 1664, but it was not accepted for publication until 1667. Under the terms of his agreement with the publisher he got five pounds down and was to be paid five pounds for each succeeding edition of fifteen hundred copies. In all he got ten pounds, and after his death his widow sold her rights in the poem for eight pounds. The book was received coldly and with some hostile criticism; but it made little general impression, although nearly three thousand copies of it were sold during the first year.

Milton was bestirred to write a sequel by the comment of a friendly critic who asked, "Why not a *Paradise Regained?*" This was so manifestly inferior to the first poem that, for reasons suggested by Norman Douglas, Milton was always made furiously angry by hearing the first preferred to the second.

With the publication of *Samson Agonistes* in 1671, Milton achieved, in my opinion, his greatest single work. In it he wrote a solemn poetical drama about his blindness, his own despair, and his courageous triumph, in terms of the biblical story of the blind Samson. During the last years of his life, his labors were titanic; he did a vast amount of hack-work, writing a grammar and other text-books, translating and editing. He died on November 8, 1674. His widow survived him more than fifty years.

THE exaggerated esteem in which Milton's two epics are held in some quarters has been of slow growth and against much damaging criticism. Among those who attacked the tradition have been Dr. Samuel Johnson, Walter Bagehot, Samuel Taylor Coleridge, Thomas Arnold and Charles Eliot Norton. But it is a curious thing that even those who have written most sympathetically about Milton cannot help betraying their imperfect sympathy with most of Milton's work or betraying their lack of admiration for the man.

Milton had become a symbol rather than the author of a literature which we can take to our hearts. He was an embodiment of the Puritan conscience of the English races—a conscience that persists and co-exists with all freedom of the mind and spirit. Certain passages from the *Areopagitica* and from the *Defence of the English People,* isolated from their long-winded texts, will always live as remarkable examples of noble and stately prose; and they are there to be cited against the censors, the busy-bodies who seek to regulate by law the taste and morals of their fellows. Milton the Puritan has written:

They are not skilfull considerers of human things, who imagin to remove sin by removing the matter of sin; for, besides that it is a huge heap increasing under the very act of diminishing, though some part of it may for a time be withdrawn from some persons, it cannot from all, in such a universall thing as books are; and when this is done, yet the sin remains entire. Though ye take from a covetous man all his treasure, he has yet one jewell left, ye cannot bereave him of his covetousnesse. Banish all objects of lust, shut up all youth into the severest discipline that can be exercised in any hermitage, ye cannot make them chaste, that came not thither so: such great care and wisdom is requir'd to the right managing of this point. Suppose we could expell sin by this means; look how much we thus expell of sin, so much we expell of vertue; for the matter of them both is the same; remove that, and ye remove them both alike.

He was extremely conscious of sin, but he believed that the problem of good and evil should be settled individually and as a matter for one's own conscience.

DE FOE *THE JOURNALIST*

*

Nevertheless, journalism is the highest form of literature; for all the highest literature is journalism. The writer who aims at producing the platitudes which are 'not for this age, but for all time' has his reward in being unreadable in all ages; whilst Plato and Aristophanes trying to knock some sense into the Athens of their day, Shakespeare peopling that same Athens with Elizabethan mechanics and Warwickshire hunts, Ibsen photographing the local doctors and vestrymen of a Norwegian parish, Carpaccio painting the life of St. Ursula exactly as if she were a lady living in the street next to him, are still alive and at home everywhere among the dust and ashes of thousands of academic, punctilious, archeologically correct men of letters and art who spent their lives haughtily avoiding the journalist's vulgar obsession with the ephemeral.
—George Bernard Shaw, THE SANITY OF ART

C. E. MONTAGUE once wrote a novel, well remembered by many, called *A Hind Let Loose*. It is about an English journalist, cynically unconcerned with the tremendous trifles of ephemeral politics but gifted with a trenchant style, who earned a fair income by living a double life: He secretly attached himself to two newspapers which were antagonistic in politics and wrote editorials thundering for both sides, the one against the other. He enlivened controversy, because no one better knew than he the weaknesses of the two opposing arguments he put up, and thus, by a dispassionately artistic treatment, he could give an illusion of importance to issues which did not matter in the least.

Daniel De Foe was the first great editorial writer in English

297

journalism; and he seems to have set the standard in the profession of editorial writing as it is quite universally practiced nowadays. Editorial writers think nothing of switching from a Democratic to a Republican newspaper or from a radical to a conservative magazine and putting their minor convictions (if they have any) in their pockets and their abilities at the service and dictates of their employer.

De Foe was the progenitor and paragon of editorial writers. He was an artist first and foremost and, as he had early very painful reason to know, in the Whig camp as well as the Tory camp the men in control were scoundrels, and between Anglicans and Dissenters there was little to choose on the score of degrees of stupidity, selfishness and intolerance. Nominally a Whig, therefore, he did not hesitate to accept service as a pamphleteer in the pay of a Tory ministry or, even as a known Whig, to write mild editorials against the Tories so he could get into Whig counsels as a spy of the Tories. He would turn out an anonymous pamphlet attacking the standing army as inconsistent with a free government; and, when no other pamphleteer could meet his argument with any force or logic, he would do the job himself, anonymously and in the grand style.

When an unusual happening occurs in some remote place, metropolitan newspapers send reporters to the spot to investigate and write up the incident and the circumstances. In 1706 De Foe inaugurated this practice by journeying post-haste to Canterbury on his own initiative when word reached him that a particularly startling visitation of a ghost had occurred there. Quite like a trained and efficient modern star reporter (but with more talent than most of them) he investigated the matter thoroughly, interviewed the natives, ordered his notes into an artistic model of news reporting and ran it in his journal, the *Review,* under the heading, "A True Relation of the Apparition of one Mrs. Veal, the next Day after her Death, to one Mrs. Bargrave at Canterbury."

Alfred Harmsworth, Lord Northcliffe, who rose to such power in England before and during the War that he could make and break ministries through the influence of his chain of newspapers, founded his fortune on a newspaper called *Answers to Correspondents* (later *Answers*) which achieved enormous circulation by attempting to answer all sorts of questions,—historical, political, philosophical, scientific, literary or personal (such as advice to the lovelorn, and on household economy, decoration, and cooking and problems of marriage, the education of children and gardening).

This type of newspaper was first started by De Foe's friend, John Dunton, with a monthly publication called the *Athenian Gazette*. De Foe stole the idea from Dunton, started a rival publication called the *Little Review*, brought it out weekly instead of monthly, made it much brighter and livelier than Dunton's, got most of Dunton's trade, and drove the latter into bankruptcy. (No: De Foe's ethics were no more exemplary than Harmsworth's or Hearst's or Rockefeller's or Morgan's or of members in good standing in the Authors' League or of evangelists or of merchandisers or of advertisers or of anybody who is not in business for his health.)

The editorials of Arthur Brisbane, Walter Lippmann and David Lawrence, the "colyums," cartoons, news features, fiction and the staple appurtenances of a modern daily newspaper are syndicated and appear simultaneously in all parts of the country. Daniel De Foe originated that idea. He was the first to contrive to have his pamphlets issued simultaneously in various cities in England, Scotland and Wales.

Nearly all metropolitan newspapers now carry road maps and information about routes and what is seen along the way. There is the faithful Baedeker and many another guide to Europe. Chambers of commerce and railroad companies employ writers to describe the pleasures to be had and the sights to be seen by travelers to, and through, different states. Daniel De Foe was one of the first, if not actually the first, writer in England to be commissioned by a publisher to write such a guide, with maps. It required months of travel on horseback and painstaking work of observing, taking notes and reducing the material to a concise, reliable and entertaining work of information. It was called:

A Tour thro' the whole island of Great Britain; divided into Circuits or Journies. Giving a Particular and Diverting Account of whatever is Curious and worth observation, viz.: I. A description of the Principal Cities and Towns, their Situation, Magnitude, Government and Commerce. II. The Customs, Manners, Speech; as also the Exercises, Diversions, and Employment of the People. III. The Produce and Improvement of the Land, the Trade and Manufactures. IV. The seaports and Fortifications, with the Course of Rivers, and the Inland Navigation. V. The Publick Edifices, Seats and Palaces, of the Gentry and Nobility. With use Observations on the whole, Particularly fitted for the reading of Such, as Desire to Travel over the Island.

That work, as the descriptive title would indicate, was of immense value to merchants and traveling salesmen (the latter were just beginning to appear in England at that time) as well as to tourists and pilgrims.

Reports of the daily fluctuations and transactions in the stock market is an indispensable feature of a modern metropolitan newspaper. De Foe was the first to print news of stock quotations and comment on the stock market. (Robert Harley, Chancellor of the Exchequer, and Daniel De Foe were the ones who worked out the great financial scheme of the South Sea company, a bold and legitimate enterprise which wiped out the public debt; but it was so successful that it developed such a fever of speculation over all England and Europe that it finally collapsed, spreading financial ruin everywhere, as such speculative bubbles always do.)

The public appetite for scandalous gossip has never diminished since the days when the ancient Spartans were chinning about the affair between the Prince of Troy and the young wife of King Menelaus, or when the Thebans were busy swapping morsels of news and theory about the goings-on in that crazy Laius family. The *Lives* of Suetonius and the *Secret History* of Procopius, with their peep-hole accounts of the depravities of the Cæsars and of Justinian and Theodora, are there to remind us that we all like to read about naughtiness and misconduct, illicit love, disappointments of the heart and discomfiture of the emotions among the higher-ups. The late Gordon Bennett made his fortune out of the New York *Herald,* chiefly on scandalous items about members of society; and the success of Pulitzer's New York *World* and Hearst's New York *Journal* in their beginnings was the result to a large extent of piquant stories of extravagance and license amongst the rich New Yorkers who had homes in Newport. The more modern *Town Topics,* founded by the late Colonel Mann, who specialized in pointed scandal among society people, with the names concealed or left out, was the immediate precursor of the columnist gossip-monger of the newspapers. That type of journalism originated in France under Louis XIV and in England almost simultaneously, and it was Daniel De Foe who brought it to a suble perfection.

When the notorious New York murderer-bandit, Gerald Chapman, was finally caught, tried and hanged all of the newspapers devoted a vast amount of space to him and his "master-mind" exploits, and at least one newspaper did not scruple to publish a life-story of the bandit purporting to be written by him but actually written by a staff reporter. After the execution of Judd Gray of the notorious Gray-Snyder murder case, an "autobiography" of the will-less little man, written by a hack, was published in book form. This type of journalism was started by (God help him!) Daniel De Foe. When the famous English bandit, Jack Sheppard, who had escaped so many times from Newgate prison that he became a national hero, was caught, convicted and hanged, Daniel De Foe made circulation and money for his newspaper, hand over fist, by interviewing Sheppard in prison while Sheppard was awaiting execution, faking a great number of letters by the bandit, and, after the execution, manufacturing out of the whole cloth a biography which purported to be written by Sheppard himself. De Foe also made money and circulation for his sheet by his brilliant interviews with the great criminal, Jonathan Wild, interviews which Henry Fielding later pilfered for his novel, *Jonathan Wild.* De Foe wrote his entire gazette himself. The bulk of his unsigned stuff is enormous.

The "colyum" of wit, jokes, sardonic comments and japeries has become a standard daily feature of many newspapers in England, Germany, France, Spain, Italy and America. The first English newspaper was published on Dec. 2, 1620. Less than a hundred years later De Foe had originated the "colyum" idea of jests and satirical thrusts, just as he anticipated and invented practically every feature of a modern newspaper except the comic supplement, the cartoon and the rotogravure section. He even wrote literary and dramatic criticism and sports.

Robinson Crusoe was the first newspaper serial ever published!

Robinson Crusoe was the first progenitor of the fictionized account of life and adventure in strange, remote and primitive places. It was suggested to De Foe by a section called *An Account of Alexander Selkirk's living alone four years and four months in an Island* in an authentic record by Capt. Woodes Rogers published in 1718 and entitled *A Cruising Voyage Around the World.* But Rogers' account was true; De Foe's work was in the invention of his fertile imagination. He at once seized upon the idea as a fiction possibility, and wrote a story that was read round the world, translated into nearly every known language, and imitated at once by hundreds of writers in Europe in his time and by thousands of writers since.

Robinson Crusoe was really the first great novel in the English language. It established a genre and it remains preëminent in that genre. It retains that preëminence almost solely because De Foe, the journalist, was one of the greatest individual masters of prose that ever wrote in English. He knew how to make people, things, places, events live vividly in his pages. He followed and developed the prose tradition of Shakespeare * and Dekker, of the anonymous translators of the Authorized Version of the Bible, of Jeremy Taylor, Abraham Cowley, John Evelyn, Samuel Pepys, and John Bunyan instead of the prose tradition of Sir Francis Bacon, Sir Thomas Browne, and John Milton; and so helped to emancipate English prose from the heaviness of ecclesiastical Latinity and from the cacophony of Anglo-Saxon polysyllables and to make it a medium of grace, easiness, clarity, levity, naturalness and wit.

Simple people with small education could read De Foe, whereas only people with considerable learning could read Bacon, Browne, Milton or even Sir Robert Burton. And the curious point is that De Foe was a much more cultivated man and a man of sounder learning than either Bacon or Milton: he could speak French, Dutch, Spanish and Italian with fluency; he was soundly grounded in Latin and the Humanities; and as a young man he spent more than two years abroad in travel, observation and study in France, Spain, Italy, Holland and Germany. Because he did not choose to clutter up his prose with Latin tags and with allusions to Greek and Latin authors, his ineffectual enemies tried to discredit him by saying that he was uneducated. This taunt was the only one that ever infuriated him, because he knew perfectly well that he could outpoint any one of his time except Dryden and Swift, possibly, in a general examination on cultural matters. Even in these days a general dumbness, turgidity of style and an ability to pick inept quotations from Bohn's *Handbook of Classical Quotations* to give an air of learning, is quite generally held to be a mark of intellectualism superior to sense, sensibility and a knack for readable prose.

JUST as *Robinson Crusoe* set the fashion for a thousand Crusiads, *Moll Flanders* was the precursor and paradigm of thousands of realistic and romantic novels and short stories. In *Moll Flanders* De Foe exhausted nearly the whole repertory of possible plots in fiction. Let us take an example. O. Henry once wrote a story about a poor working boy and a poor working girl, unknown to each other,

* The notion is curiously widespread that Shakespeare never wrote prose. Even H. L. Mencken, himself the possessor of a prose style of great force and pungency, fell into that popular delusion when he wrote *Prejudices: Third Series*, wherein, on page 165, he says he cannot make up his mind what Shakespeare's prose would be like if Shakespeare had ever written prose. About half of Hamlet is in prose; and the proportion of prose in all the other plays is about two parts of prose to three of blank verse and song. With a few exceptions, the most famous lines of Shakespeare are in prose.

who saved their money for a vacation at a fashionable seaside resort. The girl pretended to be an heiress; the boy pretended to be a scion of wealth. They met and fell in love, each believing the other to be as represented. Dozens of variations of this plot appear in manuscript at the offices of American magazines every week; fifteen or twenty variations appear in the pages of magazines in the course of a year. Plots involving mistaken identity on the part of lovers go back to Menander or earlier; but De Foe gave it its modern form and he gave it a twist which was too realistic for O. Henry. Moll Flanders, pretending to be a wealthy widow at one stage in her adventurous career, is married to a man who pretends to be a wealthy Irish landowner. They are no sooner married than it comes out that the husband is a highwayman and that Moll is a poverty-stricken woman who is pregnant and anxious to make an advantageous marriage. They are both taken aback; but they are amused at the duplicity and separate, she to look for another husband and he to continue his precarious career as a robber. But consider the whole interweaving of plots:

Moll's mother is to be hanged for theft but defeats the course of the law by submitting to her jailer, because pregnant women are not hanged. Moll is the issue of this union. The mother is deported to the American colonies as an undesirable and Moll is brought up in an orphanage. A wealthy woman takes her out of the orphanage and brings her into her home. The woman has two sons. One of them seduces Moll; the other falls in love with her and asks her to marry him. On the wedding night the elder son contrives to get his brother so drunk that the latter will not observe his bride's loss of virginity. The couple live happily for five years and then the husband dies. Moll marries again, but her husband loses his money and disappears to avoid the debtor's prison. Moll moves to another county to escape responsibility for her husband's debts, meets a Virginia planter and goes to America with him, where, after a few years of happiness, she learns that her husband's mother is also her mother. Horrified by the incest she has committed, she leaves her husband and returns to England where she becomes the mistress of a man with whom she lives for six years. At the end of that period the honorable fellow is stricken with an illness, which his conscience tells him is a punishment for his sins. He prays for health and promises God he will lead a pure life if he is permitted to recover. Unfortunately he regains his health and poor Moll is cast out. She meets the man she thinks is a wealthy landowner, as described above, and when they part, she goes into seclusion until she has borne her child, which she places in the keeping of others while she starts out again to look for a husband. She marries a bank clerk who promptly dies. Her beauty now is gone; she finds she cannot lure men. She turns to shoplifting, and becomes a professional thief, prostitute and blackmailer. (Moll's account of her years of criminality are the most thrilling and realistic of all the episodes in this exciting book: they are the result of De Foe's careful observation as a reporter and as a prisoner, thrown among criminals, at Newgate.) She is caught in the act of shoplifting and sentenced to be hanged; but her husband, the highwayman, also turns up in prison. They both repent of their past and promise that if their sentences are commuted to deportation they will go to America and lead honorable lives. They reach Virginia, work out their indenture, find Moll's son by her incestuous marriage, become rich planters; and when Moll's husband dies, she returns to England at the age of seventy to write her story as a moral lesson to mankind.

Many nineteenth and twentieth century critics have objected to the Puritan homiletics in *Moll Flanders*. Some have accused De Foe of insincerity. They say that he wrote a realistic story of a prostitute, giving many details of her amorous and professional life, but interlarded it with moral warnings and discourses to make the whole palatable to prurient Puritans. Some have apologized for De Foe, saying that he was perfectly sincere and that he was as much of a moralist as a novelist. This may be true; but they overlook this fact: namely that *Moll Flanders* is Moll's own story and it is given to us by De Foe in her own words. Harlots are notoriously the most conventionally minded of women; they place an excessive valuation upon virtue and chastity because they feel so keenly their complete lack of these qualities. Women who live to be thirty without having won a husband or lost their virginity usually put a much lower valuation on chastity than harlots do. Do but read the Report of the Vice Commission of Chicago, 1911, wherein there are case histories of prostitutes together with interviews with them and you will find nearly all of these women have the same moral point of view as Moll and many of them account for their downfall and degradation in much the same manner as Moll accounts for hers. Or, to go higher up in the scale, read the novel *Lui* and the moral discourses which Louise Colet, who had been mistress of Benjamin Constant, Gustave Flaubert and many others, wrote when she was no longer the lascivious wench who inspired *Madame Bovary* and

Adolphe but a woman grown unattractive and piously agitated over the immorality of the age. There are many feminine counterparts of the St. Augustine of the *Confessions;* and their moral fervor increases with every year that their immoral youth recedes into the past.

De Foe gives us Moll Flanders at seventy and puts her story into her own words (that is, he says in his preface that he did so far as he dared: he tells us he had to alter the style a little and make her tell her tale in "modester words than she told it at first, the copy which first came to hand having been written in language more like one still in Newgate than one grown penitent and humble, as she afterwards pretends to be.") Every line of it sounds authentic. There is not a false note. The sentiment of the novel is native to a woman like Moll grown old. The little feminine touches on points of remembrance, even the "happy turns" of "her lewd life with the young gentleman at Colchester," are marvels of artistic intuition. De Foe gets himself entirely inside the character, quite as much as he gets himself into the character of Robinson Crusoe.

It is my feeling that *Moll Flanders* is a much more realistic novel, *psychologically,* than either *Nana* or *Madame Bovary.* The French recognized this. When the Naturalist movement was at its height in France and Zola was the literary king of the hour, Marcel Schwob, that great scholar, fine ironist and superb stylist whose mind and spirit Anatole France valued more than that of any other contemporary, made a translation of *Moll Flanders.* It was a sensational success. The French critics acclaimed it as a great masterpiece of naturalism; they condemned the English nineteenth century critics, who had been shocked by it, as hypocritical and lacking in perception. The French people took Moll Flanders to their hearts as more than a century and a half before they had taken Robinson Crusoe. French scholars became the real authorities on De Foe and the best biography of De Foe is that by a Frenchman, Paul Dottin: *The Life and Strange and Surprising Adventures of Daniel De Foe* translated into English by Louise Ragan.

THE return of Charles II to the throne of England, after Cromwellism had been left without a leader, threw everybody into such confusion that the parents of Daniel De Foe neglected to have his birth recorded in St. Giles' register. The date has been conjecturally placed by Dottin as September 30, 1660, because September 30 was the day Robinson Crusoe was cast upon the island, and De Foe "attached a superstitious importance to dates." The father of Daniel was James Foe, a candlestick maker, and his mother the daughter of an impoverished country squire. The Foes were Flemings who had settled in England to escape the persecution of the Duke of Alba. It was Daniel who added the "De" to the family name in the tide of his fortunes in 1695.

The Foes were Baptists in religion but Royalists in politics. This was a contradiction; for Charles II was Anglican in religion and he was soon to begin the persecution of all Dissenters. A complicated problem in alliances faced all Englishmen during the Restoration. Many Protestants whose fortunes had been swept away by the Civil War, welcomed the restoration of the monarchy without changing their religion. Moreover, the question with them was: Who will follow Charles?—his Catholic brother, James, or his Protestant (and illegitimate) son, Monmouth? The Whigs, largely made up of the growing mercantile class, were for Monmouth; the Anglican Tories were torn between business and religion, because Charles II favored the merchants against the landed gentry in all things, because of the rise of the chartered monopolies of the East India and Hudson Bay companies, because of the rise of the textile industry in England to an importance equal to that of the Dutch, and because a century's influx of Spanish silver and gold had established a money economy in Europe. It was hard for an Englishman in those days to decide which side his bread was buttered on. Nor did he know from one day to the next whether he would be among the persecuted or with the persecutors in the religious war.

When Daniel was two years old, Charles II passed an act which forbade attendance at any religious service except that of the Established or Anglican Church. This deprived Baptists, Presbyterians, Puritans, and Methodists as well as Catholics of all religious freedom and made nominal allies of people who were bitterly opposed in religious affiliations. It also tried the conscience of members of the merchant class, among whom were to be found both Protestants and Catholics. The Reverend Doctor Annesley, beloved pastor to the Foes, was evicted from his church and had to hold services in his parishioners' houses. Two years later even this practice was stopped by Charles who issued his Conventicle Act which forbade attendance at Dissenting meetings under penalty of deportation. The Foes had to sneak into the fields to receive their pastor's ministrations.

Then when Daniel was five years old, the Great Plague (which he was many years later to describe graphically, when a lesser plague occurred) broke out in London. A comet streaked through the sky shortly before the plague and the Dissenters interpreted the comet as a warning that God would strike the oppressors, in answer to their prayer. And when the plague came they believed their prayers had been fulfilled. The plague struck terror everywhere. All night long through the streets watchmen would knock at doors crying, "Bring out your dead." Great pits were dug and corpses piled into them. Streets and alleyways were strewn with bodies of the dead and dying. James Foe set a vinegar pot in front of his shop into which customers dropped the money for their purchases. When the plague grew worse, he stored the top floor of his house with provisions, closed his shop, and retired there with his family until the danger was over.

The plague was followed within less than a year by the Great Fire which destroyed nearly a third of London. Under the stress of these catastrophes the edicts against non-conformists in religion were in abeyance and Dissenting meetings were openly held. But the Catholics, who were in a small minority, found themselves in a worse predicament than ever, because both Anglicans and Dissenters spread reports that the Papists had set fire to the city; all robberies, rapes and murders were attributed to Catholics. As a young man, Daniel De Foe, like other Protestants, carried a "Protestant flail" (two clubs joined together with a leather thong) with which to harry Jesuits and their supposed henchmen, the robbers; for to a Dissenting tradesman all footpads were minions of the Pope.

The plague and fire were blessings in disguise to James Foe. He, his family and his shop, survived and the catastrophes left him virtually without competition. He became a butcher, joined the Corporation of Butchers and prospered greatly. He engaged Doctor Annesley as a tutor, who, among other tasks, required Daniel to attend his sermons and to reconstruct them from memory. This was Daniel's first training as a reporter: it habituated him to attention and accuracy. He was also required to copy out long passages from the Bible, and at one time when there was a rumor abroad that all printed Bibles were to be confiscated the young Daniel hastily set to work trying to copy the whole Bible in long hand. Fortunately the untruth of the rumor became known before he had got through *Pentateuch*.

Along with the instruction of Doctor Annesley there was a constant spur to analytical thought in the mind of young Daniel, arising from the family's anomalous position as Royalists, genteel and Dissenters, and also from the impact of national events. England's siding with William of Orange, newly made Stadtholder of the Netherlands in the great Protestant Coalition which beat off Louis XIV's second drive against the Low Countries, while its sovereign was pocketing Louis' bribes; the beginning of colonial empire in North America, and the ever-widening horizon of England's overseas trade,—all were discussed around the family hearth. Formal schooling began for Daniel in the hope that he would become a Dissenting minister. He was placed in an academy kept by Charles Morton, who later became a Vice President of Harvard University. The training there was surprisingly liberal and extensive for the times—geography, modern languages, shorthand, law, science, and astronomy. Morton also encouraged debates and discussions, with, however, constant emphasis on moral values and the workings of Divine Providence.

After four years at the academy, during which time he developed a contempt for the religious fanaticism of his school-mates, he gave up the idea of becoming a minister and entered service as an apprentice to Charles Lodwick, a London importer of wines and exporter of hosiery and cloth. He had decided his future was in trade, and he meant to learn Lodwick's business from the ground up. He was rapidly promoted and soon attained a clerkship. Then, it appears, his employer agreed with Daniel's opinion that he would be more valuable to the firm if he spent two years abroad studying foreign commerce, exercising his linguistic attainments, meeting and dealing with all sorts of people. Therefore, with commissions in his pocket from Lodwick and other London merchants, which would pay his expenses, he spent two exceedingly profitable years in the Netherlands, Germany, Italy, France, Spain and Portugal. On this grand tour he gathered notes and impressions which he later elaborated in his *The Compleat English Tradesman.*

He returned to Lodwick's employ, but when he was twenty-three years old he married Mary Tuffley, who brought him a dowry of 3,700 pounds sterling, with which he set up in business himself as a hosiery manufacturer, assured in advance of orders from Lodwick. He also engaged in the importing of wines and liquors. He was a successful business man from the first, in fact altogether too successful; for he spent his money as fast as he made it, took a large house, bought himself a horse and carriage, gambled and speculated and attended the races. It was a very good thing for English literature, as all the disasters which befell De Foe in his life turned out to be, that two years after he set up in business himself, Charles II, apologizing for the unconscionably long time he took in doing so, died—and at once the country was thrown again into turmoil. Charles' elder brother, James, succeeded to the throne, and the disappointed Whigs, muttering darkly about a mysterious document which would establish the legitimacy of Monmouth, had to watch their favorite slink off to Holland.

James pursued a blundering course of incompetence and stupidity which finally brought William of Orange sailing into Tor Bay as the Deliverer of England. De Foe was beside himself with joy and excitement when Parliament finally gave the crown to William and Mary as co-sovereigns. He was not astute enough to foresee that this occurrence meant his ruin. William of Orange had no sooner been crowned than the peace between him and Louis XIV was broken again by Louis, who backed James in an Irish campaign, and war was on. War-time conditions brought high insurance rates, loss of cargoes and unsettled business conditions generally. De Foe's trade was badly damaged; he had speculated inadvisedly; and he had run into debt at a most inconvenient time. In 1692 his business collapsed into bankruptcy,—a tragedy indeed in those days when unsatisfied creditors could keep a man in prison until his debts were paid, which might well be for the remainder of his life.

DE FOE, like others in his predicament, fled to "The Mint," a district in London peopled by thieves, thugs and rogues of every description and of both sexes, a district so tough that the police scarcely dared to enter it. Unwritten custom permitted a man to remain in "The Mint" before serious efforts were made to apprehend him. Meanwhile he could negotiate with his creditors and try to come to terms with them. But De Foe had discovered his gifts as a pamphleteer and while in hiding he wrote his first serious work, a collection of essays on state affairs, including a portrayal of how Whiggish policies would help improve them, entitled *An Essay upon Projects*.

This work attracted the favorable attention of William and his party and this, coupled with the success of De Foe's wife and friends in procuring him another chance with his creditors, enabled him to return to London, where he was appointed commissioner to administer the new tax on glass. William soon learned to esteem De Foe as a valuable adviser on government policies concerning revenue and business. From a rogue's hideaway he had become in a short space of time the king's private counselor. He embellished his name with a "De." He began attending the races again, bought back his horses, dined with eminent personages, and led the life of a gentleman. Moreover, he conceived the idea that he might manufacture and sell tiles cheaper than tiles could be imported from Holland. He borrowed money, built a factory, and was soon turning out tiles so successfully that he was giving employment to a hundred families, paying off his debts, and living in luxury.

It is interesting to note that De Foe as a manufacturer became wholeheartedly a manufacturer; that is, he paid slave wages and became gravely interested in the problem of increasing the efficiency and moral responsibility of the English workmen. He found that many of his men, as soon as they received their pay on Saturday night after their six days of toil from dawn till dark, made straight for the pubs, got drunk and stayed drunk until Monday morning, spending all or most of their pay and leaving their families to be supported by the parishes. The average weekly pay of his workmen was nine shillings. At Pontack's famous tavern, where De Foe went to dinner almost nightly to join in the conversation with men of mark in business and politics, he gravely discussed the problem as to what could be done to remedy a situation whereby the English workman was so sunk in drunkenness and shiftlessness that his family was a charge upon the community whereas a Dutch workman supported his family and saved money on nine shillings a week. After these discourses he was accustomed to comment upon the excellence of the dinner and wine at Pontack's which never came to more than fifteen shillings, unless one had a second bottle of wine, in which case it would be twenty-two,—or more than he paid two workmen for a full week's work.

The realities and the ironies of life did not sink into De Foe for a very long time and until misfortunes had thoroughly chastened him. During the tenure of William he sat easily as a man of affairs and fortune. In his spare time he turned out pamphlets. He had a distinct knowledge of his limitations: he knew he was not a poet, and he did not aspire to be one; but he knew he was a wit, a good versifier, and that he had a marvelous style and a quick-thinking brain. When propaganda began to spread against William as a foreigner, he rushed to the defense of his sovereign, whom he idolized all his life, even though William's kingship had at the outset brought him misfortune. In answer to a satirical poem which declared it was intolerable that a "true-born Englishman should be governed by a Dutch king," De Foe wrote his famous *True-Born English-man*.

Although it was written in a temper, it is so true that it remains a refutation of all jingoism in England or any other nation. He said that your true-born Englishman was a mixture of Roman, Gallic, Greek, Lombard, Pict, Hengist, Saxon, Spanish, Norman, Welsh, Irish, and Hibernian blood from soldiers, auxiliaries and slaves of every nation, who came to Britain for plunder, and that from these "dregs of armies" and this "amphibious, ill-born mob" came "that vain, ill-natured thing, an Englishman."

This poem was received by Englishmen with chuckles of delight. Nine editions at a shilling a copy and eighty thousand pirated copies at tuppence were sold in the Kingdom within a year. It made De Foe a considerable sum of money; but, more important, it elevated him at once into the limelight as a writer, a satirist and a wit. The Tories hated him because with one stroke he had destroyed their pretensions to true-blood gentility; he was accused of trying to break down the distinctions between classes, of contributing to the insolence of the workmen. Puny pamphleteers in the pay of the Tories, called him filthy names and said he was a fishwife whore's son begot by a Dutch sailor. All this only added to his renown. He was in the public eye and in the Tory craw.

After the accession of Queen Anne, De Foe's security was more precarious than under William, as indeed, was the security of every one in England. Nevertheless, he was very sure of himself and blithely pleased with his ability to say his mind as he pleased, to his own profit and amusement. Then in 1702 occurred a succession of events which, I believe, determined the whole subsequent history of his career as a writer. In that year he had his first great disillusionment. He learned that the majority of people don't want truth or justice; that their interests are selfish and often stupid; that nine people out of ten don't know satire when they see it; and that you may pour out your life-blood in defense of common sense, justice and humanity and get clubbed on all sides for doing so.

Under James and William the agitation against the Dissenters had died down. Under Anne it flared up again. She lent an ear to the party which was led by one Doctor Sacheverell, a bigot who was thundering every Sunday against the Dissenters. The Commons tried to pass a law forbidding non-conformists to hold meetings, but the House of Lords defeated it (a strange situation wherein the Commons majority was lined up with the Tories, and the Lords were lined up with the Whigs against the encroachments of the Established Church upon religious liberty).

De Foe got fed up with Doctor Sacheverell and wrote a satire as vicious as Jonathan Swift's later *Modest Proposal* (that starvation be prevented in Ireland by slaughtering the babies of the poor and converting them into sausages and puddings). De Foe called his satire *The Shortest Way with Dissenters.* He published it anonymously but as the work of a member of the High-church group. It was a bitter burlesque of Doctor Sacheverell's arguments and manner: he carried the reverend doctor's ideas to absurdity; he proposed that all Protestants and Catholics be caught and crucified, "and may God Almighty put into the hearts of all friends of truth to lift up a standard against pride and Antichrist, that the posterity of the sons of error may be rooted out from the face of the land forever!"

THE pamphlet was published on December 1, 1702. Neither Dissenters nor Anglicans, neither Whigs nor Tories got the satire of it. Leaders of all parties were thrown into a panic. Timid Catholics and Protestants gathered up their belongings and left town or kept indoors, prepared to be descended upon any minute by executioners under orders from Queen Anne. The Anglicans were equally perturbed, thinking that one of their number had gone too far and by that pamphlet would consolidate all Protestant sects and Catholics against the Queen and Church. Few saw the irony of De Foe's style; and when things looked pretty bad De Foe hastily published *A Brief Explanation of a late Pamphlet entitled the Shortest Way with Dissenters,* explaining that the pamphlet was not written by an Anglican but by a Dissenter and that it was meant as a satire against Doctor Sacheverell and his fellow fanatics. This cleared the air for awhile but Nottingham, Anne's secretary of state, had recognized the satire from the first and had learned of De Foe's connection with it. Consequently he issued an order for De Foe's arrest as a dangerous agitator against Church and State.

De Foe went into hiding, but kept in communication with his wife, who in his early misfortunes always stood by him with courage and tender helpfulness. A large reward was offered for information leading to his arrest. De Foe was frightened half out of his wits; he did not know whether or not he might be hanged or allowed to rot in prison. He addressed a humble petition to Nottingham, begging for mercy, saying he had no seditious designs, that the whole thing was a joke and that if he were forgiven by the Queen he would thereafter dedicate his whole life and abilities to the services of his Queen and his benefactors.

Nottingham did nothing about the petition but Robert Harley saw the letter and had an idea. Harley was Tory speaker of the House of Commons, an astute and intriguing politician. He realized De Foe's power to sway the people with his pen. While in prison De Foe was busily writing Whig pamphlets. Harley laid plans to place De Foe under obligations to him and thus to secure his service to the Tory side. De Foe had other enemies in power, including the advocate general, who was scheming to get De Foe to confess to the authorship of *The Shortest Way*. De Foe's lawyer suggested that De Foe confess and pray for clemency. This was a mistake (a good mistake as it turned out) for the judges had no sooner heard the confession than they fined him and condemned him to three sessions in the pillory. William Penn interceded for De Foe to no avail; De Foe was brought before the ministers of the court and questioned as to Whig activities, but he disclosed nothing; and finally Queen Anne ordered the sentence carried out.

Now, the pillory was a barbarous form of punishment. The prisoner was forced to stand all day with his neck and wrist clamped between two wooden blocks, with holes just large enough for the head and hands to protrude on one side while the body was on the other. The pillories were in conspicuous public places. Sadistic and insensitive people tormented the victims, throwing slime, ordure, rotten eggs, decayed vegetables at their faces.

But meanwhile the Whigs and common people were busy. The latter recognized De Foe as their champion. When he was led out the first day, the Tories found the pillory decked with garlands and flowers strewn about. A great crowd had gathered. They had declared a holiday. When De Foe's neck was clamped between the blocks, a shout went up and he was given an ovation. Wine was passed around. While awaiting sentence, De Foe had written and distributed a humorous poem, *The Hymn to the Pillory*. People recited it. De Foe was given wine. He smiled and jested with the people. He was thenceforth the hero of the hour; the demonstration for him increased as the two remaining sessions in the pillory were carried out. Around him was a sea of flowers. On the last day everybody got drunk in De Foe's honor.

The Tories did not know what to make of it, but Robert Harley, a moderate Tory, did. De Foe still had a prison term to serve out and it might be indefinite, since he could not pay his fine. Harley sent De Foe's wife money to meet her expenses and conferred secretly with De Foe. The exact terms of their agreement never became known; but De Foe was released at Harley's instigation and one of the conditions was certainly that De Foe support his policies secretly. De Foe was to continue to be known as a Whig. Harley put up the money for a weekly newspaper for De Foe, which De Foe called the *Review*. It was on this newspaper that De Foe began nearly all the journalistic innovations recited at the beginning of this chapter. His first innovation was a gossip column, called "Advice from the Scandal Club," being a weekly history of "Nonsense, Impertinence, Vice and Debauchery." Using initials instead of full names he published spicy satirical gossip about all sorts of persons in high places. To this column he added the prototype of the modern "colyum," wherein he printed a miscellany of verse, jokes, paragraphs of comment, and contributions from his readers. He added to his journalistic activities the *Little Review*, also described above. Harley meanwhile had become Prime Minister and what political support De Foe gave to any party he gave to the moderate Tories, simply by not writing in favor of the Whigs. He devoted himself to the service, instruction and amusement of the common man. In his editorials he took a high moral tone, smug and pious. In this vein he wrote some nauseating stuff, pleading for the closing of the theaters as immoral and preaching against this and that. This was hypocritical in design on his part. He, who had been in jail and in the pillory and who was even referred to by Jonathan Swift as "the fellow who was pilloried," wanted a reputation for piety and he got it.

FOR the next four years De Foe pursued a cynical and deceptive course of life as the tool of Robert Harley. And the connection between the two was known only to themselves and to some sworn secret agents who brought De Foe money and instructions from Harley. Nominally a Whig, even ostentatiously a Whig, during the first stages of the connection he allowed it to appear that his better judgment had made him independent of politics and, later, a champion of the moderate Tory party's program. As a spy for Harley he made secret journeys all over the British Isles, particularly to Scotland. He was very funny about this. He liked to dramatize himself, and his fertile imagination led him into many absurdities. He loved to mystify and so, like the sort of detective who in disguise looks more like a detective than before, De Foe changed his name and the story of the object of his visit with every town he reached. He enjoyed having people gossip and wonder about him. His job was to spread propaganda for the ministry's policies, sound out the feeling in Scotland for a union with England, learn the state of political sympathies in various parts of the country. All this he did as a confidential agent of Harley's. But as a journalist he was developing the free play of his imagination and ingenuity. He established a newspaper in Scotland, writing the whole contents of it, and almost at once became the foremost journalist in Scotland. He established several newspapers in various parts of the country and arranged to have the material he wrote appear simultaneously in all of them—the first syndication. Traveling as a Whig business man, he had difficulties in Tory centers and was once challenged to a duel by a Tory hireling whom he discomfited only to have an order issued for his arrest on a charge of having attacked a Tory admiral —an order which Harley promptly squashed.

What De Foe never knew as long as he was in Harley's pay was that Harley was secretly a Jacobite. Harley never disclosed this to De Foe, because he knew of De Foe's almost fanatical loyalty to the memory of William of Orange. De Foe in time, however, began to get into hot water. The Whigs began to suspect his loyalty and later were utterly convinced that he was in Harley's pay. He was attacked by Whig pamphleteers as well as by Tory writers; and the more succcessful his papers became, the more violent were the attacks on both sides. Dean Swift, also secretly in the pay of Harley (though a Tory and an Anglican), wrote diatribes against De Foe's newspaper. De Foe was accused on all sides of double-dealing, not without justice.

Then, as once before, De Foe let his real conscience and his art get the upper-hand, and he wrote three ironical pamphlets really deriding the Tories, Anglicans and Jacobins by an ironical and satirical thrust at them. In a paradoxical manner he pretended that it might be a good thing for England to have a Catholic government; moreover, he said that under the reign of the Pretender, Louis XIV would exercise a benevolent protectorate over England. He should have remembered from his first experience that people don't ordinarily understand satire unless it is labeled, "This is a satire." These pamphlets were just what the Whigs were waiting for; he was clapped into jail for treason on charges brought by the Whigs, whereas his pamphlets were Whiggish in the extreme and intended to make Jacobins and Tories ridiculous! When he was brought before his judge, he admitted authorship of the pamphlets but said they were written in an ironical vein. The judge read them over, could not see the humor of them, declared De Foe had lied and sentenced him to be drawn and quartered.

Things looked bad for De Foe, because Harley was in eclipse. Harley and Bolingbroke had broken because of the former's shifty ways: Bolingbroke was an out-and-out Jacobite, whereas Harley was also, but pretended not to be. After the break he turned Hanoverian. De Foe was certainly anti-Jacobite, if he was anything at all; and it was now in Bolingbroke's power to let De Foe be drawn and quartered. But Bolingbroke was a cultivated man, a wit, and a friend of Voltaire; he appreciated De Foe's gifts and knew that if he became chief of council De Foe would be a good man to have with him. Therefore when De Foe's petition for pardon came through to him from Harley, he spoke to the Queen and De Foe was freed.

After this experience De Foe had every reason to desert the Whigs; so, in gratitude to Bolingbroke, after getting Harley's consent, he discontinued the *Review* and started the *Journal,* ready to write just what Bolingbroke wanted him to write. He was just getting into his stride, when a complicated series of events happened. Harley, a staunch Jacobite, after his break with Bolingbroke, having turned Hanoverian, was deposed. Bolingbroke was expecting the job of chief of council, when the Queen suddenly took mortally ill and on her deathbed named the Duke of Shrewsbury for Harley's place. Shrewsbury was a Hanoverian.

Within a few months, George I of the house of Hanover was sitting on the English throne; Bolingbroke was out; the Whigs were in power. Harley, of course, by the turn of events, held the reins. He summoned De Foe, who was always loyal to him, and set him to work writing pamphlets clearing Harley of the charge of Jacobinism. De Foe had no recourse. There were charges against him which might be revived at any moment. For the next several years, he tried to straddle the fence, turned out pamphlet after pamphlet, got anonymous employment with a Tory paper, and then kept free from political arguments, devoting himself strictly to journalism.

During all this period, he had spent very little time at home. He liked an active life, and he had traveled about the country so much that he saw little of his family. From time to time they had been in very straitened circumstances. His wife, son and three daughters turned against him; and when he did finally settle down with them, ill and exhausted, he found them rather cold to him, especially since he had recently engaged in some very ill-advised speculation. He gave up active journalism and began to write books of pious instruction like *The Family Instructor,* which were full of advice about living quietly and peaceably at home, in domestic bliss, surrounded by one's obedient children. It may have been genuine remorse which caused him to write these platitudes, because everything he advised was almost the precise opposite of what he had practiced. But the people were still Puritan and this drivel sold well.

He was very badly pressed for money, in such straits really that the debtor's prison worried him, when he fell upon Captain Rogers' account of the adventures of Alexander Selkirk who had been shipwrecked and cast upon an island where he lived alone for four years before being rescued. This gave De Foe an idea. At the time, he was in a state of mind where he wished he were alone on a desert island. He remembered a school-mate's strange name of Crusoe. He prefixed a Robinson and took his idea to a publisher. He got an advance on the book and started feverishly to work. It was agreed with the publisher that the story should appear serially. Haste was necessary to capitalize on the public enthusiasm for books of adventure stirred up by Captain Rogers' narrative. The English of the eighteenth century did not care for fiction, especially romantic fiction. It was necessary, therefore, to put out the yarn as an authentic experience. De Foe sent the sheets to the publisher as fast as he wrote them, apparently never looking them over. In fact, it would appear that he never read the story over at all after he had written it because he never corrected its obvious errors and inconsistencies in succeeding editions. Dottin has pointed some of them out:

Robinson had stripped off his clothes to swim to the shipwreck; but when he is ready to start back to shore he fills his pockets with biscuits. He complained of having no salt for his bread; then he tried diligently to teach Friday to use salt with his meat. He had to give up keeping his detailed journal because he was almost out of ink; but twenty years later he gave the ambassadors to the Spanish wreck written instructions. He had a pipe and some tobacco yet he frequently lamented that he could not smoke. Oppressed by the night, the wolves, and the snow, why did he stop so many times crossing the Pyrenees to watch Friday's encounters with the bears? All of his dates and figures are wrong. Friday is both conventional savage and well-trained servant.

—Translation of LOUISE RAGAN.

The Life and Strange Surprising Adventures of Robinson Crusoe of York, Mariner, so true to the heart of De Foe's own imaginative experience, so authentic in homely little details, so popular in its humor and practicality, was a tremendous success. It was hardly off the press in book form before the publisher urged De Foe to rush a sequel or second volume. De Foe did so; he brought his rescued hero back to the island and sent him on various voyages. But this second volume was poor stuff. De Foe had run out of inspiration. To satisfy the publisher he had to write enough to fill out a book, so he dumped into it anything he could think of, including old moral discourses he had published and which people had forgotten. But the second volume was a great success also. Fame of the book spread to Europe. Translators began turning it into various languages and dialects. Pirated editions were brought out in England. Imitators sprang up. It started a whole literature of adventure, of which the best is Wyss' *Swiss Family Robinson* (an imitation which is preferred by some children to the original, because the idea of having a whole family cast up on an island gave the Swiss author more scope for invention of episodes which would appeal to children).

FOLLOWING *Robinson Crusoe,* De Foe turned out the *Life, Adventures and Piracies of the Famous Captain Singleton* (a misfire novel with little to recommend it), and engaged in various kinds of publishers' hack work, until, hearing about the French and Spanish picaresque novels about irresponsible rogues, he conceived the idea from which he could draw upon his experiences and contacts in Newgate prison and in "The Mint." The scheme of it, unlike *Robinson Crusoe,* obviously was worked out leisurely and in plot detail before he set to work on it. It has none of the faults of inconsistency of the better known work. He called the novel *Moll Flanders,* and it is one of his two masterpieces.

Reports of the outbreak of the plague in Marseilles stirred London to excitement and precautions. De Foe capitalized upon this fright by calling upon his childhood memories of the Great Plague, and composed his *Journal of the Plague Year.* This work brought into play all his skill as a reporter; for it was published as the authentic journal of an adult who lived through the plague, which had taken place fifty-seven years before. It remains the only good account we have of that dreadful occurrence. It is marvelously vivid, as thrilling today as the day it was written.

After this until the end of his life De Foe continued to turn out novels, guides, handbooks, a treatise on spiritism, etc., none of which is of general interest now, except possibly his faked stories and interviews with Jack Sheppard and Jonathan Wild, which he wrote as serials for *Applebee's Journal* and later published in book form, and his interesting *History of Peter the Great*. For special students there is interest in his *Political History of the Devil* and his *Compleat English Tradesman*. In fact, nearly everything De Foe wrote may be studied for style and read with a deal of pleasure, for he was a master of simplicity, clarity, liveliness and vigor; there was nothing of the academician in him. It is characteristic of him that when he was commissioned by a publisher to write a complete travel book of the British Isles, he had to read a great many books; but having digested them, he did not refer to them while writing lest they dull his style.

During his last years he lived as a great personage in a large house, surrounded by books, in the village of Stoke Newington. There he turned out some books contradictory in character; some of them were more or less pornographic, as for instance, the *Use and Abuse of the Marriage Bed,* in which he records some scandals of his day under the guise of inculcating a moral; and some of them bombastically Puritanical. He was alienated for a long time from his son, Daniel, who, it appears, wrote pamphlets against his father; and he was embroiled in a comical and pathetic squabble over the dowry with his future son-in-law which continued after Sophia De Foe's marriage. De Foe had promised the girl a house and a certain amount of money, but had engaged in some financial speculation, and having lost, was unable to pay the *dot.* His wife took her daughter's part against De Foe and held out against him until he agreed to pay the son-in-law the amount promised in installments and with interest. In his old age he turned out an extraordinary amount of writing of all sorts—commercial handbooks, treatises on commerce and taxation, pleas for a university of London, tracts in favor of British beer instead of Holland gin, schemes for trade expansion and one or two learned works of scholarship.

His last days are shrouded in mystery. Either he was suffering from hallucinations of persecution, or had real reason to believe

that some of his old creditors were ready to clap him into jail. Or perhaps he was trying to evade paying the rest of Sophia's dowry. At
any rate, he slipped away and took lodgings in an obscure district
in London, saying that his enemies were pursuing him and forbidding any member of his family to come to him (although he wrote
to them). He turned over his property to his son, which was a bad
thing to do, for his wife and daughters wrote to him that Daniel, Jr.,
was not providing for them; whereupon the poor fellow had visions
of his wife and daughters starving. He moved several times to cover
his tracks and finally ended up in a room in a boarding house in the
very district in which he was born. Alone in this room he died on
April 26, 1731, at the age of seventy-one.

The De Foes had eight children, two sons and six daughters.
Daniel, Jr., went into trade after an unsuccessful attempt to follow
the career of a pamphleteer and Benjamin is supposed to have emi-
grated to America. De Foe also had an illegitimate son, the result
of his days of splendor as a hosiery manufacturer, when he set up
a mistress because having a mistress, like having blooded horses and
a carriage, was what all men of "quality" did in those days. This
natural son, Benjamin Norton, lived principally by blackmail.

It was Carl Van Doren who, in an essay on Defoe which is used
as a preface to the Borzoi edition of *Moll Flanders,* pointed out that
Moll Flanders and Robinson Crusoe complement each other, that
"Crusoe, thrown utterly on his own resources by an accident, has
to contend with all his homely, sensible craft against the negligence
of nature; Moll, thrown on her own resources by her own behavior,
has to contend with all the watchfulness of law and order."

All denigrations of De Foe's character as a political turn-coat
seem to me not only irrelevant but to some degree untrue to the
facts. The trouble with him was that he was too honest for his
times, too frank, too much the true artist and true journalist. He
wrote a lot of stuff anonymously which he did not believe, simply
to make money; and, in writing these anonymous pamphlets (authorship of which has been ascribed to him probably on excellent
grounds) he did not mind taking both sides of the same unimportant
issue. He could make money both ways because he could write
better than anybody else; to do this gave him exercise for his logical
faculties and employment for his gifts.

But fundamentally he was a Puritan without bigotry, capable
of seeing both sides of the truth and enraged when either side was
distorted. It is significant of the stupidity he had to fight against

that the two Whiggish pamphlets of greatest force and art that he wrote got him into trouble, not with the Tories but with the Whigs, who were so stupid they took his irony literally. His misfortunes, it would appear, were his salvation: they kept him alive to the needs and aspirations of the common man and awake to the tyranny of the higher-ups. Had he continued in his success as a hosiery manufacturer, it is probable that he would have ended up as a smug, self-satisfied Tory, quite convinced that he was of superior clay (he was well on the way toward this when he added "De" to his name and, without foundation, claimed descent from Sir Walter Raleigh) much as do many people today who owe their success to accident or relentless selfishness and their "superiority" to the fact that they had a father or grandfather on the spot when there was a fortune to be grabbed or seized by mayhem and murder.

GOETHE *THE ADVENTURER*

*

THE healthiness, mental and physical, of Goethe is his out-
standing characteristic. His physical health was a natural
endowment: his mental health was attained by a long process of elimination from his consciousness of those fears and prejudices and trep-
idations, heritages from a medieval past, which beset him in his
youth. Goethe wrote *Werther* to save himself from suicide. By causing his romantic hero to kill himself, Goethe worked out, vicariously,
an impulse which was threatening his sanity. The unfortunate thing
about this is that the novel was published. It caused an epidemic
of suicides among adolescents in Europe and particularly in Germany; such is the power of suggestion in a work of art which is
sometimes only an artist's catharsis—the means whereby he cleans
out of his mind the poisons which have accumulated.

Nearly all of the major works of Goethe are the residua of this
psychic purging. If one cannot read them for vicarious experience
and in order to rid one's self of the same problems which beset
Goethe, one had best leave much of Goethe's work alone. Napoleon
on seeing Goethe remarked, "Ecce homo" ("Behold a man") and
this was almost the same remark uttered by Lincoln when he saw
Walt Whitman pass by his window. Lincoln said, "There is a *Man*."
But what Napoleon saw in Goethe and what Lincoln saw in Whitman, was, in each case, the physical aspect of an inner dignity and
serenity achieved through suffering and courageous struggle against
the disintegrative factors of an inner chaos.

Goethe was sixty years writing *Faust*. It is a poetic record of
a man's whole inner experience. It is not a unified drama; it is, as
Georg Brandes, Goethe's stanchest critical admirer, pointed out,

"one confused and conglomerate pile," inconsistent, illogical, without unity, emphasis or coherence—and like life itself, an unpredictable adventure.

DIVISION of opinion over Goethe's greatness has been constant since the days when, like a German Byron, he first burst upon the literary world. Schiller and Schlegel, his foremost contemporaries in Germany, despised *Werther* and greeted the publication of his first *Faustfragment* with a lack of enthusiasm bordering on contempt. While Goethe's popular reputation was growing in Germany and France, the more moralistic critics in England were bothering themselves by animadversions on his personal life wherein he had displayed some characteristics inconsistent with an Englishman's idea of the conduct of a gentleman. (Later Somerset Maugham in England and James Branch Cabell in America were to observe that it is impossible to write literature and remain a "gentleman": Ellen Glasgow and Isabel Paterson were to add to this the corollary that a woman cannot write good books and remain a "lady.")

Right now, in America as I write, there are two profound convictions about the worth of Goethe to the modern world, both of these profound convictions being very far apart indeed: there is the one that Goethe is the paragon of the "stuffed-shirt" (in the vivid parlance of our time); and there is the other that Goethe alone is the figure of the "Faustian Man" upon whose ideals we must concentrate to lead us out of defeatism and death. In either consideration there is little that bears upon the pleasure that the average man may take in Goethe as an artist.

"For Europe and America," wrote Georg Brandes, "he should typify not merely the deepest and broadest poetic phenomenon but also the most superbly endowed human being in general that has concerned himself with literature since the days of the Renaissance."

One may have one's reservations about that, . . . and still there rises up in my mind the months in which Goethe meant much to me. That was back in 1909 when I was carrying a route as a newsboy in Shawnee, Oklahoma. I had been directed to Goethe by Emerson and Carlyle and, since I did not read German, I took Bayard Taylor's translation of *Faust* out of the Carnegie Public Library and, through many weeks, read that book between four and five o'clock in the morning while I was eating my breakfast in the City Café. My friend "Gus" (whose real name was Constantinos Pappathakos) had been through the gymnasium in Sparta and had reached America, "land of the free," by the system of indenture prevalent at the time (and probably still prevalent) whereby a Greek lad, eager for a future, will sign over the major portion of his wages as a bootblack for a period of years to any one who will pay his fare. Gus had paid out his indenture and had prospered to the extent of being part owner of a restaurant. From Gus I was to learn more Greek than from any of the professors later in college; for Gus was able to make alive a literature he dreamed about when, as a cook responding during the day to the cry of a waiter, "Roastabif, makit two!" in the early morning he would read Æschylus and Homer to me in the original as the Greeks pronounce ancient Greek and together we translated what he read. Through many weeks I carried Taylor's translation of *Faust* in my newspaper satchel and when I reached the café for my breakfast I would read until daylight, with Gus dozing in a chair behind the counter. This reading of *Faust* led me to learn German and to enjoy in the lyrics of Goethe and Heine a pleasure that is still a sentimental memory to me.

The Faust legend is medieval; but Goethe's treatment of it is peculiarly modern. The Faust legend was old before it was crystallized in the stories which gathered about one Dr. Johann Faustus of Wittenberg in Germany during the early part of the sixteenth century. This Dr. Faustus, it appears, was a necromancer and astrologer, an erudite man who professed to be able to conjure up spirits and restore lost manuscripts of classical authors. He was also a swindler; and he used his cleverness in various ways to mulct the gullible. In consequence he got the reputation of having sold his soul to the devil. It is possible that he was a member of one of the witch-cults which flourished alongside of Christianity in medieval Europe and even flourishes in certain communities today. He disappeared under mysterious circumstances. Anonymous "biographies" of Dr. Faustus and of his disciple, Christopher Wagner, began to appear in Germany and in England toward the end of the century. The first of these in English, *The History of the Damnable Life and Deserved Death of Doctor John Faustus*, appeared in 1592. It has been modernized and edited by William Rose and published in the Broadway Series of Translations.

There are two parts to *Faust:* the first part is a lyrical tragedy; the second part is an uncharted philosophical jungle which has a

THE AUTHOR OF "FAUST"

JOHANN WOLFGANG VON GOETHE
(From the drawing by Daniel Maclise)

certain interest for those who like to follow Goethe's mind in and out of his various studies. For the general reader only the first part remains permanently interesting. Those who do not read German will find the translation by Alice Raphael into English verse the best. As Mark Van Doren has said, "Bayard Taylor's *Faust*, standard as it once was, and energetic as it still is in so many places, wears the dust of Victorian idiom, Victorian inversion, Victorian rhetoric," whereas Miss Raphael's version is that of a gifted modern poet who is also a lifelong student of Goethe.

Goethe's treatment of the Faust theme was to make it the vehicle for a drama of the emotions around the conflicting desires in the heart of man to reject or accept life. There are many ways of rejecting life without entering a convent: one may reject it simply by surrounding one's self with prohibitions and taboos, as Milton did, by refusing to accept experience, by shutting one's self up in a dream-world of philosophical consistency. The message of *Faust* is that men should have the courage to face life as an adventure and give full play to all one's possibilities: to develop fully and not one-sidedly. It is the philosophy of Havelock Ellis in *The Dance of Life* and of Elie Faure in *The Dance Over Fire and Water*. Georg Brandes has pointed out that Goethe was not a heroic character but he was a full man, and, provincial middle-class German citizen that he was, he yet lived a full life.

Johann Wolfgang Goethe (he acquired the "von" in later life) was born at Frankfort-am-Main on August 28, 1749, the son of a lawyer whose male antecedents had been smiths and tailors, and of a mother who was a descendant of the petty nobility. Johann Caspar Goethe was a stern disciplinarian, narrow-minded and pedantic. He was resolved that his son be thoroughly equipped intellectually for the battle of life, and when Wolfgang was a child he subjected him to long hours of study of Latin, Greek, Hebrew, French and English as well as of the natural sciences and the art of metrics. He also required him to write themes on what he saw and heard and try his hand at verse. This discipline had its advantages in the mental development of Goethe but it was so severe that it entirely alienated the affection of the son. And in *Faust* perhaps we get an echo of young Goethe's revolt against too much book learning in Faust's resolution to leave his study and seek passionate adventure.

Goethe was sent to study law at the University of Leipsic and he used this escape from the parental roof to make his first contacts with life. He paid very little attention to his legal studies, participated in the student activities, fell in love with a wine dealer's daughter, wrote poetry, took up painting, and read Lessing's *Laokoön* with enthusiasm as a new revelation to him. In his first freedom, however, he overdid it: under dissipation his health broke, he had a hemorrhage of the lungs and he had to return to Frankfort without taking his degree.

After two years of recuperation Goethe went to Strassburg to study law at the university. He eventually emerged with a master's degree in law, but more appropriately to his career, with a considerable body of lyrical verse, a drama, *Götz von Berlichingen,* and the idea for *Faust.* In Strassburg, too, he had come under the influence of the critic, poet and philosopher, Johann Gottfried Herder, who was the foremost leader of German thought in the eighteenth century. And in Strassburg he had his first serious love affair, with Fredericke Brion, the daughter of a pastor, and to this love we owe many of Goethe's most beautiful love lyrics.

Goethe returned to Frankfort not to practice law but to engage in newspaper work and to settle seriously into a literary career. Within four years' time he developed so rapidly as a poet that by the time he was twenty-six he was already the foremost literary figure of his time in Germany, with a popular reputation greatly enhanced by his romantic novel, *Werther,* and by the publication of his *Götz* which was highly praised by the most eminent critics. At Frankfort Goethe's two most important love affairs were with Charlotte Buff (the Lotte of *Werther*) and Lili Schönemann. His love affair with Lili was a stormy and jealous one; for Lili was a flirt with a heart as wayward and susceptible as Goethe's own. They became engaged but the engagement was broken by pressure brought upon the couple by both families.

After the affair with Lili, Goethe accepted the invitation of the young Duke Karl August of Saxe-Weimar to come to Weimar to live. The young duke and his mother-in-law were building up a literary circle around the small provincial court, and they had visited Goethe in Frankfort where they offered Goethe a post as Councilor at a salary of twelve hundred thalers annually. Goethe bought a home in Weimar and thenceforward to the end of his long life he was rarely to stir out of the quiet little town.

Goethe took his governmental work seriously: he was elevated in rank and salary and in time attained to the title of nobility and the grant of a coat of arms by the emperor, Joseph II. Many critics have considered it a blemish on Goethe's character that he should have allowed himself to become a petty noble and political functionary in a petty court; but it seems to me that for him to have done so was in keeping with the philosophy of life to which he attained—to accept life as it is, assume the duties and responsibilities of a citizen. He functioned freely and without restraint; his literary productivity was continuous and immense until the day of his death, on October 22, 1832, at the age of eighty-four.

When Goethe first went to Weimar he was a tall, handsome, graceful and passionate young man, described as looking like Adonis. He lived up to his Byronic reputation, drank and caroused and fell in love with Frau von Stein, a woman seven years his senior, married to the duke's master of horse. About his relationship with Frau von Stein—that is, as to whether that relationship was platonic or not— a great body of conjectural literature has been built up. Agreement seems now to be that for nearly seven years it was platonic; that for a brief period after that it was not; and that once the platonic nature of the relationship changed into a more intimate one the illusion he had about Frau von Stein was broken and after some violent quarrels wherein Frau von Stein exhibited bitter jealousy of Goethe's accredited mistress, Christine Vulpius, the affair came to an end with the departure of Goethe for Italy, where he remained more than a year.

Christine was a pretty, uneducated young country lass who had worked in a factory in Weimar when, at twenty-three, she brought to Goethe, then forty, a petition that he help her brother find a job. Goethe was attracted by her and at first had her visit him secretly. In the small town gossip spread and the liaison became known and a scandal. The middle-class morality of the town was not shocked, for Goethe's many love affairs were an open secret; but the social notions of the petty court circle were outraged: Goethe was deemed to have taken up with a girl who was beneath him socially. Goethe intensified the social antagonism to Christine by marrying her on October 19, 1806. For some time previous to this he had taken her into his home where he described her as his "niece" to strangers and relegated her to the position of housekeeper.

Goethe's conduct in regard to Christine is difficult to condone. The women of Weimar refused to meet her socially; and when they were entertained at Goethe's house, Christine was treated as a servant by her husband no less than by his guests; she did not appear at table at his dinners and in general kept out of sight. Madame Johanna Schopenhauer, mother of the famous pessimistic philosopher and an author in her own right, was the first to entertain Madame Goethe in her house. Madame Schopenhauer had moved from Danzig to Weimar as a wealthy widow of a banker, and a literary personage as well as irreproachable socially. But the championship of Christine by Madame Schopenhauer did not quite break down the prejudices which had grown up against the former factory girl; and when Christine died in June, 1816, she was still something of a social outcast, although her son had grown up and had married the daughter of Baron Pogisch, who had presented Goethe and his wife with three grandchildren.

The mere catalogue of women in Goethe's life is an extensive one and the history of his relationships with women has been the subject of many volumes. He was of the type which seems to find stimulation in numerous love affairs; but unlike the typical Don Juan this constant emotional stimulation did not break him. He thrived under it. What might have been the disintegration of a weaker man physically only seemed to cause Goethe to expand. The reason, however, may have been that after his first youth, he did not give very much of himself to any one, and reserved his real emotion for his writings. He achieved a serenity in life never felt by his more lyrical younger compatriot, Heinrich Heine. But Goethe was peculiarly German. It has been pointed out that he did not create a new idiom but used the dramatic structures no less than the language of classical German. And, too, Heine's temperament was Jewish, ironical and bitter against all things German, because he had been made to suffer so much in his youth through German anti-Semitism.

BYRON *THE YEARNING*

*

THE poetry of Lord Byron grows less and less readable with the years; the personality of Lord Byron continues to exercise its fascination upon the minds and imaginations of men and women. More than any writer who ever lived he left a definite impress upon his times. He colored the whole thought of Europe. He set a fashion of individual audacity, passionate yearning and pessimism which was to be the literary mood of a whole century, inspiring Goethe and a whole school of romantic poets in Germany, inaugurating the romantic movement in France and being largely responsible for the realistic reaction against the romantic excesses his personality had created.

Byron was the poet of the revolution, the lyrical heir to Rousseau's doctrine of equality and of the innocence of man corrupted by the artificial conventions of society. He defied all the conventions of his class; he attacked all the social assumptions of his period. And he was a noble lord: that accounted for much of the wonder and excitement his doings caused. His life was scandalous in the extreme and he traded on the scandal he created. This was something new. Other people led scandalous lives in the peerage but they were at pains to cover it up: they never celebrated their lapses of morals in glowing verse. They did not have that combination of genius, personal beauty, profound conviction of the value of individual liberty, capacity for enjoyment, and tendency to dramatize themselves which Byron possessed.

The eighteenth century, in England and in France, had been one in which the accepted mode, in literature and life, was one of politeness, restraint, levity, grace, ease, sophistication. The accepted

329

attitude was one in which there was no display of passion, no high enthusiasm, no exuberance. One did not, officially in life or literature, take life very seriously. This fashion led gradually to a certain sterility.

The undisciplined, savage, erratic and gifted young Byron changed all that. Poetry had become a sort of pleasant pastime, something exterior to the poet's own moods and feelings. Byron was to write an intensely personal poetry, poetry in which the man and his verse were interfused, poetry which celebrated the awakening concepts of "liberty, equality and fraternity."

Henry Blake Fuller once summed up Byron thus: "He was a bundle of discords and discrepancies—a peer but poor; gifted, but undisciplined; well born, but ill-bred; dowered with a handsome head and a hideous foot; impelled to write, but too proud—for a while—to take money; contemptuous of society, yet finding society's notice the very breath of his nostrils; always ready to puncture humbug, yet an incorrigible poseur himself; aristocratic in sentiment, yet with democratic theories; retiring to Pisa or Ravenna, yet exacting the whole European spotlight as his due; endeavoring to express himself in multitudinous verse, yet perhaps succeeding only in his letters and journals; living as a gay libertine, yet throwing away a tired, impatient life in the cause of a freedom quite other than self-indulgently personal. A century has not sufficed to bring harmony out of such discord."

George Noel Gordon Byron, later Lord Byron, came of crazy parentage on both sides. His great-uncle from whom he inherited the title was a dissolute peer who killed a man in a drunken brawl and was tried and acquitted for murder only to shut himself up in his castle, overwhelmed by debts and dissipation. His father, Captain Byron, was a notorious rake, who married a divorced woman, and when she died, married a rich woman whom he deserted as soon as he had exhausted her fortune. His mother was a hysteric, with no maternal affection for her son.

Under these prenatal disadvantages Byron was born in London on January 22, 1788. His childhood was especially unhappy. He had a club foot which made him shy and timid and full of a sense of inferiority which he later over-compensated by arrogance and athleticism. His mother, mentally wrecked by poverty and by the treatment accorded her by her husband, hated her son, banged him around and screamed at him.

Byron was first sent to a private school and later to a public

GEORGE GORDON, LORD BYRON
(From the painting by Richard Westall)

school in Aberdeen; still later to Harrow and then to Trinity College, Cambridge. As a child and youth he was beautiful, with almost a feminine beauty. He was a quiet boy, eager for affection, passionately devoted to those women who gave him the tenderness he never enjoyed from his mother. He acceded to the peerage at the age of ten on the death of his grand-uncle but this only aggravated his timidity at first, because of the poverty of his family. He was submitted to tortures in an effort to cure his foot.

He was precociously passionate and afflicted with a narcissism which caused him to fall in love with his relations who somewhat resembled him. His first passion was for Mary Duff, a cousin, and his second was for Margaret Parker, also a cousin. His love for these girls caused him intense pain and suffering; he was extremely jealous of them. His interest in them foreshadowed his later incestuous passion for his sister, Augusta Leigh, which caused his wife to leave him and which was to be so much the source of the infamy with which his name became associated. It was a scandal which for almost a century was kept from the public, but by the very fact of its being suppressed became the central factor of bitter controversy.

At Harrow he wrote some verses but until his last year at Cambridge his particular interest in life was politics and he was seriously preparing to take his seat in the House of Lords, with an ambition to become a great Liberal orator. The publication of his juvenile verses in a book called *Hours of Idleness,* however, brought down upon him such a derisive blast of criticism from the *Edinburgh Review* that he was steeled into an effort to prove his own cleverness in a satire called *English Bards and Scotch Reviewers.* Published anonymously, it attracted a great deal of attention. Byron acknowledged the authorship of the satire, and shortly thereafter, on borrowed money, he spent two years of travel in Spain, Greece and Asia Minor, gathering the impressions and the experiences which he was to weave into his semi-autobiographical verses *Childe Harold's Pilgrimage.* He was accompanied on this trip by John Hobhouse, first Lord Houghton.

All of the cleverness and excesses of Byron were in seedling in those first two cantos of a poem he later expanded. He had taken up residence in Newstead Abbey, the ancestral palace of the Byrons, and was beginning the melodramatic sort of theatricalism which was to figure so much in his career. He posed as a modern Timon of Athens, worn out with lusts, satiated with pleasures. As a matter of fact, he was healthy enough, young and full of life. His "harem of

Paphian beauties" had really been some servant girls at Newstead and probably one or two amiable women on the continent. He went up to London with the cantos of *Childe Harold* he had written to show them to his friends and get their criticism. While he was there his mother died of an apoplectic stroke before he could return to her side at Newstead. He grieved greatly over her death; for in spite of their passionate quarrels they were sufficiently alike so that toward her he had an understanding sympathy. The death of his mother was followed shortly by the death of one of his closest friends by drowning. His pessimism and despair, so much a pose before, became real after these two events and through his constant need of money.

AFTER he had finished his revisions of *Childe Harold,* Byron had the manuscript brought to the attention of John Murray, the publisher, who was immediately conscious of the merits of the poem and began to prepare the reception of it by propaganda before he published it. Byron himself was of two minds about it himself; one moment he thought the poem was good and the next he would take the criticism of his friends so much to heart that he would think it worthless.

With the publication of *Childe Harold* Byron's fate was sealed; his reputation was made. He said he woke up one morning and found himself famous. This was almost literally true. Byron's name was on the lips of every one in society; his book was on all drawing-room tables. He was the lion of the hour and invited everywhere.

Although Byron was a peer and had already made two speeches in the House of Lords this was his first contact with London society. He was taken up by Lord and Lady Melbourne and became an intimate member of their household. Lady Melbourne, who had been Elizabeth Milbanke, was a beautiful and charming woman, whose morals were of an eighteenth century libertinism and who had grown old gracefully after several liaisons in court circles which she had managed to keep from becoming scandals. Byron fell under her spell, for she was from a moral point of view all that Byron was not. She was, in fact, the most disintegrating influence in his life. Byron's code was really conventional and his moral sense highly puritanical. Lady Melbourne, with her easy attitude toward the peccadilloes of the heart, encouraged in Byron the ideals of a voluptuary.

At Melbourne House he became intimate with Lady Melbourne's daughter, Lady Caroline Lamb, who, having ceased to love her husband, William Lamb, deliberately set her cap for Byron, and was abetted in this enterprise by her mother. Byron admired and respected William Lamb, whom he considered "as much above me as Hyperion above the Satyr"; and at first he was appalled and repelled by Lady Caroline's advances. Against his inclination he yielded to her blandishments and she abandoned herself recklessly, going to Byron's house and being seen there dressed as a page. News of Lady Caroline's conduct got bruited about and the Prince Regent demanded of Lady Melbourne and Lady Bessborough (William Lamb's mother) that the affair be broken up. Byron was heartily sick of the affair already and with the aid of the two elderly women helped to get Lady Caroline and William to Ireland, where Lady Caroline, however, managed to send him passionate and indiscreet letters.

Meanwhile at Lady Melbourne's house he had met and become interested in Lady Caroline's cousin, Annabella Milbanke, only daughter of Sir Ralph Milbanke, a wealthy baronet. Byron's closest friend at that time, Thomas Moore, the poet, urged Byron to repair his fortunes by marrying Miss Milbanke and to retire to Newstead Abbey in ease and splendor. Miss Milbanke was chaste, austere and something of a blue-stocking. He paid court to her but at first she rejected his advances. She was aware of the affair between him and Lady Caroline; she was aware also of his immoral reputation and, like many women of irreproachable virtue, she conceived the notion that through her love she could redeem him.

Lady Caroline was becoming more and more importunate, threatening suicide and in other ways making Byron uncomfortable and heartily sick of her. She tried suicide by slashing her wrists before Byron at a ball and this made a public scandal; then Byron broke with her decisively and definitely.

However, his life was becoming more seriously complicated. His sister Augusta, whom he had not seen in many years, was married to Colonel Leigh, a gambler and a rake with a passion for servant girls, who had run deeply into debt and spent so much time at the races that he rarely saw his wife. Augusta came to see Byron and told him of her unhappiness. He and she became sympathetically attached to each other and went out much together. She was a Byron, with Byron's own profile, and with her he fell in love with himself. They committed the sin of Paolo and Francesca. After living with him at Newstead Abbey Augusta bore him a daughter.

Byron had talked, for his success with women had so gone to his head that he boasted of his conquests; he had even made a confidante of Lady Melbourne, who was properly horrified and told him he would never expiate that crime; but he was sure of himself. He sent Augusta home to have her child, paid her husband five thousand pounds, wrote some lovely lines about their love, and renewed his court of Miss Milbanke.

They were married on January 2, 1815, and in the following December she bore him a daughter. The next month she left her husband's house in London and returned to her father. Hers had been a disastrous union. Their differences of temperament were soon manifest; she had no liking for Byron's poetry and tried to make him give up writing it; she brought her mother, whom Byron disliked, into the household; quarrels developed; Byron took to drink; and finally introduced Augusta into the ménage. Lady Byron awoke to the situation, perceived that Byron's passion for his sister was irresistible, and after vainly trying to win his love, left him, convinced that Byron was mad. She disclosed the cause of her unhappiness with her husband to her doctor, who kept the secret, but saw that reconciliation was impossible. A formal deed of separation was drawn up, whereby he was to receive half of Lady Byron's annual income from her dowry and was to give up nothing. He wrote a rather spiteful poem, *Farewell to Lady Byron*, which he afterwards said he did not mean to publish, but which was published anyhow, and found himself out in the street, attacked in the press, a lion in disgrace. He took a new mistress, Clare Clairmont, had Newstead Abbey put up for sale and arranged to go abroad.

He went to Geneva where Clare Clairmont met him. She had accompanied another poet and his mistress on a hegira—Percy Bysshe Shelley and Mary Godwin. The poets had never met before and they immediately became friends; they were joined by Byron's friend, Hobhouse. Byron and Shelley visited the Castle of Chillon, read each other's newly finished work, discussed Chauteaubriand and Goethe. Byron took a cottage near the Shelleys and settled down to the writing of more cantos of *Childe Harold* and to the composition of *Manfred*, a dramatic narrative inspired by reading the first part of Goethe's *Faust*. Clare Clairmont presented him with a bastard daughter. She lived at the Shelley house and visited Byron at night. Byron was contemptuous of her and irritated Shelley by his caddish way of speaking of the girl. With the sale of Newstead Abbey, Byron had been able to pay off his old debts and have a considerable fortune left, augmented by seven thousand pounds in royalties from his poems, and an income from his settlement from Lady Byron. But he grew parsimonious with his access of wealth. He left his daughter by Clare Clairmont with Shelley and only after repeated requests put the child in the charge of a nurse in Vienna. He gave Clare her *congé* and wents to Venice, where he had a succession of mistresses, chief of whom, the Countess Guiccioli, who was in time separated from her husband over Byron, and who lived as Byron's accredited mistress, following him to Ravenna and Pisa and remaining with him (but as only one of several mistresses) until, urged by Edward John Trelawney, an adventurer, Byron put his liberal theories into practice by enlisting in the cause of Greek independence.

In the quieter atmosphere of Pisa Byron had done a great amount of work. He concluded *Childe Harold,* finished *Don Juan, Cain* and other poems by which he is best known. While resident at Pisa, Shelley was drowned in the Gulf of Spezia and Byron, with Trelawney, erected the funeral pyre on the shore in which the dead poet's body was consumed, Byron snatching Shelley's heart from the flames. With Leigh Hunt and Shelley, before Shelley's death, Byron began the publication of a journal in London called the *Liberal,* which ran for four issues and in which Byron's *Vision of Judgment,* a radical satire, appeared.

The extraordinary adventure of Byron's last days should be read in Harold Nicolson's *Byron, the Last Journey* or in the definitive biography *Byron,* by André Maurois, translated by Hamish Miles (this latter work is the only one which is detailed and explicit on the subject of Byron's relationship with Augusta Leigh and it contains other details avoided or unknown to previous biographers).

At the time Byron undertook to help the Greeks in gaining their independence, his unpopularity in England had reached its highest pitch. This unpopularity was in the main caused by his radical political opinions, but it had not been helped by the scandals or by the publication of a novel by Lady Caroline Lamb in which Byron figured as the hero under a thin disguise.

As a member of the London Greek committee in 1823, Byron raised some money, bought an English brig, sailed from Genoa and reached Missolonghi, where there were long delays before he saw action; the Greeks were not organized. He was made commander-in-chief of an expedition against the Turks at Lepanto, but while camped in a swamp he was seized with fever and, with his constitution badly weakened by dissipation, he was quickly carried off on April 19, 1824, aged thirty-six years.

Immediately after Byron's death, sentiment toward him in England changed. He was considered a hero; enthusiasm for the concluding cantos of *Childe Harold* and for his daring *Don Juan* mounted. His fame had already spread through France, Germany and Italy and had set the romantic movement going at an accelerated pace.

Byron's versification has liveliness of movement, speed and occasional dazzling qualities; but he was careless; he had too much cleverness and facility and there is not a great deal of his poetry which will stand the test of critical examination. His Heliogabalism was a violent reaction against British smugness. His moral disintegration was the result of his surprise and acquiescence when he found so many women eager to throw themselves at his feet. He represented something beyond himself to them, something different from the commonplaceness of existence; and that is the reason, no doubt, why his personality, callous as it was or grew to be, continues to attract the interest of the sentimental and romantic. He who had only one love affair in his life with any real tenderness in it, or with any affection or even liking for the object of his attentions, and that one extremely repugnant to civilized society, continues even in death to win the hearts of thousands of women.

BALZAC *THE HISTORIAN*

*

JUST as Hugo was the last great champion of the romantic
virtues of heroism (although he was a republican and without
a sense of humor), Balzac was the first celebrant of the new era of
democratic, capitalistic, industrial society. He was its critic and
historian also. In the work of Hugo as in the work of the medieval
romances, money and the effects of money play an inconspicuous
part in the scheme of living; even the poor, upon whom Hugo
lavishes so much agreeable sentiment, are never considered in relation to the economic system which makes them poor, but as un-
fortunates, slighted children of God upon whom the more fortunate
are constrained to exercise charity and pity.

The acquisition of money is the central passion of Balzac himself, and it is the mainspring of the characters of nearly all of his
fictional creations. He and Stendhal (whose career as a novelist
somewhat antedated Balzac's), alone among nineteenth century
novelists, did not disdain money (or profess to) or discount its
importance in the scheme of life under industrialism. Balzac was
not repelled, like so many writers of his time, by the idea that
prosperity, pleasant living, pleasant enjoyment of the amenities
might be gained by peaceful trade, instead of by pillage; that the
individual, whatever his birth, might of his own talents win to the
ease and comfort, luxury and freedom of the mind and spirit by
supplying the wants and needs of his fellow man, instead of, by
force of arms, taking what his fellows produced.

Balzac saw all the evil that this new opportunity could produce:
he saw the miser centering all his passion on the accumulation of
gold, never spending it, never making use of it and causing misery

337

to all who were dependent upon him or were subject to his lust for gold. He saw the clever *arrivistes,* winning their way to power through money by crushing and killing those less clever; he saw new artificial classes arising on a new basis of possessions; he saw, in fine, all the disagreeable and sordid factors in the new touchstone of success—money.

But he did not, like the middle class dilettantes of his period who rooted like any swine for cash, make a show of disdaining money. Money was frankly what he was after as a writer. Others wanted fame; Balzac wanted money. That he never quite attained his objective, that he wore himself out paying off old debts and died just when he had finally attained a degree of wealth, is one of the fortunate ironies of life, unfortunate for Balzac but fortunate for the rest of humanity.

For the fact is Balzac reproduced in novels every phase of the society of his time. Future students of his period will go to Balzac, and not to the historians, to learn what life was like in Paris during the greater part of the nineteenth century. He was a meticulous observer; he was a faithful reporter; and he had a sense of drama.

He created types, like Dickens, and the development of the novel during the last fifty years has been away from types and toward the psychology of the individual. Therefore the popularity of Balzac has been on the wane. Realization that Balzac contained worlds within him, that he summed up all the phases of French genius, that the body of his epigrams alone bulk larger than all the epigrams of La Rochefaucauld, La Bruyère and Vauvenargues put together and stand the closest comparison with them, that he had the gusto of Rabelais, that he had an astonishing critical gift, and that he was an incomparable analyst and historian of a whole society—all these things have been realized but tardily by the guardians of French taste and opinion. They have not been so tardily realized by the generality who have read Balzac. The intellectual, literary and artistic force of a man whose amazing bulk of compositions permitted Harry Rickel to compile that astonishing book, *The Wisdom of Balzac,* a collection of epigrams and characterizations which make Oscar Wilde seem like a sophomore; whose amazing technique has become the subject of an exhaustive study by Dr. Ethel Preston of the University of Chicago (*Récherches sur la Technique de Balzac*); and whose novels have found favor in translation in all parts of the world—is a fact one must consider in any estimate of that Gargantuan figure who wrote *La Peau de Chagrin, Les Contes drolatiques* and the *Comédie Humaine.*

HONORÉ DE BALZAC was born in 1799 at Tours, the country of Rabelais. He had many of the qualities celebrated by the creator of *Gargantua and Pantagruel:* he was stout, broad-shouldered, sanguine, inclined to fatness, a prodigious eater and drinker, coarse, clumsy, close to the soil, nearer to the peasant than to the nobility. He had full sensual lips, thick black hair, coarse as the mane of a horse, and deep brown eyes which shone with a steady luster. He was educated at the College Vendôme in Tours and, when the Balzac family moved to Paris, he was entered as a notary's apprentice with the view to his taking up the legal profession.

The law was not to Balzac's taste, however, for he had early conceived the ambition to conquer Paris with his literary gifts. He proposed a plan to his father, which his father finally yielded to: his father was to contribute a small amount for his support until he had tried out his gifts. If he was able to sustain himself as a writer, he would be permitted to go on with a literary career; if he did not, he was to take up law again.

The future creator of a teeming world of fictional types took an attic room near the Père Lachaise, and entered upon the titanic labors which were to produce ninety-six novels, any number of short stories, and literary hack-work of all kinds and finally kill him prematurely. In *Père Goriot* he pictures Rastignac, an ambitious young man, standing on the Butte above Paris in the evening, looking down on the city and vowing to conquer that city by brain and will, no matter what it cost him. In the same way we are sure that Balzac, looking out of the window from his garret over the rooftops of Paris, vowed that he would conquer Paris by the labors of his pen. He had to practice every economy. His room was cold and cheerless, drab and sparsely furnished. He worked through the night, wrapped up in blankets, and with a pot of coffee beside him. To obtain a lower price for his room he agreed to make his bed, sweep the room and keep it tidy. He permitted himself a short walk in the morning as the only form of exercise; his food was scanty— rolls, a paste of sardines and olive oil, coffee and some fruit. Later he would starve himself for days at a time and then eat enough to kill him—six dozen oysters, two whole chickens, slices of roast, salad and cheese—and wash it down with a magnum of wine.

He tried a tragedy and soon found he had no sense of dramatic technique. Time was pressing. He turned to novel writing. He had not had much experience in life, but he had read a great many novels. He turned out five novels in one year, under a pseudonym, all of which were accepted, but none of which had any considerable merit. But he got a thousand francs apiece for them. He had proved to his family that he could earn a living by his pen.

In 1825, after having turned out a mass of poor books, he despaired of winning a distinguished name for himself and conceived the first of his ideas for making money quickly. Authors are notoriously bad business men (though there are some exceptions, of course, like Bernard Shaw), but this does not prevent them from engaging in business enterprises and speculations which, in theory, are sound. Their imaginations are, in fact, precisely the sort of imaginations which are commercially important and which, channeled exclusively into the enterprises they undertake, would lead to wealth. But as a rule authors have not the application for details of business, or the critical faculty for considering their commercial ideas in relation to other factors, which make for success. Thus James Joyce, the author of *Portrait of the Artist as a Young Man* and *Ulysses,* opened the first motion picture theater in Dublin. It was a bold and enterprising idea which, and but for one thing, might have been the start of a career that would have made him the motion picture magnate of Ireland. But he opened his theater in a disreputable street, in which no respectable woman would be seen after dark. And since the success of a motion picture theater depends largely upon the patronage of women and children, Joyce's theater soon failed. Sir Walter Scott and Mark Twain are two other notable examples of authors who tried to make money with grandiose commercial schemes only to fail and find themselves heavily in debt.

BALZAC gave up writing for a time and with his meager savings started a publishing house with the idea of bringing out cheap one-volume editions of the classics; but he failed in this because he had not reckoned on the competition he would have to meet. He had also set up as a bookseller to distribute his own publications, as the result of which other booksellers declined to purchase his wares. Again on a trip to Italy, he had an idea (which later proved correct) that the silver mines of Sardinia were not exhausted and, since silver at the time was at a premium, he set about examining the mines, returned to Paris for capital, got the money needed, and applied for permission to work the mines. Unfortunately he had told others of his idea while in Italy, and one of these beat him to the concession. His idea, however, had been correct: the mines made a fortune for the man whom he guilelessly told about it.

Balzac's publishing idea had been a grandiose one, for he meant to edit the classics himself, write prefaces for them, and be his own printer, agent, distributor and bookseller. He persuaded his father to put money into the scheme. At first things seemed to work out all right, but then the booksellers combined against him; he went bankrupt and was overburdened with debts. He spent some months in a debtor's prison before he was able to make arrangements with his creditors which would allow him to pay off his debts by installments.

To pay off his debts he plunged again into writing. Writing did not come easy to him. He did not have a natural, easy facility; he could not, like his friend Gautier, hastily turn off a newspaper article which would be a marvel of felicitous phrasing while standing at a counter in the newspaper office with the editor waiting for the sheets. Balzac never learned to write easily nor did he ever acquire any charm of style. Like Theodore Dreiser in America after him, he always wrote graceless prose with only occasional lapses into felicity: like Dreiser he was not so much concerned with the way of saying a thing as with what he had to say. His style, therefore, was always somewhat distasteful to the more exacting French critics.

Gautier has given us his reminiscences of Balzac as a worker. All the world has heard about Balzac's habit of working all day and all night, keeping awake by drinking vast quantities of strong coffee. But, as Gautier reveals to us, Balzac got as much sleep as the average person requires. He merely distributed sleep over periods when other people were awake. Gautier tells how Balzac would come to his house in the early morning after working all night and, being ravenously hungry, would make innumerable sandwiches of sardine paste and fall asleep with his clothes on, asking Gautier to wake him in an hour. This Gautier would invariably fail to do, and Balzac would sleep soundly until nightfall, when he would wake up in a high state of excitability and hurl maledictions on his benefactor, crying out that he had thus lost so many thousand francs for the chapters he might have written of his novel. This performance was repeated day in and day out, and Balzac, getting plenty of sleep all the time, entertained the delusion that he did not need sleep and rarely got it, and then only when some one betrayed him into the hands of Morpheus.

Balzac turned out many novels under a pseudonym before he dared to acknowledge the work that came from his pen. Then he wrote *The Physiology of Marriage*, a Rabelaisian analysis of the institution of wedlock, which had an excellent sale but which did not help his literary reputation. He followed this by *La Peau de Chagrin*, a half supernatural, half psychological novel which some critics consider the finest of his novels. It established his reputation; it was translated into German and English. It made an impression on Goethe.

It was not until after Balzac had written his most famous classics, *Eugénie Grandet* and *Père Goriot*, that he conceived the idea of linking all his past and future novels together, with some of the same central characters reappearing from time to time, of treating every phase of contemporary French society and of calling the whole work, the *Human Comedy*. Dante had called his principal poem the *Inferno* and had peopled it with Florentines of his time. So Balzac would write an *Inferno* of Parisian society, peopling it with go-getters, misers, rakes, peasants, novelists, journalists, frivolous high society persons, bankers, actors, mountebanks. Always in debt, he struggled on with his gigantic task until at last he achieved a degree of security and a certain happiness—only to die.

In 1832 he received a letter from an unknown admirer, Countess Eveline Hanska, a wealthy Polish woman who was married to a Russian nobleman and living in the Ukraine. Balzac's life had not been chaste; he had had a mistress to whom for a while he had given a certain devotion; and he had had many ephemeral affairs which had always tortured his conscience, not for moral reasons, but because they took time away from his novels. With his unknown correspondent, however, he fell promptly in love. She seemed to understand him perfectly; later there was some tosh about "elective affinities" (started by Goethe), with Countess Hanska and Balzac as examples. They corresponded for eighteen months before they met in the spring of 1833 at Neufchatel, where they consummated their devotion. They continued their correspondence for seven years after the death of Count Hanska, Balzac begging her all the time, first to divorce her husband and marry him and, after her husband's death, to marry him since there was now no obstacle in the way. They met, during this time, once a year in Switzerland. Finally, after putting Balzac off so long, she consented and they were married in 1850, after a visit he paid her on her Russian estate.

They returned to Paris and set up in a beautifully furnished house. Balzac was a famous man. Distinguished personages called at their house. He had finally achieved the wealth he had struggled for, but he had worn his body out; he was suffering from angina pectoris. Madame Hanska, it must be admitted, was not the pure soul Balzac had conceived her as being. Indeed, she was a sentimentalist and something of a nymphomaniac. She had had lovers before Balzac and while knowing him, and she had no sooner got established in Paris as Balzac's wife than she took as a lover, unbeknown to Balzac, a young cad of a painter who liked to boast of the women he had, naming their names.

Balzac was stricken, and Victor Hugo called at the house. On the way to the dying man's room, a door was ajar and Hugo saw the painter and Madame Hanska in bed. After seeing Balzac, Hugo called for Madame Balzac to tell her her husband's condition was extremely serious. Madame Balzac appeared in negligee, much disheveled. Hugo left. A doctor was summoned. Balzac died that morning. He was fifty-one years old when he died, but he had done enough work to keep five men busy through a long lifetime. In an age when collaboration was common, and when Alexander Dumas employed a number of writers to assist him, Balzac wrote every line he signed.

Balzac's great value as a novelist lies in his depiction of types and in his minute and careful observation and detail.

VICTOR HUGO *THE ROMANTIC*

*

HATRED of the middle class, a hatred which found a variety of expression in the economic pathology of Karl Marx's *Capital*, in Flaubert's ferocious caricatures in *Madame Bovary* and *Bouvard et Pécuchet*, in the extravagances of the Symbolist poets who wished to exclude their enjoyment of beauty from average man, and in the devices of Baudelaire to *épater le bourgeois*, was a romantic convention of the nineteenth century. It was a reactionary emotion of a people who wanted a return of the pomp of kings. One sees it in Marx's sentimental ideas of feudal splendor; one sees it in Flaubert's romantic reconstruction of the savage glory of ancient Carthage in *Salammbô*; one sees it in Trotsky's pages wherein his special delight is in his rôle as Cæsar to the Soviets; one sees it in the writings of the modern American middle-class intellectuals who have embraced communism. It is all a yearning after romantic unrealities. The last conquest of the imagination will be when the generality accept the fact that human beings are human beings; and that heroes are creatures of our imagination, that power is something the mass confers upon others.

Hatred of the middle class began in France when King Louis Philippe first appeared in public carrying an umbrella. To carry an umbrella is a sign of prudence and caution; and these are bourgeois virtues; to carry an umbrella is to be prepared against any unforeseen inclemency of the weather; the umbrella is the badge and symbol of the plain citizen. Louis Philippe carried an umbrella. This was disillusioning to the populace. That admirable man, who was without pretense or theatricalism, who in his innocence of heart as citizen king attempted to establish the equality of man by friendly handshakes with all who proffered their hands when he walked along the streets, did not know that the French wanted rulers full of arrogance, pride, aloofness, contempt and ruthlessness. They wanted their rulers to ride in state, with all the accouterments of the kingly office—or they wanted no kings at all. Louis Philippe had been elevated to the monarchy through the support of a prosperous middle class in a new money economy of Europe in which capitalism had taken the place of an economy of grants and seizures possible only in a monarchy supported by a military force capable of plunder, of enforcing subjection and of collecting taxes.

When Napoleon died at St. Helena in 1821 the industrial era had begun in France. The revolution had swept away the old monopolies and privileges enjoyed by a handful of conspicuous idlers who enjoyed their power and privileges by right of family inheritance. The revolution had created new opportunities for millions who hitherto had to face the fact from birth that their lives were a hard, circumscribed lot determined by social and economic inequalities inherent in a monarchical system. With the confiscation of the vast estates of the nobles who had done nothing to earn them and with the seizure of ecclesiastical domains for distribution by the state, old inequalities were broken up.

How necessary it was that the old order should permanently pass is seen in the restoration in 1825 of the Bourbon monarchy under Charles X. All liberties were at once curtailed; the power of the press was destroyed; by a union of church and state, which restored the monasteries, a brief reign of medieval power shut out all freedom of life and movement; the censorship was clamped down with the force of the inquisition; the elementary rights of the poor were abrogated; the pomp of kings was restored under Polignac, a princely minister who believed in the divine right of kings.

This reign was brief; but with the elevation of the citizen king Louis Philippe the romantic hearts of the French, of the intellectual as well as the common man, sighed for the ermine and extravagance of conquest and levy. An aristocracy of wealth, acquired by individual effort, was created. And somehow this was deemed less honorable, less ennobling than an aristocracy created by mass murder, plunder, tyranny and extortion. Marx held this savage romantic notion; Flaubert held it; it was characteristic of the thought of the nineteenth century.

The literary artist of the nineteenth century, in contrast to the literary artist of most other periods of history, is in reaction against the tendencies of his time, even against all the actualities of his time; and I think this was largely a nostalgia for an impossible past conceived by imaginations, nurtured too well on fictions, which sought some other glories to take the place of glories which were disappearing with the twilight of the kings.

In the early part of the century the meteor of Byron streaked across the sky, to disturb the complacencies of the humdrum and to inspire the notion that the life of the individual could be glamorous and adventurous, defying all the proprieties and conventions. Here a poet had shown that romance, courage, heroism, brilliance, audacity and loose morals could be a personal achievement, not dissociated from a love of liberty, a sympathy with republicanism, and an attitude of acceptance of the brotherhood of man.

In France at the beginning of the century an official intellectual and literary attitude had been frozen into a convention that the eighteenth was the happiest of all centuries, especially the eighteenth century when the classical form of French literary expression had been formed under the patronage of Louis XIV. This was literature in the main of politeness, grace, cleverness and sophistication, wit and urbanity.

VICTOR HUGO, a profuse and titanic genius, was to change all that. He was to cause a revolution, a veritable cataclysm, by the simple effrontery of writing a poetic line which ended with a noun and beginning the next line with its modifier. This seems incredible to us now; and it is difficult for us to conceive the furore this act occasioned when Hugo's drama, *Hernani,* was produced on the night of February 25, 1830, in Paris, when *éscalier* was separated from *derobé* in the opening scene of the play. Screams, hisses and cat-calls came from the audience, to be drowned by Hugo's supporters, chief of whom was Alphonse Daudet, resplendent in a green velvet jacket, as a supporter of the new romantic revolt against the classicism of Racine. The success of *Hernani* worked a revolution in French literature. It made it possible for a writer to bring upon the stage and into the pages of his novel a laborer, a peasant, a proletarian and exhibit him as a humane and sympathetic figure capable of noble actions and emotions, and not, as such figures had been used hitherto, as comic relief, clods who were the butts of their masters' jests.

The romantic revolt paved the way for Daudet's incomparable blague in the figure of Tartarin of Tarascon; for the simple, lovable, elfin children of nature in George Sand's romances; for the teeming

VICTOR HUGO
(Lithographed from life by Maurin)

world of Victor Hugo's own *Les Miserables;* for the grandiosities of Balzac; for Flaubert's analyses of bourgeois life; for Zola's zoölogical studies of lower orders of society.

Hugo had the misfortune to live too long, and the monumental egotism of the genius who had triumphed so conspicuously in the years of his creative vigor made him, in his old age, a ridiculously pontifical great man in whom bombast had taken the place of inspiration. As a result there was a reaction against his work, from which there has never quite been a recovery. The popularity of his novels for a long time overshadowed the great lyrical genius he had displayed as a poet; and as the defects of his novels began to be generally apparent his real gifts as a poet were lost sight of. Swinburne and Saintsbury in England were alive to Hugo's genius as a poet; and Swinburne's worship of Hugo was nothing less than idolatry: in an article for the Encylopedia Britannica (now displaced for a calmer estimate) Swinburne listed Hugo first among all poets in the world and defended his position with truculence and fire. Gradually there has been growing up in France a school of criticism which may revive appreciation of Hugo as a lyric poet—"the greatest poet of France," says Saintsbury.

To English and American readers Victor Hugo is known largely as the author of *Les Miserables, Notre Dame de Paris, The Man Who Laughed,* and *Ninety-three.* They are the novels one reads, in translation, in one's childhood and youth, struggling with Hugo's windy digressions, and yet held enchanted by the atmosphere he creates, by the figures of Jean Valjean, Javert, little Cosette, Monsieur Myriel, Fantine, and the gamin Gavroche; by Quasimodo and Esmeralda and Claude Frollo; by Ursus Major and the gibbets with bodies swaying in the wind. When we grow up we are more sensitive than formerly to Hugo's faults, his false air of profundity, his reiterated antitheses, his unbridled rhetoric. It may be necessary for the race to recapture, by some miracle, the lost innocence of youth for Hugo's romances ever to become for adults what they are in the way of enchantment for young people on the threshold of life.

But no one who has read Hugo's novels can quite forget them. Like Dickens Hugo touches the heart; he awakens the emotion of pity for the lowly, the outcasts, the victims of society. Hugo had sympathy for suffering; his was a great vision of the nobility and dignity of homely loyalties and faith in one's fellows. In that Utopia, which may some day be realized, readers may turn to Hugo rather than to Flaubert, who carried too much contempt in his mind for his fellow residents on this changing planet. It may be found in that remote date that it was a more stupendous event to have given a soul to a medieval cathedral and to conjure up a whole populous age, with its superstitions, its achievements, its passions and its emotions, on an epic scale, as did Victor Hugo, than to take so many clinical pains to show the shallowness of a provincial housewife who "found in adultery all the platitudes of marriage."

Hugo had the exuberance of an uncontrolled genius; he had the abounding energy of a Titan; he was absurd almost as often as he was great; but it is foolish to deny his greatness. Some statistical minded person has found that Hugo had and used the most enormous vocabulary in literature; that he used 15,000 words against Shakespeare's 12,000 and Milton's 9,000; and he used them in a torrent. In his old age there remained to him almost nothing except his vocabulary and his vice of antithesis: there is his book, *Postcriptum de ma vie,* in which he thought to sum up his philosophy of life, and which is actually without any sense at all. It is a whole volume of words, grandiose and extravagant, which mean nothing whatever. But who having once read them can forget his Battle of Waterloo, the towers of Notre Dame, the barricades on which little Gavroche lost his life, the escape through the sewers, the sanctuary of the wooden elephant, the mad love and sacrifice of Quasimodo, the sinister stealth of Javert, the slavery of the child Cosette?

VICTOR MARIE HUGO was born in Besançon in 1802, the son of an officer in the army of Napoleon and of a daughter of a royalist shipowner in Nantes. His father was constantly being transferred from one garrison to another; so Victor's childhood was spent in Corsica and at Elba, in Spain and in the Pyrenees. It was not until the father returned to Paris as a full-fledged general after a governorship of Madrid that Victor entered upon a stable existence in Paris. He was sent to the École Polytechnique where he displayed a precocity in writing verse, made the vow that he would be "Chateaubriand or nothing" (Chateaubriand being the literary idol of the times because of his *Genius of Christianity* and his now forgotten romantic novels), and won honorable mention from the French Academy for an essay; and a year later he took a prize awarded by the Academy des Jeux Floreaux of Toulouse for a poem. At eighteen he and his two brothers started a short-lived literary magazine; and at nineteen he married a childhood sweetheart, Adèle Foucher.

During the year following his marriage Hugo published his first odes in celebration of Napoleon. These were classical in form and extravagant in epithet. He had not found his medium. It was not until 1829 that he came under the influence of the personality of Byron and wrote his *Orientales,* a book of poems in which he broke first with the French classical tradition and, choosing oriental and romantic themes, filled his verse with imagery and color.

He immediately became the center of a group, all ardently planning a revolution in literature. It was a group which consisted of Théophile Gautier, Alfred de Musset, Charles Augustin Sainte-Beuve, Louis Boulanger, George Sand, Honoré de Balzac, Pétrus Borel and Charles Nodier. There existed at that time a feeling of solidarity and brotherhood among these enthusiastic writers; they helped one another; took pains with one another's work. They met either at Charles Nodier's apartment in the Arsenal, in Pétrus Borel's garret or in the little flat in the rue Notre-Dame-des-Champs where Hugo and his pretty wife managed to live on two thousand francs a year. It was in this group that the romantic movement was planned and launched.

Hugo's contribution of *Hernani* gave the historic signal. Hugo imagined it was derived from Shakespeare whom Voltaire had called "a savage"; in reality it was the first time a plebeian, speaking the language of a plebeian (poetized, of course) had appeared on the French stage as a hero. He followed this with *Notre Dame,* under the romantic influence of Scott; but it was a novel undeniably Hugo's own and peculiar to his imagination and his abounding vitality.

Up to this time Hugo had been little interested in politics, although nominally a royalist, because his father was. The revolution of July, 1830, in which Lafayette became commander of the royal guard, Charles X was forced to abdicate and Louis Philippe of the House of Orléans was placed on the throne, made Hugo an ardent democrat. His poems for the next few years were to be poems for the oppressed, pæans to democracy, humanitarian in sympathy and in expression. "Hugo's watchword," wrote the Danish critic Georg Brandes, "was, undoubtedly, nature and truth, but it was at the same time and first and foremost, contrast, picturesque contrast, antithesis founded upon medieval belief in the confliction between body and soul; that is a dualistic Romanticism. . . . He desired truth to nature, but he believed it was to be arrived at by making nature's extremes meet, by placing opposites in juxtaposition—Beauty and the Beast, Esmeralda and Quasimodo, the courtesan's past and the purest love in Marion Delorme, bloodthirstiness and maternal tenderness in Lucrece Borgia."

Those are simplifications which are naïve to us now after we have seen the results of a good half century of the crude beginnings of the science of psychology; but they were simplifications which lent themselves superbly to drama and melodrama; and it was in melodrama that Victor Hugo excelled. Shortly after the publication of *Notre Dame* occurred the break between Sainte-Beuve and Hugo. They had been the closest of friends; the critic had been an almost constant visitor at Hugo's house. He fell in love with Hugo's pretty wife and affected a liaison with her which he was afterwards to expose in an extremely poor and extremely caddish novel. The sentimental alliance between Mme. Hugo and Sainte-Beuve was the more easily effected in that Hugo himself had strayed and had found flattery for his ego in adultery with an actress who worshiped him almost as a god.

Hugo's dramas were not conspicuous successes but they had brought him into the full glare of the limelight, and his *Notre Dame* and his poems had made him a success as a writer and a national figure. In 1841 he was elected a member of the French Academy. His paper on taking his seat in the Academy was on French history since the revolution, democratic in tenor. He went to Germany in 1842 for a period of contemplation in order to make certain the stand he should take on political questions; he returned to see his drama *Les Burgraves* prove a failure and to suffer the sorrow of the loss of his daughter and son-in-law by drowning.

In 1845 he was made a peer of France by Louis Philippe and from then until 1851 he was occupied chiefly with politics. He was a member of the constituent assembly after the revolution of 1848 and after resisting the *coup d'état* of Louis Napoleon which established the Second Empire, he was banished from France. At first he lived in Belgium and then in Jersey, where his family joined him, and still later in the island of Guernsey off the coast of England. During his banishment he wrote his *Napoleon the Little,* a violent invective against the "usurper," the lyrical satires of *Les Chatiments,* his masterpiece of poetry *Les Contemplations;* and his most famous novel, *Les Miserables.* At the big house in Guernsey where he lived with his wife and his mistress, shocked the neighbors by taking baths in the nude on the roof, and indulged in other eccentricities of a man convinced of his greatness, Hugo also wrote his prose epic, *Toilers of the Sea,* his English historical romance, *The Man Who*

Laughs, his realistic-romantic novel of the turmoil in France, *Ninety-three,* and the first series of his lyric cycle, *Legende des Siècles.*

With the end of the Franco-Prussian War and the fall of the Second Empire, Hugo was able to return home in triumph. He was by this time the Great Old Man of French letteıs, idolized by the people alike for his novels and for his republicanism. His wife died in 1868 and two of his sons died shortly afterwards. His consolation in his old age was in his two grandchildren. He died at the age of eighty-three, in 1885. His funeral was made a solemn national event; his body was exposed to view under the Arc de Triomphe; thousands passed by; and the *cortège* proceeded to the Pantheon where Hugo keeps company with the illustrious dead of France.

VERLAINE *THE MUSICIAN*

*

PAUL-MARIE VERLAINE was perhaps the greatest lyrical voice in French literature of the century which produced Hugo and Lamartine, Gautier and Musset, Baudelaire and Rimbaud, Jules Laforgue and Tristan Corbière, Stéphane Mallarmé and José-Maria de Hérédia. As a music maker he was of the company of Villon and Herrick, of Heine and Edgar Allan Poe. François Coppée has said of him that he created "a poetry peculiarly individual, an inspired poetry which is at once naïve and subtle, full of nuances, evoking the most delicate vibrations of the nerves, the most fugitive echoes of the heart—a natural poetry, moreover, indeed almost popular; a poetry where rhyme, both free and broken, preserves a delicious harmony, where tropes twirl and sing like a nursery rondo, where the verse—which remains verse and among the most exquisite—is always musical. And in that inimitable poetry he has given us all his fervor, all his faults, all his remorse, all his tenderness, all his dreams, and has revealed to us his soul, so troubled and yet so ingenuous."

That Verlaine was a poverty-stricken victim of his gifts and his appetites, a satyric, irresponsible, pitiable and unhappy creature buffeted *au vent mauvais*

> *Deçà, delà*
> *Pareil à la*
> *Feuille morte*

from low drama to confessional, from prison to bagnio, from alleyways to charity hospitals we know, and the knowledge was common property to all literary Paris of his time. Anatole France has described him thus: *C'est un vieux vagabond, fatigué d'avoir erré trente ans sur tous les chemins. . . . Il surprend, il choque le régard. Il a l'air à la fois farouche et calin, sauvage et familier. Un Socrate instinctif, ou mieux, un faune, un satyr, un être à demi brute, à demi dieu qui effraye comme une force naturelle qui n'est soumise à aucune loi connue. . . . Et Verlaine ressemble à Villon; ce sont deux mauvais garçons à qui il fut donné de dire les plus douces choses du monde. . . .*

One day, toward the end of his harried life, this old vagabond, plagued by an inconceivable vanity, took it into his head to announce his candidacy for that ornate and ribald sepulcher of mediocre talents, the French Academy. It signified the one thing which was denied him above all—and which he had no need of—respectability. This gravely comic gathering, "directed in everything by petty considerations and wasting its energy in childish tournaments, in which the flatteries that it showers upon others are only a foretaste of the compliments it expects in return for itself" had (to mention only a few) excluded Molière (because he was an actor), Proudhon, Chénier, Constant, Lammennais, Béranger, Stendhal, Balzac, Gautier, Baudelaire, Flaubert, Maupassant, Goncourt and Zola. And yet this old reprobate, who had penned the loveliest songs of his generation, nursed the hope that he might enjoy the Academy's dubious benisons, live in better comfort (and with more ample wine) on its meager pension, and end his days crowned an "immortal" by correct and orthodox rhetoricians, a sterile and emasculate body of well-meaning mutual back-scratchers.

His past, he knew, barred him. He was the "empire at the end of the decadence"; but he inhabited a greasy garret. He had refreshed and enriched French poetry with strange, intimate, ingenious and ingenuous verbal harmonies; but he was often outlandishly drunk. He was the idol and master to a group of talented poets; but he had abandoned his wife for a none too savory London adventure with Arthur Rimbaud. . . . Even the thought of Verlaine's occupying an armchair in the Academy would have horrified the prim grammarians and concoctors of pot-boilers who formed that areopagus of arid minds. His child-like habit of pulling up a frayed and dirty trouser to show the interesting coloring of his ulcerated leg would have sent them screaming from the Mazarin Palace.

So we find Verlaine in pathetic humility patching with infinite care the soiled and threadbare legend which shrouded him that he might appear acceptable in the society of these men, not three of whom were worthy, artistically, of cleaning the grime from his shapeless shoes.

In the defense which he wrote after he had filed the declaration of his candidacy with the perpetual secretary of the Academy, we read:

"Unhappily the idea came to Huysmans, in his curious book, *A Rebours,* to compare me, from a literary standpoint, with Villon. From that moment others began to improvise on the theme and, because I was poor and because in those days I had looked misery in the face, they presumed to speak of me as one whose troubles in life, whose early adventures, and even whose temperament was like that of our great poet of another century and to compare me to him. They dragged into their analogy everything, the jails, the hazy assassinations, even the nameless hovels, even the *grosse Margot.* . . . As to my poverty, it is not sordid; as to my domicile, it is not an almshouse, but a very modest chamber for which I pay dearly enough and regularly; as to the hovel . . . it turns out to be a very respectable, well-furnished hotel. . . ."

And so forth; a great and gifted man abasing himself that he might appear the social equal of M. Crapaud, Member of the Academy.

Verlaine's candidacy was not even considered.

PAUL-MARIE VERLAINE was born in Metz on March 30, 1844, the son of Nicolas Auguste Verlaine, a captain in the French army and a *chévalier* of the Legion of Honor. In 1851 the Verlaines moved to Paris, where Paul was sent to private school and later to the Lycée Bonaparte, where he took his bachelor's degree, with honors in Greek, Latin, rhetoric and literature. He studied law for a short time, but gave it up and found a clerkship in the bureau of budgets of accounts in the city administration.

In school Verlaine had already shown a precocious aptitude for verse. At the age of twenty-two he published his *Poèmes Saturniens,* which contained among other exquisite poems, all full of strange harmonies, some light and fanciful, some grave and tender, his famous *Autumn Song:*

Les sanglots longs	Long sobbing winds,
Des violons	The violins
De l'automne	Of autumn drone
Blessent mon cœur	Wounding my heart
D'une langueur	With languorous smart
Monotone	In monotone.

Tout suffoquant	Choking and pale
Et blême, quand	When on the gale
Sonne l'heure	The hours sound deep,
Je me souviens	I call to mind
Des jours anciens	Dead years behind
Et je pleure	And I weep
Et je m'en vais	And I, going,
Au vent mauvais	Borne by blowing
Qui m'emporte	Winds and grief,
Deçà, delà,	Flutter, here—there,
Pariel à la	As on the air
Feuille morte.	The dying leaf.

—Translation of BERGEN APPLEGATE.

At the time of the publication of this volume he was a member of a group of bohemian poets who met nearly every night in a restaurant in the rue de Rivoli to discuss literature and art. It was at these meetings that he formed the drinking habits which were to cause so much havoc in his life. Many men can drink moderately every day of their lives only to have their constitutions thrive under it. But Verlaine was highly neurotic and alcohol was poisonous to him. Besides joining this set of younger versifiers, none of whom, with the exception of Verlaine, ever wrote any poetry of consequence, he also became a frequenter of the salon of Louis Xavier de Ricard where he became identified with the Parnassian group which included Leconte de Lisle (the leader), José-Maria de Hérédia (whose sonnets are now classics of French poetry), Sully-Prudhomme, François Coppée and Catulle Mendès. Even with the support of this group, Verlaine's first volume attracted little notice at first, Sainte-Beuve being the only critic who saw its worth.

Verlaine's father had died the year before this book was published, and the young poet lived with his mother who pampered him in his dissipations, gave him money, and spoiled him. In 1869 Verlaine brought out another volume called *Fêtes Galantes,* which, like the preceding volume attracted the attention of Sainte-Beuve, the critic, who began to write of Verlaine as a discovery and as the most promising poet of the times. The *Fêtes Galantes* were gayer in mood than the earlier poems; they were a sort of Mozartian music unlike anything that any one had ever written in French. Typical of the mood and music is *Clair de Lune,* now found in all good anthologies of French poetry:

Votre âme est un paysage choisi
Que vont charmant masques et bergamasques
Jouant du luth et dansant et quasi
Tristes sous leurs deguisements fantasques.

Tout en chantant sur le mode mineur
L'amour vainqueur et la vie opportune,
Ils n'ont pas l'air de croire a leur bonheur
Et leur chanson se mele au clair de lune,

Au calme clair de lune triste et beau,
Qui fait rever les oiseaux dans les arbes
Et sangloter d'extase les jets d'eau,
Les grands jets d'eau sveltes parmi les marbes.

Your soul is like a landscape always glad,
Peopled by merry maskers with bright eyes,
Who play the lute and dance yet are half sad
Beneath the tinsel of their quaint disguise.

Who sing upon a strangely minor mode
Of love's success and life so opportune,
As they go tripping lightly on their road,
Mingling their songs with rays caught from the moon,

The moonlight rays so sad but O how fair!
That make the drowsy birds dream in their trees,
And sob with ecstasy the fountain clear
That from its marble bed jets in the breeze.
           —Translated by BERGEN APPLEGATE.

In the spring of 1869 Verlaine met Mathilde Mauté, the young half-sister of one of his friends. They fell in love at first sight and for her sake Verlaine began to reform his habits. She inspired him to write some of his happiest poems, notably *La Bonne Chanson*. But she was a mere child and marriage at the moment was impossible. He continued his courtship for a year and at last got the consent of Mathilde's parents to the marriage. Never again was he to be so happy; he was deeply in love; he looked upon marriage as a sacrament; and he had hopes that marriage would redeem him from his vices.

In 1870 the Prussian War began; the Germans marched toward Paris and laid siege to the city; the Commune was established; the citizens of Paris faced starvation. Nevertheless, Verlaine and Mathilde were married. They settled down in housekeeping rooms in the rue du Cardinal-Lemoine. Thus began for Mathilde Verlaine a long martyrdom, because Verlaine went into the army service in defense of the city and soon took up his drinking habits again, and by the time the war was over and order was restored, Verlaine had become so undependable that he soon lost his clerkship, which he had regained after peace was established.

Verlaine's mother had been left with a comfortable fortune by Captain Verlaine, but she took bad advice and engaged in speculations which reduced her to poverty. Paul Verlaine and his wife, who had borne him a son, were therefore in dire straits. They went to live with Mathilde's parents.

About this time occurred the really disastrous event in Verlaine's life. He received a letter from a young man who gave his name as Arthur Rimbaud; his residence, Charleville. He had read Verlaine's published work and hailed him as a genius. He also sent to Verlaine some of his poems for criticism. This sheaf of unpublished work contained some startling work; Verlaine saw in Rimbaud a new force, a new voice, a new vision in French poetry. He invited Rimbaud to visit him.

This was a great mistake. Verlaine had no home of his own in which to entertain any one; he was living on the bounty of his wife's parents. Nevertheless Rimbaud came and camped himself in the crowded apartment. He was a strange creature, tall, ungainly, dirty, ferocious in countenance, and then only seventeen years old. He was even worse than he looked; he was drunken, quarrelsome, savage. He was insulting to Verlaine's wife and her mother, and after enduring him a little while, they forced him to leave the house. With a sublime arrogance Rimbaud presented himself at the home of Theodore de Banville, the poet, announced that he was a genius infinitely superior to Banville and stated that he meant to make his home with him. Banville took the eccentric youth in, but Rimbaud's manners were so rude and his person so dirty, that he had to take measures to get rid of him. Rimbaud visited around thereafter at the homes of various friends of Verlaine, joined and dominated the group of poets of whom Verlaine was becoming the particular star. Rimbaud made one trip to Charleville to see his parents and then came back to announce that he meant to become a permanent resident of Paris.

All critics are agreed that at the age of sixteen Rimbaud was already in the full maturity of his weird genius. He dominated Verlaine, mind and soul; and in time their attachment took on a more

sinister character. Mme. Verlaine naturally was jealous and horrified. Violent quarrels broke out between Verlaine and his wife over
Rimbaud; the upshot was that Verlaine allowed Rimbaud to persuade him to leave home and go to England. The two struck out for
London, where Verlaine, with an excellent knowledge of English,
undertook to teach French. Verlaine also gave some lectures in
English, and some of his posthumously published *conferences* in
English show a surprising command of English prose idiom and
cockney slang.

But association with Rimbaud had brought about Verlaine's
almost complete moral disintegration. He alternated between extremes of adoration for his wife and remorse over the break that had
come between them, and between hate and love for Rimbaud. It
seems that Rimbaud was not by nature homosexual himself, although
Verlaine apparently was; Rimbaud simply used Verlaine to provide
him with food, lodging and drink, and took pleasure in dominating
the weak-willed older poet. Verlaine was sinking further and further
into dipsomania.

After leaving England the pair went to Brussels, where in a
drunken quarrel in a hotel room Verlaine fired two shots at Rimbaud,
wounding him in the wrist. Verlaine's wife and his mother came to
Brussels at the urgent solicitation of Verlaine who was a physical
wreck. His mother persuaded Verlaine to give up seeing Rimbaud,
and paid the latter's train fare back to Charleville. But on the way
to the station Verlaine fired at Rimbaud again. Verlaine this time
was arrested, tried and sentenced to two years in prison at Mons.

While he was in prison, Verlaine made a collection of his unpublished poems which were brought out in Paris under the title,
Romances sans paroles; and it was in prison also that Verlaine experienced his conversion or return to the Catholic faith of his childhood. In prison he wrote his famous religious poems, *Sagesse,* which
are probably the most beautiful spiritual poems ever written. But at
or about the same time he wrote some poems of unparalleled depravity, poems so indecent that no publisher in Paris of Verlaine's
time dared publish them. Verlaine was as ingenuous as a child; he
had a divine gift for song and was apparently incapable of distinguishing between the suitability of one theme and the suitability of
another. His song, as George Moore wrote in *Memoirs of My Dead
Life,* is like a robin's: "The robin confesses his little soul from a
twig; his song is but a tracery of his soul, and with the same sim-

plicity Verlaine traces his, without troubling to inquire if what he traces is good or ill."

While Verlaine was in prison, his wife procured a divorce from him. When he was freed, he attempted a reconciliation with his wife, protested that he had reformed and had been received into the church. She refused to accept his protestations. He turned to his mother and they went to live on a farm in the Ardennes where he tried to wrest a living from the soil. He was unsuccessful in this, and, in desperation he went back to England again where he taught school for a while, giving lessons in French and Latin—and drawing. (He was a proficient draftsman and had a considerable talent for caricature. Many of his sketches of Parisian cafés, his friends, and the poets around Mallarmé are reproduced in the Albert Messein edition of the *Œuvres posthumes de Paul Verlaine*.)

In 1878 he returned to France and obtained the position as professor of Latin at the College de Rethel, a post he held for a year and gave up for another attempt at farming. The scandal over his connection with Rimbaud had not yet died down; his name was under a cloud of shame; and his poetry, consequently, was but little discussed. After a year on a farm, however, he returned to Paris and published *Sagesse,* most of the poems of which he had written in prison.

This volume made his reputation as a poet. It was greeted with enthusiastic acclaim by the best critics; the book sold well, and he obtained a job as sub-editor on the daily newspaper *Reveil.* He also began to be seen around the cafés of the Latin quarter, where he joined the group of disciples of Mallarmé who called themselves the Symbolists. They published a magazine called *Lutèce,* to which Verlaine contributed some poems, some studies of the work of Rimbaud, Tristan Corbière, and Stéphane Mallarmé.

In October, 1883, after having published a collection of critical studies called *Les Poètes Maudits* and another volume of verse, *Jadis et Naguère,* he suddenly got sick of Paris, took his devoted mother to the country and tried farming again. But he was so far gone in drunkenness that one day, crazed by drink, he fell upon his mother and beat her into insensibility. He was arrested for this and thrown into prison for a month.

He returned to Paris with his mother, who had a mother's pity and love for him yet; but his malady of dipsomania grew worse and he was confined for a long time in a hospital. His mother, worn out with suffering, died in 1886, and Verlaine was alone in the world. He became the drunken vagabond described in the character of Chouette in Anatole France's *The Red Lily*. And yet between bouts of drunkenness he was composing the most beautiful poems of his career.

Gout, rheumatism and other afflictions attacked him; he was a patient from time to time in the charity wards of the hospital. He was bald and fat with the face of a Silenus. Still, from time to time he would attempt to drag himself out of the gutter, seek out a priest, confess his sins, and try to live decently and respectably. He was famous, nevertheless. His poems were quoted; Arthur Symons and George Moore, then in Paris, spread his fame in England with magazine articles celebrating his genius and describing his vagabond existence. His poems came out in successive editions; and slender volumes of his verse were published as fast as he could turn them out. He braced up for a time, made a lecture tour of Belgium, where he was greeted everywhere as a great man of letters. He was guest of honor at many banquets. He took the cure at Aix-les-Bains. It seemed for a time that he might live out his life in a fair degree of comfort. It was at this time that he set about trying to kill the legends which had sprung up about him. He gave as one of his lectures an account of himself tending to dissipate the stories that he, like Villon, was a wretched drunken vagabond who lived in a hovel. (At the moment, indeed, he wasn't.) He announced his candidacy for the Academy and paid the necessary formal calls upon the members, in the prescribed manner, driving around to their various houses in a carriage and leaving his card.

Poor, pitiable, child-like Verlaine! Such as he never get into academies. He went to all that expense for nothing. He was heartbroken when he learned that his name had never even come up for discussion. A chair was vacant, but these "immortals" elected some mediocrity as a fellow-member. Verlaine had won his own immortality. But this snub hurt him. He plunged once more into drunkenness. Happily he found a woman almost as miserable as himself, who took pity upon him and became his mistress. They had some rooms in the rue Descartes where Eugénie Krantz fed him, took care of him and received his guests—among whom were the most distinguished names in French literature.

He was stricken mortally ill in January, 1896. A doctor was summoned who looked at Verlaine and declared to Eugénie that nothing could be done: Verlaine's physical resistance was too weak to withstand any disease and the doctor had discovered by a cursory examination that Verlaine was suffering from diseases of the kidneys, stomach, lungs. He died on January 8, 1896.

Forty years after Verlaine's imprisonment at Mons, Arthur Symons met Mathilde Verlaine, the wife who had inspired the tenderest of Verlaine's love poems. They met by appointment in a Paris café. She was still, Symons wrote, despite her plumpness and her years, the young girl in countenance,

> Sa voix étant de la musique fine
> Accompagnait délicieusement
> L'esprit sans fiel de son babil charmant
> Où la gaieté d'un cœur bon se devine.

Her hair was still blonde; she still had laughing eyes above a *retroussé* nose; her spirit was still without malice; her voice was the clearest music. She told him at length about her relations with Verlaine, the meeting with Rimbaud, the unsuccessful attempt on her part to become reconciled with her husband at the instance of Verlaine's mother after his imprisonment at Mons. Then:

"Afterwards? Oh, I was very wretched. In one of his poems Verlaine spoke of my 'small, consumptive voice.' Well, it became true. I grew consumptive from grief. But I tried to react, for the sake of my son. Once he had scarlet fever—I'll never forget how miserable I was. And think, just at that time Verlaine managed to come to see the boy. My mother thought there would be a reconciliation. Not I. I knew how weak and wavering he was. I stayed in the next room and refused to see him. And I did well. He never came back. The same way with his letters. He wrote such a lot of them. For three years I kept them unopened. One of them read: 'If you don't come back soon I'll kill myself.' I didn't open the letter until three years later. Of course, he still loved me in his own peculiar way. But he was so wavering, as I have said, and so terrible. . . . I tried to forget him . . . and at last succeeded. . . . *Que voulez-vous?* . . . What was I to do? Yes, I tried to forget him."

The son of Paul and Mathilde Verlaine became a waiter in a Paris café.

That such a character and such a life should produce the enchantment that is Verlaine's verse is one of the mysteries. All critics are united on the perfection, the sublimity of Verlaine's genius. He created a new poetic language, a new music. In his *Art of Poetry*, he said, "Take eloquence and wring its neck." He shunned rhetorical devices; he wrote from the heart; he is, as Anatole France wrote, a musician of the soul. There is no mood of human feeling which he did not catch in imperishable words.

Rimbaud, who was Verlaine's evil genius and who recognized this fact in after life, wrote his terrible and fascinating *Une Saison en Enfer* (his "pagan book, a nigger book") burned his poems, turned his back on literature and European civilization, entered the world of activity as a teacher, a laborer, a dock-walloper, a soldier in the Dutch army, and finally as a trader in the Orient. After twelve years in the Orient during which time he would never discuss his poetry, he was stricken with an illness which necessitated the amputation of one of his legs, and he was shipped back to Marseilles, where he survived the operation for a short time and died.

The group, however, of which Verlaine was the most melodious voice, including Rimbaud, in Paul Claudel's words, "the savage mystic," Tristan Corbière, "the adulterous mélange of everything," and Laforgue, the consumptive who wrote poems of a supernal cleverness, a clownesque and sophisticated disillusion, was to have its influence upon all the poetry of the time, and it was also to be the principal stimulant to the work of Anglo-American poets, like Conrad Aiken, T. S. Eliot, John Gould Fletcher, and so many others of lesser talent.

DICKENS *THE HEART*

*

AFTER I had written the three words which constitute the title of this chapter, I found it extremely difficult to elaborate upon those three words. I am reminded of a story about the late Frank Moore Colby, the encyclopedist who wrote those priceless gems of sense and beauty which were collected and edited by Clarence Day, Jr., under the title of *The Colby Essays.* The story was told me by Philip Littell, a charming essayist himself. Colby and Littell were on the editorial staff of the old New York *Globe.* Hamilton Wright Mabie had died and inasmuch as Mabie was a prominent figure in literary matters of the day, it was deemed necessary to have an editorial lamenting his exit. Colby was asked to write the editorial and he said he would. Three days passed and there was no editorial from Colby. His chief inquired several times and Colby said, each time, that he was still writing it. The chief had visions of column after column on Hamilton Wright Mabie, taking up all the space he had reserved for editorials against Tammany and in favor of certain municipal improvements. He was in despair. Finally, on the fourth day, the chief said, "Frank, we can't give too much space to Mabie. Let's see what you have written. We may have to cut it to get it into the paper now." Colby handed him a sheet of paper on which were just these words, no more, no less: "Hamilton Wright Mabie conducted young ladies into the suburbs of culture and left them there."

My sentiment in regard to Dickens is the reverse of Colby's sentiment in regard to Mabie, but, like Colby after his having written that sentence, I, after having written that Dickens is the "heart" of literature, among the Titans, I find it difficult to say more. Dickens at his best, in the *Pickwick Papers, Nicholas Nickleby,* and *David Copperfield,* displays a gigantic imagination playing about the central interests of the human heart, the seat of sentiment.

What I like about Dickens—what we all like about him, I think —is that he was a free writer, without inhibitions: he wrote as he felt, with pity, humor and gusto. He was often prolix and occasionally a little dull; some of his novels of plot, such as *A Tale of Two Cities,* seem to us old-fashioned now; but his was a healthy, unhampered mind; he enjoyed life and communicated a joy in living. Dickens' humor was warm and broad and deep: he unites all mankind in his work with a robust but kindly sense of the absurdities of life. His humor deprived him of a sense of proportion; but this lack of a sense of proportion was also at the base of his humor. His distinctions between good and evil were sharp and clear-cut. To him a cruel and evil man was a cruel and evil man, not a maladjusted individual. His villains are real villains and their villainy is ingrained in their character. Dickens had lived in the direst sort of poverty and he knew that character is not so much made by conditions as that conditions are made by characters, by characters who have flint hearts and evil natures. When Dickens made war in his writings upon English prisons, wage slavery, child labor, and slum conditions it was a war against the characters who created those conditions or were responsible for their continuance.

Dickens wrote most of his books out of his own actual experience in life. He caricatured his father in the character of Micawber and portrayed his mother in the character of Mrs. Nickleby; he drew upon his knowledge of real people for his realistic distortions. He was born in Portsmouth, England, in 1812, the son of a navy pay officer, who later moved to London. Throughout Dickens' boyhood the family lived in the direst poverty. His father was imprisoned for debt; as a mere child Charles was sent out to work for two years in a blacking warehouse, where during long hours he tied covers on bottles, for nine shillings a week. His mother was an educated woman and she taught Charles to read. She even planned to establish a boarding school and Dickens tells how he was sent out with circulars to advertise the school, but nothing ever came of the plan. His education was through reading; he received little formal schooling. He was, however, precocious, gifted, and full of ambition. He taught himself shorthand and at the age of nineteen got a job as a reporter on a London daily, at first assigned to copy out legal decisions but later to have a free run as a roving reporter.

CHARLES DICKENS
(From an unpublished drawing by Ary Scheffer)

While he was employed as a reporter Dickens sold his first magazine story. It was a mere sketch. He was asked for more and after he had published nine of them he was engaged by another magazine to continue them. These pieces were brought out in book form, with illustrations by Cruickshank, under the title *Sketches by Boz*, since "Boz" was the pen-name Dickens used when he began writing. This book was immensely popular. In them were the seeds of all his later books—his heartiness, his gentle satires on the weaknesses of simple people, his distaste of the reserved and haughty types, his hatred of the cruel, avaricious, and cantankerous, his delight in the simple pleasures of life.

Shortly after this the publishers, Chapman and Hall, were about to bring out a series of colored plates of sporting life and they were looking about for some one to write the texts to accompany the plates. They contracted with Dickens to write these descriptive lines, and out of this contract grew the *Pickwick Papers*. Interest in the text outweighed interest in the drawings with the public; Dickens was encouraged to expand the sketches; he created his immortal Sam Weller; and thereafter Charles Dickens was on the way to being the most famous man in England; for with the successive monthly installments of the *Pickwick Papers* their circulation went up by leaps and bounds.

In the first flush of that rare appreciation by the public of a young author's first offerings, Dickens plunged into an orgy of work, writing the *Pickwick Papers* and *Oliver Twist*, under contract with two publishers to furnish them monthly installments. Writing constantly against a deadline, never an hour ahead of the time his copy was due at the printer's, he turned out, in four years, four serials, *Pickwick Papers, Oliver Twist, Old Curiosity Shop* and *Barnaby Rudge*. He had touched the hearts of all the people below the grade of the aristocracy and had become a popular idol.

The uppity-upper classes did not like him for many alleged reasons not germane to the truth. They said he was not a "gentleman" and did not know how to portray a "gentleman." What they meant was that Dickens had hit at the vulnerable spot of all their pretensions; he had scored a success by treating of common life; and he had endangered the source of aristocratic luxury by calling attention to the exploitation whereby that luxury was derived.

It is pleasant to reflect that, in America, this disdain for Dickens among the powerful did not exist. The Boston and New York older families, so imitative of English attitudes and manners, shared some of their cousins' feeling; but when Dickens first came to America he was welcomed like a foreign prince by all "society" and like the author of *Pickwick Papers* by the proletarian newspaper men. And later, who was to purchase and to own, he and his heirs and legatees inviolate and to preserve in a great monument—a private library—the original manuscript, in Dickens' own handwriting, of *A Christmas Carol,* except that great rugged sentimentalist, J. Pierpont Morgan? Mr. Morgan's unofficial biographer, Herbert Corey, tells us that it was the custom of that great man every Christmas Eve to get out the original manuscript of *A Christmas Carol* and read it aloud before his assembled family, which had gathered around the fireplace of that magnificent Renaissance room. Mr. Corey fails to tell us what were the real feelings of those men and women, boys and girls, who had heard that story read aloud so many times; but we must all agree that the scene that is conjured up is touching. *A Christmas Carol* has something in it about Scrooge.

Dickens returned from a visit to America and wrote his *American Notes.* He was a faithful reporter always; he saw all things as news: that was his irresistible charm and it still is. Some Americans did not like this book, because it was not a flattering account of Dickens' American experiences; but Dickens was not in the business of flattering people (that is why he was great), and when he came back to America again, on a lecture tour, he was received everywhere in a triumph exceeding the one originally accorded him. (Trumpery, dull-witted, tenth-rate English novelists, particularly of the type who try to imitate Dickens, have thought to imitate Dickens' success by saying ill-natured things about America and American culture, in a fashion which they believe Dickens wrote and spoke. But they caught only his animus and that animus in relation to things which have long been dead. Hence their remarks have been as offensive as their fictional imitations of Dickens. And they have not prospered like Dickens.)

After his return to England, Dickens made a tour of France and Italy and wrote some now forgotten pieces about his impressions of Italy. On his return from this tour he became editor and proprietor of two magazines in succession. He was a keen business man; one of the best in the whole history of letters. He did not wish to share his profits with others; so he published his own magazine, for which he wrote the contribution which would make the circulation of the magazine. He had two of these magazines, and he prospered with them. His difficulty, if one may offer a little kindly advice to one who is long dead and cannot profit by it, was that he undertook too much, and so lost his wife and his life, because he was a truck-horse for work, accepted all commissions and all lecture engagements. He took the editorship of a daily newspaper when his schedule already called for about twenty-two hours of work per day. He had to give it up, naturally, but he kept his connection with the newspaper, projected a weekly, went abroad for material, lectured throughout England and Scotland, revisited America, and returned to England to settle down in a fine old house called Gad's Hill Place, near Rochester, where he continued his unremitting labors and died, on June 9, 1870, of a cerebral hemorrhage while trying to complete the serial, then running in a weekly newspaper, *The Mystery of Edwin Drood*.

Millions of words have been written on Dickens. The bibliography of the books and essays on Dickens would fill a fat volume by itself. Dickens deserved all this attention—as a writer (perhaps not altogether as a man)—and it remains to me merely to suggest that you look into a volume of Dickens at his best to become enchanted. Does that sound presumptuous? Do you already know Dickens? Well, forgive me. You see, I am one of the few writers (according to the reports writers give of themselves) whose childhood was neglected. Nearly everybody else, it seems, had homes where there were complete sets of Dickens and families who read Dickens aloud around the hearth on wintry nights. That never happened to me. There was no set of Dickens in our house when I was a child and there was no one in our family who was addicted to reading aloud. So I missed one of those lovely incidents of childhood about which so many writers have been able to reminisce charmingly.

I console myself with the reflection that the most beautiful tribute to Dickens I have ever read was that written by George Santayana after he had discovered Dickens with shocked surprise that no one had ever discovered him before when he, Santayana, was above sixty years of age. That gentle and humane philosopher had been so long engrossed in metaphysical and abstruse problems that he was not aware that people knew Dickens, because until he was sixty he didn't really *know* Dickens himself. A volume of Dickens came into his hands, and he wolfed it up like a famished man. He read all of Dickens. When he was finished he started out to do battle with the world which had failed to recognize that Dickens was one of the salient saviors of truth and beauty that had ever been put on earth. That, I think, is evidence enough of Dickens' value; that, and that among his worshipers were such diverse figures as Dostoievski, J. P. Morgan, Anatole France and G. K. Chesterton.

SHELLEY *THE VOICE*

*

PERCY BYSSHE SHELLEY, whose speaking voice was extremely discordant ("his voice was not only dissonant, like a jarring string," wrote Thomas Love Peacock, who knew him, "but he spoke in sharp fourths, the most unpleasant sequence of sound that can fall on the human ear"), had the compensation of possessing the most intense, the most musical, lyric gift in English poetry of the nineteenth century. His very inability to utter agreeable sounds probably served to develop the acuteness of his inner ear and so enabled him, in the words he set down on paper, to utter in lovely sequence words which were perfect poetical expressions of his emotions.

Byron, who said of his own poetry that it was "the dream of the sleeping passions" and "the lava of the imagination whose eruption prevents the earthquake," too often used his easy facility at versifying as an adornment to enhance his personal attractions; he was often the show-off, the shallow poseur, the clever man; and to that extent his personality came to be much more important than what he had to say. He was the romantic in action, the animated symbol of the yearnings toward a freer expression of individuality held suppressed in the hearts of a people too tied to the earth and obedient to the conventions of earthly society. The war between the individual and society is a never-ending and relentless one. Byron broke with conformity in a wild, unrestrained, giddy triumph.

Shelley, too, was heir to all the libertarian ideas let loose by Rousseau and the French Revolution; but he was a frail, nervous, ethereal spirit, who expressed himself very little in action, and gave

369

voice to his deeper sentiments, the sentiments of his heart and mind no less than to his emotions.

He was absurd (from a mundane point of view) in his child-like reliance upon the dictates of his heart; but the progress of the world from the tedium of monotony is furthered only by the absurdities of the guileless adult children who live in their imaginations.

Shelley was definitely a product of his times, even if his poetic gift (and no one has succeeded satisfactorily in accounting for the poetic gift) was individual and for (one may say now with infirm conviction) all times. Byron was contemptuous of mankind, and liberty meant to him liberty to take what he could get out of the world, without paying, if possible. (His stinginess when he became rich through the sale of Newstead Abbey was profoundly in char-acter: he lived largely by the principle, "what's yours is mine and what's mine is my own.") Shelley loved his fellow man; he gave forth tenderness, compassion, affection. All who came into contact with him felt the force of his affection. It was, indeed, the cause of the tragedy in his life: he gave his affection simply and guilelessly even to the point of never realizing that passion may be, and usually is, jealous and terrible. There is no great love passion in Shelley: there is warmth of friendliness, intellectual passion, passion against cruelty, the passion of revolt; but not the passion of exclusive possession, of the merging of one with another, in his poetry.

Shelley was of the generation of Byron and Keats, a generation which had succeeded the period of Wordsworth and the great giants, Coleridge and Blake. Men of the older generation out-lived the great trio, Byron, Shelley and Keats, and Wordsworth and Coleridge came to take a calmer attitude toward the humanitarian ideas and aspirations which inflamed the imaginations of the younger men. Then, too, of Shelley, Keats and Byron there was an additional force to intensify their revolt against their environment: the guardians of British taste and culture were one and all a reactionary lot, contemptuous of the revolution, exponents of the Tory ideals of class and conduct, and these young poets were, or were asso-ciated with, the radical element and the radical thought which were upsetting the complacency of the British respectables of the time. Shelley, Byron and Keats were attacked and execrated by critics of the powerful *Edinburgh Review, The Quarterly, Blackwood's Maga-zine* and those who followed in the footsteps of the self-satisfied dictator, Jeffrey, who had greeted Wordsworth's *Excursion* with a critique which began: "This will never do!" They were attacked as low-born cockneys, libertines, illiterates, corrupters of morals. Such foolish attacks only served to intensify the revolt of these poets against all that their critics represented; they pushed Byron to excesses (perhaps made a poet out of him), distracted Shelley and broke Keats' spirit.

SHELLEY was born on August 4, 1792, in a cottage near Horsham in Sussex. His father was a petty squire, a Whig in the House of Commons, and the son of a testy and quarrelsome fellow who had married two heiresses and had largely dissipated their fortunes and his own and achieved a baronetcy when Percy Bysshe Shelley was fourteen. Percy was the eldest child of a delicate and beautiful mother who bequeathed to her son much of her exquisite featuring, large beautiful eyes, curly gold-brown hair, delicate sensibility, poor health and a tendency to hallucination.

He was educated privately at first, and was sent thence to an academy where he was first to show his revolt against cruelty by rages when he was beaten for being slow in learning Latin conjugations. Thence he went to Eton, where he showed his rebellious temperament again by resenting and opposing the hazing which was customary at the school. His opposition to the cruelties and indignities of hazing cut him off from his fellows, who considered him queer. When they had baited him several times, he had gone into such rages that they were afraid he would kill them with whatever missiles came to hand. He participated in none of the sports— and the playing fields of Eton were considered more important than the classroom—withdrew into himself, studied, read and made a few friends, with whom he discussed literature and political ideas.

Throughout his adolescence and even throughout his brief life, Shelley was the victim of delusions of persecution. These delusions were aggravated, it is true, by certain occurrences which flabbier boys or boys with thicker skins would pass off as in the nature of things and even up in their own minds by being as cruel to the helpless as others had been to them when they were helpless; but Shelley, with a more sensitive organization, with nerves as vibrant as a mocking-bird, exaggerated every commonplace into an intense experience. That was the penalty he paid for being a poet.

He took every slight in school, every rule of discipline as acts of tyranny, directed exclusively against him. He did not hate his teachers or even his schoolmates who exasperated him, but he did consider them malevolent beings, misguidedly afflicting him with sorrow. He lived in a world of fantasy, as an escape from the reality he knew, and on some counts it was a terrible world, because he had to give battle to thousands of demons that had no real existence. Hallucinations pursued him throughout his life: he was morbidly hypochondriacal. He fed his mind on pharmaceutical papers and essays on the treatment of disease until he began to imagine he had all of the most fantastically horrible diseases of the world. A fat old lady who sat opposite him in a stage coach (Peacock relates) caused him to imagine she had elephantiasis, that the disease was catching, and for months after that, he watched for development of the symptoms, squeezing up his skin to see if it was still smooth, watching his legs until he was sure he was out of danger.

He read Goethe, Æschylus, Shakespeare, Milton, Wordsworth, Thomson and Southey, but the literature which held a particular fascination for him was the work of an American, Charles Brockden Brown, whose macabre, hallucinatory stories enjoyed an enormous success in America at the time. Brown's stories undoubtedly also influenced Edgar Allan Poe very deeply, although I find no awareness of this in the biographers of Poe, except Hervey Allen, who barely mentions Brown but recognizes Brown's influence as one of many on Poe and suggests that Brown (whom Allen apparently had not read) be made the subject of a book of research and biography. Brown's novels affected Shelley so much, indeed, that his discussion of them with his second wife caused her to write her famous novel, *Frankenstein,* on a typical Brockden Brown theme.

I have not read the Brockden Brown novels myself, but Peacock, in his life of Shelley, has told us enough about them to give us a strong clew as to the way they affected Shelley, Mary Shelley and Poe. In the first of these novels, *Wieland,* according to Peacock, the father of the hero was a hermit who spent most of his time in a summer house where he died of spontaneous combustion! In *Ormond* there is apparently a Poe-esque idealization of feminine character. Poe rarefied his women to an excessive degree; and Shelley's idealization of womanhood was almost as other-worldly as Poe's. Brown's *Edgar Huntley; or the Sleepwalker* has something about Clitheroe, in his sleep, digging a grave under a tree; and in *Arthur Mervyn* there is a description of a pestilence, which doubtless gave Poe the notion for *The Masque of the Red Death.*

IN HIS nonage Shelley fell in love with a child named Harriet Grove, a beautiful girl his own age, to whom he disclosed his conversion to atheism, his poetic aspirations, and his adolescent ideas of the freedom which should exist between girls and boys, men and women. What he meant principally (an ancient, unconscious dodge with the timorous male adolescent) was that he would like to experience physical love with Harriet but did not want to endure the responsibilities, marriage and what-not, that went with it. Harriet found him strangely interesting; but she was not in love with him, not physically attracted to him; and so, having, in a perfectly natural feminine way, egged Shelley on until he became too importunate, she exacted a proposal of marriage out of him, a proposal which she allowed to be an engagement long enough to air her conquest to her unengaged school chums, then hied herself to her parents, discussed Shelley's adolescent social, religious and political beliefs with an air of shocked surprise, horrifying her parents (which she undoubtedly enjoyed doing) and allowed her parents to break off the engagement peremptorily, thus saving her the trouble.

Shelley, as is the way with poets, indulged himself in a brief period of self-pity and broken-heartedness, wrote some poems eloquent of his sorrow, and turned to the next girl who happened along who flattered him in his preoccupation with himself. Real stimulation to his ego, however, he had found in Thomas Jefferson Hogg when he entered Oxford. Hogg was a virile and sanguine youth, with his head swirling in Faustian dreams of the conquest of the world's secrets through chemistry, biology, philosophy. He was a militant atheist and a revolutionary with all the enthusiasm of a convert from an upbringing of middle-class Toryism, conformity and piety. He thrilled Shelley to raptures of admiration. Here, thought Shelley, was a man of the world, a robust, athletic figure who was not a dub, not a clod, but a scintillant intellect.

Hogg and Shelley became bosom companions, Damon and Pythias. Together they concocted audacities, the result of which was the issuance of an anonymous pamphlet by Shelley called *The Necessity for Atheism*. It was published at a provincial printing establishment and offered for sale at Oxford. This created a scandal. Suspicion fell upon Shelley and Hogg as recalcitrants. Nowadays, in an American college, the brighter deans would mentally label a college freshman a dullard fit only for the football team and for a career as bond salesman or broker's clerk if he failed to profess atheism, socialism, communism, or some form of decisive revolt; but in those days the university authorities were pathetic idiots who believed that beliefs can be stifled by summary displays of authority. In fine, they questioned Hogg and Shelley severely and, getting no admissions from them but plenty of contempt from the lads, fired them both from the university. We must bless these misguided college authorities; had they had sense and understanding, had they been suave and gracious and had they taken the lads into their confidence and sympathy, encouraged them, promoted them, shown appreciation for their audacity, both Shelley and Hogg might have been tamed in time into the more comfortable complacences, sent out into the world as confident Tories, destined for a certain wealth and commonplaceness.

Shelley wrote some poems after his expulsion from college (he had written some before with which his posterity is not concerned) and found himself up against parental disapproval: Timothy Shelley attributed his son's disgrace to his association with Hogg. Many parents, unfortunately, are like that: they find every reason except those they would find if they examined themselves, for believing that their offspring's failure to live up the exact opposite of themselves is the result of an outsider's baleful influence. There was an inordinate amount of Timothy Shelley in Percy and as a result Percy clung to Hogg, who was very unlike himself.

Percy took up lodgings in London after parting with Hogg, and, in company with his younger sisters, found a sweetheart in a friend of theirs, Harriet Westbrook, the daughter of a retired tavern keeper. Harriet's proctor and foster-mother was a sister thirty years old when Harriet was sixteen, who carried on a vicarious flirtation with Shelley, telling herself she was admiring his mind and furthering the consummation of her emotions by promoting the love affair which was slightly visible in the relationship between her ward and the poet.

At length, through a combination of conventional, fortuitous and emotional circumstances, Harriet Westbrook and Percy Shelley were married, and Shelley, vaguely put upon, though he did not know why, felt that his motives had been mistaken but nevertheless resolved to be chivalrous and do what the conventions expected of him. He even went through the romantic farce of an elopement, because the parents of the girl saw (or thought they saw) money and prestige for themselves in the marriage of their daughter to the heir to a baronetcy: the father of Harriet vociferously would not have a child of his married to a disgraced atheist, which meant, in truth, that he was determined that Percy should marry his daughter.

After the elopement and marriage Shelley and his wife settled down to an ordinary, commonplace, penurious existence, wherein Shelley undertook to instruct his wife with the utmost seriousness in all the most trumpery notions he had absorbed or given wing to in his own neurotic imagination. The poor child was aghast. She had married not a man but a phantom—the embodiment of an idea which could be disagreeably unromantic, quarrelsome, touchy, egotistical and not much pleasure, physical or otherwise, even though he had promptly impregnated her with a child.

Trouble arose in the young couple's household. Friends were called in to settle the difficulties, even Harriet's elder sister, even Hogg. Hogg at least was close to common human nature. Harriet found in him some one to whom she could confide her own disillusion. This put pressure upon Hogg's conscience, because he was Shelley's closest friend. But such intimacy of physique and emotions is what unmoral Mother Nature apparently diabolically waits for and there seems (we don't know this for sure) to have been a surrender of Hogg and Harriet to each other and a momentary fulfillment in each which was to throw all three asunder, centrifugally. Shelley had found platonic consolation for his marital unhappiness in another, an older woman, called in to smooth things out.

There were those violent quarrels and recriminations which are all the more violent and recriminatory when two persons in love are deceiving each other and drawing resources from outside themselves which each feels should come from him or her. Harriet became vindictive, hateful. She spent more money than Shelley had in income and ridiculed him for not being man enough to earn more. Thinking to stir his ego to a more exclusive service to herself, she threw herself into the arms of an army officer of good physique and taunted Shelley.

Shelley, meanwhile, had found a friend in William Godwin, a professed atheist, a philosopher, a student of Kant and Hegel, and a man resigned to an inactive life but hopeful of being a tutor and inspirer of sanguine youth. Godwin had been a revolutionary, execrated and condemned, and in his old age people had forgotten him, young radicals especially, and so he was living in poverty and in the dreams of his radical past. Godwin had three daughters by two marriages and the idol of his heart was the youngest, Mary, whom he himself had educated, taught to read the books he thought were the best books, taught to discipline her mind and think as he thought.

Shelley noticed Mary; Mary noticed Shelley. This meant the breakup of the Shelley household. The bitter Harriet and her child were in lodgings on which rent was long due; Shelley, finding Mary Godwin easy to talk to and intellectually a companion, proposed elopement to Europe—anywhere out of the world. Father Godwin gave them his blessing: such things were his idea of the fulfillment of his theories. With Clare Clairmont, one of Byron's many mistresses, the two, Mary and Percy, set out for the continent, reached Switzerland and took a cottage near Byron's, afterwards being burdened by the quaint domestic responsibility of taking care of Clare in her pregnancy and of Clare's child when Byron nonchalantly omitted to bear the responsibility himself.

Shelley, who was all naïve affection, wrote to Harriet inviting her to come and live with him and Mary. He saw nothing absurd in this, because he was divinely innocent. He did not know at the moment that in England he was generally held to be a satanic monster of libidinousness, a man not content with one woman at a time but who demanded a whole harem and boasted of it, by implication, in poems and prose documents on free love. He had written subversively: he was therefore a criminal.

Shelley (quaint type) got no response from Harriet and engaged detectives to learn of her whereabouts—and his child's. He was worried, no doubt, because she had tried suicide once before. His conscience bothered him. He received a report from the detective agency. The rent had been long overdue for the lodgings occupied by Mrs. Shelley and the child; the landlord was angry and had a low opinion of Mrs. Shelley and a worse opinion of her absent husband; a Major Ryan had been visiting Mrs. Shelley and had caused gossip in the neighborhood; Mrs. Shelley, Major Ryan and the child had disappeared; Mrs. Shelley had told her landlady she was moving to get rid of Major Ryan. Shelley had come back from his hegira with Mary Godwin to Switzerland to find his child and his wife. A few days later he learned that Harriet, pregnant by Major Ryan, had drowned herself in the Thames.

This was a grief for him in an overwhelming degree, for in his way he loved Harriet. It was shame and disgrace for him because the natural inference of the gossips and the newspapers was that Harriet had committed suicide because of her love for Shelley who had, so it seemed, shamefully mistreated her. But Harriet Shelley did not kill herself because of Shelley but because a concatenation of things, including the selfishness of Major Ryan, and because her own mistaken attempts to procure happiness to herself faced her in a terrible moment which she could not live out.

In three paragraphs I have spanned a long interval, of course, in which Shelley traveled, wrote poems, some of which are as imperishable as we dare say anything is imperishable, became estranged from Godwin (who feared for his daughter's happiness in her illicit union with Shelley, after everybody had learned of it), fell heir to a fortune, lost it, formed new friendships including those with Byron, Leigh Hunt and Thomas Love Peacock, learned of the suicide of Harriet after he had been summoned by her when she was in depressed spirits only to arrive too late, and had traveled, distracted, back and forth from Switzerland to England.

After the death of Harriet, Shelley married Mary Godwin and tried to get possession of his son and daughter, who were in the hands of Harriet's family. In court proceedings he was denied his paternal rights to the children but permitted to see them on stated occasions, provided he put them under the custody of suitable persons who would take care of their rearing and education. Shelley returned to England, made friends with Godwin again, enlisted himself in social work and propaganda for the relief of the wage slavery of the workers, and wrote poems expressive of his vision of the calamitous conditions in England. He and Mary Godwin (Shelley) had with them, besides a son and daughter of their own, Byron's daughter by Clare Clairmont; and Shelley was anxious that Byron should relieve him of the responsibility of this illegitimate daughter. Therefore with his wife and two children, Clare and her daughter, Shelley left England never to return. He was ill of consumption; he went to Milan, to Pisa, to Rome, to Venice, to Pompeii; his child William died; he saw Clare's child die in her mother's arms; he finished the *Cenci;* Mary bore him another son; and he spent several years of happiness and sorrow, and seemed, after an extraordinarily productive period, to be just at the start of his career when he put to sea in a small craft in the Bay of Spezia, encountered a storm, and was drowned when the boat was swamped ten miles off shore. Shelley's body was washed up on the beach and identified: he had a volume of Sophocles in one pocket and a volume of Keats in the other. Shelley's friends, Trelawney, Byron and Hunt, who had been summoned by Mary Shelley, had found the body, and by special permission they erected a funeral pyre and burned the corpse instead of burying it in quicklime.

Shelley's death occurred in July, 1822. Mary Shelley lived until 1851. Her son, Percy Florence, succeeded to the baronetcy on the death of his grandfather and died in 1889. Mary Shelley edited Shelley's unpublished work, wrote a biographical memoir of him, contributed much to the establishment of the facts regarding his life in place of the legends that had grown up in his brief lifetime.

The life, the accomplishments, in a not very bulky book of poetry of that frail Titan who beat luminous wings against the void to so much purpose, have been the subject of a mastodonic library of memoirs, biographies, semi-fictional treatments of his life, essays, explanations, attacks and refutations of attacks. Pleasant reading among all these pennings are: J. A. Symonds' *Shelley*, Dr. Garnett's biography, Trelawney's *Records of Shelley, Byron and the Author,* and André Maurois' *Ariel: the Life of Shelley.* None of these, perhaps, comes to the heart of things, no more than does Elinor Wylie's novel, *The Orphan Angel,* but when we read Elinor Wylie's own sequence of sonnets in *Angels and Earthly Creatures,* we can, if we have any quick apprehensions, know, subliminally, what Shelley was not like, nor what we are like, but what Shelley and we (if we are warmly considerate of our fellow-man) would like to be.

FLAUBERT *THE REALIST*

*

ONE of the critical delusions of the nineteenth century (a delusion carried over into the present time by the force of reiteration) was that Gustave Flaubert was supreme among dispassionate artists, seeking with infinite pains and much travail of soul for the precise word which would render a scene with such exactitude to reality that even God would approve of its fidelity. This was and is a delusion to which Flaubert contributed by his constant complaints to his friends about the arduousness of his labors and about the horrible inflictions his artist's conscience put upon him.* Gabble about the Flaubertian search for *le mot juste* became a persistent dogma among the esthetes, especially among those so far removed from contact and sympathy with ordinary life and common expression that for one to say "It is cold today" would

---

* After the death of Count Robert de Montesquieu (about whom I have written in the chapter on Proust), the Count's collection of manuscripts, autographs and books was put up at auction in Paris in 1923. About one item in the collection a teapot tempest arose. It was a letter from Flaubert inserted in a copy of *Salammbô*. Arthur Meyer, the Jewish editor of the Catholic Royalist newspaper, *Gaulois*, threatened to buy the letter and burn it in the public market place. Paul Souday attacked Meyer over the letter and adherents rallied to both sides. The letter was sold privately. Where it went I don't know. In it Flaubert authorized Montesquieu to dramatize *Madame Bovary* and said, among other things: "La littérature, d'ailleurs, n'est plus pour moi qu'un supplice quasi artificiousus et immensus phallus qui, fundam lacerans, nequidquam me juvat; anus penetratus sed nullas voluptas. Cette métaphore, peut-être indécente, pour te faire comprendre à quel point je suis en." The catalogue description gave the horrifying phrases in Latin: Flaubert wrote them in French. If the description is true, one should have said that writing was the last occupation Flaubert should have taken up. His was a more serious occupational maladjustment than that of a bookkeeper who hates figures.

startle them into strange raptures by the appositeness of the expression: they had been used to having Mallarmé express such observations in words which would take them a week to find out what he meant.

Alongside these legends about Flaubert's search for the exact word (which he would always have found if he had asked the postman or his cook) there grew up other absurdities—absurdities so great that it is a wonder that any mere common reader ever dared to pick up one of Flaubert's sour romances and pursue it with pleasant enjoyment to its always conclusive end. "Flaubert," wrote Arthur Symons, "is so difficult to translate because he has no fixed rhythm; his prose keeps step with no regular march music. He invents the rhythm of every sentence, he changes his cadence with every mood or for the convenience of every fact."

That sounds prodigious, doesn't it? But what does it say? It says M. Flaubert wrote prose and that, unlike M. Jourdain who never knew that what he set down in all innocence was prose, M. Flaubert was quite conscious that he was writing prose: he had no aptitude for verse certainly. Every prose writer has (he doesn't "invent") a rhythm for every sentence; every prose writer changes the cadence with every mood or for the convenience of every fact. Every prose writer worth his salt writes sentences with no "fixed rhythm." If he did not he would write a bastard poetry. Or he would write in a habitual monotone. No writer with any sense says to himself: "I will now write a sentence which will contain two anapests and a dactyl. The sentence after that will be made up of two spondees and a trochee. And the sentence after that will be made up of three iambics alternating with a triple stress."

Whatever the esthetes may say, Flaubert did not write that way either. What he did write came out painfully, slowly; not because he was searching for the "right word," but because all his life he was so divided in his mind between romanticism and fact, between acceptance of bourgeois life and fashionable intellectual revolt against reality, that (with one exception, which I will explain later) he never allowed himself to come simply, humbly, and of his heart into his writings.

Nevertheless that self was there, despite all that has been written about his dispassionate artistic attitude. It was there in the character and person of a chill, unsympathetic, unfeeling moralist, his mind, which is to say his intellectual judgment in fee to the "correct" intellectual attitude of his time, always triumphing over what he felt in his heart. Aside from the first, suppressed edition of *The Temptation of Saint Anthony*, and his callow but sincere first novel, *November*, Gustave Flaubert never wrote a single novel from his heart: he wrote for a coterie; he wrote to an intellectual pattern wherein the pleasure of life consisted in making bitter fun of poor helpless fellows who earned a living in trade.

A first reading of *Madame Bovary* is a rather interesting experience. A second reading of it is almost impossible. That, I think, is a test of its quality. A book that one takes to one's heart one can read and re-read, finding new beauties with each re-reading. One who loves Homer, Horace, Shakespeare, Montaigne, Cervantes, De Foe, Dickens, Tolstoi, Poe, Mark Twain, reads and re-reads them. Those who love James Stephens' *The Crock of Gold*, Anatole France's *Penguin Island*, James Branch Cabell's *Jurgen*, Norman Douglas' *South Wind*, delight to turn to favorite passages for a fifth, even a fiftieth time. There are many who re-read *Huckleberry Finn* at least once a year over a long period of years.

Madame Bovary is a dry book, without a heart and without much substance. The principal characters are uninteresting, because Flaubert does not get inside of them. They have a certain objective reality, as persons seen but not felt. The only character in the book in whom the reader becomes really interested is the chemist, Homais, who is a caricature of all that Flaubert hated in the bourgeois. Homais is the embodiment of mediocrity. He is a humorous character, but Flaubert did not conceive him with humor: he conceived him with venom. There is, indeed, only one attractive personality in all of Flaubert's novels, Mme. Arnoux in *Sentimental Education*. He shows tenderness in only one short story, *A Simple Heart*.

Madame Bovary, Sentimental Education, and the unfinished *Bouvard et Pécuchet* are all works of revenge—revenge of a man who expected too much of life and, when it failed to come up to his romantic expectations, turned away from it and against it. One cannot appreciate the nature which produced those works unless one knows Flaubert's early development. One cannot see how subjective Flaubert's so-called "objective" novels are unless one has read Lewis Piaget Shanks' *Flaubert's Youth*. Professor Shanks' book is the result of painstaking research; it explains the revolt that took place within Flaubert himself against all the tendencies of his nature and led to his suppressing every emotion, every natural impulse he had. Flaubert was seven years writing *Madame Bovary* because he set an artificial form and mood for it and to maintain this form and mood he had to be constantly at war with himself. He was a hysterical neurasthenic and *Madame Bovary* was the means whereby he achieved calm.

As A youth, like nearly all of the men of his generation, Flaubert was profoundly affected by the hero of Chateaubriand's romantic novel, *Réné,* and by the personality of Byron. Romantic pessimism was the rage; like Byron, Flaubert wrote apostrophes to Sin and Satan, sighed for the voluptuousness of the Orient, kept a human skull on his desk. His youthful correspondence is full of puerile extravagances: "I was born to be emperor of Cochin-China, to smoke pipes 36 fathoms long, to have 6,000 wives and 1,400 minions, scimitars to cut off the heads of people whose faces I don't like, Numidian mares and fountains of marble; and I have nothing but immense, insatiable desires, an atrocious ennui and yawnings without end"—and, "I would have liked to annihilate the creation and fall asleep with it in the infinite of nothingness; why could I not awaken among the flames of burning cities! I would have liked to hear the rattling bones that crackled in the fire, to cross rivers filled with corpses, to gallop over prostrate nations and crush them with the four iron hooves of my horse, to be Gengiskhan, Tamerlane and Nero."

He was also the victim of a typical nineteenth century delusion cherished by the literary, that to be a writer, an artist, was the only thing worth while in life; that any other means of earning a living or of doing one's work in the world was somehow base and ignoble. There was hardly an untalented scribbler in all France and England who did not imagine that he was superior to a great surgeon, a great chemist, a great jurist, a great inventor, a great legislator,—and Flaubert, no less than much smaller fry, throughout his life heaped contempt upon all the other professions and employments of men. From his earliest letters to his last he was always harping on the importance of the writer. Even in his old age we find him writing to George Sand: "It is we and we alone, that is to say, the literary men, who are the people, or to say it better: the tradition of humanity." In that same letter he also reiterates his other preoccupation: "Hatred of the bourgeois," he writes, "is the beginning of virtue. But I include in the word bourgeois, the bourgeois in blouses as well as the bourgeois in coats."

In other words, to hate one's fellow man—the workman in the blouse and one's neighbor in a coat—was a religion with Flaubert.

Words such as I have just quoted from him we smile at as sophomoric when uttered by a very young man with a decadent pose;
they are intolerable in an adult. They are the words of a sentimentalist who conceals his sentimentalism behind an unpleasant
mask.

GUSTAVE FLAUBERT was born in Rouen on December 12, 1821. He
was the son of Achille-Cléophas Flaubert, chief surgeon of the city
hospital, himself the son of a veterinary whose father and grandfather had been blacksmiths. On his mother's side Flaubert was a
descendant of a noble family in Normandy. His mother took intense pride in her ancestors and she bequeathed to Flaubert a
tendency to neurasthenia and a disdain for common people. She
was, however, a devoted mother and it was largely because of the
affection which existed between mother and son that Flaubert never
married.

He was spoiled by his mother and his nurse and was not sent
to school until he was eight years old. He had been taught to read
at home, however, and decided at the precocious age of nine to be a
writer after having read Goethe's *Werther* and the poems of Byron
in translation. He planned a series of novels and even acquired titles
for them. When he went to school, he paid little attention to his
studies, but read romances and poetry incessantly. At the age of
thirteen he wrote a play, a sketch of Byron, a short story in imitation of Lewis' *Monk* and another in imitation of a horror story by
Merimée, and other juvenilia. He was preoccupied with the fantastic,
the horrible and the morbid; he devoured Scott and decided to
write a series of historical romances in the manner of Scott but
embracing legends of Normandy.

At a precocious age also he had a disdain for every one who
was not a writer and at the age of nine he made a collection of the
commonplace and foolish remarks of his father's patients, a collection foreshadowing his compendium of fallacies and superstitions
in *Bouvard et Pécuchet*. As a youth he was tall, handsome, blond,
blue-eyed, slender and graceful.

He experienced his first love at the age of thirteen, a puppy
affair full of romantic ardors, for a sixteen-year-old English girl,
Gertrude Collier, to whom he confided his literary ambitions. His
next love at fifteen was more serious. Indeed, he never quite got
over it. At the beach in Touville he met and fell passionately in
love with Mme. Maurice Schlésinger, who was then twenty-six,

married and the mother of a baby. Over and over again, in *November*, in *Sentimental Education* and even in *Madame Bovary* he was to draw upon his experience in relation to Marie Schlésinger. She never encouraged him; she was happily married, although Flaubert fancied that her husband was stupid, boorish and unworthy of her. He mooned outside her window, cherished every feature about her; he even tells us in his Memoirs that he pictured to himself what she was like beneath her clothes and "I could see Maria in her bed, and then I stopped, for the rest made me shudder." He made other visits to Touville in the summers to see her and on one of these occasions he found not her but her husband and his mistress. This incident seems to have had a profound effect upon Flaubert for from that moment on till the day of his death he was preoccupied with the word "adultery," finding in it a fascinating horror.

At seventeen he lost his innocence in a peculiarly disagreeable manner. "Taunted by schoolmates and ashamed of his chastity," writes Shanks, "urged on by the daring that pride gives the imagination, Flaubert now 'took in hatred' a woman who 'offered herself' to him, probably a servant of the family." His reaction to the experience was one of extreme distaste and disappointment. Unfortunately it set the nature of all his future reactions to sex experience also; for he would go to brothels only to come away in disgust with himself; and with the several mistresses he had before Louise Colet he never seems to have had any beauty or poetry or sentiment in love.

In 1840 Flaubert's father sent him to Paris to study law and he put in five years of occasional attempts to master the subject only to give it up and give his time entirely to literature. In 1845 he settled down at Croisset, near Rouen, with his widowed mother in an old house overlooking the Seine. This was to be his home until the end of his life. With one of his friends, Maxime du Camp, he traveled through the near East, visiting Egypt, Palestine, Constantinople, Athens and Malta. Thereafter he rarely stirred out of Croisset, except for week-end visits to Paris to talk with Turgenev, Daudet, Renan, Taine, the Goncourts, Zola, and Gautier. In 1858 he made a brief visit to Tunis to study the site of ancient Carthage when he was gathering material for *Salammbô*.

He never married and the only sentimental affair of his adult life was a curious one. It was an affair which lasted eight years and was with a woman who apparently had made up her mind to become, in turn, the mistress of all of the foremost literary men of her time. Her name was Louise Colet. Her career is one in which are mixed the elements of comedy, irony and melodrama.

Mme. Colet was a vain and pretty daughter of a provincial drawing master, and at an early age her head was filled with romantic notions about the lives of women of the great world.

She was, in time, married to a humdrum, unemotional but understanding little music master whose incompetent income spelled dismal failure for the dreams of social success and elegance she had so ardently and hopefully cherished. There came, however, an opportunity for her to make an effort to move into the world she wanted to enter. She saw an announcement of the French Academy's annual prize award of 2,000 francs for the best poem submitted in a contest. With much labor she wrote a flamboyant and metrically defective poem on the history of Versailles, which, bad as it was, was deemed somewhat less terrible than the forty-nine other poems submitted. It was a contest which attracted only amateurs, because of the conditions imposed and the smallness of the cash award.

Mme. Colet's decision to call upon all the members of the Academy personally and thank them for awarding her the prize inaugurated her career. She put on her prettiest hat, hired a cab and called first upon the philosopher Royal Collard. M. Collard was a practical joker as well as a philosopher. He saw through Mme. Colet, but he was appreciative of her physical attractions—in an immune and impersonal sort of way. He must have chuckled to himself as he pictured what would happen when his friend the austere and distinguished philosopher, Victor Cousin, was subjected to the coquettish wiles of the fluttery little mushhead whom the Academy had been ill-advised enough to award a prize for poetry. Diabolically he told her that thanks were not due him, because her most enthusiastic supporter, the one, indeed, who had swung all the votes in her favor, was no less a person than Victor Cousin, the foremost French philosopher, the exponent of Kant and Hegel, the friend of Mill and Austin, a frequent guest at Mme. Récamier's, and the man who had been loaded with all the academic honors in the power of the French to give.

A point to remember is that Cousin's reputation had hitherto been spotless. Handsome, distinguished, charming and witty as he was, husband-hunting mothers with marriageable daughters had despaired of him and beauteous women had tried to flirt with him in vain. He had conserved his energies and emotions to the greater glory of the human intellect. A man with the air and address of a cultivated man of the world, he had prescribed for himself the chill regimen of an ascetic scholar. But at the first smile and curtsey from Mme. Colet he fell. Within two weeks after their first interview she was his mistress. And this meant also that she was received as a favored and important figure in all the literary and social salons of Paris.

Mme. Colet, like many another pretty woman, attributed her success no less to her literary talent than to her personal charms. She continued to submit poems which were regularly crowned by the cynical and easy-going Forty Immortals of the French Academy, who had only to notice that the poems were signed by Cousin's sweetheart to award her the prize. On one occasion Mme. Colet had put off writing her poem until the day before the close of the contest. She invited Flaubert and his friend Bouilhet to her house, locked them up in a room with rum and tobacco and said they weren't to be let out until they had written the prize poem for her. At midnight they had not yet written a line, when, suddenly, in desperation, one of them seized a volume of Lamartine and dictated about two hundred lines from it at random while the other copied them down. This selection from Lamartine was innocently submitted by Mme. Colet under her own name, and the Academy duly awarded the prize to her and bound up and printed, according to its custom, a de luxe edition of the work. Anatole France, who relates the story, sardonically excuses the Academy for its apparent lack of familiarity with Lamartine by saying that the Immortals never read the literary work for which they award prizes.

MME. COLET's acquaintance with Flaubert began one evening in 1846 at a party in the studio of the sculptor, Pradier. Nothing was known of Flaubert at the time except that he was "the son of a country doctor, that he had independent means and lived in the country, three miles from Rouen, and that he was writing a book." He was tall, handsome, heavy and shy. Pradier pointed him out to Mme. Colet: "Ce gros garçon là. He is going in for literature. You should be able to give him some good advice." Mme. Colet, in her divine egotism, thought she would be able to give Flaubert some pointers also. She engaged him in conversation, told him a few things about literature she thought he stood in need of knowing, and within a week she was his mistress.

It was the first time, probably, that she was ever in love, and the only time. But the relationship was not one which reflects credit on Flaubert. During the eight years of their intimacy, he never gave her a dime, or anything else much, so far as we are able to learn; he came up from Rouen to Paris for a day once every two months and returned with an expedition and punctuality which distressed Mme. Colet. She hinted in her letters that she would like a new pair of shoes, an article of finery, or a bit of jewelry, but he, who wrote her voluminous letters every night (letters which when collected are twice the bulk of *Madame Bovary*), was either too clever or too stupid to take the hints. When her husband died, she suggested that they might now get married, but he wrote back, with frank sincerity or callous duplicity, that he was much too disagreeable a person for any one to live with and would not marry her under any circumstances. Exasperated by this indifference, she tried to torture him with jealousy, but so much more did his art mean than life to him that even this was without its desired effect. She sent him the devoted and passionate letters Cousin and other admirers wrote to her, and he replied that this was sweet evidence of her devotion to him—that she should permit him to share her intimate correspondence was an earnest that he was the only one in her life who mattered. At her wits' end, she became jealous of phantom rivals. When he inadvertently praised the good looks of other women, she forthwith accused him of being in love with them. When he asked her to post a letter to a married friend of long standing, she nagged him for weeks with accusations that this woman had been his mistress for years and that he visited her in secret. Finally, she became jealous of his armchair, for which he had been unwise enough to confess a fondness. "Is it possible," Flaubert wrote in bewildered incredulity, "that you reproach me even for the innocent affection which I feel for an armchair? If I were to mention my boots to you, I think you would be jealous of them. Come, come, I love you very much all the same." Recalling the most famous sentence in *Madame Bovary*, it was Flaubert and not Emma Bovary who "found in adultery all the platitudes of marriage."

There is ample proof in his letters that Flaubert loved Mme. Colet; they are tender, affectionate, passionate even. But he expected too much of her. For him, art was everything; for her, art (as she understood it) was only a convenient means toward obtaining social recognition and pin money. For Flaubert art was the lever of Archimedes; for her it was a burglar's jimmy for prying open exclusive doors. Their romance foundered on the rocks of this disparity of temperaments. She was determined that he marry her and he wouldn't marry her, and that was an end of it, for, as he brutally told her: "Truly, if I saw you every day perhaps I should love you less. You live in the back parlors of my heart and only come out on Sundays." No woman wants to live in the back parlors of her lover's heart. It cannot be pretended that Flaubert got much out of his love, for his was a temperament which made it impossible to get much out of life, whose actuality he distrusted; but it did give him the material for *Madame Bovary*. And in reviewing the history of him and Mme. Colet it is not difficult to learn why it is that that "impersonal" novel does not leave an ineffable impression of having related the whole truth; that, in fine, it seems to the judicious to be more than a little unfair to Emma Bovary. Flaubert, may I whisper it, was more than a little unfair to the only woman who ever came into his life, and in his relationship with her he was something of an ass.

After Flaubert, Mme. Colet had no more lovers, but it was not her fault that she did not. She tried to supplant George Sand in the affections of Alfred de Musset, but failed rather ignominiously and related to Baron Plautel, with sublime conceit, "If I had known him (Musset) as a young man I should have made him the greatest poet of the French language." You see, Mme. Colet was duped by the romantic fallacy that women are the "inspiration" of poets, novelists and dramatists, whereas, as in her own case, the most any woman ever offers a man of genius in the way of inspiration is a model for certain caricatures not flattering to the model. Art and life are separate matters, and if any woman ever discovered that for herself it should have been Mme. Colet. Fortunately, perhaps, for her own self-esteem, that knowledge was kept from her.

Louise Colet never had much except vivacity and good looks; but, as Alfred Henry Lewis has said, she was the sort of woman who could collect without even a tambourine. She got what she was after, she gratified her most soaring ambition; she was the mistress, in turn, of some of the foremost thinkers and literary men of her century; she was a confidante of Mme. Récamier, even though she later abused that confidence by publishing the intimate correspondence of Benjamin de Constant and Mme. Récamier; she moved in the great world of French society and letters and she rounded out her years in the happy illusion that although she was no longer beautiful she was a person of literary consequence, an adornment to French letters and a friend and advocate of the cause of liberty. In this last claim she was forgivably ridiculous, for she was, between us, much more concerned with inspiring respect for the name of Louise Colet through advantageous publicity than she was with human rights. The Church, which she had the audacity to challenge as a feminist and Voltairean, ignored her with a patronizing good will that was galling. She never got over it.

It is a satisfaction to all right-thinkers to learn that with age and experience and vanished good looks Mme. Colet's character was refined and that she achieved high moral standards and an intolerance of evil. She spent her last days hounding the prostitutes of Italy and France, decrying the degeneracy of the age and exposing with jeremiads the lamentable prevalence of adultery among the peasants of Sicily.

It will be observed that Flaubert's only considerable love affair was with a silly woman. He was a romantic who never matured. Tortured in his youth by the desires of the flesh, his head was turned by Byronism and romantic novels. Highly neurasthenic, he suffered from a nervous breakdown in 1843 which caused him to develop a hate for everything he had loved before. Up until that time the gay life, the artistic life of Paris had meant everything to him; after that he hated Paris and all that Paris had once represented to him. Almost like a hermit he settled down to the painful toil of conquering every humane and sentimental impulse within himself. Out of distaste for his own character he created *Madame Bovary*. The one novel he wrote which has great warmth and feeling in it, the first version of *The Temptation of St. Anthony*, he repudiated and rewrote entirely. The second version is distinctly inferior to the first.

Flaubert died of a stroke of apoplexy in his fifty-ninth year. He was a giant who never took any exercise and abused his constitution by over-eating, over-drinking and working through all hours of the day and night. It was for a long time thought that he was epileptic; but Réné Dumesnil has satisfactorily refuted this. Professor Shanks has the right of it when he says that Flaubert's genius was lyrical (this is seen in his earliest work and particularly in the first version of *The Temptation of St. Anthony*) but that Flaubert deliberately stifled his lyrical gifts and gave us his minutely observed, hard and bitter pictures instead. Flaubert was a Titan, in his way, a deluded Titan deceived by both of the literary fashions of his time, Byronism and Realism. The best that was in the man is to be found in his correspondence, particularly his voluminous correspondence with his friend, George Sand, to whom he was much more akin in sentiment than he ever permitted himself to believe.

WHITMAN *THE PROPHET*

*

DISPUTE as to whether Walt Whitman was a poet or not crops up in nearly every discussion of him. It is like the argument as to whether or not Alexander Pope was a poet. Of course both of them were poets. They were poets of a special kind as all great poets are. There is no one nowadays who denies that Keats is a poet, despite those critics of his time who called him an "illiterate cockney"; and yet there is a vast amount of Keats' verse which is as inferior in quality as the worst in Whitman.

Robert Louis Stevenson had the right of it in his *Men and Books* when he wrote: "He (Whitman) conceived the idea of a literature which was to inhere in the life of the present; which was to be, first, human, and next American; which was to be brave and cheerful as per contract; to give culture in a popular and poetical presentment; and, in so doing, catch and stereotype some democratic ideal of humanity which should be equally natural to all grades of wealth and education, and suited, in one of his favorite phrases, to 'the average man.' "

Whitman's poetry is as surely poetry as are the books of the Old Testament which voiced the highest aspirations of the Hebrew people. Whitman is, in truth, the poetical prophet of democracy. This concept of "democracy" is a hope and aspiration toward which we are, or seem to be, striving. It is not yet an achievement. Wide differences exist in our republic between the degrees of freedom enjoyed by people; class and caste differences still exist; prohibitions and inhibitions, social conventions and prejudices continue to make a mockery of the idea of a brotherhood of man. But with the degradation of the democratic dogma which came about in an era of anarchic

391

industrialism, Whitman kept the faith that men would some day be free and equal, and he sang that hope in rhythmical, joyous and vigorous lines which are an encouragement to the spirit. He rejected the poetry of Byron and literature like that of *Werther* and *René* and called it the "Literature of Wo." Theirs was a literature outside of his experience and he believed it to be a literature outside of the experience of any average American man. He believed that such poetry and such literature should be shunned as being the cause of sorrow and of developing in the reader a warped mental attitude toward the realities of life. Revolting from all prettified poetry written under a culture based upon class and privileges, he invented a form and a poetical expression entirely new, entirely individual.

At its best Whitman's poetry is an exalted song of a healthy and hearty enjoyment of life, of pleasure in manual work, of the freedom of the body and mind. In the best sense it is ecstatic. Whitman at his best is, from the conventional point of view, least "poetical" in the sense that Longfellow is poetical. I do not hold with those who seek to argue that Whitman was a poet by citing his famous poem on Lincoln, *When Lilacs Last in the Dooryard Bloom'd*, for that opening line, so celebrated, is false to Whitman's method and spirit. "When the last lilacs bloomed in the dooryard" would have been nearer to his accustomed idiom and the line would have been easily turned into the meter of Longfellow's by another transposition, "When lilacs last bloomed in the dooryard." After that first line, the poem becomes nobly poetic in Whitman's best vein.

WALT WHITMAN was born at West Hills, Long Island, New York, in 1819. His father was a carpenter. Walt (or Walter, as he was christened) was educated in the public schools of Brooklyn, and in his youth he learned carpentry and printing. He taught school for a while and began writing pieces for the local newspapers, largely about the wild life of Long Island, sketches of the countryside and of the beaches. At twenty he was editor of a country weekly in Huntington, Long Island, and he was a reporter for a year on the Brooklyn *Eagle*. During these years he read Shakespeare, Goethe, Byron, Rousseau, Hume and Gibbon, but he came to feel that these writers gave him less than Dickens, Melville, and Thoreau. As a reporter for the *Eagle* he wrote book-reviews and dramatic criticism, and to the *Eagle's* columns began to contribute his first attempts at poetry, the experimental work in the technique he was to develop. These poems celebrated the rise of cities like Brooklyn and New

WALT WHITMAN
(From the etching by Thomas Johnson)

York, and they also celebrated Whitman's hope for a development of a wide feeling of brotherhood in the building of the new democracy.

For several years Whitman disappeared from Brooklyn and wandered about the South and Middle West. He visited New Orleans and seems to have spent considerable time there, and it was in New Orleans that he later boasted of having become the father of an illegitimate child or of several. The facts about Whitman's love life have never been threshed out, although Emory Halloway in his *Whitman, An Interpretation in Narrative,* believes that Whitman not only had a love affair in New Orleans but that he had several. Many commentators, however, have believed that Whitman boasted of love affairs he never had and of illegitimate children to cover up the fact that he was homosexual and incapable of falling in love with . woman. About this point I have the opinion that these commentators are right and that much of the distaste which we feel for some of the "friendship" poems of Whitman is due to his abnormality. But even despite the evidence of many extremely affectionate letters he wrote to his friend, Pete Doyle, and the indications, I believe Whitman told the truth when he answered John Addington Symonds' direct question as to whether he was homosexual or not. Whitman denied it with vehemence and expressed horror for such aberrations. It is possible that his tendencies were wholly unknown to him, that he sublimated them into his poetry, and that his horror was real. He was brought up in a Puritanical home; the whole *mores* of his time were such as to rule out even the possibility of such a thing occurring to oneself.

Whitman returned from his wanderings in 1850. He had gone away a stalwart young man, handsome and athletic and beardless. He returned aged beyond his years and bearded. He became interested, on his return, in the question of slavery and in the economic panaceas which were rife at the time and ran for a short while an organ of the Free-Soil party called *The Freeman,* after which he returned to carpentry and to the doing of odd jobs to earn a living.

In 1855 he collected and published his poems under the title, *Leaves of Grass.* His fame as the result of these poems was not immediate, but of slow growth. It penetrated to England where Whitman's genius some twenty-five years later was recognized by Algernon Charles Swinburne, Robert Louis Stevenson, John Addington Symonds, Edward Carpenter and Havelock Ellis, all of whom, to the surprise of many American critics, hailed Whitman as a creator, poet and prophet in extravagant terms. In France, even later, a Whitman cult grew up, and a school of poetry came into being under the banner of the Whitmanists, headed by Émile Verhaeren.

Whitman did not serve as a soldier in the Civil War, but after his brother was wounded in the second year of the war he volunteered as a nurse and served in the hospitals of Washington and behind the lines in Virginia. He developed an infection from gangrenous wounds which was to leave him paralyzed during the last years of his life. After the war he was given a clerkship in the Interior Department but the controversy over the frankness of Whitman's poems had developed and some sacrosanct official in the department dismissed Whitman as an immoralist. However, he was reinstated after much controversy as a clerk in the Treasury Department, where he served until he had a paralytic stroke in 1873. He never received a pension because of opposition to his poems in official Washington. After living for a while in Philadelphia, enjoying a few years of productivity and growing fame both here and abroad, he settled down in poverty in Camden, New Jersey, where a Mrs. Mary Davis took pity on him and lived with him as his housekeeper through his long disablement. Pilgrims came to the house of "The Good Gray Poet" as to a shrine—writers and poets. His poverty in his last years was alleviated from time to time by subscriptions organized by Rossetti in England and by Burroughs, Traubel and others in America. He was attended during his long last illness by famous physicians, such men as Drs. Osler and McAlester, who honored the man and the poet. He was suffering toward the last from numerous ailments, including tuberculosis, and he died on March 26, 1892, after an attack of pneumonia.

WHITMAN never quite became the poet of the people that he wished to become. He has never been popular in the sense that Robert Burns was popular. But that is perhaps because the people no less than the official torchbearers of civilization have not yet emerged from the eighteenth and nineteenth century inclination to regard literature as something like wax flowers under glass.

POE *THE INVENTOR*

*

IT HAS been the persistent claim of several generations of critics in France and in England that Edgar Allan Poe has never been appreciated in his native land. Legends about America's neglect of Poe sprang up abroad which have never died down; but the truth is Poe enjoyed during his brief and unhappy lifetime much more fame, popularly and otherwise, than that which many of the French poets who were drawn to Poe enjoyed in Paris. Baudelaire, speaking of "barbarous, gas-lit America," which had allowed Poe to die in pathetic and poverty-stricken circumstances, was only transferring to Poe and to the United States the misery he felt because of the neglect of his own genius.

Nevertheless, there is a certain validity in the assertion that the real significance of Poe has never been felt quite so strongly in American literary history as that significance has been felt in France. Certain French critics do not hesitate to claim Poe for French literature, just as certain German critics of the last century decided that Shakespeare's true genius was German and not English and claimed him as their own along with Goethe, Schiller and Heine.

Poe, even yet, is an isolated phenomenon in American letters, whereas his work, translated into French, affected a whole current of thought and fathered an impressive school of writing. The French poets of the Symbolist movement took Poe as their major prophet. Mallarmé, teacher of the school, translated *The Raven* and other poems; Charles Baudelaire, the chief poetical adornment of the school, translated (or rather re-created into French) Poe's prose work and saluted him as the Homer of the Literature of the Decadence. Poe also originated the modern detective story, and among French writers he found his first disciples in this genre.

Poe never founded a school of writing in America; he had but one successful American imitator—Henry James. But also he had only one successful imitator in England—Robert Louis Stevenson, who drew upon Poe's study of a dual personality, *William Wilson*, for the inspiration of *Dr. Jekyll and Mr. Hyde* and upon Poe's *Gold Bug* for certain phases of *Treasure Island*.

But it is probably precisely because Poe was a unique phenomenon in American literature that he found fewer imitators than even did Walt Whitman, who was likewise unique. Also no one has imitated Vachel Lindsay, who created a form and idiom all his own.

Just now there is a revival of appreciation of Poe in France and in England, inaugurated largely by the extremely high estimate put upon Poe's genius by Paul Valéry, the poet-essayist-philosopher, who succeeded to the chair in the French Academy left vacant by the death of Anatole France. Valéry tells us in his *Variety* that Poe's *Eureka* was the first book to make him understand the passion of the scientist or of the mathematician for his work. He tells us that the fundamental idea of *Eureka* "is a profound and sovereign idea"—the doctrine of relativity anticipating Einstein, a philosophy of perception, and a doctrine through which we may one day reach the solution of the mystery of life.

Poe's mind was a mathematician's mind. The logical pursuit of the inter-related laws governing a hypothesis fascinated him. He was profoundly concerned with the relation between illusion and reality and with how the one merges into the other. He tried to erect laws which would solve this riddle. His prose tales are worked out with a mathematician's passion. His poems, or at least some of them, have that pure beauty which Edna St. Vincent Millay once said in a beautiful sonnet is inherent only in problems in geometry. Nevertheless music and sense are united in Poe's poetry to an extent much greater than shallow critics have been ready to grant.

There have been some students of psychiatry who have considered the case of Poe and have arrived at the conclusion that he had a psychic trauma. This tells us nothing. Poe wrote *To Helen, The Raven, Ulalume, The Gold Bug, The Fall of the House of Usher*, and many another story and poem between, which I think the world will not willingly let die; and, in the most impalpable of these there may be some intimations which future scientists will recognize as rare intuitions. If not, we, as mere ordinary readers, may enjoy them anyhow.

EDGAR ALLAN POE was born in Boston on January 19, 1809, while his parents, who were members of a troupe of stock company actors, were playing at the Federal Street Theater in that city. His mother was of a family of actors; his father was the son of an army officer. When Edgar was still a baby his father disappeared. What became of him we do not know; for Edgar's mother never disclosed the truth about the matter. She, herself, however, continued to play the boards as a vivacious and beautiful young leading woman, supporting her two children (she had already given up one for adoption) until 1811 when she fell ill in Richmond, Virginia, while the stock company was playing there, and, after a long illness, during which she was poverty-stricken, died.

In Mrs. Poe's last illness she was visited by some of the ladies of the best families in Richmond who had admired her work on the stage, and among these was Mrs. John Allan. Mrs. Allan, who was childless herself, took the boy, Edgar, and Mrs. William Mackenzie took the girl, Rosalie, into their homes. John Allan at the time was a keeper of a general store. His wife urged him to adopt the child legally, but at the moment he was embarrassed for ready cash and did not wish to complicate his responsibilities by making an orphan his legal heir.

Nevertheless, as a member of the Allan household, Edgar Allan Poe grew up a beautiful, sturdy, brilliant, spoiled child. There existed between foster-father and him one of those strange psychological relationships wherein the extent of the real closeness of spirit between them was to be gauged, as the relationship between Byron and his mother, by the extent of the conflict between them. They seemed to hate each other and probably did, but their hatred was only the reverse of the shield which showed a deep affection between them.

John Allan took the child, Edgar, on one of his trips to Scotland and England, and Edgar attended a grammar school at Irvine, Scotland, for several months and a private school at Stoke Newington, London, from 1817 to 1820. On Edgar's return to Richmond he was entered in a private school. Even at that age, eleven, Edgar had revealed the shy, morbid tendencies which were to mark his life. At fifteen he fell violently and, of course, hopelessly, in love

with Mrs. Jane Stith Stanard, the young mother of one of his
school-mates, and his memory and idealization of her was to continue to be a potent psychic force in his life. The best-remembered
of his poems, probably, *To Helen,* expressed what Mrs. Stanard
meant to him. When she died, a few years after his first meeting
her, Poe was inconsolable and, if his own story is to be believed,
he went night after night to the graveyard in which she was buried
and wept over the mound beneath which her corpse lay.

He grew up in Richmond as a typical young Southerner of
good family of the period and was entered at the University of
Virginia. He had written some verses as a mere child, and the writing of verses and the reading of novels occupied much of his time
at the university. But, while he was in college there developed that
strained relationship with his stepfather. Mr. Allan wished to dominate him and, not succeeding, withdrew the too liberal allowance
he had been accustomed to give the boy. Edgar Poe was a slim,
handsome and graceful youth who nevertheless was afflicted with
a painful sense of inferiority. He took immense pride in his personal
appearance and address to overcome this sense of inferiority.

John Allan learned that Edgar read novels, such as *Don Quixote,*
the romances of Scott, and the mystery yarns of Charles Brockden
Brown. He forbade Edgar Poe to read novels, and particularly did
he object to Poe's reading Byron, of whose personal life he disap-
proved. Balked and exasperated by his foster-parent, Edgar developed two solaces and distractions which he was to abuse—
gambling and drinking. He also had one or two love affairs, one
of them peremptorily broken off by the young miss when she learned
that Edgar Poe's desires were physical. This experience may have
had much to do with the neuroses affecting Poe's later sexual life;
for, as an adult in marriage, his love life was abnormally not of
the flesh.

(Hervey Allen in his exhaustive, two-volume *Israfel: the Life
and Times of Edgar Allan Poe* has credibly accounted for Poe's
a-sexual nature in a way which, I think, disposes of the hypothesis
that Poe was afflicted with a psychic trauma which caused him
to marry a thirteen-year-old girl and worship her until her death
not as a physical being but as something unearthly. Mr. Allen has
established that before Poe's marriage to Virginia Clemm he had
become addicted to opium and he explains that one of the effects
of opium is gradually to deprive one of sexual desire and potency.)

At the University of Virginia, Poe's love of luxury and his

mania for gambling brought about a bitter contest of wills between him and his foster-father. In the end, Poe was disowned by Mr. Allan and forced to leave the university, owing some $2,500 in gambling debts and many tradesmen's bills which John Allan refused to pay, taking the stand that Edgar Poe was not his legally adopted son and that he was not responsible for the wayward youth's debts.

Under an assumed name, Edgar left for Norfolk and joined the artillery division of the United States Army. After serving a considerable period in the barracks, where he made friends among some officers and disclosed his identity, he schemed to get an appointment as a cadet at West Point. At first John Allan refused to sponsor his foster-son's ambitions but at length decided that West Point might reform Edgar and provide a self-sustaining career for him.

Edgar Poe was at West Point from June, 1830, to February, 1831, probably the most impossible cadet ever registered at the academy. Legends exist in West Point, strictest of disciplinary institutions, that Poe was a wizard at mathematics but, like James McNeill Whister, who followed him and like him created legends, everything a West Point cadet should not be. A story goes that he appeared once for full-dress parade in tar-bucket, dress tails and boots, but with no shirt or trousers whatever, thus almost causing a stroke of paralysis in the commandant; but these stories are not substantiated.

Poe was expelled from West Point within eight months after his arrival on five charges in courts martial. But while there he had written *To Helen, The Sleeper, The Pœan, Fairy Land* and *The Valley of Unrest*, all poems indicating the maturity of his poetic genius. Poe went from West Point to New York in disgrace and certainly without the financial support of his foster-father. His life at that period cannot be accounted for except in faint traces which reveal the fact that he was often on the point of starvation.

He traveled about from New York to Boston, to Philadelphia and to Baltimore and finally back to Richmond, doing some newspaper work and living we don't know how. In 1833 the Baltimore *Saturday Visitor* offered a prize of $50 for the best short story submitted in a contest and Poe won it with *The Ms. Found in a Bottle*. About this time Poe found two friends in John P. Kennedy, a Baltimore lawyer, congressman and novelist, and in T. S. Arthur, renowned as the author of *Ten Nights in a Bar-room*. Among the letters preserved to us of Poe's life at that period were pitiful requests from Poe for the loan of sums of money. It was in Baltimore, too, that he met the two women who were to occupy the larger part of his remaining life, Mrs. Maria Poe Clemm and her daughter Virginia. Mrs. Clemm was the younger sister of Poe's father, a widow who kept a boarding house where Poe occupied an attic room. Toward Poe Mrs. Clemm adopted a motherly attitude from the first. It was in Mrs. Clemm's house, according to Mr. Hervey Allen, that Poe, who had given up his drinking habits for a long period, took to opium as a solace to his tense nerves. He also appears to have tried laudanum (possibly in imitation of Coleridge, the great English poet critic to whom Poe owed so much in the way of esthetic and critical standards) and on one occasion attempted suicide by an overdose.

Living at Mrs. Clemm's Poe married Virginia Clemm, when she was only thirteen years old, in 1835. She was the inspiration of his "Ligeia," his "Eulalia"; she was his "Eleanora," "Berenice" and "Annabel Lee." Shortly before the marriage, Poe had been recalled to Richmond by the death of John Allan, to participate in the Allan legacy. Having left Mrs. Clemm and Virginia behind in Baltimore, Poe took up residence in a boarding house; he found himself welcomed back into the city and his gambling debts forgotten; and, after he had contributed a poem to the *Southern Literary Messenger,* Poe was invited to join the staff of that magazine as sub-editor. His employer soon found that he could leave the editing of the magazine to the young poet and devoted his time to traveling about the country drumming up subscriptions. But Poe was developing a psychosis which made him prey to a thousand fears, no doubt aggravated by his separation from Mrs. Clemm and Virginia, the upshot of which was that Poe lost his job, hastened back to Baltimore and (since he had already attained a literary reputation) set out with his child-bride, mother-in-law and very little money for New York. Poe's *Narrative of Arthur Gordon Pym* was being serialized in the *Southern Literary Messenger* at the time and, on the strength of this tale no less than on the brilliantly incisive book reviews and critical essays he had contributed to that magazine, Poe's reputation was in the ascendancy. He was asked to contribute to various literary publications and he settled down in cramped lodgings at the corner of Sixth Avenue and Waverley Place. All prospects brightened—except for one thing. Poe had gone to New York in January, 1837, and a few months later the country was in the grip of a panic, following the failure of the state banks which had been issuing "wildcat" paper money after the collapse of the Bank of the United States. Some of the magazines Poe counted upon for support suspended.

Nevertheless he managed somehow to live and to frequent literary society where he met Washington Irving, William Cullen Bryant, Fitz-Greene Halleck and lesser lights. During that awful summer of 1837, in lodgings at 113¼ Carmine Street, Poe was developing that special genius of his for the macabre and sinister. "No one, not even Coleridge," writes Hervey Allen, "had so successfully exploited the psychology of fear. Coleridge always left off where beauty refused to follow; with Poe in the realm of prose, there were no confines to horror whatsoever, and he was artistically successful in overstepping the former frontiers. Only some of the drawings of Leonardo da Vinci approach the delineation of the emotions and the details which he describes."

Next year Poe and his little family took up residence in the then literary capital of America, Philadelphia, home of *Godey's Lady's Book* and other magazines of national repute and circulation, where, after a season of prosperity, he became co-editor of *The Gentleman's Magazine,* to which he contributed *The Fall of the House of Usher, William Wilson, To Iolanthe in Heaven,* and other work in prose and poetry, including his always notable literary criticisms. To this period belong also his embroilments with the literary big-wigs of the time. Among the Boston and Concord group of philosophers, poets and essayists it must be admitted that there was a great deal of log-rolling—Whittier, Holmes, Emerson, Longfellow, Thoreau, and the rest (Lowell excepted) were exceedingly sure of themselves and disdainful of all literary reputations which sprang up in other cities. Poe resented this and in his resentment began to attack with merciless argument the most sacrosanct idol of the whole group—Longfellow.

Poe spent five years in Philadelphia, and they were the happiest, most productive period of his life; there he was an editor, a much sought after contributor to magazines; there he derived much from his old eccentric friend, the Rev. Holley Chivers (whose biography, *Thomas Holley Chivers* by S. Foster Damon, should be read as much for sheer entertainment as for a fascinating study of the times); there he met Dickens; there he published *The Gold Bug,* which won him a $100 prize, and *The Murders in the Rue Morgue;* there he rode on the crest of a wave of popularity for a time and dropped to the depths largely by reason of his own weak-

ness for drink; there he encountered the evil and envious acquaintance of Rufus Griswold, who was later to do his reputation so
much harm by writing a biography of Poe.

It was in Philadelphia also that Poe wrote the first draft of
The Raven, which he tried unsuccessfully to sell to *Graham's Magazine* when Virginia and Mrs. Clemm were actually starving. Within
a few years Poe had gone to the top of success and gone back to
the bottom again. He and Virginia went to New York, sent for Mrs.
Clemm after they had got established and then Poe scored a sensational success shortly after his arrival by writing his newspaper
hoax about a Mr. Monck Mason's having crossed the Atlantic in
a flying-machine. So realistic was this yarn in detail and circumstance that everybody believed it; the circulation of the penny
newspaper, the *Sun*, went up; Poe's reputation was revived. Remy
de Gourmont, the French critic, cites *The Balloon Hoax* in refutation of the notion that Poe's genius was not peculiarly American.
This intellectual practical joke, Gourmont wrote, is a species of
humor found nowhere except in America—it was the type of thing
which allies Poe to Mark Twain.

Thenceforth Poe was to be associated with the literary world
of New York. Virginia was consumptive and for her health the Poes
moved first to a house at 184th Street and Broadway (where he
completed *The Raven*) and later to the cottage in Fordham which
is still preserved as a Poe museum. He was a lion, though a somber
one and always without money; and he was besought by a bevy
of women with whom he entered into platonic relationships, notably
Frances Sargent Osgood and Mrs. Anna Cora Mowatt.

During the summer of 1846 Poe was ill and poverty-stricken,
unable to work. Autumn and winter came on and he still could earn
no money. Virginia was dying in the cramped little bedroom in the
Fordham cottage: the three of them had gone without food for days
on end; there was no way of keeping the whole house warm; Mrs.
Clemm begged food from the remote neighbors; Virginia complained
of the cold; more blankets were piled upon her; and on a morning
in late January she was found dead, apparently smothered to death
in her weak efforts to get warm.

That loss spelt the doom of Poe; he lived on and wrote and
lectured, sporadically attaining success and falling back into drunkenness and penury. He was imprisoned once and once charged with
forgery. He braced up for a time, ceased to drink and went on a
successful lecture tour. On September 29, 1849, he landed in Balti-

more by boat from Richmond. There was an election campaign going on. He had drunk too much at a farewell banquet for him in Richmond and apparently was in a stupor when he arrived in Baltimore. He seems to have been shanghaied as a "floater" to vote in the coming election and plied with drink. In one of his lucid moments Poe sent word to a doctor he knew and when the doctor arrived Poe was helplessly drunk in a barroom. The doctor got Poe to the Washington hospital where pneumonia, complicated by alcoholism, rapidly developed and, wishing to die, begging the physician to kill him, he died on October 7, in his fortieth year.

For a long time, and perhaps even unto this day, Poe's genius was obscured by over-emphasis on his drinking habits. Longfellow, who was unofficially America's poet laureate, had never been seen drunk and had never been harassed by poverty. But, also, though Longfellow had a valuable gift for imitative rhyming and a touching ability to put platitudes into verse, he had no genius such as Poe's. Any psychiatrist worth his salt nowadays will tell you that Poe died as much from writing poetry as from drinking; that the mental constitution of Poe, which led him to make the speculations in *Eureka* which Paul Valéry regards as probably the profoundest philosophy in literature, was also the mental constitution which made drink necessary to him. With his fragile nerves, his quivering sensibility, it is probable that he would have gone insane if he had not had recourse to the deadening effects of alcohol. Poe, it is admitted, did not drink for pleasure; the smell and taste of wine or spirits were repugnant to him. He drank for oblivion. But in the few years his mind was undulled and functioning, what an amazing lot of strange, unearthly beauty he created! What curious penetrations beyond the veil of reality seem to have been vouchsafed to him! He is of the company of Coleridge and Blake, among the miraculous madmen of poetry and art.

DOSTOIEVSKI *THE ANALYST*

*

NIETZSCHE said that Dostoievski was the only psychologist from whom he had ever been able to learn anything; and perhaps in general it may be said that no other novelist has portrayed with such insight and understanding those subtle and profound workings of the mind under emotional stress. *A Raw Youth* is a prose *Hamlet* in which the sufferings of a sensitive adolescent under the blind cruelty of life are portrayed with an emotional intensity which is lyrical and dramatic. An excellent case might be made out for saying that *The Brothers Karamazov* is the profoundest study in character in the whole realm of prose fiction.

Most of Dostoievski's novels are morbid in the same way that several of the plays of Shakespeare are morbid; but just as all of our knowledge of the diagnosis and treatment of disease comes from the study of pathological conditions of the human body, what little we have been able to learn about the mind and the subconscious, about the part memory plays in our emotions and in all our reactions to life, comes from the study of the sort of morbid psychology in which Dostoievski excels.

Modern Soviet Russia has officially condemned Dostoievski as "defeatist" and his novels there are under a ban. This is ironical; for Dostoievski, more than any other Russian novelist, helped to stir up revolt against the feudal conditions of autocratic Russia in his *House of the Dead* and in *Crime and Punishment:* he served four years at hard labor in a Siberian penal colony for seditious activities; and he was once almost worshiped by the whole mass of the Russian common people as the prose-poet of their sufferings and aspirations.

In English and French criticism two extremely divergent views of Dostoievski's worth have been expressed. There is the view of George Moore that Dostoievski was only a concocter of melodramas and horror stories "with psychological sauce," and there is Maurice Baring's sweeping pronouncement, "His genius soars higher and dives deeper than that of any other novelist, Russian or European." Somewhere between these two opinions the average reader's opinion may be found. Dostoievski wrote novels which are tragical in the extreme; but there are also to be found in his books pages of humor like Gogol's or Dickens'. He wrote many pot-boilers, and it is probable that a canon of his best work narrows down to *The Brothers Karamazov, A Raw Youth, The House of the Dead, Crime and Punishment, The Idiot,* and *The Possessed.* In each of these novels the characters come alive in his pages with such vividness that, once any one has read them, certain characters remain unforgettable.

FEODOR MICHAELOVITCH DOSTOIEVSKI was born in Moscow on October 30, 1821, the son of an army surgeon of Lithuanian origin, and of a Ukrainian mother. Both parents were devout Catholics. His father, upon whom Dostoievski drew for some aspects of the character of Old Karamazov, the buffoonish and profligate father of the *Brothers Karamazov,* was a drunken, brutal and avaricious scoundrel, whose savage mistreatment of his serfs caused them finally to murder him.

Feodor as a child was brilliant and sensitive but morose and epileptic. He read almost incessantly and, like nearly all Lithuanians, he had a linguistic gift which enabled him to read widely in English, French and German. He studied at the College of Engineers in St. Petersburg and upon his graduation received an appointment in the state department of Military Engineering. He was engaged in work he did not like but he stuck to it doggedly because at the time that was the only source of support he had in view. His youth, which he has brought vividly before us in several of his novels, were extremely unhappy; he had neither the inclination for the ordinary social pleasures of students nor the means of gratifying them if he had. It was while he was in school that he had his first epileptic fit, on hearing of the murder of his father. At night, after his duties for the day were over, he read Schiller, Goethe, Balzac and Racine and began to dream of earning a living by his pen.

His first connection with the literary world was as translator for a publishing house. This enabled him to meet some of the great Russian writers of the time, such as Turgenev, Sologub and Nekrassov. His first attempt at a novel of his own was *Poor Folks,* written in imitation of Gogol. The book was a commercial success; but it was not well-received by the critics. As popularity of the book increased and its sales mounted, Dostoievski was made the object of much abuse. Even Turgenev contributed to this disparagement of his younger rival, by writing a burlesque poem ridiculing Dostoievski. This was a great humiliation to the young writer, for he had admired Turgenev almost to idolatry and the affront he suffered by this poem was something that clung to him throughout his life: he never forgave Turgenev and, in later years, developed a bitter hatred for the man, a hatred matching that of Tolstoi, who also began by idolizing Turgenev and ended by disliking him intensely.

The success of *Poor Folks* sent Dostoievski into a furious grind of literary activity, wherein he turned out novels in imitation of Balzac, Dickens, George Sand, even Sir Walter Scott, all the more feverishly ground out in that he had already contracted his passion for gambling which became a passionate vice for him and caused him much misery. He had taken it up innocently enough in a mistaken notion that through gambling he could relieve his poverty. It became later on a passion like drink or satyriasis, wherein he sought oblivion from worry and illness in the distraction offered by the intense concentration offered by play for money.

When he was twenty-eight years old he became involved in one of those revolutionary plots of the period in Russia which were continually being unearthed by the secret police. Among the group of intellectuals of which Dostoievski was a leader there had been some talk of fomenting a revolution to overthrow the czar and set up a republic. Incriminating literature was found in Dostoievski's rooms; he was arrested and thrown into the Fortress of Peter and Paul, where after a trial which dragged wearily through the months, he was sentenced to be shot. Nicholas I refused to sign the order of execution, but contrived a diabolical punishment. He arranged that Dostoievski should be allowed to spend the last hours of a condemned man with all the sinister accompaniments of the death sentence, led out to the scaffold and the halter placed round his neck. Then at the last moment when the trap was ready to be sprung, he contrived to have the official actors in his hideous farce present, as a last-moment reprieve, a document showing the clemency of the czar. He was condemned to penal servitude for life and sent to Siberia.

Dostoievski's life is so intimately and realistically detailed in his novels that *The House of the Dead* and *Crime and Punishment* should be read for the record of his four years in a convict camp. Aside from those novels we have no other records except those of the young Swedish military genius, Baron Wrangel, a native of the Baltic Provinces who was sent to Siberia as a military governor and who there met Dostoievski and invited him, during the last year of Dostoievski's stay in Siberia, to live at his house.

While still in prison Dostoievski met the woman who was to become his first wife. She was the wife of Captain Issaieff, who was stationed in Semipalatinsk, which was the town of the penal colony to which Dostoievski was condemned. A certain amount of freedom of movement was allowed the convicts in Siberia. They were required to do back-breaking manual labor during certain hours and they were under surveillance; but they were permitted, if they were socially acceptable, to visit at the houses of officers. The military command and state officials cultivated the society of many of the convicts, so many of whom were cultured intellectuals; and in this way Dostoievski became a welcome guest at the residence of the Issaieffs.

Captain Issaieff was suffering from consumption and a few months after meeting Dostoievski was ordered to another Siberian settlement where he died. Madame Issaieff began writing to Dostoievski letters exaggerating the state of her poverty and playing upon Dostoievski's sympathy, of which he had an inordinate amount. He received money occasionally from his relatives and his publisher and he sent it all to the widow. His interest in her was that of friendship and he had, in fact, been advised by doctors and friends not to marry on account of his epilepsy. Nevertheless Madame Issaieff pursued him with letters, tried to make him jealous by telling him of a suitor, and, failing in this, threatened suicide. Dostoievski went to see her. The upshot of it was that he returned to Semipalatinsk with her as his wife. She was part Negress, part French and part Russian, and an idle and frivolous type of the sort often found among those brought up in the monotonous surroundings of a remote military post.

Dostoievski engaged a tutor for his wife's child at her request. He did not know it until years later, but this was a ruse of hers to get her lover into her house. At length Dostoievski was permitted to return to St. Petersburg, where he resumed his novel writing. He published *The House of the Dead,* which he had written in Siberia, and it was a great success. Even the new czar was said to have wept tears over it and to have made some effort to repair the injustice of the penal laws.

Then Dostoievski's wife developed galloping consumption and that terrible woman in an agonizing hour of torturing cruelty revealed to him in all the repugnant details how she had been unfaithful to him, how her lover had slept with her the night before the marriage. She did this in her mad rage upon hearing that her lover, whom Dostoievski had brought back to St. Petersburg with him, had tired of her and had left her, although Dostoievski did not tell her this. This was a crushing experience for Dostoievski. Some years later he was to torture himself by dictating the scene in detail to the young woman who was to become his second wife. It is the most dramatic episode in *The Eternal Husband,* and thereafter the sufferings of a betrayed husband, who is aware that he himself is considerably responsible for his betrayal, becomes a poignant note in many of his novels.

This awful and hateful confession killed Dostoievski's love, and although he sent money to the wife, who hated him until her death, he fell in love, passionately for the first time in his life, with a young woman student, who, after flattering her vanity awhile with the devotion of a now celebrated novelist, ran away to Paris with a lover and was pursued thence by Dostoievski. There occurred a comic-opera drama of passionate absurdities, with Dostoievski at forty displaying the young lover's temperament he had never shown when he was younger; with the theatrical young woman plying back and forth between her French lover and Dostoievski, threatening suicide and driving Dostoievski mad. The real point was that her French lover was unfaithful to her and would not show the love she expected of him, and she was using Dostoievski as a foil, to rouse her lover's jealousy. Dostoievski was slow in learning this; when he did, he returned to Petersburg cured of passion.

Madame Dostoievski died and Dostoievski withdrew from society, writing his books and living in dreary lodgings with his stepson, who looked after his accounts and ran his house for him. One day a young and pretty stenographer, Anna Snitkin, called at Dostoievski's house in answer to an advertisement for a writer of shorthand. She was gifted, well-educated, sympathetic and charming.

She became Dostoievski's secretary and to her he dictated, day after day, the first drafts of his novels. Five months after their first meeting she became his wife, and there began for her a long martyrdom to his passion for gambling, a martyrdom which she carried with better grace than did Countess Tolstoi, for she not only bore with Dostoievski's sufferings but understood his malady; and when she came to publish the pathetic and beautiful story of her life with the novelist it was a work of infinite tenderness and love. She bore Dostoievski two children, a boy and a girl, one of whom, Aimée, wrote one of the best of the Dostoievski biographies, however biased it is against the Bolshevists.

The Dostoievski home was, ordinarily, a model of domestic happiness, spoiled only by the strained relations between Dostoievski's step-son and his own children. Madame Dostoievski was an efficient and kindly mother and a mother to her husband no less than to her children. They traveled; Dostoievski was received everywhere as a famous man; but frequently they were in direst poverty because Dostoievski's insane passion for gambling would lead him to throw away in one session at the roulette wheel all the money he could get in advance on royalties—the very money on which his wife had counted to settle old debts and pay the household expenses while Dostoievski was writing his next book.

He developed a surprising talent for lecturing; he became one of the chief adornments of Countess Alexis Tolstoi's salon; he published novels with regularity and success; he quarreled with Turgenev and to a lesser extent with Tolstoi, who failed to appreciate his genius, whereas Dostoievski appreciated Tolstoi's genius as a writer but had many reservations about him as a man of sense and honor; and after a troubled and disquieting life he died of a hemorrhage in a brief illness during which he was surrounded by people who loved him, in January, 1881, in his sixtieth year.

He was given the most elaborate funeral ever held in Russia. Peasants, tradespeople, students, priests, workmen and members of the nobility followed the cortège to the burial ground.

Before the services at the Church of the Holy Ghost a crowd so huge had gathered that Mme. Dostoievski had difficulty in getting inside the church. Her way was barred by a police officer. She explained that she was Dostoievski's widow and that they were awaiting for her arrival for the mass to begin.

"You are the sixth widow of Dostoievski who has tried to get in," said the policeman, according to Aimée Dostoievski who was with her mother. "No more lies. I shall not allow any one else to pass."

But, happily, those in charge of the services were on the lookout for Mme. Dostoievski and the children and they came in a run and enabled them to get through the crush into the church.

TOLSTOI *THE PAINTER*

*

PROBABLY the greatest individual example of the novelist's art is Tolstoi's *War and Peace*. In that book Tolstoi undertook to paint a picture of a whole epoch, not in the manner of a historian like Gibbon, not in a series of novels like the *Comédie Humaine* of Balzac, but in a single novel peopled with living characters in every phase of European as well as Russian life, from peasant to Napoleon, and to make you see them go about their daily affairs and participate with them in momentous events; and also with all this drama to give you a unified sense of the whole of a social cataclysm. In that novel he painted for us a tremendous canvas of war and peace in which each figure is as pulsatingly alive as a portrait by Rembrandt, and three dimensional rather than two.

Tolstoi was a master story-teller who never realized that he was a writer until he was a grown man and who took up writing because he was bored with life and in debt. His first form of writing was that of keeping a diary, a habit which he continued through life. He got the notion of doing this by reading a translation of a biography of Benjamin Franklin which referred to Franklin's diaries and gave extracts from them. Tolstoi had an extremely nervous constitution, and he early became introspective and deeply concerned with himself and with the inconsistencies of his nature. He was religiously disposed, and yet he was a constant victim of his violent passions and given to restless debauches. In his diaries he probably exaggerates these tendencies somewhat; but the reason is evident: he felt a great sense of sin and shame at his inability to conquer his physical nature and rid himself of his besetting sins of drunkenness, gambling and concupiscence. Writing proved to be

411

his salvation. Once he began to direct his vast, almost superhuman energy into the channel of creative writing, his battle with himself became less violent. He always had a severe conscience which bothered him greatly, and in his after years, when the stream of his energy was dwindling, he dwelt with unnecessary regret upon the indulgences of his youth and turned so excessively religious that he lost all sense of proportion, tried to live the life of an early Christian and renounced all of his novels as pernicious. There was, if there was ever in any one, a demon in him, and that demon was the possession of a great genius. In him there was in high degree the things that were stirring in the soul of the Russian people which finally burst through the feudalism of Russian autocracy and established the tremendous experiment of communism. Tolstoi's social conscience was as deep as his moral conscience; and he, born a nobleman, perceived, perhaps a little pervertedly, the injustice of the system wherein men like himself were permitted to live in idleness, luxury and dissipation upon the products of the labor of the great mass of people who were kept in barbaric and medieval slavery.

Leo N. Tolstoi was born in 1828, about one hundred and thirty miles south of Moscow, Russia, on the estate of Yasnaya Polyana, which, together with eight hundred serfs, his mother had brought to Count Nicholas Tolstoi as a dowry. She was a daughter of a rich Prince Volkonski, whom the future novelist's father had taken as wife in a marriage of convenience, because the fortunes of the Tolstoi family, all of them soldiers and landed proprietors, had been dissipated to a large extent by extravagances, which ran up debts and brought about sales and foreclosures. Tolstoi's mother was well educated, a skillful musician and apparently a woman of great grace and intelligence, but no beauty. Leo was the youngest of four sons, and he had a still younger sister whom Marya Volkonski bore before she died, when Leo was two years old.

The early upbringing of Leo and the other Tolstoi children was largely given over to a pious aunt whose constant reading was the *Lives of the Saints,* and to a strange person, Marya Gerasimovna, who made pilgrimages to holy shrines dressed as a man, and who was a nun. This woman was taken into the house on the birth of Leo's younger sister, because of a vow to God made by his mother that, if she were permitted to bear a daughter, she would make the first pilgrim that came along the road godmother to the child.

These two women undoubtedly had a vast influence in giving Leo Tolstoi that religious cast of mind and that profound sense of sin which later were to color his thought so completely. His first reaction to their teaching, and to the too religious atmosphere they gave the house—they entertained great numbers of religious fanatics, monks and nuns, and rarely permitted any real gayety—was to become as irreligious as possible. He avowed atheism and Nihilism and, when he escaped to St. Petersburg as a young man, he gave himself up to every form of dissipation. But in his reminiscences of his childhood he tells us that he had a deep, spiritual passion for his aunt and wept at the caress of her hand.

He was educated by private tutors on the family estate, after the fashion of the children of all nobles, and was taught to speak French and German fluently. His childhood seems to have been especially happy; he and his brothers were all on excellent terms; he wrote that "all who surrounded me in childhood, from my father to the coachman, seem to me to have been exceptionally good people"; and he was a blithe, energetic, good-mannered and gentle lad. He was not studious and read but little. When he was eight years old he conceived the notion that he could fly and in trying to do so he plopped to the ground from the upper story of a house and sustained a slight concussion of the brain.

When he was only five or six an interesting event occurred. He fell violently in love with a girl several years older than himself and in a fit of jealousy once shoved her off a porch, which crippled her for a long time. The woman he later married was that girl's daughter. Prosperity was not continuous with the Tolstois and for years in Leo's youth the family was badly pinched for money; at one time they moved from the estate into Moscow to save expense; and another time a drouth laid such waste to the lands that horses and cattle starved. In 1841 the family moved to Kaza; Tolstoi and his brothers were each given a serf as his own, as valet and bodyguard, and the boys were entered at the university. Leo thought to prepare himself for the diplomatic service and to that end entered for courses in Oriental languages as well as in mathematics, history, and literature. His favorite brother, Serge, who afterwards became a hopeless drunkard, and he, however, cared little for the discipline of university courses, and soon were initiated into the revelries of life in a college town.

Tolstoi, however, was convinced in his own mind—and so wrote in his diary at that time—that a youth should have a serious purpose in life; that he should discover as early as possible what that purpose is, and subject himself to discipline toward the accomplishment of that definite purpose. Unfortunately he had no distinct idea of what he wished to do. We find him at that time, however, beginning to read and comment upon Dickens, Gogol, Sterne, Turgenev, Pushkin and Rousseau. He failed to obtain his degree at the university, and for the next five or six years of his life lived a discontented existence, going from extremes of asceticism to extremes of dissipation, and rushing back and forth between the estate of Yasnaya Polyana and Moscow or St. Petersburg. He and his brother Serge were given much to venery. Serge's special weakness was for gypsy girls, and Leo, acting as a sort of moral guardian for his elder brother, sought to take Serge away from these girls by inducing him to enlist with him in the regiment of cossacks who were fighting the Asiatics in the Caucasus. He and Serge joined a battery of artillery, but they did very little fighting; theirs was mainly garrison duty and Tolstoi after eighteen months did not get the commission he had hoped for. He had given way to his passion for gambling and was desperately in debt, several times on the verge of suicide and writing frantically in his diary about his dissatisfaction with life and his desire to improve himself. Desire tortured him and he yielded to it, only to have his conscience flay him afterward. He was about to lose his estate, or feared he might, because of his debts, and he wrote in his diary that he would hate to lose the estate whatever were his opinions about the system which gave him serfs and land.

This is significant, since about this time (1853) he had become convinced that "the common people are so far above us by the work they accomplish and by the privations in their lives, that it seems wrong for one of us to write anything bad about them." He had already begun to believe that he might earn some money by writing novels and had started to work on a story. But he had no faith in himself and did not believe he could ever write as well as some of his contemporaries, notably Turgenev. Then he suddenly came upon Stendhal's *La Chartreuse de Parme* and this book was a revelation to him. Stendhal had seen that war was a chaos and that "in actual war there is no embellishment" and that soldiers going to their death understand nothing of the scene in which they are engaged. And so he had written. Later Tolstoi was to follow Stendhal's example in his treatment of war.

The war in the Crimea broke out in 1853, between Russia and Turkey, and within less than a year England and France joined the Turks against Russia. By that time Tolstoi had rejoined his battery and reached promotion to the staff of a general. Part of his service was taken up with drinking, gambling, women and inaction, with interludes of music, the theater, and writing. He had also begun to take notes and to observe for literary purposes. He was developing his technique, although he had not yet sold a story. He did get his baptism of fire, however, participating in several engagements, and he records frankly that he was terribly frightened and that he behaved badly. Soon, however, he had got so interested in writing his *Sebastopol Sketches* that he had "nothing to reproach myself for." The Sebastopol studies are realistic; they do not paint war as heroic but as ugly, terrifying, ruthless and as a return to savagery. He sent his articles to a monthly magazine called *Contemporary* in St. Petersburg. They created something of a sensation and gave Tolstoi assurance. There was some trouble with the censorship, but the war ended in the defeat of Russia; liberalism was springing up on all sides; the movement to free the serfs was under way; and Tolstoi returned to St. Petersburg to become a member of a liberal literary circle.

He was, however, arrogant and touchy; he delighted to contradict people; and on one occasion his manners were so bad in this respect that Turgenev left a dinner party in disgust. He also challenged a fellow officer to a duel for some fancied affront; but nothing came of it. He became a friend of Turgenev's, but it was a stormy friendship, finally breaking up altogether, for, although Turgenev was the older man and was patient and kind, Tolstoi insisted upon quarreling with him every time they met.

After the Crimean War Tolstoi continued in the service of the army, drawing pay as an officer. His estate was heavily mortgaged; the movement for the emancipation of the serfs was gaining ground; and Tolstoi drew up a proposal to grant his serfs their freedom in a plan by which the estate would be converted into a village commune, each household receiving twelve acres of land free and the householders paying for the rest in small annual payments and assuming the mortgage. But the peasants had heard that the new Czar was going to free them after the coronation and they suspected Tolstoi of fraud and refused to sign the contract with him. It is quite possible that Tolstoi's scheme *was* disingenuous, because he was in debt, could raise no money without further mortgaging the property, and the scheme *would* give him cash.

Meanwhile Tolstoi had become the father of an illegitimate son, whose mother was a peasant girl. (This natural son grew up to be a servant for one of his legitimate half-brothers.) Tolstoi also tried to settle down, and he paid court to a young noblewoman to whom he wrote many ardent letters but to whom he never proposed. He continued to write sporadically for publication and with ferocious condemnation of himself in his diary. Then he traveled abroad, visiting Paris, Baden-Baden, various cities in Italy, and London. He returned to Russia; quarreled with Turgenev (the episode is so silly that it should be read in full in Aylmer Maude's *Life of Tolstoy*); and established a school, which was raided by the police on suspicion that it contained seditious literature. And then the most important thing so far in his life occurred, his meeting with Sophie Behrs.

Mademoiselle Behrs, her sister and her mother, were visiting relatives on a nearby estate, and stopped for a few days as guests of Tolstoi's sister. Tolstoi was supposed to have been paying court to Sophie's elder sister, but on the occasion of this visit he saw that Sophie was keeping out of the way so that Tolstoi and her sister might be together; whereupon he declared to her that she was under a misapprehension and began paying court to her. Sophie made light of his advances, and his pursuit became more ardent. He followed her to the neighboring estate where she visited and even into Moscow, without any response from Sophie.

On September 12, 1862, Tolstoi records in his diary: "I am in love, as I did not think it was possible to be in love. I am a madman; I'll shoot myself if it goes on like this." Next day he added, "Tomorrow as soon as I get up, I shall go and tell everything or shoot myself."

On September 16, he handed a written proposal of marriage to Sonia (or Sophie). Miss Behrs was the daughter of a court physician in Moscow. She was pretty, well educated; she had graduated with honors in literature and had seen some of her work published; she spoke Russian, French, German, Italian, and later, English.

The couple were married on September 23, and they settled on Tolstoi's estate where, during a long period of stable and happy married life, Tolstoi wrote, first *The Cossacks* and then his great masterpiece, *War and Peace*. The Countess bore him thirteen chiluren, four of whom died. At first she helped her husband with his manuscripts, proofs and copyrights. With the increase of the family her domestic duties exhausted most of her strength.

A rift appeared in 1874 when Tolstoi lost three of his children and the aged aunt he had so loved and admired since his boyhood. He began to look for consolation in some faith he could cling to. "His seeking for truth became acute," wrote the Countess Tolstoi in her *Autobiography*, translated by S. S. Koteliansky and Leonard Woolf. "He contemplated hanging himself. . . . A spirit which rejected the existing religions, progress, science, art, family, had been growing stronger and stronger in Leo Nikolaivich and he was becoming gloomier and gloomier."

This quest was something she could not understand. He had changed and she had, of course, not followed in his steps. She was practical, engaged in household duties, trying to keep her family together. The rift widened. Tolstoi, spurred on by his gadfly, became cruel: "At one time he thought of taking a peasant woman, a worker on the land, and of secretly going away with the peasant to start a new life; he confessed this to me." He did go away, one night when his poor wife was racked by the pains of childbirth: "At four o'clock in the morning, Leo Nikolaivich came back, and without coming to me, lay down on the couch downstairs in his study. In spite of my cruel pains, I ran down to him; he was gloomy and said nothing to me. At seven o'clock that morning our daughter Alexandra was born. I could never forget that terrible June night."

Tortured with the idea that he should live a true, early Christian life, give away his money and property to the poor and work the land, peasant fashion, he proposed this singular scheme to his wife. She thought, quite properly, that it was madness, feeling that it was well enough for him to be quixotic, but she, whose strength had been wasted in childbearing, would thereby be forced to add to her cares the drudgery of washing and cooking and tilling the land.

Tolstoi's earnestness gave him no peace and he compromised by doing foolish and theatrical things: he cobbled his own shoes, whereas the labor he put upon that could have earned him, if he had used the energy in writing, many pairs of shoes, better made. He was also depriving a cobbler of that much of a chance to earn his bread. He also refused to use his more up-to-date plows and farm machinery and instead used wooden plows and hand-hewn flails and rakes. Moreover, he found a sympathetic ear in one Chertkov, a man who appears, from Countess Tolstoi's testimony, to have been a sinister, if not a designing, figure who aided and abetted the tormented old man in his withdrawal from his family.

Of Chertkov, Countess Tolstoi became extremely jealous. She confesses obliquely to prying through Tolstoi's papers and eavesdropping. Tolstoi proposed to deed over all he owned to her, and she, with a bit of theatricalism, cried out: "So you wish to hand over that evil to me, the creature nearest to you! I do not want it and shall take nothing!" Of course, though the property was evil in Tolstoi's eyes, it was not evil in her eyes; and the reader feels that she played here her last trump and lost. The end was tragic. Tolstoi went away. Tolstoi's record of the episode in the notations he made on the train should be read side by side with his wife's story in her autobiography.

THROUGHOUT the tragical life story which Countess Tolstoi wrote there runs an unreasonable cry of injustice. The unhappy woman felt, when she wrote, that life had been cruel to her (and it had been); but she felt also that she had been willfully and cruelly injured by Tolstoi and others. Toward the end of her recital, there is a typically feminine sentence—her final triumph of revenge: "I shall not describe in detail Leo Nikolaivich's going away. So much has been written and will be written about it, but no one will know the real cause. Let his biographers try to find out."

In her diary, which she did not originally intend for publication she wrote, on January 26, 1895: "No one will ever know that he never gave his wife a rest and never—in all the thirty-two years —gave his child a drink of water, or spent five minutes by his bedside to give me a chance to rest a little, to sleep, or go for a walk, or even just recover from my labours."

Toward the end of his life, moreover, he was continually surrounded by flatterers and parasites, who pretended to be his disciples more often than they were; most of them were lazy good-for-nothings, who merely made more work and trouble for Countess Tolstoi. Again, even in his old age, Tolstoi was inordinately jealous of her. He was always inordinately jealous of her, for that matter, and tortured himself with the idea that she had been unfaithful to him or had always secretly loved some one else. From these tortured imaginings he wrote the story *Anna Karenina,* in which his wife believed he had portrayed her and made her out an adulteress. (It appears that a sentimental attachment for an old friend of her youth was as close as she ever came to unfaithfulness to Tolstoi in word or deed.) She was jealous of the love her daughter Alexandra had for the old man. In fine those two old people tormented one another, until at last the weary old man, after a heated quarrel, gathered up some manuscript and a few belongings, left the house in the early hours of the morning, stumbled his way to the stables and ordered a coach. His daughters and his physician followed him, and the physician got into the coach with him. Tolstoi had decided to visit his sister at the Shamordin convent. He went third class, in a car which Mr. Maude says was crowded, smoky and over-heated, and from this Tolstoi caught pneumonia. He visited his sister at the convent, and after spending a day there, he was joined by his daughter Alexandra, who meant to go wherever he went. They set out in a third class coach again for Rostov; he was going to leave Russia. But he became so ill that it was necessary to remove him from the train. When his wife found out that he had been taken ill and was at Astapovo, she hired a special train and rushed to him. But Chertkov, Dr. Makiviski, his eldest son Serge and his daughter Alexandra refused to admit her. Nervous exhaustion rather than pneumonia killed the old man, according to Mr. Maude. The last words in his diary were: "I see our plans have failed... *Fais ce que dois, ad*.... It is all good of others, and chiefly of myself."

The problem of keeping him alive with injections was under-taken by his physician, but this ultimately failed and Tolstoi breathed his last on November 20, 1910. He was delirious shortly before the end and kept crying, "It's time to knock off... all is over.... This is the end, and it doesn't matter."

One should not waste too much time pitying Countess Tolstoi. Like Tolstoi, she dramatized herself in her personal relations with the novelist; and, though her life was at times a hell, it was inter-esting and there were moments of happiness that should have over-balanced all else. Tolstoi was mad with the madness of genius; he was capable of the cruelty of heedlessness; he was pitiable in many respects. He was driven by the gadfly of genius, and he was the victim, as much as she was, of his striving to express his vision of life and the truth as he saw it. Much of his thinking was childish; but it was a vague thinking *toward* something that was not childish at all. And in *War and Peace* and *Anna Karenina* he has left us two great novels, two great pictures of a whole society, faithfully and truthfully depicted. His dramas and some of his lesser stories and novels will I think fade with the years. But his pitifully sincere confessions and records of his great struggle for knowledge of him-self and enlightenment about life, truth and justice (the *Childhood, Boyhood and Youth, My Religion, My Confessions,* and even his strange thesis, *What is Art?*) will always hold an interest for those who like confessional literature. And his wife's *Diaries* will also always be classed among the great intimate personal records of the ways of genius; for Countess Tolstoi could write well also. And one of the finest biographies in the language, is Aylmer Maude's *The Life of Leo Tolstoy*.

MARK TWAIN *THE FIRST AMERICAN*

*

THE most important single event in American literature occurred when Mark Twain wrote the opening paragraphs of *Huckleberry Finn*. That was the first employment of an American idiom in an unquestioned work of genius. It was not the first time that an American idiom had been used; it was not the first time it had been used by Mark Twain: it was simply the first time it had been used in a literary masterpiece which was immediately classifiable as a classic of the language.

Other events of importance were:

The publication of Walt Whitman's *Leaves of Grass*.

The publication of Dreiser's *Sister Carrie*.

The publication of John Macy's *The Spirit of American Literature*.

The publication of H. L. Mencken's *The American Language*.

The first appearance of a short story by Ring Lardner in *The Saturday Evening Post*.

The publication of Vernon Parrington's *Main Currents of American Thought*.

The moment when Sinclair Lewis decided to take a year off from writing according to a commercial formula, in which he had become adept, in order to write a book (*Main Street*) which he thought would be a failure.

The moment James Branch Cabell conceived the idea of the Biography of Manuel and his descendants.

The publication of Mark Van Doren's anthology, *An Autobiography of America*.

421

Of lesser importance, but of significance, in the evolution of a definite American literature were: William Dean Howells' *Rise of Silas Lapham;* Harold Frederic's *Damnation of Theron Ware;* the tenure of Finley Peter Dunne as a creator of the opinions of Mr. Dooley and Mr. Hennessey; E. W. Howe's *Story of a Country Town;* Stephen Crane's *The Red Badge of Courage;* Willa Cather's *O Pioneers;* the posthumous appearance of Emily Dickinson's poems; the founding of *Reedy's Mirror* in St. Louis, which published, among other things, Edgar Lee Masters' *Spoon River Anthology;* the phenomena of Elbert Hubbard, Percival Pollard, Ambrose Bierce and James Huneker; the apparition of Carl Sandburg and Vachel Lindsay; the decision of Ellen Glasgow to continue to be a novelist, let Richmond say what it would; and the publication of the posthumous collection of *The Colby Essays,* wherein there are some of the best of that incomparable humorist-thinker's distillations of sagacity and mother wit.

It is the mark of a healthy man and of the free man that he expresses himself naturally, spontaneously, with emphasis, point and clarity. That is why slang, when it is natural slang and not a clever invention, is so much more picturesque and to the point than a dessicated, "literary," polite language. A too polite language is a language of fear. The fear is not of giving offense, because you can give offense in the politest phrases in the world (the French wits made of the French language a medium for clever insult, thereby emphasizing the cleverness and destroying the natural impulse which prompted it), but the fear of being socially incorrect. The fear of being socially incorrect is, at bottom, a prostitution of self. It is a selling of one's character at the very cheapest price—the social valuation which some one else puts upon you not by what you are but by the correctness of the language you use. Christine Vulpius, whom Goethe made his wife, as we have seen in the chapter of Goethe, wrote letters in which she misspelled words and her diction was not of the petty court circles of Weimar, therefore she was shunned and snubbed by the brummagem dukes and duchesses of that dreary town. But what is worse, there has been a succession of biographers and critics and biographico-fictioneers with class and caste notions who have been aghast that Goethe should have married such a creature. Goethe was a wise man and he had known many women intimately. It may have been his opinion that Christine had more character than any woman he had met, that she was the only woman he knew in all Weimar who was a natural person.

THE peculiar genius of America has been in a democratic give-and-take, of an independence of spirit and of a humorous attitude toward the conditions of life. It has been fought down by social hypocrisy, by false standards as to what constitutes good literature, by a deliberate falsification of feeling, by a deference to ideas of good taste.

Mark Twain struggled against these things all his life; and it is my belief that he succumbed (after years of healthy heartiness) to the pessimism of his last years precisely because the opposition had been too great: his friend Howells, dean of American literary criticism at the time, benignly drew Twain's teeth time after time by friendly counsel; Mrs. Twain joined in with Howells; H. H. Rogers, the Standard Oil millionaire, who took Mark Twain under his wing as a friend and financial adviser,—all these helped to restrain the naturalness of the genius. Twain resented it, deep within himself, and therefore turned to an escape in a rather juvenile sort of pessimism, written not in the vernacular but in the most acceptable choice of words in high socio-literary circles of his time.

IT IS necessary to realize that Mark Twain was not only typically American, but a middle-western American the greater portion of whose life was spent on the shifting frontiers. Born Samuel Langhorne Clemens on November 30, 1835, in Florida, Monroe County, Missouri, he grew up in the river town of Hannibal, where his father kept a general store. He was apprenticed to a weekly newspaper publisher when he was twelve, worked as a pilot on the steamboats which plied the Mississippi, prospected for silver in Nevada, edited a weekly newspaper in California, and in other ways was identified with the adventurous common life of an expanding new country. When he became famous as a popular writer his genius was recognized even by literati in high circles. Drawn to him particularly was William Dean Howells, who had spent his boyhood in the middle west, had been a printer like Mark Twain and had come later under the domination of the "genteel" tradition of the eastern seaboard, a tradition which was slavishly imitative of the English. Howells, like many another, tried to tame Twain into writing like the "correct" middle-class English authors, subservience to whose tradition had emasculated Howells' own prose. For a long time Twain was considered a mere buffoon. He tells us in his *Autobiography* that a president of Vassar treated him like a menial when he had gone to the university to give a lecture. Up until the present time, in fact, a great many of the "authoritative" critics who have written about Twain have considered it necessary to apologize for his "vulgarity," the very quality which made him great. Twain was divinely vulgar, and when the *vulgus,* or the common people, overthrow the sham conventions of etiquette by which a small minority maintain their "aristocratic" pretensions and their economic dominance, Twain will receive the greater homage to which he is entitled.

In order to understand Twain versus Back Bay Bostonism, it may be necessary for the reader to recall the chapter in this book on Latin literature. The corruption and abuses of democracy began within less than a century after the founding of the republic. The American republic followed the general pattern of the Roman republic. The same corruption of the official, "literary" language occurred in America as occurred in Rome. The "correct" language was a language of dissimulation. But, all the time, there was a refutation of this "correct" language in the vernacular, Mark Twain was at war with the "correct" language and the "correct" attitude all his life. His protest against regimentation for profit is registered in his masterpiece *Huckleberry Finn,* and *The Golden Age,* even in *A Connecticut Yankee at King Arthur's Court.*

Mark Twain's autobiography appeared fifteen years after his death. Twain originally intended it not to be published until a hundred years after his death, but as it grew in manuscript he modified his vision of it and published portions of it in magazines. It is significant, however, that the autobiography was withheld and that Twain's literary executor and biographer, Albert Bigelow Paine, has not yet felt that the time is come wherein the full, unhampered expression of Mark Twain may be made known without danger to Twain's fame. It was not until 1931, when C. Hartley Grattan came to write his essay on Mark Twain in *American Writers on American Literature,* edited by John Macy, that an intelligent attitude toward Twain's genius began to be entertained in American criticism. Hitherto there had been two schools of criticism: that in which Twain's genius was accepted with too many reservations about his vulgarity and that in which his work was made the subject of a social protest and his life displayed as a series of frustrations in which he never quite realized his capacities.

Mark Twain wrote everything he was capable of writing and he met with singularly little resistance in saying what he had to say. That Van Wyck Brooks is correct in contending that Mrs. Clemens toned down a considerable number of passages is borne out in Twain's autobiography, but that Twain resented this is not apparent in the autobiography. Nor is it readily apparent that in her excisions she was not wise, for his exuberance often led him into intemperate outbursts; in his rebellion against stupidity, cruelty and intolerance he sometimes defeated his own purposes by resorting to the equivalent of swearing. And swearing is not an expression of ideas, it is a release of feeling.

We will have to destroy the concept that literature is like wax flowers under glass and not a vital coördinate of life before we can realize what a debt we owe to men like Mark Twain. The common run of humanity recognizes this debt but only vaguely and inarticulately; a literate and articulate minority recognizes the debt only with a vain and envious side glance and with an eye toward what is acceptable. In this there is death of the spirit.

THROUGHOUT Twain's adult life he was obsessed by the idea that origin of man's misery and unhappiness was in the sense of sin, remorse and a guilty conscience. It is the theme of *The Mysterious Stranger,* wherein his revulsion against the sense of sin makes him the devil's advocate. Possibly this was because his own sense of sin was enormous. He had it when he was a child; it darkened his days for him. He relates a series of dismal tragedies he witnessed as a boy, the usual sordid tragedies that few hamlets are free from. There is both irony and pathos in his musings upon these terrors of his childhood:

"My teaching and training enabled me to see deeper into these tragedies than an ignorant person could have done. I knew what they were for. I tried to disguise it from myself, but down in the secret deeps of my troubled heart I knew—and I knew I knew. They were inventions of Providence to beguile me to a better life. It sounds curiously innocent and conceited now, but to me there was nothing strange about it; it was quite in accordance with the thoughtful and judicious ways of Providence as I understood them. It would not have surprised me, nor even over-flattered me, if Providence had killed off that whole community in trying to save an asset like me. Educated as I had been, it would have seemed just the thing, and well worth the expense. Why Providence should take such an anxious interest in such a property, that idea never entered my head, and there was no one in that simple hamlet who would have dreamed of putting it there. For one thing, no one was equipped with it.

"It is quite true, I took all the tragedies to myself and tallied them off in turn as they happened, saying to myself in each case, with a sigh, 'Another one gone—and on my account; this ought to bring me to repentance; the patience of God will not always endure.' And yet privately I believed it would. That is, I believed it in the daytime, but not in the night. With the going down of the sun my faith failed and the clammy fears gathered around my heart. It was then that I repented. Those were awful nights, nights of despair, nights charged with the bitterness of death. After each tragedy I recognized the warning and repented; repented and begged; begged like a coward, begged like a dog, and not in the interest of those poor people who had been extinguished for my sake but only in my own interest. It seems selfish when I look back on it now.

"My repentances were very real, very earnest; and after each tragedy they happened every night for a long time. But as a rule they could not stand the daylight. They faded out and shredded away and disappeared in the glad splendor of the sun. They were creatures of fear and darkness and they could not live out of their place. The day gave me no cheer and peace, and at night I repented again. In all my boyhood life I am not sure that I ever tried to lead a better life in the daytime—or wanted to. In my age I should never think of wishing to do such a thing."

THERE is no hope for him; he was born and he died that way—a great, fine-spirited, earthly, noble, gifted, dynamic, quixotic and interesting man, a Prometheus among pygmies, an intelligence functioning with marvelous clarity and vision. And don't deceive yourself that he did not know how great a figure he was: "I told Howells," he writes, "that this autobiography of mine would live a couple of thousand years without any effort and would then take a fresh start and live the rest of the time." Of the truth of this statement I have perhaps less doubt than he had. "I intend," he says further, "that this autobiography of mine shall become a model for all future autobiographies when it is published after my death, and I also intend that it shall be read and admired a good many centuries because of its form and method. . . . I hit upon the right way to do an autobiography: Start it at no particular time of your life; wander at your free will all over your life; talk only about the thing which interests you for the moment; drop it the moment its interest threatens to pale, and turn your talk upon the new and more interesting thing that has intruded itself into your mind meantime. Also make the narrative a combined diary and auto-biography. In this way you have the vivid thing of the present to make a contrast with memories of like things in the past, and these contrasts have a charm which is all their own."

That is truth, certainly, of the autobiography. The book is formless. It follows no chronological order. Reminiscences of his childhood are interrupted by comments upon events of the day, diary entries mingle with stories, jokes, anecdotes, comments and details of his family life. He will include a clipping of a newspaper account of some happening and perhaps devote a chapter to it; he quotes from his little daughter's biography of himself—a quaint and charming and intelligent piece of writing—and he will tell how his wife wrote him a note and put it in the vest pocket he would be fingering, reminding him not to wear his arctics into the dining room at a fashionable dinner.

"It is wrong to try to split him (Twain) into two fragments—part humorist, part pessimist," writes Grattan.* "He was both because of an ambivalent emotional equipment and the two parts joined in Pudd'nhead Wilson's maxims as they joined time and again in his passing remarks to be found in the letters and in A. B. Paine's biography and in, for example, *The Man Who Corrupted Hadley-burg.* This story would have delighted Henry James, Senior, for it is a gorgeous and humorous protest against what James called 'moralism' in contrast with Christianity. 'Moralism' was ostentatious goodness without true roots in personality. Just as crooks wear fine clothes and an engaging manner, so victims of 'moralism' show the world pious minds and scrupulous conduct about which they protest much. Mark Twain hit at this sort of thing, the particular offense being an ostentatious honesty."

Some English dunce presumed to correct Twain's copy for an introduction he had ordered by substituting listless formal words for Twain's living language, and Twain wrote a remarkable essay on style by way of resenting the impertinence. "The idea! That this long-eared animal—this literary kangaroo—this illiterate hostler, with his skull full of axle grease, this . . . I could have said hundreds of unpleasant things about this tadpole, but I did not even feel them."

* *American Writers on American Literature,* by Thirty-seven Contemporary Writers, edited by John Macy.

IN THE Mark Twain autobiography there is this pathetic story about Mark's failure to humanize the Boston Back Bay tradition even in company with his friend John Hay:

"I arrive at the application now. That Sunday morning, twenty-five years ago, Hay and I had been chatting and laughing and carrying on almost like our earlier selves of '67, when the door opened and Mrs. Hay, gravely clad, gloved, bonneted and just from church and fragrant with the odors of Presbyterian sanctity, stood in it. We rose to our feet of course—rose through a swiftly falling temperature—a temperature which at the beginning was soft and summerlike, but which was turning our breath and all other damp things to frost crystals by the time we were erect—but we got no opportunity to say the pretty and polite thing and offer the homage due; the comely young matron forestalled us. She came forward, smileless, with disapproval written all over her face, said most coldly, 'Good morning, Mr. Clemens,' and passed on and out.

"There was an embarrassed pause—I may say a very embarrassed pause. If Hay was waiting for me to speak, it was a mistake; I couldn't think of a word. It was soon plain to me that the bottom had fallen out of his vocabulary, too. When I was able to walk I started toward the door, and Hay, grown gray in a single night, so to speak, limped feebly at my side, making no moan, saying no word. At the door his ancient courtesy rose and bravely flickered for a moment, then went out. That is to say, he tried to ask me to call again, but at that point his ancient sincerity rose against the fiction and squelched it. Then he tried another remark, and that one he got through with. He said, pathetically and apologetically:

" 'She's very strict about Sunday.' "

HAD Mrs. Clemens been allowed to edit the autobiography her sense of artistic values might have caused her to blue-pencil the elaborate prelude and end the anecdote with Hay's pathetic sentence, and so leave the story in all its tragic simplicity, instead of encumbering it with a jarring jocosity. But then again, she might have cut the whole thing out as being indiscreet or in bad taste or from a false idea that she would save her husband from humiliation. She was always trying to save him from humiliations—"which ought to have humiliated me, but didn't because I didn't know anything had happened. But Livy knew; and so the humiliations fell to her share, poor child, who had not earned them and did not deserve them. She always said I was the most difficult child she had. She was very sensitive about me."

That she saved him from other humiliations of a considerable import comes out in his frank account of the failure of his publishing house. His liabilities exceeded his assets by 63 per cent. "I was morally bound for the debts," he writes, "but not legally. The panic was on, business houses were falling to ruin everywhere, creditors were taking their assets—when there were any—and letting the rest go. Old business friends of mine said: 'Business is business, sentiment is sentiment—and this is business. Turn the assets over to the creditors and compromise on that; other creditors are not getting 33 per cent.' " He was plainly inclined to heed this advice, but his wife said: "No; you will pay a hundred cents on the dollar." Still undecided, he sought his friend, H. H. Rogers, who agreed with Mrs. Clemens, pointing out that his reputation would be seriously damaged if he did not pay his creditors in full. When they had made up his mind for him there was nothing left for him to do but go to work, and posterity is the gainer by a number of books he might not have written, because on his own confession he was inclined to shirk, and went into various business ventures hoping to make enough money to give up writing for a living.

MARK TWAIN died in Redding, Conn., in 1910. He had achieved a Doctorate of Law at Oxford along with Edith Wharton, and that is the supreme irony of his life, because the Oxonian tradition had been all that he was in rebellion against in literature and Mrs. Wharton was the very antithesis of him in all things. One is happy to record that he was childishly delighted in being granted a certificate of learnedness in literature. "I never expected," he said, "to cross the water again, but I would be willing to journey to Mars for that Oxford degree." ... Well, people are people and the vanities of men are childlike.

ANATOLE FRANCE *THE SKEPTIC*

*

A NATOLE FRANCE and Remy de Gourmont are, I am pleased to consider, among the most emancipated intelligences the world has produced. Their sound reason and sanity stand out distinctly in a world of stupidities, hopeless muddling, confusion of issues, wrong emphasis, duplicity, hypocrisy, sentimentality, intolerance, and petty vanities. They were contemporaries until 1915, when Remy de Gourmont died at his desk of a cerebral hemorrhage —the very death he had attributed to the journalist in *Une Nuit au Luxembourg*. They were almost neighbors. Gourmont inhabited a modest apartment lined with books on the fourth floor in the rue des Saints-Pères, a short distance from the *Mercure de France* of which he was the brain; Anatole France made his home in a magnificent and richly furnished house in the Villa Saïd. (The Villa Saïd is the name of a dead-end street off the Avenue du Bois de Boulogne.)

They were both ironic skeptics, "working the same side of the street" with incredible unconcern for each other: only once in his volume of work does France mention Gourmont—in a cursory review in the *Temps* of Gourmont's small study of the Latin poetry of the Middle Ages; and Gourmont repays the compliment by referring most casually to France only four times, I think, in his great body of critical work. France, by grace of his sense of humor and his warm humanity, achieved world renown and a popular success. His royalties were enormous considering the nature and excellence of his work. He was burdened with honors. Remy de Gourmont remained until his death a man known only to a few select and appreciative minds. He subsisted upon the sparse royalties of his numerous books and upon his advising editorship at the *Mercure*.

These peers in the realm of skepticism met only twice—shortly before Gourmont's death. Mutual admirers had endeavored to bring them together. Finally Andrè Rouvyère, the artist, visited France with this purpose in view. He brought Gourmont's name into the conversation. France expressed a desire to meet him and asked Rouvyère to bring Gourmont to the house in the Villa Saïd. Rouvyère was dubious about suggesting to the proud hermit of the rue des Saints-Pères that he discommode himself to make a pilgrimage to France, the universal celebrity and member of the Academy. He told Edouard Champion of France's invitation and Champion took it upon himself to escort Gourmont to Villa Saïd.

France paid his guest several polite compliments and talked at random, apropos of nothing, on erudite subjects. Gourmont, who was ill at ease in the presence of others and who was afflicted with an impediment of the speech which made talking difficult, said little. The visit was brief. Gourmont was overjoyed when France accepted his invitation to visit him in return.

Not long after France repaid the courtesy, Rouvyère was in Gourmont's apartment. The philosopher and poet was still vain over the fact that France had visited him. With a slow voice, swelling with pride, Gourmont said, as if speaking of a god: "He came to see me.... He sat there... in that very chair you are now occupying."

No WRITER, ancient or modern, has been more industriously Boswellized than Anatole France, and yet few first-rate writers have been more unfortunate in their biographers. Much attention has been paid to what he said in the privacy or the semi-privacy of his home, especially after he had grown old, famous and garrulous: still, no one bothered to ascertain the date of his first marriage, or indeed, more than to guess (incorrectly) that this marriage was only a brief and unfortunate affair. The marriage endured all of eight years: it was fruitful of a daughter, a number of books, and of a cynicism toward love and marriage that lasted throughout France's life.

Although James Lewis May went to live at France's country home near Tours for the express purpose of writing a biography, his book is wholly unsatisfactory, treating of France's married life in a paragraph, omitting all mention of Madame de Caillavet, and telling nothing that might not be gleaned from France's semi-autobiographical novels and the French *Who's Who*. Thus far, the best biography of France in either French or English is *Anatole France;*

The Mind and the Man by Lewis Piaget Shanks, a professor at Johns Hopkins University, who never met France and who depended almost entirely upon France's writings for his source materials. The memoirs, reminiscences and biographical sketches that have appeared since France's death have been (some of them) informative or suggestive, but in the main mere tosh or downright misstatements of fact. The reports of France's familiar conversations by J. J. Brousson, Paul Gsell, Nicolas Segur and Charles Le Goff are all delightful. So little was actually known from print about France's life that several months after his death a controversy was waged in *L'Œuvre* in Paris as to the exact location on the Quai Voltaire where France was born.

Some of the questions left unanswered by those who have written about France were: (1) To whom was France first married, what was she like, how long did the marriage last, and what were the reasons for the separation and divorce? (2) When did France first meet Madame de Caillavet, what was the status of her relationship with her husband, how old were she and France, and what was the basis of the attachment between them? (3) Just how much did Madame de Caillavet contribute toward gaining literary recognition for France? (4) Just how much did she collaborate with him on his literary work, how many prefaces and articles did she write to which he signed his name?

This last question, in especial, has been a mooted one, many extravagant claims being made by Madame de Caillavet's devoted admirers—among them the amazing assertion that the best phrases in France's work were written by Madame de Caillavet. The fact that France had signed his name to at least one article written by Madame de Caillavet became public property after the death of Marcel Proust, when it was learned that the preface with which Anatole France had given his imprimatur to the first published book by Proust, *Les Plaisirs et les Jours,* was actually written by Madame de Caillavet and that France himself had never been able to make head or tail of Proust's syntax.

This news, of course, led to conjectures on the part of students of Franciana as to the precise number and nature of the texts signed by France which had really been written by Madame de Caillavet. I, for one, had been puzzled by the essay in *La Vie Litteraire* on Jules Lemaître. The first part of the essay sounds like a burlesque of France's Olympian courtesy; the middle part is a stiletto thrust made with elaborate unction; and the last part is, almost word for

ANATOLE FRANCE

word, several paragraphs from an article France had written some time previously on the subject of criticism—the very paragraphs which, used as a preface to the first published volume of *La Vie Litteraire,* contain the famous pronouncement, "A good critic is one who relates the adventures of his soul among masterpieces."

It was not humanly credible that any one, man or woman, who had been privileged to write, however much or little, of the writings signed by the most famous literary man of his generation, should be so lacking in vanity as to leave no record of the contribution. Madame de Caillavet did everything within her power to add to, rather than to detract from, the glory of Anatole France; but she was no exception in this matter. She left evidence in letters of her contributions to the work signed by France, even down to the paragraphs from her hand that are included in *Thaïs.*

These letters appeared in a source book of the first importance, without the author's ever knowing that it was a source book. It is a book so wretchedly written that the author apparently could not find a Parisian publisher to bring it out, and had to issue it at her own expense; and when it was reviewed, apparently no French critic had patience enough to wrestle with its flat and awkward French long enough to discover that it was the most valuable of all the biographical documents that have come to light about Anatole France.

The book is *Le Salon de Madame Arman de Caillavet* by Jeanne Maurice Pouquet. When I say that it is the most important biographical work that has been published on France, the statement will probably be a great surprise to Madame Pouquet, since she was so little conscious of the biographical value of her book that she quotes extracts from letters without dating them, and sets forth extremely pertinent information for a purpose which is not, in her mind, primarily concerned with France.

Madame Pouquet (who was the widow of Gaston de Caillavet), and her mother-in-law, Madame Arman de Caillavet, were on terms of affection and sympathy that are rare in such relationships. Gaston de Caillavet had become estranged from his mother over the propriety of her liaison with France; but his wife had, and retains, for his mother an admiration and affection bordering on adoration.

When Madame de Caillavet knew her end was near and was crying out, like the Cumean sybil, that she wanted only to die, she turned over to her daughter-in-law a packet of letters to be opened long after her death and disposed of as her daughter-in-law saw fit.

Her words to Madame Pouquet were that when her son, Gaston, read those letters, he might begin to understand his mother and warm his heart to her; but meanwhile she was too old and weary and heart-broken to reason with him herself.

The book, then, by Madame Pouquet is an act of *belle-filiale* devotion; but it contains source material of the first importance to biographers and practitioners of biographical criticism. Madame Pouquet clears up many problems concerning France's career, and, without intending to do so, supplies a great deal of information which has previously been lacking in relation to the man and his work.

It turns out, for example, that Madame de Caillavet wrote the article on Lemaître which France signed, and that she did it with malice prepense. She was annoyed with Lemaître for not deserting the table of Madame de Loynes for her own, when those two former friends conducted rival salons.

Shortly after the review was published, Lemaître came to Madame de Caillavet's house to dinner. France was there. Lemaître for some time avoided reference to the review, but finally his irritation overcame his reticence and he uttered some reproaches to France. France stammered explanations and excuses. "At any rate," answered Lemaître, looking alternately at France and at Madame de Caillavet, "you did not write the article. It is well written, but you didn't write it. I am very curious to learn the identity of him . . . or her . . . whose prose style and intelligence you estimate so highly that you permit that person to employ your signature." Madame de Caillavet avowed modestly that she often helped M. France when he was pressed with work.

Lemaître discontinued coming to Madame de Caillavet's house; but the review did not make a breach between France and Lemaître: Lemaître retained a profound affection and admiration for France throughout his life. Textual evidence of letters in Madame Pouquet's book further disposes of the gossip repeated (in a rather mangled manner) by the Princess Radziwill to the effect that Madame de Caillavet prevailed upon Lemaître to write the enthusiastic review of *Le Crime de Sylvestre Bonnard* which gave the first impetus to France's literary fame. Lemaître wrote the review before France had ever been introduced to Madame de Caillavet.

Indeed, it was Lemaître who first brought Anatole France to Madame de Caillavet's house. Her first impression—and one which continued for some time—of France was that he was a frightful bore and a total loss at a dinner table; nor could she, who was impatient with bores, understand why Lemaître insisted on bringing France there. At the time, France was gauche, ignorant of social usage, and his excessive timidity and shyness aggravated his affliction of stammering. She was abrupt and rude to him. In time, however, she began to take an interest in France, and finally began to drop Lemaître, who had been her particular lion, and set about remolding France into a lion nearer to her heart's desire.

France first began coming to Madame de Caillavet's soirées in 1882, almost a year after the publication of *Le Crime de Sylvestre Bonnard*. Madame de Caillavet had been married in 1868, so it is safe to assume that she was at that time about thirty or thirty-one years old. France was thirty-eight; he had been married about eight years.

Arman de Caillavet, it seems, was a fatuous sort of fellow who reverenced the aristocracy, espoused the royalist cause, spent a large part of his time trying to establish a noble ancestry for himself, and, being a vintner, had labels for his bottles engraved reading Château-Caillavet in imitation of the famous Château-Lafitte and Château-Margaux. Madame was democratic and interested in men of mind and spirit rather than in men of lineage. When her husband busied himself going through old documents in the attempt to establish his ancestry, she was happy, because "when he is occupied with that sort of foolishness, he leaves me in peace. I encourage him in it."

Meanwhile Anatole France and his wife were on even worse terms. *The Wicker-Work Woman*, it turns out, is largely autobiographical. Madame France was the grandniece of the celebrated miniaturist, Guérin; she, like Madame Bergeret in *The Wicker-Work Woman*, had an excessive pride in race, looked down upon her bourgeois and scholarly husband as both low-born and ineffectual and ruled him absolutely. When they were first married she was a ravishing beauty, with marvelous feet and hands, and very blonde tresses. The Comtesse de Martel, who knew them in those early years, relates that France, who wore a beard, and Madame France, looked more like father and daughter than man and wife. But later Madame France grew fat and lost most of her teeth. Madame de Caillavet invited the Frances to her house in the country, and relates in a letter that France was always trembling and stammering before his imperious spouse. Whatever he suggested doing, that would Madame France veto. In order to be alone with France for a few minutes Madame de Caillavet had to contrive ingenious deceptions.

Later Madame de Caillavet gave France some Genoese velvet hangings which had been left over from a house she formerly occupied, and he engaged an upholsterer to put them up on the walls of his study. Madame France was jealous over the gift and countermanded the order. A quarrel ensued. It was France's first assertion of independence. Later he returned to the house to find the dressmaker's dummy in his study again, after his having ordered that it was not to be stored there any more. He smashed it and threw it into the courtyard in the manner described in *The Wicker-Work Woman*.

In the course of another quarrel Madame France called him a word which struck at his pride more poignantly than any other conceivable—a word which France forebore to mention in *The Wicker-Work Woman* and one which does not occur, I believe, but once or twice in all his work—a highly significant fact, for it is a favorite epithet with the French. She called him a cuckold. He forthwith moved out of the house to a hotel without stopping to change from his dressing gown and skullcap and never returned. He divorced his wife in 1891.

Madame Pouquet suggests, without stating, that there was truth in the unforgivable epithet. If this is true, certain parts of *The Wicker-Woman* take on a new significance in the interpretation of the mind of Anatole France and the point of view which became characteristic of him. From the evidence in *My Friend's Book, Little Pierre,* and *The Bloom of Life,* there is every reason to believe that as a child and youth France was a delicate, timid, shy and sensitive boy, who early began to take refuge from life in books. His head was filled with romance and his heart overflowed with sentiment. He worshiped a sturdy youngster who was the reverse of himself and who was a juvenile epitome of the man of action; and iron sank into his soul when that boy did some trifling thing which revolted the youthful Anatole's sense of honor. Almost a baby, he fell in love with an adult woman whom he discovered to be deceiving her husband (this episode is implicit, not only in *My Friend's Book,* but in Brousson's record of his conversation with France), and romantic disillusion sent him more definitely to his books.

In the light of Madame Pouquet's book, we may take *The Wicker-Work Woman* as the record of the period in France's life when he was beginning to reconcile his romantic illusions with reality. It was quite late. France was in his middle thirties. He had not yet been emotionally awakened. He subscribed to the illusion, propagated by those who have troubled themselves to become articulate without being effectual, that the life of the mind and spirit insures an inner serenity impossible to those who busy themselves with the vain rewards and pleasures of a workaday world. A studious and scholarly bourgeois himself, he had married a healthy, beautiful and imperious woman who had great pride in her antecedents and never let him forget it. The more she lost respect for him, the more studiously did he apply himself to scholarship and literature.

She did not reckon that the worm would turn, especially when turned by a pretty and intelligent woman, and the episode of this turning is recorded with dispassionate fidelity in *The Wicker-Work Woman*. The whole event is majestic, primitive and human. Willa Cather, in appropriating the major phase of the story for the most effective part of *The Professor's House,* missed its entire intellectual significance and turned it into a wistful bit of pathos. Miss Cather wept and drew tears over a situation which Anatole France, a year or so after he had actually experienced it, was able to describe with almost alarming good-nature and perspicacity. He recognized himself to have been, during the period of his marriage, not a little fatuous and inept and, having later gained some sense of life, he was able to envisage the whole episode with candor and understanding, even if with a sentimental tenderness over the plight of the piddling Monsieur Bergeret, a stuffed-shirt, though an appealing stuffed-shirt, if there ever was one. He had taken another tack, and with a vengeance. Fidelity, virtue, chastity, became for him synonyms of idiocy. With his natural bourgeois sentiments, he was simply unable to fathom the situation in which he had been placed. He was an accepted lover in the de Caillavet household, several points beyond what he had been able to aspire to, either financially or socially; the husband in the triangle was not merely indifferent but benign; and he was under the thumb of a woman more imperious than his wife, since she was able to make him write (which he liked to do) instead of come to bed (which was foreign to his ascetic notions of the fitness of things).

Nothing could possibly be imagined more disturbing psychologically than the relationship between herself and him that Madame de Caillavet had engineered. He was talented, scholarly, physically ripe and a noodle. A prolonged regimen of asceticism, in the name of learning, had made him a sensualist of most attractive outward semblances; and it is evidence of Madame de Caillavet's good sense that she had picked France instead of Lemaître (who was under the domination of Madame de Loynes, ten years his senior) while she had a husband who spent his evenings going through documents relating to the antiquity of his family.

France was tractable and he had talent. Madame de Caillavet had a superb sense of occasion. She knew that with a little effort on her part and on France's he would become the foremost literary glory of their country, and that her own glory would not be forgotten in subsequent accounts of it.

She chose him as a potential literary lion of a series of soirées designed to discomfit her anti-Dreyfusard rivals; and she played her game with admirable efficiency. Before France was divorced, she engaged, and entered into contracts for, articles which France was to supply to *Le Temps*, *L'Univers Illustré* and for the *Neue Freie Presse* of Vienna. He was to write, not only a weekly article on books, about which he knew a great deal, but also, for the Austro-Hungarian weekly, an article on French politics, about which he knew only what he was able to infer from Clemenceau's articles and from what his political friends told him. Until after the success of Thaïs, he signed his articles in *L'Univers Illustré* with the pseudonym "Gerôme."

The aim of Madame Pouquet's book is to establish the platonic character of France's relationship with Madame de Caillavet, and although the circumstances would ordinarily discredit the theory, there is a tiny little to lend weight to Madame Pouquet's contention. After his divorce, France came to live at Madame de Caillavet's house; and she made him work a certain number of hours every day. He was naturally lazy, and in his letters asserts again and again that if she had not held the task-mistress' whip over his head, he would have accomplished little or nothing. She was better versed in modern languages than France and she translated articles which she thought might be of interest to him. She did most of the research work in the libraries which was necessary for his novels; and she helped him now and then to give a better twist to a phrase or to elaborate an idea which he had evolved in his meditations.

"Madame de Caillavet had only one aim in life: the furtherance of the literary work and fame of Anatole France," writes Madame Pouquet. When he was not with her, she made him report regularly on the progress of his work. She made up (I use the word advisedly, since they usually consisted of scissors and paste work of newspaper clippings, with a few paragraphs of comment) many of France's political articles in the Vienna *Neue Freie Presse;* she wrote the preface to Proust's first book, the preface to a book by Houssaye, part of the preface to a de luxe edition of *La Princesse de Clèves,* the essay on Lemaître, about a page in Thaïs, and she was responsible for certain paragraphs and phrases mentioned in the letters included in Madame Pouquet's book.

New light is thrown by Madame Pouquet on the Argentine episode. After more than twenty years of intimacy, Madame de Caillavet and France began to get on each other's nerves. Madame de Caillavet was unreasonably (or rather reasonably, if we are to take seriously France's amorous boasts in Brousson's book) jealous. They quarreled violently; terrific scenes were enacted; and they agreed finally to separate. France, who had no talent for public speaking, accepted a lecture engagement in Buenos Ayres.

On the way over, he fell in love with an Argentine actress, young enough to be his granddaughter. Whether blinded by France's glory to his age and decrepitude or whether prompted by a shrewd sense of publicity, the actress played her part in the liaison only too well. She went about publicly with France in the Argentine, and the old man was silly enough to appear with her at a reception given in his honor and to introduce her as Madame France. The women of the Argentine knew better and they stayed away from his lecture to a woman. The occasion was a fiasco. Only men were present (for the sensual Latins have a strict code of propriety): France talked badly, as usual, with much stammering and inaudible articulation. But the rumor was returned to Madame de Caillavet that the Argentines had got together to honor "Monsieur et Madame France."

On seeing these words in a newspaper clipping the poor lady fell at once into a jealous decline; she told her daughter-in-law that life was a heartless deception and that she wanted only to die; and when M. France returned, she received him with a terrific blast and carried him off on a motor trip. France, who had taken his secretary, Jean Jacques Brousson, to the Argentine, believed that it was Brousson who had made the trouble by sending Madame de Caillavet the clipping about "Monsieur et Madame France," and gave Brousson the boot.

The wound suffered by Madame de Caillavet was never healed. She died brooding on human ingratitude; and France wrote to a friend, Dr. Aunis, a letter full of eighteenth century protestations that, with the death of Madame, his own life was ended.

He lived, however, fifteen years more, and published eight more books, some of which are among his very best.

Although Anatole France was forty-four years old when he took up his post as literary critic for the *Temps*, he had only just begun the career which has made him almost universally recognized as the greatest literary figure of his time. He was then still in his imitative and formative period. He had recently published two books of first rate importance, *The Crime of Sylvestre Bonnard* and *My Friend's Book*, but his great work lay ahead of him. His collection of severely chiseled Parnassian poems written when he was an ardent disciple of Leconte de Lisle, the prefaces he re-wrote to new editions of French masterpieces, the biographical sketches, literary studies and the fiction he tried until the time he was forty, were the products of a long apprenticeship in letters before he had determined his attitude and perfected his style.

When he began work as literary critic for the *Temps*, France's manner of expressing himself had reached the point where it was pure Renan. Hitherto he had taken life and the world of ideas with the utmost seriousness. He had filled his head as a boy in his father's bookshop on the Quai Malaquais and as a youth on the staff of the Senate library, with a vast amount of reading; and his earlier literary essays had the cocksureness and the fervor we associate with young men. They also were somewhat academic. Renan taught him urbanity and gave him a taste for dilettantism. Montaigne, his second master, so thoroughly convinced him that one's personal feelings of the moment were the only data which one might record with any surety that France was enabled later to come off in flying colors after a battle with Brunetière on the essential merits of subjective and objective criticism. Renan had taught France urbanity, and Montaigne, with his reiterated "What do I know?" and with his answer to all things, "Perhaps," had taught France skepticism. After this it was not difficult for France to announce that (so far as he was concerned) criticism was the "adventures of a soul among masterpieces" and that when he was writing about Shakespeare, Racine, Goethe or Pascal, he wanted his readers to understand that he was writing about himself apropos of these masters. He disarmed his critics utterly and endeared himself to the hearts of men when he added, "The occasion at least is excellent enough."

When France began to write for the *Temps* he became immediately conscious that he was writing for a large audience with whom he had, perforce, to be extremely tactful if he was to hold his job and not alienate his readers. The urbanity he had learned from Renan and the skepticism he had acquired from Montaigne stood him in good stead. He adopted a formula which was an amalgam of Renan and Montaigne, whereby he might, if he wished, convey to the more subtle of his readers that the work of the author he was discussing was trash and the author himself an idiot, and to the more obtuse of his readers that the work was a masterpiece and the author a compendium of wisdom and virtues. Thus he satisfied everybody (or, rather, most people and not everybody, as I shall later point out), held his job and said pretty much what he wanted to say. It is a formula I should recommend to every one who writes for the public, but it also is a formula which I should be hard put to if called upon to describe. First of all, it is an attitude of false humility, an insinuating attitude of mind, a way of worming one's self into another's confidence and respect. It is the reverse of the Olympian and dictatorial attitude, although it is often Olympian and dictatorial. It is the effort to reach the hearts of men and women on the plane of a universally shared sentiment. And that plane is most advantageously and expeditiously reached if the ascent is facilitated with a little unction.

France is not without unction of the most creditable and intelligent sort. It is the quality in him which gives all his work that charm which pleases all who read him, even his adversaries and antagonists. It is a rarefied and heavenly tolerance. It is a deliberate shutting of the eyes to imperfections, ignorance and stupidity in order to contemplate the important fact that we are all really ignorant human beings, here for a brief while, consumed more or less with curiosity and fated to die before we have really learned anything.

That is the sort of mind that makes friends, but it is not the sort of mind which succeeds in more than being amiable in the world. Progress, or, rather, that change we designate as progress, is achieved by fanatics. France, for all his urbanity and dilettantism, contains something deeply imbedded in him which is fanatical. It is a form of idealism which persists in spite of his inveterate mockery, his cynicism and his clear-eyed view of reality. He would like to make the world a better place to live in, even if it means to readopt some of the ideals which have been outlived. For himself he has a special fancy for the eighteenth century, and prefers it to the nineteenth, in which he takes it as a misfortune that he has had to live. This is a romantic sentimentalism on his part which we find hard to reconcile with his public career as a Socialist and Drey-fusard, an anti-royalist and anti-clerical; for the eighteenth century was the century when the principles of equality and democracy were most in abeyance and when culture was the privilege and the exercise of the very few at the expense of the toil of the many.

No one, so far as I know, has traced with proper patience and application the development of France as a writer. This is all the more curious in that France has himself exposed, even talked of, that development with entire candor. Most writers who have chosen France as a subject have remarked on his indebtedness to Renan and Montaigne—a very obvious indebtedness which France has been scrupulously paying off with interest by beautiful tributes to these masters.

What I have in mind especially is his indebtedness to Heine. I have a suspicion that his acquaintance with Heine began during or after the period of his tenancy on the *Temps,* and from his acquaintance with Heine, I believe, date his great satirical books, *Penguin Island, The Queen Pedauque, The Revolt of the Angels* and the books in the series of *Histoire Contemporaine.* I shall tell you why I think so. In the first place, he has acknowledged in his later work a very obvious indebtedness to Heine, the most Aristo-phanic of the spirits of the nineteenth century, the most cultivated, sensitive and sardonic of all German writers. Any one reading the fourth volume of *On Life and Letters* will realize that France, after four years, had run the formula he had acquired from Renan into the ground; that compromise and urbane complaisancy had become a stereotype with him, and that without new mental fertilization he was in danger of becoming a rubber stamp, a very beautiful, grace-ful, impressive rubber stamp, but a rubber stamp none the less. It was agreeable to his readers and to himself to begin by asserting that some one was a "good," "pious," "worthy," "unselfish" soul and then proceed obliquely to make him out neither good nor pious, neither worthy nor unselfish; indeed, to mock at him and still em-brace him with a human sympathy and with a benign implication that we are all ignoramuses, and that, therefore, the superior men stand essentially on the same low plane as the inferior men. But after France had been nearly four years at it it began to get tedious. You know, too far in advance, what to expect. It is all too much a reiterated, well-bred monotone. The pungent thoughts, the shrewd comments, the delightful observations have begun to come out as subordinate and casual reflections, almost surreptitiously, as if they were the bastard children of respectable platitudes. The pleasure to be had from the fourth volume of *On Life and Letters* is only to be had when France forgets that he must be amiable and considerate in the presence of a very mixed audience. It still remains the sort of thing which no other critic has ever approached in sweetness of temper, depth of information, breadth of cultivation and serenity of mind, but it shows the imprint of a formula which, persisted in, would have ruined France for further creative effort.

Heine, I feel sure, set him off on another track. He did not lose what Renan and Montaigne had taught him, and he never deserted the clarity, simplicity, directness and ironic crystallization of a thought which he had learned from Renan, and his fidelity to Montaigne never let him forget that his own personality in all its trivial and profound aspects, all its activities and emotions, is the only proper medium through which to judge of life itself. However, I am sure that Heine fanned the dying embers of fanaticism in him, and called him to the service of satire and critical irony. A Heinesque bitterness and acid intolerance, though urbane and sweetened, comes into the two books which are to follow that *Thaïs* which was written under the Flaubertian influence, much as if Renan and Montaigne had collaborated upon another *Temptation of St. Anthony*. I refer to *The Queen Pedauque* and *The Opinions of M. Jérôme Coignard*.

Meanwhile, it is instructive to us who write for the papers to consider the career of Anatole France as literary reviewer for a Paris newspaper. He was the most tactful, the most considerate, the best informed, the gentlest, the best endowed man who has ever held such a job. And yet he had his difficulties. He sacrificed much to expediency, he deliberately adopted a tone of humility, he rarely criticized adversely or distributed blame, he wrote for the most part about books he had a special liking for, and he took care not to touch upon topics where his opinion might start a controversy. And yet he was continually in hot water. The sincerity of his praise concerning no man is so convincing as that of his praise of Calmann-Levy, the editor of the *Temps,* who hired him to write these pieces, and who retained him as critic through all the envious and dissatisfied clamoring for his hide.

None of us now reading the piece he wrote for the *Temps* about Leconte de Lisle on the occasion of that poet's election to the Academy would be struck by anything except the magnificent humor and the critical justness of it. We should not feel that Leconte de Lisle had been maligned or belittled, but that a pompous and a limited poet who was very popular at the time had been fairly estimated and had been tendered much more consideration than we should now feel was necessary. It was possibly in bad taste (as people without any taste whatever employ that term) and it was certainly irreverent; but it was also one of the most delicious bits of characterization that it has ever been my pleasure to read. France knew his man intimately; indeed he had entertained a certain reverence for him and had been a disciple of his in his youth, and this article was written with a heavy trace of that affectionate sentiment we feel toward people we have come to know and love very well without failing to take cognizance of their weaknesses. But, none the less, that article caused France and his employer considerable annoyance. It evoked a public retort and all sorts of subscribers in the *Temps* wrote in to tell the editor that if he didn't get rid of that smart aleck France they would cancel their subscriptions to the paper. Even financial and political considerations were brought to bear, but M. Calmann-Levy was wise enough as a business man and a publisher to know that he would gain rather than lose by retaining a writer who was read with so much attention.

Cultivate his public as he might with good-humored tolerance, deference and smiling courtesy, France did not escape censure. M. Déscaves, piqued by the fact that France had failed to consider his work worthy of a week's article, protested that France gave no consideration whatever as a literary critic to the work of contemporaries, and that in the same week that Huysmans' *La-bas* was published France elected to discuss the writings of a man long dead. Déscaves lied, for France was in the habit of discussing the work of contemporaries whose work interested him. He wrote about and criticized the novels of Paul Bourget, Guy de Maupassant, Gyp, Maurice Barrès, the Goncourt brothers and Pierre Loti. On the occasion of new editions of their work he wrote about Flaubert, Balzac, Hugo, Gautier, Verlaine. He used the new works of serious scholarship for points of departure in beautiful and pertinent speculations of his own. And he did not omit to give his analyses and opinions concerning the work of the Symbolists whose poetic aims were far removed from what his own had been—Charles Le Goffic, Jean Moréas, the popular balladists and the cabaret versifiers. He left Déscaves and his ephemera to the other reviewers, and wisely ordained that Déscaves should survive in men's memory largely by virtue of his having protested against Anatole France. This is a negative sort of immortality, like that of being registered under the Bertillon system, but M. France, remembering that Ephialtes, who traitorously led the Persians over the secret approach to Athens, and that ignoble person who set fire to the library of Alexandria, would not be insensitive to the irony of it.

Among France's deficiencies as a critic must be counted his indifference to and his patronizing attitude toward the Symbolists. This led him to a complete dismissal, except for a review involving the medieval Latinists, of Remy de Gourmont, the only writer of France's time in France whom France might have counted among his intellectual peers. They were both Epicureans and skeptics and possibly this may account for their attitude toward each other (for, after all, they were human): still, in France's elaborately deferential preface to the second volume of *On Life and Letters,* I divine, I believe, a man who is a little too sure of his popular support and who feels that he can be at once delightful and arrogant without seeming to be so. It was rather petty of him deliberately (as I believe) to misspell Rimbaud's name and to refer to him with an Olympian condescension as Raimbault; to align Rimbaud and Ghil (whose name he also misspelled), and then to make out that both Ghil and Rimbaud (and by inference all their followers, including Verlaine and Moréas) were victims of a physical and mental malady of interest to pathologists, and that, by inference, their work was of no interest to his readers; these pettinesses and his ignoring of Gourmont are the only ones I can discover wherein France used his position to advantages which were personal or which appear to be so. Such a record is exceedingly rare, and if you will read Anatole France you will see how rare it is, for no one so accurately and so honestly as he has endeavored to expose the motives of other men with so much understanding of good humor and sympathy.

ANATOLE FRANCE, taking as his model Ernest Renan's *Souvenirs d'enfance et de jeunesse,* wrote *Le Livre de mon ami* ("My Friend's Book") in 1885; fourteen years later he wrote *Pierre Nozière,* and thirty-three years later he wrote *Le Petit Pierre.* In these beautiful and tender books he recalled his childhood so vividly and with such feeling that they will remain always, I think, the books by France which will find favor with every one who reads them. One may lack a sense of humor and have no taste for irony and so find *Penguin Island* beyond one's capacity for enjoyment; one may find *The Gods*

Are Athirst too destructive to one's illusions; one may find (like the College of Cardinals) that *La Vie de Jeanne d'Arc* is antipathetic to one's religious beliefs; one may be shocked by *La Rôtisserie de la Reine Pedauque* ("At the Sign of the Queen Pedauque") or by *Les Contes de Jacques Tournebroche* ("The Merry Tales of Jacques Tournebroche") ; one may think Anatole France a satyr, a sensualist and a skeptic with quite horrid views about the justice of the social order; and yet with any or all of these handicaps, one who reads *My Friend's Book,* and *Pierre Nozière* and *Little Pierre* must, inevitably, fall happy victim to France's charm as a writer.

From those books and others, one gathers these facts:

The man who is known as Anatole France was born and baptized Jacques Anatole François Thibault. In Paris they say that a man who should choose Anatole as a first name when he might have chosen Jacques and who called himself France was courageously defying all the gods of convention there may be; for "Anatole" in Parisian slang is synonymous with "booby" and "France," of course, is what the nation calls itself: in our country it would be like taking as a pen-name Hiram America. But M. Thibault was from Anjou and there the name François is always abbreviated to France. "Old France," as his friends called him, kept a bookshop at Number 9 Quai Voltaire and in the flat above this bookshop Anatole France was born on April 16, 1844. From the upper stories of this house one could look out, through the plane trees on the quai, across the Seine at the Louvre, almost directly opposite, and, toward the north, see Notre Dame. Down the street a way was the Mazarin palace, first home of the Academie Française. Back of "Old France's" bookshop and to the northeast a bit were the many buildings of the Sorbonne; not far away was the Odéon and the Faubourg Saint-Germain, the Luxembourg Gardens and the Boulevard Saint Michel. Anatole France, then, was born in the heart of Paris.

"Old France" was a typical bookseller; he preferred to read books rather than to sell them; and, royalist Catholic that he was, he had stout opinions about the sad state of human affairs in which he found himself, and he made his shop a rendezvous of disgruntled fogies who did not value very highly the opinions of those who championed the revolution and the republic. Young Anatole used to listen (with later profit) to these fiery denunciations of the democratic régime.

Young Anatole was entered at the Jesuit college, Stanislas. He was a timid and rather backward child, humbly full of admiration for those of his classmates who were energetic, physically powerful, and clever. As for himself he read incessantly, day-dreamed about Cleopatra and (also) about the saints: he aspired to write a history of the world in forty volumes.

He matured slowly. He was indolent. His father wished him to prepare for a profession, but there was no lucrative profession he had a taste for; so his father let him idle about the shop, waiting on customers, reading books, scribbling imitations of the books he had read and letting his youth slip away. Anatole helped his father prepare catalogues, bibliographical notes and other works of research; he did some publishers' hack work; and he wrote some poems as an ardent Parnassian.

He lived at home and made little effort to support himself until he was thirty years old, when he got a job in the Senate Library. He resigned after a disagreement recounted below. After that he earned some money by writing prefaces to popular editions of the classics— prefaces now included in the collection called *The Latin Genius.* Then he married and lived with his wife for eight years. He published some poems and stories and definitely set out to write a book which might win the notice of the French Academy. This book was *The Crime of Sylvestre Bonnard.* It was copied after *The Attic Philosopher* and the sentimental novels of Georges Ohnet. "It is the most insipid and tedious of all my books," France told his secretary, J. J. Brousson. "I wrote it to win a prize of the Academy." It actually got him elected a member of the Academy. Jules Lemaître launched the novel with an enthusiastic review; the popular demand for it was, and is, inexhaustible.

One night Anatole France and Jules Lemaître returned to France's home, France found the dressmaker's dummy again stored in his study in contemptuous defiance of his wishes, and, in a rage, threw the thing out of the window into the courtyard. After the quarrel that followed, he moved out of the house at once, never to see his wife again.

He met Mme. de Caillavet, in the manner described above and became, in time, not only her accredited lover but a resident in her house, an arrangement to which M. de Caillavet did not seem to object at all. Mme. de Caillavet had a salon—and all French successes used to be hatched in the salons of Paris. Mme. de Caillavet remade France socially and kept him at work. The conventions were observed, however. The arrangement was common knowledge; and yet, on the evenings when Mme. de Caillavet had people in to dinner and wanted Anatole France to roar as a lion, poor France had to dress, descend by the back stairs, and enter the front door of his only home in the guise of a tardy guest.

Jean Jacques Brousson, who became France's secretary at the time France was doing the research for his *Joan of Arc* and remained with him in that capacity until the episode of the lecture trip to South America, has given us several glimpses of that interesting household in his book of France's intimate life and conversations, *Anatole France en pantoufles,* which has been translated into English by John Pollock under the title, *Anatole France Himself.* One of the best is this:

Three o'clock strikes.
"Enough of play," says Madame. "Come to work!"
She goes up to the second floor. Anatole France, behind her, mounts without enthusiasm. He looks like a boy being taken by his nurse to school.

Between the linen cupboard and Madame's bedroom is a huge room, well-lit and with but little furniture.

From the ceiling is suspended a little boat, the model of a yacht. It recalls the votive offerings that sailors hang after a storm from the vaulted roofs of chapels. Two windows. No paper on the walls, but papers everywhere else. On the mantelpiece lie books and note-books and proofs, and proofs and note-books and books lie pell-mell on the carpet. It is June, but the fire is lit and the room is like a hothouse. Madame seats herself at a little school-desk between the fireplace and the wall, opposite the window.

On her desk are a bunch of flowers, a bag of chocolates, and a box of sweets. She and her sulky little dog, with its red morocco collar and gold bell, have ensconced themselves in a befringed and betasselled low Louis Philippe armchair.

Anatole France strolls nonchalantly to his writing-table on the other side of the fireplace in the window corner. He instals himself in a kind of Gothic throne covered with a maze of heraldic devices. On the table, which is in the same Gothic style that hails from the Faubourg St. Antoine or the chapel of Dreux, is a medley of objects. Here is a reproduction by some electric process of the silver goblet found at Bosco Reale with a ring of dancing cupids and skeletons. There are seals, match-boxes, boxes of pens, and of throat lozenges; there again, a Breton doll, a ghastly crystal inkpot, the sort of penwiper you might win in a raffle embroidered with beads and flowers, and here a crystal paper-knife and a crystal paper-weight, all complete, a schoolboy's leather pen-box with the Eiffel Tower and a captive balloon painted on it, medals, and two or three pairs of scissors and a huge pot of gum, and an astonishing metal penholder with the monogram A. F. on it surrounded by a sprig of ivy, just like the presents people give to children being confirmed. Behind his head is a set of pine book-shelves. On one, within reach of his hand, are Littré, Godefroy, Darmesteter and the *Grande Encyclopédie.* Above is a complete set of Renan. Below is a row of folio volumes— Lacurne de Sainte-Palaye, Moreri, and so on. Behind the others, red in the

face and breathing hard, comes Monsieur. His writing-table is in front of
Anatole France's, at the other end of the room, near the other window.
Between the windows is another set of shelves of white wood, full of books.
The writing-table is of the American variety. Monsieur sits down heavily on
a cane-bottomed armchair with an indiarubber cushion in it.

Madame is eating a sweet. She throws one to Anatole France, who
catches it in the air. Monsieur grumbles. He doesn't like being left out.

France. "In this world one must know how to cry. There is a Spanish
proverb that says: 'The babe that doesn't cry gets no milk.' You cried and
Madame offers you the milk of lovingkindness."

Monsieur. "Much I care for your rubbishy Spanish proverbs." He
takes the telephone. "The market is appallingly weak."

Madame (lisping with the sweet in her mouth). "How are Rio Rintos?"

Monsieur. "Down. Still falling."

Madame. "You bought, I suppose?"

Monsieur. "Of course."

France (echoing). "Of course."

The irreverent spirit of the playboy persisted in France up
until his very last years. He told Brousson that the only advantage
in having fame was that it permitted one to do what one likes; that
he being a member of the Academy and a writer of renown could
wear in season and out his old gray felt hat and attend the opera
wearing bedroom slippers if he wished; and that it also gave him a
certain standing with the police force.

After the Dreyfus affair, in which France joined hands with
Zola and took the stump as a Dreyfusard, France never attended
the meetings of the Academy because the Academy rejected the
candidacy of Zola. Previously he attended the meetings largely to
have fun with the serious graybeards. One day discussion of the
definition and uses of the word "ring" came up for the dictionary
the academy was compiling. Discussion at length was about to close.
The oldest and most dignified member was half asleep. France
jogged his elbow and whispered in his ear: "They have forgotten
Hans Carvel's ring." Not knowing what he was saying the old man
arose from his seat, still half asleep and cried out: "You have forgotten Hans Carvel's ring!" The academy was aghast and horrified:
Hans Carvel's ring refers to a lewd story in Rabelais.

With the publication of *The Opinions of M. Jérôme Coignard,*
wherein France comments upon French politics and politicians of
the period and gives to the abbé's utterances a universality, France
really struck his stride. He was to continue this through *The Elm
Tree on the Mall, The Wicker-Work Woman, The Amethyst Ring,*
and *M. Bergeret in Paris,* putting his comments this time into the

mouth of M. Bergeret, member of the Institute. He turned aside to write *Crainquebille,* the pitiful story of the miserably poor, which was an attack upon the inequalities of the law. His sympathies were always with the outcasts of society. He had spoken of the laws "which forbid the rich as well as the poor to sleep under bridges, beg or steal."

He also tried again in *Histoire comique* to compete with Paul Bourget in a novel of Parisian society. And he wrote a great number of charming short stories, of which the most famous is that masterpiece of irony, *The Procurator of Judea,* wherein Pontius Pilate in his old age cannot recall the episode of Jesus and the crucifixion— to him it was only one of many brushes with the cantankerous Jews he had had as Roman governor of the province of Judea. His masterpiece, however, and the work most characteristic of his thought, his humor, his art, is *Penguin Island,* published in 1908. Ranking high in the France canon are *The Gods Are Athirst,* a novel of the French Revolution wherein he expresses his disillusion that social justice may be established by carnage, and *The Revolt of the Angels,* an ironic comedy on revolutions.

France was given the Nobel Prize in literature. He gained world renown. Before his death, however, the inevitable reaction set in against him who had been celebrated so long and so continuously. He is certainly among the immortals of literature, but it will probably be a few years yet before a new generation arises to find in his work that pleasure which was almost universally enjoyed by readers before the World War.

France died at his country home, La Béchellerie, near Tours, on October 12, 1924, calling in his last delirium several times for his mother. Living with him at the time was his grandson, Lucien Psichari, son of his daughter Clothilde. Lucien's father had been killed in the war and his mother had died in 1919.

DURING the last years of his life Anatole France frequently complained that he had lived too long; and certainly the somatic death of no great man was ever awaited with a more extraordinary exhibition of impatience on the part of those who expected to profit in one way or another by his demise.

The very reluctance of France's physique to comply with his expressed wish to give up the ghost caused considerable inconvenience to some of the more expeditious among those who were chafing at his persistence. The old man's health rallied once during the two months of his mortal illness and it seemed, for a time, that he might remain alive indefinitely; whereupon Cres et Cie. had to stop the presses which were already grinding off copies of *Anatole France en Pantoufles,* by Brousson, who had given his master his word that he would withhold the book until after France's death.

And a false report from Tours announced France's death a day before it actually took place; whereupon the impetuous young *Surréalists* who had prepared the malignant pamphlet, *Un Cadavre,* attacking France, had to scurry around Paris to suspend its sale when more reliable news came that France was still conscious.

Once the illustrious old fellow had circumvented the plans of those who showed too great an urgency in wanting him to shuffle off. He married his faithful housekeeper, who had ministered to him since the deaths of the tyrant Josephine and Mme. de Caillavet, and thus invested her with the major control of his estate. The master of that estate is now the former butler to Mme. de Caillavet, who had known France's widow when they were both servants in the same household. Thus destiny has contrived to make it possible for Anatole France, in death, to realize more concretely his dreams of communism and democracy than he found occasion to realize in life.

WHEN France was first seized with his fatal illness a great many persons were stirred to a feverish activity. Besides the usual newspaper obituaries and tributes, prepared long in advance, no less than twenty signed magazine and revue articles were able to appear in Paris within a week after his burial. Five books of reminiscences and reports of France's informal talks were announced for publication. Politicians, to whose ideas and activities he had been hostile, seized the opportunity to profit by doing honor to the celebrated man, and before he had breathed his last, had laid plans for an elaborate funeral procession. André Breton, Philippe Soupault, and Drieu de la Rochelle arranged for the printing of *Un Cadavre* and sat up nights biting their pen nibs in search of brilliant phrases of contempt to lay upon the grave of the foremost European man of letters.

Dr. Schott, an erudite and eccentric San Francisco physician, left for Paris to be on time for the funeral. A cranial specialist stood by waiting with saw and scalpel to get inside of the dying man's skull and thus win a little kudos by announcing his findings after examining the convolutions of France's brain. Dressmakers sent bordered cards to Mme. France at La Béchellerie, and florists held consultations with the concièrge of the Villa Saïd. And a priest sat in the reception room of the early seventeenth century house near Tours hoping vainly to hear a summons to France's bedside to hear his confession, see the sign of repentance and apply the blessed sacrament to get the dying atheist into heaven under the auspices of Mother Church.

At last the white-edged black canopy with the great white "F" at its center was stretched from the roof eaves to the ground at the house in the Villa Saïd. Valets to the members of the Academy laid out their full-dress clothes. *Un Cadavre* appeared on the kiosks. The Minister of Public Instruction put the finishing touches to his speech, perhaps recalling with a feeling of uneasiness that the man whom he was to eulogize had said the Minister of Public Instruction was incapable of writing or speaking literate French. The magnificent and preposterous cortège filed down the Champs Elysées, putting money into the pockets of funeral contractors who were on the right terms with the Commissioners, and the body lay in state under the Arc de Triomphe de l'Étoile.

Time came when the populace had filed past the dead visage of the bearded old man, the Minister of Public Instruction was asking his friends if the speech came off all right, the funeral contractors were celebrating their business coup in a bistro, and indignant journalists were indicting editorials expressing horror at the bad taste of the *Surréalistes*. The eccentric Californian stood in the shadows while tipsy Gauls juggled the coffin banteringly and lowered it into the grave by the light of two lanterns held by the sacristan. A short parley and Dr. Schott was able to carry away as a souvenir the two lanterns that had lighted Anatole France's way into the realm of Persephone.

PROUST *THE INVALID*

*

WHEN Anatole France had grown old, famous and fatigued, he was continually besieged by young authors to launch their first books for them with a preface which would draw the attention of the critics to work that might otherwise go unnoticed. Courteous and amiable as he was, it was impossible for him to read all these manuscripts or books in proof and comply with the requests. Sometimes he would refuse altogether, pleading illness or pressure of his own work; other times, however, obligations of friendship imposed upon him the duty of allowing his name to be used in sponsoring the fledgling stuff of some young poet or dilettante in prose in whose home he had been entertained or who was an adornment of Madame de Caillavet's salon.

Marcel Proust was a young man of fashion, with a peculiar neurotic brilliance and a sedulous prococity in the etiquette of the drawing-room, who, though half Jew and the son of a bourgeois doctor, had, through charm and persistence and tact, got himself into the most exclusive circles of fashionable and literary Parisian society. He had found favor in the eyes of Madame de Caillavet by his feline strangeness, by the way in which he would reward people with bushels of flowers for the slightest favor, by the way he would arrange himself on a cushion at her feet and look up at her with glowing eyes of attention and admiration, and by the way he would be infinitely exact in all the attentions and courtesies due her guests. Moreover, Anatole France had dined at least once at the Proust flat in the boulevard Haussmann on the invitation of young Marcel—no doubt reluctantly and as a result of persistent nagging on the part of Madame de Caillavet. And when he had gone there he had been mystified: young Proust had sent away his indulgent family, brought into his service the best caterer in Paris and had served in the tasteless middle-class dining room of the Prousts a magnificent dinner, perfectly ordered, prepared and served—to some of the most notable persons in Paris, including the Comtesse de Noailles, Henri de Régnier, the Princesse Mathilde, the Baronne Alphonse de Rothschild, the Comte Robert de Montesquiou and a sprinkling of lesser lights of the arts and fashion.

One day Madame de Caillavet brought to France's attention a small collection of miscellaneous sketches, portraits, and articles which Marcel Proust had contributed to magazines and which France's own publisher, Calmann-Lévy, was about to bring out under the title, *Les Plaisirs et les jours*. The style was precious, finicky, strained; the subjects uninteresting to France. No doubt there was some urging on the part of Madame de Caillavet and some protests on the part of France, at the conclusion of which he told her to write the preface herself as she had done several times before on such occasions (she was fairly skillful in imitating France's phraseology), to tell him what the book was like, and he would work in a characteristic phrase or two of his own and sign it. Madame de Caillavet wrote a preface and submitted it to France.

The one phrase definitely identifiable as Anatole France's in that preface to *Les Plaisirs et les jours*, although the whole has France's unctuous charm and cadence without quite having France's spirit, is: "In him there is something of a depraved Bernardin de Saint-Pierre and an ingenuous Petronius."

Without ever being able to read Proust, in Proust's early over-refined stage or in Proust's later highly involved syntax (so foreign to France's clarity and simplicity), France nevertheless, by a brilliant intuition, hit precisely upon the most accurate and enlightening characterization of Proust as a writer. Proust was a depraved romancer with a heart not unlike that of the author of *Paul and Virginia* and he was a wondering, wistful and inquisitive satirist and historian of the upper levels of a decadent French society whose mind and purpose was not unlike that of the author of the *Satyricon*.

In the posthumous final volume of *The Remembrance of Things Past,* Marcel Proust tells us that after he had become superficially acquainted with Parisian society it dawned upon him that here was a unique opportunity afforded him to write something which would be a sort of combination of the *Memoires* of Saint-Simon and of the

Arabian Nights. Every class of French society, down to the dregs depicted by Zola and Carco had been treated in fiction, except that strange, sick society of curious beings, descendants of the nobles of France, who inhabited the Faubourg Saint-Germain and to whom the only realities and values left in life were in the childish game of excluding people from their houses and their acquaintance. It was a gossipy, idle, eccentric, pitiable set, thrown in so much upon themselves that they had developed strange complexities, vices and methods of torturing one another and an elaborate *cheveaux-de-frise* of codes, customs and manners as a protection from the outer world and to create for themselves an illusion of the importance of living.

This society, so near extinction, so sick that its only escape from itself was to mingle and merge with the stupider servants and the lowest criminals (the only classes with whom they had anything in common) had had no historian, no analyst, because they were one and all devoid of talent or intellectual qualities and even of education. "I had been among society folk enough to know," writes Proust, "that they, not the electrical workers, are the real illiterates." The very highest, most exclusive of all families, the Courvoisiers, were so completely devoid of talent and sensibility themselves, that they were positively shocked to hear that one of their few intimates had entertained some one described as "intelligent," for to a Courvoisier it was like boasting that one had had a murderer in to dinner. The Guermantes moved among their priceless collection of Monets and Manets, which conveyed no esthetic meaning to them; Madame de Villeparisis had known Balzac and Hugo and all that these two writers meant to her was that Hugo's manners were bad and Balzac had a red handkerchief; and the most "intellectual" of these descendants of nobles declared she would not permit a certain young woman to enter her doors because "she recites Aristotle. I can't permit such things in my house." (The young woman, as a matter of fact, was given to reciting passages from a French translation of Aristophanes.)

Proust had come to know these people better than any other class; they had fascinated him; he had studied them closely, curious to learn every detail about them, their individual phrases and clichés, their mannerisms, their ways of betraying themselves, their temperaments, their vanities, their egotism, their pleasures, their vices, the morbid sadness of their unhappy lives—and he resolved to be their portrayer, historian, analyst, satirist and moralist. He seemed to feel instinctively that this society was to be swept away, destroyed: the images of Pompeii, Sodom and Gomorrah, the first destroyed by the elements, the other two by the wrath of God, continually presented themselves to his mind, and he felt that a picture, a record of an analogous modern society was worth preserving. "The frivolous life of an epoch after ten centuries have passed over it is worthy of the most scholarly research," he once wrote.

Meanwhile, through nearly twenty years, he had not only made that society part of himself, the source of his pleasure and stimulation and the satisfaction of his curiosity, but had loved and suffered in it. He had felt and watched, like an acute and sensitive scientist, the emotions of this society, his own as well as theirs; he had studied the manifestations of desire (there is some justice in the criticism that Proust himself never experienced love); and he had explored, with the intensity of a neurasthenic, the fluidity and relativity of time, the inconsistencies and unpredictability of facets of personality, the influence of memory upon one's conscience and actions. And so, "when it comes to studying the laws of character, one can do this quite as well on a frivolous as on a serious subject, just as a prosecutor can study the laws of anatomy precisely as well on the body of an imbecile as on that of a man of talent, for the great moral laws, like those governing the circulation of the blood or renal elimination, vary but little with the intellectual worth of the individual."

In order to describe what one has known and seen and felt and loved, he said, it is necessary to withdraw from it, and then, having concentrated upon the plan of the work one has contemplated, to let memory, and the associations of memory, flow freely in an imaginary reconstruction. "I had already come to the conclusion," he said, "that we are not at all free in the presence of the work of art to be created, that we do not do it as we ourselves please, but that it existed prior to us and that we should seek to discover it as we would a natural law because it is both necessary and hidden." He did not manufacture, or follow a formula, least of all did he attempt to produce an intellectual work. He did not work from theory: "From this comes the vulgar temptation for the writer to produce intellectual works. A grave lack of feeling! A book in which there are theories is like an article from which the price mark has not been removed." He wrote from the depths of both his consciousness and subconsciousness, true to the record of his knowledge and experience.

To do this Proust had almost to invent a new language and a new syntax. Since the days of Voltaire and Racine the logic and form of the French language had become perfected and fixed. It had become a marvelous medium of clarity, simplicity, lucidity and urbanity; but it was made up almost entirely of clichés. Certain fixed rules had been established for saying certain things, to depart from which was not to write good French. From Montaigne, through Renan, to Anatole France the French language, in the great tradition, had reached its absolute limits in its purest expression of the characteristic of French thought, which is its logic. All that could be said had been said in that classic medium. But with the dawn of the twentieth century—and more apparently with the beginning of the World War—something new had come into the world, new ideas, new investigations, new interests, new regions of the mind and soul to be explored; and this called for a new syntax in Proust, for he had something unique to say.

He was not exercising a too conscious control over what came out of the reservoir of his feelings, judgments and impressions, a control always regarded by the French as necessary to preserve the classic purity of the language. He got away from the literary formula. He often said he would have preferred to write in German, as a language more resourceful than French, or failing German, to write in English, which he also considered more flexible, suggestive and capable of expressing shades of meaning impossible in French. He therefore wrote a French more like German in its syntax than like classical French, often placing the verb at the very end of an extremely long sentence, as being the logical place for it for the development and emphasis of what he was saying, and stringing out an idea to prodigious sentence lengths with subordinate clauses, parentheses, qualifying phrases and explanatory hesitancies (a practice frequently found in English literature but almost never in French literature).

THE hero of *Remembrance of Things Past* is a monster and a madman; and he is the symbol, as well as the most dazzling and horrifying figure, of the decadent society he represents. He is a man sick with all the maladies of his class and station. He has an insane pride of race (the chief topic of conversation among the people of the society Proust depicts is family and family connections); he has a paranoiac sense of importance; he is at once the epitome of politeness and extremely brutal in his arrogance and rudeness. He has a certain native intelligence and a cleverness plus an unimpeachable nobility of ancestry which permits him to rule, like so many vassals, the curious automatons of his clan; and he is a wretched man, suffering from an incurable malady of perversion, the victim of a thousand fears and apprehensions that he will be found out, sensitive to the slightest, most careless phrase or glance which suggests to him that he is despised and loathed; he is the pitiful, conscious victim of the scum of Paris who for money pander to his vices and humor his pleas for affection by pretense, loathing him all the time.

It is a fantastic and enthralling world, peopled by strange, fascinating, amusing and monstrous people that Marcel Proust has introduced to us. It is, indeed, a new *Arabian Nights,* in which the characters are not Orientals but descendants of those idle and vicious nobles of the Court of Louis XIV, who are described with malice, wit, zest and truthfulness in the *Memoires* of Saint-Simon and with such vigor and frankness and healthy repugnance in the letters of Elizabeth-Charlotte of Bavaria, Princess Palatine, who was the wife of the brother of Louis XIV. (A selection of these letters has been made and translated by Gertrude Scott Stevenson under the title *Letters of Madame.*) As sheer entertainment, once the reader has begun to follow the careers of Swann and Odette, the narrator and Albertine, the Guermantes, Madame de Villeparisis, the Verdurins and Charlus, there is probably no more absorbing reading in literature. One may be repulsed somewhat by Proust's ideas of love and even wearied by minute details he gives of the hysterical manifestations of attraction, repulsion and jealousy and yet derive a healthy enjoyment from the neurotic adventures of Proust's characters. One may or may not derive from Proust that vivid sense of the importance of gesture, manner, inflection, choice of words, which he meant to give his readers and by which, with his hypersensitive nervous organization, he seemed to know what was going on in a person's mind behind the spoken words or even before they were spoken. One may find in Proust few of those metaphysical perceptions, intuitional profundities and resoundings of the depths of the subconscious which some critics claim to find in him; but once one has a grasp of the fact that Proust has a magnificent and human story to tell, one will find him incomparable.

I have, by the way, a suggestion for those who have never read Proust. In the first place, even if one reads French easily, it is best not to read him in the original, but in the superb transfusion into English made of the first six parts of *Remembrance of Things Past* by the late C. K. Scott-Moncrieff. In Scott-Moncrieff's translation Proust reads better than he does in French, as Proust himself realized. A bilingual French man of letters, familiar with English through studies at Oxford and Harvard, told me that it may be necessary to re-translate Proust from Scott-Moncrieff's English version back into French to secure for Proust the audience which the intrinsic *entertainment* value of his work possesses. After the death of Scott-Moncrieff, the final volume of the long work, entitled in English, *The Past Recaptured*, was attempted by Stephen Hudson, and that is the version published in England. It is extremely bad. The American publishers, however, intrusted the translation to Frederick Blossom with very happy results. It is more literal, closer to the text than is Scott-Moncrieff; Dr. Blossom even reproduces Proust's slips of grammar and occasional carelessness in leaving out words; and, while it is not a recreation of Proust into an English masterpiece like Scott-Moncrieff's, it is an excellent translation. My suggestion to the person who has never read Proust or who has tried to read him and found him difficult, is to begin with the last volume, the one translated by Blossom. There Proust tells entertainingly and at length just what he set out to do; he tells in straight narrative form about his early life, how he became interested in aristocratic society, how he got into it, how he met Charlus, how he felt there was a book in him that he must write, how he got the idea for his long novel, what problems he set for himself, how he analyzed the truth of other writers in relation to himself and resolved to improve upon the "reality" of these writers, how he withdrew from society on account of illness and how that illness enabled him to carry out his designs—how, indeed, toward the last he knew he was soon to die and how his only anxiety was that he should complete his work before he breathed his last.

Also in that volume, Proust brings all of the threads of his narrative together, though not precisely as he promised to do: for it was part of his art and intuition, as he explained, that life is fluid and unpredictable, that characters change through events and accident, and that until the creations of his imagination died or he died, they would have an unpredictable life. But in this book, we do see the principal characters of the first volumes grown old, some of them hideous, all of them victims of frustrations, accidents or lusts; those most arrogant and sure of themselves in the first volume most pitiably brought to grief in the last; those too put-upon in the first part, ostracized or condemned, like Odette and the new Duchesse de Guermantes, later in triumph, all things changed and changing, and an ineffable sadness over it all. Terror and tragedy develop in this satire; and there is a nightmarish description of the depths of degradation to which Charlus descends. Having read this final volume, one can go back to the first volumes, *skip the first thirty or fifty pages* and take up the story of the remembered childhood of Marcel Proust, a delicate and affectionate boy who worshiped his mother, was pampered by her; who was misunderstood by a practical father who nevertheless indulged him in his whims; who suffered from asthmatic attacks which made him an invalid all his life; who conquered society by will-power, grace and charm; who studied that society like an entomologist and who went to bed in a cork-lined room, wrote a masterpiece—and died.

Marcel Proust was born in Paris on July 10, 1871, the son of a Catholic physician, who became commissioner of health for the city of Paris, and of a Jewish mother of some beauty, sensibility and charm. From Proust's very earliest remembrance there existed an affectionate tenderness between mother and son, so great that even as a growing boy he could not go to sleep unless she had kissed him and stroked his head after he had gone to bed. He was frail, delicate, high-strung; he gave away easily to great floods of tears. When his mother told him stories from books of fairy tales he threw himself so much into the sufferings of the hero or heroine that he shook with emotion. As a child he visited his relatives in the country, and his childhood among the woods and springtime flowers, the trees which he thought had souls and personality, recurred to his memory in later years as the only hours of pure contentment he ever had.

He was sent through a preparatory school, the Lycée Condorcet, where he seems to have learned little because he was out of school so much on account of his health and because he was a dreamy child who preferred to read books of his own and his mother's choosing. He learned a great deal of classical and symbolist French verse by heart; and he lost himself in Madame de Lafayette, Hugo, Dumas and a French translation of Dickens. Upon his graduation, he went up for his term of military training. He was pampered in the service as elsewhere because of his bad health, and, exempted from strenuous occupations, he devoted himself largely to reading and writing, and to acquiring a slight familiarity with English. He wrote some descriptive juvenilia and vaguely dreamed of a literary career; but as soon as his military training was over, his father wanted him to enter the diplomatic service and, to prepare him for it, he prevailed upon him to enter the school of law and political science at the Sorbonne. His chosen subjects did not interest him, but the lectures of Henri Bergson on philosophy, metaphysics and psychology did, and these lectures he attended with assiduity. Bergson, who became Proust's friend and later a relative by marriage, exercised a profound influence upon his thinking, especially in relation to the subconscious and to memory associations. He also instilled in Proust an interest in metaphysical subjects which was not quelled until Proust met and came under the influence of the skeptic, Anatole France, who convinced him that all efforts to explore the world beyond the boundaries perceived by the senses result either in madness or despair.

Proust did not take his degree in law but instead spent much of his time at the Sorbonne, either at lectures in philosophy and psychology or in the libraries reading. He also tried to write, attended the theater, and made the acquaintance of young literary aspirants like himself, such as Henri Barbusse, Robert de Flers, Daniel Halévy and Ferdinand Gregh,—and developed his already precocious mania for society.

In his adolescence, Proust tells us, the world of rank and fashion was the center of his imagination and dreams. Out of the pages of romance and history he had conjured images of princesses of unearthly beauty and grace and princes of charm and wit. Moreover by going into the Avenue du Bois de Boulogne he could see these enchanted persons, hereditary bearers of all the dignity, glory, beauty and chivalry of France—the Prince de Sagan, the Prince de Ligne, the Comtesse of This, the Duc of That, driving by in their carriages, mayhap with Edward, Prince of Wales, His Highness King Leopold of Belgium, the Prince of Monaco, Austrian Archdukes, or *the* Grand Duke of Russia. (It is amusing to observe that in his anxiety to learn all he could about royalty and nobility, titles, precedents, lineage, and etiquette, Proust seems never to have learned foreign distinctions and to his dying day imagined there was only one Grand Duke in Russia. He seems to have confused the title with that of the heir apparent.)

As a youth Proust read up on the etiquette of the aristocracy. He had princes pointed out to him and he studied their dress, their manner, their gestures. What is more, he would dress himself in all the elegance he could command, stroll in the Avenue of the Bois and, upon encountering a prince, princess, duke or duchess whom he recognized from pictures in the society press, he would lift his hat and execute the salutations he had learned from books. The women thought him a little mad, this frail, pale, childish dandy, but interesting and amusing, and they acknowledged his salutes, paid attention to him, racked their brains in wonder as to where they had ever met him. That was what Proust wanted.

Somehow while yet in his teens, he wangled an invitation to the salon of Madame Straus, where he quickly made the most of his opportunity by impressing his hostess with the aristocratic grace of his manner, his febrile wit, and his air of eccentric dandyism. It was there that with a group of young men, with literary tastes and no outlet for their faltering talents, he helped to found a little magazine which ran a few issues before its collaborators ran out of money and material. Léon Blum, later Socialist leader in the Chamber of Deputies, was one of the editors and contributors; Robert de Flers, who later became a fashionable playwright, was another; Henri Barbusse, who was later to write *Under Fire,* was still another. Proust contributed some sketches of famous mistresses of noble lords and of historical women of quality—dreadful stuff altogether.

His mother encouraged him in every whim and his father, convinced that his son would never amount to anything, gave up the training and education of Marcel as a bad job, yielded to his wife's demands that the youth be supplied with adequate spending money, and thought no more about him. Marcel's first passion was for a woman of rank much older than himself, whom he had not met but whom he followed on the streets, stepping into doorways to get a glimpse of her as she passed by or devouring her with his eyes as she rode by him in her carriage. His next passion *seems* to have been for a young girl his own age whom he met on a beach at a seaside resort (I say *seems,* for the feminine character, Albertine, may not have been of the sex represented) at a time when he felt a violent need for love of some one. Seeing a group of young girls he fell in love with all of them at once and only with difficulty made a choice among them. Albertine in the book is depicted as being sanguine, frivolous and a tease, amused by the passion of Proust and, as he says, knowing that he could not provide her with the sensual pleasure other admirers could, she yielded to him largely out of curiosity and thereafter tortured him with her infidelity, her casualness, and her failure to respond to the intensity of his feeling of love. In short, he was not loved. (Connoisseurs of the psychology of aberration may read in the Albertine and Gilberte episodes more than I am willing to; but Gilbert and Albert are common French first names, while these names with feminine suffixes are not.)

THE most influential man in all Paris society in the Eighteen-Nineties was Count Robert de Montesquiou. He knew everybody considered worth knowing in the society of the Faubourg Saint-Germain and, to a lesser extent, in the world of the theater and the arts also. He was the last male descendant of one of the oldest families in France, and he never tired of reminding people of the fact. He was, even as a young man, a grotesque creature, a sort of decadent Ward McAllister, the familiar of royal highnesses as well as of descendants of the older and the parvenu aristocracy of France. He was almost a phenomenon and a prodigy in his circle: he could read, not just simple, elementary sentences, which most of the aristocracy could manage, but even sentences of a certain complexity and length. Moreover, he had a degree of literary, musical and artistic yearnings, some cultural appreciation, a slight feeling for music and poetry; and he had a mimetic talent, enabling him to write a few eccentric verses in imitation of Mallarmé, of about the same quality, I should say, as those Harry Thaw would write if he were to study the verse of Amy Lowell. He fancied himself a literary man and wrote one novel which I have read, *La Petite Mademoiselle*, which reads as though it might have been written by an especially deficient scullery maid who nevertheless could read the novelettes in *Le Temps* and *Le Journal* and was especially interested in items about the *bon-ton*.

That there should be in the highest circles of the society of the Faubourg Saint-Germain a representative of that society who had a vocabulary of more than three hundred words and could use them in something more than social correspondence wherein every phrase is stereotyped, gave Count Robert an enormous reputation within his circle and without. It was at the end of the century and, in literature and art, decadence, languor, exhaustion were in fashion. Verlaine had sung, "I am the empire at the end of the decadence," and he might have added, "after me the deluge"; for a taste for the horrible, the depraved, the eccentric had set in. The Symbolist movement, wherein poets tried to attain in words "the condition of music," to suggest refined states of sensibility, came to the front to bewilder the bourgeois. Madmen abounded in the arts; Gérard de Nerval led a pet lobster tied with ribbon about with him; Baudelaire rubbed a green salve into his scalp to save him from baldness and word spread about that he had dyed his hair green. Baudelaire, in fact, profited by this notoriety and, for the ears of those at nearby tables, once told of having eaten the flesh of boiled infants and of having found it a great delicacy. Word went about that the Black Mass was being celebrated with orgies in the shadows of St. Sulpice and of Nôtre Dame. Van Gogh, a maniacal master-painter, cut off his ear and sent it to a friend as a sign of repentance for a fancied wrong. Gauguin, in the first stages of paresis, left civilization to go native in Tahiti, to send back curious distortions in rich color and, by taking a native mistress, to spread syphilis among the islanders. Maeterlinck, the Belgian, captured the imaginations of members of the French Academy and of clubwomen in Pecos, Texas, with medieval stage romances in which all the characters spoke as though they either were drugged or were somnambulists. The Princess Chimay posed in negligée for the penny press and eloped with a gypsy violinist who ended his days in the slums of New York. Anna Gould, the American heiress, married Count Boni de Castellane, the acme of Paris nobility. The salons of Mesdames de Loynes, de Caillavet and Straus elected the candidates for the French Academy. Oscar Wilde, bloated and drooling, was rotting in Paris, surrounded by young idolators like Robert Ross and André Gide. Félicien Rops was etching his mordant cartoons of prostitutes. Odilon Redon was making his terrible and pathetic pictures of the misery of the Paris poor. The scandal involving the German Kaiser and members of his military high command in perversions was in currency. And in Parisian aristocracy there was discovered a person who read books—most ghastly aberration the aristocrats could conceive of.

Immediately the fame of this freak, Count Robert de Montesquiou, spread; legends sprang up about him, grew, took on color, became fantastic. As early as 1884 Joris-Karl Huysmans, a punctilious bourgeois functionary in the ministry of the interior, with a clever gift for strained epithet, who had begun as a disciple of Zola, had heard of the legends about Montesquiou and patterned a hero after these legends in the figure of Des Esseintes in a cerebral novel called *A Rebours*. This Des Esseintes is pictured as the last descendant of an ancient family, who sums up in his tainted body all the excesses of his ancestors, all the febrility of their noble temperaments. At thirty he had not only tried and become weary of every vice, but had experimented with every stimulant to his fatigued sensibility. He builds a Udolpho's palace, surrounds himself with books of all the authors of the Latin and French decadence, all the strange new paintings of the moderns—and has opinions about them. (This gives Huysmans an opportunity to give his verdicts on Flaubert, the Goncourt brothers, Verlaine, Rimbaud, Corbière, Laforgue, de l'Isle-Adam, Mallarmé, Hello, Moreau, Redon, Dégas. In attributing preferences in decadent and medieval Latin to Des Esseintes he conveyed to Remy de Gourmont, among so many others, an impression that he was a Latin scholar; however, Huysmans told Gourmont that he got his titles and descriptions out of library catalogues.)

More important to the point of this chapter, however, the Des Esseintes of *A Rebours* has his memory awakened from time to time by reading a sentence from a book, by the faint odor of a perfume, which recalls vividly to him and in detail impressions of his active life which are more real to him in memory than they were when they occurred. That is the scheme followed by Proust. Des Esseintes recalls his search after sensual pleasures, his affairs with an acrobat, a ventriloquist, a woman who is a monster of depravity; he recalls his Neronian banquets, his bizarre escapades in society, his ancestry, the life, art and opinions of his times!

Who is quite willing to say that Marcel Proust is not a product of the mind of that macabre little clerk in the ministry of the interior, Joris-Karl Huysmans, whose imagination led him to picture in detail the obscenities of a Black Mass which he had never seen, who in remorse embraced the Catholic Church with fervor (with so much the fervor of a convert, indeed, as proved very troublesome to the Church, and sent word to Anatole France to repent of his writings and seek the bosom of the Lord before it was too late. Whereupon France replied: "To M. Huysmans my compliments, and tell him M. France suggests he have his water examined." Who shall say that life did not imitate art in the case of *A Rebours* and Proust, and that Proust did not get his notion of the remembrance of things past, not from Henri Bergson, but from the occupation of a fictional character?

Nevertheless, Count Robert de Montesquiou, who suggested Des Esseintes to Huysmans and Charlus to Proust, was Proust's idol in his youth. More than anything else in his youth, Proust wanted to gain entrée into the exclusive aristocracy of the Faubourg Saint-

Germain. That he succeeded is only further proof that with sufficient resolution and tenacity any one can do whatever one most
wishes to do. The set he meant to become familiar with contained
people whose whole sole reason for existence was sustained by the
limited number of persons to whom they permitted themselves to be
introduced, who snubbed princes who were not of the royal blood
and remained proudly adamant against the ingenious devices employed by countesses to be invited to their houses. Proust was half
Jew and wholly bourgeois; he had, in the society sense, "no family";
except for his marvelous eyes, he was unprepossessing, he was small
in stature, perverse, and without noticeable talent. The odds were
mightily against him; but he got what he wanted: he learned the
higher circles of Parisian society inside and out, and at last was profoundly disillusioned.

Proust's first step toward the conquest of aristocratic society
was to model himself in every conceivable fashion after his idol,
Count Robert de Montesquiou. Count Robert chose to ride in a
certain kind of open carriage, with a certain kind of horse, with a
driver in a certain kind of uniform, and to make his appearance on
the boulevards on certain occasions. This Proust would do also.
Count Robert appeared at the Ritz at a certain hour, displayed a
certain demeanor, wore a peculiar kind of flower in his lapel, always
addressed the *maître d'hôtel* in ordering his dinner, examined the
wine brought to him in a certain manner, sipped his wine thus and
so and ate his food in a singularly hoggish manner. This Proust also
would do. Count Robert maintained his reputation as a Beau Brum-
mell by saying that any one could pay a tailor to make one look
like a well-fitted dummy, but it took a genius like himself to "compose" a costume from the bargain counters in miscellaneous hand-
me-downs at the Trois Quartiers, a cheap department store near the
Madelaine, patronized largely by the lower bourgeoisie. So Proust
bought his trousers from one scrambled counter at the Trois Quartiers, his waistcoat from another, his jacket from another, his shirt
from this one, his shoes, cravats, spats and so forth from others—
as exactly like Count Robert's as he could find them.

In time Proust contrived to meet Count Robert, who was rude
to him at first, that being his customary mode of advance and attack.
(Charlus' malady, Proust explains to us, prevented him from ever
extending his hand first for fear that it might be refused by some one
who knew his secret; his appearance of snobbery was from fear, not
from arrogance. He once, in fact, lost his heart to a seven-foot

Senegalese but the poor fellow did not know how to contrive to meet the grinning Negro.) In time Count Robert took young Proust under his patronage. He told him he would train him in etiquette, social behavior, taste; he would introduce him into the most exclusive circles of society; he would make him socially. And he did. The older man fascinated and bewildered young Proust. Proust knew how Count Robert had contrived to make the fame and fortune of brilliant young composers, violinists, painters, etchers, by drawing the attention of society to them. (Read Proust's account of the fête Charlus got up for Morel's performance of an unpublished masterpiece of music, a fête that made the reputation of the composer and the musician, obtained fine notices in the press—and further purposes which were not æsthetic for Charlus and several others.)

If the attempted seduction of the narrator of *Remembrance of Things Past* by Charlus (one of the most amazing scenes in all literature) has any correspondence in fact in the relations between Count Robert and Proust, it was a very long time before Proust knew the reason for Count Robert's violent outbursts of temper, accusing Proust of ingratitude, ordering him out of the house and then, when Proust meekly and bewilderingly obeyed, running after him with tears streaming down his face and begging the youth to forgive him. That, though he did not know it then, was Proust's first real glimpse of the psychology of the evil of the Cities of the Plain.

As a guide and proctor for Proust in society, however, Count Robert was invaluable. Count Robert knew the lineage of the aristocratic families, which was something that many of the leading members of these families did not know themselves, their ignorance, as Renan said, giving one a rough idea of the infinite. The names, illustrious in the history of France, which Proust had carried in his heart since childhood, associating them with poetry, great deeds, estates, regions, the court of the Sun King, were soon to become familiar to him, borne by quite ordinary flesh and blood, with certain distinguishing mannerisms and habitual, almost automatic activities, polite, distracted and quite dull. (In reproducing literally the appalling attempts at witticism occasionally attempted by the brighter members of the aristocracy, Proust writes an implied comment on George Meredith's ideas of the conversation of dukes and duchesses. Meredith, who wished to conceal the fact that he was a tailor's son, attributed to the aristocratic figures of his novels the sort of conversation which, as Frank Moore Colby said, is to be heard nowhere, except possibly in a gathering of intellectual Jews, and least of all among hereditary dukes and duchesses.)

Proust gained entrée into the literary salons as well and he developed into a literary dilettante. He translated Ruskin's *Sesame and Lilies* and *The Bible of Amiens* (poor translations with the words picked painfully out of the dictionary), and wrote some parodies and imitations in an inconsequential volume called *Pastiches et Mélanges*. He contributed occasional pieces to the newspapers and to the literary magazines. But generally he was accounted a failure by the members of his literary generation, a mere *boulevardier*, a society sycophant; only Edmond de Goncourt and the bluestockings had any faith in his literary future.

When his father died in 1903, Proust inherited a considerable fortune, which enabled him to entertain on a still more extravagant scale at his home and at Foyot's and the Ritz, to exercise his almost embarrassing generosity (he was always urging money, expensive gifts and flowers on his friends and tipping waiters and cab drivers five times too much in fear of not tipping enough), and to carry on his butterfly life. Leon Pierre-Quint describes Proust at twenty:

" ... large, black, brilliant eyes, with heavy eyelids that drooped slightly to one side; a look of extreme gentleness, fastening a long time on the object it fell upon; a voice still more gentle, breathless a little, and somewhat drawling, verging on affectation yet always avoiding it. Long hair, black and thick, falling sometimes over his forehead, hair that was never to have a white thread amongst it. But it was to the eyes that one always turned back, immense eyes ringed with mauve, weary, wistful, of extreme mobility, eyes that seemed to leave their orbits to follow the secret thoughts of the speaker. A continual smile, amused and inviting, hesitated and then fixed itself motionless on his lips. His complexion was dull, but then fresh and pink, and in spite of his fine black moustache he gave one the impression of an overgrown child, indolent and over-observant."

(From *Marcel Proust: His Life and Work*.)

His asthma caused him to dress in woolens, and wear a heavy cape or overcoat even in summer and to bundle up like an Eskimo in winter, for fear of catching cold. His father was a famous physician and, unless Marcel's asthmatic condition was wholly neurotic, he might have cured him; but Marcel would have nothing whatever to do with doctors, had no faith in them, and like all true hypochondriacs, drank all sorts of nostrums, tried all kinds of crank remedies, and during the last years of his life subsisted largely on caffeine, pills, quack medicines and veronal.

This brilliant son of a doctor, who held a chair of hygiene at the Sorbonne and was city commissioner of health, did everything to kill himself it is possible to imagine. He kept himself shut up in an air-tight, cork-lined room in which the air became foul and almost completely devoid of oxygen; lying in bed, month after month, he wrote with the feeble electric light glaring into his eyes from the center of the room. His bed was rarely made and he wouldn't bathe for fear of taking a cold; he ate almost nothing and by taking caffeine he would stay awake three days and nights in succession writing and then, after thus stimulating his heart, he would depress it by doses of veronal. He wouldn't see a doctor when he had pneumonia and of pneumonia he officially died; but he probably also died of heart trouble, tuberculosis, and a completely ruined interior economy.

The death of Proust's mother in 1905 was a great blow to him. Soon after that he retired from society, took a barn-like flat in the Boulevard Haussmann and began to fill the note-books from which he was later to write his masterpiece. He had an intelligent and devoted housekeeper named Céleste, who dressed him, fed him and waited on him in the sparsely furnished room he lived in. (The rest of the flat, except for Céleste's and her husband's room, was either empty or used as a store-room for the family furniture.) Céleste's husband was a taxi driver, who stationed his cab outside the door every night at ten, because Proust never went out in the daytime and never earlier than eleven.

Proust's movements were secrets from many of his friends. It is certain, for one thing, that he was an unusually successful speculator on the Bourse, that he followed the price movements of stocks closely and was astute in calculating from the financial news the probable rise or fall of prices. Thus, although he was always complaining that he was ruined by some fractional move in stocks and professing a lack of money, he had augmented his fortune considerably; he entertained on a lavish scale from time to time, loaded his friends with gifts, and tipped like an American bonanza miner millionaire. He made a mystery of himself nevertheless, refused to see people when they called and received his friends only at night. He would be seized with a desire for conversation at two or three o'clock in the morning, send Céleste in a cab to get a friend out of bed and bring him to see him. In this way he was a great nuisance to his friends and after a while many began to avoid him. Yet he was the soul of generosity; he spent almost nothing on himself, never even troubling to have his room made comfortable, whereas he would order a feast at a famous restaurant for a host of friends, and eat a snack at home so he would not have to bother about eating while enjoying their companionship.

For six years he lived and wrote mostly in bed, never speaking of his work, until he had finished *Du Côté de Chez Swann (Swann's Way)*, the first part of his long *Remembrance of Things Past*. During those six years he had not only dropped out of sight, but had become practically unknown in the publishing world. He sent the manuscript to his old publisher, Calmann-Lévy, who declined it. He sent it to the new and enterprising firm, La Nouvelle Revue Française, presided over by Jacques Copeau, André Gide and Jean Schlumberger. In order to get special attention for the manuscript the Prince Bibesco gave a dinner for Proust inviting the editors; but none of them knew or remembered him except as a society snob, who occasionally wrote "little things." Jacques Copeau told me that no one in the office read the manuscript. They glanced at it, but it was an enormous pile of sheets, all in scrawling handwriting, with many interlineations; it seemed to be about nothing and in very bad style. They sent it back. Friends took matters in hand; but to no avail. One publisher wrote to one of these friends that he might be dense but he couldn't see any point in a writer's taking up thirty pages to describe how he turns over and over in his bed.

In short, *Swann's Way* was finally published at the author's expense. It fell flat. Paul Souday, of *Le Temps*, was the only critic who recognized any merit in it. Two years passed by and Jacques Rivière of the Nouvelle Revue Française, heard of the book through a friend, got a copy, read it and, believing he had just discovered a masterpiece, rushed to the office to announce his discovery only to learn that the "N.R.F." had turned the book down. Rivière said to Copeau and Gide, "Then the only thing left for us to do is either to jump out of the window or get the succeeding volumes from Proust and serialize it in the magazine." The editors called upon Proust in a delegation, offered profound apologies and begged for an opportunity to publish the succeeding volumes. They got some material for serialization; but this had scarcely got under way, when the War came on and the magazine was suspended, while nothing except war books was published for five years.

Proust continued to write, feverishly and against time, against approaching death. In 1918 the "N.R.F." brought out, by agreement with the original publisher, its own edition of *Swann's Way*, followed shortly by *A l'ombre des jeunes filles en fleurs* ("Within the Budding Grove"). A Proust cult sprang up. Wires were pulled and Proust was awarded the Prix Goncourt. Fame at last—the thing Proust had striven for since he gave up society. He gave a big dinner at the Ritz, spending all his prize money, and went back to bed, turning out in succession the other volumes of the series, in a cramped position, writing on loose sheets of paper, with no bed table or support for them, with a cheap pen dipped into a gummy ink bottle, crumbs, medicines, sheets of paper piled all about him, and himself dressed in two suits of woolen underwear and wearing knitted bed socks. He had just finished the last corrections of the manuscript of the last volume when he was seized with pneumonia. He would allow no doctors to see him, not even his own brother, Dr. Robert Proust. He died in great agony on November 18, 1922, in his fiftieth year. Shortly before his death he and his old friend, the Comtesse de Noailles, were both awarded the cross of the Legion of Honor, a reward which gave him immense satisfaction. Already his fame had spread in England where he had found enthusiastic admirers in Joseph Conrad, A. B. Walkley, Clive Bell, Stephen Hudson, Arnold Bennett and C. K. Scott-Moncrieff, the translator who recreated Proust in English.

Proust was an invalid, the historian and analyst of a sick society. It is a mistake, a superficial judgment, to think of Proust as a snob because he chose to write about snobs. The snobs from whom he drew his masterpiece hated and reviled him for betraying their tragic insipidity. Like Lenin, Proust pronounced a terrible moral judgment. It is small wonder that Proust is read by Soviet intellectuals. This depraved Bernardin de Saint-Pierre, this ingenuous Petronius did write his *Arabian Nights*, which had in them the authenticity of the *Memoires* of Saint-Simon.

GEORGE MOORE *THE MAN OF LETTERS*

*

THOSE who undertake to teach young men and women how to write should cherish the name of George Moore as a challenge against the repeated assertion that writers are born and not made. Moore is the most conspicuous example I can recall of a man who became a great prose artist by virtue of perseverance alone. He showed, in the beginning, even in the late beginning—after he had nearly a dozen books to his credit—no natural talent for writing. He had at the first only a vanity which was appeased by scribbling, at a moment in the history of Anglo-French culture when even among the English it was beginning to be conceded that a man who displayed genius in the field of literature was not really declassed but somehow set apart from his fellows in a flattering light.

If Moore had genius in those days it was a genius for imitation. He had gall, surely, and a prodigious conceit which was not balked by any curbing quality of self-criticism. He wanted to be a writer and it seemed to him that what he wrote was literature. He was thrilled by Baudelaire in much the same fashion as a schoolgirl is thrilled by a movie star; and he wrote *Flowers of Passion* in much the same spirit that animates the schoolgirl who loads her eyelids with blue bismuth and her eyelashes with mascara. The career of Alfred de Musset seemed to him a splendid skyrocket, bursting into the gorgeous pyrotechnics of the famous *Confessions;* and with Baudelaire and a fashionable boredom to give Moore the cue of affected ennui, he wrote his own *Confessions of a Young Man,* perhaps the callowest book ever signed by a name with any literary pretensions in the English language. It is a book which is a joy to read if only for the malicious pleasure of discovering how ludicrous

472

a donkey a young man can show himself in all seriousness to be. What was not George Moore posturing as a very precious esthete in that book was second-hand opinion picked up in the Paris cafés frequented by writers, just as in *Modern Painters* what was not George Moore in another rôle of make-believe is a great deal of not wholly assimilated art theory caught from the lips of artists and critics in the Impressionist studios. Yet even in these books we have the seedling of a temperament which flowers into the artist; for the artist is a person who resolutely gives over all else in life to his art.

After Moore had first paid Zola the tribute of professing to be revolted by his work, he next paid Zola the tribute of imitating him. This was in the beginning of Moore's period as a writer of realistic novels, a period which lasted until he had produced nearly a dozen in that genre, all of them, except *Mike Fletcher,* according to the Moore-ites, fine, finished and soundly realistic. I cannot speak with authority on this point, for I have read only two of Moore's realistic novels, *A Mummer's Wife* and *Evelyn Innes.* The others I have set aside among those numerous books of generally attested merit which I hope some day to get around to reading. But from those two samples I know that, good as Moore was in that stage of his literary career when he was realistic and realistico-romantic, he had not really struck his literary stride; he had not produced work which is unique in our literature.

There are, in Moore's later works, several pieces of literature which are unique. In the trilogy, *Hail and Farewell,* he originated a new method—a method which W. B. Yeats, one of the great literary artists of our time, thought good enough to take as his model when he came to write his own reminiscences in *The Trembling of the Leaf.* In substance, *Hail and Farewell* is George Moore touching up, like an artist, the scenes and episodes he remembers; it is the Irish Literary Renaissance and the interesting figures in it, acting upon the playful imagination of George Moore. In style, it is a lucid and refreshing narrative method, compounded of conversational idioms and exact imagery. It sounds informal, spontaneous, to the point, from the spirit; and it has charm, delicious malice, roguish humor. It is probably more exact than an exact history would be (presuming that such a history could be written), and it is literature to which the manner has given distinction.

Memoirs of My Dead Life is the most delectable and delicate piece of pornography in our language; indeed, it is one of the few examples we have of pornography which is at the same time fine literature. It is pornographic in that it has no other intention than to entertain and that it is indelicate in material; the instruction it imparts is not pious; its moral "message" does not exist; it is sensuous and sensual in form and matter. It can offend no one, I believe, who is not pathological; it can give the judicious only amusement and delight. It is apart from the Anglo-Saxon tradition in that it is a departure from the tacit agreement that love shall always be treated tragically, but it is in a great tradition, of which even Homer now and then partook.

In *Avowals* Moore revived conversation as a literary form, and gave to that form, I think, more charm than any one before him. *Avowals* is one of my favorites, if not my favorite, among the Moore books. When it was first published in a limited subscription edition a great number of collectors of erotica returned the book to their booksellers because they had bought it under the impression that, because it was issued in a limited edition, they were getting something choice in the line of facetiæ. There is nothing of the kind in *Avowals;* the imaginary conversations between Moore and Edmund Gosse are for the most part on the subject of literature; but they are conversations which are not weighted down with erudition and recondite allusions as in Landor; they are humanly and humorously interesting and they are written in a prose which is a miracle of grace, beauty and clarity.

A literary artist is privileged to choose any material he can transmute by the alchemy of clarity and distinction into the fine metal of literature. He need not have any point of view—except his own. Moore has been accused of naughtiness, and he has been accused of blasphemy, too, for having used legendary material in *The Brook Kerith,* which a certain sect of Christians cling to as an article of faith. But, again, it is not ultimately a question as to whether Moore offended one sect of Christians when he might just as easily have offended another sect; but whether in writing *The Brook Kerith* he produced a fine piece of literature. It is my impression that he did.

In *A Story-Teller's Holiday* he drew materials from numerous sources, from the Talmud and from the story of *Daphnis and Chloë,* from folk-tales and from tavern gossip, from libels against the church and from churchmen themselves, and he made from these materials a series of yarns which, whatever else may be said of them, are told in exquisite style. Moore has mastered the art of prose to such a fine degree, indeed, that he can, and often does, write beautifully about nothing at all. In one of his conversations I remember he said substantially that a young man paid him a visit in Ebury Street and told Moore that he was happily married—that and nothing else—and yet he made of this small episode a beautiful and charming thing. That is the achievement of an artist.

Outside of his books George Moore has had no life to speak of. What little life he has had he has confessed with extraordinary candor and not a little artistic dressing up in *Confessions of a Young Man, Memoirs of My Dead Life* and *Hail and Farewell.* He has consistently refused to disclose the date of his birth in *Who's Who,* but Susan Mitchell in her delightfully malicious monograph on Moore (which she wrote to avenge Dubliners for the fictional portraits of them in *Hail and Farewell*) fixes the date as 1852. He was the eldest son of George Henry Mayo of Moore Hall, an ancestral estate in the County Mayo. He was brought up a Catholic but from youth onwards he made the Church the object of a perpetual revolt, ever conceiving the absurd notion he tells us about in *Hail and Farewell* that the Catholic religion had never produced a first rate writer.

Susan Mitchell thus describes him in his youth: "... a man of middle height with an egg-shaped face and head, light yellow hair in perpetual revolt against the brush, a stout nose with thick nostrils, grey-green eyes, remarkable eyes, a mouth inclined to pettishness, lips thick in the middle as if a bee had stung them. He had champagne shoulders and a somewhat thick, ungainly figure, but he moved about a room with a grace which is not of Dublin drawing-rooms. Afterwards, seeing George Moore in the street, I found he was the only man in Dublin who walked fashionably." In Dublin, Miss Mitchell tells us he is described as "an over-ripe gooseberry," "a great big intoxicated baby," "a satyr," "a boiled ghost" and "a gosling"; but after telling us this, she says sardonically that she is not satisfied with these descriptions; "they are florid and untidy." He has now (she was writing in 1916) "a face dear to the caricaturist and in itself at times a caricature: the yellow hair, the fat features, the sly smile, the malice, the vanity." One of Manet's most famous portraits is of George Moore; and other great painters have found his features interesting enough to paint.

Moore published in his callow youth two slender volumes of exceedingly bad poetry under the frightful titles, *Flowers of Passion* and *Pagan Poems,* insincere nonsense which he imagined to be daring and of the school of Swinburne. Possessing an independent income, he went to Paris, where he lived for a number of years, idling principally, picking up impressions, frequenting the studios and cafés, and ostensibly studying painting at the Atélier Julien. He made the acquaintance of nearly everybody in the literary and artistic world. Manet, Dégas, Daudet, Verlaine, Zola, Turgenev, Flaubert. He read Balzac, Gautier, Daudet, the Goncourts, Flaubert and Zola, and the poets, Baudelaire, Mallarmé, and others of the Symbolist school. He also read Thomas Hardy, Henry James, George Meredith, seeking in each what he could find for his own use as a writer. He established some journalistic connections in London and wrote the articles which he later included in *Impressions and Opinions* (1890) and *Modern Paintings* (1893).

When Moore was in Paris the decadent movement was at its height and he at least imaginatively threw himself into the fashion. He posed as a decadent with Neronian tastes, wrote about having a pet python and professed to adore blue china; he celebrated absinthe and sin. But Miss Moore says: "Perhaps the Latin races can sin gracefully; the Irish cannot. And Mr. Moore's sinning? He cannot escape from his birthright, Lough Xara set her seal on him, 'islands lying in misted water, faint as dreams.' As Silenus he is a poor thing. His leer is so much 'make-up' and it is the more revolting because he is naturally sincere. He has no genius for the gross."

That is to take Moore too seriously: Moore's accounts of himself in the rôle of a decadent are to be read with the appropriate smiles of incredulity and amusement that any one can so shamelessly display himself a booby. Much of the enjoyment of Moore's many confessions, as a matter of fact, is to be found in the ridiculous character he gives to himself in prose which no one has equaled for lightness and limpidity.

With the publication of *A Modern Lover* in 1883 Moore's life in contact with people and events was ended. After 1883 he settled down in a flat in London and thenceforth devoted himself exclusively to his career as a writer. He went back to Dublin for a short period to participate in what has been called the Irish Renaissance and he helped Lady Gregory and W. B. Yeats to establish a theater in Dublin which would produce the work of Synge and other peculiarly Irish dramatists. He was the associate also of James Stephens, author of *The Crock of Gold* and *Demigods,* of George Russell (AE), John Eglinton, and Oliver Gogarty. But his residence in Ireland, as always, was for the purpose of gathering material for his imaginative autobiography. After that he was to return to Dublin on several occasions but principally his residence has been in Ebury Street in London.

After the publication of *Lewis Seymour and Some Women* he was sued by a man who bore the name of Lewis Seymour. He had to pay damages and this event, combined with brushes with the censorship, caused him to issue his books only in private editions for subscribers. He has revised his work in so many editions, writing new prefaces nearly every time, that a complete collection of all the various editions of Moore's work would fill an enormous amount of space in one's library. There is no writer in the history of literature who has been more exclusively the man of letters than George Moore is. There is no one who has written with greater charm, whether his work be as light as it is in *A Story-Teller's Holiday* or as grave, well-documented, deeply imagined and thought out as in *The Brook Kerith*.

CODA

*

THE prevailing social spirit of the literature of the late nineteenth century may be said to have begun with the publication of Henrik Ibsen's *A Doll's House* in Norwegian in 1879. Three years later a translation of that play by Miss Frances Lord appeared in English. It was not the first of the social plays of Ibsen after he had turned away from lyric drama (the first was *Pillars of Society*, published in 1877), but it was the first to set thousands of heads spinning with the impact of a new idea. That idea, in its simplest form, was that women had souls of their own. It is quaint to reflect nowadays upon how unquestioningly men and women in western Europe and in America accepted the orthodox Mohammedan dogma of the inferior nature of women, of the purely physical quality of woman's endowment and her relative unimportance in the scheme of things, down through the centuries to the dawn of the twentieth. We have seen how Milton held the masculine doctrine that man alone should seek God and that women should seek God through man. Woman's place was considered to be not only in the home but under the dictates and subjection of man.

THE apparition of a Queen Elizabeth brought nothing to the minds of people regarding the independence of spirit and judgment which might reside in the bosom of a woman. And, most curious irony of all, it was when England was ruled by a fiercely capable, extraordinarily self-willed and intelligent woman, Victoria, that the tyranny of woman's subjection to man became most intolerable and that all the man-made conventions with their sentimental emphasis on home and motherhood and on the necessity for paternal rule and discipline were so abused in practice that among men, first, and then among women, there arose a revolt so emotional and so violent that the aim of the revolt came to be to wipe out the family and the home and the institution of marriage altogether.

For a woman to write novels, essays, or plays was considered (at least officially and outspokenly) an aberration in the nineteenth century. One forgot Sappho; one forgot that in *La Princesse de Clèves* Madame de Lafayette had written the first psychological novel; one forgot Margaret of Navarre, who was at once a queen, an exquisite poet, and a romancer; one forgot Mrs. Aphra Behn—or considered them freaks. Amatine Dupin, Madame Dudevant, found it almost obligatory to write under the masculine name, George Sand, and Mary Ann Evans did not dare court disdain from masculine critics and conventionally minded women by writing under her own name but put out her novels under the pseudonym, George Eliot. Charlotte and Emily Brontë braved the storms of outraged masculinity by writing from their feminine hearts novels bravely true to feminine emotions and signed their books by their own names only to be overwhelmed by the obloquy of male prigs and hypocrites in high places who forgot or did not forget with what serene and masterly truth and malice Jane Austen had exposed to ridicule all such posturing male nit-wits in *Pride and Prejudice* and *Sense and Sensibility* at the beginning of the century. Ellen Glasgow, a beautiful girl with a brilliant brain and a great talent for writing exquisitely of life as she saw it, scandalized not only all Richmond, Virginia, and all America but all England as well by a novel called *The Descendant* in 1897 and made her reputation as much by the scandal of a woman's thinking of things women were not expected to think about as by the fine merits of her novel.

In America, one of the most precious lyric poets the world has ever known, Emily Dickinson, had to yield to the convention which required her to be an old maid if she did not accept the proposal of marriage of some lug she did not love, and pen out her sorrow in poignant poetry which she dared not publish while she was alive lest it betray to the world that she had a heart not in docile subjection to decorum. She loved a man who was married.

In a Norwegian village a lyrical Viking who had turned pessimistic and truculent and savagely prophetic, hating all the abuses of a money economy wherein corruption flourished, wrote some plays which were masterpieces of showmanship and of technical construction, and these plays revolutionized the thought of Europe and of the whole western world. One saw dramatically presented in the plays of Ibsen that nearly all of the man-made conventions, which were supposed to insure the progress and stability of society, were really wrecking the souls of men and women, spreading disease and death through callous and cruel mercenary means and ends, destroying character and true inner sense of decency, making an obscene farce of marriage, motherhood and communal life. In a dominant masculine world, men were playing both hands against the middle and losing all (without knowing it) for a fatuous egotism.

The revolution Ibsen caused was basic and momentous, a thousand times more important than a political revolution or an economic revolution; for a political revolution merely affects a change of privileges, and an economic revolution merely affects the distribution of wealth, whereas the revolution inaugurated by Ibsen affects the most vital of all things—the love and relationship between men and women. That revolution is not complete; Australian women novelists still find it expedient to publish their work under masculine pseudonyms; impassioned feminists over-emphasize the significant trifles like inequal wages and the habit among women of using their husband's names after marriage; the liberation which women felt with the challenge of Ibsen led many to contract unsanctified unions, not because they were in love but as a matter of duty, thus laying up heartbreaks for themselves, but in all the extravagances of the feminine revolution there was a pent-up and explosive emotion against a long inequality and injustice to one half of the human race, the half that is a necessary complement to the other half.

Women revolted and continue to revolt against the idea that they are the mere instruments of men; they revolted against the apparent biological law which seemed to make them the passive agents in the continuation of the race and in the expression of love. Henrik Ibsen made them conscious of the ignoble situation which the conventions of man-ruled society placed them. We get, in literature, a lyrical expression of this liberation of the feminine spirit in the joyous, ecstatic, confident sonnets of Edna St. Vincent Millay and in the daring splendor of some of the poems of Elinor Wylie. In the work of these two poets, who have written sonnets equal in beauty, depth and music to any ever written in the world, later generations, I believe, still see that, with those two poets, something new and vital and prophetic came into the world. With them, as with Sappho, the feminine voice dared to speak in feminine accents and character and spirit and not according to the manner masculine vanity ruled that they speak.

THE social revolution precipitated by Ibsen gathered force in England with the publication of George Gissing's *New Grub Street* in 1891, and of Samuel Butler's posthumous novel, *The Way of All Flesh* in 1903. The first was a somber, realistic and bitter challenge to the sentimental tradition, best expressed in Dickens, that poverty is charming; and the second was an enormous quantity of dynamite discharged in the midst of the British family. *The Way of All Flesh* denied, with great emphasis and point, that fathers should be obeyed and respected whether they were worthy of respect and obedience or not; and the novel did this not by argument but by indirection: it was a veristic and verifiable picture of British home life under the placid austerities of outward decorum. Behind nice manners before visitors we perceived a hell; and this hell was a concomitant, and a derivative, of this same front of nice manners, carefully erected, this front, under the guidance of the doctrine that father should rule in the home, mother should keep her virtue and her place in the kitchen (or as a parlor adornment), first-born son should have too much and later born sons too little, daughters should stifle their feelings until father had sized up the young man's prospects and approved of them before consenting to his daughter's marriage. But human beings are individuals, mothers, sons and daughters (as well as fathers) and whatever outward signs they gave of conformity which utterly wiped out their individuality were only a poor indication of the rebellion within.

Bernard Shaw was one of the first writers of facility and genius who, looking back upon a childhood in which he had no awesome reverence for his father, and looking closely at his own slight capacities as a pater familias, augmented with a great rush of brilliance and technique in dramatic composition the audacious abstractions he had derived from Butler, Ibsen, and, to a lesser extent, Nietzsche and Marx—a mixture more apparently adulterate than actual.

The Fabian Society was formed in London by a group who seriously imagined that all the horrors of living were attributable to the fact that some few people have a lot of money and a great many have none at all. This is a false assumption, with a certain basis in fact and exploited to the limits of any theory in the economic pathology of Karl Marx, who neglected to observe that he lived in a relatively complete happiness and in concord with his wife and children on almost no money whatever, who also neglected to observe that the story of Christ and His disciples was not conspicuously a money relationship, and who also neglected to observe that among the peasants of Ireland who were oppressed beyond endurance a sweet acceptance of the beauty of life under poverty had flowered into song and literature happier far than that achieved by the most successful London novelist who was deriving stupendous royalties from pretty pictures of the status quo. I don't mean to fall into the sentimental doctrine that riches do not bring happiness: I merely mean to indicate riches or poverty have no precise relationship to happiness or its reverse.

It had all been a long accretion of accepted false notions. Swift, as only one among so many who had preceded him, had said that nine-tenths of happiness consisted of having money and he did not know what the other tenth consisted of, and this notion had been behind the motive which propelled Balzac to "conquer Paris" by an assault of many novels only to achieve a great contribution to literature and to die in unpleasant circumstances just when, for the first time in his life, he had got out of debt. Bernard Shaw was to say that the only vice was poverty, and, as a professed Socialist and vegetarian, teetotaler and cagy fellow, he carried on a correspondence with Ellen Terry which shows him up in a curious light as a smart chap, desperately trying to get on in the theatrical world and quite willing to use a woman to help him by paying her rhetorical court which she, with divine wisdom, understood and condoned.

CONSPICUOUS in the Fabian Society meetings was a young scientist and romancer who was, at the same time, an intuitive genius always a few days or a few months (happily for himself, not a few years) ahead of the rest of the world in perceiving what the majority of mankind were thinking about,—what was in the air. This was H. G. Wells, a journalist par excellence, a journalist so good that it is a pity he was not journalist enough. It was his habit to burst into the Fabian Society meetings in a fever of excitement. In his stammering and unpleasant voice he demanded that something be done immediately about this or that—about illegitimate motherhood, child labor, inequitable laws, military preparations, education of the young, or what not. Shaw sardonically observed that Wells was always demanding that something be done about something but never had any notion as to just what.

That was Wells' métier as a social philosopher-novelist, after he had left the entertaining trade of being a cracking good concocter of scientific mystery yarns à la Jules Verne. Babbitt on Patmos that he was, he wrote a series of challenging novels about divorce and marriage, education, politics, religion, war, economics and what not —all extremely apposite in their challenge for the moment, all badly written from a precisionist point of view, all alive, vibrant and readable. Diverse posterities may choose to find piquant or instructive some of those novels in which Wells mixed adultery (as if it were a new subject) in about equal proportions with exhaustive discussions of the "vital" problems of the day. But, as Anatole France reminded us, you and I and any man or woman we brush against in the subway or encounter on the street are posterity. We are the posterity of Menander and Milton; and do we quite live up to what Milton expected of us when he dedicated himself to the composition of a form of literature which should be cherished by us and not meant for the vulgar ears of those of his times whom he scorned? Posterities to come may find piquancies in the novels by Wells in which he threw all his ardor into the resounding of great "problems" of the hour; but such posterities which happen to discover him will, I think, value him for *Tono-Bungay, The New Machiavelli,* and, more especially, for *The Island of Dr. Moreau.*

John Galsworthy came to eminence in this Ibsenian revolution, and he depicted in pleasing pictures the crumbling of a squirocracy in his saga of the Forsyte family. He saw, with some not quite warranted trepidation, a decay of pleasant manners and of a middle-class noblesse oblige which country gentlemen had adopted toward their underlings; and in this he was a bit on the wrong side of healthy sentiment and the heart of truth; but he made it up, to his cost as a re-readable artist, by artistic fervor in behalf of a reform of the penal laws and a reconsideration of the statutes on divorce.

Arnold Bennett, too, was drawn into the vortex of this revolution stirred up by Ibsen and carried on by Butler and Shaw. And he wrote one masterpiece, *The Old Wives' Tale,* which had nothing to do with the revolution at all. He also was a man who wrote his very best stuff, after that masterpiece, under the impression that he was turning out pot-boilers and mere newspaper pieces. His notebook jottings and things tossed off in newspaper columns, and collected under the titles *Things Which Have Interested Me* and *More Things Which Have Interested Me,* wherein he recorded the lively and unpremeditated impressions of the things he saw and experienced, will continue, like Pepys' *Diary,* to be relished by a posterity which will find the Clayhanger series a strained striving after an effect achieved gracefully and with ease, as sheer entertainment, by George Moore in *Evelyn Innes* and *A Mummer's Wife.*

Nevertheless, in English literature, Wells, Bennett and Galsworthy were a trio, proctored somewhat by a positively amazing Irishman, Bernard Shaw, who changed the point of view, colored the attitude, channeled the expression of a whole generation, socially and politically. Alongside of them were several independent artists working quietly rich lodes of ore. They were, to name but a few, Joseph Conrad, William H. Hudson, George Meredith, Thomas Hardy, Henry James, Ford Madox (Hueffer) Ford. Hardy was an older independent, primarily a poet, the author of the only considerable epic in English, *The Dynasts,* and a defeatist naturalist as a novelist who wrote *Far from the Madding Crowd, Tess of the D'Urbervilles* and *Jude the Obscure,* which are still impressive and dramatically poignant, however we may wonder why their author was considered, at the time he published them, satanic and evil.

Conrad was a Pole, whose second language was French, articled as a ship's master in the English merchant marine at a time when he knew very little English. He had sought his British certificate because Poland was not a maritime nation and France was overcrowded with competition in a slender field. Conrad wrote stories in his master's cabin of sailing ships against the time when he would be forced to retire—for money. He wrote his stories painfully: he was never able to think easily in English, and so often he would formulate what he wanted to say in French and translate it into his own meager knowledge of English. To the day of his death his accent in English was foreign and this was a positive indication to those who knew him that the words he set down in English sounded differently to his inner ear than they did to the inner ear of his English readers. This was a fortuitous happy defect; because in reading a Conrad story one encounters a strangeness, almost mystical and certainly effective, which the author did not consciously strive at. He was never preoccupied with effects. He was preoccupied with one tremendous fact, and this is that men are whipped, broken and defeated by their own ideals. It is a mistake to imagine that Conrad wrote "sea stories." Comparatively few of his stories are directly concerned with the sea: they are, nearly every one, concerned with the tragedy often inherent in man's idea of himself and of what is expected of him. He wrote one short story, *Youth,* which is, by common consent, one of the world's masterpieces of short-story writing; and it is, symbolically, about that determination one has in one's courageous youth to win out, whatever the obstacles.

Meredith, anxious to forget that his father was a tailor, wrote about dukes and duchesses and about a brilliant aristocracy which had no more relation to the facts of that aristocracy than a *chanson de geste* had to the exploits of a feudal plunderer; and he endowed this aristocracy with a wit and intellectuality in conversation which, as Frank Moore Colby pointed out, is to be found only among intellectual Jews—which is to say Jews without money. Meredith created, however, a world of interesting people of his own and he analyzed their souls with a particularly bright malice in *The Egoist* and in *The Ordeal of Richard Feverel.* In his *Modern Love,* a poetic distillation of the same ideas expressed in *The Egoist,* Meredith set a standard for an artistic realization of grace in living which he imagined to be possible to those of the upper reaches of economic security, and so set a false notion of a goal to attain to—a goal, by the way, which members of the upper reaches of British economic security rejected as impossible of attainment: their vocabularies of five hundred or six hundred words largely concerned with the slang of hunts, grog, hounds and horses did not embrace the scintillant, drop-stitch vocabulary Meredith had invented for them.

Henry James, a fat, wistful remittance man with a passion for elegance to obscure the affront to his delicacy that was borne in on him by the fact that his grandfather was a highly successful merchant (or man in trade) in Syracuse, New York, and by the hauteur of Boston Back Bay society too flagrantly contemptuous of his origins, shook the dust from a "vulgar" America and removed himself to England, where through a long period he braced English aristocratic society and, in novels, gave a profound psychological significance to the manner in which a duchess accepted a cup of tea from a younger, remote cousin of a son of a man with whom she had had, in her dim past, an irregular affair. Through several novels, too, Henry James rationalized, in an absurd and idiotic manner, his own flight from an America in which his healthy and brainier and more common-sense brother, William, had not only found himself perfectly at home and at ease but had written some works on psychology which even today place him among the great psychologists of all time. Henry James created heroes in his novels whose great psychological and moral problem was whether or not to live in America and accept its vulgarities or make one's home in England or France, where one could have the right chintz for one's rooms and talk precious nonsense about Renaissance art. Henry James' idea of culture was that of a prim and not too bright finishing-school girl, and he never got out of it. Nevertheless he did have a certain undefined, unapprehended groping toward form; he said a few things with a certain hesitant grace; and in *Daisy Miller* and *What Maisie Knew* he wrote two novels almost as profound as *Gentlemen Prefer Blondes* by Anita Loos. In *The Turn of the Screw* he wrote a really creditable mystery story. His highbrow fame, however, rests upon a critical acceptance of the pompous and pathetic social values he placed upon himself.

One doesn't forget *Green Mansions,* or *Idle Days in Patagonia* or any of the works of Hudson (if one has read them) any more than one forgets Doughty's *Arabia Deserta,* or Burton's *Arabian Nights* or Fitzgerald's Omar, or *Alice in Wonderland.*

Meanwhile there was Chekhov in Russia, getting at a core of reality with the clinical sense of the physician-surgeon that he was and with the fidelity to the record of a conscientious journalist; and there was Gorky coming up from the depths, picturing the tragedies of the miserables, and later forgetting, like a Socialist who has fallen heir to a fortune, his origins, his birthright, what he knew, almost as soon as he became famous, and having to revert to it in his old age, when the cataclysm of the autocracy brought about the end of feudalism in Russia. In Italy there was D'Annunzio, a tiny, sensuous, and ugly dandy with a burning energy, who ensnared Eleanora Duse and Ida Rubenstein, and who made capital of his amorous triumphs in rapturous novels like *The Flame of Life* and *The Triumph of Death.*

On the Halsted Avenue street car line in Chicago there was an immigrant conductor, Knut Hansun, who had known the extreme limits of the physical pains of hunger and, like so many of his compatriots in Norway, had been disillusioned after setting forth to the promised land of America, and this street car conductor was to write a prose epic of his people, of the peasant and of the peasant transformed into the American farmer in *Growth of the Soil.*

In Ireland, a spark ignited by a German scholar who had interested himself in the dead language, Gaelic, led to the founding of a school of Irish writers in which, happily, all the members cordially hated each other and so created, each on his own, *Riders to the Sea* by J. M. Synge, the poetry of that W. B. Yeats who became an Irish senator and won the Nobel Prize, the *Ulysses, Dubliners* and *Portrait of the Artist as a Young Man* by James Joyce, the ribald poems of Oliver Gogarty, the delicate beauties in prose and poetry of the elfin Padraic Colum, and (dearest to the hearts of humble persons who enjoy humor, fantasy, sweet-natured kindness and wit) James Stephens' *The Crock of Gold* and *The Demigods* (two books I turn to with the same pleasure in anticipation and satisfaction that I find on repeated hearings of music by Bach, Mozart, and Brahms).

The spirit that was abroad and came to expression in Ibsen, Nietzsche, Dostoievski, Tolstoi, brought a new phase of literature into being: the novel of one's inner self as opposed to the surface appearance of self. Dostoievski was the forerunner of this type of fiction; but all who followed after him were not necessarily readers of Dostoievski. There was, for instance, the untamed, natural, neurotic man, incapable of thinking in orderly logic but gifted with a holy urge to express what he felt (not in his head but in his heart; or rather, "in the belly," as he expressed it). This was D. H. Lawrence, by all accounts a saintly man, who had so profound an effect upon those who came into contact with him that they almost worshiped him. He was a son in the most poverty-stricken class in England, the colliers, and he wrote a novel called *Sons and Lovers* which, I think, readily takes its place among the great novels of the world. He was a shy ascetic, who was married when he met and fell in love with the Baroness von Richthofen, sister of the German ace aviator, and ran away with her. He wrote sensuous, erotic poetry but with a choice of words which would not offend prudish tastes; and in the short, distracted years left to him before he died of tuberculosis, he made, of his marital experiences and out of the very depths of his consciousness, novels of strange and terrifying beauty, coming closer perhaps than any other novelist to the nerve-edge of our inner experience. No realist has ever written a realistic novel: to do so is impossible. Lawrence comes closest to those realities which are really incommunicable. He is uneven and sometimes bizarre; he wrote some novels which are wholly outside an ordinary man or woman's experience; but as a novelist he had intimations usually found expressed only in the work of the great lyrical poets.

In America, the Promethean figures who came up in literature after Mark Twain in a slow emergence from colonial, sycophantic genteel subservience to England, were Theodore Dreiser and James Branch Cabell. These two men are so extremely unlike in literary aims and purposes, taste, style, and personality that I doubt if either one could read the work of the other without actual unsympathy. It is interesting to note that when Cabell reviewed the accomplishments of his contemporaries he included Willa Cather, Ellen Glasgow, H. L. Mencken, Joseph Hergesheimer and Sinclair Lewis, but omitted discussion of Dreiser. The reason is, perhaps, that he is temperamentally incapable of reading Dreiser; and (though I say this without any warrant in anything Dreiser has ever said or written) Dreiser is temperamentally incapable of reading fifty pages of Cabell.

But, no less, I think that Dreiser and Cabell are the two most important literary figures in America of our time and that both of them have achieved the distinction of being classics during their lifetime. In any comparison between a single important novel by Dreiser and a single important novel by Balzac I think that the American will stand out as superior in power, depth of understanding, fidelity to scene and observed truth, more comprehensive in imagination. And Cabell's *Jurgen* is unique in the world's literature. It has taken its place, I think, among the singular and great masterpieces which have spun out of a richly endowed, wise, critical, and humorous subconscious. Analytically and philosophically it is, I think, the deepest, most prophetic, and most beautiful work of the creative imagination of our period.

A rich and varied indigenous America is in the making with the work of the lyric fantasist, F. Scott Fitzgerald; the proletarian panoramas in multichrome by John Dos Passos; the aggressively masculine and unsentimental stories in a concise, steel-sharp and steel-hard idiom of Ernest Hemingway; and in the scarifying studies of morbidity and the "normals" of American life by William Faulkner. All these have builded more or less upon the ground cleared by James Huneker, H. L. Mencken, Sinclair Lewis, and Sherwood Anderson after the Titan, Dreiser, had strode through the forest of American imitations of the "genteel" British tradition. For a study of these new developments I should refer one to Carl Van Doren's *Contemporary American Novelists* and Joseph Warren Beach's *The Outlook for American Prose.*

INDEX

*